THE INSIDERS' GUIDE TO
Tucson

THE INSIDERS' GUIDE TO

Tucson

by
David Barber
and
Chris Howell

Insiders' Publishing Inc.

Published by:
Insiders' Publishing Inc.
105 Budleigh St.
P.O. Box 2057
Manteo, NC 27954
(919) 473-6100
www.insiders.com

Sales and Marketing:
Falcon Distribution Services
P.O. Box 1718
Helena, MT 59624
(800) 582-2665
www.falconguide.com

•

FIRST EDITION
1st printing

•

Copyright ©1998
by Insiders' Publishing Inc.

•

Printed in the United States
of America

•

All rights reserved. No part of this book may be reproduced in any form without permission, in writing, from the publisher, except by a reviewer who wishes to quote brief passages in connection with a review in a magazine or newspaper.

Publications from The Insiders' Guide® series are available at special discounts for bulk purchases for sales promotions, premiums or fundraisings. Special editions, including personalized covers, can be created in large quantities for special needs. For more information, please write to Insiders' Publishing Inc., P.O. Box 2057, Manteo, NC 27954, or call (919) 473-6100 Ext. 241.

ISBN 1-57380-051-1

Insiders' Publishing Inc.

Publisher/Editor-in-Chief
Beth P. Storie

President/General Manager
Michael McOwen

Creative Services Director
Giles MacMillan

Director of New Product Development
David Haynes

Managing Editor
Dave McCarter

Regional Advertising Sales Manager
Greg Swanson

Local Advertising Sales Representative
David Popke

Project Editor
Amy Baynard

Project Artist
Carolyn McClees

Preface

Welcome to Tucson — the Old Pueblo.

There is much here to explore and appreciate in this, the oldest continuously inhabited city in North America. While Phoenix to the north is Arizona's seat of government, Tucson is the state's cultural center. A scan of our Arts and Culture chapter will satisfy even the stuffiest patrons of the arts who may have believed an Old Wild West cow town couldn't possibly have anything to offer.

It's understandable. After all, much of what America and the world believes about the Old West comes from movies that were filmed in the area and at the 1939 movie set, Old Tucson Studios. John Wayne filmed *Rio Bravo*, *El Dorado* and *Rio Lobo* there, kicking off what is now a $130 million movie industry for Arizona. Though we treasure our Wild West, American Indian and Mexican heritage, Tucson isn't all Stetsons and cattle talk.

The University of Arizona continues to expand the intellectual environment here and is currently on the cutting-edge of optics, astronomy and medicine. The brain power of Tucson has ranged from transplant innovations to alternative medicine to contributions for the recent exploration of Mars.

Tucson's economy is on an upswing. Economic forecasts estimate the creation of thousands of new jobs in 1998 in positions ranging from entry level to technical to corporate VPs. At the same time, the area's unemployment continues to hover around 2.9 percent. And though wages are not rising, fringe benefits are increasing, with some companies offering full fringe benefits for 20-hour-per-week jobs. The papers are full of want ads and the unemployment low, so who will fill the jobs? Maybe you.

But Tucsonans aren't all work and no play. This is, without question, a laid-back city. Dress in business, as well as recreation, is casual. Despite the triple-digit temperatures in the summer, the dry air is comfortable enough to allow more outdoor activities than visitors from the Midwest or East Coast might think possible. And we enjoy few things better than dining or relaxing on the outdoor patio or in the courtyard of practically any one of Tucson's restaurants or cafes.

The city's unique location in the desert makes for a daily picturesque environment unmatched by other Southwestern cities. Surrounded by majestic mountain ranges that contain county, state and federally protected lands, Tucson sees more than its share of pink and purple rock cliffs during our seemingly endless string of beautiful sunsets. The sky is so bright and clear and blue you'll write home about it. Our sunsets and scenery have drawn artists from all over the world to capture the beauty on canvas and in photographic print.

Most people are surprised by just how much green space we have in Tucson. After all, it is the desert, right? Besides the simple beauty of the natural desert area, the city is dotted with parks, offering everything from small lakes and rose gardens to picnic areas and golf courses. And in the winter when we want snow, it's a mere hour's drive to Mt. Lemmon in the Santa Catalina Mountains.

Believe it or not, cuisine isn't limited to steaks and chili. Tucson boasts a wide range of restaurants, many highly rated, fine dining experiences with their own unique twists on Southwestern, Italian, French and Continental cuisine. Needless to say, we also think we have the best Mexican food north of the border.

No matter what your appetite — outdoor recreation, awe-inspiring landscapes or the perfect enchilada — Tucson has something to satisfy it. So pack up your gear and this guide and begin your exploration of the Old Pueblo.

About the Authors

D.A. Barber

While attending college in upstate New York, David Barber had two loves: music and writing. After performing as a singer-songwriter throughout New England for six years, he moved to Los Angeles on a whim. But when his first published freelance feature won a Los Angeles Press Club Award for the *L.A. Weekly*, he knew what he wanted to do.

In succeeding years, Barber not only wrote for a variety of local and regional publications, but his radio reporting appeared on National Public Radio, California Public Radio, Canadian Broadcasting Commission and a number of syndicated commercial radio news shows. He also produced a call-in talk show in Los Angeles and a weekly radio newsmagazine on NPR's KCRW-FM in Santa Monica for two years.

When he returned to New York state, he helped start a statewide travel magazine that focused on the state recreational canal system; wrote for a weekly entertainment newspaper; and worked as news director at a commercial radio station and as a features writer for the daily *Utica Observer-Dispatch*.

In the course of his freelance career he's covered presidential news conferences, interviewed Ansel Adams and Edward Abbey, toured offshore oil rigs, tagged along on ocean research ships and produced full-length Public Radio documentaries. His material has appeared in numerous national magazines, including *New Age Journal*, *Ecology Digest*, *Communities Journal* and *Backpacker*.

In Tucson, Barber has written for every major publication in the region, including the *Tucson Weekly* and *Tucson Citizen,* and his features on life in the area appear regularly in the monthly *Desertleaf*. While program director for a local public radio station, he produced two weekly radio programs: one on the area arts scene and another on outdoor recreation. The connections he has made with his radio programs and writing have made him a true Tucson *Insider*.

Chris Howell

A transplanted Easterner who has lived in and loved Arizona for nearly 15 years, Chris Howell is thrilled to coauthor *The Insiders' Guide® to Tucson*.

On her first (and fateful) visit to the desert Southwest, she landed in Phoenix on a sunny, warm December day. In less than a year, Phoenix became her new home, followed seven years later by a move to Tucson.

Howell grew up on the shores of Lake Erie in Erie, Pennsylvania, and graduated from Pennsylvania State University. (She remains an avid and loyal fan of Penn State's winning football team and its longtime coach Joe Paterno.)

With a desire for adventure and new experiences, she headed for Chicago and soon found both a city to love and the start of her career as a wordsmith, working as an editor for the educational publishing division of Rand McNally & Co. Next she was an editor with Blue Cross Association and then a public affairs generalist with American Hospital Association.

While in Chicago, she earned a master's degree in marketing communications from Roosevelt University. But after living through 10 years of Chicago's ferocious winters, and despite loving the big-city life, she longed for a milder climate.

Phoenix became her new home, where she worked in marketing and public relations positions before relocating 100 miles south to Tucson. Howell eventually started her own business, TeeCee Creations, to provide writing, marketing and fund-raising services. She has written articles for Tucson Newspapers, Inc. (*Arizona Daily Star*) on subjects including allergies, senior fitness and the Tucson performing arts scene. For another client, Positive Promotions, she has written publications on health and safety topics.

Chris lives in the Tucson Foothills. Gardening, decorating and travels around Arizona and the Southwest occupy much of her free time, along with the all-important Saturday afternoon Penn State football games broadcast in the fall.

About the Researcher

Rita Connelly has lived in Tucson for more than 20 years, and during that time has seen it grow from a small Southwestern city into the sparkling metropolis it is today. A graduate of the University of Arizona, she majored in English and earned a degree in secondary education. She has written on many topics, but the focus of her work is food, food, food. Her articles have appeared in *Pool & Spa Living Magazine*; *Grill & Barbecue Business*; *Broker*Agent Magazine* and numerous local publications. She lives halfway between the University and the mountains with her husband, John, and daughter, Riene.

viii • ACKNOWLEDGMENTS

The moon rises quietly over the desert.

Acknowledgments

Chris . . .

I, too, was once a newcomer to Tucson. In fact, when I first arrived in Arizona, I knew nary a soul and absolutely nothing about my new surroundings (except that it was warm and gorgeous). In the nearly two decades since, I've learned much about my adopted homeland, which is one reason it was my good fortune to be selected by Insiders' Publishing to convey Tucson's treasures and pleasures to lots of other tourists and newcomers.

During the course of writing all about Tucson — its natural world, transportation, campgrounds and RV parks, shopping, attractions for grownups as well as kids, golf, sports, education, air force base, neighborhoods and real estate, retirement living, and daytrips and getaways to surrounding areas — I also found out there was much to learn. For example, I discovered something as seemingly basic as what Arizona's state flower is (but you'll have to read the Daytrips and Weekend Getaways chapter to find out) and learned that golf courses have strange things called signature holes and bentgrass greens.

But I also learned that it takes a great deal of help to pull together this amount of information, especially when the subject matter is totally foreign to me (such as, you guessed it, golf).

For starters, hundreds of total strangers took their time in person and over the phone to answer my countless questions. One of my first contacts was a woman at the Metropolitan Tucson Convention and Visitors Bureau who, with her delightful accent and even more delightful smile, enthusiastically talked to me about many Tucson topics. So to all those people at stores, government offices, airports, schools and many more places who took the time to educate and inform me, a big thanks.

But it was some dear and wonderful friends who made it possible for me to complete this project. Vini Lacsamana, who knows both golf courses and Tucson better than the rest of us know our Social Security numbers, spent hours filling me in on both. Lynn and George McLean, also golf aficionados, did their utmost to help me see what they see in the sport. Juan (actually John) Wolfe, the ultimate computer guru, also did his utmost to try to transform my meager knowledge of the machine into something workable. And real estate guru (and lovely person) Barbara Hodges was my inside connection to Tucson's real estate scene and diverse neighborhoods. Nancy and Roger Ingersoll enlightened me about shopping (that was Nancy), introduced me to Mexico many years ago and listened often during my months of work on this book. Shelly and Ed Berger, parents extraordinaire, gave me great insight into things kids like to do in Tucson and also imparted knowledge about real estate (that was Ed).

A big thanks also to Rita Connelly, who helped us authors by taking on the research for several chapters in this book and went above and beyond the call of duty. My thanks also to Insiders' Publishing for selecting me to write about this land I love and to this book's always patient and pleasant editor, Amy Baynard.

And to borrow a line from Hollywood's Oscar awards, I thank my parents, who among many other things gave me the opportunity to attend college and somewhere along the way discover my talent with the written word.

Finally but foremost, my gratitude to the person who helped me the most (and also happens to be the best person I have ever known) my love, Bob Scheuneman.

David . . .

I'd like to give special thanks to the people of Tucson and everyone in this great city who helped with this book. Most of all, I'd like to thank my editor, Amy Baynard, and the publisher of Insiders' Publishing, Beth Storie, for pushing me to my limits.

Rita . . .

This project was great fun — I learned something, met lots of new people and earned some money . . . what more could you ask for? I especially want to thank Nickie M. Aiken, friend and photographer extraordinaire, for sharing her photos for The Natural World chapter; Ray McKee, from the City of Tucson Parks and Recreation Department, for all the great photos from his files (thanks to his boss, Barb Hayes, for her assistance in where to get started with the Parks and Recreation research); thanks to all the wonderful people at Tucson Arts District Partnership for their friendly help whenever I called or stopped by; thanks to Pat Perry at the Metropolitan Tucson Convention and Visitors Bureau, Jamie Eggolt at Old Tucson Studios, Nancy at The Gaslight Theater and to all the other people who kindly shared their slides and photos. An added thanks to Dawn Moriarity at Congregation Anshie Israel, Dan Bronson at Regina Cleary Center and Douglas R. McKinley for their information for the Worship chapter. Thanks to writer Chris Howell; she was great to work with and offerd a ton of support along the way.

Finally, a big thanks to my husband, John Connelly, and my daughter, Riene, for their encouragement, support and input through this project.

A Special Thanks . . .

Insiders' Publishing would like to thank Rita Connelly for providing the photographs and contributing to the research of *The Insiders' Guide® to Tucson*.

Table of Contents

History 1
Area Overview 7
Getting Here, Getting Around 15
Accommodations 27
Bed and Breakfasts 41
Campgrounds and RV Parks 49
Restaurants 57
Nightlife 85
Shopping 95
Attractions 115
Kidstuff 131
Festivals and Events 143
Arts and Culture 155
The Natural World 181
Parks and Recreation 193
Golf 207
Bicycling 219
Spectator Sports 229
Davis-Monthan Air Force Base 241
Daytrips and Weekend Getaways 247
Neighborhoods, Neighboring Towns and Real Estate 267
Education and Child Care 285
Healthcare 297
Retirement 307
Media 321
Worship 329
Index of Advertisers 332
Index 332

Directory of Maps

Tucson and Surrounding Area xii
Downtown Tucson xiii
Tucson Bike Trails 218

Tucson and Surrounding Area

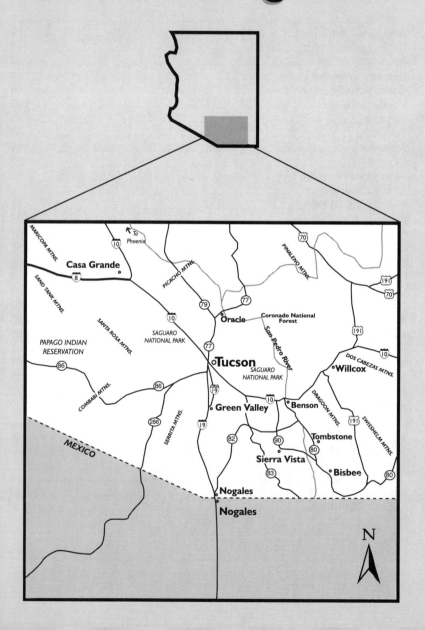

Downtown Tucson

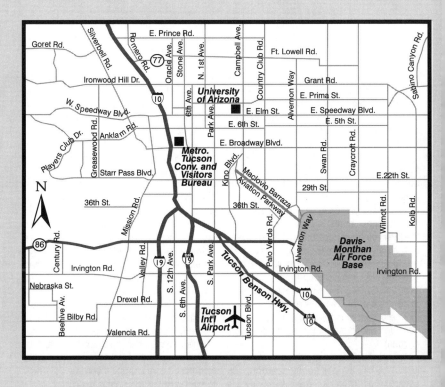

How to Use This Book

Maybe you're visiting Tucson on a family vacation or business trip. Perhaps you've just relocated to Tucson or plan to soon. Or maybe you're a "snowbird" — the term Southwesterners use for winter visitors who take flight from the snow states to spend all or most of the winter in our inviting valley. No matter why you're here or how long, you'll find this the most thorough and interesting guide to the city and surrounding areas available.

The Tucson area is alive with unique and fascinating flora and fauna, with a multitude of outdoor recreation offerings, with restaurants, attractions, nightlife and lodging to suit any taste and budget and with sports for everyone from bleacher bums to birders to bicyclists. We'll tell you how to get there, what you'll see, how much it will cost and impart some Insiders' facts (and well-founded opinions) to help you choose wisely among the vast array of things to do, see and experience in Tucson. We even give you a complete primer on crossing the border to Nogales, Mexico (not to be confused with its stateside neighbor Nogales, Arizona).

Tucson's city limits are actually rather limited. The city proper comprises only 125 square miles. Therefore, much of what you'll see and do in Tucson is located in the metropolitan area of Pima County that surrounds the City of Tucson. So even though we say "Tucson" on this book's cover and throughout its pages, keep in mind that we are really referring to a metropolitan area of approximately 500 square miles that extends from one mountain range to another. Like most Southwestern cities, Tucson has developed outward rather than upward. You'll find very few high-rises here, but you will find a lot of land to traverse getting from one attraction on the far east side, for example, to another "way out west." Just be patient. With our help you will get there, and it will be worth the trek.

Each chapter of this book covers a specific topic (or combines related topics). We think we've covered every subject that would be of interest and value to any traveler or newcomer. It's easy to zero in on restaurants if sating your appetite is on your mind; or on our Golf chapter if you're longing to hit the links; or how to tune in a country-western radio station as you drive down Interstate 19 to the border. If you're just arriving to Tucson by air, turn to our Getting Here and Getting Around chapter and find out how to get where you're going in town — without breaking any rules of the road along the way. Read the Natural World chapter and you'll soon know as much as Tucsonans about the strangely fascinating cacti, our summer monsoons and the four mountain ranges that surround the valley of Tucson. If you're looking for a Spanish-language newspaper or how to find National Public Radio, dial in the Media chapter. And don't skip the History chapter if you want to know the origin of Tucson's name and lots more.

Within each chapter, the information typically is subdivided to help you easily find a specific type of cuisine, a place to shop for American Indian jewelry or pottery, or nearby nightlife if you're staying in the downtown area. Places are listed alphabetically within each chapter or subsection of a chapter.

You won't be in Tucson long before you hear or see some strange-sounding words. Many of our words for places, streets and natural things

HOW TO USE THIS BOOK • xv

are from the Spanish or American Indian languages. Tucsonans are accustomed to them, but you might not be. So in several chapters we include a pronunciation key of foreign words used in that chapter. You'll want to take the time to learn the correct pronunciation.

You'll notice that, throughout this book, we tell you that we only list area codes with phone numbers if they differ from the 520 area code. But you will see the 520 preceding the phone number in certain listings. In these cases, our inclusion of the 520 means that the call is considered to be "long distance" when dialed from Tucson, even though it's still within the 520 area code. (Except for the Phoenix area, which is area code 602, all the rest of Arizona is in area code 520.) So in cases where you must dial the area code from Tucson, we indicate that by including the 520 along with the seven-digit phone number. Expect to be charged for the call accordingly. (If you dial the seven-digit number only, a recording will announce the error of your ways but may not be helpful enough to tell you the way to correct it.)

If we'd included everything in the Tucson area, this book would be far too weighty to travel with you in a glove compartment, briefcase or backpack. The philosophy of Insiders' Publishing Inc. is to cover the best and the brightest of what a city has to offer. And while we have made every effort to be accurate and include all the highlights of Tucson, we're only human. If you find mistakes in our book, if you disagree with something we've said, if you'd like to recommend additions or changes in future editions or if you'd like to compliment us on a job well-done, we would appreciate hearing from you at our corporate offices:

The Insiders' Guide® to Tucson
P.O. Box 2057
Manteo, North Carolina 27954
or at our website (www.insiders.com).

Scientists uncovered the largest Southwest settlement of the Late Archaic period along the Santa Cruz River.

History

Early Tucsonans

The Tucson area is one of the oldest continually inhabited cities in the United States. Scientists once believed that the Hohokam were the first people here, but the theory was disproved in 1997 when scientists uncovered the largest Southwest settlement of the Late Archaic period along the Santa Cruz River. The settlement dated back to the Cienega phase (800 B.C. to 150 A.D.). The Cienega were farmers in a time dominated by nomadic hunters and gatherers. They grew corn, beans, squash and tobacco. They traded with others throughout the Southwest for shells and other trinkets that they then used in making jewelry. The settlement's 171 pit dwellings, storehouses and communal structures are believed to have been occupied between 760 B.C. and 200 B.C., several centuries before the better-known Mogollon, Anasazi and Hohokam cultures.

The Hohokam occupied an area along the Santa Cruz River (known then as the Rio de Santa Maria) near what is now downtown Tucson from 600 A.D. to 1450 A.D. They irrigated and farmed the area for 700 years. The Hohokam were a dominant culture in the Southwest and built 200 miles of canals in the Phoenix area to irrigate their crops. They also settled the Tucson area's riverbanks. Hohokam is a Tohono O'odham word meaning "those who have vanished," and anthropologists still debate their disappearance. Some have suggested that the Hohokam may have been the ancestors of the Tohono O'odham, who currently live in the area.

Other Indian tribes followed the Hohokam into the area, settling along the Santa Cruz River and farming the valley. The Tohono O'odham clustered at the foot of Sentinel Peak (now known as "A" Mountain, named for the large "A" built of rocks and painted by University of Arizona students in October 1915). The Tohono O'odham incorporated this prominent volcanic "black mountain" when they named their village Stjukshonso (pronounced "Chukson"), meaning "spring at the foot of dark mountain." Stjukshonso evolved into the name Tucson after European settlers arrived.

Spanish Discovery

Spanish explorers Cabez de Vaca, Maros de Niza and Vasquez de Coronado swept through the Southwest in search of gold almost a century before the Pilgrims landed on Plymouth Rock. Niza was sent by the Spanish Viceroy of Mexico to search for the fabled Seven Cities of Cibola (which he never found), but his reports back to Mexico led to Coronado's famous expedition and "discovery" of the area in 1540 (the Coronado National Forest was named for this early explorer). Coronado found several groups of Indians living peacefully and farming the fertile river valley, and he also found the nomadic Apache, who were less friendly. As many more treasure-seeking expeditions came north through the area from Mexico, word continued to get back to the Spanish Empire. It wasn't until the late 1600s, however, that Europeans established any settlements.

When Jesuit Padre Francisco Eusebio Kino, "The Priest on Horseback," arrived to the area, the Tohono O'odham were thriving in a village at the base of Sentinel Peak, farming the fertile valley of the then-flowing Santa Cruz River. Kino, an explorer, cartographer and scientist, established a mission in the area. He taught agricultural techniques and introduced Christianity to the area natives.

Father Kino established a number of missions in the Southwest, including Mission San Jose de Tumacacori, south of Tucson near Tubac, and San Xavier del Bac, "the White Dove of the Desert," located 19 miles south of downtown. San Xavier still stands today. A statue honoring Kino on horseback now graces Kino Boulevard near the Lewis C. Murphy overpass in Tucson. Duplicate statues stand in the Mexican city and state of Magdalena and Sonora and in Italy, which was Kino's homeland.

Kino was more interested in the San Xavier del Bac mission and spent little time in the Tucson Indian village, so the natives were spared the restraints of mission life for half a century. Kino died in 1711, and visits by other priests were infrequent at best.

In 1757 Bernardo Middendorf, a German-born Jesuit, arrived to build a new mission at the village. This mission was short-lived as four months later some 500 Apaches attacked from the mountains and destroyed the site; Middendorf barely escaped.

Five years earlier, the Spanish army established a presidio at Tubac, about 40 miles south of Tucson where a Jesuit mission had been created in 1691. In 1762 the Spanish army tried to reinforce Tucson against Apache attacks by moving the Sobaipuris Indians (relatives of the Tohono O'odham) from the San Pedro River to the village on the Santa Cruz River. Because they were on the San Pedro, the Sobaipuris were receiving the brunt of Apache attacks; yet, by moving what had become Tucson's first line of defense against the Apaches, Tucson actually became more vulnerable to raids.

It wasn't until 1775 that the Spanish army made the decision to move the garrison from Tubac to Tucson. Lt. Col. Don Hugo O'Conor arrived in Tucson and with Father Francisco Garces selected a presidio site. Plans for the Presidio of San Augustin de Tucson included a 12-foot adobe wall for defense against the Apaches. Construction was slow going: By November 1779, the walls were only 4 feet tall. A force of some 375 Apaches attacked Tucson only to be driven off by Capt. Don Pedro de Allande, the fort's commandant. In May 1782, another 600 Apaches attacked the Spanish fort but once again were repelled by Capt. Allande. After these two failed attacks, the Apaches and the Spanish settlers formed a peace that would last until the 1830s.

The Spanish army completed the presidio in 1783. It consisted of a walled garden and more than 20 buildings, including a two-story convent, a chapel, barracks for soldiers, stables and a granary. The presidio covered about 12 acres and included the downtown area outlined by Church Street on the east, Washington Street on the north, Main Avenue on the west and Pennington Street on the south — basically the heart of today's downtown business district. Some historians believe it's the only walled city in our nation's history, and it's from this structure that Tucson gets its nickname: The Old Pueblo.

Mexican Rule

The Mexican Revolution bypassed Tucson for the most part, and the Spanish flag continued to fly until Mexico gained her independence from Spain in 1821. For the 65 European settlers in the presidio, it only meant changing their flag — life went on as usual. Farming, sheep and cattle ranching and trapping in the mountains continued with limited contact with the outside world. What did change was residential development outside the walls of the presidio. Lacking a seaport for the transportation of goods in the early 1800s, the area depended on the Mexican port of Guaymas from which goods were transported by wagon, creating a new business of "freighters" in the Old Pueblo.

INSIDERS' TIP

The Tucson-based Arizona Historical Society sponsors annual tours of many Sonoran-area missions established by Father Kino. The museum, at 949 E. Second Street, houses an extensive research library and archives. Call 795-4043 for more information.

HISTORY • 3

This statue in Fort Lowell Park memorializes the soldiers who were early settlers of the fort.

A United States Territory

When the United States signed the Gadsden Purchase in 1854, some 30,000 square miles of Arizona and the Southwest became part of the United States' New Mexico Territory. However, Tucson remained a Mexican garrison until March 1856 when the Mexican army packed up and left. It wasn't until November that U.S. Dragoons rode into town and raised the U.S. flag atop the Miles Mercantile Store. For the next few years Anglos and American goods began arriving in the area. These relations between Mexicans and Anglos formed the backbone of today's rich culture.

In 1858 the Butterfield Overland Route brought the first stagecoaches to Tucson, making it one of 16 stations in Arizona. By 1860 the city's non-Indian population had grown to more than 600, but many were rough characters who had been chased out of California. Tucson quickly gained a reputation as a law-

INSIDERS' TIP

The 1904 City Directory listed 25 saloons that served the city with wide-open gambling 24 hours a day.

less Western town. Street fights were daily events, and most people carried weapons. A plaza whipping post was established to dish out punishment since there was no jail.

The outbreak of the Civil War called American federal troops from all over the frontier back East. Their departure left the settlers defenseless against the Apaches, who had resumed their attacks in the 1830s. Tucson, encompassed by its adobe walls, became one of a few territorial refuges for miners and ranchers in the area. When 200 mounted Confederate soldiers arrived from Texas on February 28, 1862, Tucsonans greeted them happily — but not for long. Word came that 2,000 Union California volunteers under Col. James Carleton would soon arrive from Yuma, so the Texans retreated home. On May 20, 1862, Union Col. Joseph R. West took possession of Tucson.

By the time Lincoln gave Arizona territorial status and named Prescott the capital, Tucson's reputation for gambling, prostitution and filthy streets was common reading in Eastern newspapers. But despite the lawlessness, Tucson had garnered enough political clout by 1867 to force a vote to change the territorial capital from Prescott to Tucson. The Old Pueblo was the capital for 10 years until the power of northern mining interests helped return the title to Prescott.

During this decade, Tucson fast became a "city" and a bustling business and transportation crossroads. The population in 1869 was 3,200 people. By 1872, a public school had been built. Tucson had two flour mills, four livery stables, two hotels, two breweries and numerous saloons. Roulette wheels turned 24 hours a day until 1905. The first Southern Pacific railroad train arrived in March 1880. That same year, the state's first hospital, St. Mary's, was built in Tucson. The city's first telephone rang in 1881, and gas-operated street lights were turned on for the first time in Tucson on March 20, 1882. Suddenly Tucson was a bit less "Wild West." Ironically, that same night Wyatt Earp shot and killed Frank Stilwell at the Tucson railroad station, taking revenge for his brother Morgan's death in Tombstone earlier that week.

The influx of more white settlers led to intensified attacks on the surrounding area by the Apaches. U.S. troops constructed Fort Lowell to protect Tucson and nearby ranchers. The raids ended in 1886 when Geronimo, the last great Apache leader, surrendered. The fort was deactivated in 1891. Remnants still stand in Ft. Lowell Park in what is now central Tucson. The "fort" is listed on the National Register of Historic Places.

Building a University

Due to a grant of $25,000 from the Thirteenth Territorial Legislature in 1885, Tucson agreed to establish a university — the first in a territory that had no high schools. Though politicians believed the university would bring economic benefits, the citizens wanted to be returned to territorial capital status. After all, a university might have a negative influence on the city's gambling.

The city's territorial legislators left for Prescott to force a vote to return the capital to Tucson. But in an unfortunate chain of events, inclement weather delayed them. When the legislators finally arrived, they found that Prescott had already won. Tucson was tossed money for a university as a consolation prize. When the delegation returned to Tucson, they were pelted with rotten fruit and vegetables.

The city fathers convinced a pair of wealthy gamblers and a saloon owner to donate land for the university, which they did — with a catch. The land was situated as far away from downtown gambling saloons as possible to keep away any high-minded influences. The spot was 3 miles across the desert. By 1891 "Old Main," as it's known today, opened its doors on about 40 acres of land to 32 students and six faculty members. Today, more than 35,000 students are enrolled at the University of Arizona, and the campus, once in the middle of the desert, is now in the heart of the city.

A New Era and A New State

By 1886, Geronimo and his band of renegade Chiricahua Apaches had been exiled to Florida, ending the official Indian Wars (of almost 30 years) with the "Blue Coats" in this part of the west. That was the beginning of the end for "Wild West" Tucson. In 1896 the first mule-driven streetcars started running, and the following year the first "horseless carriage" sputtered down the dirt streets. By 1906 the mules were replaced with electric streetcars, making a 3-mile loop from downtown to the University.

On a territorial level, Arizona had begun its battle for statehood driven by lawmakers in the territorial capital, which was finally relocated to Phoenix in 1889. The battle ended on February 14, 1912, when President Taft made Arizona the 48th state. Tucson's population was 13,125.

Along with the new status in the country came a new frontier — flight. Aviation came to Tucson on February 17, 1910, when barnstorming pilot Charles Hamilton flew his biplane a mere 900 feet above the ground to thrill spectators. In 1915, 19-year-old Katharine Stinson, a daredevil pilot, delivered the first airmail to the city. But these were just tastes of what was to come. The aviation age arrived in Tucson formally when the city built the nation's first municipally-owned airport in 1919. In 1927 Charles Lindbergh dedicated Tucson's next airport, the Davis-Monthan Field — today an Air Force base. By the 1930s the U.S. Army Air Corps was using Davis-Monthan Field; they finally took it over completely in 1940 and separated the two air fields into commercial and military uses.

By 1920 the population had grown to 20,292, and the first of many resort hotels had been built to draw Easterners to Arizona's warm, dry climate. Many came to these elaborate resorts hoping the climate would cure tuberculosis. In 1931 the electric trolley cars were replaced by gas-powered buses, just like a "real" city.

Hollywood discovered Tucson in 1939 when movie producers built what became Old Tucson Studios as a set for the epic movie *Arizona* (see the Attractions chapter). Since then hundreds of movies, television shows and commercials have been made there.

Tucson's population boomed during World War II. People were seeking military employment. The military had taken over Davis-Monthan Field as a base for training pilots to fly B-17 bombers. After the war, the U.S. Army Air Corps officially became the United States Air Force; the name of the base was changed to Davis-Monthan Air Force Base. Huge hangars were built for B-24 bomber modifications (see our chapter on Davis-Monthan Air Force Base.)

By 1950, the population was 55,454 in the city and 118,034 in the metropolitan area. The increase in population is attributed to the return of many servicemen and their families to Tucson after the war as well as the advent of air conditioning. In the 1960s and '70s the city focused on developing the arts. In 1967, the Arizona Theater Company was founded here as the state's only professional resident theater company. The state's only resident opera company, The Arizona Opera Company, was founded in 1972 and based in Tucson. Three years later the Tucson Museum of Art was built near the original presidio in downtown Tucson.

During the 1980s, highly technical businesses began moving to Tucson, led by aviation-related technologies. The metropolitan area's population grew a whopping 22.6 percent with a population figure of 431,988 in 1993. During this period Madison Avenue advertising agencies began using the deep, saguaro-studded desert to sell everything from cars to beer to jeans to credit cards. The constant romantic image of the West in print and TV ads spurred growth in Arizona's population as many Easterners left their homes to discover the new promised land.

In recent years gambling has returned to Tucson in the form of Indian casinos. In 1992 after a bitter fight with the now ousted Governor Fife Symington over the 1988 Indian Gaming Regulatory Act signed by President Reagan, the Tohono O'odham opened one of the state's first reservation casinos south of the city. Today, Tucson has two Indian casinos (see our Attractions chapter).

Tucson has maintained its relationship with nearby Mexico as a trading partner. The passage of the North American Free Trade Agreement signed in 1993 helped Tucson and Arizona expand their international market.

As Tucson rolls through the 1990s, the city watches major expansion and breakthroughs at the University of Arizona, including participation in the space program and major optics and agricultural research. And the University's Integrated Medicine Center, established 1997, is the first in the nation. The University is also pushing for a future Technologies Park to draw spin-off business to the Old Pueblo's newfound obsession: high technology.

But despite the growth and influx of high-tech industry, the blend of American Indian, Hispanic and European cultures can still be felt throughout the city.

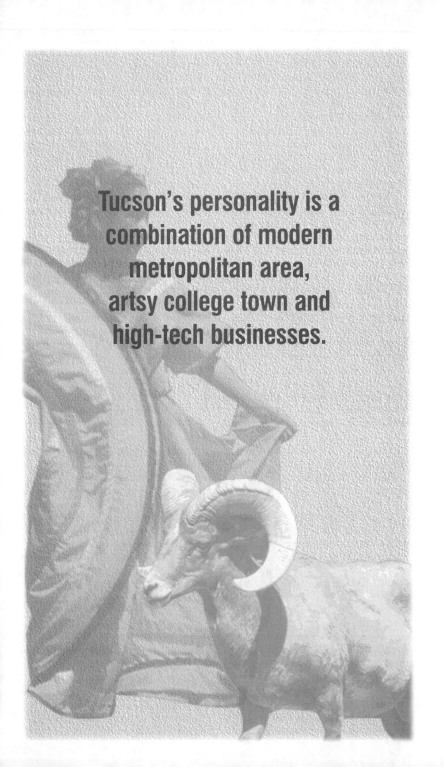

Tucson's personality is a combination of modern metropolitan area, artsy college town and high-tech businesses.

Area Overview

By all definitions, you can't get more Sunbelt than Tucson, Arizona. The city's personality is a combination of great climate, modern metropolitan area, artsy college town, incredible landscapes, classy resorts and high-tech businesses, all intersecting with a cultural heritage that has been molded by influences from Spanish, American Indian, Mexican and Anglo pioneers. With the Mexican border just 60 miles south, the area continues to embrace its Mexican heritage and be influenced economically by its neighbors south of the border. Tucson is the county seat of Pima County, a 9,240-square-mile area larger than the state of Massachusetts and Arizona's entryway to trade with Mexico. It is only a few hours drive to two of Mexico's foremost commercial cities: Hermosillo and Guaymas. Tucson is also a four-hour drive to what is considered "Arizona's Beach," Puerto Penasco, or Rocky Point, in Mexico.

From its roots as a Spanish presidio along the Santa Cruz River, where downtown now lies, to the metropolitan area of today, Tucson has been a classic study in planned urban sprawl, stretching east and north. The urbanized area covers more than 412 square miles, with the City of Tucson covering 125 square miles. The area sits on a sloping plain between 2,000 and 3,000 feet above sea level in a basin surrounded by the Santa Catalina Mountains to the north and northeast, the Rincon Mountains to the east, the Santa Rita and Sierrita Mountains to the south and southeast and the Tucson Mountains to the west. It's this combination of relatively high altitude and surrounding mountain ranges that contributes to Tucson's dry climate. The city also lies in a zone that receives more sunshine than any other section of the United States, resulting in 350 sunny days per year. And though the temperatures can reach more than 100 degrees in the summer months (expect about 140 days with temperatures above 90 degrees per year), the low humidity keeps it pretty comfortable. On the other hand, an hour's drive up Mt. Lemmon in the winter months brings you to a ski area that is located farther south than any other ski area in the United States, giving you the opportunity to ski in the morning and bask by your Tucson pool in the afternoon.

The Old Pueblo has much to boast about. The University of Arizona has been ranked 10th among research universities by the National Science Foundation. The Metropolitan Tucson Convention and Visitors Bureau has won seven Gold Service Awards for the past seven years as one of the best convention and visitors bureaus in the world. Pima Community College is the largest multicampus community college in Arizona and the fifth largest in the nation. The University of Arizona Wildcats basketball team made history in 1997 by winning the NCAA championship. Also in 1997 The Tucson Hispanic Chamber of Commerce was named the best Hispanic chamber in the west (excluding California) by the United States Hispanic Chamber of Commerce.

What most people know about Tucson, and Arizona in general, is the impression they've gleaned from the more than 200 movies, TV programs and commercials that have been filmed in the area, but there is much more to Tucson than dusty trails, cacti and ghosts of banditos.

Geographic Growth

What started out as a small presidio evolved first to a series of barrios multiplying slowly across the valley and then an urbanized sprawl stretching north to the base of the Santa Catalina, west to the Tucson and east to the Rincon mountains. This is fairly typical of cities in the desert Southwest, and Tucson continues the tradition of stretching out, instead of building up with East Coast-style high-rises.

Tucson's growth can be read in layers, like studying the geologic record left by soil deposits. The layers are reflected in the architecture. The move to barrios outside the original presidio can be seen in the adobe houses within the city's oldest neighborhoods. The post-World War II explosion in population is reflected in the '50s-style apartments and houses in the central/University area of town.

During the 1980s, Pima County's population grew by 25.8 percent, well above the national average of 10 percent during that time period. Growth during the 1990s has included modern homes in the Foothills and northwest with numerous gated communities of town houses that seem to go up in a matter of months. The city, aware of the inevitable expansion, initiated the Livable Tucson Vision Program within the city limits in 1997. It's a futuristic program in which neighborhoods are asked to submit blueprints for how the city should grow and prioritize topics the city should concentrate on, such as crime, traffic and development. The program began in late 1997 and is designed to help city government deal with the impact of growth on Tucson's established neighborhoods.

While in Tucson, you will no doubt hear the terms "growth" and "water issues" used in the same sentence. Tucson is the largest, if not the only, city in the country that relies totally on ground water. The underground water table has dropped 200 feet in portions of central Tucson since heavy pumping began in the 1940s. Though it's estimated that Tucson has about 100 years of water left below the surface, the problem was supposed to be solved when the massive canal system known as the Central Arizona Project (CAP) began shipping water south from the Colorado River in 1993. When the project finally brought water into local homes, consumers complained about the treated river water's odor, taste and color. The CAP water was even corroding pipes in homes and city water mains. In November 1995, Tucson residents voted to cut off CAP water for use in homes and require the river water to be used only for mining and farming operations and to recharge the ground water. This has brought Tucson full circle to relying totally on ground water for the immediate future.

By far the fastest growing area in metropolitan Tucson is the northwest, outside the city limits. From retirement communities to gated town-house complexes to plush resorts, the northwest is considered to be the last frontier for development in the Tucson area. The other area seeing much activity is the southeast, where the Science and Technology Park is located. Two new planned-community developments are slated for this area.

Growth brings traffic, and several main roads in the Foothills area are already overcapacity, prompting Pima County to begin a $485 million, decade-long road widening project in that area. In fact, numerous street upgrading projects go on almost continuously in metropolitan Tucson as the area deals with its increasing traffic woes. Luckily, it's not really that bad, but with the projected growth of the area, officials aren't waiting for gridlock to act. According to Pima County, by the year 2020, Tucson's traffic will be similar to that of Phoenix in 1980. Today, Phoenix deals with daily gridlock and has constantly been in violation of federal air pollution standards due to the high volume of traffic. Tucson has not been in violation of the air standards since 1988, and officials want to keep it that way so we can all breath easier.

The People

Tucson has been a cross-section of American Indian, Spanish, Mexican and Anglo inhabitants since its early days. Today this unique mix of cultures gives the area its flavor. The city is not so much near a border as it is within a borderland, and Mexican-American culture permeates Tucson. The 1990 census put Pima County's population of Hispanic origin at 25 percent, but the Census Bureau took a lot of heat for that ridiculously low number. Unofficial estimates put the number closer to 37 percent.

The area is home to two major Indian reservations: the Pascua Yaqui Tribe on 895 acres

---

www.insiders.com

See this and many other **Insiders' Guide®** destinations online — in their entirety.

Visit us today!

The domed Pima County Courthouse is one of the most recognizable and beautiful buildings in Tucson.

with 9,000 members, and the Tohono O'odham Nation on 2.8 million acres with nearly 19,000 members. Both reservations operate Indian gaming casinos — Desert Diamond Casino and Casino of the Sun — that have helped life at these underfunded reservations tremendously, despite the State of Arizona's numerous past attacks on the concept of Indian gaming statewide (see our Attractions chapter).

Tucson is a well-educated community, with more than 80 percent of the population having earned a high school diploma or higher, compared to the national level of 66 percent. In addition, 23.3 percent of the area's working population has a bachelor degree or higher and 9 percent has a graduate or professional degree.

Today, standing in a line at a bank, don't be surprised if you're surrounded by someone in a military uniform; a rancher donning blue jeans and a cowboy hat; a lawyer attired in a three-piece suit; an American Indian artist with exceptionally long, beautiful black hair; a green-haired rock musician; a Mexican-American businessman; and a blond California transplant. The contrast is typical of Tucson's growing population. And as the September 1997 issue of *Condé Nast Traveler* magazine pointed out when it ranked Tucson as the friendliest city in the country, everybody is welcome in the Old Pueblo.

Working in Tucson

Tucson has always had a reputation for being a low-wage town, and because of that city officials have been actively drawing high-tech businesses that offer high paying jobs. But the jobs currently being created by the relocation of companies and new start-ups continue to offer relatively low wages compared to other areas — an average of about $24,000 per year — despite the fact that Tucson ranks in the top-10 out of 300 metropolitan areas for overall wage growth per

INSIDERS' TIP

Tucson's entire downtown area is uniquely compact. So much so that you can actually cover the whole district on foot many times over in an afternoon. If you have business downtown, don't be afraid to park and walk — you won't have to go far.

employee. The reason for the discrepancy is a labor surplus and a low unemployment rate. Yet people are willing to work for less money just to stay in this fast-growing, sun-drenched Southwestern city. To add to the paradox, Tucson continues to be one of the least affordable housing markets, ranking among the 50 worst in the country based on the continuing high cost of an average single-family home.

But job production remains on the upswing. A July 1997 report from DRI/McGraw-Hill ranked Tucson 13th out of 114 major metropolitan areas for job creation "over the next five years."

Southern Arizona's Top-10 Employers

1. U.S. Army Fort Huachuca
2. University of Arizona
3. State of Arizona
4. Tucson Unified School District
5. Davis-Monthan Air Force Base
6. Pima County
7. Hughes Missile Systems
8. City of Tucson
9. BHP Copper
10. HealthPartners of Southern Arizona

— According to "Star 200," *Arizona Daily Star*, March 1997

Economy

Tucson's proximity to the Mexican border has always had an impact on the region's economy. In fact, Arizona's exports to Mexico total close to $2 billion a year, and since 1988, the state's exports to Mexico, Japan and France have increased by 150 percent — more per capita than New York. Tucson is the gateway to Mexico, leading to the city being named one of the top-10 cities in North America for international companies by *World Trade Magazine*. With the passage of the North American Free Trade Agreement in January 1994, Tucson's status as a global gateway to Mexico and South America has only been enhanced, positioning the area to export its expertise in industrial equipment, telecommunications, electronics and financial services.

The military too has always had a strong presence here and, over the next few years, Davis-Monthan Air Force Base (which continues to avoid any base closings lists and is home to the 355th Tactical Training Wing, the nation's only A-10 training facility) will be spending $25 million to extend its main runway, as well as building a new control tower and fire substation. The construction will result in Pima County and the City of Tucson spending $13.2 million in contracting crews to realign Valencia Road in what is expected to be one of many road widening projects throughout the region over the next decade.

And while Tucson's proximity to Mexico and its relationship with the military has afforded it many economic advantages, Tucson's pro-business organizations acknowledge that an estimated 80 percent of local business can be roughly defined as "small businesses." The entrepreneurial spirit is alive and well in Tucson.

The Greater Tucson Economic Council (a partnership between Pima County, the City of Tucson and the business community) has targeted specific kinds of industrial clusters for relocation to the area, which has resulted in the creation of more than 4,000 jobs in the last two years. These include defense/aerospace, health/biomedical, optics, environmental technologies and software/information systems. When you include jobs created by local busi-

INSIDERS' TIP

Tucson's carefree lifestyle is reflected in the attire of its residents — casual, yet practical. In the summer you'll want a wide-brim hat and sunglasses, and on winter evenings, the temperature can drop by more than 30 degrees, so you may need a jacket.

nesses, Tucson has seen more than 16,000 new jobs over the past two years. According to the Tucson Chamber of Commerce, there are currently 27,000 businesses located in Tucson.

The area has become one of the top five locations in the country for telemarketing operations and is becoming known as Optics Valley, due to the more than 50 innovative optics businesses that have sprouted up in the area. Environmental technology is another fast-growing segment of Tucson's relocated companies. In late 1997 there were already some 31 companies, with an estimated 50 companies expected to be here by mid-1998. The growth of these companies in Tucson is a direct result of the planned American-Mexican border cleanup that is part of the NAFTA agreement. The companies will be providing technical expertise to border towns for upgrade of sewer systems and removal of toxic dumps.

The University of Arizona has been instrumental in Tucson's high-tech growth, establishing the Science and Technology Park on the southeast side of the metropolitan area just off Interstate 10 near Houghton Road. This complex was built by IBM in the late 1970s and, at its peak, employed 5,000 people. When IBM pulled out much of its operation in 1989 and 1990, it left behind about 1,000 workers and a $13 million state-of-the-art, 345-acre complex of 12 buildings. The site is self-sustaining, with its own water wells, a railroad spur, sewage treatment plant, power plant, a gray water system to recycle water for toilets and landscaping, recreation center and cafeteria.

In 1994 the University of Arizona acquired the site (considered the largest real estate deal ever in Tucson), establishing the Science and Technology Park. With very little marketing, the University was able to lease space out to a variety of technology-related companies. Today, some 4,000 people work at the Park, including Hughes Missile Systems, IBM and many smaller software and information systems companies. The goal is to create a world-class research park, much like the Research Triangle Park in North Carolina and the Stanford University Research Park in California to function as a support site to incubate high-technology businesses.

Tourism

In its 16 years, The Metropolitan Tucson Convention and Visitors Bureau has gone from securing 104 conferences and group meetings to drawing 680 conventions of 300,000 people — having a $152.6 million impact on the community. The year-round sunny weather is a big draw for those planning their annual conventions, and Tucson has become a favorite spot for those gatherings.

Encouraged by these numbers, resorts and accommodations have spent millions of dollars either renovating or building new hotels to woo convention organizers as well as tourists. In the Foothills, all the area's plush resorts have seen multimillion dollar upgrades during the past two years including the Sheraton El Conquistador, at $5 million; the Westin La Paloma, at $5.3 million; the Loews Ventana Canyon, at $2.8 million; and The Lodge at Ventana Canyon, at $15 million (see our Accommodations chapter).

Tourism in Tucson today is a $1.54 billion industry accounting for 12 percent of the area's workforce. Many come to see the area's natural wonders, such as Saguaro National Park (2 million people per year), Sabino Canyon Recreation area (1.5 million people per year), Mt. Lemmon (1.4 million people per year), Arizona-Sonora Desert Museum (600,000 people per year) and Old Tucson Studios (500,000 people per year). But annual events attract their share of the crowds as well. The Pima County Fair normally draws about 400,000 people each year and generates approximately $4 million for the

INSIDERS' TIP

Though a great place to live, Tucson has one downside: The November 1997 issue of *Ladies Home Journal* ranked Tucson the eighth worst out of 200 cities for bad hair days. The *Journal* cites the area's extremely low humidity and occasionally breezy afternoons as the reason (El Paso was ranked the worst).

San Xavier del Bac is known locally as "The White Dove of the Desert."

community. At the end of the year, some 45,000 fans pour into the Arizona Stadium for the annual Copper Bowl, recently renamed the Insight.Com Bowl. The Tucson rodeo draws 55,000 people, and the rodeo parade — the world's longest nonmotorized parade — sees an estimated 100,000 people line the streets.

Downtown Revitalization

Tucson actually has two distinct business districts: Downtown Tucson and, on the Eastside, the multibuilding Williams Centre and its cluster of office and bank buildings. But downtown Tucson still remains the hub of activity centered around Congress Street and Stone Avenue. The Downtown Development Corporation has been working hard over the last five years on downtown revitalization, historic preservation and industrial development. Like many American cities, Tucson's downtown core went through a slump during the 1960s and '70s, when retail businesses pulled out of the decaying area in favor of the ever-expanding urban malls as Tucson stretched out over the desert. The city's response was to focus on the area as an Arts District. Created in 1988, the Downtown Arts District is an idea that has taken off, and today more than 600 cultural events are presented in downtown Tucson each year (see our Arts and Culture and Festivals and Events chapters).

The city is going forward with a long-term revitalization plan, since the office vacancy rate in the downtown area is relatively high. Two exciting construction projects have already broken ground in the downtown area.

The first is the $4 million, 15,000-square-foot Southern Arizona Regional Visitors Center, to be located just off Interstate 10 at the Congress Street/downtown freeway exit. This complex will be the new home of the Metropolitan Tucson Convention and Visitors Bureau with interpretive exhibits from the Forest Service. The Forest Service will share offices at the new site with other natural-resource organizations, such as the National Park Service, Bureau of Land Management, Arizona State Parks, Arizona Game and Fish, Pima County Parks and Recreation Department, City of Tucson Parks and Recreation Department, Arizona State Lands Department and the Arizona-Sonora Desert Museum. The offices will be known collectively as the Tucson Basin Resource Managers. This new visitors center, expected to be opened by September 1998, will serve as a one-stop shop where people can get not only information on area attractions, but also camping permits, licenses, campground and hotel reservations and information on outdoor recreational opportunities in the area.

The second major revitalization project in downtown Tucson is the construction of a new, 413,000-square-foot federal courthouse, expected to be completed in August 1999 and located on four acres at the corner of Granada Avenue and Congress Street. The $70 million, six-story, L-shaped, Evo A. DeConcini U.S. Courthouse and Federal Building will be the largest structure in downtown Tucson, though not the tallest, and is the first major construction in the area in a decade.

Sustainable Tucson

A quiet revolution has been taking place in the Old Pueblo that has made Tucson a leader in sustainable technology advances and given the area national recognition as being eco-friendly.

Ever since the world's first conference on solar energy took place in Tucson and Phoenix in 1955, the city has slowly embraced alternative energy and building technologies. Whether it's low-tech bicycles, straw bale construction, solar heating or advanced technologies like electric cars, photovoltaic cells that turn sunlight into electricity, or planned, eco-friendly communities, Tucson is considered on the cutting edge of the sustainable technology movement.

The area has become a showcase for turning sunlight into electricity. At Tucson Unified School District's Cooper Environmental Science Camp in the Tucson Mountains, Colorado-based Solar Energy International has held workshops since 1995, resulting in the installation of enough photovoltaic cells to power the campus today. Now the site pays virtually nothing for electricity.

In 1997 the city's electric utility, Tucson Electric Power (TEP), announced a $5 million investment in an equal partnership with Denver-based Global Solar Energy to build a high-tech manufacturing plant for the next generation of solar cells. The cost will be a third of existing photovoltaic technology. The state-of-the-art plant, completed in 1997, is located at the site of the Tucson-planned, eco-friendly community of Civano, near University of Arizona's Science and Technology Park.

Though it has barely broken ground, the Civano "solar village" has already received worldwide attention, not to mention city funding. The 818-acre residential and commercial development at South Houghton and East Irvington Roads is expected to have 2,600 homes and more than 700,000 square feet of commercial space. The concept of this village is that many of the people who will live in the state-of-the-art, energy-efficient homes will also work there, making commutes into the city unnecessary. The environmental construction techniques include alternative building materials, such as rammed earth, straw bale and even recycled water for landscaping. A third of the community will be dedicated as natural, open space containing community orchards, linear parks and an 18-hole, environmentally friendly golf course. The business center on the site continues to target ecologically oriented technologies.

Tucson is also one of only four cities in the country chosen to introduce General Motors' first production electric car, EV 1, in late 1996. Today, you'll see numerous blue parking spaces reserved for electric cars only, with a recharging station. Since most of the major car makers are expected to release their own versions of electric cars over the next two years, Tucson will be used as a test market for more and more of these high-tech, alternative vehicles.

The City of Tucson is also the home of the nation's first FHA-funded straw bale house. As the home of one of the authors of *The Straw Bale House* book and headquarters of one of the country's most active straw bale building companies, the area has seen a flurry of straw bale construction, including a building at the Girl Scouts' Hacienda Environmental Education Center (which also uses photovoltaics for electricity). Straw bale is new to the Southwest. The construction technique allows homes to stay cool in the summer's 110-degree heat. Since the City of Tucson changed the uniform building code in January 1996 to allow straw bale within the city limits, straw bale is being used for everything from homes to perimeter walls around residential properties.

With the introduction of high-tech companies, innovative construction projects and the University's scientific advances, Tucson is where the Old West meets the New West.

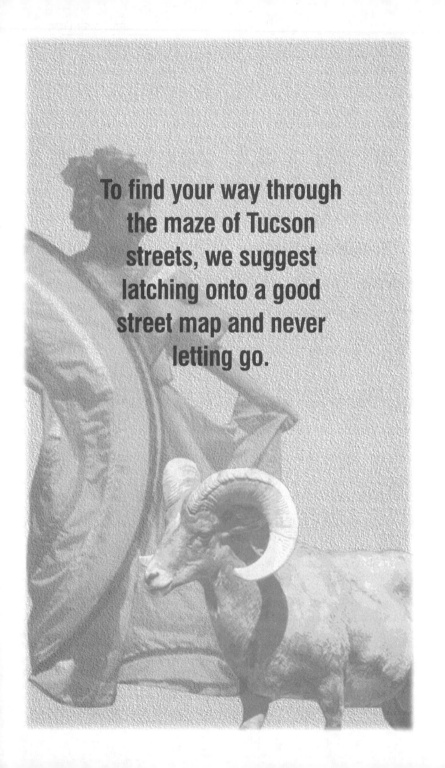

To find your way through the maze of Tucson streets, we suggest latching onto a good street map and never letting go.

Getting Here, Getting Around

Like most Southwestern cities that are spread out rather than up, Tucson is awash with cars. As of 1995, Tucson-area drivers logged an astounding 17.6 million miles a day behind the wheel. Cars are such a part of daily life that public transportation has taken a backseat. And despite being so car dependent, Tucsonans don't have many interstates or freeways to carry them all around — there are just two, and they only help if you're traversing certain parts of the area. Otherwise, drivers must use the crowded surface streets, stopping at nearly every intersection for lights. But despite these shortcomings, Tucson is fairly easy to find your way around, and there are alternatives to driving. (Getting around on bike paths is covered in the Bicycling chapter.)

But before we tell you all the ins and outs and tricks of getting around the metro area, we'll tell you the ways to get here. (About the only mode of transportation you can't take to get to the Old Pueblo is a boat.) And we'll tell you how best to get from your arrival point to where you're going in Tucson.

Whether you're traveling to or from Tucson or traveling around the valley, keep in mind that Tucson's busiest season is the "winter," specifically from October to April. That means airports, buses and roads will all be more congested then. It also means that, if you can tolerate the heat, getting here and getting around can be a much more pleasant experience in the summer.

Getting Here

By Air

While Tucson International Airport is the major air artery into the city, we should tell you that it's not the only place you can arrive or depart by air in Tucson. But to use one of the other airfields, you'll need to be a pilot yourself or have one to fly for you. There are three private airfields serving the Tucson area: the executive terminal of the Tucson International Airport and just adjacent to it, Ryan Airfield to Tucson's southwest and Avra Valley Airport in northwest Marana.

Tucson International Airport
7250 S. Tucson Blvd. • 573-8000, 573-8001

Many major domestic airlines serve Tucson International Airport, and those that don't can probably get you into Phoenix, a short flight or less-than-two-hour bus or car ride away. **America West Airlines**, (800) 235-9292, and **Southwest Airlines**, (800) 435-9792, are the two major airlines with flights in and out of Tucson. **Reno Air**, (800) 736-6247, also flies here as do three Mexican airlines — **Aero California**, (800) 237-6225, **AeroLitoral**, (800) 237-6639, and **AeroMexico**, (800) 237-6639. The 100 flights each day in and out of Tucson In-

---

INSIDERS' TIP

If you plan on stopping on the terminal road to drop off or pick up a passenger, make sure you make it brief and stay in your vehicle or risk a ticket or tow.

ternational encompass about 50 cities across the country and major Mexican cities like Hermosillo, Guaymas and Mexico City. If you're flying to or from Mexico, you'll go through U.S. Customs in the international wing of the airport.

There are some real pluses to arriving at Tucson International Airport (beside the obvious one that it's probably your destination). Flights rarely are encumbered by weather delays. The airport is fairly small and uncongested compared to behemoths like Phoenix, LA or Chicago, so flight delays are not as common. Another plus is that passengers can usually get into and out of the airport with ease. (Our primer on navigating the airport is located in the close-up of this chapter.)

The airport has both short-term and long-term parking lots, the former very close to the terminal for ease of lugging the luggage or finding an arriving traveler. Both lots charge $1.25 an hour, and long-term is $5.50 for each 24 hours. If you're parking long-term, you'll probably save money at one of the private parking lots just outside the airport, which will shuttle you to or from the terminal. Several of these lots are on Tucson Boulevard, the main road into the airport, and cost about $3 a day.

Ground transportation — taxis, shuttles, limos or hotel vehicles — will drop you off or pick you up right in front of the terminal, and the locations are well-marked with signs as you step out of the terminal's lower (baggage) level.

Airport passengers have several choices for ground transportation. **Sun Tran**, Tucson's public bus system, provides service to and from the airport every hour, so check with the terminal information centers or Sun Tran, 792-9222, for information. Many hotels provide complimentary airport transportation for their guests, so either ask ahead when you make your hotel reservation or stop at the hotel reservation board in the lower terminal level for direct phone service to some hotels. While you may have a tough time finding a taxi anywhere else in Tucson, they're very available at the airport. They have a flag drop rate that includes the first mile plus a per mileage charge after that (unless you're going beyond 25 miles of the airport, in which case it would be a flat fee). Expect to pay about $20 between the airport and central Tucson. Taxi fares include baggage and extra persons going to the same location. **Arizona Stagecoach**, 889-1000, operates a door-to-door van service to and from the airport. You can call them in advance for information or go to the reservation desk in the terminal's lower level.

Many car rental agencies are located in or very close by the airport. If they're off the grounds, they'll have shuttles to and from the terminal. They include **Alamo**, 889-6762; **Avis**, 294-1494; **Budget**, 889-8800; **Dollar**, 573-8486; **Enterprise**, 295-1964; **Hertz**, 294-7616; **National**, 573-8050; and **Value**, 889-9596. It's obviously best to reserve your car before your trip to Tucson, but if you didn't, merely walk up to one of the car rental ticket counters on the lower level and see if anything's available.

If you want the luxury of limousine service, several in Tucson will transport you to or from the airport. Information on this service is available at the airport as well as later in this chapter.

> **FYI**
> Unless otherwise noted, the area code for all phone numbers listed in this guide is 520.

Executive Terminal
Tucson International Airport, 7081 S. Plumer Ave. • 573-8128, (800) 758-1874

Operated by Tucson Airport Authority and connected to Tucson International Airport, the executive terminal is the busiest of the three private fields, primarily because of its proximity to the airport and the city. It has access and facilities for all kinds of aircraft, from two-seaters to million-dollar jets. Aircraft services available include fuel, overnight parking, a weather briefing room and lavatory cleanout but no maintenance or repair services. (These are available at neighboring businesses, as is flight instruction.) There's a pilots lounge in the terminal, plus car rentals, taxi and limo services and a restaurant. The terminal can also reserve cars and hotel accommodations and provide Mexico insurance. At this airport, there are no landing fees for privately owned aircraft, but commercial (cargo or for-hire) craft will pay $1.28 per the aircraft's maximum gross capability landing weight. The UNICOM number is 122.95. Those in the know say that this is a popular spot for the rich and famous (or

GETTING HERE, GETTING AROUND • 17

infamous) to land and step out of their aircraft into a waiting limousine without curious observers ever observing them.

Ryan Airfield
9700 W. Ajo Wy. • 883-2921

Ryan Airfield, also operated by Tucson Airport Authority, lies at the western end of Valencia Road where it intersects with Ajo Highway in a fairly remote area about 15 miles from Tucson International Airport. Services here include fuel, overnight parking at $3.50 and a restaurant that's open from 6 AM to 8 PM. Maintenance, repair and lessons are available at private businesses adjacent to the airfield. There are no landing fees. Tower hours are 6 AM to 6 PM and until 8 PM in summer. There is no UNICOM, but radio frequencies are 125.8 for air and 118.2 for ground control.

Avra Valley Airport
11700 W. Avra Valley Rd. • 682-2999

Avra Valley Airport, operated by Pima County, is in the town of Marana, about 5 miles west of I-10, and may be most convenient to residents of Tucson's northwest. Services include fuel, overnight parking ranging from $4 to $8 depending on aircraft size, car rental, restaurant and pilots lounge (with showers). There are no landing fees, and a private flight-based operator on-site provides maintenance, repair, lessons and charter flights. UNICOM is 123.0.

Charter Services

If you prefer private to commercial flying and don't have your own wings, several companies operate charter services. They'll take you to other cities for business or pleasure or on flights of fancy, such as over the Grand Canyon or whale-watching in Mexico's Sea of Cortez. **Double Eagle Aviation**, 294-8214, is conveniently located near the executive terminal and has a wide range of services for charter and private flying. **Tyconic Air Taxi and Charter Service**, 883-4823, is based at Ryan Airfield and has helicopter flights over the Grand Canyon and excursions to popular spots in Arizona and Nevada. Operating out

18 • GETTING HERE, GETTING AROUND

of Avra Valley Airport, **Tucson Aeroservice Center**, 682-2999, has full charter services as well as special tours. All three service Mexico and Canada as well as the United States.

By Train

Amtrak
400 E. Toole Ave. • 623-4442

We hope that by the time you read this Amtrak still exists — one never knows. Tucson's Amtrak station is downtown, actually at the northwest corner of 4th and Toole avenues. Although open daily, the station keeps very strange hours, primarily corresponding to trains' arrivals and departures. Amtrak's *Sunset Limited* brings passengers into Tucson from points east or west three days a week and departs from Tucson to the east or west three days a week. Strangely, Amtrak no longer serves Phoenix, so it operates a bus service between Tucson and Phoenix (as well as Flagstaff and the Grand Canyon) to bring passengers to Tucson for the train. The bus route also serves to connect two Amtrak lines — the one through Tucson and another train line further north that goes through Flagstaff.

Parking is available at the station and nearby on the street, but none of it is secured or advisable for the long term. The safest bet for long-term parking is a nearby city garage for about $8 a day. Ground transportation from the train station is convenient since it's located downtown and only a stone's throw from Sun Tran's Ronstadt Transit Center at Pennington Street and 6th Avenue. Beyond the city bus, you're likely to find taxi cabs either at the train station or the bus transit center. For a rental car, you'll need to call one for a pickup since none are within walking distance of the train station

or in the immediate downtown area. The train station is also only a block from the Greyhound bus terminal, 2 S. 4th Avenue.

By Bus

Greyhound
2 S. 4th Ave. • 792-3475

If you follow the age-old saying "leave the driving to us," you'll be arriving or departing Tucson by Greyhound bus at the terminal, located at Broadway Boulevard and 4th Avenue. Spanish is spoken here and nearly all the signs and schedules are in Spanish as well as English. The terminal is clean if not beautiful and has a restaurant, games, lockers and armchair pay-TVs. Signs say "No Loitering," and they seem to be strictly enforced. Taxis are usually waiting outside. The city bus terminal is a block away at Pennington Street and 6th Avenue.

Greyhound serves all points north, south, east and west of Tucson, including Nogales and several other cities in Mexico. So, for example, you can get to or from Las Vegas, Los Angeles, Texas or Phoenix from Tucson. For the convenience of airline travelers, Greyhound also has 18 trips a day between Tucson (the Greyhound terminal) and the Phoenix airport.

By Car

If you're driving to Tucson from points west, such as California or western Arizona, you'll probably be traveling east along Interstate 8, which meets up with Interstate 10 just south of Casa Grande and about 70 miles north of Tucson. From that point, I-10 east will take you southward right into Tucson. If you're driving from points north like Flagstaff or Phoenix, I-10 eastbound will deposit you in Tucson. If you'd rather take the scenic route than the fast route,

---

INSIDERS' TIP

In Arizona, drivers generally are allowed to turn right on red after stopping, but some intersections, especially around schools, have signs saying it's not permitted.

GETTING HERE, GETTING AROUND • 19

Airport Primer

Tucson's only commercial airport, Tucson International, isn't one of the giant, sprawling airports of the country, which most folks consider a definite benefit. It's a small, pretty airport with award-winning landscaping and art exhibits throughout. Covering more than 5,000 acres, the airport is not owned by the city but is run by a volunteer authority (Tucson Airport Authority) and funded from landing fees and the various vendors that operate there.

Established about 60 years ago, the airport now serves about 1.5 million passengers a year, the majority of whom use it during the peak season from late fall through early spring to arrive at our sunny destination. The terminal recently was remodeled to improve the lower level entryways, security checkpoints and concession areas. If you've ever been to the new Denver airport, you may recognize a similar sight outside the Tucson terminal, but on a much smaller scale — those white tent-like coverings that replace roofs and provide cover as well as an unusual architectural detail. Located just west of the airport (but accessible via Plumer Avenue) is the Executive Terminal for private aircraft and the Arizona Air National Guard.

If you have the time, the airport offers a number of tours that will take you into areas not seen by the average traveler. There's a self-guided tour for which you can pick up a map at the Information Center on the lower level. Along the way, be sure to notice the collection of more than 45 works by southern Arizona artists that dot the terminal. Another tour is the "tennis shoe" terminal tour that takes you behind the scenes for about 90 minutes beginning at 9 AM on Wednesdays. Tour-takers must be age 16 or older. There's also a Saturday Ramp Tour that includes visits to the fire station and control tower. Several other tours are geared to younger people (see our Kidstuff chapter). All

— continued on next page

The food at Tucson International Airport comes from some of the best-known local restaurants.

of the tours are free, but reservations are advisable. Call 573-8100 for tour information and reservations.

To get to the airport, take Tucson Boulevard south, about a half-mile past Valencia Road. This is a rarely congested road that becomes the airport, with numerous hotels and private parking lots lining it. The airport itself forms a circle with parking in the center and splits into upper and lower roadways at the terminal building. The lower roadway goes to the arrival (baggage claim) level of the terminal and the upper to the departure (ticketing) level. The terminal building also has a small third level that houses an El Charro restaurant and a Southwest gift shop. (See our Restaurants chapter for details on El Charro.) The upper level of the terminal has two wings, or concourses, where airline gates are located as well as other services such as food, lounges and newsstands. The international building is just before the main terminal and is easy to access from the roadway.

The airport is handicapped-accessible, and you'll find well-marked phones, restrooms and information booths throughout the terminal, plus the obligatory shops, newsstands, lockers, ATM machines, mail boxes, stamp vending machines, lounges and restaurants. Smoking is permitted only in the designated lounges. The information centers on the baggage-claim level will help you find (page) someone, while lost and found on the main level will help you find something. They also provide TDD and fax and copy services. House phones throughout the terminal will connect you to important help, such as paging, lost and found and medical assistance.

If you've forgotten to pick up an all-important Arizona souvenir during your Tucson visit to take back to the kids or a coworker, don't despair. The airport has plenty of shops with Southwest goodies, such as pottery, pistachios and cowboy paraphernalia, plus turquoise jewelry, T-shirts and even hats emblazoned with "But It's a Dry Heat." All in all, you'll find the airport user friendly with all the services to make traveling as convenient as possible.

exit I-10 early and head for Sacaton or Coolidge, which will take you to Ariz. Highway 87 and past the Casa Grande Ruins National Monument, then connect up with I-10 again.

Mexico is about the only point south of Tucson, so if you're coming from that direction you must be coming across the border, in which case Interstate 19 will carry you north into downtown Tucson. Or take the scenic path, Ariz. Highway 82 north to Ariz. Highway 83 north, which will connect with I-10 east of Tucson, so take it west to the city. Traveling from the east, such as from New Mexico, the major route into Tucson is I-10 westbound. This part of I-10 goes through some lovely country, including a boulder-laden area called Texas Canyon and past the farmlands around Willcox, Arizona.

If you're traveling from Colorado or northeastern Arizona and its fascinating Indian reservation spots like Canyon de Chelley National Monument or Window Rock, the fast option is to take Interstate 40 east into Flagstaff, then go south along Interstate 17 and I-10 to Tucson. For scenic routes, there are many choices including Ariz. Highway 77, which goes through the White Mountains and eventually becomes Oracle Road into Tucson, or U.S. Highway 191, a very scenic road winding through forest lands that eventually connects with I-10 east of Tucson.

Getting Around

OK, you've arrived. Now how do you find your way from one end of the 500-mile valley that's metropolitan Tucson to the other and all points in between? Well, it won't be by boat or by fast transit (like trains), but it could be by car, bus, taxi or limousine. Here's how to find and use the various forms of in-town transportation and how to get around the streets if you're the driver.

Navigating the Streets

In one sense, Tucson is fairly easy to navigate by car. If you get to know the four mountain ranges that are strategically placed at the four compass points, you'll be able to ascertain north from south and east from west from nearly any spot in the city. At the very least, learn to recognize the Santa Catalinas, and you'll know where north is. And much of Tucson, especially the central area, is laid out in a grid system with streets one mile apart and running directly north-south or east-west.

But there are more than a few chinks in this armor that can confuse even longtime Tucsonan drivers. For example, there are the streets that inexplicably change their name somewhere midstream. Or natural obstacles such as washes, rivers or mini-mountains (and manmade obstacles such as an air force base) that simply won't let a street pass through or over them, so it just stops. There are streets that go in any direction but straight and twist and turn until you're almost dizzy trying to stay on course. And then there's the myriad of strange names for streets, many of them coming from the Spanish language — as tricky to read as pronounce.

To find your way easily through the maze of Tucson streets, we strongly suggest latching onto a good street map and never letting go. Another wise piece of advice is to plot out your trip in advance, especially if you're driving to some obscure street that may sound like several other streets unless you speak Spanish.

And speaking of Spanish, particularly if you don't, keep in mind that many Tucson street names include a Spanish word that means street, way or place. Among them are *calle*, *camino*, *placito*, *via*, *avenida* and *paseo* — with an abundance of "del" and "de" words tossed in. Street names can be frustrating to newcomers, but with patience you'll get as proficient at deciphering (or ignoring) them as Tucsonans are.

Main Thoroughfares

Our primer on land travel begins with the two biggest streets, the two interstates or freeways. **Interstate 10** comes down from Phoenix heading east (which actually seems like south) into Tucson and skirts the western side of the city. Near downtown, it curves abruptly and actually begins heading east, then skirts the very southern part of the metro area to points east, including eventually New Mexico. The other freeway is **Interstate 19**, which has its starting point about where I-10 curves to go east. From there, I-19 heads directly south past Green Valley and eventually right to Mexico. (The signs on I-19 give distances in kilometers not miles.)

The interstates are handy if you're traveling to Phoenix, New Mexico or Mexico, or along the western or far southern parts of the metro area. Beyond that, drivers must tolerate surface streets and lots of stop-and-go traffic, even to get from, say, the far northwest to the east or from the foothills to downtown.

So if the interstates won't get you where you're going, you might want to know about some of the major streets that cross town. Starting up north, **Ina Road** will take drivers from the far west, actually I-10 and beyond, all the way to the mountains in the east, but it changes names — first to Skyline Road and then to Sunrise Drive. **River Road** is another west-to-east option, but it terminates well before the interstate on the west and goes only to Sabino Canyon Road on the east. Nonetheless, it's a good route, albeit curvy in spots, and comes with views. Other major east-west streets are **Grant Road**, **Speedway Boulevard**, **Broadway Boulevard**, **22nd Street**, **Golf Links Road**, **Ajo Way**, **Irvington Road** and **Valencia Road**, all of which run parallel to each other and are major byways lined with all manner of commercial enterprises.

Major north-south streets, beginning on the

INSIDERS' TIP

If you really must fly into or out of Phoenix instead of Tucson, Arizona Shuttle Service, 795-6771 or (800) 888-2749, operates hourly buses in both directions seven days a week. It's a convenient way to get between the two cities in about two hours and for about $20 one-way. Reservations are advisable.

22 • GETTING HERE, GETTING AROUND

The Rillito turns into a raging river during monsoon season.

west side, include **Oracle Road**, **Stone Avenue**, **Campbell Avenue**, **Alvernon Way**, **Swan Road**, **Craycroft Road**, **Kolb Road** and **Houghton Road**. Some of these streets end abruptly, usually because of natural or man-made barriers. Swan and Craycroft roads, for example, are stopped in the south by the air force base. Tucson International Airport is the southern end for streets like Park Avenue and Campbell Avenue (which for part of its route is called Kino Boulevard).

A Road by Any Other Name

Quirks are common with Tucson's streets. For example, 22nd Street, a major east-west thoroughfare, changes to Starr Pass Boulevard west of I-10. Fifth Street becomes 6th Street and then St. Mary's Road and finally Anklam Road as you travel west. Pima Street turns into Elm Street near the Arizona Inn. And there's a Pantano Road and a Pantano Boulevard, and they run next to each other, so who knows which is which. Of all the street quirks in Tucson, however, the strangest may well be the place where Wilmot Road becomes Tanque Verde Road and Grant Road becomes Kolb Road, and they all intersect and go off in different directions. This is a very busy area to boot. Again, consult your trusty map and plan ahead.

And if you're looking for any rhyme or reason to the use of terms such as "street" or "avenue" or "boulevard," forget it. Many roads are tagged with boulevard, but you may never see one along its length. The use of numbered roads can be confusing also: We have 5th Street and 5th Avenue and 6th Street and 6th Avenue, for example, and often they intersect. Just remember that in the case of numbered roads, the avenues run north-south and the streets run east-west.

Rules and Warnings

You won't be on Tucson streets long before you notice that the main ones at least have a left turn lane down the center, indicated by yellow lines. This is a fairly easy concept even for newcomers — turn left from the center turn lane. Except there are a couple of exceptions, and you'd best know them in advance or risk the wrath of Tucson rush-hour drivers or even a collision. In order to improve rush-hour traffic flow — traffic going into central Tucson in the morning and coming out of it in the late afternoon — a couple of these main east-west streets transform the left turn lanes into rush-hour lanes. In other words, you can't make a left turn at all and the left turn lane becomes a traffic lane. This only happens from 7 to 9 AM going west and from 4 to

6 PM going east, and only portions of two major streets are affected: Grant Road and Broadway Boulevard. These are called reversible lanes (or suicide lanes by some folks) and, when they're in effect, orange pylons or flashing warning lights above the street remind drivers. If you're confused, just stay off those streets during rush hours, and you won't even have to try figuring it out.

And if that's confusing, try figuring out the address numbering system in Tucson. We'll explain it but make no guarantees that it makes sense or that you'll get it. First, the point of origin for addresses in Tucson is Stone Avenue and Broadway Boulevard. In other words, Stone Avenue is the dividing line for east versus west streets and Broadway Boulevard for north and south streets (everything north of Broadway is called north something street and so forth). That's not terribly difficult, but read on. When you are on an east-west street looking for an east address, you'll find odd building numbers on the north side of the street and even addresses on the south side. But once you cross Stone Avenue and are in the west streets, the exact opposite is true — the odd numbered addresses are on the south side and the even on the north.

And guess what happens to the north-south streets? When you're on a north-south street that's north of Broadway Boulevard, the odd address numbers are on the west and the even on the east. But south of Broadway Boulevard, the switch takes place and odd numbers are on the east side of the street and even on the west. And making matters worse is the fact that only about every third building (at best) in Tucson even has a visible address number. Finding your destination and driving at the same time can be a real challenge.

Another caution about Tucson streets pertains to rain storms. We have them infrequently, but they can be fierce. In a flash, a simple dip in the roadway or a low spot where a wash or arroyo crosses the road will fill up with rushing water and can careen vehicles downstream with no warning. So when you see a "Do Not Cross When Flooded" sign, pay heed.

As a final caution for driving Tucson's streets, be aware that many downtown streets are one-way, even though they may be two-way streets beyond downtown. Stone Avenue, for example, becomes strictly southbound as it goes through downtown, while Congress Street is westbound and Broadway Boulevard becomes eastbound during their downtown paths. Again, refer to the trusty street map before you turn on the ignition.

Parking

Driving and parking — you can't have one without the other, so here's the mostly good news on parking your vehicle in the Tucson environs. With two primary exceptions, parking is usually very accessible and free. Nearly every business and major attraction has ample parking, and there's almost never a charge. The two notable exceptions are downtown Tucson and the University, where people congregate, buildings dominate and land for parking is scarce. So if you're attending one of the many events or attractions in either of these areas, you'll probably have to hunt for an available space and pay once you find it. Both areas have metered street parking, but it's not easy to get. Both also have numerous pay parking garages and lots at about $2 an hour with daily rate specials. The University publishes an annual campus parking map, and a guide to downtown parking is available at the Tucson Visitors Bureau or city offices.

Rental Cars

The major national car rental agencies are represented here and most are located at the airport (see the listing for the Tucson International Airport previously in this chapter) but also have additional locations around town. It's often possible to rent a vehicle in Tucson and drop it off in Phoenix (or vice versa) without the typical steep drop-off charge, which is a big help if you're using the Phoenix airport. As is true in most large cities, you'll find a number of car rental companies that aren't the "biggies" — they're local but usually offer the same types of vehicles and rates as the national ones do. Some of these are operated out of car dealerships. Check the Yellow Pages under "Auto Renting" and "Auto Leasing" for the many car rental options in Tucson.

If you're renting a vehicle and plan to travel south of the border, however, be advised that you're unlikely to find any rental vehicle that you can take to Mexico. (If the border town of Nogales, Mexico, is your destination, you can easily park in the United States and walk a block or two to the border crossing and into Nogales. Check out the Daytrips and Weekend Getaways chapter for all the details on going to Mexico.)

Riding the Bus

Tucson has only one form of public transit: The **Sun Tran** bus system, 792-9222. It'll get you to and from many places, but it's by no means as frequent or as comprehensive as bus transportation in major cities in other areas of the country. That's why there are so many cars and drivers in Tucson (or maybe it's vice versa — Tucson doesn't expand public transportation because everybody drives anyway). And Tucson buses travel mostly within the city limits even though much of Tucson lies beyond the city. Here are some of the bus basics.

For starters, let's talk about where the buses stop. They only stop at designated bus stops, of which there are about 2000, indicated by a sign. The sign will tell you which route (by number and name) stops there and whether an express bus also stops there. Many stops are covered, which is good news if you're a summer rider or just don't want to wait in the fierce sun, and most are wheelchair-accessible.

Sun Tran has several features that make it a usable system for the disabled, plus Sun Tran operates a separate Van Tran system just for the disabled, 798-1000. Many Sun Tran buses are lift-equipped for wheelchairs and are marked with the international wheelchair symbol on the door. Some buses accommodate people who have difficulty stepping up. Sun Tran produces special guides for people with vision disabilities, operates TTY/TDD phone service, 628-1565, and accommodates guide dogs. If you're in need of special assistance, chances are Sun Tran can accommodate you.

Sun Tran also caters to drivers who want to park and ride and bike riders. There are about two dozen locations where you can park a car for free and then take a bus to your destination. They're listed in the Sun Tran Rider's Informa- tion Guide. For bike riders, Sun Tran buses are equipped with bike racks on the front (although they only carry two, so it's first-come first-served), at no extra charge. They also rent monthly bike lockers ($2 per month plus a key deposit) at designated locations and have bike racks at designated bus stops.

Once you've figured out how to find a bus stop, you'll need to know how to get where you want to go. It can be complicated, so your best bet is to call Sun Tran, 792-9222, and they'll give you specific instructions (in Spanish if needed). Or pick up a Sun Tran Rider's Information Guide, which you can get just about anywhere, including grocery stores and libraries. The guide tells you everything you always wanted to know about Sun Tran. Another option is to go to one of the three transit centers, which have information booths as well as covered waiting areas, restrooms and telephones. They're also major transfer points for buses. The Tohono Tadai Transit Center is located on Stone Avenue just north of Wetmore Road; the Roy Laos Transit Center is at Irvington Road and S. 6th Avenue; and the Ronstadt Transit Center is downtown at Pennington Street and 6th Avenue.

> **FYI**
> Unless otherwise noted, the area code for all phone numbers listed in this guide is 520.

Fees

To ride the bus you'll need exact change or a fare pass. The regular fare is 85¢. Youth (younger than 18) pay 60¢, kids younger than 5 with an adult ride free, and seniors, disabled and low-income riders carrying a special ID pay 35¢. Transfers are free, but you need to request one when you first get on the bus. It's good for one hour in the same direction (in other words, it won't work for a return trip).

If you're a regular rider, the pass may be the way to go. There are several varieties, such as a monthly pass for $24, a student pass for $16, an economy pass for seniors and qualified low-income riders for $10.50, as well as monthly express passes, University passes and booklets of 20 rides. Passes are available at lots of places, including Sun Tran, so call or refer to the Sun Tran Rider's Information Guide for where to get one. They're also available by mail.

Hours and Special Events

Sun Tran buses operate from 5:15 AM to 10:45 PM Monday through Friday and from 6:15 AM to 9:45 PM on Saturdays, Sundays and holidays. Not all bus routes operate all these hours, however, so check the schedule or call Sun Tran. The Van Tran system for disabled riders operates the same hours, but it's an advance reservation system and is explained fully in the Pocket Guide to Van Tran, available at Sun Tran and the Tucson Visitors Bureau among other places.

Even though Sun Tran may not exactly cover the land and may not operate buses every 10 minutes (or even close to that), they do have a number of special runs that make it easy to get to some major events. These shuttle fares will take you to and from basketball, football and some baseball games, Winterhaven for Festival of Lights, the Gem Show and the rodeo. (See the Festivals and Events and Spectator Sports chapters for information on these outings.) Check the *Rider's Information Guide* or call Sun Tran for details.

Catching the CAT

Folks who attend or work at the University of Arizona have another tran option — the University's Cat Tran shuttle, its name taken from the school's Wildcat nickname. It operates from 6:30 AM to 8 PM Monday through Friday but not usually during semester breaks or on school holidays. It's free to riders showing the appropriate ID, and route maps are available at the University.

Taxis and Van Services

This isn't New York, LA or Chicago, folks, so hailing a taxi isn't even in the vocabulary here. About the only places you can expect to see a taxi ready to take on a passenger are the airport, bus and train stations and possibly major event venues such as the Tucson Convention Center. And except for the airport, even these locations aren't a sure bet. So plan on calling for a taxi if you need one.

Tucson has less than a dozen taxi cab companies plus several private transportation services operating on-call vans. Taxi rates aren't regulated in Arizona, so they vary widely — we recommend shopping around. Most taxis use a flag drop rate plus mileage charge for shorter trips and a flat fee for longer ones, such as from Tucson to Green Valley. Extra charges usually are not levied for more than one passenger going to the same destination. Several taxi companies can accommodate Spanish speaking passengers, including Fiesta Taxi, Golden Eagle Taxi and Yellow Cab. Several also have wheelchair cabs available including Allstate Cab Company and Yellow Cab. The major taxi companies serving the area are **Allstate Cab Company**, 798-1111; **Ameri-Cab**, 797-7979; **Checker Cab Company**, 623-1133; **Fiesta Taxi**, 622-7777; **Golden Eagle Taxi**, 889-0000; **Handicar**, 881-3391; and **Yellow Cab**, 624-6611.

As an alternative to taxis, several companies operate private van or car services. Some accommodate either individual passengers or groups while others are strictly for groups. They typically have flat rates per hour or by destination and may offer tours, special services to businesses and other limousine-like services. These companies include **Arizona Stagecoach** (airport shuttle), 889-1000; **Christopher Robert Corporation**, 529-7400; **Courier Transportation**, 624-6455; **Diamond Sedans**, 795-8070; **Foothills Luxury Sedans**, 750-0365; **Michel Livery and Tours**, 444-1630; **MS Transportation** (groups only), 327-4674; **Metro Taxi and Shuttle**, 444-1221; and **Safe Ride**, 746-3398.

Limousines

They claim you need not be rich and famous or know Robin Leach to rent a limo, but at $50 to $100 an hour (plus gratuity), it helps. So if luxury is your lifestyle or if you just want to be pampered on occasion, Tucson has plenty of limousine services — about two dozen. They'll drive you in everything from town cars to stretch limos that look more like a boat, and some also have vans and mini-coaches. The more vehicle and the more amenities you desire, the more it will cost. Some have special rates for the Tucson and Phoenix airports. Check the phone book's Yellow Pages under "Limousine" for all the options, but here are a few: **A&A Limousine Service**, 622-6441; **Cactus Limousine**, 298-6471; **Sunset Limousine**, 573-9418; and **Starr Limousine**, 326-0812.

He said he'd take me to a desert oasis
where a glistening pool reflects the sunlit sky
and lush gardens invite quiet moonlit walks.

I didn't think there was such a place.
Sometimes it's nice to be wrong.
SunStone.

SunStone
guest ranch

2545 North Woodland Road, Tucson, AZ 85749 • 520-749-1928
(Near Tanque Verde and Catalina Hwy.) • www.azstarnet.com/~sunston

Accommodations

Lodgings in this former cowtown are expanding, with many considered among the best in the nation. Noted for their "elite status" among resorts and spas are Canyon Ranch (one of the top-10 spas in the country, according to the 1997 Zagat Survey, a national survey of travel professionals) and Loews Ventana Canyon.

For visitors who wish to be pampered, check the Resorts and Spas section of this chapter for facilities that offer a totally upscale experience. Though there has not been a new resort built in the area in a decade due to a real estate recession in the late 1980s and early 1990s, five more megaresorts are planned over the next five years, mostly in the fast-growing northwest area.

Many Tucson lodgings follow the two-room guest-suite trend geared toward business travelers. These accommodations typically have a separate bedroom and living room with kitchen and two televisions. For those who prefer to stay at a bed and breakfast, we have added a separate chapter to deal with this kind of accommodation. And the term *casita* should be added to your vocabulary if you're choosing a lodging in Tucson. This is the Southwestern term for a guest house or bungalow.

All listings include a toll-free reservation telephone number when available, as well as the local number and a symbol indicating the price range.

Most establishments offer the choice of smoking or nonsmoking accommodations as well as rooms that are handicapped-accessible. We've tried our best to note when an accommodation is the not the norm; however, we suggest that if you have special needs or requests, you convey them to the accommodation when making your reservations.

Price Guidelines

The following price codes indicate the cost of a one-night, double-occupancy stay during peak season. (Peak season usually runs from October to April.) The codes do not include a 9½-percent tax within the city limits or a 7½-percent tax in Pima County, which includes the Foothills. Virtually everyone accepts credit cards (we only note the ones that do not), but pets are another story, so it is best to call.

$	Less than $50
$$	$50 to $95
$$$	$95 to $145
$$$$	More than $145

Visitors to Tucson should be aware that, unlike in other parts of the country, you'll pay the most during the winter months — generally between October and April. It's difficult to find rooms during February — a ringing endorsement of the popularity of the Gem and Mineral Show and the Tucson Rodeo, which both draw attendees from all over the world. If you are planning to be in Tucson during February, book as far ahead as you can.

Summer is when you'll find the best rates, since many travelers avoid the area's 100+-degree heat between May and September.

INSIDERS' TIP

Don't be afraid to ask your hotel or resort for a complimentary ride to your destination. Most offer such a service, though they don't always promote it.

Hotels and Motels

The Arizona Inn
$$$ • 2200 E. Elm St. • 325-1541, (800) 678-8946

This historic hotel is a local favorite. Created in 1930 by Mrs. Isabella Greenway, a community leader and Arizona's first congresswoman (1933-1936), the first-class inn sits on 14 acres of gardens surrounded by vine-covered walls. Listed on the National Register of Historic Places, the 83 rooms are classy and quiet in one of the city's nicer neighborhoods but still close to everything. Clay tennis courts, outdoor swimming pool, fountains, indoor/outdoor dining, a library in the main sitting room and a piano lounge add to the inn's elegant atmosphere. It has even been listed in the *Ten Best Country Inns of America* and the *300 Best Hotels in the World*. Even if you decide not to stay here, at least stop by for a visit. Classical guitarists perform nightly in the dining room. (See our Restaurants chapter for dining information at The Arizona Inn.)

Best Western Executive Inn
$$$ • 333 W. Drachman St. • 791-7551, (800) 255-3371

Conveniently located just north of downtown off I-10, this new facility offers 129 spacious rooms, 54-channel cable TV, heated spa, pool and children's wading pool. La Fiesta Dining Room and a lounge featuring a happy hour and weekly entertainment are on site. The banquet facilities can provide space for up to 250 people.

Best Western Ghost Ranch Lodge
$$ • 801 W. Miracle Mile • 791-7565, (800) 456-7565

This long-established 8-acre site is known for its cactus gardens and lush grounds. It's a mile from Interstate 10 and just north of downtown Tucson. Mountains serve as a backdrop for the pool area. Among the 81 rooms with cable TV, radios and phones are 11 cozy one-bedroom cottages with kitchen and private patios. Other room sizes vary; many come with refrigerators, and all are on the ground floor. A coin laundry, restaurant, lounge, whirlpool and shuffleboard facilities are on site.

Best Western Inn
$$$ • 7060 S. Tucson Blvd. • 746-0271

This is the closest hotel to the Tucson International Airport, with 147 rooms, free cable, pay movies, heated pool, Jacuzzi, putting green and lighted tennis court. A perk for the business traveler: The hotel can arrange for audio, video and computer equipment in its conference suites.

Best Western InnSuites Hotel
$$ • 6201 N. Oracle Rd. • 297-2935, (800) 554-4535

Located 5 miles east off I-10 at the Orange Grove Road exit in the fast-growing northwest area, this facility offers 159 one- or two-room suites with refrigerator, microwave oven, coffee maker, hair dryer and free HBO. The larger suites have a kitchenette and separate living room for extended stays. Included in the price is a complimentary buffet breakfast, morning newspaper and afternoon social hour at the poolside cafe. There is also a landscaped pool and spa area, two lighted tennis courts and a fitness center.

Best Western Royal Sun
$$ • 1015 N. Stone Ave. • 622-8871, (800) 528-1234

At the corner of Speedway Boulevard and Stone Avenue, Best Western Royal Sun is a half-mile from the University and offers a few more amenities than most hotels, including a VCR in each room, Jacuzzi, heated pool, res-

---

> **FYI**
> Unless otherwise noted, the area code for all phone numbers listed in this guide is 520.

> **INSIDERS' TIP**
>
> When you stay in the city limits of Tucson, a percentage of the room surcharge goes to support local arts organizations, making Tucson one of the most well-funded cities of its size for fine arts.

ACCOMPANIMENTS • 29

MORE OF WHAT YOU NEED, WHEN YOU NEED IT!

HAWTHORN SUITES LTD.℠

Amenities
- Courtyard rooms and suites.
- Suites include kitchenettes for long term stays. Guest laundry facilities.
- Complimentary breakfast each morning.
- Complimentary cocktail reception each evening.
- Voice mail and data port telephones. Business services available.
- In-room coffee makers, movies, microwave, wetbar and refrigerator.

Entertainment/Recreation
- Heated pool and spa. Gas grills.
- Championship golf, tennis and health club privileges nearby.
- Nearby shopping. Restaurants within walking distance.
- Meeting facilities available.

HAWTHORN SUITES LTD.℠
7007 East Tanque Verde Road,
Tucson, AZ 85715
Ph. 520-298-2300
Fax 520-298-6756
Toll Free 1-800-527-1133
www.hawthorn.com

---

taurant and exercise room. Of the 78 rooms, 20 suites include a refrigerator and a whirlpool tub.

Candlelight Suites
$$$ • 1440 S. Craycroft Rd. • 747-1440, (800) 233-1440

Located near Davis-Monthan Air Force Base, this hotel offers 70 two-room suites with kitchenette, queen-size beds, free continental breakfast, cable TV, pool and laundry facilities. Candlelight Suites allows pets.

Clarion Hotel
$$ • 6801 S. Tucson Blvd. • 746-3932, (800) 526-0550

A half-mile from the airport, the hotel's 194-units include TV, direct-dial phones and, in some cases, refrigerators. Also available are a heated pool, spa, coin laundry, fitness center, continental breakfast and complimentary beverages in the evening. The hotel offers transfers to the airport.

Clarion Hotel and Suites — Santa Rita
$$$ • 88 E. Broadway Blvd. • 622-4000

In the heart of Tucson's Arts District downtown and near the Convention and Visitors Center, this high-rise hotel offers microwaves and refrigerators in all 162 rooms. The restaurant/lounge is known for its Mexican food (look for Cafe Poca Cosa in the Restaurants chapter). The hotel has a pool, spa, fitness center and guest laundry facility. There is a free continental breakfast.

Cliff Manor Inn
$$ • 5900 N. Oracle Rd. • 887-4800, (800) 223-5369, Ext. 298

Cliff Manor offers 60 king- and double-rooms and 12 casitas with kitchenettes, direct-dial telephones and in-room movies. Bring your racket, clubs and dancing shoes — the inn offers access to tennis courts and golf courses as well as a dance club. The spa and pool have great views of the mountains, and every Sunday from 10 AM

30 • ACCOMMODATIONS

Tucson's resorts are little pockets of heaven on Earth.

to 2 PM a brunch buffet is served. There's a restaurant on site.

Country Suites By Carlson
$$ • 7411 N. Oracle Rd. • 575-9255, (800) 456-4000

Most of the 100 suites and 57 studios have kitchenettes. The hotel also has a putting green, pool, whirlpool and a courtyard for relaxing. Every morning you can expect a free continental breakfast and weekday newspaper, and on Tuesdays the hotel hosts a cookout for guests.

Courtyard by Marriott
$$$ • 2505 E. Executive Dr. • 573-0000

These 149 king- and double-rooms and suites offer everything you'll need when not lounging by the landscaped courtyard and pool. A spa, fitness room, laundry rooms, restaurant and lounge are all on site. Courtyard has an airport shuttle and conference rooms that can accommodate up to 40 people.

Days Inn
$ • 222 S. Freeway • 791-7511

Just off I-10 west of downtown Tucson, this inexpensive facility has 122 rooms and offers guests free continental breakfast, large pool and spa, laundromat, meeting room for up to 50 people and even copy/FAX services.

Days Inn has a number of discounts to government, military and AARP members.

DoubleTree Guest Suites
$$ • 6555 E. Speedway Blvd. • 721-7100, (800) 222-TREE

Each of these 304 two-room suites includes an extra large bathroom, two vanities, two TVs, two telephones, refrigerator, coffee maker and wet bar. Larger suites have fireplaces, dining rooms and hydro tubs. On the grounds guests can use the oversized heated pool, fitness room or the courts at the nearby Center Court Tennis Club. Hungry? DoubleTree has a full-service restaurant.

TUBAC GOLF RESORT

Exclusive, historic 45-room resort located in the lush Santa Cruz Valley only a 40-minute, scenic drive from Tucson International Airport. Contemporary Southwestern units including 18 suites with fireplaces. Championship golf, tennis, swimming, hiking and world-class birdwatching. Minutes from Southern Arizona's major attractions and Old Mexico. Small group meeting faclities to 60 persons.

One Otero Rd. • P.O. Box 1297, Tubac, AZ 85646 • (800)-848-7893 • http//www.arizonaguide.com/tubac

DoubleTree Hotel
$$ • 445 S. Alvernon Wy. • 881-4200, (800) 528-0444

This 10-story, 295-room hotel is centrally located to attractions, shopping, the University and business districts and is across the street from Reid Park Zoo and two 18-hole golf courses. The resort-style hotel has three tennis courts, a pool, a spa, an indoor/outdoor restaurant (open until 11 PM), a lounge and an exercise room. For business travelers, rooms for meetings and banquets accommodate 10 to 1,200 people.

Embassy Suites Hotel and Conference Center
$$$ • 7051 S. Tucson Blvd. • 573-0700

Embassy Suites offers complete convention facilities. Some of the 204 deluxe, two-room suites have kitchenettes. Start your day with a complimentary continental breakfast, a swim and an hour in the exercise room. The hotel also offers monthly rates and complimentary beverages each evening and has a restaurant and lounge on site. Embassy Suites is near the entrance to the Tucson International Airport, so, of course, shuttle service is available.

Embassy Suites Hotel Broadway
$$$ • 5335 E. Broadway Blvd.
• 745-2700, (800) 362-2779

Each of Embassy's 142 suites has a private bedroom and separate living room with sofa sleeper, kitchen, microwave, refrigerator and coffee maker. Two telephones with dataports and voice mail, as well as in-room movies on two TVs, help you keep in touch with the outside world. Guests also receive a complimentary cooked-to-order breakfast, included in the cost of the room, and a two-hour "Manager's Reception" each evening with snacks and beverages of your choice. The restaurant has outdoor seating, and the lounge offers billiards and a big-screen TV for the times you're not enjoying the outdoor pool, spa or fitness center. Among the business services is free transportation within 5 miles of the hotel, which includes the University of Arizona and Davis-Monthan Air Force Base.

Hampton Inn
$$ • 6971 S. Tucson Blvd. • 889-5789

With 125 rooms, Hampton Inn also offers hospitality suites with separate bedroom and living room, as well as a heated pool, spa, in-room movies, coin laundry and continental breakfast. The hotel also has an airport shuttle.

Hawthorn Suites
$$$ • 7007 E. Tanque Verde Rd.
• 298-2300

Sixty-two of the 90 rooms here are studio suites, with microwave oven, refrigerator, a king-size bed or two double beds, sleeper sofa, cable with free movie channels, Nintendo and free local calls. Each stay includes a poolside continental breakfast and a complimentary happy hour (from 5:30 to 7:30 PM). You can hangout at the pool or relax in the outdoor spa. For those with business on their minds, this hotel offers a 750-square-foot meeting room that can hold up to 60 people.

Holiday Inn City Center
$$ • 181 W. Broadway Blvd. • 624-8711

In the center of downtown Tucson, this 309-room complex hosts a number of major convention events while still offering individual travelers a homey experience and the luxury of a large metropolitan hotel. A heated pool, fitness center, popular restaurant and lounge are within this high-rise, which is near government buildings and the arts district. The Tucson Convention Center is just across the street.

Holiday Inn Express
$$ • 2803 E. Valencia Rd. • 294-2500

A new 95-room facility near the airport, Holiday Inn Express specializes in large functions while still offering all the usual room amenities one would expect from this hotel chain. A restaurant, lounge, pool, spa and laundry facilities are on the premises.

Hotel Congress
$$ • 311 E. Congress St. • 622-8848, (800) 722-8848

Established in 1919, this brick and marble building was constructed to provide accommodations to Southern Pacific railroad passengers traveling through Tucson. Its 40 rooms on the second floor overlook Congress Street's arts district. The hotel's claim to fame involves the infamous John Dillinger gang, which was captured here in 1934. Today, the hotel's first floor caters to Tucson's artists' and writers' scene with a 24-hour cafe and the locally popular Club Congress, featuring live bands and disc jockeys (see our Nightlife chapter). The rooms were restored in 1985, retaining the original 1920s-era charm. This is not just a historic hotel, it's an experience.

Hotel Congress is across the street from both the Amtrak and Greyhound stations. It also operates a youth hostel, offering rooms for $45.

Hotel Park Tucson
$$$ • 5151 E. Grant Rd. • 323-6262, (800) 257-7275

This desert oasis should drop the name "hotel" and call itself a resort — it's that classy. Decorated in Southwestern colors and Santa Fe-style furniture, many of the 216 rooms overlook the courtyard. The courtyard's amenities include a pool, exercise room, steam room, sauna and Jacuzzi — all well-designed for privacy. The site features a lounge by the pool that is open for breakfast and two restaurants, including the Ranchers Club of Arizona, known for its authentic Western grilled fare.

Howard Johnson Lodge
$$ • 1025 E. Benson Hwy. • 623-7792, (800) 972-9154

Near I-10 and Ajo Way, this motor lodge offers 136 rooms and executive suites, some with private balconies overlooking the courtyard, pool and spa. The full-service restaurant is open until 10 PM, and the lodge offers 24-hour complimentary shuttle service to the airport and University of Arizona.

InnSuites Hotel
$$ • 475 N. Granada Ave. • 622-3000

Just off I-10 at the St. Mary's Road exit, this 297-room hotel sits on 11 acres with a lush garden courtyard, Olympic-size swimming pool, spa and children's playground. For the business traveler, the site has meeting spaces for 10 to 1,450 people. The hotels offers two-room executive suites, studios and even a Presidential Suite, with oversized jacuzzi and living room. Each room includes a microwave and refrigerator, free HBO, Nintendo games and a complimentary breakfast buffet.

La Quinta Inn
$$ • 665 N. Freeway • 622-6491, (800) 687-6667

Just off the I-10 freeway at St. Mary's Road near downtown, La Quinta Inn is a new facility that offers in-room movies and video games, a free continental breakfast, computer-friendly dataport phones, same-day dry cleaning, guest laundry facilities and a heated swimming pool. Some of the 133 rooms also have a microwave and refrigerator.

AUTHENTIC ARIZONA

This historic 40-room desert enclave has been a Tucson landmark for more than 60 years.

Recently restored with the addition of Cielos, a world-class dining experience, the Lodge is now an acclaimed Sonoran retreat conveniently located near the University of Arizona and major area attractions.

LODGE ON THE DESERT

306 North Alvernon Way • Tucson, Arizona 85711   800.456.5634   T 520.325.3366   F 520.327.5834

La Quinta Inn and Suites
$$ • 7001 S. Tucson Blvd. • 573-3333, (800) 531-5900

Located one block from the airport, this new facility offers 143 rooms and eight two-room suites with separate sitting and sleeping areas, double vanities, microwave, refrigerator, desk and speaker phones. All rooms have computer-friendly dataport phones and voice mail to make your business traveling easy. You can also take advantage of the heated swimming pool, whirlpool, exercise facility, meeting rooms for up to 75 people, guest laundry and same-day dry-cleaning service. The complimentary continental breakfast offers a choice of cereals, fruit, pastries, bagels and juices.

Marriott University Park
$$ • 880 E. 2nd St. • 792-4100, (800) 228-9290

This new nine-story atrium hotel, which features 250 guest rooms and a Presidential Suite, is next to the Main Gate Center of the University of Arizona, on the corner of Tyndall Avenue and 2nd Street. The hotel also has a concierge floor, for those who may need a haven during the relocation process, and 69 "Rooms That Work," which are specially equipped with dataport phones, VCRs, work spaces and voice mail. The Saguaro Grill is in the atrium, and the hotel also has an outdoor pool, whirlpool, sauna and fitness center. It's just seconds from restaurants and shopping. The Marriott is a perfect choice for parents visiting their young scholars at the University.

Plaza Hotel and Conference Center
$$ • 1900 E. Speedway Blvd. • 327-7341, (800) 843-8052

The Plaza Hotel and Conference Center is at the busy intersection of Speedway Boulevard and Campbell Avenue, across from the University of Arizona and University Medical Center. It's a newly renovated, seven-story hotel that offers 150 rooms, a pool, dining room, a lounge with entertainment and a big-screen TV, underground parking, room service and a variety of convention and banquet services.

Quality Hotel and Suites
$$ • 475 N. Granada Ave. • 622-3000, (800) 446-6589

These 297 rooms, including 10 suites, on 12 acres have a resort-like feel due to a lush courtyard and heated Olympic-size swimming pool. The El Centro Bar & Grill is worth a visit even if you don't stay at the hotel. There are 12 meeting rooms for up to 600 people or banquets for up to 800 people.

Ramada Palo Verde
$$$ • 5251 S. Julian Dr. • 294-5250, (800) 228-2828

Just off the I-10 exit at Palo Verde Road, these 153 rooms and 20 two-room suites are just minutes from Tucson International Airport (ask about the hotel's shuttle service) and include a microwave, coffee maker, refrigerator and wet bar. The comfortable mezzanine overlooks the swimming pool where you can enjoy your free continental breakfast or an evening cocktail and meal at the lounge or the restaurant. There are also four separate courtyards, each with its own heated spa.

Smuggler's Inn
$$ • 6350 E. Speedway Blvd. • 296-3292, (800) 525-8852

Do you think that Tucson is about as far away as you can get from a Caribbean lagoon and gardens? Well, think again. The 150 units at Smuggler's Inn range from single rooms to suites, and all have private patios overlooking the pool, spa and putting green. The free tennis and cable TV will keep you busy when you're not hanging out in the restaurant/lounge.

Sumner Suites
$$ • 6885 S. Tucson Blvd. • 295-0405, (800) 747-8483

All suite, all the time. Each of these 122 suites has a refrigerator, microwave oven, coffee maker, clock radio, two telephones with dataports, in-room voice mail system and a desk. Also included is a complimentary continental breakfast buffet, complimentary daily newspaper, laundry facilities, swimming pool and fitness center. There are meeting rooms available for up to 150 people.

Viscount Suite Hotel
$$$ • 4855 E. Broadway Blvd. • 745-6500, (800) 527-9666

A favorite buffet lunch spot (even for nonguests), this four-story atrium hotel includes 215 elegant two-room suites with two TVs, two telephones and a living room with a desk. The larger Presidential Suites include refrigerator, microwave oven, two bedrooms, two baths, bar and big-screen TVs. Besides the breakfast buffet and complimentary transportation to the airport, the hotel has a pool, spa, sauna and workout room. The Atrium Cafe is a local favorite, as is Wilbur's Executive Sports Bar & Grill's evening Happy Hour. For more elegant dining, try the Oxford Club. If you're a business traveler who requires just a bit extra, the Viscount is worth exploring.

Wayward Winds Lodge
$$ • 707 W. Miracle Mile • 791-7526

One mile off the Miracle Mile exit of I-10, Wayward Winds Lodge has been family-owned and -operated since 1958. It offers lodge-style motel rooms, suites and apartments with kitchenettes. All 41 units open onto a landscaped courtyard featuring a heated pool, enclosed recreation room, outdoor shuffleboard and a great view of the mountains. Covered parking and a continental breakfast are included.

Windmill Inn at St. Philip's Plaza
$$$ • 4250 N. Campbell Ave. • 577-0007, (800) 547-4747

Windmill Inn at Campbell Avenue and River Road offers 122 two-room suites with wet bar, microwave, desk, three phones, two remote-controlled color TVs, refrigerator and sleeper sofa.

INSIDERS' TIP

Sports fans will be happy to know that $1 per day of their car rental cost goes to support spring training activities. The teams that come to Tucson include the Colorado Rockies, Arizona Diamondbacks and Chicago White Sox.

ACCOMMODATIONS • 35

Each morning you'll awake to complimentary coffee, pastries and a daily newspaper. The hotel also offers a free bestseller lending library, guest laundry facilities, meeting rooms for up to 300 people and an outdoor pool and spa. Guests are provided with bicycles to explore the nearby Rillito River Bike Trail. Stay here and you'll be near some taste-bud temptations: Look for Cafe Terra Cotta and Oven's Restaurant in the Restaurants chapter for details.

Guest Ranches

If you want an experience a bit more like staying with a large group of friends without the "hotel" atmosphere, a guest ranch may be what you are looking for. Some offer true "cowboy" adventures, with horseback riding and cookouts. Others are more like summer camp, with swimming, tennis, volleyball, horseshoe tossing and plenty of pampering.

Some ranches have rooms with individual kitchens and telephones, while others offer only the basics for those wanting to escape material trappings. Whether you're a weekend cowboy or a vacationing corporate executive, the following ranches can accommodate you.

Flying V Ranch
$$$ • 6810 Flying V Rd. • 299-0702

This 1908-era ranch offers five housekeeping cottages, which range from single to two-bedroom units with ranch-style decor. The tranquil atmosphere near Ventana Creek in the foothills of the Catalina Mountains is great for bird-watching, hiking or just relaxing in the pool area. Nearby are two major golf resorts, Loews Ventana Canyon Resort and The Lodge at Ventana Canyon.

The Flying V Ranch is behind the Loews Ventana Canyon Resort, 7000 N. Resort Drive. To find the ranch, turn left at the resort's west parking lot.

Lazy K Bar Ranch
$$$ • 8401 N. Scenic Dr. • 744-3050, (800) 321-7018

Located 16 miles northwest of downtown Tucson in the Tucson Mountains at an elevation of 2,300 feet, the Lazy K Bar Ranch has offered a true Western atmosphere since 1936. Each of its 23 rooms has a private bath but no telephone or TVs to disturb you. On the property are two lighted tennis courts, heated pool, spa, shuffleboard, horseshoe court and a corral with horses for every level of rider to use during the guided rides through the desert. The dining room and bar are cheerful, and a spacious library offers a selection of all types of books or a space just to sit and visit. Saturday is steak cookout night at the ranch, served outdoors near a 10-foot waterfall. The ranch also offers airport transfers.

Lazy K Bar Ranch is only open from September 15 through June 15.

Sunstone Guest Ranch
$$$ • 2545 N. Woodland Rd. • 749-1928

This large facility built in the late 1800s is on the far Eastside of Tucson among 11 acres of lush grounds, with a pond, sitting areas shaded by some of the oldest mesquite trees in Tucson and a swimming pool. After sitting idle for two years, the property was opened in 1994 as a guest ranch.

Among its four separate buildings are the "Honeymoon" room with a king-size bed and 10 rooms with queen beds. They all have a distinctive Southwestern flavor with antique furnishings and picture windows with great views of the grounds. With on-site catering facilities, Sunstone can host corporate retreats, business seminars, weddings and private parties of all types.

The room rates are based on double occupancy and include a light breakfast of pastries, fresh fruit, cereals, juices, coffee and tea. An advance deposit is required with your reservation. Smoking is permitted only in outdoor areas.

Tanque Verde Ranch
$$$ • 14301 E. Speedway Blvd.
• 296-6275

Established as a cattle ranch in 1868 and transformed into a dude ranch in the 1920s, this 640-acre facility offers individual Western casitas, three swimming pools (including one indoors), gourmet dining, five tennis courts, a health spa and more than 100 horses (Arizona's largest riding stable) for daylong pack trips through the Sonoran Desert. The ranch is in the foothills of the Rincon Mountains on the far Eastside near Saguaro National Park East and Tanque Verde Falls. Ranch staff will take you on guided nature hikes from the ranch through the park.

White Stallion Ranch
$$$ • 9251 W. Twin Peaks Rd.
• 297-0252, (888) 977-2624

Step back into movie history at White Stallion Ranch. Located on 3,000 acres of secluded desert near the Tucson Mountains and Saguaro National Park West, the site served as the location for the filming of many scenes from the movie *High Chaparral*. This working Longhorn cattle ranch offers an inside view of the day-to-day life of real cowboys. Though closed from June through October to guests, the rest of the year you'll enjoy a heated swimming pool, indoor hot tub, ping-pong, volleyball, basketball, tennis courts, shuffleboard, billiards, horseshoe courts, horseback riding, hiking, cookouts, moonlight bonfires with a cowboy singer and even astronomy programs with its large telescopes. When you are not hanging out in the large library, you will find yourself exploring the saloon, dining room or petting zoo of miniature horses, fallow deer, bighorn sheep and pygmy goats. Peacocks and guinea hens run free on the ranch, so watch where you step.

> **FYI**
> Unless otherwise noted, the area code for all phone numbers listed in this guide is 520.

Wild Horse Ranch
$$$ • 6801 N. Camino Verde • 744-1012

Located 15 minutes from downtown Tucson in the northwest, this 20-acre site offers horses, llamas, riding and hiking trails, a swimming pool, a cantina, tennis courts and banquet facilities in a desert setting. All rooms are on the ground level, rustic in decor with outside doors.

Resorts and Spas

Canyon Ranch Spa
$$$$ • 8600 E. Rockcliff Rd. • 749-9000, (800) 742-9000

If a total health and fitness vacation experience is what you want or need, look no further than Canyon Ranch Spa. The world-famous 70-acre complex offers choices you won't find anywhere else. Besides deluxe accommodations and three gourmet meals a day, the Health & Healing center has health professionals and full-time physicians who offer 50 fitness classes daily. Or you can consult directly with any of the spa's nutritionists, exercise physiologists, movement therapists and psychologists. Also offered are activities such as boxercise, tai chi, yoga, squash and racquetball. Then treat yourself with a massage, herbal wrap, cleansing facial or other body treatments. Canyon Ranch offers special Health & Healing packages that range from four- to seven-night stays. No tobacco or alcohol products are allowed at the facility. Also, children must be at least 14 years old to participate in any activities or use the facilities.

Hacienda del Sol Guest Ranch Resort
$$ • 5601 N. Hacienda del Sol Rd.
• 299-1501

This resort opened in 1929 as a preparatory school for girls. When it was turned into a guest resort in the mid-1930s, it became the favorite spot for Hollywood types like Clark Gable, Joseph Cotton and Spencer Tracy. From the 1950s to 1970, it operated as a private club. It reopened to the public in 1983 on its 34-acre desert site. The 30 rooms and five casitas sit on a slope in the Catalina Foothills. You walk downstairs to get to the pool and spa area. Each room is individually decorated, but the general decoration and construction follow the 1930s deco style. The guest lobby has a lovely library, bridge tables and a cozy fireplace. Outdoor activities include horseshoes, tennis, croquet and horseback riding.

The Grill at Hacienda del Sol is open for lunch and dinner daily (see our Restaurants chapter).

The Lodge at Ventana Canyon
$$$$ • 6200 N. Clubhouse Ln.
• 577-1400, (800) 828-5701

This 600-acre private golf resort and lodge has 49 guest suites with private balcony/patio, spiral staircase to the two-bedroom loft and a complete kitchen. Nestled in the Ventana Canyon area of the Santa Catalina Mountains, the two 18-hole golf courses have won *Golf Magazine's* "Silver Medal Award," and *Links Magazine's* "Best of Golf Award" (see our Golf chapter). The fitness center is open around the clock, and the 12 lighted tennis courts, saunas, whirlpool spas and swimming center give guests plenty to do. The resort also has 50 meeting rooms. The Hearthstone dining room and Sierra Bar offer panoramic views of the mountain range, golf course and the desert creatures who make their homes around the resort.

Loews Ventana Canyon Resort
$$$$ • 7000 N. Resort Dr. • 299-2020, (800) 234-5117

On 93 acres above Tucson, this 398-room golf and tennis resort has eight lighted tennis courts, a pool, a spa, five restaurant/lounges and two Tom Fazio-designed PGA championship golf courses (see our Golf chapter). At the foot of Ventana Canyon, this resort also offers a complete range of wet and dry massage; wrap, facial and aromatherapy treatments; 24-hour room service; and bike rentals. Check out our Nightlife chapter for details about the entertainment the resort offers.

Omni Tucson National Golf Resort and Spa
$$$$ • 2727 W. Club Dr. • 297-2271, (800) 528-4856

Offering 167 rooms and 15,000 square feet of banquet space, this golf resort is nestled in the foothills of the far northwest Catalina Mountains. Besides the European-style spa and fitness center, there are also 27 holes of championship PGA golf (see our Golf chapter), two heated pools, whirlpool, sauna, steam room and tennis. Your choice of dining includes the casual Fiesta Room or the elegant Catalina Grille.

Sheraton El Conquistador Resort and Country Club
$$$$ • 10000 N. Oracle Rd. • 544-5000, (800) 325-7832

The Sheraton is one of the largest golf and tennis resorts in the West with three golf courses, two pro shops and 31 lighted tennis courts. With 434 rooms, 30,500 square feet of meeting space and six restaurants, this resort hosts many local events. The Last Territory Steakhouse serves "Tucson's Best Cowboy Steak," and the Sundance Cafe features casual dining and "Tucson's Best Sunday Brunch." Both of those bests were bestowed by *Tucson Weekly* (see

INSIDERS' TIP

Looking for romance? Loews Ventana Canyon Resort has a few rooms with Roman Tubs — tubs large enough for two people.

38 • ACCOMMODATIONS

A winter storm can produce several inches of snow, even on the desert floor.

our Restaurants chapter). Strolling mariachis complement the Mexican dishes at the Dos Locos restaurant. You might want to just relax by the pool or lounge in the newly renovated rooms that make you feel right at home. (See the Restaurants chapter for more information about The Last Territory Steakhouse.)

Starr Pass
$$$$ • 3645 W. Starr Pass Blvd.
• 670-0500, (800) 503-2898

Very Southwestern in decor, this modern championship golf resort offers one- and two-bedroom casitas with open-beam ceilings, full kitchens, two baths, washer and dryer, fireplaces, patios and Mexican saltillo tile floors, all within walking distance to the clubhouse and views of the city lights. The full-service restaurant and fitness center add to the experience. The golf facilities offer both group and private instruction to players of all levels, and the pro shop is known locally as one of the finest (see our Golf chapter). Starr Pass is just a few miles west of downtown and is the only resort in that area.

The Westin La Paloma Resort
$$$$ • 3800 E. Sunrise Dr. • 742-6000, (800) 937-8461

This 487-room resort offers a 27-hole Jack Nicklaus Signature golf course, which was named one of the top-75 Resort Courses in the country by *Golf Digest* (see our Golf chapter). If golf isn't your favorite physical activity, the Westin also has 12 tennis courts, indoor racquetball, three swimming pools, a wet-and-wild water slide and waterfalls, an aerobics center, Nautilus room and children's play area. One of the pools even has a swim-up bar for drinks and sandwiches. There are also five restaurants, two lounges and 42,000 square feet of meeting space. Some of the suites come with wood-burning fireplaces, sunken hot tubs, patios and well-stocked refrigerators.

Westward Look Resort
$$$$ • 245 E. Ina Rd. • 297-9023, (800) 722-2500

Westward Look (built in 1912) was Tucson's first resort. On 80 acres in the foothills of the Catalina Mountains, these 244 rooms have great city views from their patios or balconies above Tucson. Two restaurants offer either elegant dining or a casual ambiance and good food as well as varied musical entertainment by local groups. There are also eight tennis courts, three pools and spas, a Wellness Center and fitness club and 11 meeting rooms accommodating up to 300 people. Small pets are allowed.

Tucson offers a wide variety of bed and breakfasts, from Spanish-style ranches to contemporary homes.

Bed and Breakfasts

When one thinks of the Southwest, the idea of a traditional bed and breakfast may seem slightly odd. After all, the traditional bed and breakfast is usually an East Coast mansion steeped in early American history. Well bucko, you're in for a shock. Tucson offers a wide variety of bed and breakfasts, from Spanish-style ranches to contemporary homes.

Many of Tucson's bed and breakfasts are operated by people who really know the area and its history, so don't be afraid to ask. The area's bed and breakfast operations are mostly located around the University and in the historic downtown district, or on the outskirts of town among the flora and fauna of the Sonoran Desert. A tour of the in-town structures is a study in elegant, historic architecture ranging from 1880 adobe homes to Victorian mansions through the late 1920s. Wherever you stay, count on the innkeeper to know the whole history of the building, including its past owners and what historic figures may have passed through.

For the bed and breakfasts in the outlying desert areas, your stay will be a lesson in wildlife and panoramic sunsets. Most offer hiking trails into the nearby mountains that surround Tucson. The innkeepers at these establishments will gladly take you on a tour of their property and point out desert life and points of interest.

Unlike the hotels and resorts, the room prices for bed and breakfasts generally stay the same all year. However, the guidelines we mentioned in Accommodations still apply: May through September is a slow time in Tucson, so there is the possibility that rates will be lower. And February, with the Gem Show and the Rodeo, is not the time to be caught in town without a reservation.

Price Guidelines

Each listing here includes a symbol indicating a price range for a one-night, double-occupancy stay. Though experiences at Tucson bed and breakfasts vary, you can assume a few basic facts: no smoking, no children, no credit cards, no pets and a two-night minimum stay on weekends. Of course these rules can change from accommodation to accommodation. Issues such as handicapped accessibility, smoking policy, children, etc., are worth investigating beforehand to avoid any complications during your stay. One easy way to deal with reservations, questions and the like is by using one of two bed and breakfast reservation services that do take credit cards and have toll-free numbers: **Arizona Trails B&B Reservation Service**, (888) 799-4284; or **Advance Reservations & Old Pueblo Homestays**, (800) 333-9776.

$	Less than $55
$$	$55 to $85
$$$	$85 to $110
$$$$	More than $110

Adobe Rose Inn
$$ • 940 N. Olsen Ave. • 318-4644, (800) 328-4122

A historic 1933 home, the Adobe Rose Inn offers three lodgepole-furnished guest rooms with double beds, two of which have a cozy fireplace and stained-glass windows. Or you can choose one of two private cottages.

INSIDERS' TIP

The owners of local bed and breakfasts usually know a lot about local history, activities and events, so be sure to spend some time talking with your hosts.

The guest rooms and the cottages feature cable TV and a private bath. The Inn also has a pool and a spa. The Adobe serves a basic American breakfast of eggs, toast, fruit and cereal. This is a great choice for visiting Wildcat parents, as the University is only a couple of blocks away.

The Big House
$$ • 629 N. 7th Ave. • 623-1907

This historic prairie-style home, built in the early 1900s for Don Carlos Jacome, was designed by Senor Pesquiera. Jacome was one of the signatories of the Arizona Constitution on February 14, 1912. The Jacome mercantile store was well known in southern Arizona and northern Mexico until it closed in 1980. Each of the five rooms has a private bath and a work table in case a laptop computer is part of your vacation plans. In fact, the site includes a conference room and offers limited secretarial services for an extra charge. The rooms are bright and spacious. French doors from the living room lead to the breakfast area that looks out onto a huge porch. The inn is convenient to the University.

The Cactus Quail Bed and Breakfast
$$$ • 14000 N. Dust Devil Dr. • 825-6767, (888) 825-6767

This Spanish-tiled ranch about 10 miles north of Tucson off Oracle Road offers spectacular views of the Santa Catalina Mountains and rooms decorated with a rustic Southwestern flavor. The largest room ("The Bunkhouse"), which can sleep four, has a loft and a private bath. The other two rooms ("The Pueblo" and "The Hacienda") have double beds and share a bathroom. The rooms have TVs and VCRs. Expect the best in Southwestern cuisine for breakfast, including Mexican eggs and tortillas. Ask owners Marty and Sue Higbee about horseback riding opportunities through Pusch Ridge Stables. The Cactus Quail is convenient to Biosphere 2 (see our Attractions chapter).

Car-Mar's Southwest Bed and Breakfast
$$ • 6766 W. Oakahoma St. • 578-1730, (888) 578-1730

Surrounded by a romantic desert setting, this bed and breakfast at the western base of the Tucson Mountains offers three guest rooms with private courtyards and baths. These spacious rooms are uniquely decorated with lodgepole and saguaro rib furniture, much of which was designed by the owners. Rooms also contain queen-size beds, a phone, TV/VCR, microwave and refrigerator. A pool and hot tub offer a relaxing vantage point for viewing the sunset. Car-Mar is short for Carole Martinez, the bed and breakfast's innkeeper. Stay here and you'll be minutes from Old Tucson Studios and the Arizona-Sonora Desert Museum (see our Attractions chapter.)

Casa Alegre Bed and Breakfast
$$$ • 316 E. Speedway Blvd. • 628-1800, (800) 628-5654

This 1915 bungalow-style home is centrally located between downtown and the University of Arizona. You'll be surrounded by wood: The inn is room after room of beautiful hardwood floors and mahogany cabinetry. Make the most out of your vacation by relaxing your cares away in the pool or hot tub. Inside, all five rooms have private baths; outside, the grounds are covered in lush gardens. A full traditional breakfast is served between 8 and 9 AM.

> **FYI**
> Unless otherwise noted, the area code for all phone numbers listed in this guide is 520.

INSIDERS' TIP

There may well be an increase in the number of bed and breakfasts in Tucson due to city zoning changes made in 1996, which have encouraged these small business establishments. If you've ever thought of starting your own bed and breakfast, Tucson might be the spot.

Tucson's Favorite B & B's

Bed and Breakfast
Tucson, Arizona

Enjoy the flavor of an old Spanish hacienda in a peaceful, secluded desert setting with mountain views attractive to nature lovers and romantics.

Phone: (800) 982-1795 **Fax:** (520) 722-4558 **E-mail:** hacdd@azstarnet.com
URL: http://www.azstarnet.com/~hacdd/Index.html

"Your Arizona Home"

○ Luxurious comfort
○ Sumptuous breakfasts
○ King-size beds
○ In-room TV/VCR

The Cactus Quail
Bed & Breakfast

In the shadow of the Santa Catalina Mountains, just north of Tucson, The Cactus Quail Bed & Breakfast offers guests a singular experience. From the spectacular views outside to rustic elegance inside, The Cactus Quail truly represents the desert Southwest.

The Cactus Quail - Marty & Sue Higbee, Proprietors
14000 N. Dust Devil Drive, Tucson 85739   Toll-free (888) 825-6767
(520) 825-6767 Fax: (520) 825-4104   http://si-systems.com/cactusq/index.html

ELYSIAN GROVE MARKET
A BED & BREAKFAST INN

Located in an Historic Barrio, next to Tucson's downtown arts district, Elysian Grove Market B&B Inn is a charming, historic adobe built in the 1920s as a corner market. The four bedrooms are furnished with art, tribal rugs & comfortable antique beds. The garden is filled with cacti, mesquites, flowers, hummingbirds and fountains.

400 W. Simpson Tucson, AZ 85701   (520) 628-1522
http://www.bbonline.com/az/elysiangrove/   Innkeeper Deborah La Chapelle

The Congenial Quail is a centrally located in-town oasis. An inviting 1940s ranch house secluded on 3 acres. Theme bedrooms furnished with eclectic decor and original art beckon you. Savor your gourmet Southwestern breakfasts in morning sunshine as it filters into the Arizona room. For over 25 years, these educators have enjoyed a life of academics, travel, art, and a passion for foods and want to share this with you.

Laurie & Bob Haskett
4267 N. Fourth Avenue, Tucson 85705
Toll-free (800) 895-2047   (520) 887-9487

Casa Tierra Adobe Bed and Breakfast Inn
$$$ • 11155 W. Calle Pima • 578-3058

Located on 5 acres of secluded Sonoran Desert on the western side of the Tucson Mountains, the rustic adobe hacienda offers spectacular views of the mountains and is surrounded by saguaro cacti. Casa Tierra ("earth house") features more than 50 arches and entryways with vaulted brick ceilings and an interior arched courtyard. The area is only minutes from the Arizona-Sonora Desert Museum, Saguaro National Park West and Old Tucson Studios. The rooms include private baths, small refrigerators, microwaves, patios and private entrances. In the morning you will be treated to a full vegetarian breakfast, along with home-baked goods, fresh ground coffee and a variety of herbal teas. The site is great for birding and hiking or just relaxing in the hot tub.

Catalina Park Inn
$$ • 309 E. 1st St. • 792-4541, (800) 792-4885

This 1927 mansion near the University of Arizona is your chance to vacation in true elegance. The three rooms and one suite are decorated with antiques, and all include a phone, TV and private bath. Take some time to enjoy the perennial and rose gardens. In the morning a breakfast of eggs, toast, potatoes, juice and fruit and a newspaper will be delivered to your door.

The Congenial Quail Bed and Breakfast
$$-$$$ • 4267 N. 4th Ave. • 887-9487, (800) 895-2047

This 1940s ranch house sits on 3 acres of desert a short drive north from the University area and downtown. Each of the three guest rooms has its own distinctive personality, and you will have access to the spa and outdoor patio for relaxing under the sun or under the stars.

The Castaway Cottage has its own bath with Talavera tile, a queen-size bed, a private yard and a patio away from the main house. When you're not exploring Tucson, you can explore the cottage's unique mystery and science-fiction library. The Little Golden Classic is the perfect place for your kids with a single bed (they'll get you another if need be). And the American Homestead feels like you're staying at your grandparents' house with its antique furnishings. The latter two rooms share a Mexican-tiled bath.

You'll start your day with coffee, fruit and a Southwestern frittata served on the Arizona Room's porch. Owners Laurie and Bob Haskett will welcome you, and they do accept major credit cards.

Corona Ranch
$$ • 7595 E. Snyder Rd. • 907-2501

Formerly the El Rancho del Corona, a prestigious dude ranch that hosted guests from all over the world during the 1920s and '30s, the current site has four spacious guest rooms facing a large courtyard on 20 acres near Sabino Canyon. There is also a two-bedroom guesthouse. Each room has a refrigerator, coffee maker and Southwestern decor. Although a phone is available to guests, there are no phones or TVs in the rooms. The property is nestled among mesquite and saguaro. There are plans to have up to nine rooms available in the future. A continental breakfast offers breads, muffins, fruit, juice and coffee.

What is unique about Corona Ranch is that it also offers a large banquet hall with a huge fireplace that can serve 300 indoor guests and an adjoining patio with seating for 250 people, making it ideal for secluded corporate events, weddings or parties.

Coyote Crossing Bed and Breakfast
$$-$$$ • 6985 N. Camino Verde • 744-3285

Nestled in the eastern foothills of the Tucson Mountains, this getaway offers three rooms, each with a private entrance, king-size bed, air conditioning, full bath, ceiling fans, cable TV, coffee maker and refrigerator. You can enjoy the patio and pool or relax by the Grand Room's cozy fireplace on those cold desert nights. All the rooms contain a king-size bed. It's located about a mile west of the intersection of Ina and Silverbell roads.

Day Star Farm Bed and Breakfast
$$ • 3312 N. Riverbend Cir. East
• 886-6461

This adobe-brick, mission-tiled ranch house will take you back to the Tucson of the 1940s and '50s. Located in the Northeast foothills near Sabino Canyon, this quaint horse ranch offers large rooms. "The Girls Room" has two queen-sized beds, private bath, wicker furnishings and a brick fireplace. "Becky's Room" has a large bath, sleigh bed and antique furnishings. The site also includes a pool.

El Adobe Ranch
$$ • 4630 N. El Adobe Ranch Rd.
• 743-3525

Located within a short walking distance of Saguaro National Park West in the Tucson Mountains, El Adobe offers five private casitas with complete kitchens, fireplaces, phones, TVs and air conditioning. Unlike traditional bed and breakfasts, El Adobe does not offer breakfast, but instead allows visitors to cook in their private, nonsmoking quarters.

El Presidio Bed and Breakfast
$$$ • 297 N. Main Ave. • 623-6151, (800) 349-6151

For historic Old Mexico ambiance near downtown, consider this 1880s adobe mansion. It's a vacation for all the senses. Eyes and noses are enraptured by the beauty and fragrances of the gardens; ears and fingers revel at the gentle music and cool current of the fountains. Taste buds are treated to a full breakfast; the menu changes but often has stuffed French toast, bacon, fruit and juice. Three luxury suites have private baths, TVs and phones. El Presidio is within walking distance of the Tucson Museum of Art and the city's historic presidio district.

Elysian Grove Market Bed & Breakfast Inn
$$-$$$$ • 400 W. Simpson St. • 628-1522

Elysian Grove was originally built as a grocery market in 1924 near the Museum of Art in Tucson's historic barrio. The adobe-brick complex was purchased in the 1960s by Debbie LaChapelle who converted it into an inn. The original meat locker with its 12-inch fuchsia doors was transformed into a kitchen. (The room appeared in the movie *Boys on the Side* starring Whoopi Goldberg.)

The inn offers four guest rooms, which share two baths, and two separate two-level suites (one with a kitchen), each with a Mexican-tile bath, fireplace and entrance into the backyard garden. The rooms are decorated with American Indian and Mexican art and have antique beds. The 16-foot ceilings loom over oak floors, and the garden is home to cactus, mesquite, fountains and plenty of sitting space where you'll enjoy your breakfast of Mexican pastries, fresh fruit, cheese and coffee.

Hacienda del Desierto Bed and Breakfast
$$-$$$ • 11770 Rambling Tr. • 298-1764, (800) 982-1795

This Spanish-style hacienda sits on 16 acres in the Rincon Mountain foothills near Saguaro National Park East and offers three rooms able to accommodate up to four people. Each room has a double bed and hide-a-beds as well as a private bath, kitchenette, TV/VCR, telephone and private entrance. In addition, a large casita has two bedrooms, a full kitchen, living room, bath and a private, outdoor hydrotherapy spa. Breakfast includes fruit, cereal, hard-boiled eggs, homemade muffins, coffee and juice. Well-behaved children are welcome.

Inca Dove Bed and Breakfast
$$ • 1341 W. Liddell Pl. • 797-7004, (800) 299-1747

This cosmopolitan home with antiques and Southwestern decor is conveniently located near restaurants and shopping. The four rooms vary in size and include a two-bedroom guesthouse equipped with a wet bar, refrigerator, microwave, coffee pot, toaster, two private baths and a patio. For breakfast, expect Wisconsin cheese and jams, fresh fruit, breads, muffins and, a specialty of the house, Inca Dove Breakfast custard. The inn is near I-10 at Ina Road.

The Jeremiah Inn Bed and Breakfast
$$-$$$ • 10921 E. Synder Rd. • 749-3072

Located in the eastern foothills near Sabino Canyon, this 3.3 acre desert retreat offers three rooms in a contemporary home. All rooms include a queen-size bed, private bath, TV, telephone and outside entrance. Guests can enjoy nearby golf or horseback riding or take a dip in the pool or spa after a breakfast of fresh baked breads and muffins, fruits and juices served in the dining room, poolside or in your room.

La Posada del Valle
$$$ • 1640 N. Campbell Ave. • 795-3840

This 1929 Santa Fe-style adobe and stucco mansion is surrounded by gardens and orange trees. Across the street from University Medical Center, the inn has five guest rooms with private baths and private entrances. Rooms are furnished with antiques and period pieces from the 1920s and have views of the Catalina Mountains. In the morning expect a gourmet breakfast with eggs, fruit and breads. In the afternoon guests gather for high tea. Wir sprechen Deutsch! (The owners are German.)

The Meyer House
$$$ • 562 S. Meyer Ave. • 629-0361

Located in the historic Barrio Viejo (Old Neighborhood) and within walking distance of the Tucson Convention Center and downtown, The Meyer House has two restored adobe casitas, each consisting of a living room, a bedroom with fireplace, full kitchen, private bath and patio. The private patios open into a courtyard garden with a fountain, pond and swimming pool. A large breakfast with freshly baked bread and a newspaper are brought to your casita.

The Peppertrees Bed and Breakfast Inn
$$$ • 724 E. University Blvd. • 622-7167, (800) 622-7167

You might not expect Victorian mansions in the Old West, but this 1905 inn offers just that. It's an oasis of tranquility near the main gate of the University of Arizona and within walking distance to shops, museums and restaurants. The name comes from two large California peppertrees that dominate the front of the inn. Restored and furnished with antiques from the innkeeper's family in England, there are seven rooms, including two guesthouses. Each guesthouse has two bedrooms, a living room, dining room, full kitchen and a private patio. A gourmet breakfast is served in the dining room or on the patio, which you can enjoy while you browse through the owner's own locally published cookbook, *Breakfast at Peppertrees* (1996). Owner Majorie Martin has loaded the book with favorite breakfast dishes, such as baked goods, cookies, fruit dishes and everything else you can think to have for breakfast. Stories of the inn are also contained in her book, which is available at the inn or local bookstores. Guests of the Peppertrees enjoy a breakfast of home-baked breads and coffee cakes, cereal, fresh fruit and a main course that changes daily.

Rancho Quieto Bed and Breakfast
$$$$ • 12051 W. Ft. Lowell Rd. • 883-3300

This inn 20 miles west of Tucson has a unique architectural style of massive beams and Saguaro Viga ceilings. Three suites have kitchens, private baths, fireplaces, queen-size beds and patios. There is a rooftop terrace for star gazing, and the grounds include several cookout areas, remote hideaway spots and three pool areas. Guests are welcome to gather in the main building for television viewing or access to a piano. The breakfast menu changes daily, but French toast, scrambled eggs, bacon, muffins, juice and coffee make regular appearances. The site is also available for corporate parties, weddings and receptions. It's 4 miles west of the Arizona-Sonora Desert Museum.

Rocking M Ranch
$$ • 6265 N. Camino Verde • 744-2457

If you travel with your horse, Rocking M Ranch may be the spot for you. On 10 acres adjacent to miles of trails within the Saguaro National Park West, this bed and breakfast has six covered corrals with automatic water for keeping your horse ready for a ride at nearby riding stables or on open trails (no stallions please). Rocking M has four rooms available. Two rooms have a queen-size bed and private bath. The remaining two rooms share a bath; one has a queen-size bed, the other has two single beds. During the week, a continental breakfast is served, and on weekends a full breakfast including eggs, toast, fresh fruit and coffee begins the day. A boot-shaped pool and heated spa round out the luxuries. Since Rocking M Ranch doesn't use the bed and breakfast reservation service, you'll need to contact the Ranch directly.

Sahuaro Vista Guest Ranch Bed and Breakfast
$$ • 7501 N. Wade Rd. • 579-2530

This bed and breakfast sits on 30 acres of the Tucson Mountains near Saguaro National Park West. It offers picturesque hiking trails and is located near public riding stables. The 10 double rooms and four suites all have private bathrooms, televisions and telephones. Guests can enjoy a large swimming pool, Jacuzzi, hammocks and sunny patios. Within the main house (circa 1931) is a library, fireplace, public telephone and baby grand piano. A full breakfast of eggs, potatoes, pancakes, muffins and juice is served from 7:30 to 10 AM.

Shadow Mountain Ranch Bed and Breakfast
$$ • 8825 N. Scenic Dr. • 744-7551, (888) 9-SHADOW

This 5,500-square-foot, U-shaped hacienda sits on 6½ acres of prime northwest Tucson Mountain property and offers its guests a traditional Spanish-style courtyard, a pool with rock waterfall, spa and easy access to I-10. The main building houses a Jacuzzi, sitting room with grand piano and two guest rooms, each with a queen-size bed and private bath. The separate 1,200-square-foot "Desert Villa" offers two bedrooms, two bathrooms, a fireplace, full kitchen, private entrance and patio. Guests can gather for an informal continental breakfast in the morning and then head out to various nearby hiking trails, the Arizona-Sonora Desert Museum, Old Tucson Studios or Tucson Mountain Park. The owners can arrange horseback rides during your stay.

Triple B "BBB" Bed & Breakfast
$$ • P.O. Box 91414, Tucson 85752 • 744-8770

Near Ina and Thornydale roads just five minutes off I-10, this contemporary home is located within the fastest growing area of Tucson. What makes this two-room site different is the breakfast: The owner features a full breakfast highlighting Southwestern prickly pear juice products as a specialty (she's working on a cookbook). You'll savor crepes topped with prickly pear syrup, egg burritos and home-baked sweets. Your room will seem like a step back into an Old Tucson adobe, complete with Southwestern furniture and wall hangings.

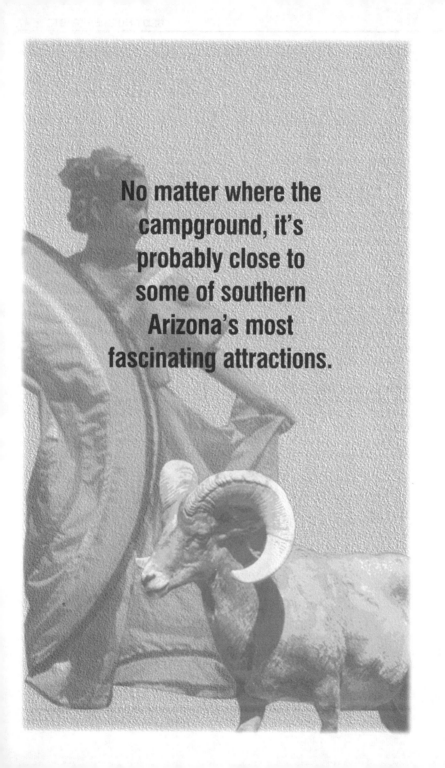

No matter where the campground, it's probably close to some of southern Arizona's most fascinating attractions.

Campgrounds and RV Parks

The best thing about camping in the Tucson area is that, no matter where the campground, it's probably close to, if not surrounded by, some of southern Arizona's most fascinating attractions. The second best thing is that camping around here offers something to suit just about everyone's taste — from low-lying desert dotted with cacti to high mountains covered with conifer forests and from back-country camping to fairly posh RV resorts.

In this chapter we cover all the public campgrounds and several of the best private sites close to Tucson as well as a number of the best camping areas in each direction away from Tucson — except east. Tucson's east — actually the Rincon Mountains — only offers back-country camping, and it's accessible only by hiking or horseback. (But if that's your style, contact the Saguaro National Park's Rincon Mountain District at 733-5153 for details on these campsites and the required permits.) We only include an RV park if it also accommodates the "old-fashioned" type of camper — in a tent. And we hasten to add that rates are subject to change and seem to do so quite often.

To get the most out of this chapter, you should use it hand-in-hand with several other chapters of the book, especially The Natural World, Attractions and Parks and Recreation chapters. The Natural World chapter, for example, contains lots of additional environmental information on the areas in which you're camping, such as Madera Canyon, the Tucson Mountains and Mt. Lemmon. It can also familiarize you with the unusual flora and fauna you're likely to see no matter where you set up your tent or RV. The Attractions chapter gives details on the many sites you may want to visit from your campground base. And since many of the campgrounds are in or near park lands, the Parks and Recreation chapter will give you a more complete picture of what awaits you in and around these camping areas.

If you're a first-time camper or RVer in Tucson, there are two things you should keep in mind when using the campground descriptions in this chapter. Below the name of the campground is an address or city where it's located. If only an address is given, that means it's in metro Tucson. If a city is listed, that means it's the city closest to the camping area. For example, Bog Springs Campground is listed as Green Valley, Arizona; while the campground is near Green Valley, it's also a ways away in the Santa Rita Mountains. So consider the "city" indicator just a general description of the location.

Our second piece of advice relates to the 520 area code. Throughout this book we tell you that we only list area codes with phone numbers if they differ from the 520 area code. However, this chapter contains a number of campgrounds that are far enough from the Tucson metro area to be considered long distance by phone, even though they're still in the 520 area code. So in cases where you must dial the area code if you're calling from Tucson, we indicate that by including the 520 along with the seven-digit phone number. (If you dial the seven-digit number only, a recording will announce the error of your ways but may not be helpful enough to tell you the way to correct it.)

Now you're ready to dive into the fun part of this chapter — our picks of some of the best places to pitch your tent or park your RV in and around Tucson. So pack up your gear, supplies and sunscreen and get ready for your adventure in the great outdoors.

Bog Springs
Forest Service Rd. 70, Green Valley • (520) 281-2296, 670-4552

At the western side of the steep Santa Rita Mountains and about 30 minutes south of Tucson — not counting the extra time it might take to traverse up the forest service road for 13 miles — is this 15-acre campground in and operated by the Coronado National Forest. The campground is just below Madera Canyon, one of the premier birding spots in the Southwest. You'll be driving past plenty of century plants, yuccas and barrel and prickly pear cacti, and if it's spring or fall, they may be in full bloom or showing off their colorful fruits. You'll also wind through pecan groves and across grassland sprinkled with mesquite trees. At the campground's 5,600-foot elevation, you'll be surrounded by juniper, oaks and sycamores and hear the soft tumbling of Madera Creek.

If you're in an RV, keep in mind that the limit is 22 feet and the campground loops, though paved, are steep and twisting. There are 13 tent or RV sites with no hookups at $5 per night per vehicle. Near the campground entrance are several shaded picnic areas with grills as well as restrooms but no showers. Bog Springs is open all year for 14-day stay limits. Winter nights at this elevation can get quite cold, but summertime camping can be a comfortable diversion from temperatures on the valley floor below. It's a popular place, and spaces cannot be reserved in advance.

If you happen to run out of some basic supplies or food, Madera Canyon even has a small store or two, but it's iffy whether they'll be open, although more likely in summer. Many trails take off from here up toward the Mount Wrightson wilderness — more than 70 miles of them throughout the mountain range. Or you can save your hiking shoes for another time and simply hike around Madera Canyon and along the creek. Another option is to take the bus tour to the Smithsonian Astrophysical Observatory at the top of Mount Hopkins from the observatory's ground-level visitors center. And nearby, you'll find attractions like the Titan Missile Museum and the outstanding golf courses of Green Valley.

To get to Bog Springs, take I-19 south from Tucson to Exit 63 (Continental) and head east on Forest Service Road 70 for about 13 miles.

Cactus Country RV Resort
10195 S. Houghton Rd. • 574-3000, (800) 777-8799

If you're looking for the amenities of a resort but still want to bunk in your own tent or RV, Cactus Country RV may be the spot. This private RV complex covers 3 acres on Tucson's far southeast, close to the Santa Rita Mountains, the Santa Rita Golf Club and the Pima County Fairgrounds. You can stay for a day, week, month or a season and have access to electricity, heaters, air conditioners, cable TV, restrooms, dump station, heated pool, whirlpool, shuffleboard, recreation room and laundry facilities.

And all of this is in a serene desert setting surrounded on all four sides by state land. Cactus Country sits on a hill from which you can see not only the nearby Santa Ritas but also the Rincon and Santa Catalina Mountains to the north and unobstructed sunset views to the west. The resort offers mature vegetation, paved roads and gravel-covered spaces.

Of the 265 sites, many of which are tree-shaded, 260 are for RVs at $25 a day, and five are for tents at $15 a day. You'll pay less per day for longer-term stays. Many of the extras listed above require an additional fee. Cactus Country is open all year, and the busiest time is January through March, when RV spaces require a two-month minimum stay.

From Tucson, take I-10 east, exit at Houghton Road and go north about a quarter-mile.

Catalina State Park Campground
11570 N. Oracle Rd. • 628-5798

The closest campground to Tucson is also one of the best. Located in the Santa Catalina Mountains on Tucson's northwest, Catalina State Park covers 5,500 acres at elevations

---

FYI

Unless otherwise noted, the area code for all phone numbers listed in this guide is 520.

Nothing can compare to a desert sunset.

ranging from 2,650 to 3,000 feet. There are plenty of nature trails in the park and, for the more serious hiker, trails extending up the mountains into the national forest. Highlights of the park include Romero Canyon with its falls and clear pools shaded by sycamore and oak trees, ruins of the pit houses left by Hohokam Indians, and the nearby Pusch Ridge wilderness, home to desert bighorn sheep. And from this location, nearly every attraction in and around Tucson is less than an hour's drive away.

Spacious campsites pleasantly arranged amid groves of mesquite trees await road-weary travelers. All 48 sites have paved parking pads and 23 have electrical hookups. Facilities include wheelchair accessible restrooms with showers. The overnight fee at this year-round campground is $9 ($14 with hookup), and maximum stay is 14 days. Reservations are not accepted, so it's best to show up early in the day (it's open at 7 AM) during the busy winter season for a campsite. Catalina State Park is about 9 miles north of the city limits.

Crazy Horse RV Campgrounds
6660 S. Craycroft Rd. • 574-0157

The owner calls this "a good old down-to-earth RV park with dust." (He means the kind of desert dust a crazy horse would kick up, or in the absence of such an animal, a windy desert day.) In other words, it's comfortable with all the basics but not fancy. The basics consist of 154 sites for either tents or RVs, full hookups (electric, water and sewage), restrooms, showers, a laundry room and a pool that may or may not be heated in winter. The main road is paved, but the spaces aren't, and trees are few, which no doubt contributes to the dust in the air. They welcome both kids and pets but do have rules about noise levels in an attempt to keep the park as peaceful as the surrounding desert.

The daily fee of $20 is all inclusive, and weekly, monthly and seasonal rentals are available as well. Crazy Horse is open all year but their peak season is January 15 to March 15, and you must reserve before January 15 to get a space during this time.

Located in the southeast of Tucson at I-10 and Craycroft Road, Crazy Horse is close to the Pima Air and Space Museum on Valencia Road and no more than 60 minutes away from any other attraction in the metro area. A truck stop and convenience store are close by.

Gilbert Ray Campground
Kinney Rd., Tucson Mountain Park
• 883-4200, 740-2690

Of the two units of Saguaro National Park (east and west), the west unit is the only one with a nearby campground. On the west side of the Tucson Mountain range and not very far from downtown Tucson is the vast 20,000-acre Tucson Mountain Park, where this campground is located. Its proximity to Tucson and to some great attractions means that this popular campground, though large, often sports the "full" sign (it's first-come, first-served). In addition to Saguaro National Park, both the Arizona-Sonora Desert Museum and Old Tucson Studios are nearby. So is the 6-mile Bajada Loop Drive where you'll see Indian petroglyphs. Wildlife is abundant here despite the number of humans around. You'll see the typical varieties of thorny vegetation, lots of birdlife and probably a coyote or mule deer or two. An excellent visitors center can give you a complete orientation to the park and its trails and sights.

Operated by Pima County Parks and Recreation Department, the campground has 175 sites — 25 for tents and 150 for RVs, including 146 with hookups. (If you're driving an RV, be advised that you'll need to take Kinney Road into the area because RVs are not permitted on Gates Pass Road.) There are wheelchair-accessible restrooms and a dump station but no showers. Volunteer attendants are on duty during regular business hours in the winter season but usually not during the slower summer season. The fees are $6 to $9 per night for a maximum of seven days.

The easiest way to get here is to take Ajo Way west to Kinney Road and then head north to the campground. The scenic route is Speedway Boulevard to Gates Pass Road, then south on Kinney Road. RVers must take the easy way.

Lakeview
Ariz. Hwy. 83, Sonoita • (520) 378-0311

Fishing might be the reason you choose this campground, but the camping is superb also. It's located at 130-acre Parker Canyon Lake, where the cottonwoods, willows and marsh grass — not to mention the sight of water — might fool you into thinking you're not in Arizona. It's not recommended for swimming (algae and reeds would slow your progress across the lake), but bring your fishing gear along and see if you can land any of the lake's rainbow trout, large-mouth bass, sunfish or catfish for a tasty dinner. Lakeside, there's a store, a marina and boats for rent.

Operated year round by the Sierra Vista Ranger District of the Coronado National Forest, the 64 campsites on 50 acres in the shadow of the hulking Huachuca Mountains accommodate either tents or RVs with a 32-foot limit. There are restrooms but no showers, dump station or RV hookups. Maximum stay is 14 nights at $10 a night. At an elevation of 5,400 feet, summer nights will be heavenly and winter nights on the cool side.

INSIDERS' TIP

Just like almost everything else in Tucson, the "winter" season (generally October through March) is usually the busiest for most camping and RV areas. But that means bargains are often available to summer campers, such as two free days with 14 (for a maximum 16-day stay) at Catalina State Park campground.

The easiest way to get here from Tucson is to take I-10 east to the Patagonia/Sonoita exit and then head south on Ariz. 83, an all-weather but unpaved road, for about 30 miles.

Mt. Lemmon

Tucson's own "sky island," Mt. Lemmon is also Tucson's most diverse outdoor recreation area. Along 25 miles of steep and curving roadway up to a 9,000 foot elevation, sights and sounds include full-blown pine forests, see-forever views, biking, skiing, fishing, picnicking, hiking, wildlife watching and camping. For Tucsonans, it's akin to making a short drive to Canada. So it's a very popular place year round. In summer, it's an escape from the heat down below, in fall a spectacular foliage show, in winter a test of winter driving skills and a close place to hit the ski slopes, and in spring a blooming treat for the senses.

All of these delights await campers and so do four forest-service maintained campgrounds, three open in the summer and one in winter. And for the brave among you, wilderness camping is permitted on Mt. Lemmon a quarter-mile or more away from campgrounds. For information on any of the four campgrounds, call 749-8700 or 670-4552.

But before we get to the campground descriptions, here are some things you should know to keep your Mt. Lemmon experience safe and rule-abiding.

• Bears live here too and they're attracted to food, so keep yours well-covered and hidden — that means tightly sealed and in your car or one of the bear barriers.

• Your own pets must be on a leash.

• You can fish at Rose Canyon Lake, but you can't get a license on the mountain.

• If a summer is particularly dry, the forest service may temporarily ban all fires, so have a backup for your charcoal-broiled steaks or hot dogs.

• Gas up the vehicle in Tucson since there are no stations on the mountain.

• At the top in the village of Summerhaven, you'll find stores and restaurants.

• Trail maps for the mountain are available at the Sabino Canyon Visitors Center (on Sabino Canyon Road), so get them before you begin your trek up the mountain.

• Some of the campgrounds have a daily fee and all have a 14-day stay limit.

• And most importantly, keep our precious environment clean and undisturbed — a good thing to remember no matter where you're camping.

The Catalina Highway (or Mt. Lemmon Highway) begins at Tanque Verde Road about 5 miles east of Sabino Canyon Road. (See the Natural World chapter for phone numbers to check on Mt. Lemmon road conditions and fire restrictions.) In late 1997, the National Forest Service instituted a recreational fee for the Santa Catalina Mountains, which includes Mt. Lemmon. If you're camping or otherwise recreating, it now costs $5 a day per vehicle, $10 a week or $20 for an annual pass. You can purchase passes at a booth on the road just before Molino Basin from 10 AM to 6 PM Monday through Friday and 8 AM to 6 PM weekends. After hours, a sign will instruct motorists to pay at another location, or get them at Sabino Canyon Visitors Center on Sabino Canyon Road before heading for Mt. Lemmon.

Molino Basin

Despite its location in the Santa Catalina Mountains, this campground is actually closed during the summer months (mid-April through mid-October) due to the heat (no, that isn't a typo). That's because its southern exposure, even at an elevation of 4,500 feet, makes it warmer than, say, Catalina State Park on the northern slope of the same mountain range. Conversely, the same conditions make wintertime camping here great at an elevation that normally would be uncomfortably cold.

Molino Basin is the first of four campgrounds on Mt. Lemmon operated by the Catalina Ranger District of the Coronado National Forest Service. About 10 miles up the highway from Tucson, it nests in a deep "V" between two granite ridges in the mountain. This is a great area to get the kids treasure hunting for "jewels" — the sandy washes in this basin composed of metamorphosed granite are rich in silvery mica flakes and tiny burgundy "sand rubies," better known as garnets. The area offers great scenic views, rock climbing and hiking. You'll even spot a few saguaros, which generally don't grow above 3,500 feet.

The campground covers 65 acres and has 49 sites for tents and RVs up to 22 feet for a daily fee of $5. There are restrooms but little else, so be sure to have drinking water on hand. Campsites cannot be reserved in advance.

General Hitchcock

At milepost 12 and an altitude of 5,800 feet, General Hitchcock is the second Mt. Lemmon campground, the smallest and only open for the summer season (mid-April through mid-October). The 13 campsites will accommodate either tents or RVs of no more than 22 feet for $5 a day but can't be reserved in advance. There are restrooms but no showers or hookups.

Rose Canyon

If the idea of lakeside camping and casting for your dinner appeals to you, this is the campground to choose. Only about a block from the campground, the 7-acre Rose Canyon Lake is stocked with several varieties of trout and surrounded by tall green pines. The campground is at milepost 17 with paved loops winding through a number of campground sections and ending at the lake's parking lot. It's only open from mid-April to mid-October, and this oasis at 7,500 feet is very popular with Tucsonans escaping summer's heat. Campsites for tents and RVs number 74. There are wheelchair-accessible restrooms but no showers, no hookups and no RVs longer than 22 feet. The fee is $9 per day on a first-come basis.

Spencer Canyon

The last and highest of the mountain's campsites is at milepost 22, has an elevation of 7,800 feet and is only open mid-April to mid-October. It has 77 campsites for tents and RVs shorter than 22 feet and wheelchair-accessible restrooms but no hookups or showers. The fee is $8 a day.

The campground is laid out in four levels, all connected by paved roads. Keep in mind that activity at this altitude can be a real strain for lowlanders and confirmed couch potatoes. But if hiking and rock climbing are not your cup of tea, the village of Summerhaven is nearby, along with a few shops, restaurants and probably a cup of tea that will suit you.

Patagonia Lake State Park
Ariz. Hwy. 82, Patagonia
• **(520) 287-6965**

Patagonia Lake, not far from Arizona's southern border, offers fun on the water as well as a nicely laid out campground. The 260-acre lake features fishing, boating, a sandy beach, a store, a marina with boat rentals and even a high pedestrian bridge with a scenic view. Although rainbow trout are stocked in the lake, you're more likely to hook bass, sunfish, crappies and catfish in this warm-water fishery. The lake also offers southern Arizona campers a rare treat — water skiing, jet skiing and wind surfing are allowed here (but during the summer, only on weekdays). As you might guess, Patagonia Lake is a very popular spot for water-deprived folks in this area.

Situated on one of the gentle slopes above the lake, the year-round campground has picnic areas, restrooms and showers that are wheelchair-accessible. Of the 115 campsites, 34 have hookups and 13 are boat accessible only. Rates are $10 or $15 with hookup for a maximum of 15 days. Campsites cannot be reserved in advance.

To get here from Tucson, take I-10 east to Ariz. Highway 83, go south to Ariz. 82 and continue south 7 miles past the town of Patagonia. Nearby is Patagonia-Sonoita Creek Preserve, a 312-acre wildlife sanctuary of the Nature Conservancy open to the public. And the border town of Nogales, Mexico, is only about 40 minutes away.

Peppersauce
Forest Rt. 38, Oracle • 749-8700, 670-4552

This is a superb campground for several reasons, not the least of which is the story (or perhaps tall tale) of how its name originated. The story goes that Louie Depew, who was hooked on pepper sauce — hot sauce — lost a bottle of it in the wash and was upset for the rest of his days at the campsite. And whether you believe that or not, once you see this spot you will surely believe that it's a sight to behold.

Start out in Oracle, Arizona, which is about

> **FYI**
> Unless otherwise noted, the area code for all phone numbers listed in this guide is 520.

20 miles north of Tucson, head east-southeast on Mt. Lemmon Road, or Forest Route 38. (This is the north side of the Catalinas, not the Mt. Lemmon Road that goes from Tucson.) After the pavement ends, you'll pass through dry desert laden with ocotillo, cholla and barrel cacti for about 5 miles. Suddenly you'll top out on a hill, and a few hundred yards below you'll gaze upon a grove of giant sycamores shading the Peppersauce campground. The roots of this giant green canopy are nourished from Peppersauce Springs, a short distance up the wash, or arroyo, from the campground. This cool retreat from the surrounding heat makes for a great summer camp experience, but it is open all year. It probably comes as no surprise that Peppersauce is a very popular spot.

Peppersauce is operated by the Catalina Ranger District of the Coronado National Forest Service. There are 24 campsites for tents and RVs up to 22 feet at a daily rate of $5. Restrooms and water are available but hookups are not, and the stay limit is 14 days. Campsites cannot be reserved; if it's your lucky day, you'll get a campsite, although it's worth a phone call to ask.

Picacho Peak State Park
I-10, Exit 219, Picacho • (520) 466-3183

Once you see the rocky pinnacle 35 miles north of Tucson known as Picacho Peak, you'll always recognize its dramatic and distinct shape from afar. Along its slope is a state park of the same name. (And speaking of names, the word "peak" could easily have been left out since that's what "picacho" means in Spanish.) Rising 1,500 feet above the desert floor, the peak is thought to be 22 million years old — four times as old as the Grand Canyon. It is also the site of the westernmost battle of the Civil War, fought between a dozen Union and 16 Confederate soldiers. Rains permitting, in mid-March the park explodes with traffic-stopping displays of wildflowers — acres of golden, purple and magenta blooms. Within the 4,000 acre park are 7 miles of hiking trails and a scenic drive.

Rest assured that, even though Picacho borders the very-busy I-10 connecting Phoenix and Tucson, the campground is far enough removed — about 2 miles west of the freeway — so the noise doesn't intrude. Campers have access to 97 sites, 12 with hookups, for $8 and $13 per night. Maximum stay is 14 days, and maximum trailer size is 30 feet. The year-round campground has wheelchair-accessible restrooms, and nearby are showers, a store, restaurant and gas station. The city of Casa Grande is about 20 minutes away if you have the unstoppable urge to outlet shop or if you need any major services or supplies. At only 2,000 feet, camping is comfortable here in winter but a bit warm in summer.

Drive west from Tucson on I-10 about 40 miles to Exit 219 — you can't miss it.

Visitors and residents of the Old Pueblo do not subsist on tortillas and T-bones alone.

Restaurants

In recent years, Tucson chefs have really stepped up to the plate, so to speak, when it comes to offering Tucsonans diversity in dining. You'll still be able to find the best Mexican food this side of the border, and mesquite-grilled steaks continue to play an important role in the restaurant scene. But believe us when we tell you that visitors and residents of the Old Pueblo do not subsist on tortillas and T-bones alone.

Grills, bistros and cafes are making a strong showing as is Asian cuisine in all its glorious forms, including some outrageous Pacific Rim offerings. Fine dining is alive and well with continental, American, French and Italian in the mix. The University is another influence, of course, so you will find enough brewpubs, breweries, coffeehouses, diners, All-American burger joints and pizza parlors to keep you well fed for months.

Dress for the most part is casual, but some places still require a gentleman to wear a tie. We've noted in the listings when this is the case. Call the restaurant if you are unsure about a dress code.

We've divided the restaurants by cuisine, but many of them could easily be placed in more than one category. You may want to scan the entire chapter to get a full view of what the area has to offer.

The headers include All-American; American Southwest; Asian/Middle Eastern; Breweries & Brewpubs; Burgers, Sandwiches and Such; Coffeehouses & Cafes; Fine Dining; French; Get It and Go (great places to pick up dinner after a day of fun that should satisfy just about any craving); Greek; Healthy, Vegetarian and Alternative; Italian; Mexican; Pizza; Seafood (yep, we do have seafood and very good seafood at that); and Steakhouses (which include places for great prime rib and racks of rib). Although franchise restaurants can be found citywide, we have included only local chains.

Along with descriptions of the food and the ambiance of the establishment, we'll also throw in extra information to educate, such as the history of the eatery or the building in which it is housed; to advise, such as parking tips for places near the University or downtown and the necessity of reservations; or to recommend, such as signature dishes or favorite entrees of regular patrons.

Having said all that, we wish you good dining.

Price Guidelines

The following dollar-sign codes indicate what you will pay for a dinner for two, excluding appetizers, cocktails, dessert, tips and taxes. You can assume that most restaurants take major credit cards; we only make note of those that do not.

$	Less than $15
$$	$15 to $30
$$$	$30 to $50
$$$$	More than $50

All-American

Don's Restaurant
$ • 350 W. Roger Rd. • 888-0585

Don's is the kind of place all those new diners are trying to emulate. Strictly open for breakfast and lunch, Don's offers good food, fast and friendly service and a very casual atmosphere. You can eat at any one of the tables or booths or sit at the counter and watch the waitress hustle as you admire all of the Washington Redskins' souvenirs on the walls.

Breakfast portions are large (you can even get grits on the side), and the biscuits and gravy come with or without eggs. Lunch specials include chicken fried steak with mashed potatoes and gravy and a vegetable. The burger baskets are the real thing.

You may want to bring home a souvenir T-shirt or hat with Don's emblazoned across the front: The "O" is an egg sunnyside-up.

The restaurant is located in the Target shopping center on Oracle Road at Roger Road.

The Egg Connection
$ • 3114 E. Ft. Lowell Rd. • 881-1009

This popular breakfast and lunch spot has recently expanded its hours to serve dinner on Friday and Saturday nights, with dinner specials such as all-you-can-eat fish fries or chicken dinners.

But it's as a breakfast place that The Egg Connection earned a reputation. Servings are plentiful, and the coffee is hot and strong. Try the biscuits and gravy or the pancakes for a filling and tasty meal. You won't be disappointed whatever time of day you eat here.

Located in a strip mall on the corner of Ft. Lowell and Country Club roads, The Egg Connection is easy to find.

Gus Balon's
$ • 6027 E. 22nd St. • 748-9731, 747-7788

If you're looking for honest, All-American food, Gus Balon's is the place. All the breads are homemade, the eggs are fried in butter, and every day more than 20 homemade pies are on the menu. Kids can enjoy a jelly omelette or a good old pb-and-j sandwich. Grownups might like to try a breakfast special or a baked-ham sandwich. Expect a wait for breakfast and lunch, the only meals served.

Little Anthony's Diner
$$ • 7010 E. Broadway Blvd. • 296-0456

Little Anthony's is Tucson's original retro diner. After several moves over the years, this '50s-style eatery has finally settled in on the not-so-far Eastside. While not located directly on the street (it's in back of The Gaslight Theatre, another entity owned by the Terry family — see our Arts and Culture chapter), Little Anthony's is still relatively easy to find.

There will be no surprises here: big juicy burgers (the names are rock 'n' roll related), tasty sandwiches, thick shakes and malts and even wet fries (french fries served with brown gravy on the side). Pizza, actually Grandma Tony's pizza, another restaurant owned by the same folks, rounds out the menu. The wait staff is young and friendly with plenty of energy. Kids get a kick out of the DJ spinning those Golden Oldies at dinnertime while the grownups wax nostalgic over all the '50s memorabilia that hangs on the walls.

> **FYI**
> Unless otherwise noted, the area code for all phone numbers listed in this guide is 520.

It's great place to take the kids for a relatively quick meal. Little Anthony's is open for lunch and dinner on weekdays and adds a breakfast shift on Saturdays and Sundays.

Marlene's Hungry Fox Restaurant
$$ • 4637 E. Broadway Blvd. • 326-2835

At your first glance of the menu, you might think the prices at the Hungry Fox are a little steep, but on closer examination you'll find out why — all the eggs are double-yolked, which means you get two eggs for every one egg you order. What a deal!

The Hungry Fox looks like a cozy country kitchen with antiques and reproduction pieces on high shelves that run along the walls. The room is bright and cheerful, just like the waitstaff.

Open for breakfast and lunch seven days a week, the Hungry Fox closes at 2 PM. On Friday evenings it reopens at 5 PM to serve home-style dinners until 8 PM.

American/Southwest

Buddy's Grill
$$ • 4821 E. Grant Rd. • 795-2226

Buddy's Grill is the oldest restaurant in the Metro Restaurant string of great places to dine. The menu is filled with seafood dishes as well as prime rib, steaks and chicken. You can get oysters on the half shell, shrimp cocktail and a seafood sampler, with shrimp, oysters and hickory-smoked salmon from the oyster bar. The shrimp and Dungeness crab cakes are

PAPAGAYO RESTAURANT
"Serving Tucson Over 25 Years"

Tucson's Finest Mexican Cuisine
Delicious Margaritas

Foothills
4717 E. Sunrise Dr.
Swan & Sunrise NE Corner
577-6055

4th Generation Tucsonans
The Mazon & Perez Families

Major Credit Cards Accepted

East
7000 E. Tanque Verde Rd
in Santa Fe Square
721-6249

---

offered as an appetizer or as an entree. You can also get burgers, sandwiches and salads.

The atmosphere at Buddy's is comfy and fun, and dress is casual. Reservations are strongly suggested for dinner.

Buddy's is centrally located in the front of Crossroads Festival Plaza and serves lunch and dinner daily.

Cafe Terra Cotta
$$$ • 4310 N. Campbell Ave. • 577-8100

Cafe Terra Cotta is Tucson's most celebrated restaurant. With reviews in all the major food magazines and accolades such as "One of America's 50 not-to-be-missed restaurants," according to *Condé Nast Traveler*, Cafe Terra Cotta is in the vanguard of contemporary Southwestern cuisine.

Right in the center of St. Philip's Plaza, the restaurant's muted, Southwestern colors contrast with the bright colors of the art on the walls. High ceilings and large windows create an airy open feeling. The patio dining is some of the best in Tucson, and that's saying a lot.

The chefs continue the tradition of founder Donna Nordin's fresh innovative fare. Signature plates include large prawns stuffed with goat cheese served on a tomato coulis or sesame-seed crusted ahi tuna with bitter greens and pinon-herb rice. Unique side dishes include orzo or black beans, and pizzas are made daily in a wood-burning oven.

There is a take-out section as well as a catering service, and Chef Nordin has developed packaged mixes and condiments that you can prepare at home.

Lunch and dinner are served seven days a week. Reservations are suggested for dinner.

The City Grill
$$ • 6350 E. Tanque Verde Rd.
• 733-1111
The Metro Grill
$$ • 7892 N. Oracle Rd. • 531-1212

These two contemporary grills are owned by Metro Restaurants. The decors are similar with lots of copper, slate and open grills visible from just about any seat in the house. The menus are similar, also. Appetizers, entrees, pizzas and house specialties are wood-fired or spit-roasted. The sesame-seared fresh ahi tuna is only one of the mouth-watering specialties. The grilled portobello mushroom sandwich served with herbed mozzarella and cilantro aioli is a local favorite. Both sites have bars that feature nightly specials. Cigars are sold and can be smoked in the bar area only.

The City Grill is located along Restaurant Row where Tanque Verde Road meets Pima Street. The Metro Grill is in a shopping plaza at the corner of Oracle and Magee roads. Both are open for lunch and dinner daily. Reservations are recommended for dinner.

Cushing Street Bar & Grill
$$ • 343 S. Meyer Ave. • 622-7984

Located in the Barrio Historico, the Cushing Street Bar is a must for the antique lover. For starters, the building itself reeks of history. The front room was the general store in the 1880s, while other rooms, which surround the brick patio, served as a home for a wealthy neighborhood family. These side rooms, which can be rented for private parties, are small but give a true sense of history with their saguaro-ribbed ceilings and thick adobe walls. Take a close look at the wood and glass cabinets that reach to the ceiling. Over the matching bar you'll notice a fabulous cut-glass chandelier that, along with the art deco statue of Cleopatra holding a lamp, came from a mansion in Mexico City. These pieces are as beautiful as they are unique.

House specialties range from blackened tuna to country-style ribs and porcini chicken to lamb sirloin. Interesting pasta dishes, sandwiches, burgers, antipasto salad and chicken quesadillas are just a small part of Cushing Street's menu. The patio is one of the finest in town.

Cushing Street Bar is open for lunch and dinner Monday through Saturday and serves dinner only on Sunday.

Dakota Cafe & Catering Co.
$$ • 6541 E. Tanque Verde Rd. • 298-7188

An innovative mix of New American and Southwestern cooking makes the Dakota a favorite Trail Dust Town dining spot (see our Shopping chapter). The decor is as hip as the menu: Colorful walls are decorated with paintings by local artists, a heavy wooden bar adds a touch of the past, and the small dining room is divided into two areas, which adds coziness to the modern atmosphere. Menu choices may include ravioli with chipotle cream sauce, pork tenderloin in a brandy pepper cream sauce or sauteed beef tenderloin. The menu always features a Fish of the Day as well as appetizers, soups and salads. Vegetarians will be happy to know that the Dakota serves entrees to suit their tastes, and certain meals can be prepared vegetarian-style. The restaurant has a full bar, and espresso and desserts are prepared on the premises daily.

Dress is casual. You can dine indoors or on the patio. Lunch and dinner are served Monday through Saturday. Catering is available.

Fuego
$$$ • Santa Fe Square, 6958 E. Tanque Verde Rd. • 886-1745

Chef Alan Zeman has always had a reputation as an innovative and bold chef, and the menu at Fuego, his Eastside eatery, reflects that. Ostrich is always on the menu, and the ingredients used in preparation include ancho chiles (the food at Fuego is HOT!), wild mushrooms, bleu cheese and dried cranberries. Appetizers are flambeed, even polenta, and the Soup of the Moment attests to the freshness of the ingredients. Fuego also holds events such as dinner theater packages and cooking classes with Zeman. The Chipolata Lounge serves an abbreviated version of the dinner menu and has live entertainment.

You'll be talking about your dinner at Fuego for weeks. Dinner is served nightly in the elegant dining room or on the patio.

The Grill at Hacienda del Sol
$$$$ • Hacienda del Sol Guest Ranch Resort, 5601 Hacienda del Sol Rd. • 299-1501

Brunch here is not an all-you-can-eat, stand-in-a-long-line affair. Instead, fresh-baked pastries, melon and strawberries, freshly squeezed orange juice and coffee or tea are served with a choice of appetizer, a choice of entree and, for dessert, Chef's Creations in Miniature. Appetizers are unique, including the carmelized ruby grapefruit. Entrees include a gulf prawn and crab frittata and maple-pecan glazed apple and chicken sausage.

But Sunday brunch isn't the only attraction. Dinner offers entrees with a definite American flavor — wood-roasted rack of Colorado lamb and grilled Pacific salmon. Enjoy dinner in the rustic, Western dining room or out on the patio with its great view the sunset. Lunch and dinner are offered daily.

Janos
$$$$ • 150 N. Main Ave. • 884-0426

Award-winning chef Janos Wilder continues to be a leader in Southwest cuisine. Located in a historic adobe home, which was recently saved from demolition by a wise City Council, Janos offers the best and the brightest in Southwestern dining with a French influence. That influence is seen in the changing seasonal menu, which allows for use of only the freshest ingredients.

If the high prices scare you off, take advantage of the Summer Samplers offered Tuesday through Friday evenings during the summer. The prices are nicely reduced. Dinner is served nightly, and reservations are strongly suggested. You can find parking in the neighborhood, but expect a short walk.

Maxwell's Restaurant
$$ • 1661 N. Swan Rd. • 326-5454

While it is hard to categorize this restaurant, it is definitely a midtown favorite for the business crowd. Both in style and in substance, Maxwell's meets the needs and wants of anyone who needs to grab a quick bite or wants to enjoy a leisurely lunch. Burgers, sandwiches and pasta dishes with ever changing sauces will delight. The small dining room is bright and pleasant, with art by local artists hanging on the walls (all the art is for sale); the patio is cool and shaded, even in the summertime (misters help).

Maxwell's is located in an office building on the corner of Swan Road and Pima Street. It's open Monday through Friday for lunch, Thursday through Saturday for dinner and Saturday and Sunday for brunch.

Oven's Restaurant
$$ • 4280 N. Campbell Ave. • 577-9001

Oven's has been called "one of the best bistros in town" by a local food critic. The menu includes handmade pastas, salads, light fare and Oven's specialty — wood-fired food. Order the angel hair pasta cakes with goat cheese, scallions, roasted peppers and avocado pesto or try the grilled polenta served with a mushroom ragout, marinara, gorgonzola and pine nuts. Oven's is known for its wood-fired pizzas. The Arizona Harvest pizza has a whole wheat crust topped with roasted corn, poblano chiles, summer squash, red peppers, tomato and goat cheese. For chocolate lovers there is a Serious Chocolate Sundae with Brownie.

On the patio overlooking St. Philip's Plaza, Oven's serves lunch and dinner daily as well as a Sunday brunch at which the full menu and daily specials are available. There is also a wine bar that serves more than 40 selections.

Presidio Grill
$$$ • 3352 E. Speedway Blvd. • 327-4667

The bar at Presidio Grill is straight out of a 1920s Midwestern tavern, complete with a black-and-white tiled floor, a mahogany bar and tall tables with stools. The dining room is a bit of bistro, and the Metro Room, which is used for private bookings, is ultramodern.

The Presidio Chicken, sauteed in olive oil with poblano peppers, browned garlic and prosciutto on a bed of linguine, topped with roma tomatoes, basil and parmesan, is a winner. And so is the restaurant with cheers from food magazines and awards (39 and counting) from the likes of *Wine Spectator*. Hard to believe you can find all of this at a resurrected strip mall on Speedway Boulevard. And while great care is taken in the preparation of the menu, this place is not fussy; casual and comfy is the motto here.

Lunch and dinner are served every day. The lounge is cigar-friendly.

Ric's Cafe
$$ • 5605 E. River Rd., #121 • 577-7272

Fresh seafood and patio dining go hand in hand here. Ric's, located in River Center plaza, is a great place to stop during or after a long day of shopping or on Sunday morning for breakfast. Salads run from the unusual ceviche to Caesar salad, and the chef prepares a creative soup of the day. Signature dishes include the Cajun combo, a grilled filet mignon and blackened shrimp, and Sonoran chicken roulade, chicken filled with roasted peppers, poblano chiles, spinach, sun-dried tomatoes and Romano cheese rolled in a corn tortilla and topped with a green chile sauce. The setting is American Southwest and casual. Patrons appreciate the friendly service and reasonable prices.

Ric's is open daily for lunch and dinner and on Sundays for breakfast.

The Third Stone Bar and Grill
$$ • 500 N. 4th Ave. • 628-8844

This relative newcomer to the Fourth Avenue scene is fast becoming a favorite. While well-respected as a venue for blues and rock music (see our Nightlife chapter), The Third Stone also offers new twists on old standbys. The grilled chicken sandwich, for example, is served on focaccia with roasted garlic aioli, roasted peppers and mushrooms. The Sidewinder Burger is topped with roasted red, green and yellow bell peppers, Swiss cheese and guacamole. Other goodies include a veggie burger, hummus dip, bruschetta and the Third Stone's Black Bean Chili.

The color scheme is very chic with deep reds and purples throughout. Old posters from long-ago rock and blues concerts hang on the walls.

The full bar has a wide assortment of seasonal beers. The Third Stone serves lunch and dinner daily.

Tohono Chul Tearoom
$$ • Tohono Chul Park, 7366 N. Paseo Del Norte • 797-1711

Sitting on the patio at Tohono Chul Tearoom, you'll forget that just a little more than a block away lies one of Tucson's busiest intersections, Ina and Oracle roads. That's because the restaurant is set amid the quiet serenity of Tohono Chul Park, a little oasis of desert in the ever-expanding city (see our Attractions chapter).

You have a choice of two patios that are divided by the indoor dining area. On the larger patio you'll find views of the park and maybe a critter or two. The smaller patio offers the serene sounds of a trickling fountain. The food, prepared by those associated with Cafe Terra Cotta, is every bit as good as any found there. The menu is well-balanced, including such favorites as chicken salad, quesadillas, club sandwiches and, for dessert, flan.

Breakfast, lunch and dinner are served daily as is high tea. At high tea you will be offered a choice of teas and little tea cakes, scones and biscuits. After your meal, take a minute to browse through the gift shop, where you'll find hundreds of handcrafted and imported items.

Asian/Middle Eastern

AZ Stixx
$$$ • Broadway Village, 3048 E. Broadway Blvd. • 323-3701

AZ Stixx is an Oriental bistro with a perfect fusion of Asian cuisine and upscale attitude: Salads are wok-seared, the "Really Rockin' rolls" are stuffed with nutty tiger shrimp and the duck is served moo shoo-style. Another innovative touch is the special menu that changes weekly instead of daily.

The decor is a tasteful blend of East and West, and the bar offers a wide assortment of beer and wine. The back patio is a delightful place to spend an evening. Lunch and dinner are served daily.

Firecracker
$$ • 2990 N. Swan Rd. • 318-1118

Firecracker is located in Plaza Palomino on the corner of Swan and Ft. Lowell roads. The exterior of the building complements the interior in color and style. The outside is painted fiery red with yellow accents and gray pillars. The interior walls are painted in pale yellow; the color seems to catch the sunlight that streams through shuttered windows. Large paddle fans hang from the ceiling, and pillars of birch trees add a unique touch. The Asian/Pacific Rim-influenced menu stands out from other restaurants in town. Watch the chef prepare wok-charred fresh salmon or the house specialty Fireworks Chicken. Hot! Hot! Hot! Sushi is also available, and the bar serves saki and Japanese beers. Take advantage of the Sunset Dinners, which are served between 4:40 and 6 PM daily. Although the full menu is not offered during these times, many items are featured at reduced prices.

Firecracker, which is open seven days a week for lunch and dinner, is fast becoming a favorite, so it is wise to make reservations for dinner.

Golden Dragon
$$ • 6433 N. Oracle Rd. • 297-1862
$$ • 6166 E. Speedway Blvd. • 512-1922
$$ • 1145 N. Alvernon Wy. • 325-5353
$$ • 4704 E. Sunrise Dr. • 299-8088

These four Golden Dragon Restaurants offer consistently good Chinese food. Lunch is a real deal with a choice of many entrees served with egg flower soup, fried wonton and fried rice, all for less than $5 per person. Or try the lunch and dinner buffet offered seven days a week.

For dinner try General Tso's Chicken or the two-flavored shrimp with moo shoo pork, which are local favorites. Service is fast and friendly. All locations are open seven days a week for lunch and dinner.

New Delhi Palace
$$ • 6751 E. Broadway Blvd. • 296-8585

New Delhi specializes in vegetarian and nonvegetarian Indian food, which has been voted the best Indian food in Tucson for almost 10 years, according to a *Tucson Weekly* poll. The owner takes pride in the masalas and curries. For the vegetarian a good bet is the Bengan Bharta, gently seasoned roasted eggplant. Nonvegetarians will delight in any one of the curries, especially satisfying when washed down with a cold beer served from the full bar. New Delhi is open daily for lunch and dinner.

Sakura
$$ • 6534 E. Tanque Verde Rd.
• 298-7777

An interesting combination exists at Sakura, which is both a sushi bar/teppan-style restaurant and a sports bar. The rooms are separate, but whichever side you choose we're sure you'll enjoy yourself.

Decorated in traditional Japanese decor, the dining room offers a show with your dinner: The trained chefs dazzle diners with flashing knives and fire right at the table as they prepare fresh seafood or New York steak teppan-style dinners. Kids may enjoy the show, but lunchtime is probably a better time to take them here.

The sports bar is a favorite with Eastsiders, offering TVs, dining and dancing. While lunch and dinner are served every day in the restaurant, lunch is available in the bar during weekdays only. It's on the east side of Restaurant Row on Tanque Verde Road.

Samurai
$ • 3912 N. Oracle Rd. • 293-1963

Samurai is known for Japanese fast food. But don't confuse "fast food" with bland or greasy. Actually Samurai serves some of the best sushi and teppan-style food around.

The bowls (dons) are the way to go. The yakisoba beef, chicken or pork, is hot and tasty, and for sushi try the California roll. If you want a bigger meal order a bento plate, which is any of the bowl offerings served with goyza dumplings. Miso soup and green tea ice cream are seasonal favorites.

Samurai may be hard to find, tucked behind San Francisco Bar and Grill just south of the corner of Oracle and Roger roads, but it's worth the search. Samurai is open daily for lunch and dinner.

Breweries & Brewpubs

Breckenridge Brewery & Pub
$$ • St. Philip's Plaza, 1980 E. River Rd.
• 577-0800

Breckenridge Brewery & Pub offers casual atmosphere, great food and an assortment of handcrafted beers. It also features a martini menu, single malt scotches and a cigar menu. Although not brewed here, hard cider is available.

Much of the food is made with the brews including the Stout-Laced Meatloaf. A specialty of the house is the Jerk Ribs, tender ribs prepared jerk-style, not barbecued. Seafood, steaks and chicken are also available. For appetizers the bartenders recommend the Mile-High nachos, tricolored tortilla chips black beans, olives, tomatoes, cheese and salsa. For dessert, they suggest Chocolate Suicide, a three-layer chocolate cake with fudge icing in a puddle of chocolate sauce, topped off with whipped cream.

The cool interior is open and bright, and the vats are visible from both levels of the restaurant. Patio dining is also available.

Breckenridge Brewery is open seven days

a week for lunch and dinner. And while the menus differ slightly, all efforts will be made to prepare a dinner entree at lunchtime if you just have to have one.

Gentle Ben's Brewing Co.
$$ • 865 E. University Blvd. • 634-4177

Located in the heart of the University area, Gentle Ben's is both a new and old brewery. Originally, Ben's was in an old house just two blocks from the University's Main Gate. But as the University grew, Ben's rebuilt down the street.

The restaurant offers great salads, several different burgers and its version of great brewhouse sandwiches, which are named after songs by The Grateful Dead. The Peggy-O, for example, is a garden veggie burger served with avocado and Jack cheese, and the St. Stephan is grilled pastrami, Ben's homemade coleslaw and Swiss cheese on marble rye.

While you wait for your meal, enjoy a stroll past the glass-enclosed vats of the brews ranging from a Red Cat Amber Ale to an Oatmeal Stout. Some beers are seasonal; the menu explains each type of beer.

Parking is at a premium. Note that the metered angle parking along the three blocks in this area is back-in only!

Nimbus Brewery
$ • 3850 E. 44th St. • 745-9175

Ben Franklin once said, "Beer is living proof that God loves us," and the owners of Nimbus Brewery have adopted this philosophy (the quote is part of their logo). Nimbus beers, which are brewed in small 10-gallon batches, are the only local brews sold at other beer parlors.

In a warehouse district off S. Palo Verde Road, Nimbus Brewery is a little tricky to find: Head east off of Palo Verde Road and then turn left into the driveway of a series of small warehouses. The atmosphere is very casual. Food is limited to cold, but big, sandwiches, which are served at lunch and dinner daily. Live music is featured Thursday through Saturday.

Pusch Ridge Brewing
$$ • 5861 N. Oracle Rd. • 888-7547

With five handcrafted ales, this newcomer to the brewpub scene is holding its own. But the name is a little deceiving. Located between River and Rudasill roads on Oracle Road, it is a good 10 miles south of Pusch Ridge. The casual atmosphere is ideal for a brewpub. The staff will take the time to explain the nuances of each of the brews and which beer best accompanies a particular menu offering or vice versa. Pusch Ridge Brewing serves burgers and sandwiches for lunch and dinner daily.

> **FYI**
> Unless otherwise noted, the area code for all phone numbers listed in this guide is 520.

Burgers, Sandwiches and Such

Baggin's
$ • Campbell Ave. and Ft. Lowell Rd.
• 327-1611
$ • 5056 E. Broadway Blvd. • 327-8718
$ • 6342 N. Oracle Rd. • 575-8878
$ • 5407 E. Pima St. • 795-7135
$ • 2741 E. Speedway Blvd. • 327-4342
$ • Church and Pennington Sts.
• 792-1344

Turkey is big at Baggin's; in fact, the majority of the sandwiches have turkey as the main ingredient, but you can still get other fresh sandwiches and salads. A regular favorite is the Sundowner, which is stacked high with turkey and all the goodies you might find at Thanksgiving dinner including cranberry sauce, stuffing, lettuce and mayo. Non-turkey favorites are the Almost Reuben, a hot pastrami sandwich, cole slaw and Baggin's spe-

---

INSIDERS' TIP

Summer is a great time to sample the fine dining establishments without spending a fortune. Many offer reduced summer rates in late afternoon and early evening.

Whether you desire a little sun or a little shade with your meal, Tucson's restaurants can accommodate you.

cial dressing on marble rye, or the chicken salad, which is chunks of chicken in a creamy dressing served on a bed of greens. A recommended side dish is the Chinese sesame noodle salad flavored with soy sauce and sesame seeds. All orders come with a homemade, chewy chocolate chip cookie.

The decor features Southwestern touches, wooden tables and saltillo tiled floors. Baggin's is open seven days a week for lunch or dinner. The downtown location on Pennington Street is only open for lunch Monday through Friday.

The Big A
$ • 2033 E. Speedway Blvd. • 326-1818

When the widening of Speedway Boulevard lead to the demolition of the original Big A, regulars at this University area favorite were bummed. The Big A was going to be rebuilt across the street from the original site, but would the collegiate atmosphere be lost?

Luckily there was nothing to fear. The new Big A is every bit as comfortable and laid-back as the original, and all the college banners and memorabilia can still be found hanging from the walls.

The Big A is noted for its burgers — 10 different choices including Canadian bacon, bleu cheese and pineapple. Anything else you order — hot dogs, salads or desserts — will be tasty. Beer, wine and mixed drinks are available, but try the lemonade for a cool, refreshing treat. The restaurant is self-serve.

The Big A is open Monday through Saturday for lunch and dinner. Park in the lot adjacent to the building.

Bison Witches
$ • 326 N. 4th Ave. • 740-1541

The sandwiches are really big here and offer more for the taste buds than the usual ingredients. A house favorite is The Green Turkey Sandwich, which has turkey breast, fresh avocado, bacon, cream cheese, alfalfa sprouts and the house honey dressing on your choice of white, wheat or dark rye breads. The Wildcat is piled high with beef, turkey, melted Gouda, lettuce and a splash of Bison Witches' Russian mustard. For the kid in you, try the grilled pb-and-j sandwich. Soups are served in bread bowls, and chips come with all meals. After dark, this is more bar than restaurant, so lunch may be a better choice if you've got kids in tow. Lunch and dinner are served daily, and cold beer and mixed drinks are available from the full bar.

The Bum Steer
$$ • 1910 N. Stone Ave. • 884-7377

You know you're in for something different at The Bum Steer the second you step in the door. First, you won't know which way to go — up? down? And then there's all the stuff — signs, car parts, tools, toys and even an airplane (yes, we said airplane) — hanging everywhere and every which way!

With the All-American menu, choice of video games and all that stuff to look at, it's a great place to take the kids for lunch or an early dinner (it turns into a college bar later in the evening).

Check out the burgers or dogs or try the Caesar salad. Wait service is available but not all the time. You also can order directly at the kitchen window. Two bars — one on the top most level, the other down below — offer daily beer and mixed drink specials. The Bum Steer is open daily for lunch and dinner.

eegee's
$ • Tucson Mall, 4500 N. Oracle Rd. • 293-9250
$ • 7102 E. Broadway Blvd. • 885-8502
$ • 2510 E. Speedway Blvd. • 881-3280

The story behind eegee's is the American dream come true: Two guys with no money and a great idea succeed. Back in the early '70s, two college students were looking for a way to earn some money. One of them remembered the Italian ices that had been a big part of his childhood in New York City. They came up with a recipe for lemon ice, sold them to high school and college students and the rest, as they say, is history.

The lemon ices remain the mainstay of the menu (there's nothing like an ice cold eegee's on a hot summer's day). Other flavors are offered monthly. Hot and cold sandwiches, or grinders, are available. eegee's is open for lunch and dinner daily. There are 15 locations throughout the Tucson area. Check the Yellow Pages for a complete listing.

Geronimoz' Restaurant & Bar
$$ • Geronimo Hotel, 800 E. University Blvd. • 623-1711

This cozy restaurant and bar was one of the best things that came out of the renovation of the Geronimo Hotel years back. Serving juicy burgers, other All-American fare and more than 50 kinds of beer, Geronimoz' is a fun place to stop on UA game days. At night, the downstairs room holds an attraction for the college set with pool tables, video games and music. The atmosphere is casual; the bar and restaurant look like a tavern you might find in upstate New York.

Geronimoz' is open daily for lunch and dinner with late-night dining for those so inclined. Parking can be a drag, but there is a pay lot one block east and a half-block south; get your parking card validated so you can receive some free parking time.

Pat's Drive In
$ • N. Grande Ave. at W. Niagara St. • 624-0891

Pat's chili dogs are known citywide, especially by those folks who were teenagers in Tucson during the '50s and '60s. It was a great place to take a date after a school dance or a movie. Today Pat's still serves inexpensive, good food for lunch and dinner daily. Great care is taken to ensure customers get the kind of food they remember. And just because the dogs are the highlight here, don't shun Pat's burgers, fries or onion rings. All have been named favorites in area polls year after year.

Parking can be tricky. There are a few spaces right on the lot, or you can try parking on a side street.

The Sausage Deli
$ • 2334 N. 1st Ave. • 623-8182

University students and faculty flock to this tiny eatery for some of its most unusual sandwiches, made with quality cold cuts, cheeses and breads. The Susie Sorority is turkey with havarti on whole wheat with tons of mayo, tomato and sprouts, and the Artichoke Reuben uses chokes instead of Sauerkraut to top off the hot corned beef (the regular Reuben is called the Reuben Goldburger). All sandwiches can be served submarine-style. Lunch specials come with a choice of Saguaro chips or one of the deli salads. Beer, sodas, juices, tea and lemonade are available. Party subs come as small as 2 feet and as long as 6 feet. Sausage Deli is open seven days a week for lunch and dinner.

Shari's First Avenue Drive-In
$ • 2650 N. 1st Ave. • 623-5385

You really won't believe the prices at Shari's. They're something out of the 1960s. But then, so is the food. The burgers are juicy, the fries hot and greasy (good greasy, that is) and the shakes thick and cold. Shari's also has hot dogs, onion rings and other drive-in fare. Even the building looks like it must have 30 or 40 years ago.

Order your meal at a window or use Shari's one concession to the modern-day world — the drive-up window. Then wait at one of the two tables out front. Even on busy days the wait isn't long.

Coffeehouses & Cafes

The Aroma Caffe
$ • 346 N. 4th Ave. • 623-2088

On the south end of N. 4th Avenue, you will find a nifty little coffeehouse that offers a little bit of France tossed in with a healthy dose of American hipness. Open in the early morning and offering baked goods, omelettes and crepes, the Aroma Caffe is a neighborhood favorite. Enjoy a latte in one of the two indoor eating areas or take it to the streets and sit at one of the sidewalk tables.

Artwork by local artists is displayed and changes often. One recent "show" featured local schoolchildren's creations. Light musical entertainment is offered some evenings. The Aroma is open daily from early morning to late evening.

Cafe Magritte
$$ • 254 E. Congress St. • 884-8004

Cafe Magritte was one of the first cafes on the scene when downtown began making a comeback as an arts district. It remains a favorite with the arts crowd today, although at lunchtime the lawyers and county workers can be found here, too.

The menu is fun and chic, including the tuna sandwich with olive tapenade served on a crusty French bread and the Pablo Pollo, lettuce, chicken, black beans, tomato, cheese, red onion and sour cream topped with the house cilantro-lime vinaigrette.

Lunch and dinner are served Tuesday through Sunday with late-night hours on Friday and Saturday. This is a popular spot during Downtown Saturday Night, so get here early if you want to be seated before all the fun starts.

Parking will cost you. Try a metered spot on the street or one of the pay lots that are spread throughout downtown. Meters run 25¢ per 15 minutes; lots run up to $5 per day.

Cafe Paraiso
$ • 820 E. University Blvd. • 624-1707

Cafe Paraiso is located on University Boulevard in the Geronimo Hotel complex just east of Euclid Avenue. This small but quality coffeehouse has counter service where you can get coffees, teas, soups, sandwiches, salads, quiches and bagels. The chicken salad sandwich, with seedless red grapes and walnuts, is especially good and served on your choice of bread. There is a daily soup that can be served by the cup, the bowl or with a full sandwich or half sandwich.

Cafe Paraiso is open seven days a week

INSIDERS' TIP

Tucson has two restaurant rows — one on Tanque Verde Road running from E. Speedway Boulevard to Sabino Canyon Road; the other running along S. 4th Avenue where many Mexican restaurants are located.

from early morning until late evening. You'll find parking on University Boulevard — metered, back-in, angled — or in the pay lot behind the complex.

Cafe Sweetwater
$$ • 340 E. 6th St. • 622-6464

Located on the corner of 4th Avenue and 6th Street, Cafe Sweetwater is a great place for people-watching, especially if you are seated at a window table along 4th Avenue. The food ranges from pasta and crepes to potato cakes and seafood. Jazz is offered weekend nights. The cafe is open for lunch and dinner Monday through Friday and for dinner only Saturday and Sunday. There's a small parking lot behind the restaurant.

The Casbah Tea House
$ • 628½ N. 4th Ave. • 740-0393

Although this tiny place is actually a tea house, it does offer a hefty assortment of coffees. Food is strictly organic vegetarian and vegan with a Middle-Eastern twist. Items on the menu include gypsy stew, a homemade red lentil stew spiced with coconut curry and served over basamati rice. The Casbah also offers spanakopita, a fajita plate made with seitan and veggies as well as fresh baked goods.

The decor is unlike any you might find around town. The walls and floors are covered with Persian rugs and banners, and the chairs are low, about 4 inches from the ground. The room opens to a cool, shady patio in back. Entertainment includes belly dancing nightly on weekends.

The Casbah Tea House is open from early morning until late evening seven days a week. It is located behind the Creative Spirit Gallery on 4th Avenue.

The Cup
$$ • Hotel Congress, 311 E. Congress St. • 798-1618

For a true sense of downtown Tucson, spend an hour or so at The Cup. Whether it's for breakfast, lunch or dinner you will see the full spectrum of the downtown scene, from the city movers and shakers to those who are just passing through.

The menu is mixed: Mexican, Italian and East Indian entrees are on the menu daily along with good old American food like club sandwiches and garden salads.

The Eggs in Hell — eggs with chiles, salsa and tortillas — are highly recommended if you like it hot. The mocha is some of the best in town. The Cup is open daily.

Parking is typical of downtown — some metered spots, a few pay lots and a very few spaces in back of the building.

Cuppuccino's Coffee House
$ • 3400 E. Speedway Blvd. • 323-7205

This midtown coffeehouse is always busy. Located in Rancho Center, Cuppuccino's has good coffee, good eats and a warm, cozy atmosphere. It's a great place to wile away an afternoon sipping coffee or tea, enjoying stimulating conversation with friends or reading the latest bestseller. A variety of coffees is offered as well as teas and Italian sodas. The baked goods range from bagels to ooey-gooey sticky buns, and the sandwiches and salads are always fresh.

Hours vary: Monday through Thursday Cuppuccino's is open early and closes at 10 PM; weekend closing is at midnight; and on Sundays the staff gets to sleep in a little bit since opening hour isn't until 8 AM.

The Dish
$$ • 3200 E. Speedway Blvd. • 326-1714

Within weeks of its opening night, The Dish had made a name for itself as a hip, European-influenced eatery. Located behind The Rum Runner (Tucson's largest wine store, detailed in the Shopping chapter), The Dish has a great wine list. Creative chefs take common ingredients and turn them into uncommon entrees. The menu is divided into "Big Dishes," "Little Dishes," "Simple Salad" and "Fancy Salad." An example of a Big Dish is citrus-glazed salmon with crispy leeks, and from Little Dish offerings you can choose crab and goat cheese fritters or corn and scallion custard.

Dinner is served Monday through Saturday, and reservations are strongly suggested.

The Epic Cafe
$ • 745 N. 4th Ave. • 624-6844

As you approach the Fourth Avenue shopping district from the north, the first eatery you'll see is The Epic Cafe. Located on the corner of

4th Avenue and University Boulevard, The Epic has been named the "best cafe for everything" by readers of Tucson Weekly.

In addition to lattes, espresso and other coffee drinks, The Epic has an eclectic array of food such as pita pizzas, tuna with capers sandwich, hummus plates, spanakopita, soups and salads. Desserts are changed frequently and are always the perfect way to end a meal here.

While it is open early seven days a week, the hours are a bit unusual for a coffeehouse — doors close around 6 PM.

The Grill
$ • 100 N. Congress St. • 623-7621

The Grill is a favorite hangout for the young, artsy, downtown crowd because the interior is an honest to goodness real old-fashioned diner, complete with a semicircular counter and booths, an eclectic menu and 24-hour service. You can get typical diner fare, such as fluffy pancakes and tuna melts, but The Grill also has some upscale choices, including spinach ravioli with tomato cream sauce and grilled shrimp in sweet red pepper sauce.

Iguana Cafe
$$ • 210 E. Congress St. • 882-5140

For a little taste of Cuba, stop in at the Iguana Cafe located in the heart of downtown. While it is small and cheerful, the cafe is known for Monster Sandwiches, which are served on home-baked Cuban bread. The salads are "Grande," too, and sweets are baked daily in the ovens. Drinks can be juices, soft drinks or libations from the full bar.

Open Monday through Saturday for late breakfast, lunch and dinner, there are special late hours during Downtown Saturday Night.

The Village at Coffee Etc.
$$ • 2830 N. Campbell Ave. • 881-8070
$$ • 6091 N. Oracle Rd. • 544-8588

Coffee Etc. may not really appear to be a coffeehouse, but since it has made its reputation serving some of the finest coffee in Tucson (voted Tucson's best in Tucson Weekly since 1984), we thought it best to put it here. More like a cafe, Coffee Etc. serves some great omelettes, hot and cold sandwiches, burgers and salads. House specialties, called Village Delights, include chicken or shrimp Alfredo and the San Juan, which is the house version of taco salad.

Gift shops, with cards, candles, mugs, jewelry and other curios, can be found at both locations. Coffee Etc. also roasts its own beans and sells them on the premises. Teas and coffee-making equipment are available, too.

Both sites are open 24 hours a day, seven days a week.

Fine Dining

The Arizona Inn
$$$ • 2200 E. Elm St. • 325-1544

Casual elegance is the way to describe the ambiance in the dining room at this historic inn in central Tucson. The signature breakfast is eggs Benedict, but you can also find Southwestern- and Asian-influenced entrees at lunch and dinner, including the fish of the day, steamed in a bamboo basket with ginger and leeks, and the mesquite-grilled quail.

The views of the beautiful grounds are legendary as is the daily high tea, which is served in the elegant library directly across from the dining room. The Arizona Inn dining room is open for breakfast, lunch and dinner daily and offers an outstanding Sunday brunch.

Anthony's in the Catalinas
$$$$ • 6440 N. Campbell Ave.
• 299-1771

Whether you're looking for city views or mountain views in a fine dining experience, you can find them both at Anthony's in the Catalinas. You may not even have to make a choice as to which you'd prefer. This is foothills dining at its finest.

The dining room is elegant with a pianist playing nightly. The service is outstanding, and the food will bring you back again and again. The appetizer list is quite extensive, with such items as escargot de chef and Anthony's pâté maison. The entrees include a pasta du jour, veal dishes, chicken, seafood and steak, but for a memorable meal try the lamb Wellington. Anthony's prides itself on the large wine selection from its cellar. The cocktail lounge sells quality cigars to go with an after-dinner cognac. The owner of Anthony's also owns several cigar emporiums in town.

Reservations are strongly suggested. Anthony's in the Catalinas is open Monday through Friday for lunch and dinner but only serves dinner on Saturday and Sunday.

Charles
$$$ • 6400 E. El Dorado Cir. • 296-7173

Everything about Charles is elegant: the long, tree-lined driveway, the cobblestones under your feet at the entryway, the rich tapestries, the sculptured garden, the high-backed French chairs, the tuxedoed waiter's preparation of Caesar salad at your table and oh, did we mention the veal Oscar and tournedos de boeuf? Charles is housed in the former estate of heiress Florence Pond. Often compared to an Italian villa, the home has lost none of its charm in the conversion to a restaurant. The sculptured gardens can be enjoyed before, during and after your meal.

Entrees are carefully prepared, with some, such as the rack of lamb or the Chateaubriand Bouquetiere, flambeed at your table. Service is impeccable. And the wine cellar has one of the largest selections of wine in the city.

Dinner is served Tuesday through Sunday; there is also a Sunday brunch. Charles offers Early Bird Specials from 4 to 6 PM. Reservations are strongly suggested.

The restaurant is off Wilmot Road, just north of Speedway Boulevard on the east side of the street.

Cielos
$$$$ • The Lodge on the Desert, 306 N. Alvernon Wy. • 325-3366

Located in the newly renovated Lodge on the Desert, Cielos is already receiving rave reviews. Paella, lobster and pheasant grace the menu, all prepared by Chef John D. Harings. Appetizers, breads and desserts are also outstanding. Entrees are served to the table under ceramic domes, a special touch.

The dining room is elegantly styled, and during the daytime light seems to fill the room (Cielos does mean sky, after all). Breakfast, lunch and dinner are served here daily.

Flying V Bar & Grill
$$$ • **Loews Ventana Canyon Resort, 7000 N. Resort Dr. • 299-2020, (800) 234-5117**

"Imaginative" and "spectacular" are just some of the accolades The Flying V has received from diners and restaurant reviewers alike. Golfers also enjoy it as a 19th hole because it has an excellent view of the golf course at the resort.

The decor is Southwestern with lots of copper and leather; the menu is also Southwestern but with an added Latin touch. Starters reflect this fusion with such offerings as chilled and grilled shrimp served with jicama, avocado and a tequila aioli and the squash blossoms served with artichokes, goat cheese and sun-dried tomatoes in an ancho chile sauce. Entrees are just as unusual: The grilled salmon burrito is only one of the interesting choices. Tapas, which are served all day, are also on the menu. The Flying V is open for lunch and dinner Tuesday through Sunday.

The Gold Room
$$$$ • **Westward Look Resort, 245 E. Ina Rd. • 297-1151**

If you're wondering where to celebrate that special occasion, be it an anniversary, promotion or what have you, The Gold Room is a good choice.

After several remodelings over the past few years, this elegant dining room is now similar to the layout it had some 20 years ago. Raised banquettes provide a breathtaking view of city lights and some truly romantic ambiance.

> **FYI**
> Unless otherwise noted, the area code for all phone numbers listed in this guide is 520.

INSIDERS' TIP

There's nothing like a warm, fresh flour tortilla. Pick up a dozen at any of the tortillas factories in town. Two favorites are Grande Tortilla Factory at 914 N. Grande Avenue, 622-8338, and La Mesa Tortillas at 7823 E. Broadway Boulevard, 298-5966.

The selection of eateries in Tucson ranges from grab-it-and-go cafes to fine dining restaurants.

The food is innovative and tastefully prepared with ostrich, buffalo and venison serving as the bases for several of the entrees. Steak, seafood and fowl are on the menu, and entrees are changed on a regular basis. Service is top shelf, as expected. All your needs, such as assisting in choosing a wine from the extensive wine list, will be met by the well-trained staff.

Please note that this is one of the few places in town where casual dress is discouraged. Men will need to wear a tie. Dinner is offered nightly. Breakfast and lunch are also served.

The Tack Room
$$$$ • 2800 N. Sabino Canyon Rd. • 722-2800

The Tack Room has long been (since 1973) a five-diamond restaurant and for good reason: impeccable service, an outstanding and creative menu and a setting that is both Western and white-tie. Located in an old adobe house tucked back off the road, it is easy to find — look for the giant sign in the shape of a cowboy boot out front. The boot may be a bit misleading (this isn't a cowboy steakhouse by any means), but you couldn't ask for a better landmark.

Signature dishes are the slow-roasted duck (actually, The Tack Room does duck just about better than any place in town) and the rack of lamb Sonora.

Dinner is served Tuesday through Saturday, and reservations are suggested.

French

Ghini's French Caffe
$ • 1803 E. Prince Rd. • 326-9095

Ghini's offers a taste of France at a petit price. Open for breakfast and lunch only, Ghini's has omelettes, sandwiches, salads and desserts from the adjacent bakery.

The omelettes are made with three eggs and stuffed with such goodies as potatoes, onions, cheeses, bacon, garlic and herbs provencale. Salads are fresh; both the salade nicoise and wilted spinach salad stand out among several flavorful choices. Sides include homemade pâté maison, scalloped potatoes and French onion soup. And if you're in the mood for just a sweet treat and a latte, Ghini's can accommodate you. The restaurant is open for breakfast and lunch Tuesday through Saturday.

Penelope's
$$$ • 3071 N. Swan Rd. • 325-5080

Proprietor Patricia Sparks invites you to "enjoy the soul of France in the heart of Tucson" at her restaurant. Set in an old adobe ranch house, the menu offers both classic French and country French dishes. You can choose to eat in the garden or sit by the fireside where stained-glass windows add to the charm.

Start your meal with escargot à la bourguignonne; follow it with a Salade de Dieux, which has fresh fruit, pine nuts and avocado on fresh greens with a raspberry vinaigrette. For the entree, we suggest the filet mignon with Bordelaise sauce. Don't forget dessert — the mousse is wonderful!

Penelope's is open for lunch and dinner Tuesday through Friday and dinner only Saturday and Sunday. There is a prix fixe menu or an à la carte menu.

Get It and Go

Chow Bella
$$ • 2418 N. Craycroft Rd. • 290-0773

When you want to have a unique meal without the fuss of going out to eat, take a trip to this midtown gourmet shop. You will find such goodies as Sicilian meat loaf, vegetable lasagne, tortilla torte and individual pizzas. There are plenty of interesting salads and sides, and the desserts are especially sinful. Try the brownie, if you dare.

Chow Bella is small, with the majority of the space taken up by the open kitchen. If you get there at the right time of day, you can watch the daily specials being prepared. Because of the emphasis on fresh ingredients, the offerings are changed daily.

Chow Bella is open Monday through Saturday from late morning to early evening. You'll find the restaurant on the east side of Craycroft Road, just north of Grant Road. Pay attention — it's easy to miss. The building also houses a Southwest decorating store, a barber shop and an insurance office. It's right behind the Circle K store on the corner.

Feig's Kosher Foods Market & Delicatessen
$ • 5071 E. 5th St. • 325-2255

Feig's Kosher Foods Market & Delicatessen has been in business for more than 50 years. Serving strictly Kosher sandwiches and deli foods, Feig's prides itself on the high quality and reasonable prices it offers.

Catering is a speciality. The deli plates are as good as those found in New York City. The Nova Lox Party Platter includes bagels, cream cheese, Bermuda onions and tomatoes. All platters are beautifully garnished and require an eight-person minimum. Other items on the menu are chopped liver, chicken noodle soup, kugel, latkes, knishes and gefilte fish. Whole chickens, turkeys and roast beef are available from the oven or Feig's rotisserie. For lunch there are deli sandwiches, hot dogs and homemade soup.

Feig's is open from 8 AM to 5:45 PM Monday through Thursday for breakfast and lunch. On Fridays, the restaurant closes at 3:45 PM; it's closed on Saturdays, of course. Feig's is open on Sundays from 8 AM to 1:45 PM.

Reay's Market
$$ • 4751 E. Sunrise Dr. • 299-8858
$$ • 3360 E. Speedway Blvd. • 795-9844
$$ • 7133 N. Oracle Rd. • 287-5394

Reay's is a gourmet market and so much more — butcher shop, fish monger, health food store, sandwich shop, bakery and deli. The list of items you can get here seems endless.

But if you're in a hurry and still want something with homemade flavor, stop in at any one of the Reay's markets and pick up a salad to go, veggie lasagne and a killer brownie from the bakery. Your choice of beverage is wide: everything from juices and bottled water to beers from around the world. You're bound to find something to please your palate. Reay's is open daily.

Rincon Market
$$ • 2513 E. 6th St. • 327-6653

The Rincon Market has been a neighborhood grocery store since 1928. As the neighborhood changed, so did the Rincon Market. Today, in addition to groceries, Rincon Market has a salad bar, deli sandwiches, baked goods and a wonderful prepared-meal takeout section. The offerings change on a daily basis, but at any given time you will have a choice of lasagne, tamale pie, dolmas, stuffed cabbage and an assortment of salads and side dishes. The market's roasted chicken is a favorite of harried mothers all over town: The completely cooked and well-seasoned chickens are cooked daily on a rotisserie-like contraption. The results are homemade taste without the homemade mess.

Wine and beer are available, and there is a butcher in the grocery store offering quality meats. The market is open daily.

Tony's Italian Style Butcher Shop & Restaurant
$ • 6219 E. 22nd St. • 747-1245

Step into this Eastside deli and you'll swear you're in The Big Apple. The place is small but filled to the rafters with Italian goodies. The refrigerator counter holds fresh mozzarella, strings of Italian and German sausages, cold cuts, pepperocini and marinated artichokes. There are plenty of deli sandwiches on the menu. Try The Rocky, which is filled with mortadella, prosciutto and provolone and drizzled with oil and vinegar. Or indulge in the house specialties of veal saltimbocca or spaghetti carbonara. For a quick family-style dinner, pick up a Bucket of Spaghetti and Meatballs, which can feed from two to 28 people. There are also pans of lasagne. Both come with garlic rolls.

Tony's is open Monday through Saturday for late breakfast, lunch and dinner.

Greek

El Greco's Grecian Gardens
$$$ • 4635 E. Ft. Lowell Rd. • 325-7552

El Greco's Grecian Garden serves authentic Greek cuisine with everything from hummus to baklava. Lamb dishes are a specialty with broiled lamb steak or chops, oven-roasted lamb shank and, at dinner only, roast leg of lamb. If lamb isn't to your liking, try the Chicken Solonika, chicken tenders sauteed with white wine, feta cheese, special peppers and Greek seasoning served over Greek spaghetti. Avolemongo soup is offered daily at lunch and dinner. Dinners are served with a choice of a Greek dinner salad or soup and rice or potatoes. The lunch menu is similar to the dinner menu but has kebob and souvlaki sandwiches. The desserts are outstanding; try the baklava or ouzo cake for a perfect ending to a great meal.

El Greco's Grecian Garden is open seven days a week for lunch and dinner.

The Olive Tree
$$ • 7000 E. Tanque Verde Rd. • 298-1845

With such offerings as lamb bandit — which is not unlike a Greek festival for one — it's easy to see why this place is so popular. The Olive Tree is a consistent winner in local dining polls.

The intimate dining room offers romance, while the garden patio gives the feeling of dining on the Aegean Sea. An extensive wine list has something to accompany any meal you order. The Olive Tree, in Santa Fe Square at Tanque Verde and Sabino Canyon roads, is open nightly for dinner. Call ahead for reservations.

Healthy, Vegetarian and Alternative

Blue Willow Restaurant Bakery & Poster Gallery
$$, no credit cards • 2616 N. Campbell Ave. • 995-8736

The first part of the name comes from the antique china pattern of star-crossed lovers (their story is on the menu, and the pattern is repeated throughout the restaurant). The second part comes from the nifty cards, posters and trinkets that are sold in the front shop. On busy days the wait never seems long because the store has so many fun things to look at and play with.

Omelettes are the mainstay of the menu; you can choose one of the many house offerings or make your own. Sandwiches, soups

---

INSIDERS' TIP

During the summer, patio dining is made cooler by the use of misters — lengths of piping that run the perimeter of the patio and spray a fine mist into the air. Don't worry — it's usually so dry, you won't get wet.

and salads complete the menu. The patio is famous for remaining cool on hotter days; it's tented with netting held up by little balloons.

Expect a wait, especially on weekend mornings. There's a small parking lot and limited free parking on the street. The Blue Willow serves breakfast, lunch and dinner seven days a week.

Delectables
$$ • 533 N. 4th Ave. • 884-9289

Dining at Delectables is just a little bit different than most places. Sandwiches, soups and salads are offered, but it's the Boards that bring people back again and again. These are not the ordinary cheeseboards some of the '60s crowd might remember, but top-shelf gourmet in both product and presentation.

For example, the pâté de canard à l'orange has both duck and pork pâté with pistachios, orange peel and a splash of Grand Marnier. It's served with a Greek salad, French pickles and crispy French bread. Sharing one with a friend on the patio is heavenly.

Delectables is open seven days a week for lunch and dinner.

The Garland
$$, no credit cards • 119 E. Speedway Blvd. • 792-4221

This cozy little spot on Speedway Boulevard just east of Stone Avenue has a flavor treat for vegetarians and nonvegetarians alike with such delights as fresh fruit crepes and chicken salad. The salad dressings are flavorful without drowning the greens. Rolls and breads are homemade and served warm.

The setting is an older home that has been carefully renovated into a restaurant. The tasteful decorations and efficient, friendly service only add to the comfort zone. The Garland is open for breakfast, lunch and dinner daily.

Govinda's
711 E. Blacklidge Ave. • 792-0630

Located just off N. 1st Avenue — between Glenn Avenue and Ft. Lowell Road — in the Chaitanya Cultural Center, Govinda's could have easily been placed under our Asian/Middle Eastern header: On Tuesday nights, the buffet offers Indian-style food.

Meals, all served buffet-style, are consistently good here. Dine indoors and enjoy waterfalls, fountains, gardens and exotic birds that add serenity to your dining experience. Patio dining is also available.

Lunch and dinner are served Wednesday through Saturday.

Terra Nova Restaurant and Bakery
$$ • 6366 E. Broadway Blvd. • 790-7700

Located in the El Mercado shopping plaza on the corner of Broadway Boulevard and Wilmot Road, Terra Nova has a large vegetarian following, even though nonveggie entrees, including chicken, beef and seafood, can be found in abundance. Both sides of the table, so to speak, are good; it's a great place to join friends who may not all share the same dietary habits.

The eatery is open, garden-like and larger than it appears. It's open for breakfast, lunch and dinner seven days a week.

Italian

Capriccio's
$$$ • 4825 N. 1st Ave. • 887-2333

The name means "something out of the ordinary," and Capriccio's is just that.

Northern Italian cuisine is the focus at this restaurant. The roast duckling, crispy and succulent with the flavors of Grand Marnier and green peppercorns, is a house specialty. Pasta dishes lean toward the unusual including ravioli con vitello, which are pasta pillows stuffed with veal and duck liver pâté, and zuppa di pesce, a seafood soup in a tomato broth served on angel hair pasta that will delight your taste buds. Choose from a wine list that rivals other lists in town.

The dining room is intimate and decorated with wood paneling and mirrors. The wait staff

---

INSIDERS' TIP

Discount coupons for many area restaurants can be found in area phone books, the newspaper and other local publications.

is knowledgeable and efficient. Dinner is the only meal Capriccio's serves; the restaurant is closed on Sunday. Seating is limited to 50 each evening, so it's wise to make reservations.

Caruso's
$$ • 434 N. 4th Ave. • 624-5765

Caruso's may well be one of the city's oldest restaurants. In fact, the Zagona family has been serving great southern Italian food to Tucsonans at the same location for more than 50 years!

There's no surprise to the success of the place. The food is scrumptious, the ambiance charming and very Italian and the prices reasonable. The Lasagne el Forno, made with homemade noodles and baked to perfection, is a house specialty, and all your Italian favorites are served. Your waitperson can help you choose from the many wines offered, which are available by the glass or the bottle. You may dine indoors or on the patio: Each choice has its charm.

Caruso's is a great place to dine after a long day of shopping on Fourth Avenue. The restaurant is open Tuesday through Sunday for dinner only. No reservations are accepted. You'll find limited parking on the street, but unlike downtown it's free.

Daniel's
$$$ • St. Philip's Plaza, 4340 N. Campbell Ave. • 742-3200

A cornerstone restaurant in St. Philip's Plaza, Daniel's offers contemporary northern Italian food in a most romantic setting. If you want to win the heart of that certain someone, make reservations for dinner at this award-winning restaurant.

Start with an antipasto of zuppa del frutti de mare, seafood soup; follow that in true Italian style with a pasta course, perhaps the spaghetti con funghi (mushrooms), and then for an entree order the salmon con griglia, salmon on sauteed spinach with carmelized tomato sauce. Por dulce (that's dessert) the torta di tarufo liqueftatto, an individual chocolate cake served warm from the oven with a melted chocolate truffle inside served on a vanilla sauce, is not to be missed. Proprietors Jimmy Bruer and Jeffery Fuld open the doors to their four-diamond restaurant seven days a week for dinner only.

DaVinci's Italian Restaurant and Pizza
$$$ • 3535 E. Ft. Lowell Rd. • 881-0947

Those of Italian descent agree that DaVinci's is the place to go for a real taste of Italy. DaVinci's has been voted Tucson's favorite Italian restaurant for many years in several different polls. The extensive menu, with everything from spaghetti and meatballs to eggplant parmesan, is just one of the reasons. The warm continental atmosphere is another, and the large portions probably have something to do with it, too. If you can't make up your mind what to order, try the Mezzo e Mezzo, a plate of spaghetti and ravioli. Seafood and veal dishes are superb and often come with a side of pasta. There is also a Bambini menu for the kids, and pizza is available in four sizes ranging from 10 inches to 20 inches.

DaVinci's is open for lunch and dinner Monday through Saturday.

Gavi
$$ • 7865 E. Broadway Blvd. • 290-8380

In the short time Gavi has been open it has developed a reputation for delicious Italian dinners that offer something more than the usual fare. Set in a storefront in Broadway Plaza on the corner of Broadway Boulevard and Pantano Road, Gavi may not look too impressive, but one taste of the spaghetti florentina, spaghetti with a spinach cream sauce or the chicken saltimbocca will convince you otherwise.

The menu is extensive with spaghetti, manicotti, lasagne, ravioli, eggplant, shrimp, mussels, veal and much more. The sauces are diverse also: marsala, marinara, florentina, primavera, alfredo, cacciatore and several cheese cream sauces. Most of the pastas can be prepared with any one of the sauces. The calamari salad and the eggplant salad are unique starters, and picking a wine to go with any part of your meal won't pose a problem.

The owners are Italian soccer fans as evidenced by the posters, pictures and soccer jerseys that adorn the walls. Outdoor dining is available, but it is limited to the area in front.

Gavi is open for dinner only seven nights a week, and there are extended hours on Friday and Saturday.

Scordato's
$$$$ • 4405 W. Speedway Blvd.
• 624-8946

The Scordato family is well-known in Tucson for its many fine restaurants, but it's this original restaurant that people talk about when they say "Scordato's." Dining at Scordato's, with its desert setting, impeccable service, classical music and wonderful smells, is a special experience. This is one of the places in town where you may want to dress up a little.

While any of the classic Italian meals such as clams in white sauce or pasta marinara are delicious, veal dishes are Scordato's specialty. Your waiter may recommend the veal stresa, which is a veal cutlet stuffed with prosciutto ham and mozzarella cheese and sauteed in a white and marsala wine sauce. There is a fresh fish of the day as well as an assortment of scampi dishes. Beef, chicken and pork entrees are also available. If you're there on a night when Scordato's is serving Osso Buco, you should give it a try. Bellisimo!

You will have no problem choosing a wine to go with your meal: Scordato's has southern Arizona's largest wine selection. The knowledgeable staff will assist you in making an appropriate choice.

Scordato's is open Tuesday through Sunday for dinner only.

Vivace Restaurant
$$$ • Crossroads Festival, 4811 E. Grant Rd. • 795-7221

While it is an Italian restaurant, with Osso Buco, polenta and pastas on the menu, it may better be classified as New Italian for its innovative preparation. Owner Daniel Scordato's creative talent comes from a long family history of serving fine Italian food to Tucsonans. And even though this trattoria is located in the Crossroads Festival plaza, you can still enjoy a romantic dinner or a business lunch.

The food is prepared in a kitchen that's open to diners' views. For lunch Vivace has pastas, sandwiches, salads and specialties such as pork tenderloin sauteed in lemon caper sauce with vegetable pasta or a warm duck salad with spinach. Vivace's dinner menu is an expansion of the lunch menu. Start with grilled artichokes vinaigrette for an appetizer, and then try crab-filled chicken breasts or shrimp sauteed with garlic wine sauce. Pizza is on the menu, too. Daily specials offer reduced rates on some entrees.

Vivace's has a full bar with an extensive choice of wines by the bottle or the glass.

Vivace is open for lunch Monday through Saturday and for dinner daily. We suggest reservations.

> **FYI**
> Unless otherwise noted, the area code for all phone numbers listed in this guide is 520.

Mexican

Cafe Poca Cosa
$$$ • 88 E. Broadway Blvd. • 622-6400
$, no credit cards • 20 N. Scott Ave.
• no phone

These two restaurants are very much the same and yet so very different from each other. The bigger restaurant in the Clarion Hotel on Broadway Boulevard changes its menu twice daily at lunch and dinner, depending on what's available at the market. The smaller restaurant, a half-block to the north on the opposite side of the street, serves a set but delicious menu for breakfast and lunch. The decor at both locations is similar, with brightly colored walls, hand-painted furniture and Mexican knickknacks everywhere. Both offer special touches such as homemade house dressing brought to the table in a bottle to toss on the fresh greens that accompany each meal.

Poca Cosa is a favorite of the legal crowd downtown: The federal courthouse is right next door. The crowds fill the place quickly at lunch; you may be asked to share a table with a stranger at the smaller location. Don't be shy.

Parking is tricky; a metered lot is across the street (from both places) with more pay lots within a few blocks' radius; street parking is very limited. The Broadway Boulevard location serves lunch and dinner Monday through Saturday; the other location serves breakfast and lunch Monday through Friday.

Club 21
$$ • 2920 N. Oracle Rd. • 622-3092

Club 21 is located where Oracle Road meets Miracle Mile. In business since 1946, it serves Mexican and American food, but stick with the Mexican for a real treat. The chimichangas are especially delicious and big! To go along with that big chimi, try the "El Gigante," one of Tucson's largest and most delicious Margaritas (an "El Gigante" is the perfect cure for those 100+ degree summer days). The full service bar also serves ice cold cerveza — that's beer to all you gringos. The adobe brick walls are decorated with serapes, velvet paintings and other Mexican folk art.

Club 21 serves lunch and dinner but is closed Mondays. The family also takes a well-deserved vacation sometime during the summer and closes the restaurant.

El Charro Cafe
$$ • 311 N. Court Ave • 622-1922
$$ • El Mercado, 6310 E. Broadway Blvd. • 745-1922
$$ • Tucson International Airport, 7250 S. Tucson Blvd. • 573-8255

Regularly voted Best Mexican Restaurant by the *Tucson Weekly* readers' poll, El Charro Cafe is a Tucson treasure. In the historic downtown El Presidio district, the building itself is an 1896 adobe house on the National Historic Register. The business is the nation's oldest Mexican restaurant continuously operated by the same family (since 1922), and the food reflects the tradition.

In 1922 Monica Flin opened a one-room cafe that was so popular she needed larger quarters. It was a true, low-budget enterprise. She would take an order from a customer and run out the back door to buy the ingredients from the local grocery. When the customer paid, she would run back and pay the grocer. Like all great ideas, it worked.

The restaurant was briefly located at the Temple of Music and Art, but she soon moved to what is now La Placita Village on Broadway Boulevard. By the time Tucson's 1960s urban sprawl changed the face of the city, Monica (now in her eighties) had gone home to the family house on Court Avenue, the current location of the long-running restaurant.

Though Monica died in 1972, the restaurant continues to stay in the family, run by her niece, Carlotta Flores. The restaurant celebrated its 75th anniversary in 1997.

The menu includes topopo jalisciencse and Monica's famous chimichanga, carne seca and baked fish tacos, which are known nationwide at Mexican restaurants that actually use Monica's recipes. In the early days, a combination plate would go for 15¢. Today, all the entrees are less than $12; El Charro could charge more and people would still pay. Maybe it's their wide selection of tequila and perfect Margaritas. Maybe it's just the food.

All three restaurants are open for lunch and dinner daily.

El Minuto
$$ • 354 S. Main Ave. • 882-4154
$$ • 8 N. Kolb Rd. • 882-4154

This longtime downtown landmark is known for its carne seca and refried beans. While many restaurants in town serve low-fat cooking, El Minuto has stuck with the more traditional methods — maybe not heart healthy but certainly worth falling off the diet wagon for.

The dining area is decorated with Mexican curios, chile strings and hand-painted flowered trim on the turquoise and pink walls. Serapes are used for curtains. Eat indoors or sip a Mexican beer as you soak up the historical ambiance of the neighboring barrio from the patio.

Located across from the Tucson Convention Center, it's a great place to stop before or after an event. There will be a wait on weekends, so get there early. While you wait, take a short walk to the shrine, El Tiradito, next door (see our Attractions chapter).

The Eastside location on Kolb Road is just north of Broadway Boulevard and Pantano Road, and the food is every bit as delicious. Lunch and dinner are served daily at both locations.

John Jacob's El Parador
$$ • 2744 E. Broadway Blvd. • 881-2808, (800) 964-5908

You might wonder if a Mexican restaurant with a non-Mexican owner could survive the competition in Tucson. But that's exactly what the Jacobs family has done, and done well, since 1946.

The food is unique. Try the crab nachos

78 • RESTAURANTS

Outdoor cafes and patios fill with revelers for Downtown Saturday Night.

appetizer or the Pollo Fundido, seasoned chicken rolled in a flour tortilla that is lightly fried and topped with chili con queso. The International Enchiladas, which are also highly recommended, consist of a chicken enchilada with tomatillo sauce, a seafood enchilada with a white sauce and a carne seca enchilada with the house's special sauce.

Lush plants and a skylight give the feeling of eating in a tropical paradise (it's a beautiful place for a wedding). Several private dining rooms can be used for meetings or special functions, and El Parador also provides catering services.

The restaurant is open Monday through Saturday for lunch or dinner, and on Sundays, a brunch is served. Stop in The Cantina, El Parador's bar, at Happy Hour weekday afternoons.

El Saguarito
$$ • 7216 N. Oracle Rd. • 297-1264

El Saguarito bills itself as "The Healthy Mexican Food Alternative," but don't let that fool you into thinking that the food can't be good. It lacks nothing in flavor; the secret is canola oil and a wealth of family recipes.

Try the calabacitas, which are zucchini baked with chiles, cheese, tomatoes and onions. Light and flavorful, it's the perfect thing when you crave Mexican food but want to heed your diet. Or sample the chicken mole that's served with rice and beans. And if you're feeling slightly adventurous, try the Nopalitos Colorado. Nopalitos are prickly pear cactus pads, usually served sliced, which resemble green beans. El Saguarito also serves a full slate of usual Mexican goodies. You can choose a mixed dinner, a combination plate or order à la carte. El Saguarito is known for the variety of salsas it serves with each meal. The Pico de Gallo, small chunks of tomatoes, chiles and onions mildly seasoned, is a good choice.

El Saguarito is definitely a family kind of place. You can order a Fajitas Family Pack or take home a dozen tacos or tamales from the special take-out menu. Be prepared for a wait as this is a very popular northwest restaurant, which is open for breakfast, lunch and dinner Monday through Saturday.

El Torero
$$ • 231 E. 26th St. • 622-9534

Finding this longtime south side favorite might be a little difficult, but we'll give you an Insiders' tip: As you head south on 4th Avenue watch for a mural of a bullfighter, then make the next right onto 26th Street. The second building from the corner is El Torero.

The first things that will catch your eye in

this brightly lit restaurant are the long wooden bar, the high ceilings and thick adobe walls. The place may seem a bit noisy, but don't let that change your mind. Even on busy nights, you'll be seated quickly at one of the many tables, and you won't notice the noise.

Anything you order will be outstanding, but try the carne seca plate. You'll get a heap of seasoned shredded beef with Mexican rice and refried beans. A warm flour tortilla accompanies the meal. To eat this in true Mexican style, tear off a piece of the tortilla (making sure you cover it up again to keep it soft and warm), plop on some carne seca, a dollop of beans and some salsa. The tortilla soup is another favorite as is the topopo salad, a corn tortilla slathered with beans and topped with a mountain of lettuce, slices of chicken, avocado, tomatoes and cheese. It really doesn't need any dressing, but there is a vinaigrette available at your request.

El Torero is open every evening except Tuesday for dinner. Lunch is served early, on those same days, and the kitchen closes at noon.

La Parilla Suiza
$$ • 2720 N. Oracle Rd. • 624-4300
$$ • 5602 E. Speedway Blvd. • 747-4838

With two La Parilla Suizas in town, diners can enjoy authentic Mexico City-style food, which differs from Sonoran cooking in that many of the entrees are grilled. A grill is located in the center of the restaurant, so you can watch your dinner being prepared. Popular entrees here are the fajita dishes and fish tacos. The Margaritas really hit the spot.

This company owns 18 restaurants in Mexico. Tucsonans are thrilled La Parilla Suiza decided to build two here. (There are also two in Phoenix.) Open seven days a week for lunch and dinner, the restaurants usually have good crowds at both times.

Mi Nidito Cafe
$$ • 1813 S. 4th Ave. • 622-5081

The wait at Mi Nidito on many evenings can be as long as 45 minutes, but most people don't mind because they know eventually they'll get to enjoy some of the best Mexican food South Tucson has to offer. Mi Nidito has been voted the best Mexican food in several newspaper polls for many years.

The decor hasn't changed much over the years, nor has the food. Mexican tile, whitewashed walls and a fake palm tree in the back of the restaurant are not unlike decor in restaurants on the other side of the border. The large and crispy flautas are topped with lettuce, guacamole, sour cream and a sprinkling of Mexican farmer cheese. The menudo is highly recommended, although you'll hear discussions over which is better — the white or the red. Stick with the red if you like it spicy hot.

Mi Nidito is open for dinner every night except Mondays.

Papagayo
$$ • 840 E. Ft. Lowell Rd. • 622-8233
$$ • 4717 E. Sunrise Dr. • 577-6055
$$ • 7000 E. Tanque Verde Rd.
• 721-6249

Papagayo has been serving outstanding Mexican food for more than 25 years; the Ft. Lowell Road location is the original site.

Before your meal order a cheese crisp, a large flour tortilla topped with cheese and then broiled; add chile strips or guacamole for an extra treat. Diners can choose combination plates, burros, tacos, chimichangas, quesadillas, flautas and tamales. There are also soups and appetizers such as chimichiquitas, a combo platter of minichimichangas. Desserts include flan and almendrado, a light meringue colored like the Mexican flag and topped with a sweet almond sauce.

On certain evenings, usually weekends, strolling musicians play traditional Mexican canciones (songs). While not quite a full mariachi band, the music is a special touch.

The Ft. Lowell site has a beautiful patio with a bougainvillea canopy and fragrant flowers. It's so sheltered you almost forget that just on the other side cars are whizzing down Ft. Lowell Road at a pretty fast clip. The restaurants are open every day for lunch and dinner.

Sanchez Burrito Co.
$ • 1060 N. Craycroft Rd. • 747-0901
$ • 2530 N. 1st Ave. • 622-2092
$ • 2526 E. Broadway Blvd. • 795-3306

When Reynaldo Sanchez returned to Tucson after many years as a successful restaurateur in California, his plan was to retire. Instead, he opened Sanchez Burrito Co. Today, there are three Sanchez Burritos owned by Reynaldo's daughter, Dahlia.

All restaurants serve the same menu, but each offers a different service: The Craycroft Road site offers a full-service restaurant with a full bar; the original 1st Avenue site has only counter service and booths and serves beer; the place on Broadway is take-out only and does not serve beer. Sanchez Burrito is the home of "The Giant Burrito," and that's no exaggeration (you'll need a knife and fork to eat this monster). All burritos come filled with refried beans and your choice of carne asada, carnitas, machaca, chicken or veggies. If you order it Sanchez style — topped with enchilada sauce, cheese, sour cream and guacamole — you'll have enough to take home for lunch the next day. All three locations are open for lunch and dinner daily.

Pizza

Brooklyn Pizza
$ • 534 N. 4th Ave. • 622-6868

Brooklyn Pizza is not the place to take the boss to make a good impression, which is a shame since that means he or she will miss out on great New York pizza.

The decor might be called funky. There are a dozen mismatched '50s Formica-topped tables. The walls are painted a deep yellow and covered with artwork. And the music is everything from '50s hits to alternative rock.

When your pizza arrives, you'll swear you're in Brooklyn. The sauce is thick, the toppings are all high quality, and the crust is the perfect blend of crispy and chewy. Toppings include artichoke hearts, chicken, eggplant, feta cheese, ground beef, meatballs, ricotta, spinach and other more common toppings.

You can also have pasta with marinara sauce, garlic knots, cheese or any of the pizza toppings. The hero sandwiches are imaginative. Try the Florentine or the Vatican Veggie.

The restaurant serves lunch and dinner daily and has late-night hours. Beer and wine are available. Brooklyn Pizza delivers; it will even deliver beer.

Grandma Tony's Pizza
$ • 3773 W. Ina Rd. • 744-2441
$ • 3967 N. Oracle Rd. • 292-2929
$ • 4404 E. Grant Rd. • 321-4404
$ • 970 E. University Blvd. • 884-7833
$ • 7878 Wrightstown Rd. • 886-4461
$ • 5855 E. Broadway Blvd. • 571-7678
$ • 7010 E. Broadway Blvd • 885-7117
$ • 2451 S. Harrison Rd. • 721-6600

Grandma Tony's is brought to you by the same people who own Little Anthony's Diner and The Gaslight Theatre. With eight locations in town, it'll be no problem to find one near you.

> **FYI**
> Unless otherwise noted, the area code for all phone numbers listed in this guide is 520.

The menu is small, but all the food is tasty. The pizzas, of course, are the centerpiece. Toppings are the standards with a few unusuals thrown in, including pineapple, artichoke hearts and jalapeno peppers. You can have a salad and breadsticks to go with the pizza.

The 7010 E. Broadway site is the home of The Gaslight Theatre (see our Arts and Culture chapter). While you enjoy one of the rollicking melodramas there, you can munch on a pizza. Grandma Tony's has a successful delivery business because of its numerous locations, but eat-in dining is available at all the sites. No alcohol is served with the exception of The Gaslight Theatre location.

Grandma Tony's is open seven days a week; ask about the daily specials.

Magpie's Gourmet Pizza
$$ • Speedway Blvd. and Swan Rd.
• 795-5977
$$ • Broadway Blvd. at Pantano Rd.
• 751-9949
$$ • 4th Ave. and 5th St. • 628-1661
$$ • Ina and Oracle Rds. • 297-2712

Magpie's was the first pizza place in town to offer gourmet pizza. The restaurant offers several specialty pizzas, such as The Godfather, which has mozzarella, provolone, Swiss, Romano and cheddar cheeses and Italian sausage, Canadian Bacon and capicolla. Regular crust, sourdough crust or whole wheat crust with a choice of sauces — pesto, olive oil and garlic or regular tomato sauce — are available. Toppings are numerous and include roasted green chiles, sun-dried tomatoes, fresh spinach or zucchini and pepperocini. With all of this to offer, it's no wonder Magpie's pies have been named "Best Pizza in Tucson" eight years in a row.

For the health conscious, Magpie's has lite "r" pizzas made without mozzarella or provolone cheeses. Low-fat or cheese substitute are available at no extra cost. You also have several choices of calzones and fresh salads.

Seating is limited; the majority of Magpie's business is delivery or take-out. A unique feature to the take-out menu is the Take & Bake pizza. Call ahead and order your pizza to be picked up. Then instead of getting a hot pizza at the restaurant and having a cold pizza by the time you get home, you get an uncooked pizza that you can pop into your oven. Magpie's is open for lunch and dinner and has late-night hours.

Zachary's
$ • 1019 E. 6th St. • 623-6323

Zachary's has a reputation for cold beers and humongous pizza. The beers come from all over the world. In fact, Zachary's had a large beer selection long before it became trendy. Dress is very casual, and families are welcome.

Pizzas are 2 inches thick and come loaded with toppings, including the standards as well as broccoli, artichoke hearts, fresh tomatoes, jalapenos, spinach, proscuitto and pineapple. The Big Z is the house specialty. Meat lovers will want to try the T Rex, which comes with pepperoni, sausage and ham. For veggie lovers, the staff recommends The Uptowner. The salad dressings are homemade. Insiders' tip: Due to the size of the pizzas, the wait once you've ordered can be almost an hour, especially on nights when there is a UA game.

Zachary's is open every day for lunch and dinner.

Seafood

Keaton's
$$ • 7401 N. La Cholla Blvd. • 297-1999
$$ • 6464 E. Tanque Verde Rd.
• 721-1299

Keaton's is known for the fresh seafood it has flown in daily from the coasts and the Gulf of Mexico. Clams, oysters, salmon, roughy and crab are all staples. The steamed oysters platter is a treat at Keaton's as are the crab cakes. You can also get steak, prime rib and pasta. Service is excellent and swift.

There are two Keaton's in town, one in the backside of the Foothills Mall and the other on Restaurant Row. Both offer the same quality menu, pleasant service, large selection of imported and domestic beers and patio dining.

Keaton's is open daily for lunch through dinner with late-night dining, after 10 PM, in the bar only. Keaton's takes reservations, but they are not necessary.

Kingfisher
$$$$ • 2564 E. Grant Rd. • 323-7739

Kingfisher bills itself as an American regional grill, which means the featured food comes from all regions of America, but the accent is on seafood in every way, shape and form. Diners can select from three or four types of oysters flown in daily from the Northwest, the East Coast and other briny places. And if you don't know one oyster from another, your knowledgeable waitperson will explain the subtle differences. Fresh fish specials change daily; all are cooked with attention to detail and are free of heavy sauces. Salmon is a staple, but that's not to say the steaks and other entrees aren't good here. The kitchen grills up a pretty mean steak. The wine list is large and varied enough to find a suitable match for any choice of entree.

The decor is modern but cozy. Reservations are suggested. Lunch and dinner are served, and Kingfisher is one of the few places that serves until midnight seven days a week.

Maine Course
$$$ • 5851 N. Oracle Rd. • 887-5518

Maine Course's decor is reminiscent of a restaurant you'd find in say Maryland or, okay, Maine. Wood paneling, nautical decorations and subdued lighting make you forget that you are in the middle of the desert, and the smell of melted butter only adds to the coastal ambiance.

The house specialty is, of course, live Maine lobster, with lobster tail and King Crab legs as other house favorites. The lobster is served either saltwater boiled or grilled. Sizes and prices vary according to the market. The kitchen has a fresh fish of the day, and salmon and clams (when available) round out the seaside portion of the menu. For the meat lovers, Maine Course has prime Angus New York Steak and chicken dishes. A full-service bar is available

The restaurant is open nightly for dinner. Reservations are recommended.

The Solarium
$$$ • 6444 E. Tanque Verde Rd.
• 886-8186

The Solarium was one of the first restaurants in the Eastside Restaurant Row on Tanque Verde Road. It was also one of the first quality seafood places in town. The fact that it's still one of the more popular spots in Tucson attests to its greatness.

The architecture here is striking with multilevels, lots of glass, golden polished wood and plants. A patio circles the restaurant at the upper level. The lounge is on the third level.

While the emphasis here is on seafood, including daily specials, the prime rib will please the meat lovers in the crowd. Lunch is served Monday through Friday until 2:30 PM when the restaurant closes. The Solarium reopens at 5 PM for dinner, which is served seven days a week. Catering and banquet services are also available.

Steakhouses

El Corral
$$ • 2201 E. River Rd. • 299-6092

El Corral has long been a Tucson tradition when it comes to where to take out of town visitors for prime rib. There's not an evening any day of the week or season of the year when the outside patio isn't comfortably filled with people waiting for a table. Don't be dissuaded by the wait: It's reasonable, even in peak season. You'll have just enough time for a beer, wine or highball or two from the bar.

El Corral's claim to fame is prime rib, but the ribs are also a great choice. The prime rib comes in several cuts and sizes, and the ribs come as a full rack or half rack. Sides include the usuals, such as choice of potatoes or pilaf, but Insiders know that the tamale pie is the way to go. This fluffy, soft corn bread is slightly sweet and studded with mild green chiles and kernels of corn. Top the meal off with a tableside tossed salad with the house Honey Italian dressing and such trimmings as sunflower seeds, croutons, mushrooms and fresh cracked pepper and you will walk away more than satisfied.

The ambiance here is totally Tucson — casual, comfortable and slightly rustic Southwest. Several dining rooms and close tables add comfort instead of a crowded feeling. You'll see diners in their Sunday best and others who look like they just stepped off the golf course. Service is also a plus — quick, knowledgeable and friendly.

El Corral serves only dinner nightly and does not take reservations.

Hidden Valley Inn
$$ • 4825 N. Sabino Canyon Rd.
• 299-4941

When this longtime Tucson landmark burned to the ground a few years back, few locals doubted it could ever be rebuilt. Happily, the Hidden Valley Inn is back serving lip-smacking mesquite-grilled steaks and ribs and looking much as it did before the fire.

The outside resembles a Wild West town, and the Crystal Palace Dining Room is filled with cowboy gear such as lassos, horseshoes and wagon wheels. It's a cross between an 1880s saloon and a museum.

Steaks range in size from the Trail Boss T-Bone to the Tenderfoot Filet Mignon. The Iowa pork ribs are oven-baked and plopped on the grill to get just a hint of mesquite. Fish and seafood are available. There is entertainment in the saloon Thursday through Saturday.

The Hidden Valley Inn is open seven days a week, but it does not take reservations.

The Last Territory Steakhouse and Saloon
$$$ • Sheraton El Conquistador Resort and Country Club, 10000 N. Oracle Rd.
• 544-5000

This is a fun place with a truly Wild West

flair. So even if you aren't staying at the Sheraton El Conquistador Resort, it's worth the drive.

The first thing you'll notice is the faux Western town in front of the restaurant. If you're lucky you'll catch a Wild West show shoot out. (Regrettably, there is no set schedule for these shows). The second thing you'll notice is the mouth-watering smell of steaks cooking on the mesquite grill. The dining area is a large barn-like room, sporting Western gear hanging from the walls and a fire in the fireplace. Live music is offered nightly, and the waitresses are dressed as dance hall girls. Stop in on a Friday or Saturday night and the same person serving your meal will be performing in a can-can show. The dance hall gals sing and dance, much to the delight of the crowd.

The Last Territory's servings are more than ample. The steaks are tender and well-seasoned with a true taste of mesquite. Barbecue baby-back ribs are another specialty, and fresh seafood is available. As with most cowboy steakhouses, the fixins' include potatoes, beans, bread and salads.

The restaurant serves dinner nightly. Reservations are suggested.

Lil Abner's Steakhouse
$$$ • 8500 N. Silverbell Rd. • 744-2800

Oldtimers in Tucson can remember when the drive out to Lil Abner's Steakhouse was a trek. The road was dark, narrow and winding, but it was always a treat once you arrived. Today, the ride doesn't seem so long due to all the development in this part of Tucson and the wider, well-lit road, but there is still a treat at the end. Lil Abner's has some of the best mesquite-grilled steaks around. And the atmosphere is about as cowboy as you can get. Dinner on the patio means beautiful desert views, especially at sunset, the smell of your dinner on the grill and the twang of Western music, which is offered on Fridays and Saturdays with blue grass picking on Sundays.

Other entree selections include beef ribs, pork ribs and chicken, all cooked on the grill, of course. Sides include your choice of cowboy beans or potato. All meals come with a small salad.

Lil Abner's serves dinner nightly.

OK Corral
$$ • 7710 E. Wrightstown Rd. • 885-2373

Don't miss the turn off to the OK Corral or you'll miss out on great mesquite-broiled steak, ribs (pork and beef), chicken and some of the best prime rib in Tucson. OK Corral has been at the same site for 30 years. It's only been recently that the road in front of the restaurant was moved to create the Tanque Verde Road overpass. Here's a hint: Stay in the far right lane as you head east on Tanque Verde and watch for the signs that mark the exit to Wrightstown Road.

The interior is a slice of cowboy heaven with large wooden tables covered with red-checked tablecloths, wood paneling, antiques and, in the center of it all, a huge mesquite grill.

Steaks come in seven sizes and several cuts, and there are four cuts of prime rib. Pinto beans, salsa, salad and bread accompany each meal. The drinks are hefty, too, and the beer is ice cold.

OK Corral is open seven days a week for dinner only. Banquet and catering services are available.

Pinnacle Peak Steakhouse
$$ • 6541 E. Tanque Verde Rd.
• 296-0911

If you have a friend who has horrible taste in ties bring him (or her) to Pinnacle Peak. Anyone who walks in sporting a tie will promptly be the center of attention as the waitresses begin clanging cowbells and all action stops. Then, snip! snip!: A waitress cuts off the tie and hangs it from the ceiling where it joins hundreds of others. Yep, this place takes casual dress to a whole new level.

Located in Trail Dust Town on Tanque Verde Road, Pinnacle Peak is a Tucson tradition for big mesquite-grilled steaks. A range of steak is offered from the smaller 1 pound T-bone to the monster 2 pound porterhouse. Ribs, barbecue chicken and fish are also available. Sides include the cowboy staples of beans, taters, salad and bread. Try the apple cobbler for dessert, if you have room that is, and then enjoy a stroll through Trail Dust Town. The shops here are unique, and the kids may want to ride the scale model train that runs the perimeter.

Pinnacle Peak is open nightly for dinner, but expect a wait (especially on weekends).

You're bound to find something in Tucson to suit your nocturnal cravings.

Nightlife

If nightlife to you means live music, you'll find a full slate in Tucson, including rock, country, jazz, alternative, dance, blues and acoustic performances. The major live music clubs are clustered along Fourth Avenue and the connecting downtown area and in the 5000 block of Speedway Boulevard. Club crawlers find the Fourth Avenue area the best way to spend a night on the town: It has outlets for jazz, rock, blues and acoustic music, as well as small pubs, alternative dance, all-night cafes and even belly dancing. The Fourth Avenue area draws everyone from college students to professionals, while the downtown area is a favorite hangout for the young, alternative, pierced-body crowd.

To get a taste of both downtown and 4th Avenue, we recommend that you check out Downtown Saturday Night. Held the first and third Saturday of each month from 7 to 10 PM, the family event, which hosts street musicians, vendors and clowns, usually has a different theme each week. Live performances are featured in the main bus station parking lot at Pennington Street and 6th Avenue. It's a great opportunity to see downtown's art scene at its best and to mingle with a good cross-section of Tucson inhabitants.

The strip along Speedway Boulevard contains a cluster of clubs for the bit-older-than-college-age clientele, all within walking distance of each other. This area boasts the Chicago Bar and Berky's, both of which book a variety of musical acts seven days a week and draw a remarkably mixed clientele. You'll also find The Cage (a huge radical dance club) and TD's Showclub (a fancy exotic dancer bar). Speedway Boulevard is also the address for The Loft Cinema, one of Tucson's alternative art movie houses, as well as a number of smaller pubs, restaurants and cafes.

Over the last two years, microbreweries have popped-up in Tucson and moved to the top of the list of trendy places to see and be seen. Other hotspots include the alternative movie scene, with The Loft showing artsy foreign films and The Screening Room specializing in independent productions and the works of local producers. Multiscreen cinemas are strategically located around the area, so you never have to drive too far to catch a first-run film. For the coffeehouse crowd, there is no shortage of places to sip espresso and listen to a local singer-songwriter strum a guitar and croon a tune. (For an extensive list of gourmet coffeehouses, see our Restaurants chapter.)

Much of Tucson's nightlife relates to the area's strong art scene, with numerous theatrical productions, ballets, operas and symphonic music presentations. We also have a strong literary base that has resulted in a number of regularly scheduled evening poetry readings at various venues, from coffeehouses to bookstores. Look to our Arts and Culture chapter for information about these nighttime pursuits.

Dining in Tucson can be a total nightlife experience, with many restaurants offering live music ranging from jazz to piano and classical guitar to strolling mariachis. Cafe Sweetwater, Arizona Inn and most of the resorts in the foothills are good examples of this sophisticated entertainment. We will explain the entertainment fare to you in this chapter but invite you to flip to our Restaurants and Accommodations chapters for more information on these establishments.

A Few Ground Rules

Tucson is not a late city. Most bars stop the music and the alcohol at 1 AM and close at 1:30 AM. A few even close at 1 AM. In the state of Arizona, you must be 21 years of age to consume alcohol, and Tucson's clubs won't let you in the door without a picture ID. Cabs don't really roam the streets here, but if you need one, the clubs are more than happy to call one for you. Arizona's drunk driving laws are very strict and strongly enforced with random roadblocks — especially on holiday weekends, so it's better to pay the money for a cab than spend a night in jail.

Credit card acceptance varies. All of the clubs we've listed here accept credit cards, but if you deviate from our roster, be aware that you may run into a cash-only establishment.

Cover charges often depend on the popularity of the entertainment and whether the band playing is an out-of town-act. Generally, you'll pay between $2 and $5. In the listings that follow we've tried our best to let you know which clubs charge. Our best advice if you're strapped for cash or you just don't believe in paying for entertainment is to call before you head out the door.

Keeping up with the current status of Tucson's nightlife isn't easy, since clubs come and go, change names, start and drop live music, burn down, remodel or simply fall out of favor. *Tucson Weekly* (distributed free every Thursday) offers an extensive listing of clubs, art openings and other nightlife activities. Also on Thursday, the daily *Tucson Citizen* offers a special pull-out calendar section, as does *The Arizona Daily Star* on Friday. Between these three weekly editions, you're bound to find something to suit your nocturnal cravings.

The following listings are broken down into general categories, but nothing in Tucson is written in stone. In any given week, a club could have bands playing rock one night, blues the next and reggae the following evening. And unless we tell you otherwise, these clubs have full bars.

Acoustic Music

Arizona Inn
2200 E. Elm St. • 325-1541

One of the city's most elegant spots and conveniently located near the University of Arizona, the Inn offers classical guitar music in its main dining room on Friday and Saturday evenings. In the classy Audubon Lounge, you can relax in overstuffed chairs and sofas while listening to a pianist play nightly until 10 PM. (For more information on the Arizona Inn, check the Accommodations and Restaurants chapters.)

Coffee Plantation
845 W. University Blvd. • 628-4300

An evening at this small gourmet coffee enclave near the University of Arizona makes for a nice alternative to the rock clubs and noisy bar scene. Sip an espresso and munch on fresh baked goods as singer-guitarists perform Friday and Saturday evenings.

Cushing Street Bar & Grill
343 S. Myer Ave. • 622-7984

Located near the Tucson Convention Center, this bar and grill is known for one of the best Happy Hour menus in town. In fact, at Cushing Street, Happy Hour comes twice a day, from 4 to 6 PM and from 10 PM to midnight. The covered-patio dining area offers comfortable seating and gas heaters on cold evenings. Music ranges from acoustic singer-songwriters to full rock or jazz bands on Friday, Saturday and Sunday evenings. The large wooden bar stretches across one wall inside; wooden tables with individual lamps are the seating option. The mixed crowd here ranges from artists to lawyers. It's also a popular spot for long lunches. (See our Restaurants chapter.)

Alternative Music

Airport Lounge
20 E. Pennington St. • 882-0400

Don't head for the airport in search of this lounge! It's actually in downtown Tucson in a windowless basement beneath the Plaza Pub. With a decor of brass and mirrors and painfully low ceilings, this new club has been an immediate hit with downtown lounge lizards seeking an eclectic range of live music on Saturdays. The cover charge ranges from $2 to $5.

Club Congress
311 E. Congress St. • 622-8848

This eclectic club, in the historic Congress

> **FYI**
> Unless otherwise noted, the area code for all phone numbers listed in this guide is 520.

Hotel, has risen to the forefront of the downtown night scene since it sponsored a Halloween party in 1985. Today, the pierced-body and artist crowds hang here for dancing and live music. On Mondays it's '70s disco; Tuesdays, acid jazz and hip-hop; Wednesdays, '80s retro; Thursdays, alternative rock; and for the weekend — live bands. Don't forget to bring a few bucks for the cover charge: It usually runs from $2 to $5.

Double Zero
121 E. Congress St. • 670-9332

With live alternative bands Thursday through Saturday, Double Zero is one of downtown Tucson's newest clubs for the young and hip. Red-brick walls, cement floors, two pool tables and a few sofas adorn this stripped-down spot, which is all about music. Even when no bands are playing, it's loud, it's noisy, it's fun and it's about $2 to $5 to get in the door. The very dangerous Double Zero Long Island Ice Tea certainly does its part in contributing to the atmosphere.

The Shelter
4155 E. Grant Rd. • 326-1345

Open since 1994, the decor in this round concrete building can only be described as "early JFK," with a mix of black velvet, Elvis and Marilyn Monroe. The crowd is painfully hip and very eclectic. They sip drinks at the bar or in booths while a strange collection of tunes plays on the stereo, and the television shows classics such as '60s James Bond movies. There is occasional live music or a DJ on Tuesdays and two pool tables, but the draw here is the ambiance and the cocktails. Drinks are serious business here: Bartenders only offer top-of-the-line libations and never use pre-fab mixes or disperse alcohol from a gun.

Jazz

Cafe Sweetwater
340 E. 6th St. • 622-6464

Located on the corner of 4th Avenue and 6th Street, this classy little restaurant offers one of the few venues in town to hear real jazz. The peach-and-teal lounge seats only about 50 people, so it's best to get there early since the lounge fills up fast. The live jazz groups perform on Wednesdays, Fridays and Saturdays and range from fusion to bluesy to traditional. Drinks are a bit pricey, but there's no cover charge. The club is comfortable and populated by jazz enthusiasts of all ages.

Cottonwood Club
60 N. Alvernon Wy. • 326-6000

Located at the Cottonwood Cafe, the Cottonwood Club offers live jazz combos and dancing on Friday and Saturday nights. Though jazz is near and dear to the club's heart, the music featured varies. During the week, there's '70s and '80s Retro Night on Wednesdays and West Coast Swing Dancing (complete with an instructor) on Tuesdays.

Olé!

For those who have an urge for the sounds of Old Mexico, a few of Tucson's restaurants and bars offer some of the best mariachi music you'll hear north of the border. Here we list a few of these eateries and when the singers in sombreros perform.

El Charro Cafe, 311 N. Court Ave., 622-1922 (Friday); 6310 E. Broadway Blvd., 745-1922 (Tuesdays and Thursday through Sunday).

El Mariachi Restaurant, 106 W. Drachman St., 791-7793 (Friday and Saturday).

El Parador, 2744 E. Broadway Blvd., 881-2808 (Saturday).

La Fuente Restaurant, 1749 N. Oracle Rd., 623-8659 (seven days a week).

Rock

Berky's Bar
5769 E. Speedway Blvd. • 296-1981

A favorite spot for the older rock-and-blues crowd, Berky's offers live bands seven nights a week. The cover charge varies widely, so call ahead for that evening's rate.

Boondocks Lounge
3360 N. 1st. Ave. • 690-0991

This funky club and pool hall has two

separate bars, a dance floor surrounded by tables and a horseshoe bar with a good selection of beers in bottles and on tap. Live music runs Friday through Sunday with a variety of music from rock to blues. It's dark, and the crowd varies depending on who's playing. This is a great little place to shoot some pool on an off-night or hear some of Tucson's best local bands. You'll pay $2 to $5 to get in the door.

The Chicago Bar
5954 E. Speedway Blvd. • 748-8169

With bands seven nights a week, this has been one of Tucson's most popular spots since its beginnings as a blues club in 1972. A widely mixed crowd packs the place almost every night. The dance floor is well-used (as are the pool tables), and Tucson's most popular bands play this venue, including rock, funk, reggae, blues and R&B. It's funky and grainy — a smoky bar without the smoke. Patrons usually stroll in and out, crossing the street to Berky's or The Cage. The cover charge is usually $2 to $5.

O'Malley's
247 N. 4th Ave. • 623-8600

With a very large bar, late-night snacks and a separate club for live bands, this is a popular weekend college hangout. Live music is featured Thursday through Saturday, but O'Malley's sees business all week long. Patrons are drawn in by the airy high ceilings, outside patio and several pool tables. On weekends, don't be surprised to see people waiting in line to get in. O'Malley's cover charge ranges from $2 to $5.

Third Stone Bar and Grill
500 N. 4th Ave. • 628-8844

Third Stone is one of the many clubs on Fourth Avenue for those who like to club crawl. It's relatively new and offers live music Tuesday, Wednesday, Friday and Saturday for those willing to part with $2 to $5 for the cover charge.

Comedy Clubs

Laff's Comedy Club
2900 E. Broadway Blvd. • 323-8669

In the tradition of New York comedy clubs, Tucson's only nightspot for a good chuckle is open Thursday through Sunday. The full dinner menu offers everything from Mexican food to steak. The club hosts touring as well as local up-and-coming comics. The cover charge is around $8.

Country-and-Western

Bushwacker's Dancehall and Saloon
4635 N. Flowing Wells Rd. • 887-9027

Bushwacker's is your basic country-and-western dance club with line dancing and live music Wednesday through Saturday. The band usually remains the same all week. It's a good spot to break in those cowboy dancing boots you just bought. Bushwacker's cover runs from $2 to $5.

Cactus Moon
5470 E. Broadway Blvd. • 748-0049

This hot top-40 country-music dance club does not offer live music, but it does offer nonstop country hits, line dancing, a free buffet of finger foods during Friday Happy Hour (starting at 5:30 PM) and a variety of drink specials. The notorious Men's Tight Ass Contest is the highlight of Ladies' Night every

---

INSIDERS' TIP

In Arizona, you must be 21 to purchase or drink alcoholic beverages. And alcohol cannot be sold between 1 and 6 AM Monday through Saturday and between 1 AM and 10 AM Sunday. So if you want champagne with Sunday brunch, don't shop for the bubbly before 10 in the morning.

---

www.insiders.com
See this and many other Insiders' Guide® destinations online — in their entirety.
Visit us today!

Downtown Saturday Night draws crowds to the Arts District on the first and third Saturdays of each month.

Wednesday. All this can be yours for a low cover of $2 to $5. The Moon doesn't shine Monday and Tuesday.

Chaparral Lounge
7850 N. Oracle Rd. • 297-5419

Though more of a neighborhood bar than country-and-western mecca, the Chaparral Lounge, in the northwest area of the city, is a 20-year-old institution for the local cowhands. Three pool tables, a handful of tables and a bar that sits 20 are the lounge's attributes. The Lounge serves strictly bottled beer, with nothing on tap, and the jukebox is heavily populated with Willie, Waylon and other classic country-and-western artists.

Dance Clubs

Ain't Nobody's Bizness
2900 E. Broadway Blvd. • 318-4838

Done in salmon and seafoam with plenty of art prints and neon Marilyn Monroe, this is a primarily gay establishment where the girls hang out. Weekly theme nights and a wooden dance floor add to the fun. For those who want a quieter moment of conversation away from

INSIDERS' TIP

When attending an event where parking is at a premium, watch the signs and don't assume you can get away with any "creative parking." You may find your car has been ticketed, or even towed.

the noise, there is a smoke-free lounge. Above the dance floor is a soundproof alcove with a distinctive Victorian flavor where you can kick back and watch the action.

Boom Boom's
2520 N. Oracle Rd. • 623-6969

Recently renovated, this is the home of the Thursday Night Playgirlz Cabaret — considered the best drag show in Tucson. The club has a dance floor divided by sections of chain link fence and a variety of overstuffed chairs, sofas and retro-style lamps. A second room sports red walls and a huge red velvet curtain hanging on the back wall. The crowd is mixed and of a variety of ages. Boom Boom's is frequented primarily by gay patrons but welcomes everyone with its theme nights, including Latin Dance on Friday, country-and-western music on Saturdays and karaoke on Wednesdays and Sundays.

The Cage
5851 E. Speedway Blvd. • 885-3030

This cavernous dance club sports glowing wall art, loud music, computerized dance-floor lights and, of course, cages. The 20-something crowd arrives late here, usually after club-crawling. Domestic beers are only $1, and mixed drinks are $2.

Hours
3455 E. Grant Rd. • 327-3390

A 10-foot neon pink triangle dominates the dance floor of this gay club, which is open to both men and women. The club is smaller than most, but there's a cozy patio with a rock fountain.

IBT's
616 N. 4th Ave. • 882-3053

Voted the Best Gay Bar in 1997 by readers of *Tucson Weekly*, this Fourth Avenue institution draws both gay and straight clientele. The attraction is funky techno, top-40 and hip-hop dance music that booms nonstop. The bar is separate from the moderate-sized dance floor area, and there is also a fairly large outdoor courtyard. Be aware: Thursday is Cruise Night, also known as underwear night, with drink specials for those who dance in their skivvies.

The Outback
296 N. Stone Ave. • 622-4700

The Outback is one BIG place, with a gleaming bar that seems to go on forever, numerous pool tables, a giant dance floor, a second-level bar area and a separate club with live bands on Tuesdays and Saturdays. The dance music here runs across the contemporary scale, and occasionally there are theme nights. The club is also known for booking national acts that have had their heyday but are still popular in an underground kind of way — enter The Village People.

On weekends, expect long lines. Unlike The Cage, patrons aren't as pierced and are usually a bit more well-dressed. The club is within walking distance (two blocks) of downtown's numerous nightspots.

Karaoke Rules!

For those whose idea of a good time is belting out a tune, Tucson has more than its share of karaoke bars offering the opportunity to be in the spotlight almost every night of the week. Here is a quick list of those clubs, and which nights you can be a star.

Big Al's, 5801 S. Palo Verde Rd., 294-9496 (Wednesdays, Thursdays and Sundays).

Boom Boom's, 2520 N. Oracle Rd., 623-6969 (Wednesdays and Sundays).

The Depot, 3501 E. Ft. Lowell Rd., 795-8110 (Sundays).

Famous Sam's, 2480 W. Ruthrauff Rd., 292-0492 (Tuesdays, Wednesdays and Thursdays); 3933 E. Pima St., 323-1880 (Fridays and Sundays).

Fenderskirts, 140 S. Kolb Rd., 722-1214 (Mondays, Wednesdays and Thursdays).

Good Times Restaurant & Lounge, 8495 E. Broadway Blvd., 886-4949 (Thursday through Saturday).

Grubsteak, 2851 W. Valencia Rd., 578-9009 (Thursdays).

Joe and Vicky's, 3700 N. Oracle Rd., 888-1900 (Tuesdays and Saturdays).

Mr. Catfish, 2660 W. Ruthrauff Rd., 292-9001 (Tuesdays and Thursday through Saturday).

Nevada Smith's, 1175 W. Miracle Mile, 622-9064 (Saturdays).

O'Hanlon's, 20 W. Ft. Lowell Rd., 888-8649 (Fridays and Sundays).

Old Town Restaurant & Saloon, 5200 S. Palo Verde Rd., 889-3344 (Thursdays and Fridays).

Pack-em-Inn, 22 W. Drachman St., 624-5956 (Wednesdays and Saturdays).

Rock-It Bar & Grill, 5001 E. 29th St., 747-7047 (Tuesdays and Wednesdays).

Salty Dawg, 6121 E. Broadway Blvd., 790-3294 (Tuesdays, Fridays and Sundays).

Brewpubs

Breckenridge Brewery & Pub
St. Philip's Plaza, 1980 E. River Rd.
• 577-0800

With huge shiny brewing tanks rising from the first floor to the open second-floor dining area, you know the beer is fresh. Breckenridge also serves dinner nightly and offers live music on Sunday evenings. The crowd here ranges from chic professionals to college students, and the atmosphere is open and airy. (See our Restaurants chapter).

Frog & Firkin
874 E. University Blvd. • 623-7507

This British-style pub has a variety of import and micro beers and serves pizza along with the usual pub fare. But Wednesdays are a hoot with Frank Sinatra Night. Live bands croon hit after hit, and in honor of Old Blue Eyes, $8 gets you a plate of pasta, a glass of wine and a cigar!

Gentle Ben's Brewing Company
865 E. University Blvd. • 624-4177

One block west of the University of Arizona main gate, Gentle Ben's is Tucson's original microbrewery pub with seven brews ripe and fresh for the sipping. It also serves lunch and dinner daily. (See the Restaurants chapter).

Pusch Ridge Brewing
5861 N. Oracle Rd. • 881-7547

Known for their chili, this brewpub just began brewing its own beers to complement the hard-to-find selection it has on tap, such as Crop Circle Wheat and Steam Pump Porter. (See the Restaurants chapter.)

At the Movies

Moviegoing continues to be big in Tucson, with 11 first-run theaters and two alternative film houses catering to the habit. The city's largest theater at 16 screens is Century Park 16, conveniently located near I-10 on Grant Road. Unfortunately, there are no large, ornate single-screen theaters left in Tucson, a result of growth and urban renewal, but there are current plans to revise at least one old theater house in downtown Tucson.

The *Tucson Weekly* and both daily papers in the city devote a lot of space to reviewing films and printing schedules, so it will be easy enough for you to find what you're looking for. One of the first-run theaters, Crossroads Festival, 4811 E. Grant Road, 327-7067, runs movies that have been out for a while but charges substantially less than theaters that run new releases. You'll find that all the theaters have recorded messages to let you know what's playing, and most theaters have special matinee prices for showings early in the day.

American GKC Cinema
4690 N. Oracle Rd. • 292-2430

This theater has six screens showing first-run movies that have been on the circuit for a while. All seats are a $1.50. It's behind Tucson Mall.

Catalina Cineplex
2320 N. Campbell Ave. • 881-0616

Catalina Cineplex shows new releases on six screens. Ticket prices are $7 for adults and $4 for children 3 to 11 and seniors. At or before 6 PM Monday through Friday, all shows are $4. This reduced price is also available for the first afternoon showing on Saturdays, Sundays and holidays.

Century Gateway 12
770 N. Kolb Rd. • 792-9000

Twelve screens show all the newest releases at this theater between Speedway and Broadway Boulevards. Tickets are $7 for adults and $4.25 for children and senior citizens. All tickets are $4.25 for shows at or before 6 PM on weekdays and 2 PM on weekends and holidays.

Century Park 16
1055 W. Grant Rd. • 620-0750

Located just off Interstate 10 at Grant Road, this 16-screen cinema charges $7 for adults and $4.25 for children and seniors. All seats are $4.25 for shows at or prior to 6 PM weekdays and 2 PM weekends and holidays. The cinema is the only one in Tucson that has THX sound.

Crossroads Festival
4811 E. Grant Rd. • 327-7067

At the Crossroads Festival shopping center, this six-screen theater's tickets are $2 all the time for movies that are new, but not first run.

De Anza Drive-In
1401 S. Alvernon Wy.
• 745-2240

This is Tucson's only drive-in theater. You will need an FM car or portable radio to enjoy the show. Admission for the four-screen theater is $5 per person (children younger than 12 get in free). Show up on Monday night and save yourself a few bucks — tickets are $2.50.

El Dorado Cineplex
5925 E. Broadway Blvd. • 745-6241

This cineplex, across from Park Mall, shows first-run films on six screens. Tickets are $7 for adults and $4 for children 3 to 11 and senior citizens. All tickets are $4 for shows beginning at or before 6 PM Monday through Friday and for the first matinee showings Saturdays, Sundays and holidays.

Foothills Cineplex
Foothills Mall, 7401 N. La Cholla Blvd.
• 742-6174

These six mall cinemas offer $4 tickets for screenings at or prior to 6 PM Monday through Friday and for the first showing Saturday, Sunday and on holidays. For all other shows, admission is $7 for adults and $4 for children 3 to 11 and seniors.

Valencia Vista
265 W. Valencia Rd. • 746-1823

A first-run theater, Valencia Vista has four screens and charges $1.50 per person for all showings.

> **FYI**
> Unless otherwise noted, the area code for all phone numbers listed in this guide is 520.

Alternative Cinema

Tucson has two theaters known to offer foreign, art and independent films. The University of Arizona also presents a number of films and documentaries at various locations on campus, and when it does, the shows are usually well-advertised in the local newspaper calendar sections.

The Loft Cinema
3233 E. Speedway Blvd. • 795-7777

With three screens, this is where you can satisfy your urge for foreign and art films, including a regular midnight screening of *Rocky Horror Picture Show* on Saturdays. Recent offerings have included *Love Serenade* and *The Disappearance of Garcia Laroca*. Tickets are $6 or $3.75 for seniors and students with ID.

The Screening Room
127 E. Congress St. • 622-2262

A small, 90-seat theater with an art gallery in the lobby, The Screening Room is known for independent productions, both from local producers and internationally-known filmmakers. The theater, in the heart of the downtown arts district, sponsors a weeklong film festival every April that screens everything from full-length films to short documentaries (see our Festivals and Events chapter). Ticket prices vary but are usually around $7.

Adult Showclubs

Curves Cabaret
2130 N. Oracle Rd. • 884-7210

This unpretentious topless club is open daily until 1 AM and has reasonable drink prices. The cover charge runs from $2 to $5.

Sunset Strip
3650 E. Speedway Blvd. • 323-8985

Open daily until 1 AM, this multistage topless dance club features continuous entertainment, food and billiards. During major sporting events, the club has drink specials and large screen TVs showing the game. Though the individual cover charge is slightly high (more than $5), you can purchase a three-month or year pass.

TD's Showclub
5822 E. Speedway Blvd. • 790-7307
749 W. Miracle Mile • 882-0650

TD's reputation as a topless showclub has rated it a vote of favor for the past decade from readers of *Tucson Weekly*. TD's has a cafe that is open for lunch and is known for its seafood, cognac and fine cigars. The Showclub regularly presents national entertainers and occasional magazine fold-out girls. You'll pay $2 to $5 to get in the door.

Ten's Nightclub
5120 E. Speedway Blvd. • 325-8367

Known for its national acts, Ten's is also know for specializing in office, convention and bachelor parties. Open until 1 AM daily, it offers lunch and dinner specials. Though there is not actually a dress code, patrons tend to be a bit more well-dressed than at other topless clubs, and the cover charge is a little higher (more than $5).

And Finally . . .

New West
4305 W. Ina Rd. • 744-7744

We are giving this club its own spot since, frankly, it defies easy classification. The massive, 43,000-square-foot complex has three separate clubs. The Gotham is a high-energy dance club, playing a mix of techno, rock and hip-hop. Also located here is Screwy Louie's, a sports bar and grill. But the main room, with a 6,000-square-foot dance floor, is primarily country-and-western music dancing. Formerly known as the Wild Wild West, the name was changed in September 1997, and the club began bringing in big-name country and rock acts such as Pat Benatar, George Clinton, Neal McCoy and Eddie Money. This is Tucson's newest nightlife offering, and it has been described as a honky-tonk Disneyland. It's huge, and no matter what your musical tastes, New West is bound to book someone you'll want to hear. Cover charges vary, so call ahead to get an estimate.

Shopping

If you're looking for names like Neiman Marcus or FAO Schwartz, you won't find them in Tucson, at least not yet. We do have malls, and we do have major department stores that are every bit as complete as those in cities of the East and West coasts.

But the best thing about shopping in Tucson is exploring the hundreds of small shops that carry items uniquely Southwest. And most folks who visit here or live here are looking for just that — things Western, Mexican, cowboy or American Indian. So in this chapter, we emphasize the gifts, clothes, food, art and home furnishings that people want to see and buy when they come to Tucson.

If you're not quite sure what "Southwestern" or regional specialty items are, here are a few tips. Chiles are big (as in popular) here and come in all forms and shapes, from the many varieties of real ones ready to be added to a recipe to the dried ones hanging on strings, known as ristras. Hanging a ristra on your door is said to bring good luck. But you can also get good luck from a dream catcher, which is an American Indian form of art made of yarn, usually crafted in a circular shape and embellished with beads, feathers or leather. Southwest Indians also make kachinas, which are dolls but probably unlike any you've ever seen. They are wood carvings, from tiny to more than a foot high, lavishly decorated with bright colors, feathers, spears and masks, bearing names such as Eagle Dancer or Crown Dancer. Other Indian art forms popular in Tucson shops are baskets, rugs, pottery and sterling silver with turquoise.

Popular items from south of the border include Spanish Colonial furniture, characterized by thick natural wood and intricate carvings, clay pottery, stoneware, iron and tin ornaments, wool rugs and colorful blankets. Much of the food considered regional has its origins in Mexico as well, such as tortillas, spices and flavorings and salsas. But Tucson also has some food specialties that grow locally including pecans, pistachios, mesquite honey, citrus fruits and sweets made from cacti.

With this briefing on regional specialties, you're ready to put on your walking shoes and explore the shopping scene in Tucson.

American Indian

Below we highlight some of the shops dealing in American Indian arts and crafts, but don't forget to check other categories, such as "Malls, Plazas and Shopping Centers," "Shopping Districts" and "Southwestern Shops" for more places to find these popular regional items.

Americas Gallery
6420 N. Campbell Ave. • 529-7002

Serious collectors will appreciate the museum quality antique Indian art here, including rugs, weavings, baskets, pottery and beadwork. Americas Gallery is closed on Sunday.

Bahti Indian Arts
4300 N. Campbell Ave. • 577-0290

This store in charming St. Philip's Plaza offers rugs, pots, sand paintings, weavings, kachinas, fetishes, sculpture and baskets by contemporary Southwest Indian artists. The shop also has books, tapes and CDs on and by American Indians.

Desert Son
4759 E. Sunrise Dr. • 299-0818

This shop specializes in Southwest Indian items including art, pottery, vases, kachinas, Navajo rugs, sand paintings and jewelry. Desert Son is closed on Sundays.

Grey Dog Trading Company
2970 N. Swan Rd. • 881-6888

You'll find Grey Dog in the lovely Plaza

Palomino along with its selection of Hopi kachinas, pueblo pottery, Zuni fetishes, Navajo weavings, jewelry, baskets and sand paintings. The store is closed on Sunday.

Mac's Indian Jewelry
2953 E. Grant Rd. • 327-3306

This shop boasts a large selection of well-priced American Indian jewelry but also has kachinas, pottery, rugs, carvings and sand paintings. It's closed on Sunday.

Morning Star Traders
2020 E. Speedway Blvd. • 881-2112

Morning Star Traders offers baskets, pottery, Navajo rugs, kachinas and a large selection of old pawn jewelry in a charming Spanish Colonial-revival building.

San Xavier Mission Shops
1959 E. San Xavier Rd. • 295-1350

While visiting the historic San Xavier Mission, you'll have a chance to shop for not only religious items pertaining to the mission, but also items such as pottery, art and baskets representing Southwest Indians, particularly the Tohono O'odham on whose reservation land the mission resides.

Silverbell Trading
7007 N. Oracle Rd. • 797-6852

Set in Casas Adobe Plaza, this shop offers native arts from both American and Northern Mexican Indians, among them the Mayo, Yacqui, Tarahumara, Zuni and Hopi. It features contemporary and antique baskets, pottery and jewelry. Silverbell Trading also has a selection of children's books primarily by and about Indians and Southwest books for all ages. The store is closed on Sundays.

Turquoise Skies
4410 S. Mission Rd. • 578-1673

It's a bit off the beaten path and seems forlorn all by itself, but Turquoise Skies is across the street from two huge adult RV and mobile home communities. The store sells items by Navajo, Hopi and Zuni Indians including rugs, jewelry, baskets and kachinas.

Gourmet Food and Spirits

It may seem like this category is unusually full (pun intended), and indeed it is. That's because Tucson offers a number of specialty food items that are great for both chowing down and gift-giving — goodies such as tortillas and other Mexican favorites, medjool dates, locally grown pistachios, prickly pear cactus candies and all manner of Mexican and Southwestern flavorings. Below are some of the best spots for finding food items for which Tucson is famous, as well as some of the more unusual places to go for other taste treats.

> **FYI**
> Unless otherwise noted, the area code for all phone numbers listed in this guide is 520.

Alejandro's Tortilla Factory
5330 S. 12th Ave. • 889-2279

The retail part of this wholesale operation offers customers not only tortillas, but also prepared foods such as burritos with a variety of fillings including chorizo, tacos, tortas, pastries and even bagged spices.

Aspen Mills Bread
5575 E. River Rd. • 299-7950

This bakery in River Center specializes in breads but has a few related goodies such as muffins and cookies. In addition to the customary breads, Aspen Mills has an amazing array of unusual ones containing fruits, cheeses, vegetables, honey and other ingredients and flavorings. If you can't decide, you're welcome to sample.

Chow Bella
2418 N. Craycroft Rd. • 290-0773

Located in an unassuming storefront in a tiny strip center, this shop is a bit hard to find even though it's on a major street just north of a busy intersection (Grant and Craycroft roads). Chow Bella offers "food for the taking," and it's all deliciously prepared and ready to consume. You can get a full meal to go here, from soup and salad to desert, or

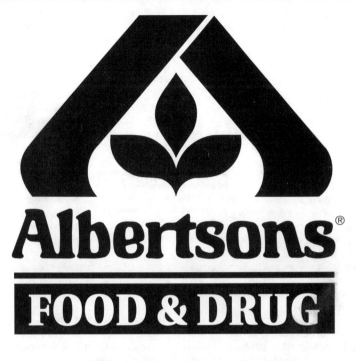

Albertsons® FOOD & DRUG

Tucson

- 6363 East 22nd Street
- 7300 North La Cholla
- 9595 East Broadway
- 2854 North Campbell
- 6600 East Grant

just an entree or side dish. Each day, there are several scrumptious entrees to choose from and a large selection of accompaniments. You won't go wrong stopping here for your family's dinner or for a picnic lunch to take to the park. Chow Bella is closed Sundays and Mondays.

El Rio Bakery
901 N. Grande Ave. • 882-9457

Located in a heavily Hispanic area west of downtown and I-10, El Rio has great Mexican baked goods plus some traditional ones. Here you'll find pan de huevo (egg bread), empanadas, pan dulce, cochinitos (ginger bread pigs, a favorite), delicious Mexican cookies and tortillas. El Rio also has some prepared take-out food such as burritos with machaca and beans, plus a small selection of grocery items with a mostly Mexican slant.

G&L Import Export
4828 E. 22nd St. • 790-9016

Tucsonans need not go to the Far East to find anything Asian — it's all right here at this large store specializing in Asian imports. It's filled with Japanese, Chinese and Middle Eastern food products in bottles, boxes, cans and bags including soy sauces, pastas, wines, seasonings and vegetables. There's also a large selection of cooking tools such as woks, tea utensils, strainers and chop sticks, and even a few Oriental furnishings and accessories.

Gourmet Emporium and Cheese Shop
4744 E. Sunrise Dr. • 299-5576

This small shop has a great wine selection, cheeses and other gourmet goodies including regional specialties. The Emporium also has a deli and will make lunches to go. It's closed on Sundays.

Grande Tortilla Factory
914 N. Grande Ave. • 622-8338

This area of Grande Avenue, just west of downtown, is a small pocket of authentic Mexican food offerings. The Grande Tortilla Factory is one of the best-known shops and has been there for 50 years operated by the same family. The tortillas are still stretched by hand, and you'll definitely notice the difference from machine-made ones. Other goodies here include masa (ground and kneaded corn kernels used in tamales), crushed pepper, dried chile pods, empanadas, manzanilla tea and menudo. The factory is closed Wednesday and Sunday.

Grossman's Bake Shop
3140 E. Ft. Lowell Rd. • 326-4626

For folks celebrating Jewish holidays, this is the place to shop. Grossman's has about two dozen varieties of bread, including Challah, ryes, pumpernickel and Lakka, as well as a dizzying array of cakes, cookies, muffins, rolls, brownies and seasonal and holiday specials. The shop has been a delicious Tucson tradition for almost 100 years. Grossman's is closed on Sundays.

Honeybaked Ham Company
5350 E. Broadway Blvd. • 745-0700
7090 N. Oracle Rd. • 544-2121

Just about every major city has one of these shops specializing in outstanding whole or half hams and offering prepared turkey, ribs and lots of side items. You can also get a

---

INSIDERS' TIP

Don't be surprised to see roadside vendors along some major crossroads around Tucson where there's enough land to display their wares. Look for them selling dried chile strings (ristras), fruits and vegetables, or art objects such as kachina dolls, rugs or metal sculpture on Sabino Canyon Road north of Tanque Verde Road, at Broadway Boulevard and Alvernon Way, or along Irvington Road west of I-10, among other spots.

Beautiful handcrafted American Indian jewelry can be found in shops throughout the city.

yummy lunch to go, but not on Sundays when the shop is closed.

Ilsa's Konditorei & Bakery
3355 N. Dodge Blvd. • 323-7101

"Konditorei" means cafe in German, so Ilsa's has both baked goods and a small cafe menu of soups, sandwiches and quiche plus espresso coffee, along with a few tables inside and out for dining. Specialties of the house include tortes of about two dozen flavors, pastries, cookies and breads. Ilsa's also does wedding cakes. The ovens are cold on Sundays.

La Buena Mexican Foods
234 E. 22nd St. • 624-1796

You'll find great Mexican food prepared daily here such as flour and corn tortillas, taco shells, green corn and red chile tamales, plus the ingredients to make your own such as masa and nixtamal. On Friday, Saturday and Sunday, the store has fresh menudo.

La Mesa Tortillas
7823 E. Broadway Blvd. • 298-5966

Folks on the Eastside don't have to be deprived of homemade tortillas because La Mesa makes them fresh daily in flour and corn. Other offerings include burros with a variety of fillings, tamales by the dozen and even a complete lunch served from 11 AM to 2 PM. The store is closed on Sundays.

Munson's Tucson Date Company
52 E. Roger Rd. • 887-2731

You wouldn't expect to see a commercial establishment in the middle of this mostly residential area, so it's easy to miss, but don't. Although dates are available year round, you might be lucky enough to get there for a newly picked crop of medjool dates, grown along the California-Arizona border. Other goodies on sale here include jellies, honeys, pecans, pistachios, candies and Arizona souvenirs. Munson's is closed on Sundays.

Reay's Ranch Market
7133 N. Oracle Rd. • 297-5394
4751 E. Sunrise Dr. • 299-8858
3360 E. Speedway Blvd. • 795-9844

Reay's (pronounced Rays) is Tucson's only combination grocery/specialty/natural foods store. The markets are upscale and pricey, but you'll find food items here you won't find elsewhere, and everything is top quality. Nearly all the produce is offered both traditionally and organically grown, and Reay's is known for it's butcher-quality meat, bakery, deli, wines and floral shop. Reay's also has a sizable selection of regional items.

Rincon Market
2513 E. 6th St. • 327-6653

This corner market and deli in central Tucson is almost an institution and a favorite of locals. The market specializes in spit-roasted chicken and have other deli delights as well, plus a complete market with butcher shop. You can take your deli food to go or dine on the outdoor patio.

Roma Imports
627 S. Vine Ave. • 792-3173

If you're cooking Italian and want authentic ingredients, shop at Roma's where you'll find pastas, cheeses, sauces, sausage, pancetta, prosciutto, biscotti, cannoli, tiramisu, olive oils, sun-dried tomatoes, olives and lots more, all imported or made on site. And to make you feel even more Italian, Roma's carries novelty items such as aprons and T-shirts emblazoned with a bit of Italy. The shop is closed on Sunday.

Rum Runner Wine and Cheese Company
3200 E. Speedway Blvd. • 326-0121

Wines and cheeses are definitely the specialty in this upscale shop, but it carries other things as well, such as homemade deli items, gift baskets, breads and regional food products. The wine selection is one of the best in the area.

Tania's Tortillas and Mexican Food
2856 W. Drexel Rd. • 883-1595

For a selection of prepared food that's as large as any Mexican restaurant's menu, stop by Tania's. It has soups, red and green chiles, machaca, carne asada, menudo, flour tortillas and lots more.

Ted's Country Store
2760 N. Tucson Blvd. • 325-3122

This place is like a homey old-time country corner store that has an updated style and an upscale selection of products. They have a great wine selection, a deli with sandwiches made to go and regional food products such as spices, jellies and honey. You'll also find the basics here.

Viro's Real Italian Bakery
8431 E. Broadway Blvd. • 885-4045

If you have a hankering for Italian baked goods like those sold in ethnic neighborhoods back East, try Viro's. Along with all kinds of breads, Viro's has sweets such as biscotti, panettone and pizzelles. The bakery is closed Sundays and Mondays.

Growing Things (or Desert Flora)

In this section, we concentrate on nurseries that specialize in things that grow in the desert, which are popular items not only for folks who live here, but also for visitors who want to take a bit of Mother Nature's unusual desert life back home.

B&B Cactus Farm
11550 E. Speedway Blvd. • 721-4687

On Tucson's far Eastside, B&B features more than 600 species and varieties of cacti and succulents from all over the world in its greenhouses and outdoor displays. You'll find desert-garden kits, container cactus gardens, Mexican pottery and hanging baskets for the patio. Take your camera along and you can photograph some amazing blooms. B&B packs plants for traveling and shipping and also has mail-order selections. The nursery is closed on Sundays.

Bach's Greenhouse Cactus Nursery
8602 N. Thornydale Rd. • 744-3333

Located in the far northwest, Bach's has hundreds of species of cacti to choose from. Whether you're looking for a cactus for your home or yard or an unusual one for a gift, you'll surely be able to find it here. It sells planted cacti gardens and will pack and ship your selections. Bach's is closed on Sunday.

INSIDERS' TIP

Parking meters downtown take only quarters. Parking lots range in price from $3 to $5 per day.

Fourth Avenue Should Be First on Your List

The trolley tracks bisecting Fourth Avenue and the weekend clanging of the Old Pueblo Trolley aren't the only things that make this a unique shopping district. The combination of eateries, services, art offerings and shops — many of them funky and fun — and the eclectic array of people frequenting them make Fourth Avenue an experience more than merely a shopping excursion. This district extends along Fourth Avenue south from University Boulevard to 9th Street, about six blocks bulging with one interesting little commercial establishment after another. Free street parking is available all along the avenue and the side streets, or you can take the Sun Tran bus.

For starters, if you're here on a weekend, stop by the trolley car barn at Fourth Avenue and 8th Street, where you can see two trolleys being restored and catch the trolley as it heads up Fourth Avenue. You might want to ride it to the other end, the University's main gate, and back before beginning your walking exploration of Fourth Avenue. Or you can get off along the route. It runs Friday evening, Saturday noon to midnight and Sunday noon to 5 PM for $1 one way (and only 50¢ for seniors and kids 6 to 12; it's free for younger ones).

But even if you're here on a weekday, there's no shortage of shopping and sights along the avenue. Thrift shopping here may be about the best in the city. You can buy, sell or trade everything from bicycle parts and washers to old lace and vintage clothing. If you're going to a shindig and need a costume, Fourth Avenue can outfit you. Other old stuff you'll find here includes furniture, jewelry, antique dolls, vintage musical instruments and funky sunglasses. Even if you're not in the market for old things, you'll have a blast just looking and remembering at places such as Hole In The Wall, Tucson Thrift Shop, Loose Change, Years Ago-Go, Kanella's, How Sweet It Was and Lost and Found Furniture.

— continued on next page

This mural welcomes visitors to Fourth Avenue.

In need of a grass skirt, Hawaiian lei, a costume or bolo tie? Try Trini Trinket's. If you're in the mood for Reggae, African or calypso music, check out Last Wax Records. Jungle Zoo has rain sticks, hand-painted masks, pre-Columbian pottery reproductions and other exotic items. If you're looking for things really Southwest, such as old cowboy hats or boots, skulls, hides, saguaro ribs and other things made from cacti, check out The Southwest Store. For cowboys, real or wannabee, there's Southwest Hatters, offering boots, belts, buckles, dusters and even chaps for men and women. Creative Ventures is a craft mall with booths and displays showing the clever wares of many local artisans and crafters.

For products made by Mexican and American Indian crafters and artisans, try Bar-JK Gifts, Piney Hollow, La Zia, Del Sol International Shop, Creations Unlimited, Gallery of Things, Pride Applied Designs and Plateaus. You'll also find one-of-a-kind jewelry, ceramics, glass and metal shops, unusual bookstores (including Antigone Books profiled in this chapter), art galleries and lots more on this avenue.

And there's no shortage of places to stop or shop for food: The Drinking Gourd, a coffeehouse and more, Nutley's Gourmet Sweet Shoppe, Food Conspiracy, a natural grocery and specialty foods store, Casa Las Rosas for Mexican foods, Caruso's featuring Italian food, La Indita Restaurant combining Mexican and Indian tastes, Cafe Sweetwater, Chocolate Iguana, The Egg Garden, but it's not just eggs, the always popular Delectables, Snack Shack, a Magpies pizza shop and even Dairy Queen.

And if all of this isn't enough to satisfy your shopping urge, twice a year Fourth Avenue closes to traffic and puts on a huge street fair with hundreds of booths offering a mind-boggling array of arts and crafts, food, entertainment and other types of fun. You'll find Fourth Avenue guides at many of the shops on the avenue or at the nearby Tucson Convention and Visitors Bureau at 130 S. Scott Avenue. For more information, call the Fourth Avenue Merchants Association at 624-5004 or (800) 933-2477.

Desert Survivors
1020 W. Starr Pass Blvd. • 884-8806

This is a favorite spot for locals for two reasons: Desert Survivors has a great selection of desert "greenery," and it's a vocational rehab program for mentally challenged adults, so your purchase helps these people maintain active and productive lives. Although you won't find cacti here, you will find nearly everything else that grows in these parts, including trees, yucca plants, agave and succulents. The nursery is open year round, except on Sundays, and has very popular semiannual sales in April and October.

Ironwood Cactus Nursery
6502 W. Ina Rd. • 744-3550

Covering 27 acres of desert 2 miles west of I-10, this nursery has a huge selection of cacti and succulents for inside or for landscaping, plus demonstration gardens where you can get ideas for your own desert gardening. Ironwood creates custom dish gardens for your own enjoyment or gift-giving. Packing and shipping are available if you want to take your purchase with you or send it. Ironwood is closed on Sunday.

Native Seeds/SEARCH
526 N. 4th Ave. • 622-5561

As unusual as the store's name is what it sells — seeds and more seeds. This nonprofit shop is heaven for the desert gardener. The shelves are lined with thousands of seeds, some of which are endangered species. And if Native Seeds doesn't have what you want, it can probably be ordered (hence the "SEARCH" in the name). The mission is to preserve and promote the traditional crops, seeds and farming methods that have sustained native peoples throughout the American Southwest and northern Mexico. (Native Seeds/SEARCH also maintains a demonstration garden at Tucson Botanical Gardens.) If you're looking for the unusual, such as blue speckled tepary beans or San Felipe Pueblo blue corn, or the more common desert lupine, sunflower or evening primrose seeds, you'll find them here, along with plenty of growing advice. Native Seeds is closed on Mondays.

Tanque Verde Greenhouses
10810 E. Tanque Verde Rd. • 749-4414

This desert nursery on the far Eastside has six large greenhouses with more than a million plants and hundreds of varieties of cacti and succulents. The selection includes Euphorbia from Africa, Mammillaria from Mexico and Organ Pipes from Arizona. You can buy a ready-to-go dish garden of cacti or have one custom designed. Employees carefully pack the cacti for air or road travel or mail them (fully guaranteed) if you prefer. If you don't have a green thumb but still want a cactus memento, the greenhouses also have sweet treats made from cacti, such as candy and jellies. Closed Sundays.

Mexican Imports

For Tucsonans and visitors who don't want to make the trek south of the border for authentic Mexican goods, Tucson has plenty to offer right here. We list some of the more popular ones, but don't forget to check in other sections of this chapter, since nearly every mall or shopping plaza has a store carrying some items imported from Mexico. Mexican products that seem to be very popular stateside include Mexican (or Spanish) Colonial furniture, pigskin furniture (called Equipale), rugs, blankets, hand-blown glassware, framed mirrors, tin and metal light fixtures and lamps, pottery, stoneware, religious statuary, Talavera, which is brilliantly painted ceramics made in the city of Puebla, and colorful wooden animals made in Oaxaca.

Antigua de Mexico
7037 N. Oracle Rd. • 742-7114

Mexican goods offered here include Equipale pigskin furniture, glassware, carved wood furniture, lighting fixtures, stone fountains and statuary, clay pottery, tin items, folk art and sterling silver jewelry. There's a location in Nogales, Mexico, in addition to this one in Casas Adobe Plaza. Antigua de Mexico is closed on Sundays.

Azteca Mexican Imports
1111 S. Kolb Rd. • 290-0024

You may not see a sign proclaiming that it's Azteca, but you will see a huge collection of pottery, fountains and chimineas at this outdoor location just north of 22nd Street.

Coleccion Mexicana
1109 N. Wilmot Rd. • 733-9022

This large store, somewhat hidden at the back of a corner shopping center, has Colonial Mexican furniture with unique wood finishing, handmade accessories, Talavera pottery, pewter, hand-blown glassware, baskets and ironwood sculptures made by Seri Indians and stoneware. Coleccion Mexicana is closed Sundays.

La Buhardilla
2360 E. Broadway Blvd. • 622-5200

In English, it means "the attic" and finds here include Colonial and Spanish baroque furniture, wrought iron, pottery including Talavera, silver and paintings. The store also carries hand-carved wooden doors and materials for restoring or building haciendas. La Buhardilla is closed on Sundays.

Que Bonita
7000 E. Tanque Verde Rd. • 721-1998

This shop specializes in Old Mexico and Santa Fe furniture and boasts a large showroom with new arrivals weekly. There's also an extensive selection of Southwestern decorative accessories, pottery and Zapotec rugs. The shop also has a unique collection of Southwestern clothing and jewelry. It's closed on Sundays.

Rascon Imports
7974 N. Oracle Rd. • 297-8358

Mexican imports you'll find here include Talavera-style pottery, Equipale furniture, mirrors framed in wood and tin, Oaxacan pots, copper pots, papier-mâché folk art and lamps.

Southwestern Shops

A chapter on shopping in Tucson just wouldn't be complete without a section devoted to regional, or Southwestern, items. Tucsonans and visitors are always interested in things grown or made in the Southwest —

chiles, whether real or artificial, salsas, sweets made from cacti, pecans, pistachios, minerals, turquoise and Mexican and American Indian arts and crafts. Here are some ideas of where to look, but many more are included in other sections of this chapter.

Arizona Earthworks Trading Company
4227 N. Campbell Ave. • 326-6068

This shop offers clay and stone pottery and accessories plus iron decor for indoors or out. Nearly everything is handmade — some are imported and others are crafted locally. It's open Wednesday through Saturday.

Cactus Cards & Gifts
5975 W. Western Way Cir. • 883-5930

If you happen to be visiting the many attractions on the western side of the Tucson Mountains, you'll be near this shop that offers lots of Southwestern goods, from T-shirts to sweets and cards to pottery.

The Dancing Gecko
2443 N. Campbell Ave. • 326-8012

This shop with the unusual name also has some of the most original and beautiful, handmade furniture and accessories around. They use local woods such as mesquite and ironwood as well as imported woods to make exquisitely crafted pieces. They also feature the collection of world-renowned mfa/eronga. The Dancing Gecko is closed on Sundays.

Discount Agate House
3401 N. Dodge Blvd. • 323-0781

For folks who want a rock, mineral or fossil without having to dig for it, this store is the answer. Here you'll find a large selection of minerals, crystals, fossils and semiprecious gems along with lapidary tools for the rock hound. The store is open Monday through Saturday.

Southwest Designs
5634 E. Pima St. • 886-5255

This shop is packed full of things Southwest, including handmade furniture, pots, wall decor, metal works, rugs and much more. Southwest Designs is closed on Sunday.

Western Wear

Both real cowboys and wannabees have a good choice of Western wear in Tucson, from hats and chaps to bolo ties and belt buckles.

Arizona Hatters
3600 N. 1st Ave. • 292-1320

This store carries a large selection of name brand hats, including Stetson, Resistol and Milano, for both men and women plus a selection of men's Western shirts and belts.

1880's Cowboy Mercantile
2559 N. Campbell Ave. • 325-2005

This shop boasts the largest selection of WAH clothing (made in Yuma, Arizona) in the area. It carries other brands as well in the form of vests, frock coats, spurs, boots and hats, even reproduction Western badges. The mercantile is open Monday through Saturday.

Cowtown Boots
5190 N. Casa Grande Hwy. • 888-0290

If you can figure out how to get here, you can choose from about 10,000 pairs of boots for both men and women made by Cowtown Boot Company, Durango, Dingo and others. It also carries Western clothing for both sexes. It's located on the east-side frontage road of I-10 just north of the Ruthrauff Road exit.

The Corral Western Wear
4525 E. Broadway Blvd. • 322-6001

Established in 1946, this western store is the oldest in Arizona. It has a complete line of Western clothes including boots and hats from manufacturers such as Justin Boots, Tony Lama, Stetson, Rocky Mountain Clothing Company and Wrangler. The Corral also carries the Pendleton brand of wool items, which are hard to find in these parts.

Western Warehouse
3030 E. Speedway Blvd. • 327-8005
6701 E. Broadway Blvd. • 885-4385
3776 S. 16th Ave. • 622-4500
3719 N. Oracle Rd. • 293-1808

Claiming to "dress the West for less," this store also claims to have the biggest selection of boots, hats, clothes and accessories for the whole family. (Employees speak Spanish.) The huge selection of straw and felt hats includes names such as Resistol and Stetson, plus they'll steam and shape it for free. The collection of boots represents practically every size and color imaginable from cowhide to exotic leathers.

Malls, Plazas and Shopping Centers

Tucson has four malls and an abundance of plazas and shopping centers — sometimes it seems like there's one at every intersection. We cover a number of the more unusual ones here.

Broadway Village
E. Broadway Blvd. at Country Club Dr. • no phone

Built in 1932, Broadway Village was one of Arizona's first shopping centers. You can still see parts of the original whitewashed adobe brick and inlaid tile structure that today surrounds a brick courtyard with trees all around. Among the unusual mix of shops and eateries here are Clues Unlimited, a bookstore of mystery and intrigue: Aroma Tree, offering all kinds of scented things; and a shop called Whimsey Designs that's full of artful creations made from silk and dried flowers. For a large and varied selection of Mexican Colonial furniture and accesories, there's Zocalo, while Primitive Arts is a gallery with fine pre-Columbian and ethnographic finds. Stacia's Bakery Cafe delights the senses of smell and taste with great baked goods and interesting lunches to take or eat there. Just across the street to the west of the main structure is a row of shops, also part of Broadway Village, including Table Talk, Coyote Voice Books and Zona Boutique.

Casas Adobes Plaza
N. Oracle and Ina Rds. • no phone

When this Spanish-style plaza was built in the 1940s, it was a shopping hub out in the boonies. Today it's in a busy section, and Tucson has enveloped it, but strolling here can still be pleasant. Look for Gepetto's Toys and Dolls, which will intrigue adults as well as kids with its array of stuffed animals, Linda Lee Indian dolls and even pogo sticks. Bullard's Hardware and Home, however, may be the most unusual shop here, or anywhere for that matter. Wander in and see the eclectic mix of goods — things for tabletops, baths, bedrooms and closets, lots of Southwest gifts and holiday decor, purses, tote bags and bathrobes — and hardware, of course. The plaza also houses a boutique, beauty salons, Marshall's Artistry in Gold, Antigua de Mexico, Reay's Market, Table Talk, Silverbell Trading and a huge and exquisite florist called Casas Adobe Flowers. For food, there's Landmark Cafe and Millie's Pancake Haus.

Crossroads Festival
Grant and Swan Rds. • no phone

This plaza meanders from Swan Road around the corner and east along Grant Road for the equivalent of several blocks. It's an eclectic mix ranging from upscale apparel stores to discount hair salons and everything in between. It houses a major grocery store, a bank, a French bakery, jewelry and gift shops, fine apparel stores, Bed, Bath and Beyond for housewares, a ski shop, a copy store, card shops and Mrs. Tiggy-Winkle's Toys (see our Kidstuff chapter). If you're looking for the only Tucson jeweler that carries Tiffany products or a certified Rolex watch dealer, Marshall's Artistry in Gold is the spot. Several restaurants are here, including the very popular Outback Steakhouse, Buddy's Grill and the upscale but outstanding Vivace. Or splurge on some real ice cream at the Marble Slab Creamery. There's also the Crossroads movie theater, which offers discounted recently released movies, but you'll need to hunt for it since it's hidden in back.

El Con Mall
3601 E. Broadway Blvd. • 327-8767

El Con was Tucson's first mall and occupies a large parcel of what is now very valuable land in a central Tucson location. Although spread out, it's all one level and therefore not as overwhelming as many more modern malls. It's anchored by several department stores including Dillard's, JCPenney, Robinsons-Mays and Montgomery Ward. In between are numerous smaller stores offering apparel, gifts, jewelry, music, shoes and much more. Bookstores include B. Dalton Bookseller and Waldenbooks. Stores specializing in regional items are Chaparral Indian Store and Indian Arts & Crafts. The Pavilion food court offers shoppers a variety of tasty options, and there's a movie theater as well. It's easily accessible by bus.

El Mercado
Wilmot Rd. at Broadway Blvd.
• **no phone**

Designed to resemble a Spanish open-air mercado (market), this plaza features a number of unusual shops plus salons and restaurants. Here you'll find a store with gifts and decor especially for cat lovers, Cele Peterson's, a fine apparel store for women that's a Tucson tradition, Maya Palace and a shop with authentic Mexican furniture and gifts, among others. The Toma El Charro Cafe is an offshoot of El Charro, Arizona's oldest Mexican restaurant (see our Restaurants chapter). Unlike most malls and plazas, this one is usually not open evenings except during the holiday season.

Foothills Mall
Ina Rd. and La Cholla Blvd. • 742-7191

This mall was having an identity crisis for years, which is too bad considering how lovely it is. Foothills Mall is distinguished by its wide Saltillo tile corridors and architectural features that give it the feeling of a village mercado. In the early 1990s, it was a full-scale mall with several large department stores and a variety of small shops, mostly upscale. Then it was almost vacant for a couple of years before new owners decided to turn it into an upscale outlet and entertainment mall. The revitalized mall now houses a Saks Fifth Avenue outlet, Barnes and Noble, Linens and Things, Mikasa factory outlet, Donna Karan Company Store, and Ross and Nike outlets, among others. Boutique shops include Berta Wright Gallery, a popular shop with a wide variety of beautiful gift and art items, Accencia for clothing and accessories, and The Sugar Plum holiday shop. For food, there's the popular Keaton's Restaurant, a new brewery and a food court with several vendors. For entertainment, the mall now has a 15-screen movie theater, a prototype Sega games section for older kids and a play area for youngsters. There are plenty of special events and entertainment at the mall as well. It's a pleasant place to shop, be entertained or just people-watch.

Kaibab Courtyard Shops
2837 N. Campbell Ave. • 795-6905

Kaibab (meaning "mountain lying on its side" in the Paiute Indian language and pronounced ki-bob) Courtyard is actually a cluster of three shops totaling about 13,000 square feet and specializing in Southwestern and American Indian goods. One is the Nambe Foundry Outlet, offering Nambeware, a shiny silver-like metal that's formed into functional art such as vases and bowls. The two others, Desert House and Kaibab Shops, sell everything from Hopi kachina dolls, Navajo rugs and Zuni fetishes to Mexican dinnerware. You'll also find clothing, furniture and folk art from Mexico and art, gifts and home accessories by local artists. If you're in the market for something reflecting the region, these shops should be on your list.

> **FYI**
> Unless otherwise noted, the area code for all phone numbers listed in this guide is 520.

Park Mall
5870 E. Broadway Blvd. • 748-1222

Tucson's second mall was built on all one level in a close-in Eastside location. Its large stores are Sears, Macy's, Walgreens and Dillard's, which are accompanied by more than 100 shops and restaurants plus a movie theater. Among the stores that offer Southwestern items are Chaparral Gifts, Desert Affair, Native Treasures, Turquoise Land and A Taste of Arizona. For books, there's B. Dalton Bookseller. The Information Booth is located just inside the mall's main entrance, which is at the center of the mall on the south side facing Broadway Boulevard. Park Mall is wheelchair-accessible and rents strollers at $1 for three hours. It's easy to reach by bus, and the mall also offers free shuttle service to major Tucson hotels.

Plaza Palomino
2970 N. Swan Rd. • 795-1177

This is one of the loveliest places to shop in Tucson, although it definitely leans toward upscale. Elegant shops, galleries and restaurants constructed of adobe with Spanish-tiled roofs surround a tiled courtyard displaying fountains, foliage and singing birds. Plaza Palomino is located near the Ft. Lowell historic district, full of old Spanish charm and a peaceful break from hectic malls. You'll find a number of boutiques, jewelry, art and home decor shops and several restaurants with patio seating so you can enjoy the surroundings. Shops specializing in Southwestern goods include home accessories at Territories, American Indian arts and crafts at Grey Dog Trading, and jewelry, art and handcrafted gifts at Enchanted Earthworks. Other than the eating establishments, it's not open evenings or Sundays. You can arrive here in luxury for free by using the Plaza's courtesy shopping shuttle that's available through Foothills Sedan Services at 750-0365.

River Center
5605 E. River Rd. • no phone

At the base of the Catalina Foothills, River Center is a pretty setting for its two dozen shops and restaurants, including a branch of the Pima County Library. Fountains, outdoor dining and views of the city lights below add to the ambiance. In addition to a major grocery and drugstore, you'll find Aspen Mills bread shop, Totally Southwest gift shop, a boutique, a wild birds shop, Tucson Trunk (a card and gift, not luggage, shop), a couple of beauty salons and several small businesses including a packaging and shipping store. Restaurants include Ric's Cafe with outdoor dining. This plaza occasionally has free jazz fests on Friday nights.

St. Philip's Plaza
River Rd. at Campbell Ave. • 886-7485

This is an upscale shopping center in a pleasant (but congested) location. The plaza itself is a series of Spanish-style brick courtyards, which make for a lovely and picturesque stroll. One of Tucson's finest beauty salons and day spas, Gadabout, is located here (they have several other locations, also). Shops include The Bag Company, Nicole Miller, West Fine Leather and Individual Man. There are art galleries, jewelry stores and several of Tucson's top eateries, including Cafe Terra Cotta, an award-winning local favorite (see our Restaurants chapter). Also located at St. Philip's is Windmill Inn, an all-suites hotel. Watch for special doings that take place here, such as jazz concerts and farmer's markets.

Tucson Mall
4500 N. Oracle Rd. • 293-7330

We're not talking megamalls like the ones in Chicago or Minneapolis, but this is certainly Tucson's largest, and it can tire your feet nonetheless. Its two levels contain more than 200 department stores and specialty shops, including Dillard's, JCPenney, Sears, Macy's, Mervyn's, Robinsons-May, Gap, Guess, Ann Taylor, Lane Bryant, Eddie Bauer, Banana Republic, Victoria's Secret, Warner Bros. Studio Store and a number of shops specializing in gifts, jewelry, home furnishings, athletic wear and shoes. Bookstores include B. Dalton Bookseller and Waldenbooks. There's something here to suit anyone's taste and budget. Kids (and adults) will enjoy riding the dragons, horses and reindeer on the carousel, while indoor fountains add a bit of tranquility to the frenzied shopping. The Food Court has more than a dozen food booths and plenty of inside seating to accommodate famished shoppers. Next to the Food Court is Arizona Avenue, a row of shops specializing in regional items from Indian and Mexican rugs to pottery to food. For more regional items, look on the upper level for Indian Village and Chaparral Indian Store. The mall has strollers ($1 per hour) and wheelchairs (free) available as well as TDD phones. And just across Stone Avenue on the mall's east is a major Sun Tran bus transit center.

Trail Dust Town
6541 E. Tanque Verde Rd. • 296-4551

To find this hidden gem of a shopping and entertainment area, look for a three-story stack of boulders with a small covered wagon on top. Trail Dust Town is a pleasant setting for finding mostly regional items in a handful of small shops that line a bricked courtyard, complete with gazebos, grass areas, colorful flowers and plenty of shady spots and benches for people-watching. You'll see facades and memorabilia of the Old West all around — a bank, apothecary store, jail, barber shop, hotel, saloon, train depot, wagon parts, posters and signs. The real stores include Wild West Outfitters, T-Line Leathers and Venture Fine Arts Gallery. Trail Dust Treasures features Southwestern gifts and novelties while Turquoise Traders has American Indian specialties such as jewelry, kachinas, bolo ties, belts and ironwood carvings. There's also a chocolate shop and the very fascinating General Store, which sells everything from old-time candy and nostalgia items to fine totem poles. For fun, take a ride on the train that circumvents the shopping area or on the carousel. Dining options here include the cowboy steakhouse Pinnacle Peak and Dakota Cafe with patio dining and Southwestern-style food (see our Restaurants chapter).

Shopping Districts

They can't really be classified as malls, plazas or shopping centers so we've labeled them shopping districts — areas around town that have a concentration of commercial establishments, mostly retail shops, that shouldn't be overlooked. These are places where you'll get a taste of Tucson history and culture along with your purchases.

Downtown

Also known as the Tucson Arts District, the downtown area is a hub of cultural, social and commercial activity, bounded roughly by Cushing Street on the south, Granada Avenue on the west, Franklin Street on the north and Scott Avenue on the east. You'll find an amazing array of shops downtown, many of them quite unusual — everything from plumbing supplies to vintage clothing and newspapers to wigs — along with numerous galleries and eateries. The main thoroughfare bisecting this area is Congress Street, where many of the stores are concentrated. On Congress Street, look for Yikes, which sells toys, wacky gifts and gags for kids of all ages; Richard Johnson's Toys and Antiques, offering imports, oddities, memorabilia and nostalgia; Red Mesa Designs, selling Southwestern and American Indian goods; Mr. Lulu's, specializing in '60s and '70s retro clothing and pop art; Bertrand's Books; and Berta Wright Gallery. Just a few blocks away on 6th Avenue, look for the fascinating Philabaum Glass Gallery and Studios, where glass is made on the spot, and Sangin, a huge hodgepodge of things from around the world and from local artisans.

This is a fun area just to window shop and people-watch, so pick up a *Downtown Guide* at the Metropolitan Tucson Convention and Visitors Bureau on Scott Avenue and see what shopping surprises await you downtown. It's accessible by Sun Tran bus, and parking is available on the street or in public lots or garages.

Lost Barrio
200 S. Park Ave. • no phone

A barrio that became a warehouse district is now a shopping district — one of the most interesting in Tucson if you're in the market for imports. These warehouse buildings along a two-to-three-block area aren't fancy, but they're packed full of furniture and accessories in wood, iron, metal, stone, fabric and glass. Much of it is from Mexico, but you'll also find work from American Indian, African and other cultures, and nearly everything is warehouse-priced. Stores here include Aqui Esta, Rustica, Magellan Trading and Apparatus. Some of the shops will also provide custom work in wood, iron and upholstery. If you want to experience a bit of Nogales, Mexico, without crossing the border, this may be the spot but not on Sundays. Parking is free on the street.

Old Town Artisans
186 N. Meyer Ave. • 623-6024

This 1850s restored adobe structure fills an entire city block in the heart of the historic El Presidio neighborhood. Reputedly, the original buildings on this site were dwellings and shops for early settlers. In keeping with Spanish tradition, the exterior wall was built on the property line with a central courtyard inside. Today, the buildings surrounding the courtyard are shops offering Southwestern folk art, American Indian tribal art and imports from Mexico. Many of the items are handmade by some of Tucson's finest artisans, yet it's all reasonably priced. If you're looking for regional items, you'll find one of the best collections all in one spot here. Old Town Artisans also houses Cocina (Spanish for kitchen) Restaurant and its delightful patio garden. While shopping, ask for a walking tour map and visit all the nearby sites reflecting Tucson's history and culture. You can park at meters on surrounding streets or in nearby public lots.

University Area

Although there's shopping almost all around the University, the most concentrated area is on University Boulevard extending about two blocks west from the main gate at Park Avenue. As one might expect, the shops and businesses here are student-oriented, but they also appeal to anyone. Besides, it's an interesting place to watch University life. Among the shops on this street are Gap, Bath and Body Works, In the Swim and Landmark Clothing and Shoes, which carries popular brands such as Bass, Teva, Polo, Timberland and Birkenstock. The corner store called University Drug seems to sell just about everything one would need for daily life. There's also a flicks and frame shop, a store specializing in comics and other cool stuff, and music, book, skate, bike and athletic shops. The shopping area just wouldn't be complete without a store selling everything University of Arizona, from clothing and hats to school supplies and calendars, and it's got that in the Arizona Bookstore. The eateries in this area, many with outdoor seating facing the street, offer a varied selection of food and refreshments with a view. There's Time Market, featuring gourmet wood-fire pizzas and a full deli; the popular Gentle Ben's; several gourmet pizza places; and Geronimoz, a popular bar and restaurant in the old pink Geronimo Hotel (see our Restaurants chapter). Metered parking is available on University Boulevard.

Bargain and Outlet Shopping

Tucson has a number of places devoted to outlet shopping and other bargain merchandise. And if you want even more choice, we point you in the direction of Casa Grande, Arizona, about an hour north of Tucson.

Mix & Match
3673 N. Campbell Ave. • 327-0399

If you prefer clothes with names such as Liz Claiborne, Calvin Klein, DKNY and Georgio Armani on the labels but don't want to pay full designer prices, this may be the place to go. It's a designer department store outlet for both men and women and claims to sell top designer fashions for up to 70 percent off department store prices.

Old Pueblo Traders
3740 E. 34th St. • 747-0800

Known locally as OPT, you might want to head here when your sore feet won't make it to another shopping spot, but you desperately need a comfy pair of Hushpuppies or Grasshoppers. OPT is like a warehouse of clothes and shoes for women, the latter including hard-to-find sizes. Actually, it's two stores across the street from each other — one is the catalog center and the other a retail store, but anyone can shop at both. Brands you'll find here, in addition to the aforementioned shoes, include Koret, Sasson, Jantzen, Playtex and Easy Spirit. OPT also has a second smaller retail store at 5851 E. Speedway Boulevard.

Tanger Factory Outlet Center
**Casa Grande, I-10 at Exit 198
• (520) 836-0897, (800) 4-TANGER**

If you're willing to drive about 45 minutes up I-10 or happen to be going to Phoenix, this is one of two outlet centers right off the highway at Casa Grande, Arizona. Its 45 stores carry everything from apparel to housewares to shoes — names such as Carole Little, Anne Klein, Mikasa, Corning Revere, OshKosh B'Gosh, Samsonite and Naturalizer. At the very next exit off I-10 (#194) is the second of Casa Grande's outlet centers, Factory Stores of America, (520) 421-0112 or (800) SHOPUSA. It's smaller but also has bargains on clothing, shoes, accessories, toys, housewares and more.

Tanque Verde Swap Meet
4100 S. Palo Verde Rd. • 294-4252

Put on your walking shoes and grab a hat and a jug of water so you'll be all set for a morning or evening of swap meeting. It's called the Tanque Verde Swap Meet because it started out on the corner of Tanque Verde and Grant roads in the days when there used to be enough land to accommodate it. It moved but retained its name. There's plenty of parking and dust, but buyers can find some good bargains and interesting items here. Most days, you'll even find vendors selling some great produce from Mexico such as tomatoes, watermelons, limes, peppers, avocados and mangos. The swap meet is only open in the afternoons and evenings Thursday and Friday, but all day and evening Saturday and Sunday.

VF Factory Outlet
I-10 at S. Palo Verde Rd. • 889-4400

Compared to more modern outlet centers, VF Factory Outlet is small. But that may be a blessing for folks who don't want to walk a mile to shop. There are no more than a dozen indoor stores, carrying apparel, accessories, luggage, housewares and party and paper products. Brand names include Vanity Fair, Wrangler, Lee, Healthtex and Jantzen. It's a bit tricky to get to, however, so look for the Ramada Inn on S. Julian Drive, and you'll see the outlet building almost adjacent to it.

Books, etc.

Although Tucson has its share of national bookstore chains, such as B. Dalton, Waldenbooks and Barnes and Noble, often located in malls, you'll also find many other bookstores, both new and used, all around the metro area. Here are a few of the more notable ones.

Antigone Books
411 N. 4th Ave. • 792-3715

This shop in the Fourth Avenue shopping district offers books by and about women and has a unique selection of nonsexist books for children. Antigone Books also has music, cards and T-shirts on related topics.

Arizona Bookstore
815 N. Park Ave. • 622-4717
1529 W. St. Mary's Rd. • 882-8772

University of Arizona and Pima College students frequent this store because it buys and sells college textbooks. It also has a great selection of UA items as well as school and engineering supplies, computer books and software and technical and general interest books. Validated parking is available behind the store. The second location on St. Mary's Road is more convenient to Pima College's west campus. Both stores are closed on Sunday.

Bertrand's Books
120 E. Congress St. • 884-1899

Located in the funky downtown shopping district, Bertrand's has a large selection of used and out-of-print books plus new books on the region. The store's specialty is science fiction. Bertrand's is closed on Sunday.

Bookman's
1930 E. Grant Rd. • 325-5767
3733 W. Ina Rd. • 579-0303

The 20,000-square-foot shop on Grant Road is a favorite of locals and University students because it's centrally located, an interesting place, open until 10 PM and full of great used materials. You'll find both hardbound and paperback used books here on nearly any subject and new books on subjects of local interest such as the desert and hiking. They also deal in used CDs and software and have a great selection of old and rare magazines but not current issues.

Book Mark
5001 E. Speedway Blvd. • 881-6350

This locally owned store has more than 200,000 new books including large children's and Southwestern sections. Book Mark also has large-print books, local and international maps and will special order titles at no additional charge.

Borders Books and Music
4325 N. Oracle Rd. • 292-1331

As the name implies, this large store has an extensive selection of both books and music. It offers discounts on *New York Times* bestsellers and has a large children's section. You'll also find specialty magazines and out-of-state newspapers here. While browsing, you can relax in the espresso cafe.

Coyote's Voice Books
Broadway Blvd. and Country Club Rd.
• 327-6560

Located in Broadway Village, Coyote's has

FYI

Unless otherwise noted, the area code for all phone numbers listed in this guide is 520.

all the usual subjects but specializes in Spanish, Mexican and Latin American language books. It also has a good selection of Southwestern and architecture books. Employees will do searches and locate any out-of-print books they don't have. Coyote's is closed on Sunday.

Fine Print
2828 N. Stone Ave. • 622-8238

This used book shop has two claims to fame: It used to be partly owned by famous author Larry McMurtry, who shows up there occasionally for signings, and it has a good collection of rare Western Americana books. The shelves hold books, many of them rare, in all subjects. Fine Print is closed on Sunday.

La Casa del Libro Bookstore
2802 E. 22nd St. • 881-2489

For folks who speak Spanish or want to, this store offers a complete selection of books and educational materials in Spanish including dictionaries and reference materials, bilingual books, religious books, records, cassettes and books in English or Spanish as a second language. The bookstore is open Monday through Saturday.

Serenity Books
2723 N. Campbell Ave. • 325-3111

As its name suggests, this New Age store offers books intended to calm and otherwise help you. Book topics include self-help, spiritualism, music, relationships, recovery and parenting. Many are available on CDs and audio cassettes. This bookstore is closed on Sunday.

Tucson's Map and Flag Center
3239 N. 1st Ave. • 887-4234

This is the top Tucson source for maps, from street atlases of Tucson and Phoenix to topographical maps and charts. The Center has travel maps of Mexico plus an excellent selection of travel guides for anywhere. If it has to do with geography or topography, you'll probably find it here, but not on Sunday when the store is closed.

Fashions

As one might expect, clothing stores abound in Tucson and you'll find them in nearly every plaza, mall and shopping center plus lots more locations around town. In other words, don't overlook the other sections in this chapter if you're looking for clothes. The men's and women's fashion spots listed below are some of the more interesting ones Tucson has to offer.

Cele Peterson's
6318 E. Broadway Blvd. • 323-9413

Cele Peterson's is practically a Tucson fashion institution, having opened the first store in 1931. The remaining store at El Mercado carries sophisticated but pricey clothing for women in both dressy and casual styles. The shop has a large collection of St. John knits. It's closed on Sunday.

Firenze Boutique
5671 N. Swan Rd. • 299-2992

Located in a small shopping plaza in the foothills, Firenze sells Italian and other European clothes, accessories and shoes for men and women. The boutique is closed Sundays.

Maya Palace
El Mercado, 6332 E. Broadway Blvd.
• 748-0817
Plaza Palomino, 2960 N. Swan Rd.
• 325-6411

This unusual fashion store for women has two locations — one in El Mercado and the other in Plaza Palomino. They specialize in fashions and accessories from around the world, along with a selection of handcrafted gift items. If you're looking for a unique, exotic, brightly colored outfit in flowing fabrics such as cotton, rayon and silk, this is the place to shop. The salespeople are friendly and will help you coordinate a total look, right down to the jewelry. Only the El Mercado store is open on Sundays.

Mills-Touche
4811 E. Grant Rd. • 795-5573

Operated for years by a Tucson family, this shop in Crossroads Festival has both women's and men's apparel, but the men's section is about twice the size of the women's. Mills-Touche offers top quality clothing and accessories with a classic style Monday through Saturday.

It's hard to go anywhere in Tucson without running into a shop that sells Southwestern apparel.

Repp Big and Tall
4045 E. Broadway Blvd. • 881-7533
4491 N. Oracle Rd. • 293-2337

For men who need sizes beyond what is typically found in department and other men's stores, this is the place to shop. Shoes can be ordered through their catalog.

Rochelle K
5350 E. Broadway Blvd. • 745-4600

This upscale shop has very current women's styles both casual and dressy. You'll find French Connection, Vanilla and other labels from New York, France and Italy here. There's also a small but unusual selection of finely crafted home accessories and linens. Rochelle K is closed on Sundays.

Savvy Boutique
5677 N. Swan Rd. • 577-9733

This boutique in a small plaza in the foothills offers women's upscale casual contemporary clothing and accessories. Labels the boutique carries include Flax and Amanda Gray. It's closed on Sunday.

Outdoors and Recreation

In addition to national chain stores offering outdoor and recreation gear and clothing, such as Popular Outdoor Outfitters, Tucson has a few specialty stores that cater to the outdoor lifestyle.

Audubon Nature Shop
300 E. University Blvd. • 629-0510

Affiliated with the Tucson Audubon Society, this shop in the University area has a wide selection of natural history books and gifts. Book subjects include astronomy, geology, birds (of course), mammals, insects, reptiles, plants and oceans. It also has educational materials and children's books on nature subjects and supplies for birders and hikers such as binoculars, field guides and hiking maps. For gift-giving or for personal use, you'll find games, greeting cards, maps, tapes and records, all with a nature theme. And for your feathered friends, you'll find bird feeders. The shop is closed on Sundays.

Summit Hut
5045 E. Speedway Blvd. • 325-1554,
(800) 499-8696

This is a local favorite for all kinds of outdoor equipment and advice, including a great selection of books and pamphlets on outdoor and southern Arizona subjects. In addition to all the outdoor stuff for sale, Summit

Hut also rents camping gear such as tents, packs, sleeping bags and climbing boots. And if you need a gift for someone who's into nature, it has T-shirts and cards.

Yesteryear's Treasures

Tucson may not have the selection of antiques and collectibles typical in older areas of the country, but this is a growing arena in Tucson, and there are many shops carrying items from yesteryear.

Antique Center of Tucson
5000 E. Speedway Blvd. • 323-0319

This indoor mall boasts 90 dealers in one location. You're likely to find everything from old typewriters and musical instruments to vintage clothing and clocks, along with all manner of antique furniture and accessories.

Antique Mall
3130 E. Grant Rd. • 326-3070

This place is typically voted "best of Tucson" by antique buffs, but you'll find much more in the way of collectibles, glassware and china here than furniture.

Canyon State Collectibles
5245 E. Pima St. • 795-1922

Whether you're hunting for movie and movie-star memorabilia or political and military collectibles, Canyon State probably has it. It also offers sports cards, old jewelry, collector plates, old toys and dolls, postcards, stamps, coins, Indian jewelry and artifacts, and Hummels, Royal Doultons and LLadros. The store is closed on Sunday.

Christine's Curiosity Shop & Doll Museum
4940 E. Speedway Blvd. • 323-0018

Nearly every square inch of this large store is crammed full of old things, from glassware and lamps to furniture and dolls and maybe even a pinball machine. It's fascinating and a find for collectors of dolls and just about anything else. Christine's is closed on Sunday.

Firehouse Antique Center
6522 E. 22nd St. • 571-1775

Nearly 40 dealers occupy this minimall, buying and selling antiques and collectibles that include books, estate jewelry, linens, sports collectibles, furniture and vintage clothing. The Firehouse also provides services such as glass repair, furniture restoration and repair and appraisals.

Museum and Miscellaneous Shops

Many of Tucson's major attractions and museums also have gift shops. Some of the more outstanding ones, or those with regional or otherwise unusual items, are Arizona Historical Society, Arizona-Sonora Desert Museum, Flandrau Planetarium, Tohono Chul Park, Tucson Botanical Gardens and Tucson Museum of Art. You're likely to find merchandise at these places, all of which are described in the Attractions chapter, that you may not find elsewhere.

There are several other shops in Tucson that don't really fit into one of the other categories in this chapter but are worth visiting if you're looking for the unusual.

Goofy Gallery
2639 E. Broadway Blvd. • 320-1488

As its name implies, you're likely to find some unusual and goofy items in this shop including nearly life-size papier-mâché animals and papier-mâché clowns. It also has more common things such as ceramics, copper fountains, hand-blown glass, sculptures and pewter decor. One room exhibits the art of area high school students, and the artwork is for sale. The gallery is closed on Sunday.

Malkia African Arts and Gifts
2900 E. Broadway Blvd. • 881-0110

Nearly all of the merchandise in this store is made by or representative of the peoples of Africa. You'll find paintings, sculpture, masks, pots, vases and lots more in both vivid colors and earth tones and made primarily from natural materials. The store is closed on Sunday.

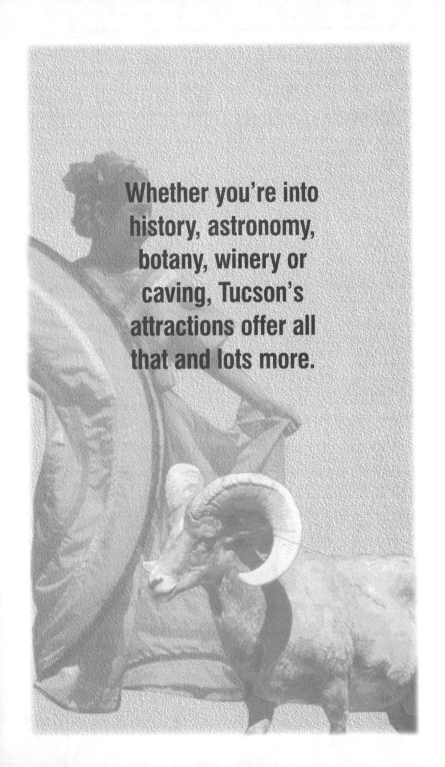

Whether you're into history, astronomy, botany, winery or caving, Tucson's attractions offer all that and lots more.

Attractions

There's little doubt that Tucson's main attractions are sun and sand — no, not the kind of sand that lines beaches, but the kind that forms in a desert. We boast 350 days of sunshine a year, and our Sonoran Desert is considered by botanists and zoologists to be one of the richest regions on earth. And there's no end to the things people can find to do given the climate and geography.

But don't wait for a rainy day to tear yourself away from that poolside lounge chair or to postpone that trek into Sabino Canyon or Saguaro National Park. For starters, there might not be one (a rainy day, that is). But more importantly, you'll miss some absolutely fabulous attractions in and around Tucson. And besides, many of the attractions are wholly or partially outdoors anyway, so you'll still be catching the rays and the desert views. Whether you're into history, astronomy, botany, winery or caving, Tucson's attractions offer all that and lots more.

Before we delve into the good stuff, however, here's a big piece of advice: Don't limit yourself to this chapter when you're looking for attractions. You'll find more great things to do and see in the Parks and Recreation, Arts and Culture, Kidstuff and Festivals and Events chapters.

Arizona Historical Society
949 E. 2nd St. • 628-5774

The historical society is actually three museums, with the main one at the UA campus. (See the Kidstuff chapter for more information on the main museum and where to park.) Its two branch museums are the Sosa-Carrillo-Fremont House and the Fort Lowell Museum. (The latter is covered separately in this chapter.) Entering the historical society's lovely old building is to take a walk through Arizona's history. Permanent exhibits include authentically decorated period rooms depicting life in the Arizona Territory, artifacts from Arizona's frontier life and its American Indian populations, and a full-scale re-creation of underground mining. Numerous temporary exhibits focus on specific times or topics in Arizona's past. And for anyone doing research on nearly anything pertaining to Arizona or Tucson, the historical society maintains an excellent library, which includes rare and unique maps and photos, that's open to the public. Docent tours are offered by appointment, and the museum is handicapped-accessible. There's also a gift shop specializing in authentic Southwestern arts and crafts and books. The historical society conducts special events and lectures year round. Admission is free, although donations are suggested, and hours are 10 AM to 4 PM Monday through Saturday and noon to 4 PM Sunday. (See our Kidstuff chapter for activities geared more for the younger set.)

At the Sosa-Carrillo-Fremont house, 151 S. Granada Avenue, hours are 10 AM to 4 PM Wednesday through Saturday. The historical society has turned this house, one of Tucson's oldest adobe buildings, into a museum. It's named after the families that occupied it from the 1860s and today is furnished in 1880s fashion with rotating displays of territorial life.

Arizona-Sonora Desert Museum
2021 N. Kinney Rd. • 883-2702

It may not be the only place you'll see cacti on your Tucson visit, but it probably will be the only way to catch a view of a Gila Monster or a cougar. So don't be fooled by this attraction's moniker of museum. It's much more zoo than museum, plus botanical garden, bird sanctuary, nature trail and even gem and mineral museum. But however it's described, it's always called one of the world's best. Allow yourself plenty of time, at least three hours, because there's so much to explore and experience here. The natural landscape is recreated so realistically that you find yourself eye-to-eye with mountain lions, prairie dogs, Gila monsters, hawks and hummingbirds. Every inch of this mostly outdoor museum is packed full of fascinating plant and animal life. One exhibit features nocturnal desert dwellers. Another gives visitors an underwater view of beavers, river otters and fish. A walk-through cave leads to a fine collection of rare and beautiful regional gems and minerals. And you'll see more reptiles and spiders than you may ever have wanted to, but they're safely tucked away behind glass. In the hummingbird aviary, one of the museum's most popular spots, hundreds of them hover about showing off their colors and flying skills. All during your walk, you'll find volunteers giving fascinating demonstrations about the creatures and plant life of the desert.

> **FYI**
>
> Unless otherwise noted, the area code for all phone numbers listed in this guide is 520.

The museum is clean, meticulously cared for and exquisitely laid out to give the best views possible of the plants and animals. It's also wheelchair and stroller friendly and both are available for free. The museum also has excellent eateries, shops that shouldn't be missed for natural history books, native crafts, bird feeders and much more, and an art gallery of artists' Sonoran desert interpretations in a variety of media.

It's open daily from 8:30 AM to 5 PM October through February and 7:30 AM to 6 PM March through September. There are shade ramadas, drinking fountains and restrooms in several locations, but be prepared to protect yourself from the sun, especially in summer. Admission is $8.95 for anyone age 13 and older, $1.75 for children ages 6 to 12 and free for younger ones. Discount coupons are usually easy to find at the Tucson Convention and Visitors Bureau, in local publications and in some stores and banks.

It's located on Kinney Road on the west side of the Tucson Mountains and can be reached via either Ajo Way or Speedway Boulevard. RVers must take the Ajo Way route to Kinney Road.

Arizona State Museum
Park Ave. and University Blvd.
• 621-6302

Enter the main gate of the University of Arizona campus and you face a lovely tree-lined street bordered by some exquisite old buildings. Two of these comprise the Arizona State Museum's north and south buildings. Its collections are recognized as some of the world's most significant resources for the study of Southwestern cultures. Included are 100,000 artifacts from archaeological excavations of the Hohokam, Mogollon and Anasazi cultures, more than 25,000 ethnographic objects documenting the cultures of both historic and living American Indians and more than 250,000 photographic images. Through the museum's exhibits, visitors discover the wonders of ancient civilizations and the contributions of living American Indian cultures. Anyone with an interest in the Southwest will also appreciate the museum's library of 40,000 volumes, including many rare titles. In the gift shop, browsers or buyers will find an excellent selection of pottery, kachina dolls, rugs, carvings, jewelry, baskets, cards, posters and books reflecting the museum's theme.

Hours are Monday through Saturday 10 AM to 5 PM and Sunday noon to 5 PM. Admission is free (donations suggested), and both buildings are handicapped-accessible. Metered street parking is available to the west of the main gate on University Boulevard, 2nd Street and 1st Street, while several pay parking lots located in the same area will cost no more than a few dollars.

Asarco Mineral Discovery Center
I-19 and Pima Mine Rd. • 625-7513

Folks who are interested in minerals or copper mining will see and learn all about them at this attraction 15 miles south of Tucson. Visitors have a choice of seeing just the Mineral Discovery Center, which is free, or also taking the open-pit mine tour, for which a fee is charged for anyone older than 5 ($4 for kids to age 12, $6 for adults and $5 for seniors).

The Mineral Discovery Center has a variety of hands-on exhibits about mining and minerals, from how ore deposits are formed and how they are discovered and mined to how the land is reclaimed after mining. A multimedia theater has presentations on mining, min-

eral resources and reclamation. There's also a display of historic and present-day mining equipment. The tour takes visitors by air-conditioned bus to an operating open-pit copper mine nearby. You'll see how the land is excavated, the massive machinery that mills the earth and extracts and processes the minerals, and the reclamation process designed to restore the landscape.

Tours take about an hour, and flat shoes are recommended because some walking will be required. Call ahead if you need arrangements for wheelchair access. The Center is open Wednesday through Sunday from 9 AM to 5 PM, and tours leave every 20 minutes. It's operated by ASARCO Inc., a worldwide mining company whose copper operations are based in Tucson.

Biosphere 2
Ariz. Hwy. 77 at Mile Marker 96.5
• **825-1289, (800) 828-2462**

We all live on Biosphere 1 (Earth), and Biosphere 2 was created to be a model of Earth, an experiment to duplicate Earth's environment and life forms and enhance knowledge of its ecosystems. When this $150-plus million model opened in 1991, eight biospherians lived here self-sufficiently in the world's largest glass-enclosed ecological laboratory, and visitors could only tour the outside areas. Although no one lives inside Biosphere 2 today, it remains a research facility under the direction of Columbia University, and visitors can now tour the human habitat, the once-sealed environment where the biospherians lived and worked. The building covers more than 3 acres and resembles something from a science-fiction movie. Visitors will see a million-gallon ocean teeming with life via both above and underwater viewing, a tropical rain forest, plus five other biomes (self-sustaining communities of living organisms) replicating earth. It's like taking a trip around the world in an afternoon.

It's best to start at the Visitors Center to get your bearings of the 250-acre campus, a map and a filmed overview of the project. A shuttle bus can take you to the areas of interest or you can walk, but be sure to have comfortable shoes and plan on at least two hours to see everything. Along the way, guides can answer questions and point you in the right direction. Or you can take a tour that begins every hour on the half-hour. You'll also find shops selling mementos of your Biosphere visit, the Cyber Cafe for snacks and the opportunity to cruise the Information Highway, and a restaurant that offers fantastic views of the Catalina Mountains and the city of Tucson. There's also a hotel for folks who want a getaway surrounded by the wonders of science and nature.

Admission prices range from $6 for children older than 5 to $13 for adults who are not Arizona residents. Arizonans pay $10. Discount

118 • ATTRACTIONS

coupons are often available at the Tucson Convention and Visitors Bureau, at other spots around the city and in local publications. Biosphere 2 is open daily from 9 AM to 5 PM. All exhibits and presentations are wheelchair-accessible, and strollers and wheelchairs are available for rent at the admission gate; rental fees are around $5.

To get here, take Oracle Road north about 15 miles and watch for the sign pointing to Biosphere 2.

Casino of the Sun
7406 S. Camino de Oeste • 883-1700, (800) 344-9435

The Pascua Yaqui Tribe was one of the last American Indian peoples to gain federal recognition by the U.S. Congress, and in 1964 the tribe was deeded about 200 acres of desert land southwest of Tucson. Today about 9,000 members of the tribe live in the area, which also houses the tribe's casino, a source of revenue and employment for the tribal members. It's billed as southern Arizona's largest casino with 500 slot machines (including nickel machines), live-action card room, bingo and Keno, plus a restaurant and grill. No alcohol is served on the premises, but nonsmokers will be glad to hear there's a nonsmoking room full of slot machines. For Bingo lovers, the casino holds afternoon and evening sessions, including Power Bingo with 25 games going at once (try to keep track of that). There's also a variety of live-action poker games, usually from 3 PM to the wee hours of the morning. (Arizona casinos are prohibited from conducting other card or table games, so poker is popular.)

As with casinos all across the United States, this place really draws the crowds, particularly on weekends. Parking is free with plenty of handicapped-accessible spots. From Tucson, go west on Valencia Road about 5 miles past I-10 — you won't miss the signs pointing the way.

Colossal Cave
I-10, Exit 279, Vail • 647-7275

If you aren't claustrophobic about being in a hollowed-out mountain for about an hour, this attraction is one of the most unusual and fascinating in southern Arizona. Actually, for an underground labyrinth, it's very comfortable, dry, well-lit and easy to navigate because of flagstone walkways and handrails. It didn't have all these amenities when prehistoric peoples used the cave, nor when it was "discovered" in 1879 or used by train robbers to hide their booty. Now on the National Register of Historic Places, Colossal Cave's history and natural beauty combine to make it a great spot to visit. It's also unique because it's the only dry, or dormant, cave in the United States, meaning that the formations are not presently growing due to a lack of water. But not to worry, the formations already extant in this crystal-filled hollow mountain are breathtaking.

The tour route is a half-mile long and takes about 50 minutes. It's led by a guide who relates the cave's history, legends and geology. You'll walk down and back up about six stories (and some 360 steps) filled with stalactites, stalagmites, flowstone and other formations, not to mention a few prehistoric markings. Unfortunately, this is not an attraction for

> **www.insiders.com**
> See this and many other Insiders' Guide® destinations online — in their entirety.
> **Visit us today!**

INSIDERS' TIP

Arizona is the only state in the continental United States that does not go on daylight-saving time in the summer. So when daylight-saving time is in effect in other states (April through October), Arizona clocks are on the same time as Pacific Standard Time, which is three hours earlier than Eastern Standard Time. During the rest of the year, Arizona is the same as Mountain Standard Time, which is two hours earlier than Eastern Standard Time.

ATTRACTIONS • 119

Tucson's Natural History Museum

Dedicated to the World's Wildlife

- Group Discounts • Hands-on Exhibits
- Exotic Gift Shop • Wildlife Theater • Lectures
- New Prehistoric Mammoth Display

Adults $6 • Children $2 • Seniors $4.75

International Wildlife Museum
Learning Fun for All Ages

On Speedway 5mi. West of I-10
4800 West Gates Pass Rd.
Tucson, Arizona 85745

Ticket Info Call
(520) 617-1439

---

people who are in wheelchairs or who have difficulty walking. It's always 70 degrees and dry in the cave.

Tours are given daily year round. They're not prescheduled, but the wait is 30 minutes at most. Meanwhile, you can enjoy the comfortable ramada, gift shop, wooded picnic areas and spectacular views at the entrance area.

The cost is $7.50 for those 13 and older, $4 for ages 6 to 12 and free for younger ones. Summer hours, in effect March 16 through September 15, are 8 AM to 6 PM Monday through Saturday and to 7 PM Sundays and holidays. Winter hours are 9 AM to 5 PM Monday through Saturday and to 6 PM Sundays and holidays. The two routes to get here from Tucson are the scenic Old Spanish Trail for about 17 miles, or I-10 east to Exit 279 and then north for about 6 miles.

Davis-Monthan Air Force Base
Craycroft and Valencia Rds.
• **750-3204**

You can read all about Davis-Monthan Air Force Base, located on Tucson's south side, in our separate chapter of the same name. But unless you have official business there or otherwise have access to the base, you'll only be able to see it by taking a tour. The tours are by bus and free on a first-come basis but are usually only offered two or three mornings a week. You'll need to call the tour phone line, 228-3358, to get all the details, which change often. The one-hour tour goes through the base, including down the flight line for a view of the array of planes using the 14,000-foot runway, but it focuses on the intriguing aircraft storage facility (or "boneyard"). Photos are allowed. If you're at all interested in the military or in vintage and modern aircraft, we highly recommend the base tour.

Desert Diamond Casino
7350 S. Nogales Hwy. • 294-7777

The Tohono O'odham Nation of about 18,000 members owns nearly 3 million square acres of land to Tucson's southwest. The reservation houses not only the famed San Xavier Mission and Kitt Peak National Observatory, but also the tribe's casino, which generates revenue for the Tohono O'odhams and employment opportunities for the community. Ways to wager at the casino include slot machines, live poker games round-the-clock, Keno and bingo. The bingo hall is huge, and sessions pretty much run all day, from morning until late at night. Beverages are complimentary, but no alcohol is served, and there's a cafe for a quick bite. Like Casino of the Sun, these are not fancy Las-Vegas style structures; they're plain and focused strictly on gambling. As with other Arizona casinos, you must be 18 to play, but you can do so round-the-clock.

Flandrau Science Center and Planetarium
Cherry Ave. and University Blvd.
• 621-4515, 621-7827

There's so much to do and see at Flandrau that adults turn into kids here and have just as much fun. For starters, a host of exhibits let visitors experience the wonders of astronomy, optics, electricity, imagination and optical illusions. Many are hands-on exhibits where you'll see moon rocks through a microscope, find out how sound and wind don't travel in a vacuum and experience the phenomena of holograms. Then visitors can walk up a stairway to the outdoor observatory and, with the assistance of a guide, look through a 16-inch telescope, gazing at planets, galaxies and star clusters. The observatory is open year round on clear nights Wednesday through Saturday, and viewing is free.

Back inside Flandrau, take in a show at the dome-shaped theater of stars where you'll be mesmerized by special effects, panoramic projections and a state-of the art video projection system. You'll sit in comfortable reclining seats as the virtual reality shows on astronomy, skylore, exploration and ancient cultures take you back through time or forward into the future of space travel. The theater also offers laser light shows, a favorite of teenagers, where laser projections explode across the dome in a rainbow of colors choreographed to popular music. Downstairs, Flandrau features a fascinating display of Arizona minerals and specimen rocks along with an informative video. And finally, Flandrau has a wonderful science store featuring science kits, posters, puzzles, star charts, books, toys, games and more — all designed to make learning about science fun.

Admission to Flandrau is $3 for adults and $2 for kids 13 and younger. Shows at the theater of stars range from $6 to $4, but the ticket also includes your admission to Flandrau. It's open weekdays from 9 AM to 5 PM and weekends from 1 to 5 PM. Evening hours are 7 to 9 PM Wednesday and Thursday and 7 PM to midnight Friday and Saturday. A metered lot for parking (25¢ for 15 minutes) is available just to the south of the planetarium across University Boulevard. (See our Kidstuff chapter.)

Fort Lowell Museum
2900 N. Craycroft Rd. • **885-3832**

Take a trip into Tucson's past and have a family day at the park, all for free. The small museum operated by the Arizona Historical Society is located in the pleasant surroundings of Ft. Lowell Park, once the site of a Hohokam Indian Village. Centuries later, a cavalry fort was erected here. From 1873 to 1891, soldiers were stationed at Fort Lowell to protect Tucson settlers from Indian raids. (It's said that the fort was built so far from town because the rowdy soldiers created a nuisance. Guess the citizens needed more protection from the soldiers than from Indians.) The museum is actually a reconstruction of the commanding officers' quarters. Here you'll find period furnishings, a photographic story of the 75 former occupants of Fort Lowell and frontier artifacts. It's open Wednesday through Saturday from 10 AM to 4 PM.

Garden of Gethsemane
W. Congress St. and Bonita Ave.
• **no phone**

As you may already know from reading other chapters of this book, Tucson's heritage includes a strong religious influence carried north from Mexico by Catholic missionaries. The signs of this heritage pop up in often unusual ways, such as the hidden treasure called Garden of Gethsemane on the west bank of the Santa Cruz River at Congress Street. It's hard to imagine that one man created these life-size carvings depicting the Holy Family, the Last Supper and the Crucifixion. The Spanish sculptor Felix Lucero vowed to do the work when he was spared on a World War I battlefield; it was his tribute to God's kindness. Today this spot is

---

INSIDERS' TIP

You may see small handmade objects with ribbons affixed to doors and statues at Mission San Xavier del Bac. Called *Milagros*, they have been placed there by people either seeking a miracle or giving thanks for one that's already been granted.

ATTRACTIONS • 121

A side altar at San Xavier del Bac displays some of the ornate and colorful trim work.

almost overshadowed by the roar of traffic on I-10, but it seems to create a sense of peace and wonder nonetheless. The gates are open daily from 9 AM to 4 PM, and there's no admission fee.

Historic Old Pueblo

History buffs wouldn't want to pass through Tucson without checking out some of Tucson's famous historical sites in and around the downtown area. Streets in these neighborhoods weren't created with car traffic in mind, so it's best to tour through history the old-fashioned way, on foot. There are four distinct districts, each with its own attractions.

One is defined by what once was the old presidio wall, which today is bounded by Pennington Street, Church Avenue, Washington Street and Main Avenue and represents 130 years of the city's architectural history. This area offers more than two dozen sites including footbridges, the Pima County Courthouse, La Casa Cordova, one of the oldest homes in Tucson and now a museum, and other old houses open to the public including the Stevens House and the Edward Nye Fish House. In the center of the more modern Tucson Museum of Art lies the Plaza of the Pioneers, honoring Tucson's early citizens.

Just to the north is the second area to tour, the El Presidio Historic District, bounded by Washington and 6th streets and Granada and Church avenues. While some of the old mansions here are still private residences, they're worth just walking by. You'll also find several, like the Manning House and Steinfeld Mansion, that have been converted into offices but still hold their allure. And be sure to take a peaceful break in the Alene Dunlop Smith Memorial Garden on the east side of Granada Avenue.

Downtown and Barrio Libre comprise the third area to tour, which is south of the presidio wall district and bounded by Simpson Street, Church Avenue, Congress Street and Granada Avenue. Here you'll find the lovely Sanmaniego House, now a restaurant; El Tiradito, the wishing shrine; and the Sosa-Carillo-Fremont House, one of Tucson's oldest adobe structures and the only barrio building spared when the Convention Center was built.

Just to the east of the barrio area is the Church Avenue district, extending to 5th Avenue. This area encompasses the lovely Temple of Music and Art; the former Carnegie Library, now housing the Children's Museum; and St. Augustine Cathedral, one of central Tucson's most striking structures dating from 1896. At the northeast corner of this area, you'll find the old Congress Hotel and an old Southern Pacific Railroad Depot now operated by Amtrak.

For an excellent site-by-site guide to these four areas, pick up a copy of the book *Yesterday's Tucson To-Day*, which has sketches of the buildings and other sites, detailed maps and brief descriptions. The book is available from the Tucson Museum of Art and Arizona Historical Society gift shops, while the Tucson Convention and Visitors Bureau has a copy you can browse through as well as a little brochure based on the book that lists all the sites in the four areas with maps. Also, check out other chapters of this book — such as Neighborhoods and Real Estate, Arts and Culture and History — for more information on the central historic areas and attractions.

International Wildlife Museum
4800 W. Gates Pass Rd. • 617-1439

Both kids and their parents have an opportunity to see and often touch more than 300 kinds of animals from around the world here. Longhorn sheep, for example, are perched along a large boulder display, showing how they live and interact in the mountains around the Sonoran Desert. Another display graphically shows the huge size difference among bears, from the smallest black bear to the grizzly. The nocturnal area depicts desert creatures of the night. Other species on display include reptiles and birds. Visitors can also watch award-winning nature films in the 100-seat theater, learn about wildlife through interactive computer displays or shop for unique gifts from around the world.

Except for major holidays, the museum is open daily from 9 AM to 5 PM and is wheelchair-accessible. Admission is $6 for adults, $4.75 for seniors and students, $2 for kids 6 to 12 and free for younger ones. It's located 5 miles west of I-10 via Speedway Boulevard to Gates Pass Road.

Justin's Waterworld
3551 S. San Joaquin Rd. • 883-8340

Water fun isn't always easy to find in the Tucson desert, especially in summertime, but Justin's has a solution. It's only open during the summer (late May through Labor Day) and only from Friday through Sunday, but it's a great family outing to escape the heat. There are water activities to suit every age, from a babies' pool to giant water slides for older kids to an adults-only pool. You can rent a water float or inner tube, play in the game room or eat at the snack bar. There's plenty of mature trees and ramadas for relaxing in the shade after a workout in the water.

Hours are 10 AM to 5 PM, and kids younger than 5 and seniors get in for free. All others pay $8.50, but it's a reduced rate if you arrive after 2 PM. Take Ajo Way west to San Joaquin Road, then go north. (See our Kidstuff chapter for more information.)

Kitt Peak National Observatory
Ariz. Hwy. 386 • 318-8726

At an elevation of 6,800 feet above the Sonoran Desert floor, Kitt Peak is in the Quinlan Mountains, which are part of the Tohono O'odham Indian reservation, on land leased to the federal government. The location, which has housed the world's largest collection of optical telescopes for nearly 40 years, is so appealing to astronomers because it's under some of the finest night skies in the world. To see this amazing collection of observatories (one of which is 18 stories tall) and telescopes, start at the Kitt Peak Visitor Center and learn the history of optical astronomy and the role Kitt Peak has had in shaping astronomical research. Then take a one-hour guided tour to see the facilities and learn how astronomers use telescopes to unlock the mysteries of the universe. At the National Solar Observatory exhibit gallery, you'll be able to watch astronomers operate the world's largest solar telescope. All of this takes place daily (except Thanksgiving, Christmas and New Year's Day) from 9 AM to 4 PM. There's no admission charge, but donations are suggested.

For a totally different experience and the chance to actually view the skies through some of the equipment, visit Kitt Peak at night or plan your daytime visit so you can stay until dark. But be aware that reservations are a must for the nighttime program (the limit is 20 people). Called the Stargazing Program, it's conducted nightly by tour guides and costs $35 for adults or $25 for students, seniors and anyone younger than 18. It lasts for 3½ hours, but you must arrive a half-hour before sunset, so the starting time varies. (To limit the effect of bright lights at night, drivers are escorted down the peak using only parking lights for about a mile.) The stargazing program uses the Visitor Center telescope dome, which is equipped with binoculars and a state-of-the-art 16-inch telescope to view planets, the birth and death of stars, nebulae and galaxies. Keep in mind that temperatures are 10 to 20 degrees cooler than in Tucson, so on winter nights it will actually be frigid. Also be aware that walking paths to several of the telescopes are steep and may pose a problem to people with cardiac and respiratory troubles.

There are no food or gas facilities at Kitt Peak. Public restrooms are adjacent to the parking lot, while wheelchairs and a handicapped-accessible restroom are in the Visitor Center. Kitt Peak is 56 miles southwest of Tucson via Ajo Way (Ariz. Highway 86) to Ariz. 386, which is Kitt Peak Road.

Mission San Xavier del Bac
1950 W. San Xavier Rd. • 294-2624

Tucsonans tend to pronounce it "Sanaveer," but the correct Spanish pronunciation is "Sahn Ha-v-yair." The full name means "mission for the Saint Francisco Xavier at the place where the water appears." (The reference is to the place where the underground Santa Cruz River rose to the surface.) But one need not know the correct way to say it or what it means to appreciate the splendor of this luminous white structure rising out of the desert floor on the land of the Tohono O'odham Indians. For two centuries, it has stood as a symbol of religion brought to American Indians by missionaries traveling from Mexico. It was the O'odham who became the skilled masons and laborers who erected the domed, vaulted and arched building of fired bricks, stone and lime mortar (or stucco) under the direction of missionary priests who had seen great edifices in Spain and Italy. From Father Kino's initial work on the foundation in 1700, it took 97 years before the church

124 • ATTRACTIONS

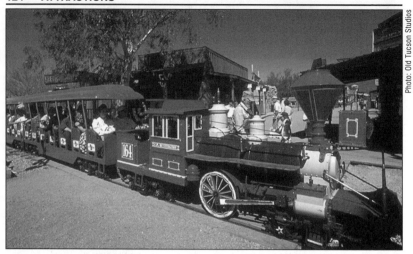

The C.P. Huntington Train arrives in the station at Old Tucson Studios.

was opened for services, and even then it was not actually completed. (Look closely and you'll see that the east bell tower has never been completed.)

Today, it is fondly called "The White Dove of the Desert," and it remains the parish church of the O'odham of the San Xavier District of the Tohono O'odham Nation. But by the thousands people of all faiths come through the mission's old dark doors of mesquite wood to appreciate its beauty and the labor of love it so obviously took to construct it.

Six generations of the same family have worked to maintain the mission's exterior, using a mixture of sand, lime and cactus juice for stucco. And although the exterior is in need of major refurbishing, an interior restoration taking six years and $2 million (mostly donated) was completed to mark the mission's bicentennial. An international team of experts refurbished 54 polychrome wall paintings and 44 statues, many made in Mexico more than 200 years ago, as part of their task. Nearly every area of the interior is covered with elaborate paintings and sculpture created by unknown artists. Throughout small rooms of the mission there are photos, documents and artifacts showing the history of the mission. A gift shop, craft store and refreshments are available on the premises.

The mission is open to visitors daily from 8 AM to 6 PM, and masses are held every day except Monday at various times. Admission is free, but donations are welcomed. It's located 19 miles south of downtown Tucson via I-19. Words can't adequately describe the mission; it must be seen.

Mt. Lemmon Ski Valley
Mt. Lemmon • 576-1400

Many chapters in this book discuss Mt. Lemmon, Tucsonans' playground in the sky in the Santa Catalina Mountains. All along the 30-mile ride to the top, activities include hiking, picnicking, camping, fishing, climbing and just enjoying the diverse scenery and topography as it changes from desert to pine forest through five distinct vegetative zones. At the highway's end, just past the village of Summerhaven, lies the ski valley, but you need not be a skier to enjoy the lift, or skyride, to the summit. The 25-minute round-trip ride of about one mile operates year round both weekdays and weekends. It departs at the base of the ski area at an 8,200-foot elevation and travels to 9,100 feet with spectacular views of the valley below and mountains as far away as Globe and Phoenix. At the base, you'll find a gift shop, mountainside patio where snacks and beverages are served, and a restaurant. For folks who'd rather glide down the slopes than ride, this is a complete ski area — the southernmost in the United States — with 15 ski runs at beginner, intermediate and expert levels, equipment rental shop and ski school (see our Parks and Recreation chapter).

If you're taking the skyride for pleasure, the ticket prices start at $6 for adults and $2 for kids younger than 12. The Mt. Lemmon or Catalina Highway begins at Tanque Verde Road about 5 miles east of Sabino Canyon Road. For road conditions (weather or construction delays), call 749-3329 or 741-4991. Although there is now a per-car user fee for Mt. Lemmon, the fee does not apply if you're going to Ski Valley.

Old Pueblo Trolley
4th Ave. and 8th St. • 792-1802

Tucson's visitors of today can step into the past on the Fourth Avenue (or Old Pueblo) Trolley. In 1906, electric street cars replaced the horse- and mule-drawn streetcars operating in central Tucson and ran until 1930. In the mid-1980s, a nonprofit volunteer group began the work of restoring trolley cars and track along 4th Avenue and University Boulevard. Now the trolley takes passengers on a one-mile journey through some of the most historic and diverse areas of Tucson. It runs between the UA main gate and 4th Avenue and 8th Street, and riders can catch it at either end and hop off along the way. At the end of the line on 8th Street, there's a car barn where you might see other trolleys being restored. It operates Friday evenings from 6 to 10 PM, Saturdays from noon to midnight and Sundays from noon to 5 PM. Kids younger than 6 ride free, kids 6 to 12 and seniors pay 50¢, and adults pay $1 for a one-way trip.

Old Tucson Studios
201 S. Kinney Rd. • 883-0100

To see a re-creation of a Western town in the 1880s, Hollywood-style, head on out to Old Tucson Studios. This popular Tucson-area attraction started out in 1939 as an elaborate set for the movie *Arizona* and was eventually turned into a frontier town replica for the public, although it continues its former life as a set for movies and TV shows. (While there, you may even see some movie or TV show being filmed.) Old Tucson Studios suffered a serious fire in 1995, and some of the original structures and memorabilia were destroyed, but it has been rebuilt and expanded. All the buildings in this town are meticulously constructed and adorned to reflect the Old West, and you'll really feel taken back in time as you saunter by or enter saloons, dance halls, a jail, a general store or mercantile, corrals, stables and wooden sidewalks. But there's lots more to do here than soak up the atmosphere and dream about the famous movie stars who may have stood on the same spot. Activities range from historical to modern day — gunfight shows, stagecoach rides, saloon revues, a gun museum, an antique Reno locomotive exhibit, gold panning, amusement rides, petting farms, magic shows, shops and restaurants.

Admission is a bit steep at $15 for adults, $10 for kids 4 to 11 and free for younger ones, but discount coupons are easy to find at the Tucson Convention and Visitors Bureau, some grocery stores and banks and other locations. Old Tucson Studios' hours are 10 AM to 6 PM daily. Of the two ways to get here from Tucson — west on either Ajo Way or Speedway Boulevard to Kinney Road — the Ajo Way route is easiest to travel. The other route leads to Gates Pass Road through the Tucson Mountains, which offers breathtaking views and scenery but is a narrow cliff-hugging road often referred to as white-knuckle pass. RVers must take Ajo Way to Kinney Road.

Pima Air and Space Museum
6000 E. Valencia Rd. • 574-9658, 574-0462

History and aircraft buffs, along with everyone else, will be enthralled by this indoor and outdoor museum displaying one of the largest collections in the world of vintage and current flying machines. Visitors will see everything from an exact full-scale replica of the Wright flyer, the first machine to fly, to the fastest, the SR-71 Blackbird, a sleek machine that flies at more than 2,000 miles per hour (or Mach three-plus in flying lingo). You'll see just about every type of aircraft flown by the U.S. military branches over the years, plus many types of private and commercial aircraft, including an Air Force One plane used by presidents Kennedy and Johnson. Visitors can go inside many of the larger ones and see navigation equipment, gunnery bays and cargo holds. Throughout the museum, interpretive exhibits inform visitors about the aircraft and about aviation's past, present and future. The museum also has a space artifacts gallery containing early space items such as mock-ups of the X-15 and Mercury space capsule.

It's open daily except Thanksgiving and Christmas from 9 AM to 5 PM, but there's no admittance after 4 PM. Kids younger than 10 get in free, ages 10 to 17 pay $3 and adults pay $6, with discounts for seniors and military personnel. Wheelchair accommodations and tours are available. If you plan to visit both Pima Air and Space Museum and the Titan Missile Museum near Green Valley, ask for a combination deal to save a couple of bucks.

R.W. Webb Winery
13605 E. Benson Hwy., Vail • 762-5777

We're not talking Napa Valley here, but southern Arizona does have a few wineries, and this is the closest one to Tucson. The R.W. Webb Winery is about 20 miles southeast of Tucson, nestled at the base of the Rincon Mountains in Vail, Arizona, where the higher elevations and summer climate are ideally suited to growing French and German varietal wine grapes. At this winery, visitors will find a lovely Spanish mission-style building whose courtyard features an olive tree, fountain, ramada and tables — a pleasant spot to bring a picnic lunch to enjoy with a bottle of award-winning wine. There's a tasting room for sampling distinctive wines rich in Southwestern flavor and character, plus a gift shop featuring regional items. And recently the winery opened a microbrewery, so beers can be sampled as well. Take an informal guided tour to see how modern winemaking technology is combined with Old World traditions to transform Arizona grapes into wines including Cabernet Sauvignon, Johannisberg Riesling and Arizona Gold Sherry.

The winery is open to the public Monday through Saturday from 10 AM to 5 PM and Sunday from noon to 5 PM. The cost of $1 includes sampling and the tour. Take I-10 east to Exit 279 north, then go east along the frontage road.

> **FYI**
>
> Unless otherwise noted, the area code for all phone numbers listed in this guide is 520.

Reid Park Zoo
1100 S. Randolph Wy. • 791-4022

Among the 500 exotic animals visitors will see at the zoo is the strange-looking, long-snouted giant anteater, an animal for which Reid Park Zoo has the most successful captive breeding program in the world. The zoo is also involved in captive breeding programs for several threatened and endangered species including the Siberian tiger, white rhinoceros and ruffed lemur. But you'll see lots more at the zoo: bears, llamas, tortoises, giraffes, zebras, elephants and lions, plus several types of exotic and more common birds, reptiles and fish. In 1997 the zoo added a new South America Habitat Loop with its very popular pair of black jaguars. All the animal residents live in environments approximating their natural habitat. Maybe you'll even be lucky enough to be in town when one of the female residents has just given birth. (The zoo staff is great about announcing these arrivals and will gladly let you know.)

To help visitors learn about the animals, there are roving interpretive stations as well as docents leading impromptu tours. On weekends, the zoo presents family-oriented slide shows and Reid-Me-A-Story for kids. The zoo has a gift shop, handicapped-accessible

---

INSIDERS' TIP

If you want to see the attractions but leave the driving to someone else, several companies offer tours of the area: Old Pueblo Tours at 795-7448, Desert Archaeology Tours at 885-6283, Off the Beaten Path Tours at 529-6090, Great Western Tours at 721-0980, Gray Line at 622-8811, Best of the West Detours at 749-5388, Arizona Custom Tours at 748-1448, Desert Paths Tours at 327-7235, Trail Dust Jeep Tours at 747-0323, and Tucson Tours at 297-2911.

There is a great hands-on museum as well as a telescope and theater at the Flandrau Science Center and Planetarium.

restrooms, snack bars and free parking. All of this takes place in the middle of centrally located Reid Park, where the facilities and fun include walking and biking paths, picnic ramadas, swimming pools, tennis courts, a lake with paddle boats for rent, a formal rose garden and a band shell.

The zoo is open 9 AM to 4 PM daily except Christmas. It opens an hour earlier in summer because the morning is the best time to see the animals being active. Admission prices are $3.50 for those age 15 and older, 75¢ for kids 5 to 14 and free for younger kids. All children younger than 15 must be accompanied by an adult.

Titan Missile Museum
I-19 and Duval Mine Rd., Green Valley
• **574-9658, 625-7736**

This museum is a National Historic Landmark because it displays the only remaining Titan II missile that wasn't dismantled after the Cold War ended and the Strategic Arms Limitation Treaty took effect. For more than 20 years from the mid-'60s to the mid-'80s, the United States had 54 Titan II nuclear warhead missiles at various locations, all ready to be launched from their underground silos on a moment's notice. The site near Green Valley was created as a museum and is operated by the Arizona Aerospace Foundation. Except for the propellants and nuclear warhead, the missile and it's huge launching arena are just as they were years ago. Some of the displays are above ground, while others are 35 feet underground, so walking shoes are required to descend the 55 steps. (People in wheelchairs or those who have difficulty walking can make arrangements to use the elevator.) Underground, visitors will walk through the 200-foot long cableway to the silo containing the Titan II missile and see the launch control center. Above ground, you'll get another look at the missile through the glass covering where the massive 750-ton roll-back silo door is partially open. You'll also see the rocket engine that propelled the 330,000-pound missile from launch to an altitude of 47 miles in just 2½ minutes, plus the reentry vehicle, a favorite subject of photographers (picture-taking is allowed).

Guided tours are offered Wednesday through Sunday from May through October. They take one hour and start on the half-hour, but it's best to call ahead and make a reservation. The museum is open daily (except Thanksgiving and Christmas) from October 1 to April 30 during the hours of 9 AM to 5 PM. During the summer months of May through September, hours are the same but it's closed Mondays and Tuesdays. Kids younger than 10 are free, ages 10 to 17 are $3 and adults are $6 with discounts for seniors and military personnel. Ask about a combination ticket if you also plan to visit Pima Air and Space Museum. To get here, take I-19 south to Exit 69 west, then go past La Canada Drive to the museum's entrance.

Tohono Chul Park
7366 N. Paseo del Norte • 575-8468

Step into this 48-acre oasis and you'll forget that the sights and sounds of the bustling city are a mere stone's throw away. Tohono Chul, meaning "desert corner" in Tohono O'odham, envelops visitors with its solitude and beauty. It's a place to experience and learn about the flora and fauna of the rich Sonoran Desert in a pleasant and attractive environment. Nature trails of .25 and .75 miles, shaded by lush palo verde trees, meander through gardens, pools, exhibits and washes. Rabbits, lizards and Gambel's quail scurry around while hummingbirds and many other varieties of birdlife fly overhead in this "aviary without walls." Plant life native to the desert surrounds the trails, much of it labeled with their common and scientific names, so you'll actually be able to identify these strange-looking growing things. Several gardens on the grounds include the hummingbird garden, designed to attract these small hovering birds, and the ethnobotanical garden, showing crops grown by early Indian settlers and introduced by Spanish and Anglo arrivals. The park's Exhibit House is a 1937 restored adobe building with art and cultural exhibits and a gift shop. Another building, a hacienda-style former residence, provides a lush plant-filled courtyard and patios for relaxing or a meal or snack in the Tea Room and Garden Cafe. At the Greenhouse, you can ask questions about desert plants and gardens and purchase native plants. The park conducts a variety of tours and holds special events like the Wildflower Festival in spring and the Night-blooming Cereus event in early summer. (See The Natural World chapter to read about this unusual flower and other desert flora you'll see at the park.)

Admission to this desert preserve is free, but donations are suggested. Free parking is available. The wheelchair-accessible grounds are open daily from 7 AM to sunset, but call for hours the buildings and other services are open. Paseo del Norte extends north from Ina Road just west of Oracle Road.

Tucson Botanical Gardens
2150 N. Alvernon Wy. • 326-9686

This small but exquisite in-town garden presents a complete primer on the amazing plants that thrive in southern Arizona. Its 5½ acres offer a shady and peaceful spot to view and learn about plants indigenous to the area plus some that normally would grow only in the tropics if not for the environment and care provided by the Tucson Botanical Gardens staff. Walking paths and garden oases are surrounded by cacti of all types, native trees, wildflowers, flowering plants that attract birds and even plants imported from tropical climates. Although the gardens are open year round with plenty to see, there are specific times of the year that certain garden areas thrive. For example, the herb garden is prolific April through June, the wildflower garden blooms March through May, cactus plants show their colorful blooms April through August, and the Native American crops garden has its yield from May through August. The folks at the Botanical Gardens will tell you what's in bloom if you call. They'll also tell you what special events are coming up, such as herb or plant sales held during the year. There's a gift shop with books and other items focusing on southern Arizona's flora and even a picnic area where visitors can bring their own refreshments and dine among the cypress, citrus and roses.

Tucson Botanical Gardens is open daily

from 8:30 AM to 4:30 PM but opens an hour earlier from Memorial Day to Labor Day. Admission is $4 for those 12 and older, $3 for seniors and free for kids younger than 12. Parking is free, but during events it fills up quickly.

University of Arizona Mineral Museum
Cherry Ave. and University Blvd.
• 621-4227

In the basement of the Flandrau Science Center and Planetarium (described previously in this chapter) is the University's Mineral Museum. Rock hounds or other folks interested in gems and minerals will appreciate this small but excellent exhibit of more than 2,000 rock and gem samples, some of which are rare and most of which were excavated in Arizona. Admission to Flandrau will also get you into the Mineral Museum, and hours are the same except the Mineral Museum is not open evenings.

Whipple Observatory
Mt. Hopkins Rd., Amado • 670-5707

It's customary to associate the Smithsonian Institution with our nation's capital, so most folks are surprised to find the Smithsonian linked with Arizona. But that renowned organization does have a facility south of Tucson — the Fred Lawrence Whipple Observatory on the top of Mt. Hopkins in the Santa Rita Mountains. A number of telescopes and meteorological instruments are located on a half-mile ridge at 7,600 feet, while the mountain's summit at 8,550 feet houses the world's fourth-largest multiple-mirror telescope. The latter is a joint project of the Smithsonian and the University of Arizona. At the base of the mountain stands the Whipple Observatory Visitor Center, which also happens to be a lovely area with walking trails, desert flora and picnic tables. From there, it's 10 miles up the mountain to the observatory on a narrow switchback road. Although the road can be traversed, at its end drivers will discover a locked gate, so the only way to visit the observatory is by taking a tour, which the observatory conducts by bus. From mid-March through November, public tours are operated on Monday, Wednesday and Friday starting at the more down-to-earth Visitor Center, which opens at 8:30 AM.

The tour begins at 9 AM with a video presentation, after which the bus travels up the mountain, returning at 3 PM. Tour-takers should be aware of the elevation, which can pose a problem to people with certain health problems. Also, some uphill walking, stair climbing and standing for 15 to 20 minutes are required during the tour. And if you're squeamish about narrow mountain roads with few guard rails, it's best to pass on the tour and learn about the observatory at the Visitor Center. Reservations are a must for the tour and only 25 people can be accommodated. Children younger than 6 are not permitted because of the tour's duration. And even if you have a reservation, it's best to call whenever weather conditions are poor, because it could be canceled. Bring a lunch along because you'll only find a soft-drink machine and drinking water at the top. They do have picnic tables. And don't forget sunglasses, a hat and possibly even a jacket — the summit is 15 to 20 degrees cooler than down below. The tour fee is $7 for adults and $2.50 for kids ages 6 to 12.

Finding the Visitor Center is a bit tricky, but you won't be disappointed, even if your plans don't call for a tour. From I-19 south take Exit 56 (Canoa Road) to the east side frontage road; head south for 3 miles to Elephant Head Road, then take Mt. Hopkins road for 7 miles to the Visitor Center.

You'll find one-of-a-kind museums, cowboy towns and Arizona's only planetarium in Tucson.

Kidstuff

Tucson is full of places where the kids will be tugging you along instead of the other way around. So when they finally get bored with the TV set or video games or pretending to be a Power Ranger or Barbie — or when they're so full of energy you'll do just about anything to tire them out — pack them into the car or hop on a bus and head for one of the great spots described in this chapter. You'll find one-of-a-kind museums, cowboy towns and the state's only planetarium. (And don't forget to check our other chapters — such as Attractions, Festivals and Events, Spectator Sports, Parks and Recreation and Daytrips and Weekend Getaways — for other ideas on fun things to do with kids.) So read on and let the kids have as much fun in Tucson as you are.

Yesterday, Today and Tomorrow

The following attractions transport kids into the past or the future as well as show them the world around them today. They're mostly educational, but that will be our little secret. Your kids will be having too much fun to realize they're actually learning something.

Archaeology For All
1000 E. Ft. Lowell Rd. • 798-1201

Kids think this is heaven — digging around in the ground, getting dirty and not getting punished for it. And all the while, they're learning something — how the Hohokam Indians once lived and how scientists find out about them centuries later. Old Pueblo Archaeology Center, a private nonprofit corporation, runs several programs including this one for kids age 5 and older (yes, that means adults, too). It has a re-created Hohokam Indian ruin complete with pit houses and real prehistoric pottery. Kids learn about how the ancient Indians lived and how to clean and interpret artifacts. (And just like real archaeologists, they don't get to keep what they discover.) Sessions are held on Saturdays September through May and last about 1½ hours, which includes the dig and a craft class. The cost for one session is $10, but Archaeology for All encourages participation in four sessions for $35. Parents can take part or just drop the kids off. Reservations are a must. (The Center also gives tours and hold digs at a real site, Sabino Canyon Ruin, that children age 8 or older can attend.)

Arizona Historical Society
949 E. 2nd St. • 628-5774

Say "we're going to the historical society" to your kids and you'll probably hear a loud moan. But say "let's go see what an old Tucson fort was like," and the response should be an enthusiastic "yeah!" The society, which is actually a museum, is fun for kids as well as adults. Youngsters can climb aboard a restored stagecoach, see a replica of El Presidio, a fort that was Tucson's first settlement, hunker down inside a traditional brush hut, view a Tohono O'odham Indian village, try on serapes and lots more. One favorite is the mine display, complete with a walk-through underground mine tunnel, that shows how early settlers here drilled for gold and silver. It's history with a fun slant, and it's free (donations are appreciated, however).

The Historical Society is smack in the midst of the University area, so street parking can be tough. However, you can park free at the big garage at the northeast corner of Euclid Avenue and 2nd Street, about a block-and-a-half from the society; just be sure to get a parking token from the Historical Society receptionist before you leave the museum to head for your vehicle. Hours are 10 AM to 4 PM Monday through Saturday and noon to 4 PM Sunday.

(See our Attractions chapter for more adult-oriented features of the Historical Society.)

Biosphere 2
Ariz. Hwy. 77 at Mile Marker 96.5
• 825-1289, (800) 828-2462

While adults are more likely to appreciate this majestic undertaking and its majestic setting, kids might think they've taken a time machine into the future or to another planet. The first thing they'll notice is the surreal, futuristic structures. Biosphere 2 is the world's largest glass-enclosed ecological laboratory. It used to be that researchers lived inside for years, so visitors could only tour the outside and peek in. Now visitors can actually go inside and see how the crews lived and how this miniature of our own biosphere, Earth, runs. A special kids' area teaches them about sound, light and other aspects of nature. There's also a restaurant and hotel, shops and hourly guided tours. It's wheelchair accessible and strollers are available to rent for $3.

Admission is fairly steep: $12.95 for adults, $6 for kids 6 to 17, $10.95 for seniors and $9.95 for Arizona residents. Kids younger than 6 are admitted free. You can usually get discount coupons at lots of local places or from the Tucson Visitors Bureau. It's about 45 minutes north of downtown Tucson on Oracle Road and open daily from 9 AM to 5 PM. (See our Attractions chapter for more information about Biosphere.)

Flandrau Science Center and Planetarium
Cherry Ave. and University Blvd.
• 621-7827, 621-4515

This may be the closest a kid will ever get to flying through outer space or touching a meteorite that actually fell in Arizona. Flandrau is the only planetarium in the state, but it goes far beyond a look at the planets. Kids can enter a cave-like display with asteroids spinning all around, experience simulated flights in space, examine moon rocks and earth minerals, see weird hologram images, have fun learning the laws of nature through hands-on exhibits, examine everyday things through huge microscopes and see a panoramic special-effects IMAX-like show in the Star Theater. They can take home science kits, posters, books and learning toys from the science store. Or they can look for planets, galaxies and star clusters in the observatory's 16-inch telescope, which is open year round on clear Wednesday through Saturday nights for free. And if you're here for an extended stay or live in Tucson, the annual family pass of $45 for unlimited visits may be the best value in town.

Flandrau is open weekdays from 9 AM to 5 PM and weekends from 1 to 5 PM. Evening hours are 7 to 9 PM Wednesday and Thursday and 7 PM to midnight Friday and Saturday. Exhibit admission prices are $3 for adults and $2 for children 13 and younger. It's $4 to $6 for the Star Theater show, but that includes your admission to Flandrau. Parking can be tough here in the middle of the University, especially during evening athletic events, so call for parking options. Insiders' tip: Try the metered parking lot directly south across University Boulevard, but take lots of quarters.

> **FYI**
> Unless otherwise noted, the area code for all phone numbers listed in this guide is 520.

Old Pueblo Trolley
4th Ave. and 8th St. • 792-1802

Take the kids for a ride on a piece of the past, the Old Pueblo Trolley, which you can catch right outside the University main gate on University Boulevard on weekends. It's a slice of the old days in Tucson and just plain fun. Recently resurrected after a 63-year hiatus, the electric street car clangs along University Boulevard and 4th Avenue. The 1-mile ride takes about 25 minutes one way, and you can get off or on along the route. Ride it to the other end, where 4th Avenue intersects 8th Street, and you can visit the trolley car barn and museum. One-way fares are $1 for adults, 50¢ for kids 6 to 12 and seniors and free for kids younger than 6. Or you can get all-day fares for a mere $2.50 (adult) and $1.25 (child) and stop and shop and sightsee all over this fascinating area. It operates Friday evenings from 6 to 10 PM, Saturdays from noon to midnight and Sundays from noon to 6 PM.

Old Tucson Studios
201 S. Kinney Rd. • 883-0100

Little bronco busters (and big ones, too) will be thrilled by the sights and sounds at one of Arizona's most popular and famous attrac-

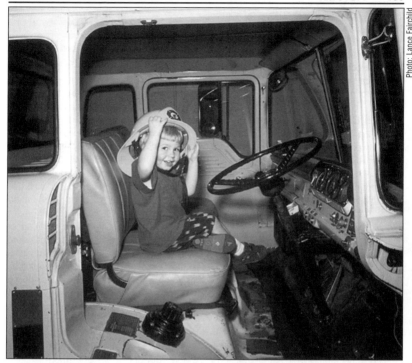

Some of the exhibits at the Tucson Children's Museum are more than life-size.

tions. It's like spending a day in an old frontier town. Kids can see spectacular stunts, trick riding and gunfights (all for pretend, of course), play a part in a saloon musical or a Western film shoot, hear old Southwestern lore or dig for treasure and pan for gold. They also can ride a stagecoach, a carnival ride or a pony.

Old Tucson Studios started out in 1939 as a movie set and later was turned into a theme attraction. It's been the site for hundreds of Western movies and TV shows, and you may even see one being filmed while you're there. This re-creation of a Western town was devastated by fire a few years ago but has been completely rebuilt. There are shops, rides, restaurants, a petting farm and saloons along with all the trappings of the Old West. It opens at 10 AM daily and goes on into the night. Gate admission is $15 for adults, just less than $10 for kids 4 to 11 and free for children younger than three. Discount coupons are easy to find around town at the Visitors Bureau and some banks and grocery stores. (See our Attractions chapter for more information.)

Pima Air and Space Museum
6000 E. Valencia Rd. • 574-0462

What kid isn't enraptured by flying machines? Within Pima Air and Space Museum's 100,000-square-foot building and 300 acres of surrounding land, there are more than 200 examples of nearly every type of flying machine ever invented. There's a perfect replica of the very first airplane, the Wright flyer, a SR-71 Blackbird that flies at Mach three-plus and set the speed record, presidential airplanes, World War bombers, helicopters and ultralights. (The museum is fortunate to be across the street from the airplane graveyard at Davis-Monthan Air Force Base, so it can get unusual planes that are retired there.) The history of aviation hangs over your head and is documented along the walls, and one of the galleries displays artifacts and exhibits about outer space.

Hours are 9 AM to 5 PM daily, and admissions are $6 for adults, $5 for seniors, $3 for kids 10 to 17 and free for younger children. This is a great place for grandparents to take the grandkids and recount their own stories of the old days of aviation. (See our Attractions chapter for more information.)

Tucson Children's Museum
200 S. 6th Ave. • 792-9985

The wonders of the world around us are captured exquisitely at this museum. It's chock-full of hands-on exhibits that transform learning into fun. Kids scamper from one interactive exhibit to another, and their delight is obvious. In the bubble factory, they can climb into a 5-foot cylindrical soap bubble. Do your kids dig dinosaurs? Here they can visit Trash Assortus Rex, who stands 13 feet tall and is the centerpiece of a board game with a recycling theme. In the fire department display, kids get to see all the equipment and even try on real helmets, rain gear and other protective stuff worn by friendly fire fighters. Another display captures the magic of how electricity works.

Exhibits throughout the museum's 16,000 square feet cover everything from nature to nutrition and from water safety to weather broadcasting. The bug exhibit offers both live and animated creepy critters. And each month there's a special event, like the Earth Day celebration, the Halloween enchanted castle and the cultural showcase where kids can learn to toss a Vaquero (cowboy) rope, roll a tortilla, weave a basket, perform a folklorico dance or make an Indian drum. It's all here at the state's only museum dedicated to children in a building that itself is a museum — the former Carnegie Library, built almost a century ago. You can even hold your child's birthday party at the museum (starting at $4.50 per person). Admission is $3 for kids younger than 16, $5 for adults and $4 for seniors, with summer "monsoon" specials and Sunday family specials. Hours are 9:30 AM to 5 PM Tuesday through Friday, 10 AM to 5 PM Saturday and noon to 5 PM Sunday. It's closed on Mondays. Kids younger than 16 must be accompanied by an adult.

Creatures, Critters and Cacti

Kids are enthralled with things that crawl, growl, bite and sting, so here are some great places where they can see the wildlife without mom or dad worrying about administering first aid.

Arizona-Sonora Desert Museum
2021 N. Kinney Rd. • 883-1380

As we've said often in this book, if there's only one place you have time to visit, this probably should be it. But don't be fooled by the name "museum" — actually it's a unique combination of zoo and natural museum that's truly world-class. Kids will be enthralled by just about everything they see — reptiles, desert insects such as scorpions and tarantulas, and wild cats such as ocelots and bobcats. The beaver and otter pond is fun to watch from above but even more exciting from below, where observers can see all the underwater antics of these furry swimmers. There's also prairie dog town, big horn sheep climbing around their mountain caves and huge walk-in aviaries, including one devoted exclusively to hummingbirds. The Desert Museum folks have done a fabulous job of providing very natural settings for all the wildlife and flora. And the volunteer docents conduct hands-on shows throughout the museum. Kids will also like the cafeteria-style restaurant, and the gift shop has lots of books and learning tools on the desert life presented at the museum. Strollers are available to rent for $3, so you can keep the little ones comfy and safe. It's hot here in summer, so be prepared or plan your visit for early in the day or the evening or go during Summer Saturday Nights when special activities are scheduled. It's open every day, and admission is $1.75 for kids 6 to 12, free for younger ones and $8.95 for adults. It's worth every penny. (See our Attractions chapter for more information about this museum.)

www.insiders.com
See this and many other Insiders' Guide® destinations online — in their entirety.
Visit us today!

Reid Park Zoo
1100 S. Randolph Wy. • 791-4022

Watching giant polar bears eating the animal version of a popsicle — a fishsicle — is just one of the treats in store for kids visiting the zoo. Though small, this well-designed zoo offers everything from long-nosed giant anteaters to lions, tigers and rhinos — Oh my! There's also jaguar, pygmy hippos, elephants, zebras, giraffes and all manner of birds in aviaries. The zoo opened a South American section in 1997 with bears, llamas, tapirs and the carnivorous piranha, plus a lush new aviary. Kids love baby animals, so be sure to ask what's been born recently. All of the 500 or so animals here live in modern, naturalistic settings, but the snack bar and gift shop are reserved for their human guests. The zoo sits in the middle of Reid Park, so it's a great place to have a picnic, ride a bike or visit the daffy ducks in the duck pond before or after you talk to the animals. If you go in the summer, go early in the day when animals are active. It's open daily from 8 or 9 AM to 4 PM. Parking is free, which also happens to be the admission price for children younger than 5. The older crowd has to pay a modest fee — 75¢ for kids up to 14, $3.50 for adults and $2.50 for seniors. All children younger than 15 must be accompanied by an adult. (See our Attractions chapter for more information.)

Get a Little Culture

Introducing kids to a little culture may not be tops on their list of things to do, but it works better if the attraction is specifically geared to youngsters. So in this section we present culture your kids might actually enjoy plus places where the little hams you have at home can go to be real actors.

Arizona Youth Theater
5671 E. Speedway Blvd. • 546-9805

So you have a budding Lawrence Olivier or Carol Channing in the house? Let them audition for one of the plays put on by kids at this theater — new talent is always welcome. Young performers stage a variety of classics and stories such as *Pippi Longstockings*, *Beauty and the Beast* and *Jungle Book*. Each is performed with a unique twist that brings smiles to even the youngest children. There are also regular workshops on a variety of stage-related topics for kids. Performances are held Friday evenings and Saturday mornings and afternoons (matinees) with ticket prices of $6 for adults and $4 for kids.

The Players
7000 E. Tanque Verde Rd. • 751-6419

The Players is an authentic theater experience for kids who want to perform and learn other staging skills. Plus it's good theater for kids by kids four times a year. The Players operates out of the Actors Theatre, but it's purely for and by kids age 5 to 16 who sign up for a session (a spring, two in summer and a fall) at $100 a month to learn all about performing in and preparing for a major production. All the hard work culminates in a play or musical performed totally by the kids that's open to the public and staged at the Actors Theatre. Past performances have included *Little Women*, *Wizard of Oz*, *Annie* and *The Secret Garden*. The theater seats 200, and it's usually standing room only, since tickets are a bargain at $3 for children and $6 for adults.

Third Street Kids
166 W. Alameda St. • 622-4100

Although focusing on kids with disabilities, this nonprofit performing arts group welcomes all children. Funded by grants and various charities, it offers youngsters through about age 16, including those with disabilities, the chance to learn and perform dance, music, drama, opera and improvisations. In addition to classes, usually held after school during the school year, the organization has two performing components. One is the ensemble company made up of "regulars" who perform at various private functions and have traveled to Australia, performed at the White House and appeared in a movie filmed in Tucson. The other component is open to kids who audition for Third Street Kids' three public performances a year, which are sometimes original plays and other times popular ones: opera, drama, comedy or musical. The community plays are usually performed in December, February and April at various venues rented by the organization and usually held on weekends running for about two weeks each. Tickets typically are $5 for kids to age 12 and $8 for adults. Watch the newspapers for information on where and when a Third Street Kids play is appearing, or call the organization. It provides a great opportunity for kids to learn skills in the arts and to perform.

Tucson Symphony Orchestra
Tucson Center for the Performing Arts, 408 S. 6th Ave. • 882-8585

Most kids aren't really into classical music, but here's a way they'll be sure to like it. And even though it's just for kids, parents will love the music and the price — it's free. The Tucson Symphony Orchestra offers six informal, interactive concerts designed to introduce quality classical music to children ages 4 to 12. Each concert highlights an ensemble of the orchestra in a presentation combining humor, storytelling, demonstrations and audience participation. They're held at the Tucson Center for the Performing Arts on the first Saturday of the month beginning in October and going through March. Call for the exact dates and times.

Munchkins in Motion

You certainly don't need us to tell you that kids love to move. From skating to tumbling, Tucson's got them covered.

Iceoplex
7883 E. Rosewood St. • 290-8800

It's hard enough to find water in Tucson, but ice?! Ice-skating in the desert may seem like an oxymoron, but it exists at Iceoplex (indoors, of course). And if you want to be somewhere in Tucson that's actually cool in summer, take the kids to Iceoplex and join in the fun. Iceoplex is open year round and has both public skating hours and lots of special things going on. The public sessions are Monday through Friday 9:30 to 11:30 AM and 1:30 to 5 PM; Saturday and Sunday afternoons from 1 to 4 PM; Friday and Saturday nights from 7:30 to 10:15 PM; and Saturday moonlight skating from 10:30 PM to 12:30 AM. Skate rentals are $5.50 for anyone younger than 12 and $6.50 for those who are older. Mommy and Me classes are offered for toddlers starting around age 2 and their moms. For the older kids, there's broomball, figure skating and hockey leagues. Skating school sessions, usually lasting four weeks, are offered for all ages beginning as young as 2.

J.W. Tumbles
7921 N. Oracle Rd. • 544-8987

Gymnastics, tumbling and sports skills are some of kids' favorite things, and they're all available at J.W. Tumbles. This isn't a free-for-all place but a structured way for kids to develop skills, build confidence and learn teamwork while having fun (and getting rid of some excess energy). Kids must commit to eight weekly sessions at a cost of $100 per month. Classes are structured by age and are kept to less than 12 kids. Toddlers as young as four months can join in (parents, of course, must accompany them). You can even throw a birthday party here.

Randolph Skatepark
200 S. Alvernon Wy. • 791-4873

Twisting and high-flying bodies along with scrapes and bangs of skateboards are what you'll see and hear at this new facility opened by the City of Tucson right behind the Tucson Parks and Recreation Department's Randolph Center. Kids — mostly teens — now have a 16,000-square-foot asphalt-paved area to call their own and strut their skateboarding skills. It includes two Bauer boxes, which for the uninitiated are platforms with ramps leading up to them and a rail along the back, one flat-top pyramid, two 6-foot quarter pipes (tall ramps used for launching maneuvers) and two grind rails. Skateboarding isn't permitted in other city areas the kids seem to gravitate to, such as downtown sidewalks and the Tucson Convention Center pavement, so this is a safe and legal alternative. In-line skating is also popular here. It's free, open daily (except holidays) from 1 PM to sundown and patrolled by security.

Skate Country East
7980 E. 22nd St. • 298-4409

Kids who like loud music and light shows accompanying their roller-skating will love Skate Country. But it's not just for kids — entire families can have a blast here. For starters, skate rentals are one price for any age: $1.50 for speed skates and $3 for in-line skates. The rink, which has good supervision, is open daily year round, but skating hours and admission prices vary. Monday through Thursday from 4 to 6 PM is called Cheap Skates because it's only $2.50. But if the whole clan is going, Sunday Family Night may be the best deal — a family of up to six pays only $9 to skate from 6 to 9 PM (additional members are $4 each). Saturday mornings are reserved for "tiny tots" when kids younger than 12 skate from 10 AM to noon for $3. Other hours the rink is open to the public are Fridays from 2 to 5 PM and 7 to 10 PM, Saturdays from 1 to 4 PM, 3 to 6 PM and 7 to 10 PM, and Sundays from 3 to 6 PM. Prices for these sessions range from $3.75 to $4.50. There's also an adult skate Thursday night from 8 to 10 PM for anyone age 18 or older for $3.50. Tornado table soccer and snacks are available.

Skate Country North
2700 N. Stone Ave. • 622-6650

This roller-skating rink is only open to the public on weekends but has a special Saturday morning session for kids age 10 and younger. Other times, it's open skating for all ages — Friday evening 7 to 10 PM, Saturday 1 to 10 PM and Sunday 1 to 8 PM. Admission ranges from $2.50 to $4.50 with rentals at $1.75. (Only roller skates are available to rent, but you can bring in-line skates.) On Friday nights, parents skate free if accompanied by a paying child. Skate Country North also has video games and a snack bar.

Just Add Water

Water parks are great finds in Tucson's desert and in summer's heat, when the whole family needs to find a cool place.

Breakers Water Park
8555 W. Tangerine Rd. • 682-2530

Kids can actually catch a wave in Tucson, but only at Breakers Water Park, which boasts one of the largest wave pools in the world. Unlike almost everything else in Tucson, however, the water parks are summer season attractions, so Breakers is only open late May through Labor Day. But that's precisely the time a splash in the cool water is most welcome. The 20-acre park in the far northwest also has five water slides and a toddler pool, so it's fun for kids of all ages. Don't forget the waterproof sunscreen.

It's open summer Saturdays and Sundays from 10 AM to 6 PM. Daily admission is $10 for adults, $8 for kids 4 to 12 and free for younger children. After 3 PM, admission is $6. No outside food or beverages can be brought into the park.

Justin's Water World
3551 S. San Joaquin Rd. • 883-8340

Justin's may not have the wave action Breakers does, but there's plenty for the kids to dive into, including nine pools and seven giant

Tuffy and friends do the Chicken Dance at a baseball game.

slides. The pirate's cove is especially for young swashbucklers (even babies have a pool here), while older ones can handle the blue twisters twin racing slides. There's also inner tubing and a snack bar. But the best part for moms and dads, beside the adult-only pool, might just be the shade. There are plenty of mature trees and ramadas for comfort while watching the kids get all wet. It's only open in the summer, from late May through Labor Day and only Friday through Sunday from 10 AM to 5 PM. Admission is free for kids 5 and younger and seniors. It's $8.95 for all others but only $6 if you get there after 2 PM. Justin's borders Tucson Mountain Park on the west side of the Tucson Mountains and is not too far from other great attractions like the Desert Museum and Old Tucson Studios.

Just Plain Fun

These are our picks for places kids will love while they get to pretend to be race car drivers, baseball champs, golf pros or even fairy-tale characters.

Discovery Zone Funcenter
6238 E. Broadway Blvd. • 748-9190

Young kids love this place where they can crawl around a maze of tubes, tunnels, ball bins and bungee rooms. A top-notch indoor playground, the center has lots of stuff to keep kids busy and having fun — places to hide, slide and climb. There are special activities for kids younger than 3. Parents might want to join in with the very little ones, so Discovery Zone provides knee pads. It's open 11 AM to 8 PM Monday through Thursday, 10 AM to 9 PM Friday and Saturday and 11 AM to 7 PM Sunday. Adults can get in for free, but kids are $6 from age 3 to 12 and $4 for those younger than 3. No socks — no service, so make sure your kids cover their tootsies.

> **FYI**
> Unless otherwise noted, the area code for all phone numbers listed in this guide is 520.

Funtastiks
221 E. Wetmore Rd. • 888-4653

If your kids are way too full of energy, give them a couple of hours here and you might tire them out, at least momentarily. The stuff to keep kids entertained and exercised runs the gamut. In addition to Tucson's largest kiddie arcade, there are two 18-hole miniature golf courses, bumper boats, single- and double-seat go-carts, bungee trampolines, rookie go-carts, Orbitron (a ride that spins riders around), batting cages and a video arcade. These attractions usually cater to older kids and teens, but Funtastiks has lots of stuff geared to the littler ones — baby bumper boats, kiddie cars and a small roller coaster to name a few.

Funtastiks opens daily at 10 AM, but some activities, including go-carts, Orbitron and bumper boats, don't open until 1 PM. The park is open late, until 11 PM Sunday through Thursday and until midnight Friday and Saturday. The rates for each activity vary, but many are free for kids 5 and younger. Funtastiks is located across the street from Tucson Mall and is surrounded by shopping and places to eat. It's also less than a half-block from a Sun Tran bus transit center that is a major transfer point with an information booth, covered waiting area and restrooms.

Golf 'N Stuff
6503 E. Tanque Verde Rd. • 296-2366

This is a lot like Funtastiks (see our previous entry) but on the far Eastside of town. In Little Indy, kids can pretend to be Mario Andretti and maneuver their own miniature racecar along a twisting track. Or they can bump around in bumper cars or bumper boats, bat a thousand in the batting cages, aim for a hole-in-one on the miniature golf courses or test their skills in the huge video arcade. Some of the attractions have minimum age requirements, so you might want to call ahead instead of seeing the look of disap-

---

INSIDERS' TIP

Grandpa and grandma can not only have fun taking kids to Tucson's attractions, but also get a senior discount at most places. And kids younger than a certain age (often 5) get into many places for free.

pointment on little faces once you're there. It opens daily at 10 AM and closes at 10 PM Sunday through Thursday and 1 AM Friday and Saturday, though outside activities like golf and rides close an hour earlier. Prices are per activity.

Malibu Grand Prix Family Entertainment Center
4002 E. 22nd St. • 790-0951

Budding Mario Andrettis, or anyone else for that matter, will be able to prove their prowess at this go-cart track in a close-in city location. For about $1.40 to $2.85 per lap, kids can race around the .5-mile outdoor track in cars their size, while adults maneuver .75-scale racecars. Kids have to be 4 feet 6 inches tall to drive their own car, or they'll need to go along with an adult driver ("adults" need to be at least 16 and have a valid driver's license). If you need to take a break from the racing, Malibu has 60 video games, for which players buy tokens, and a concession stand. It's open Wednesday through Sunday year round from 10 AM (noon on Fridays) until 10 PM or later.

Valley of the Moon
2544 E. Allen Rd. • 323-1331

The spirit of childhood was embodied by one man in this little hidden wonder. Long ago, he created rock cliffs, caves, pools and miniature gardens among the desert flora on his piece of land and called it Valley of the Moon. Then he added fantasy fairy tours and bunnyland theater, with trained rabbits. Playing the mysterious mountain gnome, he gave tours, told stories and performed magic shows that captivated his young audiences. All of this happiness he gave away for free. Now operated as a nonprofit organization, the Valley of the Moon continues the tradition of entertainment with fantasy fairy tours and special events like the Halloween haunted ruins. Hours vary, and donations are welcomed. Call to find out when activities and events are scheduled. Valley of the Moon also books parties.

Pick a Park

Parks aren't just for playing Frisbee or flying kites. Tucson has two dozen parks with tons of fun things for kids — and parents — to do. Six of the parks have swimming pools, so put on those swimsuits and jump in; they're open year round but especially inviting in the heat of summer. Swing, jump, climb and slide on the jungle gym equipment. Hit tennis balls, toss footballs or play softball. Have a family picnic under a ramada. It's all free, except for a nominal charge to swim — 25¢ daily for those younger than 17 and $1 for adults. (For a complete list of parks and what they offer, see the Parks and Recreation chapter.)

The Sporting Life

What kid doesn't like watching a bunch of grown-ups don uniforms and protective gear and run, toss, kick and slam footballs, baseballs, soccer balls, basketballs or hockey pucks around a playing field? There's plenty of opportunity for kids to both watch a sport and be a sport around Tucson.

What little baseball or softball player wouldn't jump at the chance to see a real pro baseball team? Well, several of them do their spring training right here in Tucson, so it's a great opportunity for kids and adults to get a preview of the year's up-and-coming players. The spring training season takes place in February and March, but tickets can be tough to get, so plan ahead. See the Spectator Sports chapter for details on spring training baseball.

The University of Arizona has teams in men's basketball, women's softball, baseball, football and hockey, so there's likely to be some sort of college game going on any time of the year. See the Spectator Sports chapter for all the details or call the University, 621-2287, to see who's playing when.

Kids also love watching a rodeo and Tucson has one of the best in the West — La Fiesta de Los Vaqueros, held the last weekend in February. It's a several-day event complete with a major parade that kids will love, too. See the Festivals and Events chapter for more information about the rodeo.

For kids who want to get in on the action, Tucson parks offer junior golf clinics in May and June, then kids have unlimited free golf at city courses after completing the clinic. Call the city's Parks and Recreation Department, 791-4837, or see the Golf chapter for more details. Randolph Park has junior tennis on Saturdays for kids ages 5 to 17 that includes instruction and practice time on the courts. You must register in person, but you can get information from the Parks and Recreation number listed previously. And several Tucson parks have a Saturday night teen basketball league, also called "late night hoops," for 13- to 19-year-olds (791-4870).

Pima County Parks and Recreation, 740-2690, offers lots of sports and classes for kids — swimming, BMX bicycle racing, gymnastics, Tae Kwan Do, track, golf and soccer, plus TOTS recreation for the young ones. They're held at various times of the year and at locations around the county.

Entertaining Eats

If your kids are typical, they'd rather do anything (except homework, maybe) than take time out of their busy schedules to eat. So parents are always on the lookout for places kids like to go that also happen to serve food. All the major fast-food chains are scattered around the metro area. Here are a few other fun places that might be exciting enough to lure the kids away from TV, softball or video games long enough to chow down.

Chuck E Cheese's
6130 E. Speedway Blvd. • 745-8800

The pizza, burger and salad menu isn't really the main draw here, it's the fun and games. There's something for kids of all ages. Young ones love crawling through the tubes (fondly called "human habitrails" by moms and dads used to having pet gerbils in the house), trying to stay atop the bronco busting wooden horse and watching Chuck E Cheese in the mechanical stage show. Older ones gravitate toward the Skeetball or video games. Kids can win prizes while parents can get package deals covering food and tokens (or bags of gold as they're known here). Chuck E Cheese's is open daily during afternoon and evening hours.

Little Anthony's Diner
7010 E. Broadway Blvd. • 296-0456

We guarantee moms and dads will like this place as much if not more than the kids do. It'll take you back decades to the real diners that are almost extinct now, complete with oldies on the jukebox and black-and-white checkered floors. It's got a great atmosphere with happy servers who sing and dance and give a great rendition of "Happy Birthday" to those celebrating. At any moment someone will spring up from a booth and swing to the oldies on the dance floor. There's a video room with pinball machines, and outside you'll usually find at least one beautifully preserved auto from the '50s plus a few little wooden animals for the kids to ride. The food choices are many and reminiscent of yesteryear's diners — from burgers, salads and pizzas to old-time blue plate specials such as turkey, meat loaf and fried chicken. The kids menu has burgers, peanut butter and jelly sandwiches, corn dogs (on a stick) and cheese sticks (like a stick). Little Anthony's is open daily from 11 AM to 11 PM and early on weekends for breakfast. This busy and popular spot is behind the Gaslight Theatre.

Trail Dust Town
6541 E. Tanque Verde Rd. • 296-4551

This isn't just one restaurant but several places to chow down and shop while the kids have fun. It's a lovely little plaza of shops and restaurants in authentic Old West replica buildings surrounding a trellised courtyard. It's pleasant to just stroll around, but the kids are more likely to want to ride the perimeter scale model of a real train, go panning for gold, see the gunfight shows or ride the antique restored carousel. There's an ice cream and candy shop, a general store with all kinds of old-fashioned trinkets and goodies, a cowboy steak restaurant (Pinnacle Peak) and another restaurant with pleasant outdoor seating (Dakota Cafe). As the name Trail Dust Town implies, the theme is Western but there's no dust here — just pretty walkways, real shade trees and benches for watching the goings on or the kids. Get the details on the eating establishments in the Restaurants chapter, though the kids will probably be just as happy with the ice cream and candy shops.

Toys and Other Necessities

Arizona Trains
2420 N. Treat Ave. • 327-4000

As its name implies, this store sells everything for and about model trains. It's located between Tucson Boulevard and Country Club Road north of Grant Road.

Baby's Away
No address • 615-9754

This business is more for moms and dads than babies, since it rents all kinds of things parents might find a need for, especially when vacationing. If you're looking for a stroller, high chair, play pen, crib, car seat or even a tub of toys while you and baby are away from home, here's where to call. There's no retail shop, but Baby's Away delivers just about anything to help take care of baby. Strollers, for example, are $4 a day while a full-size crib including linens is $6. If you're traveling with a baby, keep this number handy.

Boomers Childrens Boutique
El Con Mall, 3601 E. Broadway Blvd. • 323-2441

Among all the stores in the mall is this boutique that sells designer clothes and accessories for girls (sizes 0 to 16) and boys (sizes 0 to 3).

Buffalo Kids
1702 E. Prince Rd. • 881-8438

Patterned after the successful Buffalo Exchange for adults, the kids' version is a great place for quality used clothing, plus toys, athletic equipment and some furniture. Buffalo Kids buys, sells and trades.

Carter's for Kids
Foothills Mall, Ina Rd. and La Cholla Blvd. • 529-6442

This is an outlet store for all the famous Carter's kids clothes that have been outfitting youngsters for generations.

The Gymboree Store
Tucson Mall, 4500 N. Oracle Rd. • 293-2119

Despite its name (which implies athletic stuff), this is a private label clothing store for kids from birth to age 7. It sells shoes, accessories and toys. The clothing is mostly casual, mostly cotton and always bright and colorful.

Minds in Motion
3400 E. Speedway Blvd. • 795-0676

Meant to keep young minds working, the store sells books, games and educational materials for kids from birth to age 10 or so and for teachers. Minds in Motion has a large selection of books in Spanish and multicultural books.

Mrs. Tiggy Winkle's
4811 E. Grant Rd. • 326-0188

An unusual name signifies an unusual store, and that's what it is. You'll find baby toys, books, games, some clothing and quirky things (such as creepy critters and ghoulish eyes) that adults like as much as kids do.

Santa Fe Kids
Tucson Mall, 4500 N. Oracle Rd. • 293-4050

Little cowboys and cowgirls will like this store that carries Western and Southwestern stuff for kids — such as clothes, rocks, leather pouches, boots and belts, and bows and arrows.

Whiz Kids Books and Toys
1737 E. Prince Rd. • 795-3729

It isn't necessary to be a whiz kid to find something great here — recreational as well as educational games, books and toys fill the shelves.

Yikes Toys
306 E. Congress St. • 622-8807

This downtown shop, like many of the shops downtown, is unusual. There are no typical toys such as dolls, trains and video games; instead, they're best described as "old-fashioned" toys. You'll find things like plastic lizards, yo-yos, marbles, tops, scary stuff that's great for Halloween and books. It's a pleasant departure from high-tech and Barbie.

INSIDERS' TIP

Many attractions geared to kids require that an adult accompany any child younger than a certain age, often 15.

Come spring, fall and winter, outdoor fests abound.

Festivals and Events

With Tucson's 350 days of sunshine each year, it's no wonder the area hosts so many outdoor music and cultural events. Needless to say the 110 degree heat of summer and monsoon rains of July and August tend to keep events inside during the summer. But come spring, fall and winter, outdoor fests abound. The warm days and cool nights of these seasons make being outdoors a comfortable pleasure.

Annual events and festivals reflect Tucson's rich history and ethnic diversity. The Old Pueblo is where Spanish, Mexican, American Indian and rowdy frontier heritages meet the contemporary New West lifestyle — and that exciting blend of contrasts means a mix of fun.

If it's all-day music festivals you like, you'll be able to enjoy blues, folk, mariachi, pops orchestras, bluegrass fiddle contests and singing cowboys. You can catch the huge Rodeo parade or the festive St. Patrick's Day parade; a PGA golf tournament or a college bowl game; a world-class marathon or a 111-mile bike race.

Casual clothing is acceptable almost everywhere, with shorts and T-shirts the "official" dress for all outdoor events and sunscreen and water necessary accessories.

The events and festivals we present here are tried and true favorites of Tucson's residents. There are often several activities going on in the area in a single weekend, so we suggest you consult local newspapers for a complete list of the fairs, parades, exhibits and concerts offered during your stay in the city. Also check other chapters of this book, including Golf, Bicycling and Arts and Culture, for tournaments, races and performances that Tucsonans enjoy watching and participating in.

January

Jewish Film Festival
Jewish Community Center, 3800 N. River Rd. • 299-3000
Gallagher Theater, UA Student Union • 621-3192

This yearly festival, which runs from the end of December to the end of January, features films by Jewish directors, producers and writers. A wide assortment of films is shown at both venues. Often the director or subject of the film will attend. For the 1997-'98 festival, Al Hirschfield attended a special showing of the film about his life, *The Line King*. Pre- and post-film receptions were held. Other films featured were *Tell the Truth and Run* and *Can Memory Be Dissolved in Evian Water?* Tickets run $4 to $5 depending on the time of the showing (discounts are available for seniors and students). Tickets to special showings may be higher.

Parking at the JCC is easy in the front lot; parking at the Gallagher can be found at the pay lot behind the Student Union on 2nd street for about $3.

Southern Arizona Square/Round Dance and Clogging Festival
Tucson Convention Center, 260 S. Church St. • 885-5032

With thousands of participants and spectators from across the nation, this three-day celebration, held over a weekend late in the month, is one of Tucson's largest gatherings. The event offers various levels of square and round dancing as well as clog-

Annual Quilter's Guild Show
**Tucson Convention Center,
260 S. Church St. • 690-0229**

The Tucson Quilter's Guild sponsors this annual event that features more than 200 quilts, quilted garments, quilting demonstrations, antique displays, product vendors and even a raffle. Visitors to this two-day event in the middle of the month also have an opportunity to vote for the best quilt of the show, which then receives the "Viewer's Choice" award. Admission is $3 per day.

Arizona Contemporary Dance Festival
Pima Community College Center for the Arts, 2202 W. Anklam Rd. • 884-6988

This annual celebration of dance showcases Arizona dancers and choreographers from Tucson and Phoenix. The three-day event takes place at the end of the month and is cosponsored by Pima Community College and Southwest Dance. Tickets range from $7 to $15, while festival passes from $15 to $20 cover the entire weekend event.

Senior Sports Classic
Armory Senior Center, 220 S. 5th Ave. • 791-4865

Better known as the Senior Olympics, this annual event, held the last weekend of the month, is considered one of the largest of its type nationwide. Seniors ranging in age from 50 to more than 100 compete for gold, silver and bronze medals in 18 different sporting categories, including track and field, cycling, swimming and other sports. Most events take place at Tucson Parks and Recreation locations, but additional locations are also used, so call to find out where your favorite sport is being played or how to compete. Admission is free for spectators. (See the Spectator Sports chapter.)

February

Tucson Gem and Mineral Show
Various locations downtown • 322-5773

The Tucson Gem and Mineral Show is the largest event of its kind in the world. Dealers and exhibitors from all over come to Tucson the first two weeks of February to display their collections of minerals, gems, jewelry and fossils. Even leading universities and museums exhibit their finest specimens. The event offers educational activities and lectures by experts ranging from collecting to photography. Admission is $5.50 per day. Though the show lasts two weeks, only the last week is open to the public.

Climb "A" Mountain
Mission Rd. • 321-7989

The second weekend of February, teams or individuals make the 4-mile trek up "A" mountain (just west of downtown) for pledges to raise money for the Arizona chapter of the American Cancer Society. Bus rides return participants to El Presidio Park downtown for a festive celebration.

Tucson Chrysler Golf Classic
Omni National Golf Resort, 2727 W. Club Dr. • 571-0400

This PGA tournament offers a week of golf

> **FYI**
> Unless otherwise noted, the area code for all phone numbers listed in this guide is 520.

INSIDERS' TIP

If you just can't get enough entertainment, check out "Downtown Saturday Night" held year round the first and third Saturday of the month from 7 to 10 PM. The historic downtown arts district along Congress Street comes alive with mimes, vendors, musicians, magic shows and stage shows at the main bus station parking lot. Cafes, shops, galleries and restaurants stay open along Congress and around the corner on 4th Avenue.

FESTIVALS AND EVENTS • 145

Smiles are contagious at Tucson's outdoor festivals.

in the middle of the month from the world's best pro golfers to benefit a number of local youth athletic organizations. The event draws some 30,000 people per day, national television coverage and past champions such as Johnny Miller, Arnold Palmer, Jack Nicklaus, Lee Trevino and Miller Barber. Admission is $15 a day or $50 for the week. You may purchase tickets at the gate, from Dillard's department stores' ticket outlets, (800) 638-4253, or from the previously listed number. Parking is free.

If you're not satisfied just being a spectator, a Pro Am is held on the third day of the classic. One pro golfer is teamed with four amateurs. It costs $5,000 to play.

Old-Time Fiddle Contest
Reid Park, 22nd St. and Country Club Rd.
• 791-4079

In its second decade, this all-day free event is the place to be if you are a lover of bluegrass fiddle music. The mid-month competition offers cash prizes in a variety of age categories and draws players from around the country.

La Fiesta de los Vaqueros (Tucson Rodeo)
Tucson Rodeo Grounds, 4823 S. 6th Ave.
• 624-1116

Ride-em cowboy! Ranked 10th nationwide, this Professional Rodeo Cowboys Association (PRCA)-sanctioned rodeo is the largest midwinter rodeo in the nation. The late-month event kicks off with a horse-drawn parade (the world's largest nonmotorized parade) starting at Park Avenue and Ajo Way and ending at the rodeo grounds. It's so big the local TV stations preempt soap operas to offer "live" coverage of the start of "The Festival of the Cowboy." Schools even close for two days, including the University of Arizona. Daily admission is $14 for adults and $8 for children 12 and younger, but the parade is free.

March

San Xavier Wa:k Pow Wow
San Xavier del Bac Mission, I-19, Exit 92
• 294-5727

The Tohono O'odham Indians invite hundreds of American Indian dancers and craftspeople from the United States and Canada to gather at the San Xavier Mission grounds 12 miles south of Tucson for intertribal competitions in drum and dance techniques, including gourd, team, round, grass, hoop and two-step dance. You will be able to sample traditional foods and purchase baskets, silver, jewelry, rugs and pottery. Though still cameras are allowed, video cameras are not. Held in early March, there is a $1.00 parking fee, but the event is free. (Read more about the mission in our Attractions chapter.)

Tucson Poetry Festival
Various locations • 321-2163

Since 1981, this event has brought out the pros and upcoming poets of Tucson's growing literary scene (see our Arts and Culture chapter). The weekend event in early March includes readings, group sessions, panel discussions and an open mike presentation.

Welch's/Circle K LPGA Championship Tournament
Randolph Golf Course,
600 S. Alvernon Wy. • 237-8282

This week-long golf classic in mid-March offers $500,000 in prize money for pro women golfers. The kickoff event allows amateurs a chance to play with professionals and celebri-

---

INSIDERS' TIP

When you visit Fourth Avenue, check the side streets for easy parking rather than trying to park on the main street. Parking can be especially tough during the street fairs.

ties. Admission is $10 per day. General parking is free at El Con Mall at Broadway and Dodge boulevards, and from there free buses provide service to the tournament gate at Randolph Park.

St. Patrick's Day Parade and Festival
15th St. to 22nd St., 6th Ave. to Stone Ave. • 882-4343

Even in the Old West, everybody is Irish to celebrate with a bit o' green in a city founded by Irishman Hugo O'Conor more than 200 years ago. But put your greenbacks away — all the festivities are free. The parade begins at 10 AM on the 17th, and a festival carries on until 6 PM, featuring Irish music, dancing, arts and crafts, food and beverages at Armory Park, 220 S. 5th Avenue.

"Simon Peter" Passion Play of Tucson
Tucson Convention Center, 260 S. Church St. • 327-5560

Each year since 1979, this holiday tradition has brought together more than 100 amateur theater artists at the Tucson Convention Center to present a three-hour musical drama about the life and crucifixion of Christ. The production usually runs for a week in late March and is free to the public. And they are always looking for theater artists who are willing to volunteer.

April

Tour of the Tucson Mountains
Throughout the mountains • 745-2033

More than 1,000 bicycle riders tour the Tucson Mountains west of the city in 50- and 100K courses that begin and end at the main gate of the University of Arizona at Park Avenue and University Boulevard. This race usually takes place during the first weekend in April and includes a quarter-mile kids fun ride that is free to children younger than 14. Registration forms are available the first week of January, and fees are usually $25 to $45, depending on which course you choose. At the finish line, an after-race festival offers food, music and just plain fun for participants as well as those who cheered them on. The main gate is a favorite spot for spectators, but a call to the previously listed number will provide other prime viewing locations along the course.

Pima County Fair
County Fairgrounds, Houghton Rd. south of I-10 • 792-3930

The area's official county fair drew 300,000 people in 1997. It features livestock exhibits, thrill rides, petting zoo, arts and crafts, live entertainment and sports spectaculars during its 10-day run in the middle of the month. Four stages allow fair goers to sample a variety of local performers, while evening concerts include major national acts, such as Charlie Daniels and Steve Miller. Admission is $5 for adults; children younger than 12 are admitted free. Parking is $2.

Arizona International Film Festival
Various theaters • 628-1737

Sponsored by the Arizona Center for the Media Arts (which operates The Screening Room, 127 E. Congress Street, profiled in our Media and Arts chapters), this annual festival encourages the production of independent filmmaking in Arizona. The 10-day festival in the middle of the month includes screenings, seminars and workshops. International producers are invited to come and view the final products. Admission is $5 for one event or $75 for access to the entire festival.

Fourth Avenue Spring Street Fair
4th Ave. between University Blvd. and 9th St. • 624-5004

The six block-strip known as Fourth Avenue already draws throngs on the weekends to its unique shops, restaurants and nightclubs. But twice a year — the second weekend in April and the middle of December — the street is blocked off for a three-day street fair. The free event draws some 500 artisans and crafters from around the country displaying every conceivable type of wares. Live entertainment and a variety of food vendors add to the festivities. Wear comfortable shoes, and plan to spend the day. Side streets are your best bet for parking.

148 • FESTIVALS AND EVENTS

Reid Park Zoo hosts an annual Festival of Lights during the holidays.

Bank One Tucson International Mariachi Conference
Tucson Convention Center • 884-9920

This annual event in late April celebrates the blend of Hispanic music and culture. The conference, which has been held in Tucson for more than 15 years, offers a chance to hear the best mariachi bands in the world, enjoy folk dancing and observe artisan exhibits of Mexican arts and crafts. Because this is a weeklong "conference," many of the activities, such as seminars and workshops, are only for conference participants. But on the weekend following the conference, people from throughout the United States and Mexico come to enjoy the conference events that are open to the public, many of which are free. The weekend often features a parade near Armory Park, 220 S. 5th Avenue, on Saturday morning. Then there's the Festival de Garibaldi, an all-day street fair along Armory Park with music and dance performances and booths offering crafts, souvenirs and food. Throughout the weekend, the Tucson Convention Center, 260 S. Church Street, is set up with displays of Mexican arts and crafts including Mexican Colonial furniture, ironworks and pottery; there's no charge unless you decide to make a purchase, of course.

The major draw of the conference, however, is the Mariachi Concert held at the TCC, usually on Friday and Saturday nights and Sat-

---

INSIDERS' TIP

Carrying water isn't trendy in Tucson — it's a must. The convenience stores carry various sizes of bottled water, and you can get carrying cases with straps.

urday afternoon. Concert goers are treated to some of the best Mariachi bands in the world, celebrated Mexican dancers and often a major headliner such as Vicki Carr or Tucson's own Linda Ronstadt. Tickets range from $20 to $55 and are available through TCC, Dillard's ticket outlets or the previously listed number. All proceeds from the Mariachi Conference benefit a local mental health organization.

Waila Festival
Arizona Historical Society, 949 E. 2nd St.
• 628-5774

This free outdoor event at the Historical Society showcases Tohono O'odham Chicken Scratch music with bands, craft demonstrations and traditional Tohono O'odham foods. The Tohono O'odham is southern Arizona's largest Indian tribe, and their reservation is southwest of downtown Tucson. The one-day event usually takes place on a weekend in the middle of the month.

May

Cinco de Mayo
Kennedy Park, Mission Rd. and Ajo Wy.
• 292-9326

When the Mexican Army defeated the French troops at Puebla on May 5, 1862, the victory sent a ripple through Mexico that boosted national pride and international prestige. Since that time, May 5th has been celebrated by Mexicans internationally, and Tucson is no exception. The free annual festival, held the weekend closest to the 5th, features a variety of music, arts, folklorico dancers and a wide range of Mexican foods.

Tucson Folk Festival
El Presidio Park, 100 block of N. Church Ave. • 749-9770

In its 14th year, this music festival includes major national acts as well as continuous music that features contemporary folk, blues, bluegrass, folk rock, ragtime and gospel groups. Booths on hand sell arts and crafts and food. The free event is held the first weekend of the month.

June

Juneteenth Festival
Kennedy Park, Mission Rd. at Ajo Wy.
• 791-4355

This free outdoor festival celebrates African-American Independence Day, June 19, 1865, when slaves in Texas finally found out they had been freed by the Emancipation Proclamation more than two years earlier. The two-day event, held the second weekend of the month, includes gospel, rap, jazz, blues, food, fashion and arts and crafts from area African Americans.

July

Fourth of July Fireworks
Various locations • no phone

Many of the major resorts tucked away in the foothills of northern Tucson sponsor their own well-executed fireworks, but the main event for residents is the massive light show launched from "A" Mountain just west of downtown. This free spectacle can been seen from around the city, and many people gather for tailgate parties around the convention center downtown.

August

La Fiesta de San Augustin
Arizona Historical Society, 949 E. 2nd St.
• 628-5774

Sponsored by the Arizona Historical Society, this is a birthday celebration for Tucson's patron saint. The Fiesta, Tucson's oldest surviving festival, began as a religious ceremony

---

INSIDERS' TIP

The University of Arizona sponsors numerous free lectures and events during the school year. Call 621-3341 for a schedule of offerings.

150 • FESTIVALS AND EVENTS

in 1775 and flourished in the 1800s as a secular celebration. Taking place near the end of the month, you'll enjoy a variety of arts, music, food and dancing both inside and on the blocked-off 2nd Street outside the Historical Society's Museum near the University of Arizona. The event is free.

September

Music Under the Stars
Reid Park, 22nd St. and Country Club Rd. • 791-4079

The Tucson Pops Orchestra began playing in 1955. Today, the 50-piece group presents numerous concerts each year, and it continues a tradition of offering free concerts under the beauty of Tucson's night sky each Sunday at 7:30 PM during the month. Bring a blanket or lawn chair and sample the various refreshments sold by local vendors, or come early with the family and enjoy a picnic before the show.

Greek Festival
Greek Hellenic Community Center, 1145 E. Ft. Lowell Rd. • 888-0505

A three-day weekend event in the middle of the month, this festival offers homemade Greek foods plus Greek beer, wine, ouzo and metaxa brandy to sample while you enjoy live music, dancing, movies, crafts and souvenirs. Admission is $2, and the festivities run until midnight on Friday and Saturday and until 8 PM on Sunday. The festival has drawn upwards of 20,000 people in past years.

Mt. Lemmon Oktoberfest
Mt. Lemmon Ski Lodge • no phone

While it isn't Bavaria, Mt. Lemmon is the closest thing to it and offers some respite from the lingering heat that may still be present in September and October. The free festival is usually held for three weekends in late September and early October. German food, music and dancing fill your stomach and the time.

Breakaway to the Border Bike Tour
Various locations • 747-7472

Created to provide proceeds to the National Multiple Sclerosis Society and its local chapter, this 130-mile ride is considered one of the most challenging and scenic one-day cycling events in Arizona. The tour begins at the Pima County Fairgrounds, heads south to Nogales, Arizona, on Interstate 19 and returns via Ariz. highways 82 and 83 through Patagonia and Sonoita. There are also shorter rides of 70 and 30 miles. The tour loop is great if you are up to it. Frequent rest stops have volunteers suppling high-energy snacks, as well as professional bike mechanics. The tour takes place near the end of September, and there is a $25 entry fee. Participants can pick up a registration form at area retail bike shops or request one through the mail by calling the previously listed number. Prizes are given to those riders who raise the most pledges to support NMSS.

October

La Fiesta de los Chiles
Tucson Botanical Gardens, 2150 N. Alvernon Wy. • 326-9686

The Southwest wouldn't be the Southwest without red-chile ristras hanging outside doorways. The pepper is part of the fabric of Tucson's culture, and the annual harvest celebration pays homage to the chile in a garden setting. The two-day event, held in the middle of the month, offers everything chile, including crafts, food, cooking demonstrations, music and dancing. The nursery at the gardens has a variety of pepper plants for sale, and after attending this event, you'll never see the pepper in the same light again. Admission is $3 in advance and $4 at the gate. The parking lot at the Botanical Gardens has never been able to handle the 10,000 people who attend each year, so it offers a free shuttle bus from the El Con Mall, 3601 E. Broadway Boulevard. Call for shuttle times.

Tucson Blues Festival
Reid Park, 22nd St. and Country Club Rd. • 791-4079

This all-day blues fest features continuous blues music at the Reid Park band shell from morning until about 10 PM, with everything from national acts to local acoustic performers. Bring your lawn chair and relax with a cold beer and some of the great food

The El Tour de Tucson's 111-mile route crosses dry washes.

that's for sale. The free mid-month event is sponsored by the Tucson Blues Society.

November

Western Music Festival
Holiday Inn City Center, 4550 S. Palo Verde Blvd. • 825-6621

Considered the greatest Western music show anywhere, this annual celebration acknowledges the great singing cowboys such as Roy Rogers, Gene Autry and all the others who helped create this unique style of performing. Over a five-day period in the middle of the month, the Tucson-based Western Music Association presents Western musicians, seminars on a variety of topics, songwriting workshops and jam sessions that often last until 4 AM. Admission for the full five days is $75. Daily admission depends on the schedule but is usually around $10.

El Tour de Tucson
Congress St. and Granada Ave. • 745-2033

Named by *Bicycling Magazine* as one of the 10 best century courses, this annual bike race along the 111-mile perimeter of Tucson draws thousands of racers from around the world. The race begins and ends in downtown Tucson at Congress Street and Granada Avenue. Other rides include 75-, 50- and 25-mile routes. There is a preregistration fee of $50 plus a $10 processing fee before August 30th. After that date the processing fee increases all the way up to $35 by November. Registration forms are available at all area retail bike shops. The race is held the Saturday before Thanksgiving. There's no charge to cheer your favorite cyclist on to victory. (See our Bicycling chapter for more information.)

December

Balloon Glo
University of Arizona Mall, University Blvd.
• 888-2954

Hot air balloons are tethered on the University grounds, and at sundown the gas burners light up the night sky. The following morning sees a launch of many of the balloons, filling the Tucson skies with these colorful airships. This usually takes place the first weekend of the month.

Luminaria Nights
Botanical Gardens, 2150 N. Alvernon Wy.
• 326-9686

The stars of the show at this two-day event near the beginning of the month are the more than 2,000 luminarias (candles nestled in sand in a paper sack) that light the paths throughout the gardens. For more than 12 years, families have delighted in the glow of the night and the accompanying music by some 40 different musical groups who perform every 30 minutes at locations throughout the garden grounds. The candles are lit from 5:30 to 8 PM; admission is $5 for adults and $1 for children 3 to 11. Come and enjoy complimentary cookies and cider at this 5½-acre oasis in the heart of Tucson.

Fourth Avenue Winter Street Fair
4th Ave. between University Blvd. and 9th St. • 624-5004

Like the Fourth Avenue Spring Street Fair, the street is blocked off to host hundreds of artisans and crafters. The benefit of the winter fair is that it gives you the opportunity to do some last-minute holiday shopping. You'll find a variety of arts and crafts, music CDs from independent musicians, one-of-a-kind clothing, sculptures, woodworking, wind chimes, paintings and all types of food along a packed six-block stretch between University Boulevard and 9th Street. Evenings can get cool so bring a jacket.

Tucson Marathon
Various locations • 326-9383

Running from Oracle to Tucson may not seem like fun for everybody, but this race draws runners training for the Boston and New York marathons. A half-marathon and a 5K fun run and relay are also available. Registration fees vary from $40 to $55, depending on how soon you register or whether you wait until the day of the race. Expect to be pounding the pavement with some 2,000 fellow runners.

Winterhaven Festival of Lights
Ft. Lowell Rd. and Christmas Ave.
• 327-0111

After World War II, residents of this neighborhood planted an avenue of Aleppo pines, one of the few species that can survive the desert climate. For the nearly 50 years since then, these trees have been decorated by the Winterhaven neighborhood residents to create the holiday Festival of Lights. But it goes far beyond that. Throughout Winterhaven, houses and yards are decorated with some of the most elaborate holiday decorations around, and it's an annual treat that draws thousands of observers during the last 10 days of the month. On certain nights the neighborhood prohibits cars from driving through, but hayrides and tour buses make great alternatives. Hayrides are $10 per person; the bus is 75¢. Better still, walk the tour and enjoy the carolers. The sights and sounds are free.

Insight.Com Bowl
Arizona Stadium, 540 N. Vine Ave.
• 790-5510

Near the end of the month, Tucson hosts a college bowl game that matches teams from the Big 12 Conference and the Western Athletic Conference. The game-day parade is festive with floats, local dignitaries and, of course, the Bowl Queen. The parade usually starts at 2 PM on Euclid Avenue and proceeds through the University of Arizona main gate and on to the UA Mall. Tickets for the bowl range from $15 to $32. The game starts at 7 PM. (The event was formerly known as the Copper Bowl, and there's more on the game in Spectator Sports.)

FYI

Unless otherwise noted, the area code for all phone numbers listed in this guide is 520.

Music in the Canyon
Sabino Canyon, 5700 N. Sabino Canyon Rd. • 749-8700

In the eastern foothills of the Santa Catalina Mountain range, Sabino Canyon is a favorite spot for local hikers and outdoor enthusiasts. But during the second week of December, music lovers come from all over town to hear a Saturday evening concert from a variety of performers, including the Tucson Boys Chorus, Old Pueblo Madrigal Singers, jazz bands and local guest celebrities. Santa and Smokey the Bear (this is part of a National Forest) are typically in attendance, and light refreshments are for sale. Some 600 luminarias line the quarter-mile path to the stage area. Though there are no tickets required, donations are appreciated, and canned food is collected for the Tucson Community Food Bank. For those who may have difficulty making the quarter-mile walk, call ahead to arrange to be taken by wheelchair.

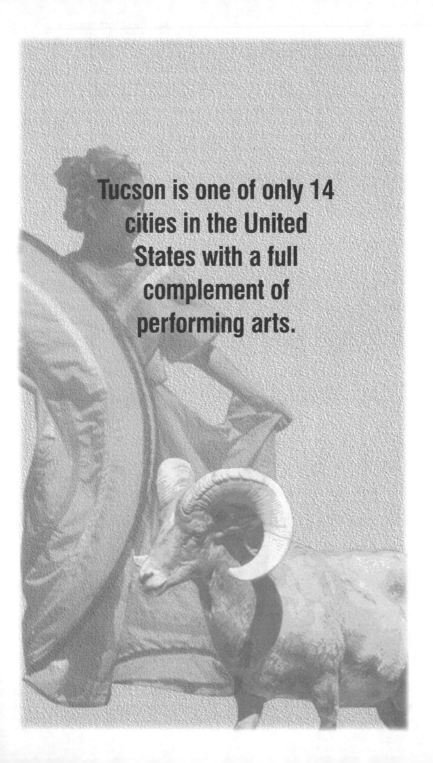

Tucson is one of only 14 cities in the United States with a full complement of performing arts.

Arts and Culture

In the early 1990s, *The Wall Street Journal* stated that Tucson "is becoming a mini-mecca of the arts in a regional renaissance." The city's cultural and arts scene includes theater, photography, painting, music, sculpture, dance and literary arts. In fact, Tucson is one of only 14 cities in the United States with a full complement of performing arts — a symphony, ballet, theater and opera. Not bad for a city of only 766,000.

But the city's cultural attractions date back to the 1860s when the Titeres puppet shows and Mexican circuses would come to town with acrobats, ropewalkers and clowns. City folks would set cactus on fire so they could watch the performances at night. The latter part of the 1870s saw the last of the Mexican circus, and during the early 1880s, Tucson saw the opening of the Park Theater in Levin's Park and Tom Fitch's 700-seat Opera House at the southwest corner of 6th Avenue and Congress Street. By 1919 the ornate Rialto Theater was completed, establishing the Theater District. The Rialto fell on hard times in the 1970s, but today is undergoing a renovation effort to bring it back to the appearance of its heyday.

In 1907, a women's group known as The Saturday Morning Musical Club began meeting to plan productions and dream of building a "temple" to music and art in the city. That dream came true in 1927 when the Spanish Revival-style Temple of Music and Art was built downtown. The Temple became the center of culture in town. Then over the years ownership changed many times, and the building fell into disrepair. The Temple was in serious trouble by the mid-1970s, despite its listing on the National Register of Historic places. On the brink of being gutted or worse, it was saved through a community effort in 1986 and a $1 million restoration effort that was completed in 1990.

In 1930 the art deco Fox Theater opened and was considered the movie theater of its day in the downtown Theater District. Though it still stands today at Congress Street west of Stone Avenue, it is boarded up and slated for demolition to make room for a high-rise. However, there is a growing faction in Tucson who wish to save the elaborate structure.

According to a 1995 study conducted by the Tucson/Pima Arts Council, the local art scene adds more than $200 million to the local economy each year and employs some 4,000 people either full time or part time. The Tucson-based Arizona Opera Company, Arizona Theater Company, Ballet Arizona and Tucson Symphony all have multimillion dollar budgets. Theater companies in Tucson produce programs that range from major Broadway plays and musicals to original works, experimental plays, multicultural works and Shakespeare in the Park.

Musically, expect to see annual blues festivals, Western music conferences, mariachi conferences, opera, symphony, pops and jazz concerts and a major annual folk festival. Dance ranges from major ballet troupes to American Indian tribal dances and from clogging festivals to Mexican folklorico. The world-class University of Arizona Artists Series at Centennial Hall brings performing artists from all over the world to Tucson, as does the Tucson Convention Center each season. The stage could be a park, a concert hall, the University of Arizona or a small, experimental theater that seats 20 people. Some are huge, professional productions while others may have no set at all — relying on the skill of the performers to convey the art.

The Tucson performing arts season typically runs from September to May. During this period the University of Arizona and Pima Community College are in session, and the snowbirds — winter visitors escaping the snow of the East Coast and Midwest — become temporary residents of the Old Pueblo, making for larger audiences. In the summer major events decrease; though the literary scene remains constant, many smaller theaters continue to perform, and the art galleries and museums remain open.

The focal point of the city's art scene is the Tucson Arts District. In 1986 the Tucson City Council approved a $5.6 million allocation to create the Arts District and save the Temple of Music and Art on Scott Avenue as the anchor facility of the district. Located in historic downtown Tucson clustered around Congress Street, the district is populated by galleries, cafes and artists' studios.

Every Thursday from September through May, the Tucson Arts District Partnership offers a free walking tour of downtown exhibition spaces featuring galleries, studios, shops, window displays, murals and the Temple of Music and Art from 5 to 7:30 PM. Call 624-9977 for tour information.

The University of Arizona campus is a fine arts mecca, with the Center for Creative Photography, UA Museum of Art, Fine Arts Complex and UA Poetry Center. The UA Theater Arts Department and Repertory Theater is one of the nation's oldest theater departments, while the School of Music and Dance has been around since 1897. Pima Community College has its own art museums and performance halls as well.

Tucson offers a wide range of theater experiences from Shakespeare to experimental to musicals. Some smaller theaters specialize in local works, many of which are produced by the Old Pueblo Playwrights (see "Literary Arts" in this chapter).

What we present here is a general overview of the arts scene in Tucson, profiling the organizations, companies and venues in the area. For specific information regarding what's being performed when, where and by whom in the city, consult *The Arizona Daily Star* or one of the other local newspapers. For ticket information, contact the number we've provided in the listing.

We begin with local and state arts organizations and then move into performing arts, where you'll find information on the venues as well as profiles of the theater groups, dance ensembles, opera companies, symphonies and chorales that entertain Tucsonans. Museums, galleries and murals take center stage in the Visual Arts section, and we round out the chapter with a look at Tucson's literary scene.

Support Organizations

Arizona Commission on the Arts
417 W. Roosevelt St., Phoenix
• **(602) 255-5882**

Though based in Phoenix, Tucson artists and organizations are eligible for grants from this well-funded statewide organization. The commission funds dance, music, visual arts and virtually everything else that is connected with arts. The annual Artist Roster includes a grant that covers the expenses of getting art or performances into schools and other venues.

> **FYI**
> Unless otherwise noted, the area code for all phone numbers listed in this guide is 520.

Arizona Humanities Council
1242 N. Central Ave., Phoenix
• **(602) 257-0335**

Based in Phoenix, this organization gives grants statewide for programs that foster understanding of the humanities, which includes interpretation and history of the arts. It funds conferences, lectures, exhibits, film and video, literary work and research.

Casa De La Cultura International
1240 S. 4th Ave. • 798-3953

This group gives arts and cultural support for the community to develop artists in all areas of art. It sponsors classes and workshops in painting, poetry, music and literature, among other mediums.

Fundacion Por Herencia Mexicana
Consulate of Mexico, 553 S. Stone Ave.
• **621-1565**

The consulates of Tucson and El Paso, in cooperation with the Secretaria de Relaciones Exteriores de Mexico, have initiated an annual series of lectures, performances, exhibitions and cultural programs in art, cinema, music, literature and history. These include mural competitions, television productions and literary seminars.

ARTS AND CULTURE • 157

National Society of Arts & Letters, Tucson Chapter
6611 N. Taylor Ln. • 628-8009

The local chapter of this 50-year-old organization is dedicated to creating opportunities for exceptional young artists in the disciplines of visual arts, dance, drama, literature and music through classes and workshops.

Tucson Arts District Partnership
2 E. Congress St. • 624-4994

The Partnership is an umbrella organization that oversees the development of the Tucson Arts District — the local arts and revitalization project. The organization offers grants to artists and organizations that have projects directly related to bringing attention to the Arts District. It also manages Downtown Saturday Night on the first and third Saturday of each month, docent-led Thursday Night Art Walks (September through May), which explore architecture as well as art in public spaces, and many of the downtown mural projects. The organization offers Art Space Loans for improving existing art space and stimulating the development of new space in the downtown area. The Partnership is also involved with developing a new Warehouse District of studios and art spaces that is still in the planning stages.

Young Audiences of Southern Arizona
P.O. Box 43606, Tucson 85733 • 624-5997

This organization believes arts are an integral part of a child's education and development. The company presents performances to encourage participation and assure that the arts are accessible to all children.

Performing Arts

Venues

Berger Performing Arts Center
1200 W. Speedway Blvd. • 770-3690

Known locally as "The Berger," this auditorium offers cozy seating for 496 with an elevated stage. It's a favorite site for promoters who specialize in alternative programs, such as acoustic music, and Celtic, eclectic, folk and traditional music concerts.

Centennial Hall
University of Arizona, 1020 E. University Blvd. • 621-3341

Located just inside the University's main gate off Park Avenue, Centennial Hall is one of the city's largest venues and the site of the UA Presents series of cultural programs (see "Music" in this chapter). The theater seats 2,500 in fixed seating facing an elevated stage.

Crowder Hall
University of Arizona Fine Arts Complex, Speedway and Park Ave. • 621-2998

Inside the Music Building on campus, this theater is located near the Speedway Boulevard pedestrian underpass east of Park Avenue. It was renovated in 1995 and now has a hydraulic lift orchestra pit and seating for 600. It's the site of the many recitals and concerts the School of Music and Dance presents during the year.

Pima Community College Center for the Arts
2202 W. Anklam Rd. • 884-6988

Located at Pima Community College's west campus, the Center for the Arts has several venues. The Proscenium Theater is a plush, state-of-the-art facility with opera house-like second-floor seating along the side walls. With 425 seats, it's the college's largest and most used venue for both college and outside community productions and concerts. When events are happening at PCC, they usually happen here. The Black Box Theater is the college's experimental space, seating 150 without a fixed stage. It is a favorite for dance performances. The slanted amphitheater seating for 130 at the Recital Hall offers a great view of the stone-backed stage no matter where you sit.

Temple of Music and Art
330 S. Scott Ave. • 884-8210

This is truly the flagship of Tucson's downtown performance venues. Built in 1927 and saved from destruction in 1986, the Temple's $2.6 million restoration was completed with an official grand opening on October 13, 1990.

158 • ARTS AND CULTURE

It's the home of the Arizona Theater Company, which performs in the Temple's 600-seat Alice Holsclaw Theater. The theater sees a variety of other performances, including music, dance and contemporary rock performers.

Downstairs, located off the Spanish-style courtyard complex, is the B&B Cafe. Upstairs, along an outdoor balcony walkway, is the Cabaret Theater, which seats 90, as well as the Temple Gallery, where various contemporary works are exhibited. The class and style of this historic building turn any performance into an event.

Tucson Center for the Performing Arts
408 S. 6th Ave. • 792-8480

Located downtown, this former 1921-era Catholic church is a small theater, only seating 250. It has been the site of the Tucson Poetry Festival (see our Festivals and Events chapter) and is the performing venue for the Upstairs Theater Company (see "Theaters" in this chapter).

Tucson Convention Center
260 S. Church St. • 791-4266

A massive group of buildings in downtown Tucson, the TCC hosts huge events, such as home shows and conferences. But there are two more artistic venues: The Music Hall, with seating for 2,221, is the home of the Tucson Symphony Orchestra and the Arizona Opera Company; the Leo Rich Theatre has 503 seats and is geared more toward chamber music recitals and concerts by contemporary and pop artists.

Theater

a.k.a. Theater
125 E. Congress St. • 623-7852

This semiprofessional company produces modern and experimental works in an intimate storefront theater in the heart of the Tucson Arts District. Considered Tucson's "off-Broadway" theater, it offers productions on a year-round basis.

Arizona Pathfinders
Hispanic Theater, 949 E. 2nd St.
• 628-5774

This small company does contemporary interpretations of historic and original plays designed to document 20th-century Hispanic culture throughout the Southwest. Plays usually have political, social or cultural content and are as much educational as they are entertaining.

Arizona Repertory Theater
Fine Arts Complex, UA Campus, Park Ave. and Speedway Blvd. • 621-1162

See this and many other **Insiders' Guide®** destinations online — in their entirety.
Visit us today!

Arizona Repertory Theater is the professional training company of the University of Arizona's Department of Theater Arts. One of the nation's oldest theater departments, it has offered performances to the community for more than 60 years. Plays and musicals are produced from November through April, with four to five productions a year.

Arizona Rose Theatre Company
Tucson Convention Center, 260 S. Church St. • 791-4836, 888-0509 tickets

Founded in 1986, this theater offers productions throughout the year at the Tucson Convention Center's Leo Rich Theatre in downtown Tucson. The company is committed to presenting high-spirited and upbeat productions that offer positive statements.

Arizona Theater Company
Temple of Music and Art, 330 S. Scott Ave. • 884-8210, 622-2823 tickets

This group has been designated as "The State Theater of Arizona." Founded in 1967 as The Arizona Civic Theater, the company staged its first productions in a small hotel in Tucson for a small number of theatergoers. In 1972 the company went professional and changed its name to the Arizona Theater Company. Later in 1978 ATC began performing in both Tucson and Phoenix.

Today, ATC mounts six professional productions per year during the regular arts season, ranging from Shakespeare and classical

ARTS AND CULTURE • 159

and contemporary dramas to musicals and works by new artists. ATC has won a number of awards over the years and in 1993 was awarded a prestigious five-year grant from the National Arts Stabilization Fund.

Arizona Youth Theater
5671 E. Speedway Blvd. • 546-9805

Dedicated to fun for children and their families, this company of children, teenagers and adults was established in 1995 to perform classic and original children's plays. (See our Kidstuff chapter).

Bianco Children's Theatre
7272 E. Inca Dove Dr. • 886-0860

Kids ages 5 to 16 make up this band of thespians that performs three or four times a year. They learn the tricks of the trade — vocal, choreography and acting skills — and dazzle their young and young at heart audiences at The Gaslight Theatre, 7010 E. Broadway Blvd.

Bloodhut Productions
1925 N. Woodland Ave. • 795-0010

When established in 1992, Bloodhut immediately made a name for itself as a touring feminist performance ensemble dedicated to presenting pieces based on women's lives. Besides touring with their work — much of it developed from improvisation — the performers also offer ongoing creative expression workshops for women.

Borderlands Theater
Pima Community College Center for the Arts, 2202 W. Anklam Rd. • 882-7406

Established in 1986, this multicultural theater company in residence at Pima Community College presents productions that reflect the diversity of the Southwest/Mexican border region. The company also provides training in production and play development. Six productions each year are offered between September and April.

Coyote Ramblers
a.k.a. Theater, 125 E. Congress St.
• 797-7779

Coyote Ramblers was established in 1995. The provocative and critically acclaimed modern works are presented in the intimate a.k.a. Theater in the Tucson Arts District. There are usually three productions per year in October, January and March.

Damesrocket Theater Company
a.k.a. Theater, 125 E. Congress St.
• 743-3650

Founded in 1995, this women's theater group has two goals: to offer plays dealing with women's issues, relationships and history and to showcase local southern Arizona talent. The company produces a wide range of works, from controversial subjects to comedies.

Desert Players Community Theater
Tucson Center for the Performing Arts, 408 S. 6th Ave. • 579-3206

Desert Players is a new theater group that stresses high-quality community theater at a reasonable price. The group typically performs four noncontroversial productions between September and April.

The Gaslight Theatre
7010 E. Broadway Blvd. • 886-9428

Tucson's only live, old-fashioned musical melodrama theater, the Gaslight is well-known in the area for its lighthearted, rip-roaring comedies. Audiences can enjoy throwing free popcorn, hissing at the villains and cheering the heroes. The majority of these year-round productions are written by local playwrights especially for The Gaslight Theatre. It's good family entertainment, accompanied by waitresses serving a wide variety of snack foods, including pizza, hot dogs, nachos, fountain treats, beer, wine and soft drinks. The food is provided by Little Anthony's Diner, which is located at the back of the theater. It's one of the best run operations in town and worth the drive to the Eastside.

Invisible Theater
1400 N. 1st Ave. • 882-9721

A very visible force in Tucson's cultural community, Invisible Theater is the city's original experimental theater (affectionately known as "The I.T."). The I.T. was established in 1971 and, for the first few years of productions, offered works from local writers. Since the late 1970s it has become better known as a "director's theater," presenting adaptations of classics, off-Broadway plays and a few musicals. The I.T. also offers Project Pastime, an educational program for mentally challenged students. The 75-seat theater's season runs September through May.

Live Theater Workshop
5317 E. Speedway Blvd. • 327-4242

This production company offers a full schedule at various local venues, as well as an educational program for aspiring artists. Since its beginnings in 1994, LTW has become an important element of Tucson's community theater groups.

Millennium Theatre Company
738 N. 5th Ave. • 882-7920

Performing and headquartered at the Historic "Y" Theater in downtown Tucson, Millennium typically offers four classic productions per year between September and December. Past performances have included *A Midsummer Night's Dream* and *A Christmas Carol*. The '97-'98 season featured *A Delicate Balance*, *Coming of Age in Soho* and *Snoopy: The Musical*.

Stewart Theater of Puppetry
3530 E. Grant Rd. • 327-3992

Founded in 1991 by the Stewart family, professional puppeteers for more than 20 years, the puppetry theater offers classic fairy tales with modern themes, using marionettes and rod puppets with movable mouths. Past productions include *The Ugly Duckling* and *The Legend of Sleepy Hollow*. Classes in puppet construction are also offered, or you can request a tour.

Third Street Kids
Tucson Museum of Art, 166 W. Alameda St. • 622-4100

Arts for All, Inc., a nonprofit organization, runs this program that began in 1985 as an after-school theater program for children with disabilities. Students ages 5 to 21 come from throughout greater Tucson and meet five times a week at Tucson Museum of Art's Education Center. There are also weekend workshops and a summer camp of the arts. The students have represented Arizona at several events including the First International Very Special Arts Festival in Washington, D.C., in 1969; the Third International Abilympics in Hong Kong in 1991; and the Fourth International Abilympics in Australia in 1995. In 1988 the group received the Meyer Marmis Humanitarian Award. Founder Marcia Berger has won numerous awards for her work leading this group. (See our Kidstuff chapter.)

Tucson Art Theater
721 N. Bently Ave. • 327-7950

Founded in 1989 by a group of actors, playwrights and directors, the Tucson Art Theater offers productions that dramatize and celebrate the life of the human spirit. The group fosters a sense of community and produces new and classic works examining the individual's role in community and family.

Tucson Parks and Recreation Community Theater
Randolph Recreation Center, 200 S. Alvernon Wy. • 791-4079

In its 10th year, the community theater presents two plays per year — a Christmas production and a Shakespeare work in June, both performed at the DeMeester Outdoor Performance Center in Reid Park. The works are performed by amateurs from around the city.

Upstairs Theater Company
Tucson Center for Performing Arts, 408 S. 6th Ave. • 791-2263

Established in 1994, Upstairs maintains the goal to be accessible to, and build audience

---

INSIDERS' TIP

The best source of theater news, especially calls for auditions, is the monthly newspaper *Tucson Theater Scene*, which can be found in most theater lobbies and bookstores around town.

A downtown dance concert is part of the Tucson Arts District Partnership's projects.

interest in, live theater. The company is committed to developing and producing original plays from southern Arizona playwrights. There are typically four productions each year between September and March.

Dance

As a pure performance art, dance in Tucson comes from different cultures as well as different disciplines. You'll find Hispanic and American Indian troupes along with companies centered around ballet, modern and experimental dance. Also, UA Presents brings in internationally known dance artists each year and has its own world-class dance department within the School of Music & Dance of the College of Fine Arts. If you check the listings of local publications, you'll even find monthly folk and contra dancing around town where everyone is invited to hit the dance floor.

Aires Flamencos
P.O. Box 44041, Tucson 85733
- **888-8816**

This nonprofit Spanish dance company educates and promotes the cultural heritage of Spanish dance arts, such as flamenco. Using Spanish folk dance, classical Spanish dances and dance dramas based on the Hispanic legends of Mexico and the Southwest, Aires Flamencos produces four programs each year in the fall, winter and spring at various locations.

Amerikan Hoodoo Theatreworks
P.O. Box 136, Tucson 85702 • 792-1994

Formed in 1989 and led by award-winning Hassan al Falak, Amerikan Hoodoo Theatreworks is one of Tucson's premier experimental theater/dance troupes. The multidisciplinary company incorporates text, theater and visual arts in its performances, which explore racism, sexism and other illnesses of modern society.

ARTS AND CULTURE

Ballet Arts Foundation
200 S. Tucson Blvd. • 623-3373

Established in 1985, the foundation provides professional training and supports a Children's Ensemble and its Ballet Arts Ensemble, a company of 18 professional dancers. The Children's Ensemble has performed in Mexico, Russia and France. The foundation also brings the art of ballet to public schools throughout southern Arizona.

Ballet Continental
3377 N. Mossy Brook Dr. • 326-7887

Ballet Continental, made up of dancers 12 and older, strives to reach out to young people throughout southern Arizona to make dance easy to understand. Classes teach discipline and classical technique. The company performs full-length ballets at locations throughout the area.

Ballet Folklorico Mexica
55 W. Adams St., Ste. 209 • 623-8200

This internationally recognized educational and performing dance group furthers the traditions of Mexican folklore and culture through education and a number of annual performances at various locations and parks around the city. The company, which is sponsored by the Instituto de Folklore Mexicano, celebrated its silver anniversary in 1996. Five productions are staged between September and June.

Barbea Williams Performing Company
P.O. Box 2775, Tucson 85702 • 628-7785

This multidisciplinary community performance company promotes African-American pride. The range of the group's work spans traditional and contemporary theater, dance, music and even poetry. Performances are held at community centers and other venues throughout the city.

Orts Theatre of Dance
P.O. Box 85211, Tucson 85754 • 624-3799

Established in 1985, Orts is one of Tucson's largest touring modern dance companies. Orts performs historical, avant-garde and contemporary dance works and has a full home season, running from September to June, that includes school-based programs. Orts is one of the only dance companies in the nation to have its dancers fly on single point trapeze. Unlike in circus acts, the low-flying, single point trapeze doesn't swing the dancers but rather allows them to spin in a circle. The group also brings master teachers and choreographers to town to conduct workshops.

Redhouse Dancers
6932 E. 4th St. • 886-7651

This American Indian cultural performing arts group was formed in the Monterey Peninsula area in 1965. The family group moved to Tucson in 1973. Along with the Navajo Nation Dancers, the Redhouse Dancers conducts information and craft classes. The group performs spectacular and colorful dances at a number of festivals, fiestas, schools and conventions throughout the area, all aimed at providing a better understanding of American Indian traditions and customs.

Tenth Street Danceworks
738 N. 5th Ave. • 795-6980

Tenth Street Danceworks is an artistic collective that was established in 1991 by a video artist, a dancer/choreographer and a dance educator. Danceworks performs primarily locally but has taken productions around the state and to the Pacific Rim area. The innovative approach explores the relationship between the dancers and computer-enhanced video images of themselves. The company also participates in a number of school-based dance programs and offers two local concerts per year.

Tucson Metropolitan Dance Company
4639 E. 1st St. • 327-0546

An annual production of *The Nutcracker* ballet using 65 local and professional dancers is the chief offering of this nonprofit community dance company. The rest of the year, members participate in classical, jazz and contemporary dance classes.

FYI

Unless otherwise noted, the area code for all phone numbers listed in this guide is 520.

Tucson Regional Ballet
2100 N. Wilmot Rd., Ste. 221 • 886-1222

This company of up-and-coming young dancers produces an annual Southwest Nutcracker that translates the classic *Nutcracker* to Tucson of the 1880s, complete with banditos and cavalry. It is a member of Regional Dance America and provides professional caliber training for talented students. All performances are held at the Tucson Convention Center's Leo Rich Theatre.

University of Arizona Dance Division
School of Music and Dance, Ina Gittings Building, Rm. 121 • 621-4698

The Dance Program at the University of Arizona offers the study of dance as an art form and as a performing art. The philosophy of the program is that dance leads to an understanding of human movement. Jazz, ballet and modern dance are offered with equal emphasis so students can experience and appreciate the diversity. As a performance group, UA dancers have been recognized for their professional productions and performances at the newly renovated Ina Gittings Dance Studio Theater.

Young Artists Community Ballet
3377 N. Mossy Brook Dr. • 326-7887

Comprising dancers ages 12 to 21 from around southern Arizona, this dance group reaches out to rural communities to introduce dance as an art form, teaching discipline and classical technique at area schools.

Zenith Dance Collective
1910 N. Dodge Blvd. • 322-9021

Established in 1991, Zenith is a group of independent choreographers who work by consensus to present dance and dance-related classes, concerts and workshops. The group's vision is to encourage individual choreographic expression and exploration with old and new forms of artistic expressions.

Music

Tucson's music scene offers everything from classical music and opera to folk, chamber, country, bluegrass, Western, blues, jazz, New Age and a variety of vocal groups and choirs ranging from professional to "kitchen musicians." Each year there are annual folk festivals, jazz festivals, blues festivals, Western music conferences, mariachi conferences, pops and symphony concerts and a bit of everything in the local club scene. (Turn to our Festivals and Events and Nightlife chapters for details.) There are also a number of music societies, which we have listed at the end of this section. And the booming cafe scene has opened its doors to performers of original music by sponsoring a number of open-mike nights. (See our Nightlife chapter for information about venues offering open-mike nights and performances by local bands.)

Arizona Opera Company
3501 N. Mountain Ave. • 293-4336

One day in 1971, 15 local musicians and actors came up with the idea of founding a professional opera company in Tucson. The following spring the city witnessed its first classical production of Rossini's *The Barber of Seville*. Over the next 10 years the company expanded throughout the state, and today it's the state's only professional grand opera company. Between October and March, the company presents five professional performances at the Tucson Convention Center's Music Hall. Past productions have included *Aida*, *La Boheme*, *Carmen* and *La Traviata*. This is the only opera company in the United States to perform regularly in two cities (Tucson and Phoenix) and is one of only four American opera companies to have produced the entire Wagner Ring Cycle.

Arizona Repertory Singers
P.O. Box 41601, Tucson 85717
• 792-8141

This 32-voice mixed ensemble brings a wide variety of choral music to venues throughout southern Arizona. Founded in 1984, the chorus performs a cappella choral music from numerous eras and countries. The group is known for its musicianship and high-energy performances. All the concerts are free and take place between October and December at a variety of locations, including Leo Rich Theatre at the Tucson Convention Center and Tohono Chul Park.

The University of Arizona Theatre Arts Department puts on a production of *Arsenic and Old Lace*.

Arizona Symphonic Winds
5201 N. Rocky Ridge Pl. • 577-2410

A community ensemble of some 60 musicians, the group has been performing at a variety of venues throughout Tucson since 1986. Arizona Symphonic Winds regularly presents the Evening of Music series at Udall Park in September, May and June, as well as offers other concerts between September and June at locations throughout the city. This group allows emerging artists a chance to develop their talents through performance and education.

Bwiya-Toli
P.O. Box 85274, Tucson 85754
• 882-7620

Established in 1979, this six-piece Latin American music ensemble plays traditional Latino instruments and regularly performs at such events as La Fiesta de Los Chiles, Tucson Folk Festival and La Fiesta de San Augustine. (See our Festivals and Events chapter for details on these celebrations.)

Catalina Chamber Orchestra
P.O. Box 64831, Tucson 85728
• 327-4721

Established in 1990, the 35-member orchestra was formed to provide an outlet for the area's young professional musicians as well as talented amateurs. Each season the group performs a range of traditional and contemporary works for small orchestra. Prominent area soloists are featured, and new compositions by area composers are regularly introduced. The orchestra has also just released (spring 1998) its first compact disc.

The orchestra's Educational Outreach Program offers a Young Artists competition and concert, and its Scramble Program provides young musicians a chance to perform prior to CCO concerts.

Chancel Choir
Christ Church United Methodist, 655 N. Craycroft Rd. • 327-1116

This 110-voice choir with orchestra performs annual concerts, featuring gospel and sacred music, a Christmas operetta and a special Palm Sunday presentation, among others.

Civic Orchestra of Tucson
1400 N. 1st Ave. • 325-3002, 791-9246

Founded in 1972, this young, volunteer symphony orchestra offers free concerts at a variety of sites throughout the city. It also sponsors an annual Young Artists competition, a concerto competition open to Tucson-area students, and conducts a musical education outreach program to area schools. The afternoon performing season runs October through May and offers five to six concerts.

Desert Voices
P.O. Box 40036, Tucson 85717
• 791-9662

Established in 1988 as the Metropolitan Community Chorus, today the choral ensemble produces three major concerts between December and June. Though the group is dedicated to promoting a positive gay and lesbian presence in southern Arizona, membership is open to anyone who is supportive of the gay/lesbian lifestyle. All concerts are held at the Pima Community College Center for the Performing Arts Proscenium Theater or the Temple of Music and Art.

Eastside Artist Series
Christ Church United Methodist, 655 N. Craycroft Rd. • 299-7189

The church has a superb Schlicker pipe organ and fine acoustics. In 1979 the musical series decided to take advantage of those attributes to present concerts of classical organ music featuring world-renowned organists and Tucson musicians. It presents 10 concerts per year during the October-through-April season.

The Foothills Phil
5201 N. Rocky Ridge Pl. • 577-5304

This philharmonic offered through the Catalina Foothills School District brings adults and students together to share their love of music and seeks to motivate students to pursue the study of stringed instruments. It offers a complete orchestral experience. The orchestra presents two concerts at Catalina Foothills High School Theater, 4300 E. Sunrise Drive, in December and May.

Heavy Metal Brass Quintet
7819 S. Orchid Vine Pl. • 574-1563

Founded in 1991, this brass quintet is comprised of classically trained musicians with years of international performance experience. The group is known for its unique blend of classics and contemporary works and new compositions. The quintet performs approximately six concerts per year in Tucson at various venues between November and March.

Sons of Orpheus
9337 E. Luchnay Ln. • 621-1649

A nonprofit, nonsectarian community men's choir, Sons of Orpheus includes men of all walks of life. Founded in 1991, the choir presents concerts throughout southern Arizona that range from classical to popular and span all periods, styles and languages. It also performs with other Tucson musical groups such as the University of Arizona's Balalaika Orchestra.

Southern Arizona Symphony Orchestra
P.O. Box 43131, Tucson 85733
• 323-7166

Established in 1979, the symphony is a blend of professional and amateur volunteer musicians who offer a rich diversity of classical performances. Over the years the orchestra has premiered several new works by American composers in Tucson and southern Arizona. SASO performs five concerts per year between October and June, all at the Berger Performing Arts Center.

Tucson Arizona Boys Chorus
P.O. Box 12034, Tucson 85732
• 296-6277

Known as "Arizona's Singing Ambassadors," this 41-year-old group has become internationally recognized and tours extensively throughout North America and overseas. Dedicated to providing boys in the area with an educational opportunity as well as performance experience, the group offers 10 to 12 local concerts in Tucson between October and May at various venues.

Tucson Girls Chorus
4020 E. River Rd. • 577-6064

Founded in 1985, this nonprofit organization provides an environment where girls develop self-esteem, discipline and music literacy. Today, there are more than 250 girls involved in four choruses. It also sponsors a Summer Fine Arts Program for boys and girls grades 1 through 6. The chorus usually offers two concerts per year at the Tucson Convention Center in December and May.

Tucson Goodtime Singers
9458 E. 26th St. • 885-5983

Since it was established in 1985, this women's choir has grown to 80 voices and is affiliated with Sweet Adelines International. Four-part harmonies have won the group several awards. Tucson Goodtime Singers offers a fast-paced performance each fall with costumes and choreography.

Tucson Masterworks Chorale
P.O. Box 41885, Tucson 85711
• 321-7279

Originally formed in 1949 as the Desert Singing Guild, today's Tucson Masterworks Chorale is a professional-level community chorus that offers singers of all ages and backgrounds the opportunity to develop their talents. The group performs choral works ranging from pre-Baroque to contemporary and typically presents three concerts in Tucson per year at various locations.

Tucson Philharmonia Youth Orchestra
P.O. Box 41882, Tucson 85717
• 326-2793

A full symphonic youth orchestra, Tucson Philharmonia is based at the Pima Community College Center for the Arts. It provides symphonic training and performance opportunities to southern Arizona youth in a professional environment. Membership in the orchestra is determined each year by audition and currently comprises approximately 100 musicians ranging in age from 11 to 19 from schools around Pima County. Three to four concerts are held between November and April at Tucson Convention Center's Music Hall. The orchestra also takes a winter tour to Las Vegas and offers coaching sessions with Tucson Symphony Orchestra musicians.

Tucson Pops Orchestra
2424 E. Broadway Blvd. • 623-6292

This professional pops orchestra has been offering southern Arizona Music Under the Stars for free since 1954. The concerts take place at Reid Park's George DeMeester Outdoor Performance Center, which is named in honor of the violinist founder of TPO. The orchestra offers 10 concerts each season that feature old favorites and popular classics. The concerts are held in September, May and June.

Tucson Symphony Orchestra
443 S. Stone Ave. • 882-8585

The oldest existing professional symphony orchestra in the Southwest, TSO was founded

> **FYI**
> Unless otherwise noted, the area code for all phone numbers listed in this guide is 520.

INSIDERS' TIP

Tucson's "Cowboy Artists" continue to get state and national recognition. At the Cowboy Artists of America's 25th annual auction in Phoenix, held in October 1997, works by Tucson artists Don Crowley, Ken Riley and Howard Terpning (who was voted "Best of Show") accounted for 55 percent of the $1.5 million in sales at the fund-raiser.

in 1929. During the year TSO offers world-class guest artists and four concert series: Classics, Pops, Chamber and "In Recital." The Classics usually comprises about 10 concerts, while the remaining three series offer four concerts each between September and April. Performances typically are held at the Tucson Convention Center or Pima Community College Proscenium Theater.

University of Arizona Balalaika Orchestra
90 E. Calle Encanto • 327-4418

Founded in 1989, this is the only balalaika orchestra in America with its own dance company, the Kilinka Russian Dance Ensemble. The 25-member orchestra performs with authentic folk instruments, and the dancers and musicians are dressed in authentic Slavic costumes to promote Russian folk culture. The group performs two concerts in Tucson each year.

UA Presents
University of Arizona, Centennial Hall, 1020 E. University Blvd. • 621-3341

Each season the University of Arizona's Cultural Affairs Department brings in world-famous performers in dance, music, ballet and multicultural performances for the entire community to enjoy. The 1997 season saw performances from the dance troupe Stomp; jazz from Joe Henderson, Charlie Haden and the Kansas City All-Star Big Band; the National Symphony Orchestra under Leonard Slatkin; famed Tibetan Monks of the Drepung Loseling Monastery performing traditional music and dance; Sukay, Music of the Andes; *Kiss of the Spider Woman*; the Warsaw Philharmonic; a Korean drum troupe; and acrobats from Peking. Locally, this is one of the most anticipated concert series in Tucson due to the quality and diversity of the acts the University brings to the Old Pueblo. Season tickets or single tickets are available through the UA Box Office or Dillard's Department Stores' box offices, (800) 638-4253.

University of Arizona School of Music & Dance
Fine Arts Department, Crowder Hall • 621-1162

Numerous events are held during the school year at the School of Music, which has existed for more than 100 years. With the help of its world-renowned faculty (who are highlighted during the Faculty Artist Series), and its 500 music majors and 100 dance majors, the School of Music and Dance presents more than 300 concerts per year, almost on a daily basis. Concerts feature everything from classical recitals, jazz and opera to steel drum bands.

Music Societies and Organizations

No matter what your musical taste, there is probably a local organization you can join, a newsletter you can receive, limited discounts on concerts you can take advantage of or like-minded enthusiasts you can mingle with. Below is a sampling of the music societies and organizations in the area.

Arizona Early Music Society (AEMS)
8202 E. Snyder Rd. • 889-4310

This nonprofit group's mission is to present concerts of early music and promote related activities such as classes about various forms of early music, including harpsichord, lute, harp and violin. Annual dues are $15; members receive a newsletter. You can purchase a season ticket to the six visiting artist concerts, held at St. Philip's in the Hills Episcopal Church (4440 N. Cambell Avenue), for $65.

Desert Bluegrass Association
7878 E. Cloud Rd. • 296-1231

A nonprofit group of pickers gets together once a month and produces a monthly newsletter to inform members of upcoming bluegrass music events and news. Dues are $12 per year, which includes the newsletter. Members gather the third Sunday of each month for an informal jam, usually at a local restaurant.

International Mariachi Conference
P.O. Box 3035, Tucson 85702 • 792-9854, 884-9920

The first International Mariachi Conference was held in April 1993. Today it is an annual event offering not just concerts, but four days of workshops, exhibits and dance instruction by master musicians and dance maestros for students from all parts of the country. (See our Festivals and Events chapter.)

Tucson Blues Society
P.O. Box 30672, Tucson 85751
• 327-5593

Founded in 1984, the Tucson Blues Society is a nonprofit organization that promotes the enjoyment of blues music through concerts, a newsletter, education and by supporting blues musicians. In addition to the monthly newsletter, it publishes the "Blues Greats" calendar, which features photos of performers taken by the society's own members. The flagship event is the very popular annual Blues Festival, which is held in mid-October at the DeMeester Outdoor Performance Center of Reid Park (see our Festivals and Events chapter). Membership dues start at $15. Members enjoy discounts on some concert events and a subscription to Blues Beat, the society's monthly newsletter. It's packed with great information, articles, reviews and listings of upcoming performances.

Tucson Friends of Traditional Music
P.O. Box 40654, Tucson 85717
• 327-1779

These Tucson friends promote participation in and appreciation of traditional music and dance. The year-round calendar of concerts, dances and workshops features American, Celtic, South American and other "World Music" traditions. With a membership of more than 500 currently, it offers a monthly newsletter (TFTM News) and sponsors twice monthly contra dances with live music and callers. Annual membership dues are $12, which gets you the newsletter and discounts on some concerts.

Tucson Guitar Society
1714 E. Edison St. • 325-2180

The Tucson Guitar Society, which includes a number of University of Arizona School of Music guitar graduates, provides area guitarists with information and opportunities to meet to improve their playing and present guitar performances. It publishes a quarterly newsletter that is included in a $15-per-year membership. Or you can skip the membership and just get on the mailing list for $5.

Tucson Jazz Society
P.O. Box 85101, Tucson 85754
• 903-1265

Of all the nonprofit support organizations in Tucson, the Jazz Society presents the greatest number of organization-produced concerts in the area (about 40 per year). Founded in 1977, the Society now boasts some 2,000 members and a $200,000 budget. This handsome financial base allows the society to offer a number of concerts and festivals each year. It also maintains The Jazz Hotline, 743-3399, and a 24-hour recorded message at the number listed above. The society organizes the Tucson Jazz Orchestra and the Tucson Latin Jazz Orchestra. Some of the major events the group sponsors are the Jazz Sundae at Reid Park in October; The Plaza Suite Series at St. Philip's Plaza, also in October; and Primavera, the oldest women's jazz event in the world, in March. During the rest of the year it presents or copresents nearly 40 other events. Membership dues are $30 per year, which includes concert ticket discounts as well as the bimonthly newsletter.

Tucson Kitchen Musicians Association
P.O. Box 26531, Tucson 85726
• 881-2016

This nonprofit group's primary focus is to promote acoustic and folk music in the area. TKM produces the annual Tucson Folk Festival, a two-day event held each May that presents a variety of acoustic music styles by local and national performers (see our Festivals and Events chapter). It also produces or coproduces a number of other concerts year

---

INSIDERS' TIP

Most of Tucson's venues, large and small, can be reserved for social events or receptions simply by calling and booking a date. This includes many of the area's galleries, which provide a more intimate setting, as well as the Temple of Music and Art, for those who just can't bear to leave anyone off the guest list.

round at venues around town. As a member ($15 per year) you'll receive discounts on concert tickets, as well as a monthly newsletter.

Tucson Musical Arts Club
2330 E. Mitchell St. • 795-4921

Established in 1953, this affiliate of the National and Arizona Federation of Music Clubs promotes individual and community growth and understanding of all forms of musical arts. It encourages young musicians through scholarships, special awards and workshops.

Western Music Association
P.O. Box 35008, Tucson 85740
• 825-6621

In 1988 a group of cowboy and Western music performers gathered in Las Vegas to do some pickin'. In February 1989 members of that group started the Western Music Association to bring Western music back into the arena of public interest. Now headquartered in Tucson (you can't get much more "cowboy" than this town), the organization strives to promote, educate and support contemporary cowboy performing artists. Every November, thousands come to Tucson to participate in the Annual Western Music Association Conference, which includes performances by nationally known acts (Roy Rogers was once a headliner) as well as workshops and jam sessions (Look for the Western Music Festival in our Festivals and Events chapter).

Visual Arts

Museums

Center for Creative Photography
University of Arizona • 621-7968

Established in 1975 and located across from the UA Museum of Art, this one-of-a-kind photographic center and museum is known throughout the world for its extensive archives and collections of works by important 20th-century photographers. The center contains more than 50,000 photographs, galleries, research facilities and a library. The library covers all aspects of photography and includes more than 10,000 monographs, catalogs, books, periodicals and microfilms. Hundreds of hours of videotaped interviews and lectures by noted photographers are also available for viewing in the library.

Southwest photographer Ansel Adams and Dr. John P. Schaefer, then president of the University, conceived this center in 1974 that now houses the late photographer's complete archives. The other several dozen archival collections housed at the center include Richard Avedon, Ernest Bloch, Dean Brown, Wynn Bullock, Harry Callahan, Louise Dahl-Wolfe, Andreas Feininger, Sonya Noskowiak, Marion Palfi, Aaron Siskind, W. Eugene Smith, Frederick Sommer, Paul Strand and Edward Weston.

The center is open Monday through Friday from 11 AM to 5 PM and Sunday from noon to 5 PM.

De Grazia Gallery in the Sun
6300 N. Swan Rd. • 299-9191

Though the word "gallery" is used here, this is more a museum, since it deals exclusively with the works of the late Ted De Grazia on the site of his studio, among a sprawling cluster of adobe buildings in the foothills.

More than 125,000 people a year visit this site to view some of the more than 10,000 De Grazia paintings that deal with Spanish exploration of the Southwest, Indian lore, legends, celebrations, rodeos and bull fighting. De Grazia even designed the floor tiles, light fixtures and other decorative features throughout the gallery. Signature works are of Indian children with round faces, no eyes and flowing black hair. The prolific artist also worked in bronze, ceramics, stone lithographs, serigraphs, glassware and jewelry.

Down a path from the main building is the small, open-roofed Mission in the Sun — a chapel De Grazia designed and built himself. The chapel's walls are DeGrazia murals.

Before his death in 1982, De Grazia created the De Grazia Art and Cultural Foundation to keep the site operating. Since that time the foundation has also supported other arts organizations, including public broadcasting within Tucson.

The gallery is open from 10 AM to 4 PM daily. There is no admission fee.

Tucson Museum of Art and Historic Block
140 N. Main Ave. • 624-2333

Founded in 1924, the Tucson Museum of Art was housed at several sites in the city before the current museum was built in 1975 on the site of Tucson's original Spanish Presidio. The complex takes up an entire city block in the heart of downtown. The museum and Historic Block are currently undergoing a $2.2 million expansion that is expected to be completed by 1999, in time to celebrate its 75th anniversary.

Besides the modern main building, the site has towering shade trees, a bubbling fountain and outside sculptures that make up the Museum's Plaza of the Pioneers, with adjoining courtyards. The complex also includes five distinctive homes built between 1850 and 1906. La Casa Cordova, a restored 1850s-era home that is believed to be the oldest house in town, replicates life during that time and contains a small Presidio museum. Casa Romero is now a pottery studio, library and part of the museum's art school. The John K. Goodman Pavilion, formerly the Edward Nye Fish House, exhibits Western art. The Stevens/Duffield House, built in 1866, houses Janos Restaurant (see our Restaurants chapter). And J. Knox Corbett House, a two-story stucco-covered brick structure, is open for tours.

The Tucson Museum of Art houses a permanent collection of more than 5,000 works of art. The focus is the Americas including pre-Columbian, Spanish, Colonial, Western American and Contemporary American art. Each year it hosts 15 to 20 changing and traveling exhibitions of work in all media.

The noncredit Art School has operated for 26 years and offers classes in ceramics, sculpture, painting, drawing, theater arts, mixed-media, art history and art criticism for students 5 through 105.

Inside the main building is a gift shop offering many one-of-a-kind handcrafted ceramic, wood, fabric and jewelry items from local artists, as well as posters, books and greeting cards from around the world. The outdoor Plaza of the Pioneers is a downtown oasis that hosts concerts, block parties, art festivals, the fall Holiday Craft Market, the spring Artisans Market and more.

You could spend all day here, especially if you plan on venturing off into the surrounding Historic Block where other small artsy shops abound.

From Labor Day through Memorial Day, the museum is open Monday through Saturday from 10 AM to 4 PM and Sunday from noon to 4 PM. It's closed on Mondays in June, July and August as well as for major holidays. Admission is $2 for adults, $1 for students and free to those 12 and younger. There's no admission fee on Tuesdays.

University of Arizona Museum of Art
UA Arts Oasis, Park Ave. and Speedway Blvd. • 621-7567

Located on the University of Arizona campus, this museum is open to the public throughout the academic year, with limited summer hours. The permanent collection has more than 4,000 works, including Rembrandt, Pontormo, Robin, Degas, Arp, Piranesi, Picasso, O'Keefe and Rothko. It also has one of the Southwest's most complete collections of art from the Renaissance to the present day, thanks to a donation in the 1950s of more than 50 works by Samuel H. Kress. Most noteworthy are the collections of European and American 19th- and 20th-century paintings and sculptures. Most of the permanent collections are displayed on the second floor and are rotated several times a year.

The first floor features changing exhibits. A popular exhibition during 1997 was "The Unbroken Chain: The Traditional Arts of Tucson's Mexican-American Community."

The museum is open Monday through Friday from 9 AM to 5 PM and Sundays noon to 4 PM. From May 15 through September 1 the museum has shorter hours: 10 AM to 3:30 PM Monday through Friday and noon to 4 PM on Sundays. There is no admission fee.

Murals

Tucson sports more than 200 murals throughout the community, with more created each year, making the area's mural movement a unique visual art form in its own right.

Though wall paintings have been found in the ruins of prehistoric Indian kivas dating back

1,000 years, Tucson's modern mural movement began in the 1950s and '60s when a number of local banks commissioned interior murals — painted and mosaic — featuring historic images of Tucson and Arizona. By the 1970s, murals began showing up in different neighborhoods, following the tradition of southwest and southern California "El Movimiento" — the "People's Murals." The artists who produced them were influenced by such artists as Jose Orozo and Diego Rivera who created "Los Tres Grandes of the Mexican mural movement. Many murals rich in Mexican-American images were created on the outside walls of neighborhood centers, beginning with the El Rio Neighborhood Center. Five more were created at other centers incorporating imagery from other cultures including Yaqui, Tohono O'odham and African American.

During the 1980s financial support from the City of Tucson, Pima County, community service organizations and private businesses helped create dozens more murals in the area. Schools, realizing that getting students involved in mural projects was great for the students' self-esteem, sought funds to create murals on playground walls, ramadas and inside the school buildings. The Arizona Commission for the Arts responded with funding to send artists to schools to help the students create these murals, and today there are more than 66 murals at more than 40 schools.

Some of the more noteworthy and older murals are Bank One, 22 E. Congress Street ("Tucson's Early History," inside lobby); El Rio Neighborhood Center, 1390 E. Speedway Boulevard (seven murals inside and out); Old Pascua Neighborhood Center, 785 W. Sahuaro Street (nine murals inside and out); Tucson International Airport, S. Tucson Boulevard ("History of Southern Arizona," interior baggage level); and Pueblo High School, 3500 S. 12th Avenue (untitled, east wall).

With more than 200 murals at about 140 sites throughout Tucson, it's good to have a guide. The Tucson/Pima Arts Council (see "Visual Arts Organizations" in this chapter) offers a free pocket guide with maps to these murals. Each site is listed by address, with the name of the artist or artists who created it, plus title and date of the mural when known. These murals have become a vital part of Tucson's art scene and heritage. Hunting down examples of this form of "people's art" makes for an interesting and out-of-the-ordinary afternoon tour of the Old Pueblo.

Visual Arts Organizations

Arizona Media Arts Center
P.O. Box 40638, Tucson 85717
• 628-1737

This service and resource organization encourages the study, production, appreciation and use of all forms of film and video. It has a research library and offer programs, classes and conferences. An international film festival and art film presentations are presented at The Screening Room, 127 E. Congress Street in the Tucson Arts District (see our Festivals and Events chapter).

Arts Genesis, Inc.
1311 E. Duke Dr. • 323-0185

This nonprofit's outreach programs are meant to inspire and create multicultural and community-based arts that enrich, empower and educate the community.

Desert Artists Guild
130 W. 11th St. • 387-5045

A guild of local artists, this fine arts club strives to help artists in the community find display space for their works.

Friends of Western Art
P.O. Box 64730, Tucson 85728
• 299-1398

This support group strives to increase the awareness of Western art in Tucson and southern Arizona through its financial assistance to young and emerging artists, civic projects and Western art exhibitions.

Group for Photographic Intentions
P.O. Box 1691, Tucson 85702 • 326-6605

A nonprofit visual arts organization that provides a forum for the exchange of ideas and information about contemporary photography, GPI provides access to resources and exhibition opportunities for photographic artists.

172 • ARTS AND CULTURE

The Bard's *Much Ado About Nothing* was performed at DeMeester Outdoor Performance Center in Reid Park.

Southern Arizona Clay Artists
P.O. Box 44218, Tucson 85733
• 762-5839

This group sponsors exhibitions, lectures, forums and workshops to further the appreciation for ceramic arts. Meetings are held six times a year, and a bimonthly newsletter, listing activities, news and opportunities, is produced for its members.

Southern Arizona Watercolor Guild
4809 E. Eastland St. • 748-7440

The primary purpose of the Guild is the advancement and development of watercolor as an important painting medium. It offers workshops, monthly meetings and exhibitions.

Southern Arizona Woodworkers Association
P.O. Box 2711, Tucson 85702 • 623-4605

This is a support group that educates the public about the woodworking arts of cabinetry, furniture and sculpture. The association offers workshops and helps local artisans promote their work. It specializes in Southwestern furniture and sculpture.

Tucson Arts and Crafts Association
P.O. Box 31541, Tucson 85751
• 825-4025

The association is the largest organized group of artists in Arizona, with a membership of more than 400. It is a juried, nonprofit organization with the purpose of promoting its members in the community through a variety of shows and exhibitions.

Tucson Arts Brigade
P.O. Box 545, Tucson 85702 • 791-9359

The Brigade is a multicultural, intergenerational arts organization that offers after-school programs and stresses art as a way to promote social justice.

Tucson Arts Coalition
P.O. Box 43160, Tucson 85733
• 623-2577

TAC provides services to artists that allow them access to working, living, performance and exhibition space in southern Arizona. The coalition is also involved in educating the public about the benefits of art to the quality of life and the economic growth of the community.

Tucson/Pima Arts Council
240 N. Stone Ave. • 624-0595

The Council, a nonprofit organization, was established in 1984 and is recognized as the official arts agency of the City of Tucson and Pima County. Through grants and commissions, the council directly assists artists and organizations in developing and producing a variety of art forms. It also offers the Arts Channel on local public access TV, which is available through the cable operator Tucson Cable Inc. Here you'll see a list of upcoming events in the area.

During the year, the council offers a number of grant-writing sessions and has a small research library. The council offers a number of different "grant rounds" during the year, usually with specific themes and goals. The offices have meeting rooms and a gallery, which rotates works of local artists.

Galleries

It is not unusual to stroll into a cafe or restaurant in Tucson and see original artwork hanging on the walls for sale, especially downtown and on Fourth Avenue. Art is everywhere in Tucson, and the number of galleries and original art shops — close to 150 — increases each year. Some may not hang around for long, but they are quickly replaced with others. The Tucson Arts District Partnership also encourages "Phantom Galleries," where art turns up in a storefront window for a short period of time and then is gone.

Here we list a cross-section of the galleries in Tucson. When exploring a gallery, look for the full-color, free pocket guide *Art Life* (see our Media chapter), which lists all the galleries in Tucson and southern Arizona. *Tucson Weekly*, *The Arizona Daily Star* and *Tucson Citizen* cover galleries and art each week. In fact, most of the magazines and newspapers in town devote some space to the arts, so you'll always know what's going on. A week does not go by without a handful of openings and receptions filling the city's calendar. So if you are interested in visual arts, you'll be busy.

Access Tucson Gallery
124 E. Broadway Blvd. • 624-9833

This downtown gallery exhibits contemporary works from local and national artists.

Alamo Woodworkers Gallery
101 W. 6th St. • 882-9490

This woodworker's collective is near downtown Tucson. The gallery exhibits handcrafted furniture, pottery and sculptures by local artists.

Art!
6328 E. Broadway Blvd.
• 745-8586

Art! features fine contemporary, traditional and Southwestern art from some 40 local artists working in oils, watercolors, clay and glass.

The Art Company
3400 E. Speedway Blvd., Ste. 110
• 881-1311

The Art Company features international, national and local artists, including Larry Fodor, Marcus Pierson, Kati Roberts and Tarkay. It exhibits bronze, Southwestern paintings, serigraphs and lithographs and has an award-winning custom framing service.

The Barksdale Gallery
500 N. 4th Ave. • 884-7541

A small gallery on hip Fourth Avenue, the Barksdale exhibits photography, ceramics, paintings and folk art.

Bero Gallery
41 S. 6th Ave. • 792-0313

The Bero specializes in experimental and nontraditional photographic works, including hand-colored black-and-white photographs.

Central Arts Collective
188 E. Broadway Blvd. • 623-5883

This membership-directed gallery exhibits contemporary artwork in all media. There are also regular juried exhibitions from local artists.

Craig Fine Arts
6070 N. Oracle Rd. • 544-9466

Craig Fine Arts specializes in Western and wildlife art. It features oils, acrylics, watercolors, pastels, terra-cotta sculptures, bronzes and limited edition prints from national and regional artists including Tom Cox, Rene Tanner, Hal Empie and Tom Hill.

Desert Artisans' Gallery
6536 E. Tanque Verde Rd. • 722-4412

A cooperative gallery of local artists, Desert Artisans' features fine arts and crafts from more than 30 artists with regional or national recognition.

> **FYI**
> Unless otherwise noted, the area code for all phone numbers listed in this guide is 520.

Dinnerware Artists' Cooperative Gallery
135 E. Congress St.
• 792-4503

Established in 1979, this art space is devoted to exhibiting diverse and experimental works by local and regional artists. Each year it sponsors a major art auction that draws works from all over southern Arizona.

El Presidio Gallery
7000 E. Tanque Verde Rd. • 733-0388
4340 N. Campbell Ave. • 529-1220

Two locations offer works by the Southwest's finest artists in a wide variety of mediums and subjects.

Eleanor Jeck Galleries of Contemporary Art
4280 N. Campbell Ave. • 299-2139

Located among the upscale shops of St. Philip's Plaza, this gallery exhibits contemporary oils, acrylics, watercolors, graphics, sculpture, neon, ceramics and glass works.

Enchanted Earthworks Gallery
2980 N. Swan Rd., Ste. 140 • 327-7007

Located in the lovely Plaza Palomino (see our Shopping chapter), Enchanted Earthworks features original jewelry arts and works in clay, wood, glass, stone and mixed media by local and emerging artists.

Etherton Gallery
135 S. 6th Ave. • 624-7370

This 3,500-square-foot gallery exhibits contemporary painting, photographs, prints and sculptures. Between June and August, it is open by appointment only. Etherton also operates the Temple Gallery on the second floor above the courtyard at the Temple of Music and Art.

F.L. Wright Gallery
316 E. Congress St. • 622-3350

Located in the Tucson Arts District, this gallery specializes in early 20th-century American paintings, Mission furniture, pottery and textiles.

Marathon Art Gallery
2920 N. Swan Rd., Ste. 119 • 323-1138

Marathon features contemporary original works by more than 20 Southwestern artists including Michael Atkinson, Amado Pena, Sarah Schmeri, Michael Ives and Warren Cullar. Complimentary sun tea is served on the patio.

Medicine Man Gallery
7000 E. Tanque Verde Rd., Ste. 7
• 722-7798

This gallery displays one of the largest collections of Navajo textiles in the country as well as antique and contemporary pottery, historic Pueblo candlesticks, baskets and other Indian art. It also features works from the Taos Society of Artists. A recent expansion now includes early American Western art, specializing in well-known artists such as Peter Hurd, Marion Boyd Allen, Maynard Dixon, Joseph Henry Sharp and Tenney Johnson.

Nova Graphics Gallery
140 W. Ft. Lowell Rd. • 888-2424

Since Tucson is considered the Astronomy Capital of the World, it's only fitting that what is believed to be the only space art gallery on the planet would be located here. Opened in 1997, the gallery exhibits and sells limited edition prints and paintings — many signed by U.S. astronauts — by such space artists as Bob Eggleton, Joe Tuciarone, Don David and Robert McCall.

Obsidian Gallery
4340 N. Campbell Ave., Ste. 90
• 577-3598

Works in clay, textiles, metal, jewelry, glass, wood and mixed media are featured at this well-known gallery. Past rotating exhibits have included El Dia De Los Muertos (Day of the Dead), a multimedia exhibition featuring works by more than 30 local artists.

Philabaum Contemporary Art Glass
711 S. 6th Ave. • 884-7404

This working studio and gallery is internationally known for its contemporary glass-blown pieces. Artist Tom Philabaum's works are exhibited throughout North America, Europe and Mexico. Here at his studio you will be mesmerized by Tom and his team as they shape molten glass into sculptures. Call for specific times.

The gallery also exhibits works of several hundred other artists from all over the world. Four major exhibitions are staged annually, each with a different theme. Every spring, the gallery stages the Southwest Invitational in which glass artists from around North America are invited to work at the Philabaum studio.

Pink Adobe Gallery
222 E. Congress St. • 623-2828
6538 E. Tanque Verde Rd. • 298-5995

With one location in the Tucson Arts District and one on the Eastside, Pink Adobe has changing exhibits from local artists that include sculpture, hand-painted black-and-white photography, watercolors, paintings on wood and a variety of other media.

Rimrock West Hacienda Studio and Gallery
3450 N. Drake Pl. • 749-8774

A working studio/gallery, Rimrock West is owned by the Robbins family whose works range from the traditional to the contemporary

---

INSIDERS' TIP

When visiting the Tucson Museum of Art, be sure to venture into the surrounding Historic Block. Just across the street from the museum is Old Town Artisans, a 15-room, 1850s restored adobe complex with a courtyard that fills an entire city block. It houses traditional and handcrafted Southwestern art and crafts in all mediums by more than 400 regional artisans.

in bronze, watercolors, enamels and oil. Their work is featured in collections all over the world.

Rosequist Galleries, Inc.
1615 E. Ft. Lowell Rd. • 327-5729

For more than 50 years, this gallery has represented scores of national and international artists. Today it presents the finest in contemporary Southwestern art, traditional as well as innovative, and represent more than 60 artists.

Tohono Chul Park Gallery
7366 N. Paseo del Norte • 742-6455

Tohono Chul Park's small gallery rotates works of regional artists with about 16 changing exhibits each year. Past exhibits have included American Indian art, photography and Mexican tile art. The desert-garden park also has a gift shop, with one-of-a-kind items by local artisans and a restaurant with two outdoor patios. High tea is served in the afternoon. (See our Restaurants chapter.)

Venture Fine Arts Gallery
6541 E. Tanque Verde Rd., Ste. 27 • 298-2258

Nationally known and emerging Southwestern artists are represented here with works in oil, acrylic, pastel, pencil, watercolor, clay and bronze.

WomanKraft Castle Art Center
388 S. Stone Ave. • 624-6441

Established in 1974 to empower women artists, the center bought a building in 1992 and created the Castle, containing a gallery, studios, workshops and more. The gallery specializes in women's art and issues. One 1997 exhibition was *Visible for a Change*, paintings celebrating lesbian sexuality, by Lorraine Inzalaco. It also holds a variety of art workshops, including the Neighborhood Arts Empowerment Workshop Series.

Literary Arts

Tucson's literary art scene has been experiencing a renaissance over the past two years. The University of Arizona's Poetry Center and Tucson's annual Poetry Festival have done wonders in bringing poetry out of the literary closet and into the public's ears. In 1997 the Tucson Arts District Partnership announced the formation of a Poetry Fund to support poets and poetry readings.

Both fiction and nonfiction writing is strongly fueled by the fact that we have a number of book publishers — so many that Tucson has its own book publishing association. For poets and fiction writers looking to get published, check our Media chapter for *Border Beat*, *Coffee Times*, *Sonora Review* and *The Tucson Poet*. With such a support system in place, it's no wonder Tucson has fast become a haven for regional and national writers alike. The late Edward Abbey and Joseph Wood Krutch are writers in Tucson's past. Today, nationally prominent writers such as Barbara Kingsolver, N. Scott Momaday, Richard Shelton, Leslie Marmon Silko, Peter Wild and Jane Miller are just of a few of the names associated with Tucson's writing community.

For more than 30 years, the University of Arizona Press has been publishing award-winning books. The University also boasts the country's largest, in size as well as scope, writing program (the Creative Writing Program has been rated among the top-10 in the nation). Pima Community College also has a variety of creative writing programs, both credit and noncredit, for those who wish to expand their skills in all forms of writing.

In this section we list some literary-friendly organizations as well as book publishers that are headquartered in Tucson.

Artsreach
1800 E. Ft. Lowell Rd., Ste. 126 • 292-0209

Established in 1987, this nonprofit group conducts creative writing workshops at schools serving Arizona's American Indian and Mexican American populations.

National League of American Penwomen
5202 N. Fort Yuma Tr. • 883-6697

This organization of professional writers (and artists and musicians) meets to gain inspiration for creative work through an exchange of ideas and instructive programs.

Old Pueblo Playwrights
P.O. Box 767, Tucson 85702 • 297-3384

Founded in 1989, Old Pueblo Playwrights is

This neighborhood mural reflects multicultural roots.

dedicated to the nurturing of fledgling playwrights and screenwriters. Members bring their first-draft scripts to weekly Monday evening meetings at the Temple of Music and Art for feedback from other members. Many members have sold screenplays and gone on to win national theater awards or have had their works produced by one of Tucson's many theater companies. Each January the group presents a Festival of New Plays to showcase members' works.

Poets Alive!
5120 W. Albatross Pl. • 744-7975

This new group gets together for regular monthly meetings at various locations to read and critique each other's works.

Society of Southwestern Authors
P.O. Box 30355, Tucson 85751
• 296-5299

A nonprofit organization with more than 270 members, the Society is open to poets, novelists, nonfiction writers, essayists, playwrights and screenwriters who are published or aspire to be. The group has monthly luncheon meetings where general topics are discussed, and guest speakers are presented occasionally. In January it sponsors a large writers conference where attendees meet and talk with nationally known authors, publishers, agents and other regional writers. Keynote speakers at the conference have included Ray Bradbury and Tony Hillerman. It's $60 to join the society and then $10 yearly to continue membership.

Tucson Book Publishing Association
P.O. Box 43542, Tucson 85733
• 571-1111

Founded in 1988, this is Arizona's premier outlet for sharing up-to-date information on the business of publishing. Membership is made up of book publishers, distribution companies, editors, agents, designers, illustrators, packagers, typesetters, binders, printers, marketers and writers. Members can attend a monthly dinner meeting with speakers who address a broad range of topics related to publishing, as well as receive a monthly newsletter, a membership directory and representation in other publishing organizations such as the Publishers Marketing Association.

Tucson Poetry Festival Committee
P.O. Box 4400, Tucson 85733 • 321-2163

Since 1981 the Tucson Poetry Festival, held in March (see our Festivals and Events chapter), has provided an opportunity for hundreds of regional poets to share and perform their work for Tucson audiences. The three-day event includes readings by nationally and internationally acclaimed poets as well as workshops, panel discussions and a major open-mike event. The committee is also involved with a statewide poetry contest as well as other events for young writers throughout the year.

Tucson Screenwriting Group
Main Tucson-Pima Library, 100 N. Stone Ave. • 770-1263

Established in 1996, this group meets the third Saturday of the month at the Main Tucson-Pima Library to explore new works from its more than 25 members. The group offers feedback and an opportunity to network with other screenwriters about contacts, contests and new markets.

Tucson Writer's Project
P.O. Box 27470, Tucson 85726 • 791-4391

Formed in 1977 with a grant from the Arizona Commission on the Arts, the Project now receives an annual grant from the Friends of Pima Library to offer diverse writing workshops and seminars for county residents of all ages.

UA Poetry Center
University of Arizona, 1216 N. Cherry Ave. • 321-7760

Established in 1990, this is a nationally acclaimed resource of more than 27,000 books, periodicals and audio/video recordings housed in a historic adobe building. The center's mission is to provide a welcome environment that will "maintain and cherish the spirit of poetry" for students and the community. The library and all reading events are free and open to the public.

UA Writing Works Center
University of Arizona Extended University, P.O. Box 210158, Tucson 85721 • 626-4444

This noncredit series of courses, including creative writing, marketing, screenwriting, poetry and journalism, could help breathe new life into your writing career. The small classes are taught by encouraging and supportive instructors who are professional, established writers. The Writing Works Center also offers a Certificate Award in either creative writing or business writing, and classes are held at various locations on the University of Arizona campus.

> **FYI**
> Unless otherwise noted, the area code for all phone numbers listed in this guide is 520.

Book Publishers

Arizona-Sonora Desert Museum Press
2021 N. Kinney Rd. • 883-2500, (800) 734-8469

This press focuses on natural history and the Sonoran Desert region, publishing trade books, maps, scholarly works and brochures. Recent titles include *Desert Dogs: Coyotes, Foxes & Wolves*.

Fisher Books
4239 W. Ina Rd., Ste. 101 • 744-6110, (800) 255-1514

Fisher Books is a nonfiction trade book publisher that focuses on cookbooks, health, self-help, gardening and automotive topics, as well as distributing books for other publishers. Recent titles include *Sassy Southwest: Vibrant New Mexico Foods*, *No Red Meat*, *Desert Heat: Chronicles of the Sonoran Desert* and *Desert Gardening*. It issues a catalog every quarter.

Galen Press, Ltd.
P.O. Box 64400, Tucson 85728
• **529-6459**

Targeting health professionals, this company publishes nonclinical health-related books, primarily focusing on medical education and bioethics.

Kore Press, Inc.
101 W. 6th. St., Ste. 4 • 882-7542

A nonprofit, artist-run publishing house, Kore Press focuses on women's and community issues.

The Patrice Press
P.O. Box 85639, Tucson 85639
• **743-9842, (800) 367-9242**

This publishing house specializes in Western history books as well as audio and video tapes. Titles include *The Oregon Trail Revisited*, *Cowboy Songs*, *The Santa Fe Trail Revisited* and *First Along the Santa Fe Trail*. It issues an annual catalog.

Treasure Chest Books
1802 W. Grant Rd. • 623-9558,
(800) 969-9558

Established in 1975, Treasure Chest specializes in books about American Indian arts and crafts, Southwest history and nature. It also acts as a fulfillment and distribution house for more than 100 other publishers and issues a quarterly catalog.

University of Arizona Press
1230 N. Park Ave., Ste. 102 • 621-1441,
(800) 426-3797

For more than 30 years, the University's press has been producing popular and scholarly works on a variety of subjects by faculty and nonfaculty writers. Today, it publishes approximately 50 books a year, with more than 500 currently in print. Key areas include cultural anthropology, archaeology, history, American Indians, Western water issues, border region issues, natural history, the environment and astronomy. The massive catalog is issued quarterly.

It isn't man-made trappings like buildings that characterize Tucson, it's nature.

The Natural World

Few cities on Earth have natural settings as spectacular as Tucson's. Going from Tucson on the desert floor to its highest surrounding mountain peak is equivalent to going from Mexico to Canada in one hour, so varied are the flora, fauna and climates. It isn't man-made trappings like buildings that characterize Tucson, it's nature. You'll get to know the real Tucson in this chapter.

The Sonoran Desert covers approximately one-third of Arizona, from Tucson west into California and south into Mexico and the Baja peninsula. Out of this desert grow several mountain ranges and a remarkable array of plants, animals and natural resources — not to mention several million people in cities like Tucson, Phoenix, Yuma and in Mexico. The Sonoran Desert floor is 3,000 feet above sea level but rises to more than 9,000 feet in the mountain ranges surrounding Tucson. The City of Tucson occupies 125 square miles of this desert, while metropolitan Tucson covers 500 square miles. Pima County, wherein the bulk of the metropolitan area lies, is 9,240 square miles, almost half of which is Indian reservation.

But before you venture into this desert region, take a few moments to review the gray box below. Many of our words for plants, animals and places come from Spanish and American Indian languages. What follows is a pronunciation chart for the foreign terms. Learning how to pronounce these strange-looking words will be of great benefit as you travel in and around Tucson and through this chapter.

Pronunciation Guide

agave uh-GAH-vee
Ajo Way AH-hoe Way
arroyo ah-ROY-oh
cholla CHOY-ya
Cruz cruise
gila HEE-la
Ina Road EYE-nuh Road
javelina have-a-LEEN-uh
Mam-a-gah MOM-uh-ga
mesquite m'SKEET
nopalito no-pah-LEE-toe
ocotillo oak-oh-TEE-yo
paloverde pal-oh-VERD-ay
Pima PEEM-ah
Rillito ree-EAT-oh
Sabino sah-BEAN-oh
saguaro sah WAH ro
Tanque Verde tank-ah-VERD-ay
Tohono Chul toe-HOE-no CHEWL
vacquero vak-CARE-oh
yucca YUCK-uh

Plant Life

Perhaps the most remarkable aspect of the desert is the plant life. Contrary to popular opinion, the desert is abundant with plant life, ranging from the granddaddy of them all, the saguaro cactus, to the carpets of spring wildflower. That's because, for a desert, the

---

INSIDERS' TIP

With all the palm trees around Tucson, you might think they thrive here. But in fact, they only thrive with the help of humans adding lots of water, at least for the early years of the palm's life. They are not indigenous to the area and must be imported from more moisture-laden areas like California, Mexico or Florida.

Sonoran is fairly wet, averaging more than 11 inches of rainfall and only 17 short-lived freezing lows a year in the Tucson area.

Cacti are perhaps the most unusual and most noticeable of the desert plants. Cacti are succulents, meaning that they have an uncanny ability to store water. They also typically have a built-in defense mechanism, thwarting predators and the curious with their almost-indefatigable needles. Some of these prickers are so tiny they appear invisible, but one slight touch and the uninitiated will painfully learn otherwise. One of the neat things about cacti is their constancy. Day after day and year after year, they remain green and stable and sturdy.

Say the word cactus and what usually comes to mind is the saguaro, even if its name is usually massacred in the pronunciation. Saguaro means giant cactus in Latin, and it grows only in the Sonoran Desert. It has come to be a symbol of Arizona and even the West. It is also a protected species. Saguaros can reach an amazing 50 feet in height and weigh more than 2 tons, most of it stored water. It takes 75 years for a saguaro to even begin to grow its first arm or two, and they can grow up to 20 or more arms.

The saguaro is home to a number of desert dwellers, as evidenced by the many holes you'll see in them. Holemakers include pack rats, Gila woodpeckers and other birds. When tenants move out, others take occupancy, including elf owls, purple martins and sparrow hawks. The saguaro's insulation keeps its internal temperatures about 20 degrees cooler than the outside air, which makes it a mighty inviting dwelling to the little ones. In April or May, the saguaro cactus blooms with waxy white flowers at the tip of its arms or main trunk. The flowers eventually give way to crimson-colored fruit. For centuries, American Indians have harvested the fruit for food. How'd they do that? With very long poles.

It has become quite popular to incorporate saguaro ribs into furniture or other home accessories, but anyone who does can only use saguaros that are already dead and felled and even then only with a permit. Landscapers and developers can obtain permits to relocate saguaros, but in truth those over 12 feet rarely survive the transplant, taking three to five years to die. Although you can see saguaro cacti anywhere in the Tucson area, including many front yards, the Saguaro National Park (east and west units) has thousands, many of them giants, and is easily accessible. Read all about the national park— actually a preserved park land with units on either side of Tucson — in the Parks and Recreation chapter.

Compared to the saguaro cactus, made famous in movies, paintings and postcards, the desert's other cacti are relative unknowns. Cacti are native to the Americas and encompass over 1,000 species; in southern Arizona, we have 100 of them, each one more odd-looking than the next. The ocotillo cactus appears as a stand of tall, spindly sticks spreading upward and outward forming a V shape. And though it may seem dead, a good rain will produce hundreds of tiny bright green leaves up and down each of its spindles. In the spring, the ocotillo sprouts gorgeous red blooms several inches high at the top of its spindles. Under the right conditions, the ocotillo is truly a beauty of the desert. Another common cactus is the prickly pear, so named because its dark red fruits resemble a pear — with a lot of prickly things covering them, of course. Those brave enough to tackle the fruit make it into a variety of prickly pear edibles like jelly and candy. The prickly pear cactus itself looks like a collection of green pancakes stuck on each other. These pads are a favorite Mexican vegetable, called nopalito, albeit quite tricky to harvest. Prickly pears can be green or a lovely purple hue.

The organ pipe cactus is so called because it sprouts a clump of tall slender arms that reach skyward, resembling the pipes of an organ. It has much the same coloration and rib-like appearance of a saguaro from afar, but its shape is different and its arms much thinner and straighter. Another cactus is the cholla, of which there are many varieties. Any cactus that looks like a miniature tree — with trunks and lots of squiggly little branches covered with prickers — is probably a cholla. One type of cholla is called jumping cholla because its spiny protrusions supposedly leap off and attach themselves to unwary passersby. This

> **FYI**
> Unless otherwise noted, the area code for all phone numbers listed in this guide is 520.

is quite an exaggeration, but they will attach if bumped; then it's the victim who jumps. Another is the teddy bear cholla, named because its needles resemble a fluff of teddy-bear-like fleece, but don't be deceived by its appearance. Other cacti include the barrel and the hedgehog, both of which sprout brilliantly colored blossoms in the springtime. Remember that all cacti have needles, some more visible and ferocious than others, so it's wise to look but don't touch.

Cacti are not the only strange-looking things that grow in our desert. The agave, also a succulent, is another signature plant of the Southwest. It sprouts a rosette of thick, hard, sharp-tipped leaves out of the ground. But the agave's most amazing feature is a stalk that grows straight up from the center of the leaves, sometimes reaching 15 to 20 feet, with smaller branches near the top that sprout large clusters of flowers. Protruding majestically out of the scrubby desert landscape, this plant can easily be mistaken for a tree because of its mammoth height and shape. It has earned the nickname "century plant" because it takes so long for the plant to bloom — up to 30 years. Some species bloom only once after all that work and then die. Beyond its striking looks and amazing life cycle, the agave has another claim to fame — it's an ingredient in tequila, a liquor produced primarily in Mexico and made famous by a tasty frozen concoction as well as a song (hint: "Margaritaville").

And then there's the yucca, which look like they might have stepped out of a science fiction movie set. Unlike the agave, they have a stem or trunk on which the leaves grow — long, thin dagger-like leaves that are more often brown than green nearer the ground, giving the impression the plant is wearing a hula skirt. Nicknamed "Spanish dagger" for obvious reasons, the yucca also sprouts a stalk from its center that bears a large cluster of wheat-colored flowers in the spring. Native Americans used the tough and fibrous yucca leaves for weaving baskets, sandals and rope and its roots for soap. Although not unique to the Sonoran Desert, yuccas do seem to like it here. One of the larger and more famous varieties is the Joshua Tree, which can have a life span of 500 years and is more commonly found near the California border.

One of the oldest living things on Earth makes its home in the Arizona desert — the creosote bush. They have been around for about 11,000 years. But to be honest, most longtime residents of Tucson wouldn't recognize one if they tripped over it. That's because the creosote is more known by smell than by sight. Accompanying almost the first drop of desert rain are two distinct aromas — one is earth (or dirt or dust to some noses) and the other is the almost tar-like fruity smell emitted by the creosote that actually comes from a resinous coating on its stem and leaves. It's a smell we've grown to love and appreciate for it signals rain.

It may not be fair to introduce you to this next plant, because your chance of seeing it is slim to none. It is the night-blooming cereus, a nocturnal flower with delicate white petals and a baby's-breath-like center of yellow stamens that blooms only during a single night in June. If you happen to be in Tucson during June, contact the Tohono Chul Park, 575-8468, and you may be lucky enough to be there when this rare plant unfurls its flowers. (You'll find Tohono Chul Park listed in the Parks and Recreation chapter.)

Yes, trees do grow in Tucson. Two of the most prominent native trees are the paloverde and the mesquite. The latter has become popular among barbeque aficionados and fireplace owners as a wood with great burning qualities and a pleasant aroma. In fact, that delicious smoked steak you dined on last week in Seattle or Chicago may well have owed its distinctive flavor to an Arizona mesquite tree.

Botanically, the mesquite tree is a legume (yes, bean). It has a dark bark with twisting branches and small fern-like evergreen leaves. Many mesquites never become more than a scrub due to lack of water. But others can pass a kid's true test of a tree — is it good for climbing? Like many other desert dwellers, it has been a source of food, fuel, medicine and containers for Americans, Native and otherwise, for centuries. And the bees use the blossoms to make a delicious edible honey. It is a protected tree, and cutting is by permit only. There are several bosques of mesquite around Tucson providing lovely shaded neighborhoods for the lucky residents. (Check out our Neighborhoods, Neighboring Towns and Real Estate chapter for some tips on finding them.)

Prolific in the desert, the paloverde tree means "green stick" in Spanish, named for its beautiful lime-green bark. It doesn't have leaves and doesn't need them because photosynthesis takes place throughout the tree, but it does have thin needles (long or short depending on the variety). In fashion-world lingo, the paloverde tree would be described as monochromatic. The paloverde is at its most glorious in the spring when it is covered with a cascade of golden yellow fleece-like blooms. A street lined with paloverdes is a sight not to be missed in the Tucson spring, and it can be found almost anywhere.

Many non-native trees grow here as well, often with a little help from a garden hose. One local favorite is the citrus tree — grapefruit, orange, lemon or lime. You will see at least one of these lush green-leafed beauties growing in many a back or front yard, particularly in the midtown neighborhoods like Sam Hughes and El Encanto and in some foothills areas. (See our Neighborhoods, Neighboring Towns and Real Estate chapter for a description of these neighborhoods.) These trees give Tucsonans three precious commodities — shade, undeniably the best-tasting fruit to be had and in the spring, weeks of wafting scents from one of the most glorious aromas nature has ever created, the citrus blossom.

No discussion of desert plant life would be complete without mention of the desert broom, the nemesis of the desert as far as human inhabitants are concerned. The desert broom seems to be green when everything around it is browning from lack of water. They go to seed around November or December, and each plant produces hundreds, possibly thousands, of fluffy white seeds. (For you Easterners, picture a dandelion seed magnified about a millionfold!) The wind blows and releases them to find a suitable spot to germinate. But they also find the grass, the patio, the car's interior, the pool, the clothes on the laundry line, the screen door — anything in their path they can latch onto is covered by white fluff for weeks. We call this phenomenon "desert snow," but not affectionately. The desert broom's sole purpose seems to be to annoy people and sell brooms (the cleaning variety).

Animals and Other Things

The first thing you should know is that our animal life is prolific, in part because the desert is relatively wet and in part because it produces so many green (or brown) things for the animal population to consume and live in or under. The second thing you should know is that most of the scary sagas you've heard about the animal life are quite exaggerated. Many of our four-legged and feathered inhabitants are certainly unusual, though, and will no doubt pique your curiosity.

Among the two most fascinating bird dwellers of the Tucson area are the roadrunner and the Gambel quail. The television cartoon characterization of the roadrunner is not too far off base. It usually travels by foot rather than by flight; in fact, the roadrunner is the fastest American bird afoot, traveling at least 15 miles an hour when racing away from predators. It can reach two feet in length, mostly tail and legs with a silly-looking feathery topknot. Perhaps it comes as no surprise that the roadrunner is a member of the cuckoo family. While you won't likely find one sprinting across a city street, they are fairly easy to spot in less built-up areas.

The Gambel quail also seems to prefer feet to flight. (Fortunately for the bird and for us, this is not the quail sought after by hunters and treasured for its culinary flavor.) Its primary mark is a reddish teardrop-shaped plume atop its head. To see how popular this bird is with the human population, just enter any Southwest or Arizona specialty shop and you will find numerous man-made replicas of it — from mailbox flags to lawn ornaments to T-shirt art. But seeing them for real, especially as a family unit, is quite a remarkable sight. After the chicks are born in the spring, the family travels around the desert on foot — adult followed by perhaps a dozen tiny young, followed by the other adult — all in a row. Be careful when driving along county streets lest you disturb and perhaps even injure this marvelous procession.

The Sonoran Desert has more species of birds — about 300 — than any other arid region on Earth, making it a top spot for birders. You may not be a master spotter, but you will easily recognize hummingbirds, ravens, pigeon-like mourning doves, wrens, owls and woodpeckers. As for furry friends, you might only expect to see chipmunks and squirrels in heavily treed areas. Don't be surprised when you see them in the desert too. Other animals you're likely to spot in the rural environs include coyotes, 10-inch-high kit foxes, mule deer — so named because of their mule-ish ears — and jackrabbits with oddly elongated ears and legs. In higher elevations, you may see bobcats, mountain lions, big-horn sheep, black bears and a strange-looking pig-like creature called a javelina. This relative of the domestic pig has an elongated snout, canine-like teeth and travels in herds for protection.

But it's the reptile population that visitors to our desert find most fascinating and often most frightening. Those squiggly, sure-footed and speedy lizards can be as small as an inch to several feet in length. The variety of lizards in the desert is almost endless, and most seem to blend in invisibly with the landscape. Some have hard spine-like intrusions covering their body, or great folds and wrinkles. The Gila monster, a protected species recognizable by its black and yellow bead-like skin, definitely has the worst reputation among lizards. Despite being the only venomous lizard in the United States, it is slow and timid and has to chew into its victim to inject poison, so it's extremely unlikely for a human to be a victim. Even so, the bite would not be fatal. Odds are you will not even catch a glimpse of this shy creature let alone be bitten by one.

Another Arizona reptile with a bad reputation, albeit a bit more deserved, is the rattlesnake. Few people realize that rattlers can be found in nearly all of the contiguous 48 states. They're simply more visible here because we spend so much time outdoors treading in their territory. In truth, however, a human stands a greater chance of being struck by lightening in these parts than being bitten by a rattlesnake. And many snake bites happen because of carelessness or bravado or even intoxication (and it's not the snake who is intoxicated). The snake's rattle is a forewarning — Listen up!

Pima County is home to eight venomous snakes, seven of which are varieties of rattlesnakes, and they can be found from the high mountains to the low desert (and occasionally in a homeowner's garage). The other poisonous snake is the small and rare coral snake with colorful bands of red, yellow and black. Snakes are most active in spring through fall but can be seen anytime of the year. They are more likely to wander into urban settings during prolonged dry spells searching for water.

Our desert is home to another famous and often feared type of fauna — creepy crawlers. One of these has been the subject of horror movies and strikes fear in the hearts of most. Lumbering across a street, it looks more like a crab than what it really is — an arachnid. Yes, it's the dreaded tarantula. But unless you suffer from arachnophobia, you have no reason to fear them. Their reputation is totally unfounded and no doubt exacerbated by Hollywood's portrayal and their sheer size. They can reach a diameter of 4 inches or more and stand several inches high. But they don't jump and typically don't even sprint very far. They do have fangs but don't often bite; if they did, it would feel equivalent to a bee sting and be no more dangerous.

INSIDERS' TIP

Started in the 1930s and finished in 1950, the 25-mile Mt. Lemmon Highway, now more commonly called Catalina Highway, was built mostly by prison labor from a federal prison camp. It is the most dangerous stretch of road in Pima County, but the winding switchbacks have undergone many improvements to make the drive less fearsome but certainly just as awesome. Before starting out on the steep drive, Tucsonans usually check on the road conditions. To be aware of possible construction delays or road closures due to weather or fire danger, call 741-4991 or 573-7623.

Tarantulas are most often seen in late summer. Females stay close to the burrows they dig, so you would be more likely to see a male as it wanders around in search of a mate. In B-movies the monster tarantulas only live about 90 minutes; in real life they have unusually long life spans — males up to 10 years and females up to 25 years.

Of all the spiders in the desert — including the black widow, which can sting but do little harm, and the wolf spider, which can be quite large and amazingly fast but doesn't bite — the only variety that could inflict harm to a human is the brown recluse, which is not unique to this area. This spider's shape is similar to a black widow's except it is brown, and, other than that, not very distinctive.

Technically not a spider, the scorpion is another desert creepy crawler with a fearsome reputation that's unfounded. Their most identifying characteristics are two lobster-like claws in front and a slender whip-like tail that curves upward. They come in all sizes, from quite small to 3 inches or more in length. The smaller the scorpion, the more potent the sting. While a scorpion's sting won't really hurt a human, it can be dangerous to domestic animals like cats and small dogs. And since scorpions like to find comfort in air-conditioned buildings during the summer heat, they often turn up in living rooms or bedrooms, contributing to a thriving exterminating business in southern Arizona.

The Mountains

Rising from the Tucson valley floor are four mountain ranges that ring the city. (Actually, a fifth range is sometimes included, the Tortolitas to the northwest, but we don't want to overwhelm you.) Although they are within the Sonoran Desert, the mountains differ greatly from the desert floor that's nearly 6,000 feet below them. To the north are the Santa Catalinas, east are the Rincons, south are the Santa Ritas and west are the Tucson Mountains. The stark Tucson Mountains are so close that they almost spill into the downtown business district, while the spread of Tucson's population has reached right into the foothills of the other three ranges. But even if you never actually get up into the mountains, you certainly will notice their stark beauty and ever-changing hues of color, compliments of Old Sol as it casts its glow at sunrise and sunset.

Because of their elevation, the mountains provide cooler temperatures as well as flora and fauna different from the desert floor's. Here you will find the southernmost ski area in the United States at the top of Mt. Lemmon in the Catalinas (assuming the winter has produced sufficient snowfall). You will also find cacti and giant century plants giving way to oak, aspen and pine trees. And wildlife to be found here but not in the valley includes mountain lions, black bears, peregrine falcons and big horn sheep. You may even see some very unexpected unwild life, such as cattle roaming the open ranges of the lower mountain elevations. The proximity of these mountain ranges to the city makes Tucson a place of wonder, delight and diversity for residents and visitors alike. Each of these mountain ranges has its distinct characteristics and people playgrounds, so here is an overview of what you might see.

The name Santa Catalina, meaning Saint Catherine, comes from Father Kino, a famous discoverer whom you can read all about in the History chapter. The highest point of this 200-square-mile range is Mt. Lemmon at 9,157 feet. The Mt. Lemmon Highway, or Catalina Highway, is a dramatic road of steep canyons on one side and mammoth granite spires on the other, with many scenic stops along the way. We're not talking New England here, but the fall foliage show is still a sight, with golden aspens and red oaks displaying their vivid hues among towering green pine and fir trees. For details on how to get to Mt. Lemmon and what to do and see there, turn to the Attractions chapter.

Also in the Santa Catalinas is Tucsonans' own "special oasis." It's called Sabino Canyon and is easily accessible from the city's northeast side. Actually, Sabino is just one of several exquisite canyons in this area of the Santa Catalinas, and if you've seen one canyon you haven't seen them all because they are all so different. But Sabino is the closest, and it will satisfy nearly anyone's craving for a taste of the wilderness. The canyon is a well-developed riparian woodland of cottonwood, willow and other native trees along a cool creek (complete with waterfalls and swimming holes) and with bountiful wildlife, all meandering up the mountainside for almost 4 miles. (Details on

A cholla cactus is beautiful as well as dangerous.

Sabino Canyon, including tram information, are in the Parks and Recreation chapter.)

Other attractions in the Catalinas, but not accessible by road, include rock formations known as Prominent Point, Finger Rock, Thumb and Rosewood Point, all of which rise above the city to the north of Alvernon Way. Areas of the Catalinas that are a bit more accessible via easy hikes are Pima Canyon and the Pusch Ridge near Catalina State Park on Tucson's northwest side. Look for details on these in our Parks and Recreation chapter.

To Tucson's east lie the three peaks of the Rincon Mountains, with a top height of 8,666 feet. Unless you are an accomplished hiker, there is no easy way to ascend this range. Because the Rincons run north to south, they do offer some spectacular sights viewed from the city: glorious reflections of the sun's colors at sunset, fierce-looking clouds rumbling toward the city during summer's monsoon storms and a massive blanket of bright white when dusted by a rare winter snow.

The most popular way to experience the Rincons is at Saguaro National Park East, which offers excellent views of the Rincons, not to mention its own amazing attractions and great spots to watch the sun setting over Tucson's western mountains. Another option is to take Reddington Pass, a rugged and dusty road that offers great vistas and some Arizona cattle country scenes as well. Reddington Road is also the way to access the trail to Tanque Verde Falls. When running at full tilt after winter or summer storms, the falls in this narrow granite canyon are awesome, but the force of the water and the slippery rocks can create a dangerous combination.

The Rincons are also home to Colossal Cave, a massive underground labyrinth that gives evidence Arizona was once covered by ocean. It is one of the largest dry caverns in the world, and its end has yet to be discovered. Other than a movie theater, it also may be the only place around to experience a constant 72 degree temperature during summer's unrelenting heat. (Read about Colossal in our Attractions chapter.)

Have you ever heard of a mountain range without an "Old Baldy"? Neither have we. Ours can be found in the Santa Rita Mountains to Tucson's south. Its other name is Mount Wrightson, which tops out at 9,453 feet. With no road, this old baldy is definitely best left to the serious hiker. The second peak of the Santa Ritas is Mount Hopkins, and located at its pinnacle is the Smithsonian's Whipple Observatory. Although accessible by a narrow switchback road, there is no point in driving it because the Observatory is behind locked gates. Instead, visit the Observatory's visitors center at the south base of the mountain, and make a reservation for the bus tour to the Observatory. (See our Attractions chapter for details.) A more down-to-earth and car-friendly way to enjoy the Santa Ritas is the beautiful Madera Canyon at about 5,000 feet elevation. Here you will find easy hiking, a cool stream, nature trails and picnic spots. And the birding in Madera Canyon is exquisite, with species that are not seen elsewhere in the United States. You might see elf owls, trogons, flycatchers and up to a dozen species of hummingbirds.

To finish off the final four (mountain ranges, that is, not basketball playoffs), we visit the Tucson Mountains on the west. This range is the smallest of the four in both girth and height, but in many ways it's both more dramatic with its volcanic peaks and more people friendly with roads, trails and man-made attractions. These mountains have much to offer in rich flora and fauna. At the Mam-a-gah Picnic Area, accessible by a 20-minute hike at the King Canyon Trailhead across from the Arizona-Sonora Desert Museum, you will find the Tucson Mountains' only permanent source of water. Continue downstream on the wash and you will find an extensive petroglyph — ancient carvings in rock.

The closest spot to traverse this range, however, is at "A Mountain," the conical little mountain that overlooks downtown Tucson. Viewable from almost any high ground in Tucson and accessible by car, it derives its moniker from the big letter A painted on it by each year's University of Arizona frosh class. Officially named Sentinel Peak, this is also the sight of Tucson's annual July 4th fireworks, funds and weather permitting (see our Festivals and Events chapter for details). The Tucson Mountains can be accessed from three roads: from Ina Road to Picture Rocks Road on the north side, through Gates Pass Road from Speedway Road near downtown, or on the south side via Ajo Way. This is also where you'll find Old Tucson Studios, home of many western film shoots; Saguaro National Park West; and the exquisite Arizona-Sonora Desert Museum.

Speaking of the Arizona-Sonora Desert Museum, you may find it comforting to know that you need not necessarily spend weeks, months or even years attempting to see firsthand the vast Sonora Desert-scapes described in this chapter. It's all re-created — from birds to bears and cacti to coyotes — in magnificent form at the Arizona-Sonora Desert Museum, so if your visit to our fine city is short, make this your foremost stop. Or make it your first stop, get appropriately educated and motivated, then head out to the real world for your firsthand experiences. Get the details on this world-class museum in our Attractions chapter.

The Rivers

"Where the river runs dry" is a saying that really befits Tucson, because our rivers usually run nothing but dry. Remember, folks, this is the desert. Tucson boasts two "major" rivers: the Rillito and the Santa Cruz. The Rillito River runs east to west across what seems to be almost the center of Tucson. But in fact it forms the northern boundary of the City of Tucson; to its north actually lies Pima County, where Tucson's population continues to spread. Rillito translates to "little creek" in Spanish (we take what we can get in these parts). The Santa Cruz River runs along what is today Interstate 19, except the river was there first. In fact, it's been used as a transportation route between Mexico and points north for centuries; the fact that the river is usually dry just added to the convenience. The strangest thing about this river, however, is that it starts its course in southern Arizona, runs south into Mexico, then makes an abrupt turn and flows back north into Arizona near Nogales. It then continues as a north-flowing river for 180 miles until it reaches the Gila River.

About the only time water runs in the rivers is after heavy rains — the summer rains of July and August and winter rains in January and February. In the interim, the riverbeds are great for walking the dog, horseback riding or mountain bike riding. In fact, many miles right along the Rillito and the Santa Cruz have been turned into river parks for safe and scenic fun.

In addition to the rivers, dry washes, also called arroyos in Spanish, dot the landscape. These are natural or man-made pathways for rainwater. Tucson's soil is made up primarily of sand, clay and rock, none of which have great absorption qualities. So instead of going down, water travels along the surface, entering into smaller washes, then larger ones and eventually into the rivers. Within several days or even hours after the rains subside, the rivers and washes again run dry. Conversely, only a few hours of torrential rain will overflow these same washes and rivers, causing flooding, road closures and property damage.

Our dry washes and riverbeds perform a vital function beyond channeling the rain. They are home to much of our desert plant and animal life.

Natural Resources

While the riches of nature abound in and around Tucson, our two most prominent natural resources are water and minerals. Stand on nearly any high ground in Tucson and look toward the southwest, beyond the buildings of Tucson. You will see a large expanse of light-colored earth; this is a copper mining plateau near Green Valley. Unlike the traditional method of underground mining, pit mining requires removing all the rock layer before sifting the earth under it to mine the copper; it's obvious the growth in this industry has not come without taking its toll on the land.

Since the dawn of time, rocks and minerals have fascinated people, providing both utility and adornment. American Indians of the Southwest gathered turquoise and other stones for ceremonies and weaponry. Spaniards came into the Southwest in search of mineral wealth, although they dug only gold and silver, overlooking deposits of base metals like copper. Gold prospectors scoured "them thar hills" looking for the precious metal, and Tombstone was founded as a silver-mining town. Arizona towns like Bisbee and Globe still thrive on copper mining. And Tucson is host to the greatest gem and mineral event in the country and probably the world each February, the Tucson Gem and Mineral Show (see our Festivals and Events chapter).

With an annual average rainfall of only 11 inches (compare that to, say, New Orleans with 54 inches) and nearly constant sunshine, it's no wonder that water would be a precious resource in Tucson. Our desert flora and fauna generally make do with the water nature provides — plants by storing it internally for months and animals by resting during the day and foraging at night, often for the very plants that hold moisture. But what do people do?

In Arizona, two-thirds of the water people use comes from underground. It's been said that, even if Tucson didn't have a rainfall in five years, no one would have to turn off the tap. But as the population increases and we look for more ways to green up our surroundings, the supply will diminish. Billions of dollars have been spent by federal and state governments, including Arizona's, to divert Colorado River water as an alternate source of water. The Colorado River no longer reaches to its outlet in the Gulf of California — we are

INSIDERS' TIP

We'd bet you knew that American Indians have been digging for and using turquoise since they first arrived in the Southwest, and we'd also bet that you probably won't leave Tucson without purchasing at least one example of their exquisite jewelry. But did you also know that, today, the bulk of all turquoise comes as a by-product of copper pit mining? To see some outstanding mineral and gem collections in Tucson, visit the University's Mineral Museum at Flandrau Science Center at University Boulevard and Cherry Avenue, 621-4227, or the Arizona-Sonora Desert Museum at 2021 N. Kinney Road, 883-2702.

THE NATURAL WORLD

Roadrunners are a common sight in the less developed areas of Tucson.

using it up. But for now, at least, Tucson's water supply is adequate.

The reality is that, no matter where one lives, water is a precious natural resource and water conservation a wise human practice. Unlike some other cities in the arid Southwest, Tucson's population has largely accepted desert landscaping as opposed to trying to recreate Kentucky in their backyards. Grass lawns are still visible in older midtown neighborhoods, but newer housing communities are adopting desert landscaping or Xeriscaping, whereby native and low-water-usage plants are grouped according to their water needs to conserve water.

Natural resources have long formed the backbone of Pima County's economy, often referred to as the four Cs: climate, copper, cotton and cattle. Climate has produced a healthy tourism industry, while the copper mines of Pima County now produce over 70 percent of the copper mined in the United States. You may be surprised about the cotton, but drive north of Tucson, such as on Interstate 10 toward Phoenix, and you will see acres and acres of it growing with the help of irrigation. Cattle ranching has been an important part of southern Arizona since Father Kino first introduced the tame beasts in the 1690s. The first Arizona cowboys, or vaqueros, were American Indian or Mexican.

Although much diminished from earlier days, cattle ranches, complete with the "cowboys" who tend them, still exist, mostly in higher elevations. The flavor of the cowboy West remains strong in Tucson — from cowboy boots and Stetson hats to horseback trail riding and world-class dude ranches for cowboy wannabees.

Stargazing

For astronomers and stargazers worldwide, Tucson is known as the center of gravity. With nights that are nearly always clear, stars as bright as beacons and unobstructed mountain peaks to hold man's formidable astronomy tools, the Tucson area offers some of the best possible conditions on Earth for viewing outer space.

Three major astronomical observatories are located near Tucson: the University of Arizona's facilities in the Santa Catalina Mountains; Kitt Peak National Observatory 56 miles west of Tucson; and the Smithsonian Astrophysical Observatory on Mount Hopkins in the Santa Rita Mountains. These sites hold the most sophisticated and advanced telescopes and tracking devices created by man, some parts of which are developed by the University of Arizona. And in a more down-to-earth location, in the heart of Tucson, is the University's Flandrau Planetarium. For information on visiting these places among the stars, turn to the Attractions chapter.

Meanwhile, as you glance upward at Tucson's star-filled night skies, remind yourself that some of the world's foremost astronomers are doing the same, trying to unravel the mysteries of endless space and perhaps our own humble beginnings.

The Weather

In case you haven't already noticed or heard, Tucson has sunshine — more, it is reported, than any other place in the United States. The actual count is 350 days a year. (Lest you feel deceived, this refers to any day on which the sun shines at some time rather than days on which it shines all day.) To be sure, there are days in the summer months when Tucsonans look skyward, urgently pleading for just one cloud to pass by. The average yearly high is 82 and low is 54. The hottest months on average are June and July at 99 and the coolest are December and January at 65. If this sounds too good to be true, remember that these are averages. It is just as likely that Tucson will have a number of 100+ (or even 105+) days and a number of winter nights with temperatures below freezing, at least for a few hours.

Temperatures are the subject of a lot of talk in Tucson but so is rain. In summer, a word you'll hear often is monsoon — as in "when are the monsoons getting here" or "here come the monsoon clouds, so where's the rain?" The climatologists say using monsoon is a misnomer; a monsoon is what India or Southeast Asia experiences. But Tucsonans like its descriptive quality and aren't likely to give it up.

About mid-July, just when Tucsonans are sure they can't survive another day of 100+ temperatures, months without rain and rising humidity, the late afternoon clouds begin building up — huge, rapidly moving white and dark gray clouds tinged with reds and golds by the sun's rays still shining in the western sky. But these are fickle clouds. For days they may let forth no rain, or just a smattering of rain on some lucky sections of the mountains or valley. Eventually, they give us what we long for, along with ferocious winds, thunder, displays of lightening that are unparalleled and maybe even a sky-sweeping rainbow or two or three. With the lightening also comes the fear of fire, particularly in the mountains and foothills that have been parched for months. As inaccessible as some of these places are, the mountain fires can burn for days or even weeks, fueled by high winds and only dribbles of rainfall.

But back to our monsoon sequence. By nightfall or shortly thereafter, the rains subside and the desert is cooled off and somewhat watered down, at least briefly. Mother Nature repeats this scene, often several days a week, through July and August and often into September. And whether on any given day she will produce rain or just its trappings, only Mother Nature knows for sure; that's the way of our monsoon season. We do get a bonus with these late summer rains: Plant life that has seemed to all but die suddenly resurrects, and birds and animals of all sorts come out of hiding to enjoy the rain and have a feeding frenzy. It's like having a second spring.

Tucson may also have a second "rainy" season, typically in December and January, when average amounts are .94 and .83 inches respectively. (Yes, you read those number right — less than an inch.) These are the rains that will sometimes produce a blanket of mountain snow and, ever so rarely, a dusting of valley snow. At Mt. Lemmon, however, the average annual snowfall is 100 inches, which makes downhill and cross-country skiing possible a mere hour's drive away from the city. When these winter rains are normal and are followed by rains in March and April, we can expect a great spring show of blooms from the desert that lasts into early summer.

Tucsonans boast about the dry heat that results from our very low humidity levels much of the year. And indeed it is a benefit of our climate. On even the coolest winter days, one rarely feels cold or chilled during the daylight hours. For eight months of the year — October through May — you can simply count on beautiful weather for almost any outdoor activity.

Although Tucson has many attractions that make it a great place to recreate and reside, our weather certainly tops the list. It is the weather that makes possible so much of what we do, see and enjoy in and around Tucson. Thank you Mother Nature!

Visitors are usually amazed to find that there's more to Tucson than just desert.

Parks and Recreation

With 350 days of sunshine per year, recreation in the Tucson area means the outdoors, and with four mountain ranges surrounding metropolitan Tucson, visitors and residents alike benefit from a wide range of state and federal parks, hiking and horse trails and numerous climate zones along the heights of the mountains.

Visitors are usually amazed to find that there's more to Tucson than just desert — we do have green spaces, some outside the city and others within its boundaries. Both Pima County and the City of Tucson maintain a number of recreational areas throughout the region, ranging from small patches of lawn to small lakes. Many of these regional and neighborhood parks also offer picnicking, jogging and bike trails, swimming pools, ball fields, tennis, basketball and volleyball courts, gyms and golf courses. In fact, golf is such a large part of Tucson's recreational scene, this book includes a separate chapter devoted entirely to the subject. We have done the same with bicycling, since Tucson is considered the second most bicycle-friendly city in America. (Portland, Oregon, is number one.)

Following the concept of greenways established in other urban areas, Tucson has been expanding a series of river parks, which include jogging, bicycling and horseback riding trails that will eventually surround Tucson. Easy to get to, these linear parks offer opportunities to stretch your legs, walk your dogs, explore the dry river beds of the Santa Cruz and Rillito rivers and peddle for miles. The area's designated bike paths and bike lanes help make getting around urban Tucson safe and easy (see our Bicycling chapter).

Whether you seek recreation for fun, fitness or professional training, you'll be hard-pressed not to find what you're looking for in the Tucson area. This chapter will give you a taste of what the city has to offer. If you're more of a voyeur than a participant, check out our Spectator Sports chapter. But whatever you choose to do, have fun!

Mountain Parks

No matter what part of Tucson you find yourself in, you are virtually minutes from one of the surrounding mountain ranges, with a variety of canyons, trails, campgrounds or scenic drives to explore. Whether you are looking for a short walk or a weeklong backpacking trip, the following list offers a full range of experiences. You can obtain free materials, including maps, on these locations by calling the numbers provided.

Saguaro National Park West
W. Kinney Rd. • 733-5158

Just 2 miles north of the Arizona-Sonoran Desert Museum, this 24-square-mile National Park Service site is a bit different from the east unit in that the saguaro are thicker and younger. The 8.2-mile Bajada Loop Drive passes two picnic areas in view of Indian petroglyphs on the canyon walls above. The visitors center offers hiking trail maps and the only water and restrooms available in the area.

In the northern part of this park is an area called Picture Rocks, accessible from the northwest via Ina Road, then west to Picture Rocks Road. To get to the main entrance of Saguaro National Park West from this point by a scenic drive, take Sandario Road south to Kinney Road.

(See "Hiking" in this chapter.)

Tucson Mountain Park
Kinney Rd. • 740-2690

This 17,000-acre mountain area just west of Tucson is managed by the Pima County Parks and Recreation Department and includes miles of hiking paths, horse trails and campgrounds as well as the Arizona-Sonoran Desert Museum, Old Tucson Studios and the International Wildlife Museum (see our Attractions chapter). Though not as high as Tucson's other ranges (its Wasson Peak reaches the top elevation of 4,683 feet), this range is more sharply cut, with volcanic peak formations that stab the sky.

The two roads into the Tucson Mountains from the city are distinct. Taking Speedway Boulevard west of Interstate 10 brings you to Gates Pass Road, a curvy mountain pass that does not allow RVs, trailers or other high-profile vehicles (if you are prone to car sickness, bring a paper bag!). The other entrance is south of downtown off Ajo Way going west from Mission Road. Turn right at Kinney Road, and you'll enjoy a smooth, pleasant drive that passes numerous well-marked picnic areas, trailheads and campsites. Both roads take you through the mountain park and terminate at a vast valley on the west side of the mountains. All day-use sites close at 10 PM, except Gilbert Ray Campground, which charges for overnight use (see our Campgrounds and RV Parks chapter).

The Tucson Mountains have a long history of both prehistoric Indian petroglyph sites and mine shafts plunging downward — holes you want to avoid. And like other mountain parks in the area, you are prohibited from removing anything from the park, even rocks.

(See "Hiking" in this chapter.)

Coronado National Forest

This is going to take some explaining, so be patient. Unlike national forests or mountain parks around the country that consist of a single range, the Coronado National Forest is a series of mountains extending from southern Arizona south to the Mexican border and east into New Mexico.

This 1,790,935-acre series of scattered mountain ranges rises from the desert floor to elevations of 3,000 to 10,720 feet, creating "Sky Islands" rising from the desert. A sky island is an ecosystem existing on top of a peak that is so different from the desert floor it is literally an island of habitat with its own wildlife, weather, vegetation and seasons. In this section we describe the Tucson area spots within the Coronado National Forest — the Santa Catalina Mountains (including Mt. Lemmon), the Rincon Mountains, Sabino Canyon, Catalina State Park, Pusch Ridge and Saguaro National Park East.

> **FYI**
> Unless otherwise noted, the area code for all phone numbers listed in this guide is 520.

The U.S. Forest Service manages Coronado National Forest, and its Tucson office is at 301 W. Congress Street, 792-6483.

Saguaro National Park East/Rincon Mountain Wilderness
5700 N. Sabino Canyon Rd. • 749-8700

As Tucson grew from west to east, it was clear the mountains needed to be protected, and such was the case in 1984 when this 38,590-acre wilderness area was established surrounding three sides of Saguaro National Park East. In fact, this adjacent wilderness was established to act as a buffer to protect Saguaro National Park East. The Rincon Mountains, the range you'll see when driving east on virtually any street in Tucson, comprises a total of 58,000 acres with three main peaks: Tanque Verde Peak, Rincon Peak and Mica Mountain.

This area is not for novice hikers, as it is dominated by very rocky, steep terrain with elevations ranging from 3,600 to 7,700 feet, with no public roads. If you make it to higher elevations, expect to see the transition from desert grasslands to oak-juniper-pinon-pine woodlands. Many of the dramatic rock outcrops are virtually impossible to reach on foot or horseback and even the best traveled back-country routes are passable only by four-wheel vehicles.

The best way to enter the area is at Saguaro National Park East's visitors center off Old Spanish Trail. From there is an extensive system of more than 70 trails heading into the Rincon Mountain Wilderness.

Established in 1933 and upgraded to park status in 1992, Saguaro National Park East is the oldest of the two Saguaro National Park units (see Saguaro National Park West/Tucson Mountains in this chapter) established to protect the vast groves of old-growth saguaro cacti and the javelinas, coyotes, badgers, bobcats, Gila monsters, desert tortoise and other desert dwellers living in the area.

(See "Hiking" in this chapter.)

Sabino Canyon
5900 N. Sabino Canyon Rd. • 749-8700

Thirteen miles from downtown in the eastern foothills of the Catalina mountains, Sabino Canyon offers an easily accessible site for either quick walks or daylong hikes. The area is known not only for its Hohokam Indian ruins, but also as an oasis of cottonwood, willow, ash and sycamore trees. Sabino Creek feeds into pools and waterfalls. Pony soldiers from Fort Lowell used the swimming holes in the 1870s, and in the 1930s 3.8 miles of road were built into the canyon for better access by the local residents to trailheads at the end of the road, which lead into the back country of the Coronado National Forest.

Sabino Canyon is Tucson's most popular outdoor playground with more than 1 million visitors each year. There are several picnic areas and at least seven popular trails throughout the area. One favorite hike for Tucsonans is a 9-mile round-trip hike, an easy walk along a paved road that begins at the visitors center. The road has been closed to automobile traffic since the early 1980s, though bicycles are allowed before 9 AM and after 5 PM, except on Saturdays and Wednesdays when they are prohibited. As an option to walking up Sabino Canyon, the area also offers an open-air shuttle tram that takes riders on a 45-minute narrated round-trip into the upper canyon area. Riders have the option of getting off the tram along the way to hike and then catching another tram for the trip back to the visitors center. The tram costs $6 for adults and $2.50 for children 3 to 12. Younger children ride free.

Check in at the 2,000-square-foot visitors center before you venture into the canyon. There you will find trail maps, a bookstore and an audiovisual room for presentations on the canyon. The exhibit gallery displays focus on wildlife, vegetation and the history of the canyon.

Catalina State Park
11570 N. Oracle Rd. • 628-5798

This 5,500-acre preserve was dedicated as a state park in 1983 and is maintained by the Arizona State Parks Board. About 135,000 visitors per year take advantage of the 48 developed campsites, more than 100 picnic tables and numerous well-kept trails. For campers, wood fires are prohibited, so remember to bring charcoal. For birders, a special 1-mile nature loop winds through a mesquite bosque that provides shelter for many area birds, including golden eagles and peregrine falcons. On the higher trails, glimpses of bighorn sheep are not uncommon. There are numerous ruins of Hohokam Indian farmers, including pit houses and a ball court.

Only the entrance roads are paved, so plan to park at the visitors center at the park entrance (there's a $3-per-car fee) and pick up a trail map. The 7 miles of hiking trails lead to numerous waterfalls and pools shaded by sycamore and oak trees with elevations ranging from 2,600 to 3,000 feet. Horses are welcome on all but the nature trails, and nearby stables offer horse rentals (see "Horseback Riding" later in this chapter). For hardy hikers, the Romero Canyon trail into the Santa Catalina Mountains will take you 16 miles to Sabino Canyon or to the top of Mt. Lemmon. Though the Mt. Lemmon hike is only about 13 miles, the trail climbs 6,000 feet. (See "Hiking" in this chapter.)

Mount Lemmon
Santa Catalina Mountains, Catalina Hwy. • 749-8700

A one-hour drive up the winding Catalina Highway from Tucson takes you through five distinct vegetative and climate zones. The summit is always 20 to 30 degrees cooler than the desert floor. In fact, in the winter, Mt. Lemmon's Ski Valley is the southernmost ski area in the United States.

From Tucson there is only one way to get up the mountain: the 34-mile Catalina Highway beginning at Tanque Verde Road on the far east side of town. The first leg of the drive takes you up a curvy road with a number of opportunities to stop and view the desert floor below. During this leg of the drive you may see rock climbers clinging to the limestone cliffs or windswept pinnacles. Over all, Mt. Lemmon has hundreds of miles of trails and numerous campgrounds that range from ancient Indian sites to areas with lakes surrounded by ponderosa pine (see our Campgrounds and RV Parks chapter).

Toward the end of the drive is Summerhaven, a village where visitors can find overnight cabins, restaurants and shops. At the very end of the road is the Marshall Gulch Picnic Area and the trailhead for the Aspen Loop Trail, considered the best hike for viewing autumn colors. Other trailheads in the area of Summerhaven are located along the highway, and the major trails are well-marked, with parking areas and posted maps.

A short drive away is Ski Valley with its chair lifts and 15 trails ranging from beginner to expert (see "Skiing" later in this chapter). In the summer, chair lifts take visitors on a 25-minute ride, featuring great views of the north side of this mountain range (see our Attractions chapter).

Both the Catalina Mountains and its highest peak, Mt. Lemmon, are named for women. Father Kino, the first missionary to arrive in Tucson, named the mountain range after his sister, and Mt. Lemmon was named after Sara Lemmon, a woman who climbed the north side of the range on horseback and described bobcats, wild parrots, mountain lions, bighorn sheep, deer and bears in her journal. Today, the area supports more than a thousand species of plants and 200 kinds of birds.

Recently completed construction has widened parts of the road up Mt. Lemmon, once considered one of the most dangerous roads in Arizona (during the winter, you may need chains). For recreational use of Mt. Lemmon, you'll pay a toll: $5 per day, $10 for a weekly camping pass or $20 for a season pass. The season pass is the best deal, and the money raised is earmarked for trail and campground maintenance.

River Parks

Rillito River Park
Campbell Ave. to Flowing Wells Rd.
• **no phone**

Run, jog, walk, peddle or roll to Rillito River Park. Movement is the big draw here, and the park does not discriminate against any mode of transportation. However, there are a few ground rules: cyclists and in-line skaters may only use the north bank, while horseback riders may only use the south. Walkers and joggers may use either bank. Currently, the park is approximately 3 miles long, but there are plans to extend it to the Santa Cruz River Park. It's open from sunrise to sunset.

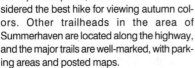

On the north bank of the Rillito, just west of Oracle Road, is the Children's Memorial Park. The center of this park is the granite-faced wall that lists hundreds of children who have died in car accidents, through abuse or by other means. Memorial services are held here frequently. The park also has restrooms, a baseball field, a playground and ramadas,

(Turn to our Bicycling chapter for more information about Rillito River Park.)

Santa Cruz River Park
West of I-10, Grant Rd. to Irvington Rd.
• **no phone**

Tucson was born on the Santa Cruz River, and today a north/south linear park cuts directly west of downtown Tucson adjacent to I-10 on both sides of the dry river. Constructed in stages since 1984, the park runs from Grant Road (north of downtown) south through the urban area around Congress Street and ultimately to Irvington Road.

Playgrounds, ramadas, mesquite-shaded picnic tables, water fountains and restrooms can be found throughout the park. The area also contains a set of arches embedded with hand-painted mosaic tiles by local artist Susan Gamble that tells the history of the river and its ancient inhabitants. Another arch facing St. Mary's Road welcomes visitors to that entrance to the river park in both English and Spanish.

Tennis and Tucson are a natural match!

Near Congress Street, an exercise course allows walkers and joggers to add to their workouts. Near the Congress Street bridge is Tucson's largest tree, a eucalyptus that is 4 feet in diameter. The park is open from sunrise to sunset. (See the Bicycling chapter for more information.)

Urban Green Spaces

A variety of urban parks are maintained by the city and county. Some parks are small green spaces with picnic tables while others are large facilities with tennis and golf courses, swimming pools, lighted ball fields, neighborhood libraries and amphitheaters. In addition the continuing effort to expand the river parks will eventually lead to a bike and jogging trail that circles the central city area. Unless otherwise noted, these urban parks are open from sunrise to 10 PM. (Also see "Handball, Racquetball and Tennis" for more information about these parks.)

Fort Lowell Park
2900 N. Craycroft Rd. • 791-2589

This historic site covers more than 10 square blocks and includes the Ft. Lowell Museum and other historic buildings from the original 1800s cavalry fort. Today, it's a major park area with an outdoor pool, small lake and lots of shaded ramadas and picnic areas. Just about any weekend you can catch a baseball, football, soccer or rugby game at one of the park's many ball fields. Tennis and volleyball courts are also open to the public.

Himmel Park
1000 N. Tucson Blvd. • 791-3276

One of Tucson's older parks and almost in the heart of the city, Himmel has lots of trees, playing fields and picnic areas. There's also an outdoor pool, a library and tennis courts.

Jacobs Park
1010 W. Lind Ave. • 791-4358

Trees, ramadas and picnic areas offer shade and relaxation at Jacobs Park, which is west of Oracle Road and south of Prince Road. The pool welcomes all with cool waters, and fields host soccer games almost on a daily basis.

J.F. Kennedy Park
3700 S. Mission Rd. • 791-4382

Six miles south of downtown Tucson at the corner of Mission Road and Ajo Way, Kennedy Park has a recently renovated area for festivals and outdoor entertainment that is the site of many annual Mexican fiestas. The main attraction here is the 10-acre lake, where fishing for bass and boating are allowed. While there is no swimming in the lake, there is a pool at the park as well as picnic ramadas and a neighborhood library.

Randolph Park
200 S. Alvernon Wy. • 791-4560

Randolph Park and the adjacent Reid Park combine to make a huge multiacre green space in the heart of Tucson. In addition to golf courses, the park has a gym, nautilus ($1 for a day pass), meeting rooms (which can be rented for between $4.50 to $9.50 per hour), basketball and tennis courts, an arts and crafts building, a performing arts center, a gallery, an auditorium and a skate park for in-line skating (see Randolph Skatepark in the Kidstuff chapter). Tennis clinics are held here every Saturday for kids 5 to 17, and a teen basketball league for kids 13 to 19 meets on Saturday nights from 7 to 11 PM. Call 791-4870 for basketball information. This park is also the site of the City of Tucson Parks and Recreation Department. (Also see our Golf chapter for information on the Randolph and Dell Urich golf courses.)

Gene C. Reid Park
22nd St. and Country Club Rd.
• 791-4022

This is the City of Tucson's flagship urban park and the home of one of the best venues for outdoor entertainment, DeMeester Outdoor Performance Center. The Reid Park Zoo is a 17-acre oasis with hundreds of exotic animals housed in realistic environments that reflect their origins (see our Kidstuff chapter). Hi Corbett Field — used by the Colorado Rockies for spring training — and a 2-acre lake make this park complex a favorite family attraction. It's a great site for picnics, paddle-boat rides among the ducks on the lake or fishing for tilapia, sunfish and bass. Take a stroll through the well-kept rose garden containing more than 2,000 plants. Combined, Reid and Randolph parks cover a .75-square-mile area virtually in the center of Tucson.

Silverbell Park
4600 N. Silverbell Rd. • 743-7284

Besides the golf course located here, this site, west of I-10 and north of Grant Road, contains a 13-acre lake capable of handling boats up to 14 feet or canoes up to 17 feet. No swimming is allowed in the lake, but anglers regularly catch bass, bluegill and trout. There is also an area reserved for model plane hobbyists to fly their gas-powered planes. (See our Golf chapter for details on Silverbell's course.)

Tohono Chul Park
7366 N. Paseo Del Norte • 575-8468

Tohono Chul Park is privately owned and located on 37 acres northwest of the intersection of Ina and Oracle roads. It's an oasis of unadulterated desert nature. Originally part of a larger cattle grazing range, the park began taking shape when date palms and citrus trees were planted in the late 1920s. The original adobe house was built in 1937, and the site changed hands several times until 1966 when it was purchased by Richard and Jean Wilson. By 1979 the couple had installed nature trails, and on April 19, 1985, they dedicated the area as a nonprofit park. Today, the nonprofit Tohono Chul Park, Inc. operates from private donations.

Some 400 species of arid climate plants are displayed here and carefully marked for strolling visitors along two nature trails (one is wheelchair accessible). The sanctuary has shaded ramadas, picnic areas, restrooms, a gift shop, a greenhouse, an art gallery and the Tohono Chul Tea Room for dining or afternoon tea inside or on the patio.

A number of events take place here — many of them fund-raising or educational in nature. Meeting rooms and an outdoor amphitheater are available for rental. Visiting the site is free, though donations are requested. For those not willing to take to the mountain parks, this is a great short walk for learning Tucson's natural history. Tohono Chul Park is open from 7 AM to sunset.

Morris K. Udall Park
7200 E. Tanque Verde Rd. • 791-4931

This park has a heated pool, ball fields, ramadas, an adult open gym and a nautilus room for ages 16 and older. The Morris K. Udall Recreation Center here offers classes through the City of Tucson Parks and Recreation Department for all ages — from children through seniors. The center also hosts soccer and basketball leagues.

Recreation

City of Tucson Parks and Recreation Department
900 S. Randolph Wy. • 791-4873

The programs and classes conducted by the City of Tucson Parks and Recreation Department could fill a book; actually, they do fill a catalogue that comes out four times a year. The pages are full of activities for everyone from toddlers to seniors in every area of interest from basketball, golf and tennis to painting, pottery and ballroom dancing.

Classes are broken into five age groups: children ages 0 to 5 years; youth ages 6 to 12; teens ages 13 to 16; adults ages 17 to 49; and seniors age 50 and older. Areas of focus include arts and crafts, dance and movement, gymnastics, tae kwon do, photography, cooking, creative writing and much, much more. The department also offers therapeutic recreation to those who are developmentally delayed; it's open to children and adults and offers similar classes as those mentioned previously as well as monthly social dances. (Call 791-4504, TDD and Voice, for information about therapeutic recreation.)

The jewel in the department's crown is **KIDCO**, especially its summer program. Running from May to July for children 5 to 12, this free program incorporates sports, games and crafts and is offered at more than 30 sites around the city. It has won praises from parents, kids and educators and serves as a model for other programs across the country. During the school year, KIDCO has an after-school program offered at schools citywide. It's free to kids currently enrolled in kindergarten through 6th grade. Hours are Monday through Friday from dismissal to 6 PM. Call 791-4845 for details.

The City of Tucson Parks and Recreation catalogue is distributed through the department's headquarters at the previously listed address as well as with the Sunday edition of *The Arizona Daily Star* four times a year.

Pima County Parks and Recreation
1204 W. Silverlake Rd. • 740-2680

Pima County Parks and Recreation maintains several parks in the area and offers leisure classes, senior and youth activities and after-school programs. Hundreds of kids have learned how to swim, how to shoot a hockey puck and how to traverse the mountain trails around Tucson in classes and programs by Pima County Parks and Rec. Call the previously listed number for a catalogue of the department's activities.

Archaeology

Old Pueblo Archaeology Center
1000 E. Ft. Lowell Rd. • 798-1201

The Old Pueblo Archaeology Center gives you the chance to get down and dirty. The group offers hands-on opportunities to dig at ancient Indian ruins. Free guided tours include the noted ruins in Sabino Canyon State Park and other locations in the area. Call for reservations. (See Archaeology for All in the Kidstuff chapter.)

Ballooning

Balloon America
P.O. Box 31255, Tucson 85751
• 299-7744

Balloon America, which has been in business for more than 15 years, operates tours from October to June. The Sunrise Tour is $135 per person, lasts about 1½ hours and includes a champagne breakfast and pictures of your adventure. The FAA-certified pilots offer pickup and return to most area resorts.

Southern Arizona Balloon Excursions
P.O. Box 5265, Tucson 85703 • 624-3599

Balloon Excursions offers tours year round that last about two hours and cost $125. Passengers enjoy a champagne brunch after their ride over Tucson.

Cattle Drives

Cocoraque Ranch Cattle Drive
6255 N. Diamond Hills Ln. • 682-8594

For those who long for an 1890s cowboy experience, this working ranch just west of Old Tucson Studios has much to offer. The daylong Western experience includes sunset horseback riding, getting your hands dirty on a real cattle ranch, hayrides, cattle drives and a cowboy cookout.

Spanish Trail Outfitters, Inc.
8500 E. Ocotillo Dr. • 751-0734

Spanish Trail Outfitters offers the same activities as other Western cattle drive and horseback companies as well as customized trail rides, off-road tours and firearms shooting at its ranch near Sabino Canyon.

Climbing

In Tucson, rock-climbing can be a sport or serious business. Most climbs in the area are off the beaten path and may require a several-mile hike before you ever strap on the ropes. Others, like the popular Windy Point along Mt. Lemmon Highway, are easy to access along roadside crags where pinnacles and rock walls hang over the highway. But if you want the real experience, consider the back-country hikes to remote areas, such as the kind led by Southwest Trekking (P.O. Box 57714, Tucson, AZ 85710, 296-9661).

Rock Climbing can be a grass roots thing with "third class" climbs that don't require ropes, or it can be highly technical, involving expensive equipment for rappelling with ropes. In fact, the area has so many year-round sites in the back country, there have been videos made here and sold worldwide. The indoor climbing gym Rocks & Ropes (listed in this section) and outdoor equipment supplier Summit Hut (5045 E. Speedway Blvd., 325-1554) both offer extensive information and maps for these locations.

Briefly, here are some sites to ask about: Esperero Spires, a 500-foot monolith at the mouth of Sabino Canyon; the east buttress of Table Mountain near Pusch Ridge; and Leviathan Dome near Oracle, Arizona, north of Tucson.

Rocks and Ropes
330 S. Toole Ave., Ste. 400 • 882-5924

Open seven days a week, this indoor rock climbing gym is not only a great place to practice and take lessons, but also to network with other climbers. The 8,000-square-foot gym offers 75 climbing routes ranging from beginner to the radical 45-degree lead cave. Rates range from $8.00 for daily use to annual family memberships of $495. The gym has a locker room and pro shop. Rocks and Ropes is open to the public from 3 to 10 PM weekdays and 11 AM to 10 PM weekends. Kids younger than 18 must get a signed waiver from their parents to use the facilities.

Venture Up
2415 E. Indian School Rd., Phoenix • (602) 955-9100

Though based in Phoenix, this group is accredited by the American Mountain Guides Association and offers two-day courses ($115) in Tucson at different times of the year. The course is geared toward people with no prior experience or as a refresher for the experienced. The program involves rappelling, belaying, crack and face climbing. Venture Up provides all the gear, including shoes, helmets, ropes, hardware and harness.

Handball, Racquetball and Tennis

There are more than 200 tennis courts in city and county parks, schools and private resorts and hotels. Most of the resorts require a membership fee that varies depending on whether you want a full membership, a golf package or just tennis, so it's best to call for information.

For the city and county parks, assume there is a need for reservations since some parks (the ones listed here) are more popular than others.

For handball and racquetball, the courts used for these sports are almost always one and the same. If you are a handball/racquetball fan, then your first stop should be the 24-hour Tucson Racquet Club listed in this section. It's one of the largest facilities in the country and the location for many tournaments the Tucson-based United States Handball Association sponsors.

Fort Lowell Park
2900 N. Craycroft Rd. • 791-2584

Fort Lowell Park has eight lighted tennis courts. The fee for daytime hours is $1.50 per person; the night rate is $4.50 per court. Time of play is limited to 1½ hours when the courts are full. Reservations are not necessary. The park also has four racquetball courts. Fees are $4 per court with unlimited play in the daytime and $4.50 per court with lights in the evening. Evening play has a 1½-hour limit.

Himmel Park
100 N. Tucson Blvd. • 791-3276

Though the park is small, it offers eight lighted tennis courts at $1.50 per person for 1½ hours during the day or $4.50 per court for 1½ hours at night.

Randolph Tennis Center
50 S. Alvernon Wy. • 791-4896

Tucson's largest city park has 25 lighted courts that cost $1.50 per person during the day or $4.50 per court at night for 1½ hours of play. The center also has 10 combination racquetball/handball courts. The cost is $4 during the day and $4.50 at night. Since these courts almost never fill up, you can play as long as you like.

United States Handball Association
2333 N. Tucson Blvd. • 795-0434

Tucson is the location of the Handball Hall of Fame and the U.S. Handball Association headquarters. The Hall of Fame contains an exhibit hall and the association's offices where it publishes a monthly magazine for members and distribute information on when and where to play in leagues and tournaments. Membership is $25 a year.

Hiking

Hiking around Tucson means trekking into one of many mountain parks or area canyons (see "Mountain Parks" at the beginning of this chapter.) Surrounded by mountain ranges as well as state and national parks, hiking trails abound over low desert hills and snow-dusted mountains. The level of difficulty can range from easy strolls to daylong marches through fast-rising terrain.

As we mentioned in "Mountain Parks," most of the major areas have a visitors center with free trail maps, so the center should always be your first stop. Areas without visitors centers usually have trailheads marked with detailed maps, highlighting your hiking options.

Some parks charge for parking while others simply have free lots near the trailhead. These have nighttime parking restrictions, but you can call for a free parking permit if you are planning to camp overnight.

Whether you'll be taking a short hike or an all-day trek, be sure you have sturdy shoes to avoid cactus thorns. And always bring more water than you think you'll need.

No matter where or how you choose to hike, always tell someone where you're going and when you expect to return. If it's summertime, avoid the excessive heat by staying home between noon and 3 PM. If you do go hiking in summer, wear a hat.

Southern Arizona Hiking Club
P.O. Box 32257, Tucson 85751
• 293-4680

If you're a serious hiker, consider contacting the Southern Arizona Hiking Club. The yearly membership fee is $15, and the club publishes a 50-page monthly bulletin with more than 50 group hikes ranging from easy to strenuous scheduled each month.

Saguaro National Park West/ Tucson Mountain Park
W. Kinney Rd. • 740-2690

One of the favorite hikes in the Tucson Mountains is the Wasson Peak Loop. Taking Speedway Boulevard 14 miles east of Tucson over Gates Pass Road and right on Kinney Road, you'll find the trailhead parking lot just across the street from the Arizona-Sonora Desert Museum. The trailhead is marked King Canyon trailhead. You'll hike north on the old jeep road for .9 miles and then approach the Mam-a Gah picnic area. Take the trail to the left and follow the narrow, rocky path along the west side of King Canyon. At this point you are about 3,200 feet above the trailhead.

Follow this trail for another 2.3 miles until you reach Sweetwater Saddle (about 3,900 feet) and the Sweetwater Trail intersection with its looming view of the western Santa Catalina Mountains in the distance. The trail continues to climb steeply and to another intersection with a sign for the Hugh Norris Trail. You are now at 4,600 feet and the end of King Canyon. Take the trail to the right, and in a third of a mile you will reach the summit of Wasson Peak and a panoramic view of Tucson at 4,686 feet.

To complete the loop, return the way you came and follow the Hugh Norris Trail along the ridge line for about 2 miles. You will encounter yet another signed junction at the Esperanza Trail. Take the left path and follow it past the old Gould Mine remains (watch for holes) and back to the Mam-a Gah picnic area, about 1.5 miles. From this location just follow the jeep trail you came in on back to the trailhead and parking lot.

Pima Canyon
East end of Magee Rd. • 740-2690

This is the westernmost canyon along the front range of the Santa Catalinas. On the eastern end of Magee Road, the trailhead is marked by a 44-car parking lot, and it should be noted that parking on Magee Road itself will get you a $55 fine, as will overnight parking in the lot without a permit.

The first third-of-a-mile entrance to the Pima Canyon trail cuts through a recently built subdivision, and hikers are cautioned to stay inside the fenced corridor through this section. There are no developed facilities in the canyon, though there is a drinking fountain at the entrance as well as an emergency phone that connects to the Pima County Sheriff's Department. The features of this canyon include steep rocky walls and great views of Tucson in the valley below. Farther along the trail at the 3-mile mark, hikers will see a change, as water becomes evident. By 5 miles, you will have climbed 2,550 feet, and if you choose to continue the full 7-mile trail to Mount Kimbell, you will have climbed another 2,000 feet.

You can camp overnight with a permit, but camping within 400 feet of the trail is prohibited during the desert bighorn sheep lambing season from January 1 to April 30. Interpretive signs along the trail explain the dangers of getting too close to these elusive animals, and in an effort to protect the dwindling herds that roam the western slopes of the Catalinas, dogs are not permitted on any part of the trail. Pima Canyon can also be approached from Pima Canyon Road at Sunrise Drive.

> **FYI**
> Unless otherwise noted, the area code for all phone numbers listed in this guide is 520.

Finger Rock Canyon
North end of Alvernon Wy. • 740-2690

The trailhead is maintained by Coronado National Forest and the Pima County Parks and Recreation Department and consists of three trails: Finger Rock, Pontatoc Ridge and Pontatoc Canyon. Though there is no entry fee, an overnight parking permit is required to camp in this area that has no developed facilities but great views.

The Finger Rock Trail is named for the close-up view of Finger Rock, a dominant landmark of the Santa Catalina mountains visible from around the city. The trail is one of the steepest in this rugged part of the mountain range. It leads hikers into the high country of the Santa Catalinas past large saguaros, steep canyon walls and sweeping views. At the 3-mile mark, a side trail leads to Linda Vista Saddle, known for its views of the entire Tucson Valley. Continuing up the trail takes you to Mount Kimbell, where the views include the other side of the mountain range north to Biosphere 2.

The Pontatoc Ridge and Canyon Trails share the same trailhead and path for the first mile before splitting farther up the ridge. The Canyon Trail goes left and leads to an area that contains several pools. The Pontatoc Ridge Trail cuts right for an easy hike to a group of flat rocks with great views of the city. Farther up the trail, it ends at the mouth of an old mine, which should not be entered. This is also bighorn sheep territory, so dogs are not allowed on this hike.

Saguaro National Park East/Rincon Mountain Wilderness
5700 N. Sabino Canyon Rd. • 749-8700

For those looking for one of the toughest hikes in the Tucson area, Rincon Peak will actually take your breath away. This is the second highest peak in the Rincon Mountain Wilderness area of Saguaro National Park East, rising 8,466 feet through the 60,000-acre roadless area.

The hike is along Miller Creek Trail, one of only five trailheads that lead into this mountain wilderness. The trailhead is located 35 miles east of downtown off Interstate 10 at Exit 297. Go north on U.S. Forest Route 35 for 16 miles and turn left at the Miller Creek Trail sign. The trail is well marked with signs along the way, and you'll pass through a gate (you must close it after you enter) where you begin your hike. At this point the trail follows Miller Creek, which is dry during the summer. You'll pass through another gate that enters Saguaro National Park East. Over the next few miles the terrain changes, and you'll pass groves of oak woodland where you may begin to see deer. This is where it begins to get steep. Soon, you'll reach Happy Valley Saddle, where the trail connects with Heartbreak Ridge Trail. It's on the left and the one you want to take. At the Happy Valley junction, pine forest becomes evident as you have climbed 1,900 feet in less than 5 miles.

Next, you'll arrive at a signed junction for the Rincon Peak Trail turning left to Rincon Peak. Though the peak isn't as high as Mica Mountain (the highest in the range), the 360-degree view is the reason you've come all this way. Enjoy the view — it's all downhill from here as you return the way you came.

Catalina State Park
11570 N. Oracle Rd. • 628-5798

This state park north of downtown Tucson is ideal for family outings and easy hikes. Seven miles of trails lead to various waterfalls and pools. The elevation changes are not as radical as other "mountain" parks. For those looking for an easy hike with good views of terrain and wildlife, the 6-mile round trip Canyon Loop Trail is just the ticket.

The trailhead is the Romero Canyon Trail, taking hikers past the looming vistas of the Pusch Ridge wilderness area of the Santa Catalina Mountains. After about a half-mile, you'll take the left turn onto Canyon Loop Trail. This trail is wide enough to allow an easy walk side by side.

When you reach the highest point (if it's spring there will be plenty of wildflowers), you will arrive at another well-marked fork in the trail. But stay on the main trail until you reach the hilltop picnic table. From here you can see beyond the park borders, with views of both mountains and valleys. It is also here where the trail makes a change from desert ironwood to oak, junipers and woodland meadows.

The path eventually reaches the Sutherland Trail intersection, looping around almost 2 miles to the main Sutherland Trail that heads back to the park's north side. You will encounter great stands of saguaros as you head back to the desert floor. It's a nice easy hike, and the park is open until 10 PM for moonlit walks.

Horseback Riding

Needless to say, this is the Old West and horseback riding is very popular. Reservations are suggested.

Conquistador Stables
10000 N. Oracle Rd. • 742-4200

Part of the Sheraton El Conquistador Resort and Country Club, this northwest Tucson facility offers guided trail rides and great wilderness rides in the hills above the valley in Catalina State Park, complete with cowboy singers and even gun fights. Conquistador Stables can arrange hayrides, cookouts and romantic sunset rides. You'll pay $18 for one hour, $32 for two hours or $25 for the sunset ride lasting 1½ hours.

Cross Creek Riding Club
3511 N. Bear Canyon Rd. • 749-3936, (800) 383-8371

In the northeast foothills, Cross Creek specializes in jumper, dressage and cross-country styles. It also offers boarding and training for horses and has been rated as one of Arizona's best equestrian facilities.

204 • PARKS AND RECREATION

Desert High Country Stables, Inc.
6501 W. Ina Rd. • 744-3789

This guided riding company offers hourly to full-day trail rides in the desert with campfire meals. It also offers hayrides and picture-taking trips. An hour ride is $18; a full day is $60.

Pusch Ridge Stables
13700 N. Oracle Rd. • 825-1664

Pusch Ridge Stables offers not only horse rentals, pack trips and moonlit rides into the Santa Catalina Mountains, but also hayrides and breakfast or steak rides for the ultimate outdoor experience. Ride fees range from $20 for one hour to $100 for a full day.

Walking Winds Stables
11600 N. Oracle Rd. • 742-4422

Walking Winds is one of the primary stables that services riders in the Catalina State Park (see that listing under "Mountain Parks" previously in this chapter). It's near the entrance to the state park and offers cookout rides. Rides run $18 an hour or $32 for two hours.

Ice Skating

Iceoplex
7883 E. Rosewood St. • 290-8800

This large indoor skating rink is open all year and offers ice skating lessons for all ages, adults-only skating, birthday parties for kids and even hockey equipment and programs. Upstairs there is a '50s-style restaurant. (See our Kidstuff chapter for hours and rates.)

Jeep Tours

High Desert Convoys, Inc.
2242-A E. Spring St. • 323-3386, (800) 93-TOURS

Explore the Sonoran Desert in World War II jeeps with personal guides. The trips are custom designed for exploring Indian ruins, ghost towns or area caves. Prices range from $45 per person for a two- to four-hour tour to $65 per person for a tour that last five to eight hours and includes lunch. Call for reservations and fees.

Mountain View Adventures
4245 N. Campbell Ave. • 881-4488, (800) 594-9644

This is Tucson's original jeep tour outfit. Mountain View specializes in group tours for special events or conventions. Tours of the Coronado National Forest last 3½ hour and are $45 for adults, half-price for children. The jeeps will pick you up wherever you like. Reservations are required.

Sunshine Jeep Tours
9040 N. Oracle Rd. • 742-1943

The area's largest jeep tour company, Sunshine takes visitors to Sonoran Desert locations. Tours of the Tucson Mountains run three to four hours. Rates are $48 for adults, $36 for kids 11 to 16 and $24 for children 4 to 10. Call for reservations.

Trail Dust Jeep Tours
1665 S. Craycroft Rd. • 747-0323

This jeep tour group can accommodate any size group for trips into the Sonoran Desert. The 3½-hour ecology trip is $45. Trail Dust also offers a 2½-hour sunset trip for $40. You must reserve a tour ahead of time.

Paintball

Paintball Headquarters, Inc.
5464 E. 29th St. • 750-1174

This group specializes in organizing paintball outings with friendly competition and state-of-the-art equipment. For $25 you get five hours of play, weapon rental and 100 rounds of paintballs to battle it out on a secret field in Marana.

Skiing

Ski Valley
Mt. Lemmon, end of Catalina Hwy. • 576-1400

Ski Valley, the southernmost ski area in North America, is only about an hour's drive from Tucson. Ascending the Catalina Highway you pass through the village of Summerhaven nestled among pines and aspens. Just beyond it is the ski area.

Three chair lifts (which are also open in the summer for sightseeing) serve the 15 runs for expert, intermediate and beginner skiers. Ski Valley also allows snowboards. Equipment can be rented at the ski-lift complex. There's also a snack bar. Across the parking lot is the Iron Door Mine restaurant with a fireplace and wonderful view of Falcon Valley north of Tucson.

The ski lift rises to 9,100 feet up Radio Ridge. A one-day lift-ticket costs $25. Skis, boots and poles run about $15, and the learn-to-ski package at the ski school costs $40.

Keep in mind that Ski Valley doesn't open until mid-December, and the season only lasts about 100 days or until the snow is gone. During the season the slopes are open daily from 9 AM to 4 PM. Skiers need not pay the user fee levied for the Catalina Highway.

Skydiving

Marana Skydiving Center
11700 W. Avra Valley Rd. • 682-4441
In the far northwest corner of the Tucson area off I-10, Marana Skydiving Center is Arizona's only public parachute training operation. The center has received national press for its world-class facility that trains first-timers as well as world champions. It offers both tandem and solo jumps for those 18 and older. Jumps start at $105.

Swimming

As we've mentioned previously, Tucson can get to be one hot place, so swimming is a popular pastime. Here we've provided the addresses and contact numbers for several pools in the area. Recreation swim hours differ at each pool and in summer and winter seasons, so it's best to call for exact times at the pool nearest you. The following swimming pools are operated by the City of Tucson Parks and Recreation. Daily admission is $1 for adults and 25¢ for children 17 and younger. Ask about multiple admission tickets and annual passes, which for a family package (two adults and two children) runs about $84. Call the City of Tucson Parks and Recreation Department, 791-4873, for information about special swim times for kids and adults or lessons.

(We also have a couple of water amusement parks in Tucson. Check "Just Add Water" in the Kidstuff chapter.)

Amphitheater High School, 125 W. Yavapai St., 791-5388.
Archer Center, 1665 S. La Cholla Blvd., 791-4353
Augie Acuna-Los Ninos Park, 5432 S. Bryant Ave., 574-0222
Carrillo School, 440 S. Main Ave., 791-4167
Catalina High School, Dodge Blvd. and Pima St., 791-4245
Catalina Park, 16562 N. Oracle Rd., 825-9011
El Pueblo Center, 5100 S. Missiondale Rd., 791-4176
Escalante Park, 6900 E. Nicaragua Ave., 791-4864
Flowing Wells Jr. High School, 4545 N. La Cholla Blvd., 690-2322
Fort Lowell Park, 2900 N. Craycroft Rd., 791-2585
Freedom Park, 5000 E. 29th St., 791-3232
Himmel Park, 1000 N. Tucson Blvd., 791-4157
Jacobs Park, 1010 W. Lind Ave., 791-4358
Jesse Owens Park, 400 S. Sarnoff Dr., 791-4821
Joaquin Murrieta Park, 1400 N. Silverbell Rd., 791-4752
Kennedy Park, 3700 S. Mission Rd., 791-4863
Kino Sportspark, 2805 E. Ajo Wy., 882-7346
Mansfield Park, 2000 N. 4th Ave., 791-4405
Menlo Park, 1100 W. Fresno St., 791-4356
Mission Park, 6100 S. 12th Ave., 791-4357
Oury Park, 600 W. St. Mary's St., 791-4186
Palo Verde Park, 300 S. Mann Ave., 791-4375
Pueblo Gardens, 2500 E. 36th St., 791-4386
Santa Rita Park, 400 S. 22nd St., 791-4165
Sunnyside High School, 1725 E. Bilby Rd., 791-5167
Udall Center, Udall Park, 7200 E. Tanque Verde Rd., 791-4004

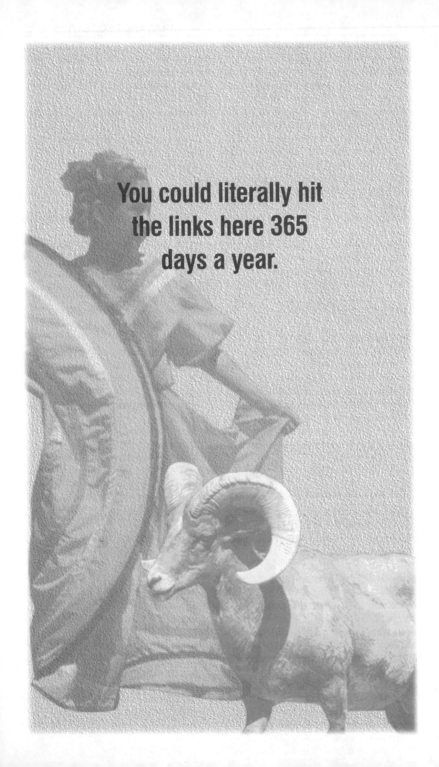

Golf

Whether you're an occasional duffer or a dyed-in-the-wool fanatic, when it comes to golf Tucson offers a multitude of benefits. (If you're a golf "widow," however, you'll no doubt view these as definite disadvantages.) The most obvious advantage is the weather, which means that courses are open year-round. Yes, you could literally hit the links here 365 days a year. Another plus is that there are very few private courses; nearly every course can be played by anyone. And as you'll see by reading this chapter, you can choose from a vast variety of course types, locations and prices — from posh resorts charging up to $160 peak season for a round with cart to municipal courses at less than $45 with cart. The county course and five municipal courses are maintained at standards that in most parts of the country are reserved for the best country clubs, so even if you're on a budget you can play on truly superb courses.

And if these aren't reason enough to get you on the links, here's one more: Summer golfing in Tucson offers some outstanding values, with prices up to half the peak winter season rates and tee times that you don't have to scramble to get. You may not want to drive, chip or putt golf balls in the midday heat, but courses are open sunrise to sunset, so you can play when temperatures are more bearable.

Whichever course you choose, be forewarned: Nearly every course has some cacti, many have lots, and they can be quite hurtful. Some golfers from Seattle, playing in Tucson for the first time, found the cactus plants to pose the biggest surprise and the biggest hazard (to life and limb). One brushed against a cholla cactus and got an arm full of stickers; the other tried to push a green, innocent-looking overhanging ocotillo out of the way only to discover its leaves were hiding some serious spikes. You can read up on these unusually deceptive plants in the Natural World chapter.

Fear not, however; grass does exist on our golf courses in the desert, though on some it's only the tees, greens and fairways that are green. The only grass that grows here in the summer is bermudagrass, but it browns out in winter, so courses must replace the grass each fall with ryegrass via overseeding. Also, the reseeding process often means that, except for the greens, the grassy areas will be brown for about a month of the year (typically September or October), and many players find this less than desirable turf. So if you're picky about the grass condition, call the course ahead of time to find out if their green grass is actually brown. (Hey! It's a small price to pay to play 12 months of your favorite sport a year.)

For visitors or newcomers to Tucson, the hardest part of the game may well be finding the golf course. Many of the courses have obscure addresses — they're on streets named just for the golf course, for example, and the street name gives no clue as to where they really are. So to help you find the links you're looking for, we include some major cross streets or other directions that will get you there with a lot less frustration. Except for the daytrip courses at the end of the chapter, the courses are listed strictly in alphabetical order, but we tell you where in the area each is located to help you decide which to play when. We also tell you which courses are semi-private, meaning that you'll need to be a member of the club or guest at the resort to play them. Courses that are strictly private are not listed here.

Most Tucson courses have four seasons for determining fees. The peak season usually runs from early January to mid or late April when the fees are steepest. Prices are lower in the fall or early winter season, usually October through December, and in the spring or early summer season (mid or late April through May or June). Lowest rates are offered in summer, generally running June or July through August or September. Nearly every course is open sunrise to sunset, which means longer playing hours in summer than in winter. At the municipal courses, driving range hours are sunrise to 10 PM with a nominal fee charged for buckets of balls.

If you're a golfer who prefers the old-fashioned way of golfing — walking rather than riding a cart — you'll need to select your courses carefully. Most courses in the Tucson area just aren't made for walking and won't even permit it; the desert terrain is too rocky and hilly or the courses are too long to reasonably walk them. If you're looking for a course to walk, watch for those that say traditional (although even that's not a guarantee you can walk it). The best ones would be most of the municipal courses plus Arthur Pack, Dorado, Quail Canyon and Green Valley's Haven and Tortuga. But not to worry, you can still get lots of walking in at other courses by keeping your cart on the cart path and walking to your shots.

Tips on Playing City Courses

You may not need a golf lesson, but if you're planning to play any of the five excellent Tucson municipal courses, we offer this lesson in how best to navigate them. It's critical that you know about the central phone reservation system for making tee times, and you also may want to know some of the great ways to save money.

Because the municipal courses are so popular, the Tucson Parks and Recreation Department, which operates the five courses, has devised an automated reservation system (for which you get 75¢ tacked onto your golf fees for the privilege of using). You can call the courses directly for any information, but they won't reserve a tee time for you. You must call 791-4336, and it's all automated from that point. (For those of you who simply won't use this high-tech impersonal approach, you do have the option of speaking with a real person from 8 AM to 5 PM Monday through Friday.) To reserve a tee time, you will need to provide either a resident card number or a home phone number (it need not be local) as well as a credit card number. Once at the course you can pay however you like, but the credit card will be charged if you're a no show. In other words, if you're a visitor to Tucson, you will need to key in a home phone number and a credit card to make the tee time; if you're a county resident, you can reserve with either a resident card or home phone number and a credit card. A resident card can be obtained by any Pima County resident at the Parks and Rec office at 900 S. Randolph Way. The card not only gives you tee time access via phone, but it also gives you a discount of about $3 off summer rates and $10 off winter rates. If you have the card, you can reserve tee times up to seven days in advance; without it, you can reserve up to six days in advance. And advance is the key word here: These courses fill up fast, more so in winter and on weekends.

> **FYI**
> Unless otherwise noted, the area code for all phone numbers listed in this guide is 520.

Another great way to save money if you're age 62 or older is the senior's card. Its discounts are slightly less than the resident's card, but you'll save a couple of bucks and even more if you have both cards. Inquire about this card at the Parks and Rec number or office listed above or at any of the municipal courses.

Arthur Pack Golf Course
9101 N. Thornydale Rd. • 744-3322

Located on the northwest side, this is the only course operated by Pima County. This combination desert and traditional course is a favorite for couples because it's a good equalizer — the short tees are well-positioned to provide a challenging game for women while the longer tees suit the men. Of the four tees, the longest plays to 6896 yards (rated 71.6) while the yardage for women's tee is 5068 (rated 67.6). It's a moderately difficult 18-hole course with wide fairways, challenging water holes and well-kept, sizable greens. City and county amateur championships are often played here. And it's often possible to just walk onto the course without advance reservations, especially in summer. For 18 holes in peak season, the cost is $28, and cart rental is $9 for one or $18 for two people. Facilities include a driving range, clubhouse and putting green. The views of Pusch Ridge at the base of the Santa Catalina Mountains are a real bonus.

Dell Urich Municipal Golf Course
600 S. Alvernon Wy. • 325-2811

This course was redesigned, renovated and renamed in 1996. It used to be the south course to Randolph North, and they were both known by the name Randolph. They are the most centrally located courses in Tucson if you're staying in the downtown area or anywhere nearby and want a great golf course that you can get to quickly. Both courses are accessed from Alvernon Way just north of 22nd Street, and they share facilities such as practice green, driving range and clubhouse. As with the other municipal courses, it would be hard to find a better golfing venue for the money, or even for more money. Of the two side-by-side courses, the 18-hole, 6633-yard (70.3 rating), par 70 Dell Urich is shorter and less challenging, but the recent renovation did add more contours. Its straightforward layout and smooth terrain make Dell Urich great for novices or a quick round of golf. Like all the municipal courses, discounts are available for residents and seniors, and you must use the automated central phone system — explained in detail in the introduction to this chapter — to reserve tee times.

The winter rate (November through May) is $44.50 with a cart. Reservations are necessary during the peak season — sometimes weeks in advance.

Dorado Golf Course
6601 E. Speedway Blvd. • 885-6751

This public course is conveniently located on the near east side of town right off a main byway. But it's also nicely secluded in the midst of a lovely, quiet residential community. Dorado is a traditional grassy course and well-maintained with bentgrass greens. You can play nine or 18 holes quickly on this executive course and only pull out your driver once or twice. Long yardage is 3751 at a rating of 58.9. During the winter peak season, it's best to call several days to a week ahead for reservations. The best deal at this course is a reduced fee of $11 for 18 holes (plus cart) after 3 PM that's available year round. There's a chip and putt area and a snack bar. The course is close to several hotels and a hidden gem of a restaurant, Charles, that's within walking distance (see the Restaurants chapter).

The winter rate for Dorado is $19 for 18 holes; carts are $9 for one person or $18 for two people.

El Rio Municipal Golf Course
1400 W. Speedway Blvd. • 623-6783

A favorite for both locals and visitors, this city course is close to downtown on the near west side just beyond Interstate 10. Ideal for the short knocker, this par 70 course measures from 5824 to 6418 yards and is rated 69.6. It has a fairly flat terrain with tight fairways, lots of trees and two small lakes. The greens are famous for being small and hard — a pitch and run setup. Facilities include a practice green, well-lit driving range and clubhouse. The oldest municipal course in Tucson and one of the oldest courses in Arizona, it was a country club before the city acquired it in 1968. Discounts are available for residents and seniors, and tee times can be made only through the central Parks and Rec number.

For 18 holes with a cart, the winter rate (November through May) is $42.50.

Fred Enke Municipal Golf Course
8521 E. Irvington Rd. • 296-8607

You'd have to look hard to find a better desert course than this one run by the city. Located on the southeast side of town on a main thoroughfare, this is a limited turf course with substantial teeing areas, large greens, well-calculated bunkers and tricky sand traps. It's target golf, calling for accuracy over distance. You can choose from four teeing areas with a yardage range of 4700 to 6809 and rating of 72.8. If you play from the back tees and plan to get a good score, you'd better be a good golfer. The heavily bunkered 455-yard par 4 number 9 hole will challenge anyone. The course offers a practice green, well-lit driving range and bar and grill for apres golf. From a couple of spots on this course you can see the Davis-Monthan Air Force Base's aircraft boneyard, a pleasant scene if you're into flights of fancy. The winter rate (November through May) for 18 holes with a cart is $42.50. Check

The Golf Club at Vistoso
955 W. Vistoso Highlands Dr. • 797-9900

Northwest of Tucson in Oro Valley is a mammoth retirement community called Rancho Vistoso, and this is where you'll find The Golf Club at Vistoso. Designed by the famous Tom Weiskopf, the longest of four tees plays to 6905 yards at par 72 and a rating of 72.1. With views of the Tortolita Mountains to the northwest and the Catalinas and city to the south, the fairways are surrounded by natural washes, giant saguaros and mesquite trees, producing a stunning and challenging target golf course.

Each of the 18 holes is named — prickly pear, double cross, waterfall, hidden green, risky and sidewinder are a few that will give you a clue about what to expect as you play them. Another unique feature at Vistoso is the excellent course book given to each player showing the full layout of each hole with lay-up and carry yardages, hazards and tee positions. Facilities include clubhouse, driving range and putting green. The peak-season rate for 18 holes with a cart is $120. You can get to The Golf Club at Vistoso from Oracle Road by going west either on 1st Avenue or Rancho Vistoso Boulevard.

Heritage Highlands Golf Club
4949 W. Heritage Club Blvd. • 579-7000

Brand new in 1997, this Arthur Hills-designed course is part of a new country club retirement community on Tucson's far northwest side. Set amidst lush natural vegetation, it's situated at the base of the Tortolita Mountains with views of the whole valley and every mountain range. The course is a loosely formed semicircle of long, angled fairways. With its variety of tee boxes and fairway angles, every game can seem totally different. It's almost like two courses in one — the front nine are flatter and the back nine more challenging and hilly. This par 72 championship course challenges the best without being too intimidating for the average player. The course measures 6904 yards from the back tee at a rating of 72.1. Its signature hole is number 13 (a blind tee shot to a plateau about 35 feet high, dropping to a long green behind an outcropping of rocks), and there are four challenging par 5s. Facilities include a clubhouse with bar and grill, driving range and putting green. The cost for 18 holes with a cart is $85 on weekends and $75 Monday through Thursday. Go west on Tangerine Road from Oracle Road (or east on Tangerine from I-10) and you'll see the course.

Lodge at Ventana Canyon Golf and Racquet Club
6200 N. Clubhouse Ln. • 577-4061

While the resort is named Loews Ventana Canyon, the golf facilities are actually down the road a bit and operated by Carefree Resorts as the Lodge at Ventana Canyon. (Confused? Just read on.) You can find lodging at both the resort and the Lodge, and in either case you receive some golf benefits over someone walking in off the street to play. The Lodge at Ventana Canyon Golf and Racquet Club is just south of Loews Ventana Canyon Resort and both are just north of the intersection of Kolb Road and Sunrise Drive in the close-in northeast foothills. (In other words, if

> **www.insiders.com**
> See this and many other **Insiders' Guide®** destinations online — in their entirety.
> **Visit us today!**

INSIDERS' TIP

Interested in saving bucks on your golfing? It never hurts to ask any course, no matter how posh, if it's offering a discount. Many have summer specials, twilight specials or two-for-one specials, particularly in non-peak season. Or ask about possible discounts available to seniors, military or kids.

The city's Junior Golf program allows kids free golf on all city courses, once they've completed classes on golf rules and etiquette.

you get to the Resort entrance you've gone too far.) The Lodge offers two distinct courses nestled against the dramatic backdrop of the Santa Catalina Mountains. In an 1,100-acre enclave, half the terrain is preserved open space providing a natural habitat for deer, rabbits, Gambel quail and other native creatures amidst the saguaros and mesquites. Winding through this secluded hideaway are two 18-hole championship courses — Canyon and Mountain — designed by Tom Fazio.

Unless you're a member of the Lodge, you basically have the choice of playing only one of the courses on any given day (it's called the "resort course of the day"). In peak season, you can reserve only seven days out unless you're a member or lodging guest. It's rather complex in case you haven't noticed, so call for an explanation if you're still confused. Whichever course is the designated "resort course for the day," however, you'll be playing on one of the best courses around, but it will cost $160 (peak season), including a cart, for 18 holes.

Canyon Course

Area golfers say it can easily take six hours to play a round of 18 on this course that offers both some incredible golfing and views amidst fine desert scenery. It winds through the beautiful Esperrero Canyon and incorporates the massive rock formation known as Whaleback Rock, where at night bobcats emerge from the desert to snooze along the green. The fairways are lush on this 6818-yard par 72 course with a rating of 72.7. This is definitely a target course where many balls are lost to the desert rough. You'll be impressed by the dramatic finish on the par 5 number 18 island green, where patrons of the restaurant may offer a round of applause if you manage to keep the ball in play.

Mountain Course

This second course at Ventana Canyon is more difficult. The obstacles inherent in its natural desert landscape make the Mountain Course one of the most formidable in the area. At 6926 yards and par 72, it's rated 74.2. The course's renowned 100-yard, par 3 #3 signature hole is hit from a peak over a ravine to the green on another peak, and the tee offers a breathtaking panorama that stretches for 100 miles across the Sonoran Desert into Mexico. This is reputed to be the most photographed hole (other than the Grand Canyon, we presume) west of the Mississippi.

Omni Tucson National Golf Resort
2727 W. Club Dr. • 297-2271

Designed by Robert Bruce Harris in 1960, this traditional par 73 course is actually three

9-hole courses, and a cart is required. Often host to the prestigious PGA tour, Tucson National covers 450 acres with expansive fairways of bermudagrass, Penncross bentgrass greens, lakes, mature trees and well-placed bunkers — a great course for the seasoned pro or novice. Several beautiful, long par 4s add to any golfer's pleasant experience on this course, which plays to 7108 yards from the long tees at a rating of 74.9. Facilities include a driving range, short game area and putting green as well as restaurant and lounge. Peak season play here is $150 for 18 holes with a cart. It's located in the northwest near the intersection of Cortaro Farms and Shannon roads, or from I-10 exit at Cortaro Farms Road east to Shannon Road, then north.

Quail Canyon Golf Course
5910 N. Oracle Rd. • 887-6161

This course, which recently changed its name from Cliff Valley Course, is the place to get your short game in shape. It's more of a recreational than professional course, with 18 par 3 holes totaling 2311 yards. Hole number 4 is longest at 165 yards, number 7 the toughest (it's long with natural obstacles), and number 14's pond is usually home to local ducks. In winter, this course charges $12.50 for 18 holes plus $12 for a cart. It's easy to find on a major thoroughfare in close-in northwest Tucson.

Randolph North Municipal Golf Course
600 S. Alvernon Wy. • 325-2811

Randolph North is the longest of Tucson's municipal courses and currently hosts the Welch's/Circle K Championship LPGA Golf Tournament in March. A favorite of locals, it's a long and demanding course that can take six hours to play. The course features a traditional country club design and is noted for its mature vegetation, tall trees and wide, expansive fairways. Greens vary from relatively flat to severely sloped or tiered and from large to small. Two outstanding holes are the 15th, a lovely hole of 200 yards surrounded by water, and the 18th, with two ponds that carry over from fairway to green. Long yardage is 6863 with a rating of 72.5. Facilities include a well-lit driving range, practice green and clubhouse.

This is a superb course located almost in the heart of Tucson and surrounded by city parks and recreational offerings.

The 18-hole fee with cart is $44.50 in winter (November through May). And don't forget to use that central reservations phone number.

Raven Golf Club at Sabino Springs
9777 E. Sabino Greens Dr. • 749-3636

When it opened in 1995, Raven was Tucson's first new golf course in 10 years. Robert Trent Jones Jr. designed this beauty of a desert golf course at the foot of the Santa Catalina Mountains to be as challenging as the rugged natural flow of the land. Instead of carving up the terrain, the design meshes with the land and its natural hills, arroyos, rocks and stands of giant saguaro cacti. So while it tests the limits of your ability, it also offers the tranquillity of spectacular scenery, including the rare beauty of nine natural desert springs (hence the course's name). Accuracy is a hallmark of this course. It will take your best and biggest hits to play the 625-yard number 11, for example.

From the longest of three tee positions, the par 71 course is 6776 yards and rated 73.2. Raven has a great driving range as well as a putting green and clubhouse. In peak season the rate is $130 for 18 holes with a cart. From Sabino Canyon Road on the northeast side of town, go east on Snyder Road to Sabino Greens Drive.

Santa Rita Golf Course
16461 S. Houghton Rd. • 762-5620

This course is at the foot of the Santa Rita Mountains on the far southeast side of the valley, about a 30-minute drive from central Tucson. Every one of the 18 holes features beautiful views of the mountains and many offer Tucson valley views as well. The course also boasts some of Arizona's most outstanding bentgrass greens. And because it's nearly 1,000 feet above Tucson, it's slightly cooler and a good choice for summer golf. Be forewarned, however, that wind is a factor here on almost every hole. Following an extensive renovation, the fairways are now on a par with the always noteworthy greens. The golf here is regarded as one of the best values around, and discounts are available for military, junior and senior golfers.

You can tee off from any of three teeing positions, with the longest at 6523 yards, on this par 72 course rated 70.2. Five of the holes are very challenging par 3s; the 250-yard number 12 is reputed to be the most challenging par 3 in Arizona, with hazards all the way and a very narrow layout. Santa Rita has a clubhouse and full practice facilities.

Rates are very affordable here: $45 for 18 holes with a cart in peak season and only $20 after 1 PM.

Sheraton El Conquistador Resort
10000 N. Oracle Rd.
• 544-1770, 544-1801

This resort on the far northwest side (in Oro Valley) offers one 9-hole and two 18-hole courses set amidst the dramatic natural landscapes and rolling elevations of the Santa Catalina Mountains. Two of the courses are pay and play (public), while the third — Sunset — is open primarily to El Conquistador Country Club members, and therefore not mentioned here.

Pusch Ridge Course

This 9-hole par 70 course gets its name from the dramatic granite ridge adjacent to the Sheraton El Conquistador Resort that towers 2,000 feet above the course. The course winds around and above the resort (on the east side of Oracle Road), offering some of the best city and mountain views to be had. A tight course that golfers describe as the best 9-hole course in the area, it runs the gamut from fast greens to long driving holes to short par 3s. Yardage from the longest of three tees is 2788 with a rating of 65.6. A putting green, plus the resort's restaurants, are available to golfers. In peak season with a cart, 9 holes will cost $35 and 18 holes $60.

Sunrise Course

The Sheraton El Conquistador's two 18-hole courses are located not at the resort, but about 3 miles away at the Country Club, 10555 N. La Canada Drive. (From the resort or from Oracle Road, take 1st Avenue to Lambert Road to La Canada.) Sunrise, the easternmost of the two courses, is open to the public. The longest of three tee choices measures 6819 yards at a rating of 72.5 on this par 72 course.

Facilities include driving range, putting greens and restaurant and lounge. Both the golf and the views from this desert course are spectacular. The peak-season fee is $118 for 18 holes with a cart.

Silverbell Municipal Golf Course
3600 N. Silverbell Rd. • 743-7284

Perched on the west bank of the usually dry Santa Cruz River, this 18-hole par 72 course has great views of both the Tucson and Catalina Mountains. Silverbell has a tight layout, wide open, flat, forgiving fairways, good-sized greens and plenty of water to negotiate. The course features 150 acres of bermudagrass that extends from tees — with a hill beyond the tee shot and water or trees lining both sides of the fairway — to greens and lots of trees. The 17th hole is reputed to be the toughest par 5 hole in the area. With three tee choices, the longest is 6824 yards at a rating of 71.4. Amenities include a practice green, well-lit driving range and bar and grill. In winter (November through April) the cost for 18 holes with a cart is $42.50. The course is situated close to downtown at the foot of the Tucson Mountains just west of I-10 and north of Grant Road on a main byway.

Starr Pass Golf Resort
3645 W. Starr Pass Blvd. • 670-0400

Once home to the Northern Telecom Open, a PGA tour stop, Starr Pass was designed as a Tournament Player's Course and is a favorite of visiting pros. Perched in the foothills of the Tucson Mountains, the rocky, cactus-covered desert terrain surrounds this course's lush grass fairways and bentgrass greens, which are kept at PGA standards year round. You'll find some tricky holes at this par 71, 6910-yard course rated 74.6. Number 15 is the signature hole and, like much of the course, emphasizes accuracy over distance. While you're hitting through the hole's narrow pass, try to envision it 100-plus years ago as a stagecoach pass (from which the resort took its name). In addition to a lovely territorial design clubhouse, Starr Pass has a great driving range and putting green. The peak-season rate for 18 holes with a cart is $106. The course is 3

Westin La Paloma Resort and Country Club
3660 E. Sunrise Dr. • 299-1500

This is terrain where golf was never envisioned possible — until, that is, Jack Nicklaus creatively forged through it, designing three 9-hole courses. *Golf Digest* rates it among the top 75 courses in the country. The three courses are named Hill, Canyon and Ridge, and they're all about equally difficult. This is definitely target golf with lots of challenges as well as great views of the Santa Catalina Mountains and the valley. At 7088 yards for 18 holes, La Paloma is rated 75.8. The course has forecaddies available for players who want someone to go ahead and give tips on lining up shots. The final hole on Canyon course ends up at a superb clubhouse. La Paloma is located in the close-in foothills on Tucson's north side, but you'll only be eligible to play these holes if you're a resort guest or a member of its country club. To play 18 holes, resort guests pay $130, which includes a cart.

Practice Ranges

If you're interested in taking a whack at some balls with your driver or putter but don't have the time to get to a golf course, you'll find several nicely equipped practice ranges around the city. All are open year round and have hours generally from early morning to 9 or 10 PM but tend to close earlier in winter months. Most have clubs you can rent or just use for the practice, and some actually sell clubs and give you a chance to demo them before you buy. Some also offer lessons. Unless otherwise noted, a bucket of balls costs $3 to $5, depending on the size, and the putting and chipping areas are free whether you're paying for a bucket of balls or not.

Family Golf Centers Inc.
8325 E. Golf Links Rd. • 290-9941

This golf center in the southeast has a driving range and putting and chipping area plus a nice pro shop and great views hitting into the Catalinas. They also have batting cages and miniature golf in case you want to take someone else in the family along while you're practicing the long ones. Take Golf Links Road east past Kolb Road.

Jack Conrad's Practice Range
1600 W. River Rd. • 293-9152

Jack has been in business 15 years and is in a great location right along the Rillito River about a mile west of Tucson Mall. He offers a driving range plus chip and putt areas and rents clubs.

La Mariposa Club
1501 N. Houghton Rd. • 749-1099

This is a membership sports and fitness center that happens to also have a golf practice range that's open to the public. You'll find a driving range as well as chip, putt and sand trap practice areas at this Eastside spot on

> **FYI**
> Unless otherwise noted, the area code for all phone numbers listed in this guide is 520.

INSIDERS' TIP

Want to help your kid get on the course to becoming a Tiger Woods? Or maybe you just want to find a safe activity for kids that gets them away from the TV and toward doing something worthwhile. Check out the city's summer golf clinics for kids up to age 18. Not only do they learn something about golf (sometimes for free), but they also get a card entitling them to play absolutely free on the municipal courses for selected hours during the summer or afternoons during the school year, and it's good for a whole year. Ask about this junior clinic program at any of the city courses.

Houghton between Speedway Boulevard and Tanque Verde Road.

The Practice Tee
4050 W. Price Club Dr. • 544-2600

This northwest facility is called "upscale" by those in the know and indeed does seem to have lots to offer, starting with 100 tee stations from which you can hit to actual greens complete with water hazards and sand traps. You'll find putt, chip and sand trap practice areas as well as lessons, clubs to rent, buy or demo and club repair. Ball buckets come in four sizes ranging from $3 to $10. Look for this facility behind the Costco/Price Club where Orange Grove Road meets Thornydale Road.

The Show
7777 E. Tanque Verde Rd. • 886-1434

Formerly called Catalina Golf Center, this range is on the east side at Wrightstown Road. They have a driving range, sand bunker, chipping and putting areas plus lessons, club repair and fitting. Batting cages are also available in case you want to switch your sport for a while.

Daytrip Golf Courses

Just 30 minutes down Interstate 19 from downtown Tucson is Green Valley, a bustling and expanding retirement community that's also become a hot spot for golf. It offers beautiful scenery set in the rolling terrain of the Santa Cruz River valley plus a number of spectacular golf courses to choose from within a short distance from each other. And after you've played to your heart's content in Green Valley, just take a swing farther south down I-19 to find courses in Tubac, Rio Rico and Nogales. You can play for days in this area south of Tucson and never play the same course twice. Good golf packages are avail-

Even the city golf courses offer beautiful mountain views.

able if you prefer to stay in the area rather than drive down from Tucson. Plan on riding, not walking, these courses.

Haven Public Golf Course and Tortuga Golf Course
110 N. Abrego Dr., Green Valley
• 625-4281

This was Green Valley's first golf course, built in 1967, and is also one of the easiest to find. Just exit from I-19 at Esperanza Road (Exit 65), go west, look for the large sign to the left of the Green Valley Social Center and untrunk your clubs. Ideal for players of all skill levels, Haven is 18 holes totaling 6867 yards (rated 71.6) from the back tees or 5811 yards from the forward tees. The Tortuga Golf Course is a 9-hole pitch and putt course. This course is an excellent choice if some of your traveling companions are just not ready for the big 18 — you can play Haven and your traveling companion can keep busy on Tortuga and everybody is happy. The Haven course is a traditional design with grass throughout and mature vegetation. In fact, you may be surprised to see large pine trees interspersed with eucalyptus and palm trees. Panoramic views of the Santa Rita Mountains may lull you into a sense of calm, but don't get too relaxed or you'll miss some shots requiring both distance and accuracy. The facilities include a driving range, putting green and chipping green plus the Palms restaurant and lounge. For Tortuga, the fee is $8 (no carts). Haven's peak-season rate is $23 for 18 holes and $8 more for a cart.

Torres Blancas Golf Club
3233 S. Abrego Dr., Green Valley
• 625-5200

One could say that this course rose out of the ashes like the legendary Phoenix bird. When developers began digging out the course in 1994, they actually uncovered a nearly complete golf course that had been abandoned due to economic conditions of the early 1980s. Under the dirt was what course developers discovered to be a masterpiece layout by Trevino Designs that needed only an irrigation system and a few refinements. The result is a 165-acre course with a traditional design reminiscent of the PGA Tour courses — the fairways are expansive and considerably wider than most modern golf courses. It stretches along the west bank of the Santa Cruz River and eventually into one of the state's largest pecan tree orchards. Four lakes and waterfall features add to the beauty and challenges of the par 72 course that plays to 7000 yards at a rating of 69.9. The peak-season fee is $45 for 18 holes with a cart. Torres Blancas is located within one of Green Valley's newer residential communities, Santa Rita Springs Development on the east side of I-19, and its Mediterranean-style clubhouse with a tower can easily be seen from the highway. Take Exit 63, Continental Road, east to the frontage road then south to the course.

San Ignacio Golf Club
4201 S. Camino del Sol, Green Valley
• 648-3468

Designed by Arthur Hills in 1989, San Ignacio already has earned accolades for its excellence and is one of *Golf Digest's* 100 "super value" courses. It is now owned and operated by Jacobs' Golf Group, parent company of the famed John Jacobs' Golf Schools. To get there, exit I-19 at Continental Road (Exit 63), take the west side frontage road south to Camino Encanto and follow the signs. The four teeing areas range from the 6288-yard professional tees rated 71.8 to the 5200-yard forward tees. No matter which teeing position you choose, intelligent decisions and accurate shots are de rigueur. San Ignacio was designed to use the natural terrain to its best possible advantage, and its superb layout makes it possible for golfers to see everything they will encounter from every tee, including the best route to the green. The fairways and rough are bermudagrass, and the greens are bentgrass. The signature hole is number 13, a 522-yard double dogleg par 5 featuring elevated tees and a double lake along the left side. As you might surmise, San Ignacio also offers world-famous John Jacobs' Golf Schools throughout the year (call 800-472-5007 for information on the school programs and packages) as well as plenty of practice facilities. And San Ignacio offers some of the most popular dining in Green Valley as well.

In peak season, 18 holes with a cart runs about $75, but the club has lots of specials.

Canoa Hills Golf Course
1401 W. Calle Urbano, Green Valley
- **648-1880**

This par 72 course is a good 18-hole choice for anyone who wants a challenge yet is fair to the average golfer. Surrounded by the natural terrain and stands of mesquite trees, the fairways are tight yet inviting. Accuracy in placing the ball is key here. The greens are generous and their bentgrass always in immaculate condition. From the long tees the course plays to 6610 yards with a 70.9 rating. Facilities include a practice range, putting green and restaurant and lounge. The rate for 18 holes with a cart in peak season is $70. To get here, exit from I-19 at Continental Road, take the west side frontage south to Camino Encanto Road and follow the signs.

Tubac Golf Resort
One Otero Rd., Tubac • 398-2211

If you're a movie buff as well as a golf buff (or even just a golf-movie buff), you may recognize this golf venue as the site for Kevin Costner's *Tin Cup*. In fact, the lake on the 16th hole was created just for the movie (we hope it poses less trouble to you than it did to Mr. Costner). Located south of Green Valley on the east side of I-19 at exit 40, Tubac is a traditional championship course that winds along both sides of the Santa Cruz River. At this spot, however, the dry riverbed to the north becomes a viable stream feeding the beautiful stately cottonwood trees that contribute to this course's appeal. The setting seems more quaint and rural than Southwest.

The work of pioneer golf course architect Red Lawrence, this par 72 course plays to 6957 yards from the back tees with a 72.6 rating. Its signature hole is the charming and picturesque number 8. The bentgrass greens have been greatly improved and enlarged to an average 6000 square feet, while the fairways have also been given a new lushness. You'll find a driving range, practice greens and restaurant and lounge at the resort, plus it's just minutes away from the delightful Tubac Village (see the Daytrips and Weekend Getaways chapter).

It's $66 for 18 holes with a cart in peak season.

Rio Rico Resort Golf Course
1550 Camino a la Posada, Rio Rico
- **(520) 281-8567, (800) 288-4746**

Continue south down I-19 to Exit 17 and you'll find Rio Rico Golf Course, one of Arizona's lesser-known gems. While the resort itself is on the west side of the interstate, the course is on the east side, meandering through rich pasture land. Golfers here have been known to think they actually were playing in the lush and rolling hills of Arkansas or Tennessee. The classic layout designed by Robert Trent Jones Sr. welcomes every player with its rolling fairways and large open greens, plus enough sand traps and water hazards to challenge the best. It is the site for many qualifying events for USGA and PGA tournaments. From its longest tees, the course measures 7119 yards, par 72 and rating of 74.4. Food and beverages are available at the course, as are a practice range and putting green. The cost for 18 holes with a cart in peak season is $75. The resort also has popular golf packages.

Kino Springs Golf Course
187 Kino Springs Dr., Nogales, Ariz.
- **(520) 287-8701, (800) 732-5751**

If you remember British film star Stewart Granger and his actress wife, Jean Simmons, you may be impressed that this course is carved out of a working cattle ranch they once owned. The original ranch house, built in 1902, now serves as the clubhouse and restaurant for the course and is peppered with photographs of the stars and their Hollywood friends.

Located almost on the Mexican border, it's situated about 6 miles east of Nogales, Arizona. Take Exit 8 off I-19 into Nogales, then Ariz. Highway 82 for 6 miles to Kino Springs Drive. (If you get to the border, you've gone too far. This Nogales, not as famous as the one just over the border in Mexico, is still stateside.) The course combines valley meadows with hilly fairways and greens in a deceptively challenging 18-hole, par 72 layout designed by Red Lawrence. From the back tees, the course plays to 6445 yards with a 69.8 rating. A reasonably priced course, the summer specials are simply amazing — like $15 weekdays and $20 on weekends, cart included. Otherwise, it's $40 for 18 with a cart in peak season.

Tucson Bike Trails

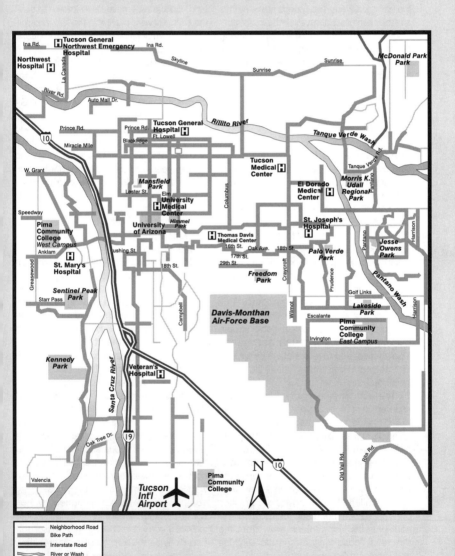

Bicycling

Interest in bicycling as an alternative mode of transportation and recreation has grown remarkably in Tucson. The increase in population, the dry weather and the growing number of bicycle events peddling into the area each year have led more and more people to choose two wheels over four.

Today, more than 3.5 percent of total daily transportation is provided by bicycles in the Tucson metropolitan area. *Bicycling Magazine* named Tucson the second best city for bicycling in the country and third best in North America in 1996. Because of this designation, we've included a separate chapter devoted to bicycling to get you up to speed.

History

In 1971, the City of Tucson designated its first bikeways, totaling some 8 miles. This was the nation's first community plan for a bikeway system, a series of designated bike routes designed to assist cyclists in connecting with other routes around the city.

In 1975, the first Tucson Regional Bikeways Plan was approved by the Pima Association of Governments, and over the next two years more than 56 miles of bikeways were added. The policy was so successful that the Bicycling Federation of America used it as a national model.

The next expansion of this transportation plan was completed in 1981. It called for all new road construction and reconstruction to include provisions for bicyclists. The city also adopted a policy to include 5-foot-wide striped bike lanes. To answer the growing interest in what Tucson had to offer bicyclists, the Pima Association of Governments began publishing the Tucson Bicycle Map in 1986. Also during this time, the Tucson-Pima County Bicycle Advisory Committee was formed to help local governments oversee bicycle project development around the area. All of the planning and policies paid off in 1994 when Tucson was officially designated "A Bicycle Friendly Community" by the League of American Wheelmen.

By 1997, the City of Tucson had its own full-time Bicycle Coordinator, and the Tucson chapter of the Greater Arizona Bicycling Association was in full gear. In April 1997 more than 2,000 commuters participated in Bike to Work Day, which is part of Tucson Bike Week and sponsored by the City of Tucson. That same year the DOT released its Five-Year Bikeway Improvement Plan. The plan calls for improvements through 2001, including some 600 miles of bikeways and expansion of bikeways along the area's river parks.

Hitting the Streets

The free Tucson Bicycle Map, which has been updated nine times since 1986, can be found at all retail bike shops and public libraries around the area. This multicolored guide lists multiuse bikeways, bike lanes and just about everything else a cyclist needs to know to peddle around Tucson.

Out on the roadways, many of the official routes are marked with large green Bike Route signs, and most have 4- to 5-foot-wide sections with white lines painted to mark the bicyclist's designated roadway. On other busy routes, streets have separate bus lanes that are shared with bicyclists.

When riding within the city, remember that bicyclists have the same responsibilities as motorists. Those responsibilities include riding on the right with traffic, obeying traffic signals, having lights on after dark and signaling before turning. There's also one additional responsibility: If you're younger than 18, you're required to wear a helmet. (And if you're older, it may not be the law, but it's a real good idea.)

In many areas, even those with good biking systems, riders still have to exercise great care when crossing major thoroughfares. But the city has alleviated that problem in some areas. For example, getting to the University of Arizona by bike may look tricky on a city map if you're coming from north of Speedway Boulevard (a main east-west thoroughfare with the best access to the University), but the city has made it simple. Crossing the six-lane road is an easy ride because of three bike routes that tunnel under Speedway Boulevard at Olive Road, Highland Avenue and Warren Avenue, all between Campbell and Park avenues.

Bike and Ride

Sun Tran, the city's bus system, has made it easy to bicycle and ride the bus with its Bike & Bus Program. Bike racks that carry two bikes are mounted on the front of the buses. Passengers unfold the rack and mount their own bike, but it's on a first-come, first-served basis since the racks only carry two bikes.

Sun Tran also rents weatherproof bike storage lockers at a number of locations for $2 a month with a $7.50 key deposit. A number of bus stop locations have bike racks for people who want to leave their bikes at the stop. All these locations are listed in the Sun Tran information guide. (See our Getting Here, Getting Around chapter for more information about Sun Tran.)

River Parks

The banks of Tucson's river systems have been in the process of being turned into recreation facilities since the first River Park Master Plan was introduced in 1976.

Since the first section of the river park was completed in 1987 along the Rillito River between Campbell Avenue and Flowing Wells Road, the city and county have been determined to build a pedestrian, in-line skating, bicycle and equestrian trail network. These well-marked two-lane, 10-foot-wide minihighways will connect all the major water courses along the Santa Cruz and Rillito rivers, Tanque Verde Creek and Panatano Wash and serve as an alternate route for bike riders to weave through the metropolitan area.

Today, two major sections of the river park system exist: the Rillito River Park and Santa Cruz River Park. Both parks open at sunrise and close at sunset, and each has amenities including restrooms, drinking fountains, parking, art work, picnic areas with bike racks and frequent switchbacks that lead down to the sandy arroyo floor. At major intersections cyclists are given the choice to go under the streets or cross them. Either way, using the river park system can be an adventure or a tranquil way of crisscrossing the urban sprawl of Tucson.

FYI
Unless otherwise noted, the area code for all phone numbers listed in this guide is 520.

Rillito River Park

Originally this east-west river park ran between Campbell Avenue and Flowing Wells Road. An addition in the early 1990s extended the park westward from Flowing Wells Road to La Cholla Boulevard, making it about 5 miles long. Future plans will extend the park to Alvernon Way at the east and I-10 at the west.

The north bank is designated for walkers, joggers, cyclists and in-line skaters, and the south bank is reserved for walkers, joggers and horseback riders. Don't make the mistake of riding your bike on the south bank; the park rangers will stop you, and you could be fined. And remember, when it comes to yielding on this well-kept bike path, bike riders are on the bottom of the food chain and are required to yield to everybody. (See the Parks and Recreation chapter for more information on Rillito River Park.)

Santa Cruz River Park

This is a very well-kept river park and the nicest way to transit the heart of Tucson. The

---

INSIDERS' TIP

When sharing the river park with your four-footed best friend, you must keep the dog on a leash no longer than 6 feet.

park runs from Grant Road (north of downtown) south through the downtown area around Congress Street to Irvington Road. There is a break from Silverlake Road south to Ajo Way, but it is easily bypassed and worth the temporary detour along Mission Road to pick up the river trail farther south to Irvington Road.

On the west bank of the Santa Cruz, near the corner of Riverside Drive and Huron Street, you'll pass a playground, ramadas, picnic tables and restrooms. There's a set of arches designed by local artist Susan Gamble that tells the history of the river and its ancient inhabitants.

Farther south along the west bank is the Garden of Gethsemane, featuring religious statuary by sculptor Felix Lucero. The sculptures were made from materials found in the Santa Cruz.

As you ride south and emerge from under the Congress Street bridge, a huge eucalyptus tree will come into view. At 4 feet in diameter, it is Tucson's largest tree. On the ride farther south you'll find restrooms, drinking fountains and opportunities to cut down into the riverbed to explore. (See the Parks and Recreation chapter for more information about the park.)

Mountain Biking

Mountain bikes seem to be the people-powered vehicle of choice on Tucson city streets. But the entire Tucson vicinity is within easy proximity to mountain and desert parks that offer great chances for off-road riding. The area's splendid scenery, moderate climate and range of elevations, from the desert floor to the 9,100 foot Mt. Lemmon, make the surrounding area ideal.

Most serious mountain bike races take place near Phoenix and in small mountain and desert towns such as Patagonia and Sonoita. The Arizona State Championship series runs from January through June at venues across Arizona and attracts some 600 to 800 racers per event. All standard NORBA age class and competition categories are offered in this series. If you plan to enter any mountain bike races, we suggest you contact the nonprofit Mountain Bike Association of Arizona (P.O. Box 32728, Phoenix, AZ 85064). This organization is the sponsor of many races sanctioned by the National Off-Road Bicycle Association (NORBA).

For maps and information on trails, check the local bike shops for a copy of the Tucson Bicycling Map. It includes designated trails in both Saguaro National Park East and West. Another map/trail guide was just released in 1997. It's the Mountain Bike Rides of the Tucson Area ($5), which can be found in many map stores and bike shops. And when you arrive at any of the mountain parks, stop by the visitors center and pickup copies of the free trail maps. Keep in mind that there are trails specifically designated for mountain biking.

The most important thing to remember when spending any time in the parks is the "Leave No Trace" ethic that has kept these areas pristine. Keep your riding groups small, and stay on the trails to avoid scarring the landscape and plant life everyone comes to admire.

For those who don't want to venture far, we describe a few of Tucson's favorite mountain bike trails, which have varying degrees of difficulty but are easy to get to. Luckily, most trails that are maintained usually have good signage to keep you on track. As you meet other riders on the trails, be sure to ask them where their favorite rides are — it's a great way to find new outlets for your off-road riding passion.

Saguaro National Park East
Cactus Forest Loop

Though there are more than 75 miles of trails in Saguaro National Park East (some of which head into the nearby Rincon Mountains), the 8-mile Cactus Forest Loop in Saguaro East is the only section of the park's trail system that is legal for mountain bikes.

To get there, take Broadway Boulevard east to Old Spanish Trail and follow the signs to Saguaro National Park East. You will pay an entry fee of about $2. Since the trail is a paved loop, you will find the trailhead no matter which way you turn past the guardhouse. Be sure stop at the visitors center for trail maps.

The trail heading north is one-way in that direction, while the loop heading south is two-way for bicycle traffic. Heading south, you'll hit the Javalina picnic area along a slight detour. This is the point where traffic becomes one-way again — from the opposite direction. Some riders take this 1.3-mile route, have a snack and then head back the other way past the visitors center to travel the entire loop. Others prefer to go north, and stop at this picnic area during the final leg of the trip to reflect upon what they've seen over the last 7 miles.

Either way, this trip through the desert forest of cacti is enjoyable, and you're bound to see a number of desert creatures lurking in the bush. The trail is accessible to beginners, but more experienced riders will enjoy it as well.

East Tucson
High Chiva Loop

This is a classic 15-mile desert ride with a few hills that crosses the normally flowing Tanque Verde Creek. To get to the trailhead, take Grant Road east to Tanque Verde Road and follow that northward (actually east) until the pavement ends (about 12 miles). You can continue on the dirt road for another 4 miles and park in a parking lot near the cattle corrals.

The trail takes a downhill run going east, where a fork in the trail appears. You want to ride to the right. By the time you reach the bottom of the hill, the trail has smoothed out a bit. From here this desert trail sees a series of small inclines for about a mile until it reaches a small peak.

INSIDERS' TIP

Tucson Police have stepped up enforcement to keep bicyclists operating under the same laws that apply to motor vehicles — that includes not riding on sidewalks.

The leaders of the pack at El Tour de Tucson push up a desert hill.

You'll go downhill from here toward Tanque Verde Creek. Take the left trail toward the creek and cross it. Expect to see water in this sparse desert setting as you continue along a jeep road toward the Rincon Mountains. The trail involves a lot of climbing here as it turns increasingly rocky. After about 6 miles, it begins to loop back to the beginning. Making it to the falls involves taking a right instead of left at the last junction. If you do so, you'll be at the falls within about a half-mile. If you don't head to the falls, stay on the jeep road. It will join Redington Road after some 4 miles where you will take a left and return to where you started.

This is a good, moderate ride with plenty of desert scenery as well as rocky climbs. Be sure to wear a helmet.

Mt. Lemmon
Lemmon Park Trail

Sometimes mountain bike riding is out of the question in Tucson's summer heat. But if you don't mind the hourlong drive to the top of Mt. Lemmon, summer will never be your bicycling nemesis again. The Lemmon Park Trail near Ski Valley at 9,050 feet is some 30 degrees cooler than the desert floor of Tucson.

To get there, take the Catalina Highway north from Tanque Verde Road. This is the only road to Mt. Lemmon. After 23 miles you will come to a junction that turns toward Summerhaven to the right and Ski Valley to the left. Go left, past Ski Valley, to Mile Post 26.5. You'll find a locked gate with a parking lot on the left. This is the trailhead.

Those who enjoy biking not only on rocky terrain, but also among towering fir trees and lush green meadows, will feel right at home. The trail starts as a winding downhill run where more professional bikers will enjoy jumping rocks and an occasional downed tree limb. From here you will link up with the Mt. Lemmon Trail, formerly the old Trico utility line road at 8,800 feet. This is where the trail starts its climb back up, with splendid views of rocky mountain vistas and the Tucson valley in the distance.

After several minutes of riding, the trail really starts to climb as you approach 9,100 feet. This is a great leg that takes you along Radio Ridge and past the top of the Ski Valley lift below. At this point, you'll follow another abandoned utility line road along Miner's Ridge and toward your descent toward Summerhaven. Coming off Radio Ridge, the trail is steep (and mostly loose rock and slippery shale) and leads into another small paved road.

This is where you'll pass Summerhaven and ride parallel to Sabino Creek's headwaters. It's known as the Upper Sabino Canyon Riparian area, and its bubbling waters draw an assortment of wildlife — from bears to birds. At this point connect with the Aspen Draw Trail that meets the paved road at the Ski area. Follow the road back to the parking area at the trailhead.

This is a great ride for a summer getaway. Other activities in the area include summer lift rides at Ski Valley (see our Attractions chapter) and shops and cafes at Summerhaven.

Information Please!

Whether you need maps or information on trails, local rider clubs or Tucson bicycle laws, the following quick reference list will help you get started. This section also highlights some of the major biking events in the area and profiles Tucson's largest bike shops.

Greater Arizona Bicycling Association — Tucson Chapter
P.O. Box 43272, Tucson 85733 • 885-8807

This local chapter of the national organization promotes interest and involvement in all aspects of bicycling. To this end, it publishes a free monthly newsletter with comprehensive tour and racing listings, legislation updates and other bicycling news. The newsletter is distributed by most of the bike shops listed under "Retail Shops and Repair" in this chapter.

The Perimeter Bicycling Association of America
630 N. Craycroft Rd., Ste. 141 • 745-2033

The PBAA is a national group located in Tucson. It organizes El Tour de Tucson every November as well as a number of other smaller events. The association publishes *Tailwinds*, a slick, color, tabloid-size free newspaper, six times a year. It's crammed with information and advertising and is distributed at area bike shops. PBAA is a membership-driven organization. Annual membership ($35) includes a year's worth of *Tailwinds* plus $5 off any PBAA-sponsored event.

Sun Tran Customer Service Center
4220 S. Park Ave., Bldg. 10 • 792-9222

City buses are equipped with bike racks. The *Rider's Information Guide* lists the times and routes of these buses as well as other useful bike info for the city bike commuter. (See the Getting Here, Getting Around chapter for more information about Sun Tran.)

Tucson-Pima County Bicycle Advisory Committee
201 N. Stone Ave., 6th Floor • 791-4372

Established in 1987, this joint committee of Pima County and the City of Tucson is a citizen advisory group of approximately 17 members, who meet each month to provide direction in decisions affecting the bicycling community. The committee also publishes *Bike Rights*, a free newsletter sent through the mail on request, as well as the *Bicycle Guide*, which lists safety tips, laws and other bike information about Tucson.

Major Events

A weekend hardly goes by without some group of riders teaming up for short or long rides as a riding club. Here we list a few of the stand-out events that draw large numbers of people and add some $5 million to the local economy. Keep in mind that an industry-approved bike helmet is always required to participate in these events.

INSIDERS' TIP
You can be slapped with a $50 fine if you are younger than 18 and not wearing a helmet while you ride.

The Tour for Tucson's Children raises money to buy helmets for underprivileged kids.

April

Tucson Bike Week
City of Tucson • 740-3345

Every year at the beginning of April, the City of Tucson sponsors Bike Week. The idea is to promote bicycle commuting as an alternative form of transportation that's good for both personal health and the health of the local environment. In 1997, some 2,000 people took to peddling to work during the midweek Bike to Work Day. The city also sponsors a free breakfast for organization and business representatives to learn how bike commuting can help their firms and their employees.

Tour of the Tucson Mountains
Various locations/University of Arizona • 745-2033

This event draws some 1,000 cyclists of all ages and abilities to participate in the 100K, 50K and Kids Fun Ride events held in early April. The best viewing area is the start and finish line at the main gate of the University of Arizona. The event routes riders through the Tucson Mountains. After the race there is usually a bike festival with food and music.

July

Tour for Tucson's Children
Tucson Convention Center, 260 S. Church St. • 791-5563

Usually held on July 4th and organized by Tucson Parks and Recreation Department, Tour for Tucson's Children is a 27-mile route as well as a 6.5-mile Family Ride and half-mile FunRide for kids. Each race starts at the Tucson Convention Center. The money raised from these rides benefits the Tucson Safe Kids Coalition Helmet Fund. In 1997, the $4,500 raised provided 1,125 helmets for underprivileged kids.

September

Breakaway to the Border
National Multiple Sclerosis Society, Southwest Chapter 626 N. Craycroft Rd., Ste. 116 • 747-7472

Considered one of the most challenging and scenic one-day cycling events in Arizona, the complete route for Breakaway to the Border runs 130 miles from Tucson south to Nogales, Arizona, and back again. There are also shorter 30- and 70-mile rides, but if you're going to do this one, go all the way. The entry fee is $25, and riders also raise pledges to support the MS organization, which gives prizes to those who raise the most. The frequent rest stops along the route provide high-energy snacks, water, bike mechanics and even medical professionals. This is not a race, so you can ride at your own pace south along Interstate 19 to Nogales, and then north along Ariz. highways 82 and 83 through Patagonia and Sonoita. The ride is held in late September.

November

El Tour de Tucson
The Perimeter Bicycling Association of America, 630 N. Craycroft Rd., Ste. 141 • 745-2033

For more than 15 years, cyclists have turned out for this tour, considered the oldest and largest perimeter cycling event in the United States with 111 miles of street route that actually circles the Tucson area. The Tour is always held the Saturday before Thanksgiving. Every year the proceeds from the race are given to a different charity, with more than $1.9 million raised since the event's inception in 1983.

Make no mistake — this is a race, and the best times are rewarded with medallions in both the men's and women's divisions. But there are also 75-, 50- or 25-mile routes and fun rides for adults and kids. The event is a big deal in Tucson, with strong police traffic support along the route for safety as well as aid stations and medical personnel. Some 4,000 cyclists, ranging from celebrated athletes from around the world to casual bikers, come out to compete or at least participate. Registration is $50, with processing fees that vary from $10 to $35, depending on when you sign up. The race begins and ends in downtown Tucson.

El Tour de Tucson has been named by *Bicycling Magazine* as one of the 10 best century (that's a 100-mile course for all you non-bikers) courses in America, and the city folk who come out to watch are very supportive.

Retail Shops and Repair

> **FYI**
> Unless otherwise noted, the area code for all phone numbers listed in this guide is 520.

Ajo Bikes
3816 S. 12th Ave.
• 294-1434

Offering a large selection of parts and accessories, this shop is best known for its wide selection of recumbent bikes — those odd, high-tech bikes with bucket seats and peddles in front of the handlebars.

Arizona Cycle & Sport
2716 S. Kolb Rd. • 750-1454

Located on the southeast side of town, this full-service shop offers the usual lifetime tune-up with the purchase of a new bike as well as free test rides. It also has a good collection of parts and accessories.

Bargain Basement Bikes
428 N. Fremont Ave. • 624-9673

Across from Arizona Stadium, this shop carries new and used bikes and is one of the best places to buy and sell used mountain bikes. It also rents bikes and surry carts and has service and parts for all the top brands. Bargain Basement will rent any used bikes it has, which includes road and mountain bikes. Mountain bikes can be rented for $20 a day, $45 for three days or $65 for a week. Call or stop in for more information about what the shop has to rent and the fees involved.

Bicycles West
3801 N. Oracle Rd. • 887-7770
7090 N. Oracle Rd. • 742-5111

Each of these locations has a full-service repair department, free monthly maintenance classes, wheelchair repairs and a full line of touring and mountain bikes. Delivery is available.

Broadway Bicycles
140 S. Sarnoff Dr. • 296-7819

One block south of Broadway Boulevard on the far Eastside, this shop has been around since 1975 and offers a full line of biking clothing, accessories, parts, tools, car racks and expert repairs on all makes. Broadway rents mountain bikes for $18 for a 24-hour period.

Catalina Bicycle Shop
2310 N. Campbell Ave. • 326-7377

Located at the busy corner of Grant Road and Campbell Avenue, this 16-year-old company specializes in Schwinn and Mongoose bikes but offers repairs on all makes. The knowledgable staff is full of great information about local events, trails and races, so don't be afraid to ask.

Cycle Spectrum
6177 E. Broadway Blvd. • 790-9394

Across from Park Mall, this shop has new and used bikes, one-day repairs and a large selection of parts and accessories. Lifetime tuneups are offered with the purchase of a new bike. Cycle Spectrum is part of America's largest chain of bike shops, so it has a huge stock.

Fair Wheel Bikes
1110 E. 6th St. • 884-9018

Around the corner from Bargain Basement Bikes near Arizona Stadium, this company specializes in pro and custom bikes — road, mountain and BMX — and used bikes. Fair Wheel offers a complete service department and rentals with pickup and delivery. Mountain bikes can be rented for $20 for the first day and $10 per additional day.

Full Cycle
3232 E. Speedway Blvd. • 327-3232

Full Cycle maintains close connections to the Southern Arizona Mountain Bike Association, so it distributes useful trail information. The shop offers maintenance classes, service packages and bike rentals. You can rent a mountain bike for the day ($20), the weekend ($35) or the week ($80). For new bike buys, Full Cycle provides a double manufacturer warranty.

R&R Bicycle
3686 W. Orange Grove Rd. • 575-2829

R&R accepts trade-ins and offers a huge selection of accessories. The shop also rents upper-end mountain bikes with dual suspension for $40 a day.

Racer's Edge Bicycles
2623 N. Campbell Ave. • 795-2453

This shop carries high-end bikes and offers a service department and free lifetime tuneups with the purchase of all new bikes. Voted "Best Bicycle Store" by readers of the *Tucson Weekly* and one of the top-100 stores in the country by *Bicycle Dealer's Showcase Magazine*, the shop carries most top-brand mountain bikes and a variety of clothing.

Sabino Cycles
7131 E. Tanque Verde Rd. • 885-3666

Sabino Cycles offers a full-service repair department, parts, accessories, clothing, rentals and bikes for all ages. Suspended mountain bikes rent for $30 for the first day and $15 for each additional day; nonsuspended bikes rent for $20 for the first day and $10 for each additional day.

Speedway Bikes
3013 E. Speedway Blvd. • 795-3339

Speedway Bikes has a complete service and repair center and carries bike clothing.

Tucson Bicycles
4743 E. Sunrise Dr. • 577-7374

In the Foothills near Swan Road and Sunrise Drive, this full-service shop is open seven days a week and offers a large selection of custom frames, repairs, parts, rentals with pickup and delivery — even wheelchair wheel repair. Tucson Bicycles also rents mountain bikes: Fees start at $20 a day.

University Bicycles
940 E. University Ave. • 624-3663

Near the University of Arizona's main gate at Park Avenue, University Bicycles offers free lifetime tune-ups on all new bikes. Mountain bike rentals are $20 for the first day, $10 for each additional day. The complete service department for all makes will keep you rolling down the road.

Two things make Tucson a strong venue for spectator sports: the nearly ideal year-round weather and the University of Arizona.

Spectator Sports

Compared to cities like Chicago and New York, which have professional teams (and sometimes more than one per sport) in football, baseball, basketball and hockey, Tucson could be considered in the minor league of spectator sports. But two things make Tucson a strong venue for spectator sports: the nearly ideal year-round weather, which attracts pro baseball teams for spring training and helps college sports thrive, and the University of Arizona, which offers nearly every sport imaginable, many of them top-ranked teams in the nation year after year.

The University's nickname is Wildcats, and you won't be in Tucson long before seeing signs, T-shirts, hats or publications touting the Cats. UA competes in at least 18 varsity sports, most of which are very spectator-oriented and provide great viewing and great fun for Tucsonans, who are faithful and supportive fans of their college teams. Unless otherwise noted, tickets for all UA games can be obtained at the ticket office at McKale Center, which is on Enke Drive just west of Campbell Avenue and a block north of 6th Street, 621-2287. Just remember that any of the ticket prices given in this chapter are subject to change.

In addition to profiling the pro teams that play here and the major college sports you can watch in Tucson, this chapter covers other spectator sports offered in Tucson such as racing and tennis. We also take a slight detour to the north to tell you about the major sports teams based in Phoenix, since it's not uncommon for Tucson residents or visitors to travel there for a pro or bowl game. And finally, we also provide a primer on the major sports playing fields in both cities so you know how to get there, where to park and what to expect.

Tucson

Baseball/Softball

UA Wildcats — Men
Frank Sancet Field, 640 N. Warren Dr.
• 621-4102

A testimony to the quality of UA's baseball program is the fact that plenty of professional baseball players have come from the team over the past 20 years. With its excellent sports reputation, UA can recruit good players, and with weather conditions conducive to lots of practice opportunities, the result is a good team and fans who come out to watch the games. The Wildcat baseball players were NCAA champs in 1976 and 1980 and play fine baseball every season, which runs from February to May. Ticket prices are $3 to $5. The playing field is at N. Warren and E. Enke drives just across from McKale Center, where tickets can be obtained. The closest parking is at the McKale parking garage to McKale Center's west or another pay parking lot just north of that.

UA Wildcats — Women
Hillenbrand Stadium, E. 2nd St. and N. Warren Dr. • 621-4920

Both women's sports and the game of softball often seem to take a backseat to more

---

INSIDERS' TIP

Dillard's department stores — located at El Con Mall, Park Mall and Tucson Mall — have outlets where tickets to a number of major sporting events in both Tucson and Phoenix can be obtained. Or you can charge them by phone at (800) 638-4253. There's a service charge added per ticket either way.

popular University sports, but this PAC-10 Conference team takes a backseat to no one. They were PAC-10 champions in 1997 and own five national titles in the Women's College World Series, so interest in the team and the popularity of the sport are definitely growing in Tucson. Home games are usually packed. The season runs from February to May, and games are played at the new 2,000-seat Hillenbrand Stadium on campus. Tickets range from $3 to $5 at McKale Center ticket office.

Spring Training
Tucson Electric Park, 2500 E. Ajo Wy.
• **319-9501, 791-4873**

You may hear it referred to as spring training or as the cactus league (the name given to pro baseball teams that practice in the cactus-laden state of Arizona), but it's the only way Tucsonans get to see major league baseball in their own backyard. It's not uncommon for winter visitors from Chicago, Milwaukee and other snowbound points north and east to descend on Arizona just for the privilege of seeing their favorite major leaguers hit, pitch and run during spring training. Over the years, many different teams (most recently the Colorado Rockies) have spent the month of March in Tucson, practicing for the upcoming baseball season and hosting other major league teams for games.

In 1998 and probably for many years thereafter, two other teams will call Tucson their spring training home: the Chicago White Sox and the new National League expansion team, the Arizona Diamondbacks. In prior years, Tucson's cactus league played in Hi Corbett Field, but 1998 also marks the debut of a new stadium — Tucson Electric Park, located along I-10 south of downtown Tucson and part of Pima County's new Kino Veterans Memorial Sports Complex. It includes an 11,000-seat stadium and separate clubhouse and field facilities for the two teams. The Colorado Rockies will continue their spring training in Tucson at Hi Corbett Field, 900 S. Randolph Way.

Between the three cactus league teams, a total of about 45 games will be played here during spring training. Tickets range from $3 for lawn seating to $14 for club seats, and season ticket packages are available. Call the previously listed numbers for information on the cactus league or tickets.

Tucson Sidewinders
Tucson Electric Park, 2500 E. Ajo Wy.
• **325-2621**

For nearly 29 years, baseball fans and anyone else just out for a fun evening of spectator sports went to Hi Corbett Field to watch the Tucson Toros, the Triple A team (also known as farm or minor-league team) housed here. Over the years, the Toros have been the farm team for the White Sox, the Texas Rangers, the Oakland A's, the Milwaukee Brewers and the Houston Astros and often finished in one of the top slots in their division. In 1996, former Toros numbering 65 were playing in the major league, and Toros gate attendance topped 312,000 for the season. It's an opportunity for Tucsonans and visitors to see the major-league baseball stars of the future.

But 1998 signals a major change in the Triple A baseball scene. Tucson still has a team but it's now the Triple A club for the new Arizona Diamondbacks (see the Phoenix section of this chapter) and is named the Tucson Sidewinders. And along with getting accustomed to a new name, Tucsonans will also be going to a new location to watch their baseball team. Instead of playing at Hi Corbett Field, Triple A baseball will be played at the new Tucson Electric Park.

One thing that's not expected to change, however, is Tuffy the mascot, who shows up at all the games and has great fun with the kids. There are also family nights and special events such as Circle K night (free tickets at Circle K stores), hot dog night (25¢ dogs), fireworks extravaganzas and Fox (KMSB-TV) Kids Club nights to make going to the game even more fun. Ticket prices (which may change with the new venue) range from $3 to $8 with kids younger than 5 free in general admission seats. About 70 games are played at home during the April-to-September season.

> **FYI**
> Unless otherwise noted, the area code for all phone numbers listed in this guide is 520.

The Pride of Arizona Marching Band entertains the crowd at half-time.

Basketball

UA Wildcats — Men
McKale Center, 1721 E. Enke Dr.
- 621-4813, 621-2287

Tucson may not have a pro basketball team, but it has one of the best of the college teams, compliments of UA and coach Lute Olson. Since the '87-88 season, UA owns the best winning percentage in collegiate basketball. This PAC-10 team has been conference champions for seven of the last 12 years, reached the Final Four in the NCAA tournament three times and won the NCAA championship in 1997. The season runs from November to March and opens with the annual Red/Blue intrasquad scrimmage for which tickets are $3.

Home games are played at McKale Center at the University, which seats more than 14,500. Your best chance for a ticket is to befriend a season ticket holder who can't get to the game. Individual game tickets may be available at the McKale Center ticket office for $14 to $20 or by phone. Student tickets are $4. As in all urban university towns, parking is at a premium and can be almost as tough to get as a ticket to the game. The closest option is the McKale Parking Garage immediately west of McKale Center.

UA Wildcats — Women
McKale Center, 1721 E. Enke Dr.
- 621-4813, 621-2287

Move over, men, the women hoopsters are gaining ground. Not accustomed to success or much of a following, the women's basketball team at UA changed all that with their best record ever in 1997 and a No. 7 seed in the West region at the 1997 NCAA Tournament. Their audience is growing along with their prestige. They play at McKale Center from early November through early March, with the NCAA tournament games immediately after. Tickets are a bargain at $3 to $4 from the McKale Center ticket office.

Fiesta Bowl Basketball Classic
McKale Center, 1721 E. Enke Dr.
- 621-2287

While the Fiesta Bowl itself is played in Phoenix, this basketball event is played at McKale Center in Tucson during the week before the New Year's Day football game. It's an invitational tournament, but the UA basketball team is usually one of the teams playing. On the first day there are two games between four teams and on the second day a consolation and a championship game. Tickets are $23 a day, meaning you'll see two games for that price, or $8 for University students. They usually go on sale around the first week of December at McKale Center ticket office or by phone.

Football

UA Wildcats
Arizona Stadium, E. 6th St. and N. Warren Dr. • 621-4917

When September rolls around in Tucson, it may not seem like fall with temperatures still hovering in the low 100s, but that's what greets the University's Wildcat football players and fans in Arizona Stadium. Sunscreen is mandatory if you're going to a day game, but fortunately most are at night. The Wildcats are in the Pacific Athletic Conference, better known as the PAC-10, and play teams such as UCLA, USC and the University of Washington. But the biggest rivalry each year is against our neighbors to the north, the Arizona State University Sun Devils, a game for which tickets are almost impossible to get. Otherwise tickets range from about $8 to $26 and are fairly easy to obtain. Parking on or near campus can be tough, so the easiest option may be the shuttle buses from the eastern end of El Con Mall at Broadway and Dodge boulevards.

Insight.Com Bowl
Arizona Stadium, E. 6th St. and N. Warren Dr. • 797-4464

For the past eight years, Tucson has hosted a bowl game (formerly called the Copper Bowl) among two college conferences — the Big 12 vs. the WAC. It takes place the week between Christmas and New Year's on a Saturday night. In recent years obtaining title sponsorship and funding has been a struggle, putting the future of the bowl game in doubt. But in late 1997, a new company came forward to be the title sponsor of the game and to rename it the Insight.Com Bowl. Tickets to the game usually range from $16 to about $40 and are available by credit card at the phone number listed above or at the ticket outlets located at Dillard's department stores in Tucson, (800) 638-4253.

Golf

Tucson hosts two major golf tournaments that draw lots of spectators. In February, it's the Tucson Chrysler Golf Classic, a PGA tournament played at Tucson Omni National Golf Resort in northwest Tucson. Spectators can watch this tourney for $15 a day or $50 for the week. Free parking is on site. In March pro women golfers come to town for the Welch's/Circle K LPGA Championship Tournament played at Randolph Golf Course on S. Alvernon Way. For this one, spectators pay $10 a day and parking is limited, so plan to take the free shuttle buses from El Con Mall. (Details on both tournaments are in the Festivals and Events chapter.)

Ice Hockey

UA Icecats
Tucson Convention Center, Church Ave. and Cushing St. • 791-4266

Tucsonans either love ice hockey (or maybe just the ice) or simply love any sport played by the University because the University's Icecats games are usually packed with a wildly uproarious audience reaching 6,000 to 8,000. One of the top club teams in the country (meaning they are not NCAA-affiliated but play in a league), the Icecats play at the Tucson Convention Center from October through February. Ticket prices range from $7 to $9. Parking is available at the TCC for $2 to $3 or free on neighboring side streets.

Gila Monsters
Tucson Convention Center, Church Ave. and Cushing St. • 903-9000

For the first time ever, Tucson got a professional ice hockey team in 1997. The Gila (pronounced hee-la) Monsters are in the West Coast Hockey League along with eight other teams. The season runs from mid-October through March with about 32 home games, all in the evening, played at the Tucson Convention Center just south of downtown. Tickets

---

www.insiders.com

See this and many other **Insiders' Guide®** destinations online — in their entirety.

Visit us today!

range from $6.75 to $12.75 and are available through Dillard's ticket outlets or from the TCC box office at 791-4266.

Racing

Horses

Rillito Downs
4502 N. 1st Ave. • 293-5011

The Rillito Racetrack is Tucson's only venue for horse racing, which takes place Saturday and Sunday afternoons, usually January through March, but the season length varies. The 88-acre racetrack is just off 1st Avenue south of River Road and is adjacent to the (usually dry) Rillito River, making it a pretty spot to watch the thoroughbreds and quarter horses run. And it's right next to Rillito Park, so you can take a picnic lunch and make a day of it. The racetrack features outside and inside seating with admission around $2, pari-mutuel wagering and a full bar and restaurant. In addition to live races, there are simulcast races, and Rillito Downs races are played at about seven or eight off-track betting sites around Tucson. Call the racetrack or check with the Tucson Convention and Visitors Bureau for free season passes. Parking is free and usually ample.

Greyhounds

Tucson Greyhound Park
36th St. at 4th Ave. • 884-7576

When the horses aren't running at Rillito, and even when they are, you can still watch races of the four-legged variety at Tucson Greyhound Park, which is open year round (except possibly Thanksgiving and Christmas days) and has pari-mutuel wagering. Live races are run four days a week — Wednesdays, Fridays, Saturdays and Sundays — usually one in the afternoon and one in the evening. Greyhound Park also simulcasts races — both horse and dog — every day, usually from about 9:30 AM to 11 PM. For the general admission of $1.50, you'll watch the greyhounds streak along from a large air-conditioned grandstand, with bars, concession stands and a nonsmoking area, or from the trackside rail. Clubhouse admission is $3, where a full-service restaurant and bar are available and reservations are advised. Call for race schedules, post times or clubhouse reservations. Parking is free at the track.

Cars

Tucson Raceway Park
12500 S. Houghton Rd. • 762-9200

Spectators who like to see stock-car vehicles speeding around a track and possibly smashing into each other or the walls should head to the County fairgrounds in southeast Tucson for the NASCAR races. It has a .375-mile high-banked asphalt track famous for its three grooves that allow three abreast racing. The main season is April to October with races every Saturday. Tickets are $9 for adults, $7 for kids older than 11 and seniors, with kids younger than 11 free. During the first three Sundays of December and January, the race park has its "winter heat" racing, which is broadcast live on ESPN television. Those tickets are $10 for everyone except kids younger than 11, who are free. The raceway has ample free parking and all the typical concessions (spectators can only bring in water in its original container).

Southwestern International Raceway
Pima County Fairgrounds, Exit 275 just south of I-10 • 762-9100

During every month of the year but December, Tucsonans can head to this drag racing track at the County Fairgrounds and see everything from professional fuel cars to novice street cars race around a .25-mile drag strip. During the winter months, events at this NHRA-sanctioned facility take place Saturday and Sunday afternoons and during the summer on Wednesday, Friday and Sunday evenings. Weekday tickets are $8 and weekends are $10 with kids younger than 12 always free. Spectators are not allowed to bring in alcohol or any glass containers, but the raceway has a full line of concessions including beer. Parking is ample and free.

Major Area Sports Stadiums

America West Arena

Located at 201 E. Jefferson Street in central Phoenix, this arena opened in 1992 and seats 19,000, primarily fans of the Suns pro basketball team, the Mercury women's pro basketball team and the Coyotes ice hockey team. Ticket prices vary with the team; for example, Mercury tickets range from $8 to $50 and are easy to get, while Suns tickets are mostly impossible to get and afford. The will-call window is at the northwest plaza level near the corner of Jefferson and 1st streets. From Tucson, take I-10 to Phoenix and exit at 7th Street. Head south to Washington Street, then west to 1st Street and south to the Arena. A parking garage directly west of the arena charges about $6 per event, but parking spaces in this area will fill up fast. Information on the arena or tickets is available at the box office at (602) 379-7800.

Arizona Stadium

This is UA's football stadium, located on E. 6th Street a couple of blocks west of Campbell Avenue. It seats about 55,000. Spectators cannot bring in any containers or alcoholic beverages, nor are they sold here during any college activity. There are a few unusual things about this stadium that the average spectator may never notice. One is that two sides of the stadium, the south and east, actually are built over dormitories. (We hope no students are trying to snooze or study during a game.) Another is the knot-hole section on the south side of the field, which is reserved exclusively for kids from 4th through 8th grades, who can obtain a seat for all home games, usually six of them, for just $8. Knot-hole tickets are available from McKale Center ticket office or through any YMCA. You can enter this stadium from just about any side, but wheelchair patrons are advised to use Gate 1. The will-call trailer is at the southeast corner near Gate 9. You'll find the typical stadium concessions between the second and third tiers and the Scoreboard Cafe on the north side of the stadium at street level. If you're not lucky enough to find parking in one of the University's nearby garages, try the neighborhood streets to the south.

Bank One Ballpark

Along with welcoming their first major-league baseball team, Arizonans will also be seeing their new team, the Diamondbacks, play in a new multimillion dollar state-of-the-art baseball field in Phoenix at Jefferson and 4th streets. Affectionately known as BOB or as Diamondtown, Bank One Ballpark has 48,500 seats, a 5¼-acre retractable roof that opens or closes in five minutes, real grass on the playing field and 8,000 tons of air conditioning. Inside goodies include restaurants, a baseball history museum, shops, interactive kiosks, countless television and video monitors and a beer garden and microbreweries. Fans are allowed to bring small coolers (although they'll be searched), lunch bags and water bottles, but beverages (alcoholic or non), thermoses and metal or glass containers are no-nos. Although Phoenix plans to build a huge parking garage nearby, parking will be a challenge given that three major sites — BOB, America West Arena and Phoenix Civic Plaza (the city's convention center) — are all a stone's throw from each other. From Tucson, take I-10 to Phoenix and exit at 7th Street. Go south to

— continued on next page

McKale Center is the home of the 1997 NCAA Basketball Champions — the UA Wildcats.

Washington Street, west to 3rd Street, then south. For information on the ballpark or tickets, call the Arizona Diamondbacks at (602) 462-6500 or (888) 777-4664.

Hi Corbett Field

This Tucson baseball field is situated in the middle of a multiacre city complex called Randolph Park that houses golf courses, parks and the zoo and can be accessed from Broadway Boulevard or 22nd Street to 900 S. Randolph Way. In the past, it's been home to the cactus-league teams that train in Tucson in spring and the Tucson Toros, the Triple A (or farm or minor-league) baseball team that now has a new name (Sidewinders), a new affiliation (Arizona Diamondbacks) and a new place to play (Tucson Electric Park). Hi Corbett Field is expected to continue to be the playing field for the Colorado Rockies during spring training. Parking is available at the field for about $2 to $3. There's also a shuttle bus from the east side of El Con Mall. For information, call Tucson Parks and Recreation at 791-4873.

McKale Center

This copper-roofed circular structure seating 14,500 is home to a number of Wildcat sports including men's and women's basketball, volleyball and gymnastics. Located just north of 6th Street and west of Campbell Avenue on Enke Drive, it's surrounded by other University sports fields including the stadium, Frank Sancet baseball field and Hillenbrand Aquatic Center. McKale is handicapped-accessible, and entry for all spectators is on the south side facing Enke Drive. Concession stands are on Level 3, and no containers can be brought into the center. McKale also houses the University's main ticket office where tickets for all sport games can be purchased. The ticket booths are outdoors on the south side facing Enke Drive, and there are metered parking spaces right there for picking up or inquiring about tickets. Phone numbers for inquiring about or charging tickets are 621-CATS or (800) 452-CATS. There's a parking garage just to the west, but don't count on getting in during a game.

— continued on next page

Sun Devil Stadium

This is Arizona State University's stadium, hence its name reflects the school's nickname, but professional and bowl games are played here as well: the Arizona Cardinals football team and the Fiesta Bowl. Located in the Phoenix suburb of Tempe, Arizona, where the University is located, the stadium seats more than 73,000 around a grass playing field. During the early half of the football season — college and pro — fans are likely to contend with 100-degree temperatures during day games, so sunscreen is de rigueur. During college games, no alcohol is sold nor can it be brought in, and containers may be checked. Beer is sold at the stadium during pro games. The ticket office and will-call are on the stadium's south end. Pay parking is available on public and private lots scattered all around the stadium, but you may have a walk from your vehicle to the stadium. Since this is a university town, before and after the game fare and fun are plentiful at numerous restaurants, bars, hotels and shops all around the stadium. If you're driving here from Tucson, take I-10 to the University Boulevard exit, then head east to Mill Avenue, then north. For information on the stadium or games, call (602) 965-3933 or (602) 965-2381.

Tucson Electric Park

This new baseball stadium is part of a new Pima County facility called Kino Veterans Memorial Sports Complex that also houses practice and playing fields for baseball, soccer and basketball. Located on Ajo Way near I-10, the baseball stadium was named to reflect the support of Tucson Electric Power Company in taking the complex from dream to reality. It's scheduled to open in time for 1998 spring training and will be Tucson's spring training home for the Chicago White Sox and Arizona Diamondbacks. It will also be the new April-to-September playing field for the Sidewinders, the Triple A team formerly known as Tucson Toros and now affiliated with the Arizona Diamondbacks. The 190-acre complex includes an 11,000 seat ballpark, 12 practice fields, three practice infields, two major-league clubhouses, a minor-league clubhouse, batting tunnels and pitching mounds. For baseball games, there are five seating levels and corresponding prices ranging from lawn seating to club seats. Beyond the great new facilities for the teams and more seating and pay parking for fans, the new stadium will have all the typical concessions for a great day or night at the ballpark. For information on the stadium or the teams, call 740-2680 or (888) 683-3900.

Rodeo

There aren't many spots in the states where you can see an authentic rodeo, but Tucson is one of them. The biggest — also one of the oldest in the nation — is Fiesta de Los Vaqueros, which takes place over several days in late February at the Tucson Rodeo Grounds, 4823 S. 6th Avenue. (For all the details, see the Festivals and Events chapter.) Another is the Desert Thunder Pro Rodeo held the third week in October at the Tucson Rodeo Grounds. It's the third largest PRCA/WPRA-sanctioned rodeo and offers live music and a chili cookoff in addition to all the roping, riding and bronco busting. Tickets are $10 for adults and free for kids younger than 12. (Call 721-1621 for information.). Parking at the Rodeo Grounds is $3 per vehicle or free on neighboring streets.

Senior Sports Classic

Each year, the City of Tucson Parks and Recreation Department holds the Tucson Senior Olympics. For about one week near the end of January, seniors from all over the area gather at a variety of sites including senior centers, city parks and adult residential communities to compete in games such as track,

SPECTATOR SPORTS • 237

The University of Arizona Women's Softball Team has won the national championship six of the last seven years.

tennis, bicycling, boccie ball, swimming, shuffleboard, golf and many more. Many of them go on to the state senior Olympics held in Phoenix and even the nationals (in l997, Tucson was the site of the national senior Olympics). For information on how to participate or when and where to go to watch the games, call Parks and Recreation at 791-4873 or 791-4865.

Tennis

Celebrity Tennis Classic
Randolph Park, 200 S. Alvernon Wy.
• 623-6165

Each year in April, about 40 celebrity players and 25,000 spectators descend on Randolph Park's tennis facilities for a weekend of sun, tennis and special events that raise money for local charities. In 1997 the celebrity host was singer, songwriter, musician and actor Rick Springfield. Celebrities who have appeared over the years include Beau Bridges, Tony Danza and Connie Stevens. For many years Michael Landon was the host, and the tournament now takes place on the Michael Landon memorial stadium court at Randolph Park. Events include tennis and golf tournaments pairing celebrities with local players and patrons, a tennis exhibition between celebrities and local media personalities and celebrity vs. professional exhibition matches. General spectator admission is $5. Parking at

INSIDERS' TIP

For definitive information on the shuttle buses that go from El Con Mall to various sport venues, call Sun Tran at 792-9222.

Randolph Park on S. Alvernon Way is at a premium so plan on taking the shuttle bus from the east end of El Con Mall (Broadway and Dodge boulevards).

Phoenix

For faithful fans of spectator sports, Phoenix isn't all that far away — less than a two-hour drive or bus trip and half that by plane. Even though most of Arizona's major sport teams are based in Phoenix, they're still considered Arizona teams; many even have adopted "Arizona" as part of their name rather than "Phoenix" to signify their statewide affiliation. So if Tucson doesn't satisfy all your cravings for sports, head on up to Phoenix.

> **FYI**
> Unless otherwise noted, the area code for all phone numbers listed in this guide is 520.

ing spring training. Seven teams currently practice in Phoenix and its suburbs: the Chicago Cubs at Hohokam Park in Mesa, (602) 964-4467 or (602) 649-8000; the San Diego Padres and the Seattle Mariners at Peoria Sports Complex in Peoria, (602) 878-4337 or (602) 878-4337; the Anaheim Angels at Tempe Diablo Stadium in Tempe, (602) 438-9300; the Milwaukee Brewers at Maryvale Baseball Park in Maryvale, (602) 759-6508 or (602) 506-5100; the San Francisco Giants at Scottsdale Stadium in Scottsdale, (602) 990-7972; and the Oakland A's at Phoenix Municipal Stadium in the city, (602) 392-0217 or (602) 392-0074. With each of these teams playing about 15 home games, baseball fans have more than 90 games to choose from during the month. Tickets are reasonably priced, usually ranging from about $3 to $12, but vacant seats are not easy to come by, especially for the more popular teams. For information on schedules or how to get tickets for any of the games, call the Cactus League office at (602) 827-4700 or (800) 283-6372.

Baseball

Arizona Diamondbacks
Bank One Ballpark, 401 E. Jefferson St., Phoenix • (602) 462-6500, (888) 777-4664

"Opening day less than a year away" was the chant heard around Arizona in 1997 as baseball fans anxiously awaited the state's first pro baseball team and its debut in the 1998 baseball season. The Diamondbacks (taken from a local menace, the diamondback rattlesnake) are a National League expansion team that has been more than three years in the making, from hiring a manager to signing players to completion of the new Bank One Ballpark in downtown Phoenix where the team will be playing. You can get a ticket for $1, but only by waiting in line the day of a game, and only 360 are sold this way. Otherwise, ticket prices range from $5.50 to $11.50.

Cactus League Baseball Spring Training

Arizona is heaven for folks from other parts of the country who are die-hard baseball fans and a bit sun-starved. For about a month each spring from mid-March to mid-April, they can watch their favorite major-league baseball teams practice and spar with other teams dur-

Basketball

Phoenix Mercury
America West Arena, 201 E. Jefferson St., Phoenix • (602) 252-9622, (602) 514-8333

The Phoenix Mercury was one of the initial charter teams in the WNBA and played their first season in the summer of 1997 at the air-conditioned America West Arena in downtown Phoenix. Attendance exceeded expectations, with home games averaging 10,000-plus fans who paid $8 to $50 a ticket. (It's a way for basketball devotees who can't get into the arena for a Suns game to see pro basketball and maybe even afford a ticket for the kids.) The season runs from mid-June to mid-August.

Phoenix Suns
America West Arena, 201 E. Jefferson St., Phoenix • (602) 379-7876, (602) 379-7900

If you don't recognize this championship NBA basketball team, you may recognize their furry mascot, "Go" the Gorilla who is as athletic and entertaining as the more famous team members and has risen to dean of NBA mascots. The Suns are a winning team, so tickets to their home games during the November-to-April season at America West Arena sell out quickly. They range from $24 to $80 per game and can be obtained through the Suns' ticket office or through Dillard's ticket office, (800) 638-4253.

Football

Arizona Cardinals
Sun Devil Stadium, Mill Ave. and Stadium Dr., Tempe • (602) 379-0102

They were the St. Louis Cardinals until they moved to Phoenix about 10 years ago. They haven't managed to muster a winning season for 13 years or a NFL championship for 50 years, but Arizona fans always have hope that their pro football team will rebound. The NFC East division team plays home games at Arizona State University's Sun Devil Stadium. Ticket prices range from $20 to $50, and they're fairly easy to get given the team's record. From Tucson, take I-10 to Phoenix and exit at University Boulevard, then head east to Mill Avenue and go north, where you'll see the crowd assembling and lots of parking lot signs with attendants pointing the way.

Fiesta Bowl
Sun Devil Stadium, Mill Ave. and Stadium Dr., Tempe • (602) 350-0900

Every New Year's Day, one of the major college bowl games is played outside Phoenix at the Arizona State University's Sun Devils' football stadium. The Fiesta Bowl is usually played between two top college teams selected by the Fiesta Bowl Committee. Tickets have ranged from $65 to $110 but are expected to increase in 1998. They can usually be obtained only through the two teams playing in the game, but if the game is not sold out, call the stadium for information on getting them locally. A number of other events take place as part of Fiesta Bowl, including the Fiesta Bowl Basketball Classic played in Tucson during the week before the bowl game (see our previous listing in this chapter).

Ice Hockey

Phoenix Coyotes
America West Arena, 201 E. Jefferson St., Phoenix • (602) 791-4266, (888) 255-7825

From September through April, Arizonans can go to America West Arena in Phoenix and watch the National Hockey League Coyotes slip and slide around on the ice, trying to score goals or block them. During the season, more than 80 games are played at the arena, and fans love them. Tickets range from $9.50 to $200 (rink side), but they sell out fast. They can be obtained through the ticket outlets at Tucson's Dillard's department stores, (800) 638-4253. Occasionally, the Coyotes play a game in Tucson at Tucson Convention Center, so call for information.

Davis-Monthan Air Force Base got its humble start as a municipal dirt runway.

Davis-Monthan Air Force Base

Over the past 70 years, some of America's most famous (and infamous) flying machines have flown the skies of Tucson. The "Spirit of St. Louis" and its pioneering pilot were here in 1927. Bombers like the B-17 "Flying Fortress," the B-24 "Liberator" and the B-29 "Superfortress" (used to drop the atomic bomb on Japan) flew overhead during the World War II years.

When the jet age was ushered in around 1953, Tucsonans could glance skyward and spot a new B-47 Stratojet or a squadron of F-86-A Sabre Jet fighters. And then came the cold war era with its Titan II missiles and silos and U-2 reconnaissance planes that flew global missions out of our Air Force base. Later years brought the F-4 Phantom fighter, and today A-10 Thunderbolts shine against our blue skies.

But long before "U.S. Air Force" was even a glimmer in anyone's eye, what is now known as Davis-Monthan Air Force Base in south central Tucson got its humble start as a municipal airfield — really just a two-man refueling station and a dirt runway. The year was 1919 when Tucson officials voted to create an airport. It all began on an 82-acre site where the rodeo grounds are today. (A plaque on the rodeo grounds on S. 6th Avenue marks the spot.) First called Macauley Field and then Fishburn Field, it became Tucson Municipal Flying Field in 1923. Tucson officials definitely had vision. Not only had they established the first municipal airport in Arizona, but hoping that it would be selected as the site for an army air base, they also began building it to military specifications under guidance from the Army Air Corps.

By 1927, their dreams were coming true. Col. Charles A. Lindbergh, fresh from his triumphant solo flight across the Atlantic aboard *Spirit of St. Louis*, came to town to dedicate the air field as an Army Signal Corps base. It was the largest municipal airport in the United States and the first to be converted to a military base. By this time, the airfield had been relocated from S. 6th Avenue — still a good way from where Tucson's population of 32,000 was concentrated — to a location farther southeast where city fathers had already bought up 1,280 acres of homesteaded ranch land. This was the Davis-Monthan Air Force Base of the future.

It was also at the 1927 dedication that two Tucson military aviators became immortalized when the airfield was officially named Davis-Monthan Airfield. The two young men may never have even met each other, but they had a lot in common it would turn out. One was born in England, the other in Tennessee, but both would eventually live in Tucson. One attended Tucson High School and the University of Arizona and served in the army at Ft. Huachuca, Arizona. The other worked on his family's Tucson ranches before joining the army. Both were military pilots when aviation was still in its infancy and both ultimately would perish in the flying machines they loved — Lt. Samuel H. Davis in Florida in 1921 and Lt. Oscar Monthan in Hawaii in 1924. Their names would grace a municipal airport, an Army air base and eventually a U.S. Air Force base.

For more than 10 years after its conversion to an Army Signal Corps base, Davis-Monthan Field continued to serve both military and commercial flights. Among the pilots who landed here were Amelia Earhart, Wiley Post and James Doolittle, along with Standard Airlines, which later was absorbed by American Airlines.

During the decade of the 1930s, the Army built the base's first hangar and operations building and added paved roads and runways. By the end of the decade, with war clouds building in Europe and the Pacific, the Army wanted to station some men and planes at the field. At the same time, city leaders wanted the federal government to take over the field in order to get additional funds for construction and the soldiers who would be stationed there. Agreement was reached — the city would move its airport to a new site (where Tucson International Airport is today) and the Army would take over Davis-Monthan Field.

At the time Pearl Harbor was attacked in late 1941, the population of Davis-Monthan Field was 2,175. One year later, the base's military population had jumped to 9,642 and the field was being expanded to the tune of $3 million by the federal government. The base's war mission was to train light and heavy bombardment aircrews who then would be deployed overseas. It had the reputation as the best heavy bombardment station in the nation. As the base work load increased and aircraft personnel were dispatched to distant shores, women from the area took on base chores ranging from driving dump trucks to serving in the Women's Army Auxiliary Corps. And for a time, the base also held a German prisoner-of-war camp.

With the war's end, the base became a "separation center," processing nearly 10,000 returning soldiers for transition to civilian life. When that job was done, the base was deactivated and all that remained was a storage site for B-29 bombers and C-47 cargo planes, better known as "Gooney Birds." But this respite would not last long. With the official creation of the U.S. Air Force shortly after the war, the base was turned over to the new branch of the service and got its official name — Davis-Monthan Air Force Base — in early 1948.

In the years that followed, Davis-Monthan would be a home base for Titan II missiles, U-2 reconnaissance forces and a series of fighter jets. Following the Strategic Arms Limitation Treaty, Russian satellites would fly overhead taking photographs of the nuclear arms and aircraft dismantled by Davis-Monthan personnel and placed in open view on the base for the satellite cameras to see. Davis-Monthan planes and people would be dispatched to serve in three more wars — the Korean, the Vietnam and Desert Storm — as well as many real or potential trouble spots around the globe.

Today, Davis-Monthan occupies 18,000 acres, employs nearly 6,000 military and 1,700 civilian personnel, and trains thousands of pilots and support personnel. But Tucsonans seem to either love it or hate it. For some residents, the thunderous drone of massive cargo and transport planes or low-flying fighter jets is nothing more than an intrusion. For others, the sound is a welcome one, signifying our nation's military might and the streamlined beauty of the world's most sophisticated flying machines. For some — like land developers — Davis-Monthan means only that valuable land cannot be turned into commercial or residential profit. For others, the lost land value pales in comparison to the base's contributions to Tucson's economy, estimated in 1992 to be more than $397 million.

Fortunately for the air base and for Tucsonans who welcome its presence here, the bulk of our residents favor it. When federal rumors of its possible closing were rampant in the early 1990s, supporters far outnumbered the picketers, and it was easy to make a case for Davis-Monthan's significance not only as a military installation, but also as an integral part of the city's lifestyle and economy.

INSIDERS' TIP

Davis-Monthan runs a speakers bureau for groups. It also can accommodate special tours for groups, such as schools. Call the Public Affairs Office at 228-3204 for information.

Five thousand aircraft are stored at Davis-Monthan Airforce Base. Locals call it "the graveyard."

With 27,000 people connected with Davis-Monthan (including military, dependents, civilians and retirees), it's not difficult to see the base's significance to Tucson and Arizona. They eat in Tucson restaurants, shop in Tucson stores, attend Tucson's events and art programs, hook up to Tucson's utilities and enroll their kids in Tucson's day-care centers and schools, adding to the city's and state's tax base with every purchase or service they consume. And if the base weren't here, many of Tucson's 13,000 military retirees (and their pensions) might not be either. Over the years, the government has pumped many millions into Davis-Monthan, often hiring local contractors for the work done on the base, from paving runways and roads to erecting hangars and housing.

Nor is the impact of the base purely economic. Davis-Monthan makes a big deal out of encouraging volunteerism. An office on the base works exclusively to help match base personnel with community volunteer assignments. Military dependents, and sometimes the military personnel as well, spend many hours volunteering in Tucson's schools, youth organizations and other agencies. And if a natural disaster or emergency occurred in the area, you can be sure the base's people and resources would be there to help the community out.

Behind its 25 miles of chain-link fence and restricted-access gates, Davis-Monthan has everything from Burger King to the Air Force's version of MASH and from an 18-hole golf course to "the world's largest parking lot." The average visitor to Tucson, and even most residents, may only be aware of the runways, airplanes and air traffic control tower — the trappings of Davis-Monthan that can easily be seen by driving along Golf Links Road or merely looking skyward. But these are just the tip of the iceberg.

244 • DAVIS-MONTHAN AIR FORCE BASE

Inside this city within a city, 3,000 people live within multiunit and single-family housing (the rest live off base), two elementary schools are run by Tucson Unified School District and a base hospital serves thousands of patients annually. There are restaurants, officers and enlisted clubs, a base exchange (BX), commissary, a post office, a youth center and a service station. For entertainment, base personnel can choose from an 18-hole golf course, a pool, movie theater, bowling alley, parks, sports fields and tennis courts, plus a library and fitness center for improving mind and body. The more than 13,000 military retirees who call Tucson home also have access to this vast array of facilities.

Although much of this military complex is out of view, even the Air Force can't hide "the world's largest parking lot" from the public eye. Only it's not for vehicles, it's for aircraft (and sundry related equipment). Maybe you caught a glimpse of it as your plane descended toward Tucson — endless airplanes lined up in perfect rows on the desert floor, as if waiting to launch a fearful invasion. They stretch for miles — colossal B-52s and Gooney Birds, scores of helicopters and sleek, fearless fighter jets. If the planes parked here belonged to another country, they would be one of the largest air forces in the world. But up close, you could see that these are old aircraft, often partially covered with a skin of plastic to protect them from the elements. These 2,600 acres on the east end of Davis-Monthan hold nearly 5,000 aircraft and tons of related equipment. It's the only storage depot like it in the country and the world.

Tucsonans tend to call it the airplane boneyard or graveyard, but officially it's the Aerospace Maintenance and Regeneration Center, or AMARC, run by the Department of Defense. In 1965, the Defense Department consolidated all Army, Navy and Air Force storage locations into this one. They picked Davis-Monthan because of the Sonoran Desert — the air is dry and the ground so hard that even a 180,000-pound B-52 can be towed over it without sinking.

And what about the fate of these flying machines? A few may someday fly again. Many are gradually picked over for spare parts. Some are flown to remote places and used for target practice. Some are purposely kept untouched so they could be put into battle on short notice if need be. Even several Boeing 707s banned by the FAA rest here, their powerful engines that were too noisy for commercial airports now stripped off for use in Air Force tanker planes. Some of the aircraft could be sold intact to a foreign government, but only after lots of red tape and only to "friendly" buyers. The majority of the planes are sold for scrap, but only after their navigational equipment and weaponry are removed. So the next time you lift up that can of soda or that garden rake, you may be holding all that's left of a 1950s military bomber or fighter.

It is quite a sight to see, this final resting place for Uncle Sam's warplanes. It even has its own celebrity row — a line of rare and one-of-a-kind aircraft, each with a sign designating its name, that are worthy of the history books and a spot in anyone's photo album. You can catch a glimpse of AMARC by driving south on Kolb Road. Or better yet, if you want to see "the boneyard" planes up close or in the lens of your camera, or a captured Iraqi tank or some of the spiffy planes on the base's tarmac, take a tour of the base. It's a free tour by bus, usually two mornings a week, but on a first-come basis. Call 228-3358 for a recording with all the details. (The

INSIDERS' TIP

Nearly 600 people work at the Aerospace Maintenance and Regeneration Center (AMARC) operated by the Defense Department on Davis-Monthan. Their job is to process in the planes arriving at this massive storage facility, protect and preserve them, keep track of what's there (all 5,000 of them), keep track of what part or plane is going out, remove parts that will be recycled and demolish the planes no longer needed. Oh, yes, and shoo away the coyotes.

call is important, since the tours could be discontinued or the time or date altered.)

AMARC is only one of the many missions going on at Davis-Monthan these days. The 355th Wing is the base's primary activity and occupant, responsible for training pilots on the A-10 "Thunderbolt," a low and slow and highly maneuverable tank destroyer. (It also happens to be a relatively quiet jet, which pleases Tucsonans who are picky about the noise level.) The 355th also conducts training for other aircrews, provides airborne command and communications and helps with Strategic Arms Limitation Treaty (SALT) compliance. It also operates one of only five air transportable hospitals (the Air Force version of a MASH unit), which on a moment's notice can be deployed to trouble spots around the globe.

Davis-Monthan also houses the 12th Air Force Command, with about 600 people assigned to it, which is responsible for the combat readiness of all tactical air forces west of the Mississippi. The base is also the site of an Air National Guard unit that flies the F-16 "Fighting Falcon" and an Air Force Reserve unit that flies search and rescue helicopters. Other federal agencies using the base include the Federal Aviation Administration, the U.S. Customs Service Air Service Branch and the U.S. Corps of Engineers. With one of the longest runways in the Air Force, Davis-Monthan is equipped to handle just about any job in the airborne military.

As with any military installation, no one knows exactly what the future has in store for Davis-Monthan. During base closures and threatened closures of the past several years, Davis-Monthan was spared and even came through with an expansion. As one Davis-Monthan spokesperson put it, "When a town is so supportive of a base and vice versa, it bodes well for the future." Tucsonans, most of them anyway, hope Davis-Monthan continues to make aviation history.

Southern Arizona has much to offer, including its proximity to Mexico.

Daytrips and Weekend Getaways

It's difficult to imagine wanting to leave Tucson, but the reality is that southern Arizona has much to offer, including its proximity to Mexico. In this chapter we give you some ideas on places to go around Tucson when you're fortunate enough to have a day or a weekend to spare.

The choices are so great that we've really only scratched the surface here. We've selected some destinations that both visitors and residents consider to be must-sees if they get the chance, plus a few others that are relatively undiscovered for those folks who would rather not mingle with the masses when getting away. Most of the weekend getaways included here are within a three-hour drive of Tucson. A few are a bit farther, but we include them because they're especially appealing destinations.

For most of the weekend getaways, we've mapped out an itinerary that highlights a number of locations, attractions and activities. You may not get to them all, but at least you'll be informed enough to make a choice about what you absolutely can't miss and what can wait until next time. Even if you're just searching for a daytrip, be sure to read the sections on getaways as well — they contain lots of ideas for daytrips. Conversely, the daytrips described here can easily be turned into getaways — we even give a few tips on how best to do that.

Whatever your destination or its duration, it's always best to call ahead and confirm the seasons and hours they're open, prices and any age restrictions, so you won't be disappointed on arrival. Likewise, contact the chambers of commerce or visitors centers for your destinations; they'll provide lots of useful information, even if you're making last-minute plans and need it quickly by phone. And last but not least, get a good map.

Daytrips

Boyce Thompson Southwestern Arboretum

This combination state park/museum/nature preserve is less than two hours from Tucson and can easily be a daytrip, or it can be combined with other sights east of Phoenix for a weekend getaway (we map out such a trip under "Phoenix and Environs"). Either way, plan on at least a couple of hours to see this site that most people fall in love with. It's a fascinating collection of arid land plants from all over the world — nearly 1,300 species to be more exact. It's also a rich riparian habitat that supports more than 300 species of mammals, birds, reptiles and amphibians thanks to Queen Creek, which flows through the property.

The arboretum, (520) 689-2811, is located near the mining town of Superior and was endowed in 1924 by William Boyce Thompson, the founder of two major mining companies in the Superior area. He established it as a research facility, but much of it is now open to the public, along with a visitors center and gift shop, self-guided nature walks, miles of easy trails, a desert lake, a picnic area and restrooms. It's open daily (except Christmas) from 8 AM to 5 PM at $4 for adults and $2 for kids 5 to 12. From Tucson, take Oracle Road (Ariz. Highway 77) north to Ariz. Highway 79, then go east on U.S. Highway 60. Ariz. 79 is also called the Pinal Parkway, a scenic drive along which the native vegetation is identified with markers.

Gila River Rafting

Those among you who aren't quite ready for the rushing white waters of rivers like the mighty Colorado will be glad to hear there's a great alternative. Since the flow of the Gila (pronounced hee-la) River is regulated, it has a consistently swift but smooth flow from May to September, even if other rivers in the state are too dry for rafting. And unlike most of the other rivers, it's not a heart-stopper raft ride. The handful of rapids add some excitement and splash but won't bowl you over. Like just about every other place in Arizona where water pours forth, the Gila is surrounded by some strikingly beautiful scenery as it meanders through rocky cliffs and high desert vegetation. In addition to being a great adventure for the whole family, Gila River rafting is cheaper and shorter than most other river raft trips. It's a 10-mile trip that costs about $50 a person, and several companies operate them.

Most likely, you'll have to get yourself to Globe, which is about two hours northeast of Tucson via Ariz. Highway 77. From there you'll probably be taken by van to Dripping Spring Wash, which is the start of the 10-mile stretch of river on which commercial rafting is permitted. After receiving a flotation vest and a safety talk, you'll jump into the large rubber raft with a guide and several other adventurous folks anxious to try it. Adults and maybe even older kids will be expected to man a paddle, but you'll get plenty of guidance from the expert on board. Your trip will last three to five hours and usually includes lunch. The journey ends around Winkleman, after which you'll be transported back to the starting point and your vehicle, no doubt a bit wet from the river and weary from the workout. Be sure to dress accordingly and protect yourself from the summer sun with sunscreen and a hat.

Considering the drive up and back and the length of the raft trip, this is a very full daytrip from Tucson, so you might want to consider staying overnight in Globe, where there are a number of lodgings to choose from. If you'd like to try a rafting adventure, here are the companies to call: Arizona River Adventures in Tucson, 318-0088; Blue Sky Whitewater in Globe, (800) 425-5253; Chandelle Travel in Tucson, 577-1824; or Whole Earth Adventures in Dripping Spring Wash, (520) 356-7522. There may be a minimum age or weight requirement for children.

Madera Canyon

Nature lovers will be enthralled by this spot 60 miles south of Tucson in the Santa Rita Mountains. It's a popular daytrip destination for Tucsonans escaping the heat in summer and for birders all year long. About 400 species of birds have been sighted here including hummingbirds and elf owls. There are about 200 miles of scenic trails, some of which hug the meandering Madera Creek, so there's something here for casual walkers as well as serious hikers wanting to explore the upper reaches of the mountains. At an elevation of 5,600 feet, Madera Canyon is covered with thick pines and is significantly cooler than the desert floor below. At the entrance to the recreation area is a small visitors center, though it's usually open only on weekends. There's also a small store that may or may not be open, so it's best to have your own supplies. Nearby is a small campground with toilets and drinking water. The canyon's Santa Rita Lodge Nature Resort, (520) 625-8746, caters to birders — all 12 rooms have bird feeders outside the windows. Madera Canyon is under the purview of the Coronado National Forest Service, so call 670-4552 for information.

To find Madera Canyon, take Exit 63 off I-19, then go east on White House Canyon Road, which becomes Madera Canyon Road. The road winds up the mountainside for about 15 miles, but it's easy to traverse by car. Just remember that this is an outdoor recreation area in the middle of a mountain, so you won't find much here beyond the bounties that nature provides.

---

www.insiders.com

See this and many other **Insiders' Guide®** destinations online — in their entirety.

Visit us today!

DAYTRIPS AND WEEKEND GETAWAYS • 249

Photo: Theresa Shea Chavez

Haggling over the price of an item is part of the thrill of shopping in Nogales.

Nogales, Mexico

This is a favorite destination for visitors and newcomers to Tucson, especially those who have never been to Mexico. It's close, easy to cross into (see our close-up in this chapter for everything you need to know about crossing the border) and an adventure for first-timers. Be aware, however, that Nogales is not necessarily representative of the rest of Mexico. As a border town, it's crowded, congested and focused almost exclusively on selling merchandise to Anglos. In fact, Anglos often have mixed reactions to Nogales. Some view it as great fun, while others are put off by the hubbub and the constant hawking of vendors trying to lure customers. One advantage to Nogales, however, is that nearly every Mexican there speaks English, so you won't have a language barrier.

Nogales is less than two hours by car, straight down I-19. It's an easy daytrip, and you'll still have several hours to shop and eat. It also can be combined into a great weekend getaway with Tubac and Tumacacori or Rio Rico (all of which are described in this chapter). It's so much easier to cross into Nogales on foot than by car that we won't even discuss taking your vehicle into Mexico here, other than to say it simply isn't worth the hassle when your destination is Nogales. As you drive south on I-19 and near the border, follow the signs "To International Border," which actually will take you into Nogales, Arizona. The freeway ends, and in less than a mile, you'll begin seeing parking lots — and attendants trying to wave you in. (An easy landmark for Anglos to recognize is the McDonald's restaurant. Consider it a sign that you're in the right spot and can park nearby.) All of these lots are within a couple blocks' walk of the border crossing, so any will do, and you can expect to pay about $5 for the day, even if you won't be there but a few hours. The parking lot attendant, or anyone else who happens to be around, will point you in the direction of the border crossing. You'll soon see the signs guiding the way for foot traffic, and before you know it you're in a foreign country. There are no border checks until your return, at which point you'll go through U.S. Customs — typically a quick process and nothing for upstanding U.S. citizens to be worried about. (Again, see the close-up in this chapter so you'll be familiar with the border process ahead of time.)

Now that you've arrived, get ready to be bombarded by vendors and by more Mexican goods than you've ever seen, all crowded together in small shops and lining alleys and sidewalks. It wouldn't hurt to practice shaking your head to signal "no" or saying "no gracias" or "no thanks" — you'll be doing it often unless you plan to buy out Nogales.

Begin walking the sidewalks and alleys looking for regional items such as rugs, blankets, glassware, tinware, wrought metal, pottery, silver jewelry, leather and so on. Most items don't have price tags, but if they do it's usually in dollars, not pesos, and dollars are the accepted currency. A few shops will not bargain and let you know; otherwise, bargaining with shopkeepers is customary and even expected. A good rule of thumb is to plan to pay about 50 percent of the initial starting price, but this can vary. Another rule of thumb: If you've done a good job negotiating the price, the item will cost you less —sometimes significantly — than if you purchased it stateside. As you shop in Nogales, all the streets look about the same, but don't worry about getting lost; anyone will be able to point you back to the starting place. Just relax and enjoy your adventure.

If you need a break from the shopping spree, here are two restaurants in Nogales to try. El Cid, on Calle Obregon, is easy to find and right in the middle of the shopping area, so just ask a shopkeeper to point it out if you don't happen upon it. La Roca (meaning "the rock" and indeed it's built into the rock in the side of a cliff on Calle Elias) is probably Nogales' finest restaurant, but it's off the beaten path and will be a walk of at least several blocks, some of it up a steep hill. Ask directions, but if you don't think you can find it anyway, you can probably find a friendly Mexican who will gladly be your guide (but tip your guide a dollar or two, please). At La Roca, you'll have a fine meal in a lovely old building, which also has a number of shops that are more upscale than most in Nogales. Restaurants and the few hotels in Nogales are also the only places you're likely to find a restroom.

Before taking your trek to a foreign country, here are a few final tidbits. It's best to plan your trip so that you leave Mexico by about 5

PM, since many of the stateside parking lots all but shut down as day's end draws near. However, if you want to stay in Nogales for dinner, just check with the parking lot before leaving your car to make sure you'll be able to retrieve it on your return. Keep in mind that, like Tucson, the busy season in Nogales is late fall to early spring, and weekends are busier than weekdays. Most businesses accept credit cards, but visitors from the United States tend to be more comfortable transacting in cash. And finally, you'll notice the word "Sonora" on lots of things, so we'll fill you in: Sonora is the name of the state in Mexico in which Nogales is located. Adios.

Patagonia Lake State Park

Water-deprived Tucsonans and their visitors will be glad to hear that the damming of Sonoita Creek 30 years ago created the largest recreational lake in southern Arizona. And there's more good news — it's less than two hours away. The 265-acre lake and the 645-acre park in which it sits combine to offer just about every type of outdoor recreation — even surfing (sorry, that's surfing over land, not water). For folks who like to catch their dinner or just fish for sport, the lake is stocked with trout in winter and with bass, crappie, catfish and bluegill the rest of the year. If you didn't bring your own, a concession at the marina rents paddle boats, canoes and rowboats, ranging in price from $5 per hour to $15 a day plus deposit. The lake even has a sandy beach for swimmers and sunbathers who just want to be reminded of the ocean. As we already pointed out, you can windsurf here, as well as water ski and Jet Ski, but not on weekends from May through October because that's when desert dwellers come here in droves. There are picnic areas, restrooms and showers, plus plenty of places for casual hikes through the rolling hills around the lake. (See the Campgrounds and RV Parks chapter for information on the campsites.) The park charges a day-use fee of $5 per vehicle. For swimming, surfing, boating and fishing in southern Arizona, take I-10 east to Ariz. Highway 83, go south to Ariz. Highway 82 and continue south 7 miles past the town of Patagonia. To reach the park by phone, call (520) 287-6965.

Taliesin West

Admirers of the 20th-century's greatest architect, Frank Lloyd Wright, won't want to miss visiting his personal winter residence and architectural school. Located in Scottsdale (the outskirts of Phoenix), Taliesin West is only about two hours from Tucson, so it's an easy daytrip. But there's so much else to do in this area that it could also be included in a weekend getaway (you'll find ideas for that elsewhere in this chapter). Perched on 600 acres of rugged Sonoran Desert at the base of the McDowell Mountains, Taliesin West is a National Historic Landmark. Like most of Wright's structures, it's both amazing and unique. He and his apprentices gathered rocks from the desert floor and sand from the washes to build this set of structures that includes his former residence, a school and an architectural firm, all linked by dramatic terraces, gardens and walkways.

If you plan to visit Taliesin West, take one of the tours. Each season, different types of tours are offered at different times of the day and for various prices, so call ahead, (602) 860-8810, for recorded tour information. For example, a morning panorama tour lasts one hour and includes the Cabaret Cinema, Music Pavilion and Wright's private office but not the residence. (This tour is $10 for adults, $3 for kids 4 to 12 and $8 for seniors and students.) Another tour — afternoon summer insights — lasts 90 minutes, costs $4 more per person, and includes the dramatic Taliesin West living room with furniture he designed. In addition to the various scheduled tours during each season, private and group tours are available but must be arranged in advance. Walking shoes and sun protection are recommended, and toddlers must be in strollers or carried. There's a bookstore with an extensive selection of Wright books and prints, works by Taliesin artists and souvenirs. For additional information or to make reservations, call (602) 860-2700. The entrance to Taliesin West is at the intersection of Cactus Road and Frank Lloyd Wright Boulevard in northeast Scottsdale.

Tubac

Just 45 miles south of Tucson off I-19 at exits 40 and 34 is a lovely little village that once was the second oldest European settlement west of the Mississippi. Today, it's a sophisticated artists' colony.

Tubac and the surrounding areas are filled with history. In the 1700s, the Spanish came north from Mexico and built a presidio (or fort) here, and the settlement of Tubac became the first European settlement in Arizona. Tubac Presidio State Historic Park marks the site of this small fort and still has its ruins. In the heart of Old Town Tubac (which is just east of the present-day shopping area), you'll also see Placita de Anza, historic St. Ann's Church, an 1885 one-room schoolhouse and the Tubac Historical Society, which offers a research library, visitors guides and self-guided tour maps. It's difficult to visit Tubac without taking in some of the shopping opportunities, but there are plenty of alternatives if shopping isn't on your top-10 list of things to do. In addition to all the historical sites, there's a 4.5-mile trail that winds south along the Santa Cruz River, and in this part of the river you'll actually see water flowing year round. The trail begins at the picnic grounds south of the presidio museum in Old Town Tubac. Throughout the year Tubac conducts many events and performances featuring music, dance, song and art. In December, for example, there's Fiesta Navidad and Luminaria Night, which celebrates the holiday season in the Mexican tradition, and in February Tubac holds its Annual Festival of the Arts, now more than 40 years old.

Intermingled with all this history and natural beauty are shops, restaurants and inns that occupy old adobe and newer whitewashed brick structures reminiscent of the earliest settlers' housing. Most of the artists and craftspeople who sell their wares in Tubac also live here, so it's truly an artists' colony. There are only about a half-dozen small streets in this entire village, but they are lined with about five dozen shops carrying everything from jewelry and pottery to sculpture and clothing. The shops offer anything and everything made by Mexican and American Indian crafters and artists, plus creations in metal, jewelry, ceramics and glass and on canvas by local as well as internationally known artisans.

The dining choices are nearly as vast as the shopping choices. At Tosh's Hacienda Restaurant, you can dine on Mexican food and Margaritas indoors or on a lovely patio. For a taste of Italy, try Melio's Trattoria. At Tubac Jack's Saloon, diners can play darts or pool while waiting for their meal or for carry-out food to enjoy at the picnic grounds in Old Town Tubac. Or take the footbridge to Shelby's Bistro or Cafe Fiesta. The Chile Pepper has cappuccino, ice cream and fountain drinks if you're just too busy to take the time for sit-down dining. For a mesquite-cooked steak, try Burro Inn Restaurant, which is a bit off the beaten path on the west side of the interstate across from Tubac Golf Resort.

Although Tubac can easily be a daytrip because it's so close to Tucson, it's also a great spot for an overnight or weekend getaway. There's certainly plenty to do in the form of shopping, gallery gazing, hiking, history learning and golfing (see our Golf chapter). If you decide to turn your daytrip into a getaway, here are a few places to bunk out. For authentic charm, try either the Tubac Country Inn, (520) 398-3178, or Tubac Secret Garden Inn, (520) 398-9371. Both are in the historic district and across the street from the presidio park. The Secret Garden Inn has a wall surrounding 3 acres of green oasis. Another spot to stay is the Burro Inn Suites (and restaurant) on the west side of I-19, (520) 398-2281.

Tumacacori

If you're going to visit Tubac, it's only a short drive to Tumacacori, the "town" that's too tough to pronounce. (Actually, it's neither a town nor tough to pronounce if you do it slowly and phonetically — Too-mah-kah-core-ee.) It's the site of a Franciscan mission built in 1795 that was regularly besieged by the Apache Indians. The ruins that are visible today include a chapel and graveyard. Visitors can also walk through a baroque church built in 1822. The site has been converted into a National Historic Park with a visitors center where you can learn all about the mission. This is a very picturesque and tranquil spot with lots of mesquite trees and a half-mile trail. On weekends, there's often a craft demonstration.

Across the street is the Santa Cruz Chili and Spice Company where you'll find spices, herbs, salsas and cookbooks plus a Western museum. Just to the north of the park is the

Wisdom Cafe, which offers Mexican fare, and to the south is an inn with a pool called Rancho Santa Cruz, (520) 281-8774, which is open year round.

Like Tubac, Tumacacori can be a daytrip from Tucson, or you can stay in this area for a weekend full of history, hiking along the river, bird-watching and shopping. Tumacacori is just south of Tubac at Exit 29 off I-19, or simply take the frontage road between the two.

Weekend Getaways

Cosanti and Arcosanti

If you're heading north to Scottsdale and beyond, these are two unusual attractions you might want to include in your itinerary. Since Cosanti is in the heart of Paradise Valley, a close-in suburb of Phoenix, it could be a daytrip from Tucson, but there's so much else to do in the Phoenix area that including Cosanti in a weekend getaway would be a much better alternative. Arcosanti, on the other hand, is a bit too far for a comfortable daytrip but could easily be combined with a weekend visit to the Prescott, Jerome and Sedona areas (and we guide you to and around these areas elsewhere in this chapter). Both of these attractions were founded by Paolo Soleri and are now operated by the nonprofit Cosanti Foundation. Soleri is an Italian architect who moved to Arizona in 1956 and has become famous for his unusual project called Arcosanti and for his spectacular bronze wind chimes.

A state historic site, **Cosanti** is at 6433 Doubletree Ranch Road, (602) 948-6145, in upscale Paradise Valley (just northeast of the Phoenix city limits). Except for major holidays, it's open daily from 9 AM to 5 PM, and it's free. Cosanti's essence is a gallery of Soleri art, but it's much more than that: a blend of desert landscaping of cacti, palo verde and olive trees with earth-formed concrete architectural structures. Suspended amidst courtyards, terraces and garden paths is the work of Paolo Soleri and his artisans — a spectacular array of bronze and ceramic wind-bells. Visitors can see how these art forms are crafted on site and pur-

Tips on Visiting Mexico

The days when Gringos were nervous at best and petrified at worst about crossing into Mexico (and often rightly so) are long gone. Today it's not much different going to Mexico from Arizona than to a neighboring state. That's because both Mexican and U.S. officials have made changes to attract tourism. But it is a foreign country, folks, so you'll need to be prepared.

Close-up

• If you're walking across the border to Nogales (which is the only way we recommend), just make sure you have something to prove your identity and citizenship for the return through U.S. Customs. A voter registration or driver's license will do.

• There are restrictions on what you can bring back into the states. For example, only one bottle of liquor per adult is allowed, some fruits and vegetables are taboo but seafood is okay, and you're required to have a prescription for certain medications that you buy in Mexico, even if they're sold over-the-counter there. U.S. Customs permits each adult to bring $400 in goods duty-free. If you're not sure, check with Customs officials at the border before you cross into Mexico, or you'll have to relinquish the "contraband."

• The border crossing is open from 6 AM to midnight daily. Keep in mind that, during daylight savings time, Sonora will be an hour behind Arizona.

— continued on next page

254 • DAYTRIPS AND WEEKEND GETAWAYS

Nogales is a great place to shop for the day.

Going to Rocky Point is a bit more complicated, because you'll be in a vehicle and driving in Mexico and no doubt staying for days rather than only hours.

• It's a good idea to buy gas on the U.S. side of the border. You'll be able to get it in Mexico, but quality and prices vary.

• Your regular insurance coverage for the car is not honored in Mexico, so purchase Mexican car insurance, either in Tucson before you start out or on the U.S. side of the border, where many signs will proclaim where it's available. It's sold in 24-hour chunks, so expect to pay about $30 for a three-day trip. Be sure to have your driver's license and vehicle documents with you. Taking a rental car across is another story, so ask at the rental agency whether they'll permit it and what you'll need.

• If you plan to be in Mexico for less than 72 hours, you won't need a passport or visa; a driver's license will do. For longer trips, you'll need a free tourist card, requiring a birth certificate or passport. (Call or visit the Mexican Consulate's Office at 553 S. Stone Avenue in downtown Tucson, 882-5595, for information or to get one.) If you plan on traveling with a minor who isn't your child, you need to have a copy of the child's birth certificate and a letter of consent signed by both parents. Also, if a child is traveling with just one parent, that parent should have a notarized letter from the other parent stating

— continued on next page

permission to take the child to Mexico, or a c[...] for the journey, have a recent (six months or le[...] this to get Fido back into the United States.

• The border crossing at Lukeville, Arizona, is [...] crossing, you may be asked to pull over by Mexic[...] bringing into the country. Searches are completely ran[...] over; if the green light comes on, just drive through. Mos[...] speak English, and usually they'll just want to look in the tr[...] should absolutely not take into Mexico is a gun; it may pu[...]

• Speed limits and mileage are posted in kilometers, and [...]ometer will usually have kilometers calibrated. Otherwise, driving in Mex[...] [n]o different, but watch for livestock crossing the roads. Stop signs, however, say "Alto."

• If you have an emergency in Rocky Point, there's a Red Cross ambulance, hospital and the Santa Fe Clinic in town.

• In restaurants and hotels, it's perfectly safe to drink the water and use ice, which are purified. But it's best not to drink from the tap, so carry or buy bottled water.

• If you're calling a phone number within Mexico, it'll be just five digits. To call from Tucson, you have to preface it with "011," representing the international code, the Mexico code and the area code for Rocky Point. Calling in the opposite direction is a bit trickier. You usually can't use a calling card from a hotel room, so you'll either need to look for signs advertising "long distance service available here" or call from a restaurant or business that will charge about $2 a minute. Or you may be able to purchase a calling card, which is the easiest method. Your cell phone may or may not work from Mexico.

• If you have any other questions or concerns, contact the Mexican Consulate Office in Tucson (listed above); one of Tucson's two AAA offices; an agency that deals in Mexican insurance such as Sanborn's, 327-1255; the U.S. Customs office; or (800) 4-SONORA.

---

chase them as well. There is also a line of "cause bells," all of which represent issues of national or global concern and sales of which go to help nonprofit organizations. (For ways to make this part of a weekend getaway, see "Phoenix and Environs" in this chapter.)

While Cosanti is a place, **Arcosanti** is a vision turned almost into reality. It could even be thought of as a prototype of Biosphere 2. Arcosanti represents a term that Soleri coined, "arcology," to describe the concept of architecture and ecology working as one integral process to produce new urban habitats. Thus, this strange-looking project of ultramodern structures built into the basalt cliffs 60 miles north of Phoenix was created as an urban "city" to epitomize Soleri's concept of arcology. It combines housing (originally for 5,000 people but never fully realized), large-scale solar greenhouses, a music center and artist workshops and galleries. Today, it's a place for students and professionals to study architecture, ecology and art in the Soleri fashion and for visitors to see this 4,000-acre experiment in urban architecture. Visitors can see the creation of Soleri wind-bells and purchase them, take tours and snack at the cafe or bakery. Be prepared to do some walking and stair climbing, since Arcosanti is built into cliffs.

For information on Arcosanti or its tours, workshops, Elderhostel or frugal overnight accommodations, call (602) 632-7135. It's open

...stmas, and
...er person. Take
...to Exit 262. To make
...eekend getaway, consider
...ight in the Verde River Valley
...Prescott or Sedona, which we de-
...be elsewhere in this chapter.

Cochise County

Southeast of Tucson is an area filled with history, beauty and tons of things to do and see. (Both Rhode Island and Connecticut would fit within Cochise County's 6,200 miles, so we're not kidding when we say it's full of treasures and pleasures.) It includes the farmlands of Willcox, some of the premier birding spots in the country, the "town too tough to die" and the mountains where the famous Apache Indian chief Cochise made his stronghold and where his successor Geronimo finally surrendered. Many of these sites could be individual daytrips from Tucson, or the area can be visited in one or two weekend getaways. For one weekend getaway, we recommend taking Ariz. Highway 80 south and visiting Benson, Tombstone and Bisbee, while a second getaway lies a bit further east and takes in Willcox and the Chiricahua and Dragoon Mountains. Read on for two trips that explore Cochise County.

Benson to Bisbee

About 70 miles south of Tucson is Tombstone, the "town too tough to die," which can be a daytrip from Tucson or combined with the other sites outlined in the following paragraphs to make a weekend getaway. From Tucson, take I-10 east to Exit 303 at Benson, then head south on Ariz. 80. Begin your adventure with a trip into the past on the **San Pedro and Southwest Railroad**, (520) 586-2266, a four-hour round-trip train ride that starts at the depot just off Ariz. 80. It operates year round, usually Thursday through Sunday, but you'll need to call for the departure times. This narrated trip takes riders into the pristine San Pedro Riparian National Conservation Area, past the ruins of a historic ghost town and through the Charleston Narrows Canyon. The cost is about $25 for adults, $15 for kids 5 to 17 and free for younger ones. Or get a family ticket for about $75. On board you'll find a beverage and snack service, and the train is handicapped-accessible.

After the train excursion, continue about 20 miles south on Ariz. 80 to one of southern Arizona's most popular and famous family attractions, **Tombstone**. This is where, in 1881, the Earp family and Doc Holliday battled it out with the Clanton boys at the OK Corral. But there's more to the old silver mining town than the OK Corral, including the Courthouse State Historic Park, the Rose Tree Inn Museum (displaying the world's largest rosebush, planted in 1885 and covering 8,000 square feet), the Birdcage Theater, the Crystal Palace Saloon, wooden sidewalks, preserved historical buildings and even a stagecoach ride down the main drag, Allen Street. Shops, saloons and eateries flourish here as well. A must-see on the outskirts of Tombstone is Boot Hill, the famous graveyard where the victims of the OK Corral shoot-out are buried, along with lots of other folks. It's perhaps too commercialized now, but you'll be able to ignore that as you walk through the cemetery reading the fascinating tombstones, which range from humorous to touching.

If your visit to Tombstone is part of a weekend getaway, some choices for lodging include the Best Western Look-Out Lodge, (520) 457-2223 or (800) 652-6772, a motel with a lot of Old West character and great views, or the Tombstone Boarding House, a bed and breakfast in two meticulously restored adobe buildings in a quiet residential neighborhood, (520) 457-3716. Stop by the Visitors Center at 315 Allen Street for maps, information and ways to save a few bucks on local sights.

INSIDERS' TIP

Mexico uses the metric system, so miles and speed limits are posted in kilometers. If you're buying the Gulf of California's famous shrimp, you'll pay by the kilo not the pound (a kilo equals 2.2 pounds).

From Tombstone, continue south on Ariz. 80 toward Bisbee. Along the way, the hikers and bird watchers among you might want to detour onto Ariz. Highway 90 west, then Ariz. Highway 92 south to see **Ramsey Canyon Preserve**, managed by the Nature Conservancy and open daily from 8 AM to 5 PM. The preserve attracts more than 170 species of birds and dozens of species of butterflies. Many varieties of hummingbird summer here, while coatimundi and white-tailed deer are among the year-round residents. Because the parking lot is small and limits visitor capacity, reservations are a must on weekends and holidays, (520) 378-2785. There's a visitors center with maps and books, and the preserve even has fully equipped, albeit rugged, cabins for overnight stays, but they must be reserved well in advance.

After your commune with nature, continue south on Ariz. 80 through Mule Mountain Tunnel to the former copper mining town of **Bisbee**, a pretty little town that hugs the steep mountainside. At one time, this old mining camp was one of the richest mineral sites in the world, and in the early 1900s Bisbee was the largest city between St. Louis and San Francisco. Eventually the mines played out, and Bisbee became an artists' colony and retirement area characterized by its Old World charm and restored Victorian and European-style buildings. Turquoise big here since it's a by-product of copper mining. To get a glimpse of what mining was like, go just beyond downtown to the Lavender Pit Mine, a huge hole that was once Arizona's largest pit mine. Or for a more authentic sample of mining, visit the **Copper Queen Mine**, (520) 432-2071, but plan on taking one of the tours offered daily and lasting about one to 1½ hours. You'll be outfitted in miner's garb and enter the shaft via a small train like the real miners rode. (The underground temperature is a cool 47 degrees on average, so be prepared.) If the underground tour ($8) sounds a bit too scary, take a surface tour ($7) by van.

And if you still haven't had your fill of mining, there's the Mining and Historical Museum across the street.

Bisbee has lots to offer besides its former industry. One of its most popular attractions is the fully restored **Copper Queen Hotel**, operating since 1902 in the heart of downtown Bisbee. You need not book a room here to wander in and enjoy its grand lobby, saloon and dining room from yesteryear. The hallways are lined with photos of the Copper Queen's early days, some depicting the celebs who have stayed here, including John Wayne and Teddy Roosevelt. Another must-see is the historic **St. Patrick's Catholic Church** built in 1917 on Higgins Hill, whose stained-glass windows are considered one of the 10 best sets of Victorian glass in the nation. In fact, all over the downtown area you'll find well-preserved turn-of-the-century brick buildings that today house a variety of boutiques, craft shops and restaurants. It's easy to park the car in one spot and then see the town on foot, stopping whenever the urge strikes for a bite to eat or a memento to buy. Stop by the Visitors Center on Main Street any day for maps and walking tour guides.

Although a daytrip from Tucson to Bisbee is long but not impossible at 100 miles, Bisbee is also a great weekend getaway by itself or via the itinerary described above. Unique places to stay besides the Copper Queen Hotel, (520) 432-2216 or (800) 247-5829, include the School House Inn, which is just what its name indicates, a schoolhouse transformed into a bed and breakfast, (520) 432-2996 or (800) 537-4333, or the Clawson House, a bed and breakfast in a fully restored former residence that's filled with art and antiques, (520) 432-5327 or (800) 467-5237.

Willcox to the Apache Trail

As a great daytrip or to start out another weekend getaway that will take you into the mountains of Cochise County, visit the farming area of Willcox. Willcox is about two hours east of Tucson off I-10, and along the way you'll go through the dramatic boulder area of the Dragoon Mountains called **Texas Canyon**. Be sure to stop for a close-up view, a bit of hiking or photos amidst this unusually beautiful terrain. Nearby at the Dragoon Road exit just south of I-10 is the **Amerind Foundation** (a contraction of "American" and "Indian"), a research facility and museum housed in a beautiful Spanish Colonial-revival building displaying high-quality exhibits that give an overview of Southwestern cultures. It's open

Wednesday through Sunday in summer and daily the rest of the year, with an admission of $3, (520) 586-3666.

Continue heading for **Willcox** on I-10 to Exit 336 north, then take Fort Grant Road, which will lead to nearly a dozen farms where kids and parents have a great time picking all manner of delicious fruits and vegetables. If you're not into picking your own, many have already done it for you and sell it freshly harvested. Willcox is most famous for its apple crops and some of the best-looking apple pies you've ever seen, but lots of other things will entice the farmer in you, including corn, tomatoes, chiles, peaches, pecans, pumpkins, melons and more. In other areas around Willcox you'll find about another dozen farms, including a couple specializing in pistachios. The harvests usually run from July through October or early November, so summer and fall are the best times to head for Willcox. The farms are well-marked from the road, or you can stop at the easy-to-spot Chamber of Commerce Tourist Information Center, (520) 384-2272 or (800) 200-2272, near the interstate exit to pick up a list of where the farms are and what they offer. The Chamber of Commerce will also send out a brochure on request.

While you're in Willcox, stop at the **Rex Allen Cowboy Museum**, (520) 384-4583), located in one of Willcox's oldest commercial buildings. This was the famous cowboy's birthplace, and the museum focuses on his life and the pioneer settlers and ranchers who shaped the West. It's open daily from 10 AM to 4 PM; admission is $2 per person or $5 per family. Willcox also happens to be about the only place in southern Arizona where it's possible to see waterfowl such as geese, ducks and cranes, especially in the winter months. You'll spot them at the Willcox ponds south of the interstate and west of town.

From Willcox, head south on Ariz. Highway 186 (the "Apache Trail") to the **Chiricahua Mountains** for an outdoor adventure, but don't plan on combining this with Willcox in one day; find a spot to stay in Willcox overnight or camp out in the mountains. Two lodging options in Willcox are Econo Lodge, (520) 384-4222 or (800) 55-ECONO, and Best Western Plaza Inn, (520) 348-3556 or (800) 262-2645. Both Willcox and the Chiricahua Mountains also have places for RVs. You can drive into much of these mountains on paved roads or well-graded dirt roads, but to really explore you'll want to do some foot travel. Your first stop might be the turnoff to **Fort Bowie**, an 8-mile gravel road that ends in a parking lot. From here you'll take an easy 1.5-mile footpath to the fort ruins, along the way passing several well-marked historic sites including a cemetery where Geronimo's baby son is buried and a picturesque four-foot waterfall at Apache Spring.

Back on Ariz. 186, continue south to the **Chiricahua National Monument**, with its thousands of rock spires and stone columns reaching skyward. Travel through the park along a winding 8-mile road to Massai Point for a spectacular view of the unusual rock formations. Throughout the area you'll find streams, maybe even a waterfall and plenty of trees, along with breathtaking views. There are places to camp and restrooms but little else in the way of modern amenities. In the summer, this getaway will be cooler than Tucson, but carry water and sunscreen; in winter, it will probably be too cold for comfort. To continue along the Apache Trail, take Ariz. Highway 181 to U.S. Highway 191 north, which leads to **Cochise's Stronghold** in the Dragoon Mountains, where the famous Apache Indian leader and his warriors evaded the cavalry easily in the canyons and cliffs of the terrain. It's now a year-round park with picnic areas, lots of historical information and hiking trails. There's no admission fee for the park. For more information on the attractions in these mountains, including camping areas, call the Coronado Forest Service in Tucson, 670-4552.

New Mexico

If you're looking for a getaway that not everyone else in southern Arizona is flocking to, consider crossing the border, but this time into another state. Take I-10 east to Lordsburg, New Mexico, then Ariz. Highway 90 north to **Silver City**, a drive of about three hours. It's an old mining town full of history — Billy the Kid roamed the streets in his youth, and miners and merchants built elegant Victorian homes here during its mining heyday. But on this getaway, we're going a bit northward, via

DAYTRIPS AND WEEKEND GETAWAYS • 259

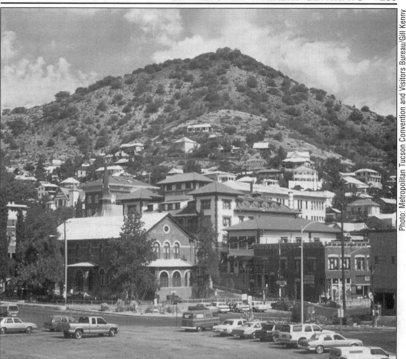

Bisbee is home to many artists and crafters.

U.S. Highway 180, to a place called **Glenwood** in one of the least-populated counties (Catron) in the Southwest. Its climate parallels the Arizona high country, so it's an ideal summer destination and great in spring and fall as well. This is land once occupied by gold and silver miners, Apaches and even Butch Cassidy and his Wild Bunch.

This getaway is truly an escape and definitely leans toward outdoor fun — canyon hikes, ghost towns and hot springs, peppered with some good old-fashioned food and hospitality. It's been called New Mexico's best-kept secret, and we're letting you in on it.

Glenwood is a pastoral community of about 200 year-round residents. For lodgings, try Los Olmos Guest Ranch, (505) 539-2311, a rustic compound of 14 rock cabins that aren't fancy but a treat to stay in and very affordable. Even pets are welcome here, for a small additional fee. The grounds are lovely and include a main lodge with dining room, pool and Jacuzzi, picnic tables, a corral with horses and even two historic attractions — the Antrim log cabin owned by Billy the Kid's family and the original Catron County Jail from the 1800s. Adjacent to the property is a fish hatchery, and everything else in the town of Glenwood is a short walk away, including the trading post across the street and the Blue Front Cafe for old-fashioned family dining. Just south of the center of Glenwood is a U.S. Forest Service office where you can get maps and recreation information on the area's hiking trails, 186 miles of trout streams, riding trails and camping sites.

A must-see attraction is the "catwalk" of **Whitewater Canyon**, about 5 miles east of Glenwood. The canyon was reportedly once a hideout for Indians and desperadoes such as Butch Cassidy, while the catwalk was built by miners in the 1800s to carry water to a remote mill site. It was rebuilt in 1961 by the Forest Service as a recreation attraction. As you walk along the very safe and easy-to-navigate metal "sidewalk" that clings to the sides of the steep canyon walls, 25 feet below you'll see Whitewater Creek as it tumbles over boulders and winds through a forest of trees. At one point on the 1-mile catwalk, stairs lead down to the creek where you can enjoy a tiny sandy beach, waterfall and wading pools. Looking skyward, you might be lucky enough to spot a longhorn sheep or two grazing near the canyon's peaks. At several spots, trails depart from the catwalk and wind up and down along the canyon. Be sure to take a picnic along and a good book — the picnic area near the entrance offers great shade and the relaxing sound of the tumbling creek.

After this visit with the beauty of nature, you might want to take a drive to the restored mountain ghost town of **Mogollon**, once the site of one of the largest gold mines in the country. But don't make this trip unless you feel comfortable navigating narrow switchback roads, because that's the only way to reach Mogollon. Traffic, however, will be almost nonexistent. No more than a few dozen people live in Mogollon today, and they've opened up shops and even a guest lodge to attract tourists. On a more down-to-earth level a bit north of Glenwood you'll find the Frisco Hot Springs — an unusual departure from typical mountain recreation — while the nearby forest of the Gila Wilderness offers fishing, hiking, bird-watching and observing the wildlife.

Phoenix and Environs

There's no shortage of things to do and see in the Phoenix area and no shortage of places to find information on them — tourist materials abound at the airport, nearly every hotel and the visitors center, (602) 254-6500. Instead of reinventing the wheel, we'll concentrate on mapping out a weekend getaway that consists of some of the attractions described in this chapter with a few others tossed in. For starters, as you head northward on I-10 (actually I-10 West), take a slight detour to the **Casa Grande Ruins National Monument**, which is accessible from Exit 194 heading toward Coolidge. Here you'll see the ruins of a Hohokam Indian settlement built in 1350 and learn what archaeologists and historians know today about this now extinct tribe. (This is true desert with little natural shade, so be prepared for the sun and heat.) After this step back into history, return to I-10 toward Phoenix.

In Phoenix, your foremost stop should be to one of the most exquisite museums in the state, the **Heard Museum**, at 22 E. Monte Vista Road in the downtown area, (602) 252-8840, or at their branch in Scottsdale, (602) 488-9817. The Heard exhibits hundreds of outstanding historic American Indian works, some dating back 1,000 years and representing almost every tribal group, past and present, of the Southwest. They also have an exquisite gift shop focusing on American Indian items and culture. From here head to north Scottsdale and visit **Rawhide,** a re-creation of an Old West town. In the middle of its 160 acres is Rawhide's Main Street, lined with stagecoaches, covered wagons, the occasional roaming sheep, zany street shows and, naturally, a gunfight or two. Visitors can take a stagecoach ride into the surrounding desert, dine on cowboy steaks or watch dance performances by American Indians. Parking is free and so is admission, but there are charges for individual attractions. It's best to call ahead, (602) 502-1880, for hours since Rawhide is open only in the evenings, beginning at 5 PM nightly, except from October through May when it's also open weekends (beginning at 11 AM Friday through Sunday). On the way to or from Rawhide, be sure to stop at Cosanti and see the famous Paolo Soleri wind-bells (see the previous listing under "Daytrips").

To continue on our getaway head back to the interstate (I-10) east to the Superstition Freeway, also known as U.S. Highway 60. In Apache Junction, take Ariz. Highway 88 north, a.k.a the Apache Trail (one of several carrying this name in the state). Here you'll see the spectacular **Superstition Mountains**, where legend has it the hidden fortune of the Lost Dutchman Mine has yet to be discovered. Stop at the **Goldfield Ghost Town** to see the area's only historic ghost town and try your luck at gold panning. Further north along the Apache Trail you'll arrive at **Canyon Lake**, one of three lakes created by dams in the Salt River. This is a gorgeous spot for just admiring the water and its surrounding canyon cliffs or enjoying a lakeside picnic. Better yet, try something totally unexpected in Arizona — a cruise on a steam-operated paddle wheeler. The Dolly Steamboat glides along the lake and its secluded inner waterways for about 90 minutes as the guide recounts legends of the Superstition Mountains. It operates daily for ticket prices of $8 to $13 with kids younger than 6 admitted free. Call (602) 827-9144 for tour times and be sure to allow several hours at Canyon Lake if you plan to include the boat cruise. For the perfect finale to this getaway, head back south on Apache Trail and east on U.S. 60 to Boyce Thompson Arboretum (see the previous listing under "Daytrips").

For places to stay on this getaway, consider Scottsdale or nearby Paradise Valley as a good midpoint. For budget accommodations, there's Days Inn at Fashion Square Mall, (602) 947-5411 or (800) 325-2525. Or try a resort that has great amenities, including a huge pool with a swim-under waterfall, but is more reasonable than most in this upscale area — the Doubletree Paradise Valley Resort, (602) 947-5400 or (800) 222-TREE. These are but two possibilities from hundreds of places to stay that are easy to locate in Phoenix area tourist guides or by just driving along the roadways.

Rio Rico

Although it's only about an hour's drive south of Tucson, Rio Rico makes a perfect weekend getaway, especially for golfers. There's blissfully little to do here besides lounge around the Rio Rico Resort and, if you're into the sport, play golf at the resort's course. (See the Golf chapter for details.) The small resort is usually a very peaceful place, unlike the busy megaresorts of the Tucson area, and offers a retreat from just about everything. Set on a hillside just off I-19 approaching Nogales, Arizona, it has a pool so large that you can easily separate yourself from other pool goers and have hours of tranquility. If you can tear yourself away from the pool, there's tennis and horseback riding and fine dining in the resort's restaurant. It's always 10 to 15 degrees cooler than Tucson, so it's even a great summer getaway. Room rates are quite affordable, too — even more so in summer. Rio Rico Resort, (520) 281-1901, also makes a great place to stay if you're touring the area of Tubac and Tumacacori, or you're stepping across the border to Nogales, Mexico, which is only about 10 miles away, and want to make a weekend of it.

Rocky Point, Mexico

Although it's quite a stretch including this Mexico destination as a weekend getaway, it just wouldn't do to keep southern Arizonans' favorite (and closest) beach a secret. Puerto Penasco is it's real name, Rocky Point a descriptive nickname, and it's about four hours from Tucson near the tip of the Gulf of California (or Sea of Cortez) — that body of water separating Mexico's continent from its Baja Peninsula. If you have three days to call a weekend, or better yet four, a drive to Rocky Point will put you on the ocean in a resort town, sort of (it's not Acapulco or Puerta Vallarta, folks, but it'll more than do for desert dwellers). There's even a bonus on top of all that sand and sun and water: As a "free zone," a visa or passport isn't required, so unworldly travelers who don't have one can still vacation in a foreign country. (Read all about the ins and outs of getting in and out of Mexico in this chapter's close-up.)

Like Nogales, Rocky Point is in the Mexican state of Sonora, and to reach it via the scenic route take Ariz. Highway 86 west from Tucson to Ariz. Highway 85 (at Why, Arizona) heading south, which will put you at the border. From there, Mexico Highway 8 goes to Puerto Penasco. Along the way, you'll go through **Organ Pipe Cactus National Monument**, a 500-square-mile preserve of huge organ pipe cacti and lots of other desert wildlife on the Arizona side of the border.

Another similarity to Nogales is that Rocky Point is very Anglicized — English is spoken

INSIDERS' TIP

When visiting Mexico, be aware that the drinking age is 18 and, like the United States, drinking and driving can land you in jail.

Take a walk through Boot Hill Cemetery in Tombstone.

by many, U.S. currency is accepted and most signage is in English, so it's easy to find your way around. Because Rocky Point has really blossomed in the past 10 or so years, there are plenty of hotels and other amenities, although one can still camp out on the beach as tourists frequently did many years ago. In addition to hotels, lodging choices include RV parks and rentals of condos and homes, some of them quite luxurious beachside vacation abodes owned by Anglos.

Before getting into the specifics of where to stay and what to do in Rocky Point, we'll provide an overview of the town. The weather is about the same as Tucson's, sometimes a few degrees warmer, which means that it may not be beach weather in months such as December or January, but spring and fall are perfect, and summer will actually feel hotter because of the oceanside humidity. But there's a solution to that problem — jump in the water. Water is all around, along with miles of white beaches, and they're all public. To the town's north is an area called Cholla Bay. With lots of beach, small beachfront houses and nightlife, this area is a favorite of vacationing college students and young adults. To the town's east is more beach, miles of it, along with a gated community called Las Conchas where Anglos and wealthy Mexicans own vacation homes and condos.

As for where to stay, choices range from a tent or sleeping bag on Sandy Beach, which cars can enter for $3 a day, to the new and pricey Plaza Las Glorias, which ranges from about $70 to $150 a night and is often packed. Other hotels include the very basic Villa Granada to the mid-level Playa Bonita, Vina del Mar and Costa Brava. There are also RV parks north or east of town starting at about $15 a night. Another choice is to rent a condo or home in Cholla Bay or Las Conchas. Reserving a hotel in advance is a good idea and reserving an RV space or private rental in advance is a necessity. For assistance, call the Sonora Tourism Office, (800) 476-6672, or look up Tucson travel agencies that specialize in Rocky Point. Another good source is the Sunday travel section of the *Arizona Daily Star*, which always has ads for Rocky Point reservation services that book private rentals and hotels.

Once you're checked into your getaway quarters, the fun begins. Seaside, you can frolic in the saltwater or on the beach, search for seashells, snorkel, fish, parasail and scuba dive. You also can rent just about any kind of fun you didn't bring with you — wave runners, Jet Skis, ATVs, parasail rides, scuba dives and even a banana boat ride in the shallow surf. (Look for the large "Tourist Information" sign for places that rent equipment, fishing boats and so forth.) Even when tourists flock in, the beaches are so broad that people aren't crammed like sardines. In town or on Cholla Bay, you can bargain for all the regional goods Mexico is famous for, including blankets, jewelry, carvings and more. But don't miss a visit to the fish market. Whether you're doing your own cooking or merely want to take some of the sea's bounty back to Tucson, you'll find large shrimp for about $7 a pound and all kinds of freshly-caught fish for about $3 a pound. Seafood is a staple of many restaurants, but there's also Italian food, burger and pizza places and, of course, Mexican food.

Your visit to Rocky Point will be most enjoyable if you remember you're a guest in someone else's country. Respect the culture and ways of the people, and don't necessarily expect things to work as smoothly or quickly as you're accustomed to stateside. Nor would it hurt to learn a few basic words or phrases that your hosts speak, such as *buenas dias* (good day), *por favor* (pronounced pore-fah-VOR and meaning please), *gracias* (thank you) and *no gracias* (no thank you). Now you're ready to head for southern Arizonans' playground by the sea.

Verde Valley

North and a bit west of Phoenix is an area called Verde Valley (named for the Verde, meaning green, River) that houses some of the state's most popular spots: the mountainside former mining town of Jerome, the historic and lovely city of Prescott and the breathtaking red-rock country of Sedona. Because this area has so much to offer and is quite different from Tucson and the Sonoran Desert, we'll map out a weekend getaway to take you there, but you'll need a long weekend — three or four days — to fit it in. The driving time alone from Tucson to Sedona, the farthest point of this trip, is four hours, and that doesn't include some must-see stops along the way.

Begin this multifaceted weekend getaway by taking I-10 west to Phoenix, where you'll catch I-17 north. For your first fascinating stop, consider Arcosanti, the urban habitat founded by Paolo Soleri and described previously in this chapter under "Daytrips." But be sure to allow enough time to drive a bit farther up I-17, to Exit 289, for **Montezuma Castle**. Don't be fooled or put off by this attraction's moniker — it's not a castle, but an Indian ruin, one of the best-preserved prehistoric cliff dwellings in Arizona. If you only have time to see one Indian ruin in the southern half of the state, this should be it. The Sinagua (Spanish for "without water") Indians built Montezuma Castle around 1125 AD. A peaceful farming people, they farmed in the valley using water from the Verde River and its tributaries and sometimes built cliff dwellings as a way to live in safety from more aggressive inhabitants of the area. What today is called Montezuma Castle was such a dwelling. (Earlier settlers erroneously thought it was built by the Aztec Indians and, thinking it looked like a castle, named it after the Aztec leader.) Today it's a national monument and a sight to behold. After parking your vehicle and entering the visitors center, you'll still have no idea what lies ahead until you walk down a pathway with a creek coursing nearby — the same water that centuries ago provided the sustenance for this small group of cliff dwellers who disappeared. The first sight of the five-story cliff dwelling is breathtaking, and the 500-acre monument itself is a lovely place of huge old trees and pathways lined with the story of these people. Montezuma Castle, (520) 567-3322, is open daily from 8 AM to 5 PM and costs $2 for anyone older than 16.

If you'd like to see more examples of ancient dwellers, both Sinagua and Hohokam, take I-17 a few miles further north to Exit 293 and visit **Montezuma Well**. This is an oasis of lush vegetation, including huge Arizona sycamore trees, where you'll see remains of a Sinagua cliff dwelling and pueblo and a Hohokam pithouse. From the Indian ruins, you'll probably want to find a spot to rest for the night before tackling the rest of this getaway. Prescott is the closest spot, Jerome the most difficult to get to and Sedona the farthest, but any will do as a base from which to explore the exciting and varied Verde Valley.

Ariz. Highway 69 west will take you into **Prescott**, a scenic city that combines the Old West and 1860s Victorian charm. Prescott was founded when gold was discovered in nearby hills and was the Arizona Territory's first capital. By then, rowdy gold miners were frequenting Prescott's now-famous Whiskey Row, and European gentry were living in grand Victorian houses. More than 500 buildings in Prescott are on the National Register of Historic Places, so history and architecture buffs will find much to explore in this city, including the territorial governor's residence built in 1864. The downtown area is where you'll find most of the historic sites, along with Whiskey Row, museums and a lovely square called Courthouse Plaza where many art shows and special events take place.

Prescott is also a great place for outdoor fun. It actually has four seasons, but they're mild; in other words, it's minus the extreme heat of the desert in summer and the extreme cold and snow common to the north. In and around Prescott, visitors can play golf, hike, climb on some of the state's best rock formations, fish, ride horses, pan for gold, watch and wager on the horse races at Prescott Downs and see the world's oldest rodeo in July. If you choose to make Prescott an overnight stop, there are many choices of hotels and bed and breakfasts, among them Forest Villas Hotel, (520) 717-1200, and The Marks House, (520) 778-4632.

Another spot you might want to consider visiting in Verde Valley is **Jerome**. While most ghost towns in Arizona have remained just that, Jerome is one of the rare exceptions. The mines around this old mining town clinging to the side of Mingus Mountain once produced $125 billion worth of copper ore, and Jerome had 15,000 residents. For several decades it was almost totally abandoned (earning it the reputation of ghost town), but today it is an enclave of artists and a National Historic Landmark.

At its 5,000-foot elevation, Jerome offers some spectacular vistas of mountains, the Mogollon Rim and the Red Rock country. The downside of Jerome is the road one must traverse to reach it. This narrow and winding switchback road up the mountain, although paved, is not for everyone. But once in Jerome, you'll find a quaint and scenic village with shops, restaurants, museums, galleries and old-time saloons. If you happen to be here for dinner Saturday or Sunday, you may be lucky enough to get reservations at one of Arizona's finest restaurants, which is only open those two days, House of Joy, (520) 634-5339. By the way, this now-famous restaurant occupies a former brothel, giving testament to the fact that Jerome was once a rowdy, albeit wealthy, mining camp. For lodging, there are several bed-and-breakfast inns, but it's best to contact the Chamber of Commerce, (602) 634-2900, in advance to find out what's open and the price of a room. From I-17, take Ariz. Highway 260 west to Cottonwood, then Ariz. Highway 89A to Jerome.

To round out your Verde Valley getaway, we've saved what many people believe is the best for last: the red-rock scenery of **Sedona** and **Oak Creek Canyon**. From either Prescott or Jerome, Ariz. 89A will take you to Sedona; otherwise, from I-17 take Ariz. Highway 179 to the Sedona exit. Be sure to include some time for seeing the surroundings because, although the town is picturesque and can keep you very busy, a walk in the wild here is like nothing you will experience elsewhere. That's because this pocket of the state was blessed with vibrant red sandstone cliffs and rock formations that display their dramatic spires and odd shapes amidst pines, sycamores, buttes and the beautiful rushing stream, Oak Creek.

Some highlights of the red rock country you'll want to include in your sightseeing are Red Rock Crossing, which is a bit off the beaten path for most tourists and therefore a more peaceful spot for frolicking in Oak Creek or hiking along an easy trail to the base of

Cathedral Rock; Bell Rock, a landmark formation southeast of Sedona on Ariz. 179; the Frank Lloyd Wright-designed Chapel of the Holy Cross; and the popular Oak Creek Canyon north of town, where slide rocks provide some serious rides down the creek for kids and adults alike. No matter where you may choose to drive, bike or walk around the Sedona countryside, however, you'll be treated to nature at its strangest and finest.

If you simply must shop and do other citified things, Sedona is a mecca for shopping, the arts, dining and lodging — and it all leans toward upscale. Tlaquepaque, for instance, is a lovely shopping center with the architecture and flavor of Old Mexico and about two dozen shops (pronounce it Tah-lack-uh-pack-ee). Throughout Sedona, you'll find shops selling everything from Southwestern items to fine clothing and home accessories. Sedona is dotted with scores of art galleries, while art exhibits, live theater and music events are regular happenings here. Sedona also has a vast array of eateries, from delis and ice cream shops to some very fine dining. And if this is where you plan to rest for a night or two, the accommodations choices are almost dizzying. There are motels, such as Days Inn, (520) 282-9166, and Sedona Super 8, (520) 282-1533, that, while not cheap in this neck of the woods, are at least affordable. Or choose from among many bed and breakfasts, including two that travel writers often call among the best in the Southwest: Cathedral Rock Lodge, (520) 282-7608, and Casa Sedona, (520) 282-2938. If you really want to splurge on a resort stay, Sedona offers some of the best. Some of the choices for luxurious accommodations are Poco Diablo Resort, (520) 282-7333; Sedona Real Inn, (520) 282-1414; L'Auberge de Sedona, (520) 282-1667; Los Abrigados, (520) 282-1777; and Enchantment Resort, (520) 282-2900.

At an elevation of 4,400 feet, Sedona is cooler than Tucson and a favorite playground of both Arizonans and tourists. It's a busy place year round but especially in summer when desert dwellers need an escape. In addition to attracting tourists for all the obvious reasons, Sedona also is said (by those who know these things) to be a "vortex" of spiritual rejuvenation; for the uninitiated, that's something like having a mystical energy, making Sedona a mecca for meditation-types. But whatever your reason for visiting Sedona — its spectacular beauty, art offerings, mystical energy or cool running waters of Oak Creek — you'll be enchanted.

For information on Sedona, call the Chamber of Commerce, (520) 282-7722, or stop by Sedona Outpost on Ariz. 179 or Sedona Information Center on Ariz. 89A for maps, tour information, accommodations and more.

Tucson, unlike many cities of its size or larger, does not have suburbs in the customary sense.

Neighborhoods, Neighboring Towns and Real Estate

Although it's the 33rd largest cosmopolitan center in the United States, Tucson may look more like an uncoordinated collection of neighborhoods than anything else. But it's these neighborhoods that give Tucson its vibrancy and distinct character and reflect its varied heritage. In these neighborhoods, some of which have grown up to become towns, you can see where Tucson was a century-and-a-half ago and where it's headed in the coming century.

In the beginning, when the Spaniards first came here from Mexico, all the neighborhoods were called *barrios* (pronounced bar-ee-yo, preferably with a roll of the tongue on the letter "r" to be Hispanicly correct). These original Spanish neighborhoods spread out from the original fort (El Presidio), but they were quite self-contained. Along with houses, they typically had food stores, woodwork and tile shops, and even money lenders, so residents rarely had to venture outside their barrio. Today, a few barrios remain, but we've adopted the Anglo terms neighborhood and community to describe their successors. In the late 1960s, Tucsonans realized that urban renewal threatened the existence of these barrios and early neighborhoods, potentially erasing Tucson's past from sight, so preservation efforts started in earnest. By the early 1980s, *Sunset Magazine* called Tucson "consistently a pacesetter in the West for honoring its architectural heritage," an effort that continues today.

Tucson, unlike many cities of its size or larger, does not have suburbs in the customary sense. There's Tucson (the city) and there's Pima County (surrounding the city), and within both are numerous neighborhoods and a few small towns, each with something a little different to offer. If we wrote about every neighborhood or community, it would be akin to trying to individually describe every cactus rising out of the valley floor. Instead, this chapter presents a primer on the metro area — from its fascinating historic ar-

INSIDERS' TIP

Many of the historic districts in and around the downtown area make for some excellent walking tours, complete with historic buildings, houses converted into museums, churches and even a shrine. Stop by the Metropolitan Tucson Convention and Visitors Bureau at 130 S. Scott Avenue for tour information and lots more on the Tucson area (including discount offers on accommodations, travel, attractions and more).

eas to the sprawling newer ones on the far edges of the valley. We try to convey the character and lifestyle, distinguishing architectural features, a few major points of interest and what the real estate scene is like.

If you're a visitor to Tucson, you'll find great information on neighborhoods to visit for their historic, cultural and design significance. If you're a new resident or plan to be, this chapter will help you see what Tucson is really like as a place to live and where you might choose your abode.

> **FYI**
>
> Unless otherwise noted, the area code for all phone numbers listed in this guide is 520.

Neighborhoods

Historic and Old Neighborhoods

El Presidio

The Hohokam Indians were the first human inhabitants of Tucson. Long after they disappeared, Spanish settlers arrived from Mexico and created what is Tucson's first neighborhood — El Presidio. They may not have known it, but they settled very near a Hohokam site. The first neighborhood started out as a fort (or presidio) called San Augustin del Tucson, covering approximately 12 acres and enclosing two plazas, a chapel, a cemetery, stables for horses and quarters for officers, soldiers and settlers. Gradually, houses were built outside the presidio walls, and eventually the walls came tumbling down. (But you can still see a Mexican barracks on Alameda Street near Main Avenue.)

As with the other downtown historic areas, the neighborhood really took off with the arrival of the railroad and Anglo-Americans in the early 1880s, their Victorian and Tudor- and Bungalow-style houses supplanting the Sonoran row houses of the first settlers. Meyer and Court streets offer examples of the original Sonoran architecture, with adobe row houses built to the front property line and open courtyard spaces in the interior. In contrast, the houses along Main Avenue reflect architectural styles introduced from the East and Midwest by Anglo-Americans — set back from the street, surrounded by yards and lush vegetation and Victorian in architectural style. The grand homes along Main and Granada avenues and Paseo Redondo Street earned this area the name "Snob Hollow" in the 1920s and '30s, coined because Tucson's movers and shakers lived there, and the area was in a topographical hollow.

Designated the El Presidio Historic District in 1975, it covers a 12-block area immediately north of today's downtown, bounded roughly by Alameda, Church and 6th streets and Granada Avenue. The district is rich with old structures, many of which have been converted into museums or professional buildings. The oldest is La Casa Cordova, now housing a Mexican heritage museum. Nearby is the Edward Nye Fish House, a typical pre-railroad Sonoran row house that now houses the Tucson Museum of Art's Pavilion of Western Art. The Steinfeld mansion at 300 N. Main Avenue, named for its residents who owned Steinfeld's department store first in downtown and then at El Con Mall, was built for $10,000 in 1899 and renovated into offices in 1979 to the tune of $625,000. The 12,000-square-foot Manning House, at 450 W. Paseo Redondo Street, was built in 1907 and occupied by a one-time mayor; today it houses offices. Other historic residences are the Corbett House, Romero House and Stevens House.

INSIDERS' TIP

Summerhaven, a village at the top of Mt. Lemmon, is surrounded by pines and firs and an occasional bear. Its cabins and homes offer a cool escape from the desert heat for both permanent and seasonal residents.

If your tour of the area makes you a bit weary of concrete and buildings, visit a lovely little oasis in the midst of it all — the Alene Dunlap Smith Memorial Garden, on the east side of Granada Street just north of Franklin. If you'd like to get in a bit of shopping or dining with your history, visit Old Town Artisans, an adobe-walled structure on Washington and Meyer streets, parts of which date back 150 years. The half-dozen shops here include items handmade by local artists and a collection of folk art. Directly across Alameda Street (the historic district's southern boundary) are El Presidio Park and the Pima County Courthouse, built in 1928 in an elaborate Moorish style with a tile mosaic dome that's a Tucson landmark.

Residential real estate in this area is scarce; only a few buildings are private residences. Most have become commercial or preserved as museums, while any vacant land has long ago been turned into commercial sites.

Armory Park

Way back when, the area now known as Armory Park began as the original military plaza of Camp Lowell (later the military camp was moved to the Rillito River area and renamed Fort Lowell, discussed separately in this chapter.) From 1880, when work on the transcontinental railroad reached Tucson, until about 1920, the Armory Park area transformed into a residential area inhabited by prominent railroad executives, affluent entrepreneurs and working class people. Like most of the central neighborhoods, the first settlers were Spanish, and their houses were typically contiguous structures built to the front property line and reflecting the Sonoran or Spanish-Mexican style. But the railroad changed all that. Anglo-Americans began migrating in and, with the help of the railroad, they imported building materials typically used in eastern housing. And also typical of the Anglo style, their houses were built in the center of lots with spacious yards all around.

Today you'll still see some of the original Spanish homes as well as an eclectic mix of Victorian, Queen Anne, California bungalow and Mission and Spanish Colonial Revival styles. Designated a historic district in 1974 (Tucson's first), Armory Park covers about 30 blocks just southeast of the central business district. It extends from 12th Street south to 19th Street and from about 2nd Avenue on the east to Stone Avenue on the west.

In addition to an actual park — named, what else, Armory Park — and a senior center adjacent to it, some of the highlights of the district are the Temple of Music and Art, a handsomely restored structure now housing the Arizona Theatre Company, the original Tucson Carnegie Library, now home to the Tucson Children's Museum, and the Tucson Center for the Performing Arts, formerly a church. Safford Middle School is an excellent example of the Mission Revival style, with plastered walls, an elaborate ornamental entry and portals.

Along with turn-of-the-century hotels, converted office buildings and even a bed and breakfast or two, the residential real estate in Armory Park offers beautifully restored homes at around $300,000 and small fixer-uppers for less than $80,000. A lovely old historic area within the Tucson Unified School District, it may not be the ideal place for families, however, because of the dense traffic, the commercial businesses intermingled with residences and the homeless population that often occupies Armory Park.

Barrio Historico

In sharp contrast to the contemporary concrete edifice right across the street known as the Tucson Convention Center, Barrio Historico dates from the mid-1850s when settlers began spreading out from the original Tucson neighborhood, El Presidio. Also known as Barrio Viejo, this historic district covers about 20 blocks from Cushing Street on the north to 18th Street on the south, and from the railroad tracks on the west to Stone Avenue on the east. While working-class Mexicans were the predominant settlers, Chinese, African-American, Anglo-American and American Indian settlers made it a somewhat ethnically diverse area.

Unlike some of the other central historical neighborhoods, the influx of Anglo-Americans and the railroad had less impact on the barrios, and they retained much of their Spanish culture and heritage, as well as the name "barrio." What did have an impact on the barrios, however, was urban renewal in the late 1960s; about half the barrio neighborhoods in the downtown area gave way to parking lots, government buildings, the convention center and other commercial structures. Barrio Historico is one of a handful of barrios that were saved from the bulldozers.

Designated a historic district in 1975, Barrio Historico is an excellent example of Sonoran style, which relied on the use of native materials — mud adobe, mesquite and saguaro — and ingenuity to adapt to the desert climate. Houses were tightly clustered, often with shared walls, to get protection from the desert heat. They were built close to the front property line so that interior courtyards would be protected from the sun by the surrounding structure. Another characteristic of the barrios is that they were self-contained — local merchants set up shop to sell groceries and staples, provide furniture and other craft works, and even give credit.

A visit to Barrio Historico is a journey back in time not only to early Tucson, but to Mexican villages or Mediterranean villages whose architecture strongly influenced the Sonoran style. It contains the largest and best preserved collection of old adobes in the West. Today the restored row houses are used for residences as well as offices and studios for artists and designers. But the most unusual site in Barrio Historico may well be El Tiradito, meaning "the little castaway" but commonly called the Wishing Shrine.

Legend has it that this outdoor adobe shrine with a soot-scarred image of the Virgin of Guadalupe was erected for a man murdered (wrongly) in a love triangle before the turn of the century. It is believed to be the only one of its kind in the United States dedicated to a sinner buried in unconsecrated ground. Now on the National Historic Register, it is said that if you light a candle there at night and it burns until morning, your wish will come true. This makeshift shrine, common in the Mexican culture, stands as a lonely reminder of the past set amidst modern paved roads, restaurants and within throwing distance of the TCC. You'll find the shrine on Main Avenue just south of Cushing Street and right next to a more modern neighborhood landmark, yet still one of the older family-run Mexican restaurants in the city, El Minuto restaurant.

For folks interested in buying in this barrio, unrestored adobe homes can be purchased for less than $50,000. This is in the Tucson Unified School District but may not be an ideal area for families with kids, because houses have no yard areas and are very close to the street, commercial businesses are intermingled with residences, and it's very close to the congestion and heavy traffic of the Tucson Convention Center.

West University

The 60-block area located between the University of Arizona and downtown is historically significant because it exemplifies the pattern of middle- and upper-class residential development in Tucson from 1890 to 1930. Thus it was designated a historic district by the city in 1984. Although some buildings reflect the Mexican style, the neighborhood's architecture is mostly European and California bungalow styles because it was settled by Anglo-Americans after the arrival of the Southern Pacific railroad.

Strolling pedestrians will pass restored bungalows and Victorian-style houses on tree-lined streets, the Fourth Avenue shopping district (and Tucson's only remaining street trolley) and, just beyond the east boundary of the district, the University's first building, Old Main. The district extends roughly from 6th Street north to Speedway Boulevard and from 7th Avenue on the west to Euclid Avenue. Today it's a mixture of older homes occupied by longtime residents and more transient student rentals, peppered with a few fraternity houses, bed and breakfasts, restaurants and shops catering mostly to students. Small homes can sell for well below $100,000, but larger ones that have been restored can bring in twice that and more.

Middle-school kids in this neighborhood can attend the very first elementary school ever built in the state, which is now Roskruge Middle School on E. 6th Street, a handsomely restored building that obviously still has old world charm and appeal (maybe not for the kids, but architecturally speaking). This school and the neighborhood are in Tucson Unified School District.

Fort Lowell

There's something about the Ft. Lowell area that just seems to silently shout "history." Maybe it's the ghosts of the Hohokam, or the imagined sounds of the battles between the cavalry post's soldiers and the Apaches, or the cracking sounds of the generations-old adobe homes handmade by early Mexican settlers. Or perhaps it's the juxtaposition of new and old — uniformed six-year-olds playing soccer games on the very park land where more than a hundred years ago uniformed soldiers may have played or where more than a thousand years ago Hohokam Indians tilled the ground to farm. Whatever the reason, this area is often said to reflect where Tucson's soul resides.

Hohokam Indians first settled and farmed this area, which is just south of the confluence of the Pantano and Tanque Verde washes and Rillito River, about 300 A.D. They were long gone by 1873, when the military began building a cavalry post to protect Arizona settlers from Apache raids — a fort that was 7 miles away from "Tucson" and connected to it by the "Fort Lowell road." Under the safety of the fort, Mexicans migrated here to farm and ranch the fertile bottomlands, and they were soon followed by Mormons.

Only a quarter-square mile in size, the district is rich in 1,500 years of history. Fort Lowell Park contains the Fort Lowell Museum (now part of the Arizona Historical Society), some remaining ruins of fort buildings and even a Hohokam archaeological site. Ft. Lowell Road, to the west of the park, offers some rambling Sonoran ranch adobes nearly hidden by lush vegetation. Just west of the district boundary is San Pedro Chapel, built in Mission Revival style and designated as the city's first historic Landmark in 1982 (and also on the state and national registers.)

In recent years, vacant land in this area has been gobbled up by home builders but even the new developments seem to reflect the character of the old — mostly stucco houses with lots of vegetation that retain the sense of quiet calm of the neighborhood. Today the area contains an eclectic mix of residences, from starter and patio homes in the low $100,000s range to luxury adobes selling for as much as $500,000 and from turn-of-the-century adobe houses to contemporary architecture. The narrow and curving E. Presidio Street is lined with newer homes but feels like an old hacienda-lined street of Mexico with walled courtyards, lush vegetation and hundreds of mesquite trees.

Located in the Tucson Unified School District, this is a great neighborhood for families — quiet, filled with history, mostly large properties and fairly removed from commercial businesses but within easy access of them. One of Tucson's foremost private preparatory schools, St. Gregory, is at the north end of the neighborhood.

Sam Hughes

First there was Sam Hughes, local pioneering merchant and civic leader. Then there was Sam Hughes Elementary School. Then there was the Sam Hughes neighborhood, bounded by Speedway Boulevard, Campbell Avenue, Broadway Boulevard and Country Club Road. Originally homesteaded by five landowners, this square mile east of the University was eventually subdivided into numerous housing projects and then combined under the rubric Sam Hughes neighborhood. It contains some of the Old Pueblo's finest examples of charming Mission Revival and Spanish Colonial homes.

This is a neighborhood that has become very popular with upscale city dwellers — people who prefer the city life to the outskirts (and the accompanying commute), along with quiet streets, older homes both restored and still needing fixing up, the proximity of the University and all it has to offer, and friendly sidewalks and streets for jogging or bike-riding. A neighborhood association was formed in 1971 to preserve the residential character of the neighborhood and fend off undesirable development. Long a Tucson treasure, the neigh-

The Sam Hughes neighborhood lies just east of the University.

borhood became a national treasure with its National Historic District designation in 1994.

Highlights of the neighborhood, in addition to the many lovely homes and relative peace and quiet, include Himmel Park and its namesake library and the Rincon Market on 6th Street and Tucson Boulevard, a favorite gathering and shopping place for the residents for years.

Among the neighborhood's famous residents are Frank Borman, who lived here before going on to orbit the moon and become president of Eastern Airlines, and Hiram "Hi " Corbett, a civic leader who brought cactus league baseball to Tucson and whose name the baseball stadium bears.

The nostalgia, the historically preserved homes and the proximity of town combine to make Sam Hughes pricey and its residents a largely liberal mix of attorneys, professors, architects and a surprising number of retirees. Served by Tucson Unified schools, this is a good family neighborhood, as long as your family conforms to the association rules and preservationist philosophy. Prices range from $100,000 to $200,000 for the handful of fixer-uppers remaining to upwards of $300,000 for the large, beautifully restored homes on 3rd and 4th streets. Houses do go on the market here but not many and not frequently. You can buy a whole lot more space for the same money elsewhere but not in a central neighborhood with this kind of commitment to the past and the future.

Pie Allen

This neighborhood owes its unusual name to pies made by one of its earliest settlers. Made from dried apples because fresh fruit was scarce here then, John "Pie" Allen's pies were a big hit and started Allen on the road to becoming a local entrepreneur and eventually mayor of Tucson. Bounded by Park and

4th avenues and by 6th Street and Broadway Boulevard, the neighborhood covers 24 blocks just west of the University. Residents formed an association in 1980, primarily to protect themselves and their historic homes from University expansion.

A building boom in the 1880s transformed the former ranch land into homes occupied largely by railroad workers. Almost every architectural style that was popular between the 1860s and the 1940s is represented in Pie Allen, and many have been restored. Several were designed by one of Tucson's most famous and distinctive architects, Josias Joesler. One of the area's vintage buildings, a Spanish Colonial Revival-style structure dating from 1928, is the Colonial Hotel at 410 E. 9th Street.

Within the Tucson Unified School District, Pie Allen boasts the oldest high school in the state, now Tucson Magnet High, which recently underwent a major renovation. Today, homes in this neighborhood are less expensive than, say, Sam Hughes homes and start at about $60,000.

El Encanto

This hidden neighborhood just west of the sprawling El Con Mall boasts some of the most elegant homes — almost mansions — in central Tucson. Sometimes referred to as the "Beverly Hills of Tucson," this neighborhood developed in the late 1920s has a strong California influence, beginning with its geometric street pattern that was a major departure from the grid pattern of all prior neighborhoods in Tucson. From a central circle, streets fan out in a diagonal pattern, making the neighborhood a bit difficult for the uninitiated to traverse. Another obvious California influence is the landscaping — hundreds of Mexican fan palms and date palms were planted during the initial layout, along with many citrus, olive and eucalyptus trees. The street pattern, combined with the lush landscaping and many walled yards and courtyards, give the neighborhood a sense of mystery and privacy.

Given the value of this real estate today, it's astonishing that the land was actually acquired free from the federal government by a homesteader 88 years ago. The first home built here with its surrounding 10 acres were purchased for $3,700 by Leroy "Jessie" James (no, not the famous outlaw), who was ridiculed for buying worthless desert land so far from town. Jessie no doubt had the last laugh when a few years later he got offers of 10 times that amount.

Today this neighborhood bounded by 5th Street and Broadway Boulevard and Country Club Road and Jones Avenue is city living at its finest. Emanating from the center circle, which boasts more than 150 saguaro cacti, are nearly 150 homes on 1-acre lots in styles including Moroccan, Spanish, Italian, Mexican and early California. About 50 are on the National Historic Register. Home prices here can reach or exceed $1 million, and there is not much turnover. It's in the Tucson Unified School District.

Winterhaven

Two things are most noticeable in this half-mile square neighborhood that extends from Tucson Boulevard to Country Club Road and Prince Road to Ft. Lowell Road — one is the lush green grass surrounding every home, unusual in the Tucson desert, and the other is the street named Christmas Avenue. The former no doubt results from the fact that a fertilizer company once occupied much of the land, its huge manure piles making for rich soil underneath. The latter signifies the neighborhood's real claim to fame — the Festival of Lights, which started in 1949, the same year the development opened, and held annually every Christmas since then. (See our Festivals and Events chapter.)

Fifty years after its founding, Winterhaven remains an attractive residential neighborhood fairly close to the University and downtown areas. It's a peaceful and comfortable middle-class neighborhood that looks like it was transplanted from back East — explained by the fact that the developer reportedly patterned it after Shaker Heights, Ohio.

You won't find land for building here, but homes on good-sized lots covered with green grass and mature vegetation start at about $150,000. It has a strong neighborhood association and lies within the Tucson Unified School District boundary.

Tucson Country Club

At one time, this enclave was considered way out in the boondocks, but with continual expansion to the east it's actually quite convenient to downtown and nearly all points in the valley. This is old-world country-club living at its finest amidst mature vegetation, lots of mesquite trees, large flat lots and some of Tucson's most prominent residents.

An exclusive, upscale neighborhood bounded by the Tanque Verde and Pantano washes on the south and west and by Tanque Verde Road on the east, Tucson Country Club is almost an island in a sea of recent development, most of it commercial. Hidden behind service stations, restaurants and all manner of shops, the neighborhood of 300 to 400 homes begins on a street called Camino Principal and winds westward to a private golf and country club. And unless you drive through the entrance area, you'd have no idea this neighborhood exists, so hidden is it and so unexpected within the busy commercial area around it.

Many of the club's homes were built in the '50s, some are newer and very few vacant lots remain, if any. The starting price approaches $300,000 and goes way up from there. It's within Tucson Unified School District boundaries, but these kids are more likely to be enrolled in upscale private schools.

Newer Neighborhoods

In the 1920s, Tucson's population topped out at 20,000. By the '60s, we were just passing the quarter-million mark. Today, we're beyond three-quarters of a million and closing in on one million in the metropolitan area. Where do all these people go? In every direction they can, including up the mountain sides.

The Catalina Foothills

Today the word "foothills" designates any area rising into any one of the mountain ranges surrounding Tucson, and as the population swells, so too do the mountain side homes. But the original foothills growth was to the city's north at the base of the Santa Catalina Mountains, an area close to the city center, offering views over the entire Tucson valley.

The Catalina Foothills area extends from River Road on the south to as high or far as anyone can build on the north and from about Craycroft Road on the east to about Campbell Avenue on the west. Here you will find exclusive gated communities such as Finisterre, Skyline Country Club and Cobblestone, the Westin La Paloma Resort and its country club housing and many custom homes on 1-acre lots. This area is also home to famous artist Ted deGrazia's studio on north Swan Road. (See the Arts and Culture chapter for details on the studio and its founder.)

Catalina Foothills land is scarce and 1-acre lots can command $100,000 to $300,000. A smaller semicustom home, built in the '70s and probably without a city view, can be purchased for a bit less than $200,000, while the most exclusive homes in the upper regions can go for $1 million plus. These desert homes are far removed from the traffic and bustle of the valley below yet close enough for a quick commute. Their appeal is bolstered by the school district — much of the area lies within the District 16 school district, usually reputed to be the best in the metro area. Many families choose to live in the foothills just for the school district, which boasts the highest test scores in the city, and homes within the District 16 boundary (versus foothills homes in TUSD) typically command a higher price.

INSIDERS' TIP

If you're a student or anyone else planning to rent in the University area, the University publishes a free annual Apartment Guide and Renters Handbook (including a child care guide). It contains some great advice on leasing plus the complete Arizona Residential Landlord and Tenant Act, a guide to University buildings and parking and lots more. Call 621-7597 for information on where to pick one up.

Sabino Canyon

Nestled into the lower Santa Catalina Mountains but farther east than the Catalina Foothills, the Sabino Canyon area is still definitely foothills land and much in demand. And it has another major draw — the Sabino Canyon recreation area. Extending north from River Road and east from Sabino Canyon Road, it is lovely desert land on the northeast side of the metro area, much of it still being developed. Although primarily residential with very few commercial businesses, major services are within easy reach.

Homes right along Sabino Canyon Road start at about $120,000 while those further east and around the world-famous Canyon Ranch Spa can reach a half-million and more. This is a booming area with choices ranging from homes built in the '70s to high-end apartments and townhomes to new golf course homes. The Sabino Canyon area is a great place for families — traffic is fairly light except for the few major roads, many neighborhoods are "neighborhoodly" with homes in close proximity, commercial establishments are almost nonexistent and much of it lies within the popular District 16 schools. (Homes south of Snyder Road are in the Tucson Unified School District but within the boundary for Fruchtendler Elementary School on Cloud Road, one of that district's finest.)

Ventana Canyon

The posh Loews Ventana Canyon Resort was the forerunner of development in this exclusive and pricey area in the foothills of the Catalina Mountains that falls between the Catalina Foothills and Sabino Canyon areas and north of Sunrise Drive. This is incredible desert land with home prices that often match. For folks who can afford it, this is the most desirable spot in the entire metro area.

Driving along Sunrise Drive near Kolb Road, you can look north into the mountains and see houses so far up they look minuscule but in reality are contemporary mansions hugging the granite mountainside. On a more down-to-earth level, lovely patio homes and single-family homes surround the golf courses of the Resort, occupied by families and retirees who appreciate the golf course views and recreation and can afford upwards of $300,000. To the east along Sunrise Drive are many developments with attractive family-oriented tract homes on streets that wind through the lower foothills and sell for about $250,000.

Ventana Canyon offers nearly every housing choice and lots of raw land, but it's all high-end — apartments, townhomes, patio homes, single-family homes and mansions. Many of the communities are gated, and they tend to be more affordable than the gated communities in the more established Catalina Foothills. This is strictly residential land with only a few commercial business starting to develop along Sunrise Boulevard. But it's accessible to all of the east side of Tucson and about a 30- to 40-minute commute to downtown or the University. And it lies within the highly demanded District 16 schools.

East

This was the most natural direction to accommodate Tucson's dramatic growth of the last several decades — the Rincon Mountains were far away, and the land was fairly flat for building infrastructure, housing and businesses. Just about anything in the vast area east of Alvernon Way and extending north to the Catalinas, east to the Rincons and south to the Santa Rita Mountains can be considered "the east." The close-in Eastside has some of the most affordable housing available in Tucson, while the closer the mountains the higher the home sites and the prices.

Nearly all the neighborhoods would be considered family-oriented; there are very few age-restricted developments here. Modest single-family homes can be had for around $60,000, but choices include townhomes and patio homes, manufactured homes and a multitude of apartment complexes. Most of the Eastside is served by TUSD except for the far east, which is served by the Tanque Verde School District.

Some of the more exclusive areas on the Eastside include Old Spanish Trail near Saguaro National Park, the Bear Canyon and Agua Caliente areas in the northeast, and the Reddington Pass area winding into the base of the Rincon Mountains. Here you will still find expanses of virgin desert along with homes built on large acreage and even some horse properties.

One of the older Eastside neighborhoods with lots of unique character is the Forty-niners Country Club on Tanque Verde Road just east of the Tanque Verde wash. Built in the '70s around a private golf course, this neighborhood features a mesquite bosque, lush vegetation due to the fertile flood-plain soil and homes built on large lots and curved streets. Although quite a distance from the city and from major services, it offers seclusion and privacy and a safe family environment. Home prices here begin near $200,000 and top out near $350,000. The 49ers is in the Tanque Verde School District, ranked one of the best in metro Tucson.

Dorado Country Club

An oasis in the midst of Tucson's close-in eastern commercial sprawl, Dorado is a lovely community surrounded by a wall that keeps it private and quiet yet within biking or walking distance of stores, restaurants, movie theaters and more. At one time, this was a gated community with a private golf course. The two gated entrances are now purely decorative, and the golf course is open to the public. The streets wind around the golf course and are lined with a variety of home types — from roomy patio homes and townhomes to exclusive single-family homes on large lots — often situated with views of the golf course. Many retirees live here, but it's also a great neighborhood for raising kids, because traffic is practically nonexistent, bicycling along the streets is safe, community pools abound and TUSD schools are nearby.

Housing prices start at about $125,000 and go to $300,000 and higher. The only rentals available are private homes.

Southeast

Rita Ranch and Corona de Tucson are two up-and-coming neighborhoods on the far southeast side of the valley with homes and lots that are quite affordable, largely because of their distance from Tucson and from major services and amenities (a minimum half-hour drive away).

Rita Ranch got its start because IBM built a huge complex here but then later moved out, leaving housing development at a standstill. It has been resurrected and more than a half-dozen builders are actively selling lots and building attractive tract homes in the $70,000 to 100,000 range. This area appeals to families who like to buy brand new but can't afford the additional $20,000 to $30,000 for the same home in a more convenient area. The land is flat, the yards are large, and the kids attend Vail School District.

Corona de Tucson, bordering the Santa Rita foothills about 7 miles south of Interstate 10 off Houghton Road, is rural desert area with real estate ranging from tract homes to custom homes on 5 acres for $300,000 to $400,000 and from townhomes along the Santa Rita Golf Course to homes on 1 acre for $100,000 to 150,000. While some of this area was developed in the '70s, much is new development and vacant land. It's within the Vail School District and a great rural area for raising a family if you can handle the distance from Tucson and from major services like shopping and medical care. Your dollar will go much further here for lots and homes than it will in any other foothills area on the Eastside.

Tucson Mountains and the West

The jagged Tucson Mountains forming Tucson's western edge are literally surrounded by real estate, even though the west side traditionally has been less popular and less populated than Tucson's east and northwest. This may be the result of the mountains themselves posing an obstacle to infrastructure development and travel. Or it may be that it's too close to downtown and some of the "less desirable" areas surrounding it. But change is in the air, and the Tucson Mountains' peaks are looking down on building activity on all sides. With Catalina Foothills lots scarce and home prices out of reach for many, the Tucson Mountains — where acre lots are available for $40,000 to $50,000 — are becoming the new foothills area. All of the Tucson Mountains area is within TUSD until it reaches the Marana School District in the far north.

The El Presidio neighborhood has experienced a renewal in recent years.

For a bird's-eye view, let's go first to the western base of the range where there are several large manufactured home communities as well as both older and newer houses, some in tract housing developments and others on large rural plots. Although close to major attractions like Saguaro National Park West, Tucson Mountain Park, the Arizona-Sonora Desert Museum and Old Tucson Studios, this area is somewhat of a trek from Tucson and accessible only by two roads — Ajo Highway to Kinney Road on the south end and narrow, winding Gates Pass Road in the middle of the range.

At the southern and southeastern tip of the mountain range our view takes in the Pasqua Yacqui reservation and the growing area around Ajo Way and Valencia Road, where housing options include modest single-family homes and apartment complexes. Traveling north to Gates Pass Road, there are more exclusive homes on large properties, many with spectacular views of the valley and the mountains. At the far north end of the mountains, around Picture Rocks Road, housing opportunities include manufactured homes, family-oriented developments with attractive tract homes, large contemporary custom homes built into the mountainside and lots of vacant land. A remodeled adobe on 3 acres can be purchased for less than $200,000.

Our final destination is the eastern side of the mountains, closest to downtown Tucson, and the most built-up side of this mountain range. Housing here includes the area around Silverbell and Anklam roads and Pima Community College's west campus, where neighborhoods are older and family-oriented and homes are in the affordable starting range of $60,000 to $70,000. Here we also see the hot new housing area called Starr Pass, anchored by a golf course and soon-to-be major resort. For thousands less than the Catalina Foothills, home buyers can enjoy saguaros and city views from golf course villas, luxury apartments and custom homes on lots starting at $30,000. Starr Pass has an eclectic mix of residents from families to retirees to vacation homeowners.

Northwest

Tucson's sprawl north of the Rillito River and across 80 square miles of desert is the vast northwest. The population was 62,000 in 1990 and 100,000 by 1995. And the numbers are still growing by leaps and bounds. The northwest region accounts for nearly 50 percent of the new homes in the metro area. Yes, this is a new area. Very little existed here before 1960, but you'd never know that driving north on Oracle Road or west on Ina Road. The number of housing developments is mind-boggling, not to mention golf courses, shopping centers, schools, churches, retirement communities, restaurants, banks and every imaginable kind of commercial enterprise. Much of the area considered northwest is unincorporated Pima County land, while other areas have incorporated into towns like Oro Valley and Marana.

Here you will find Tohono Chul Park, the Sheraton El Conquistador Resort, Foothills Mall, Rancho Vistoso (Tucson's Sun City), Catalina State Park and its Romero Falls, Omni Tucson National Golf Resort, Heritage Highlands Golf Club, Northwest Hospital, Miraval Life in Balance Resort, Green Fields Country Day School, Continental Ranch, the retirement community of Saddlebrook and the area called Catalina that runs along U.S. Highway 89 to the Pima County northern boundary.

The northwest used to be an area where affordable homes, priced at less than $100,000, were plentiful. Not so anymore. The market is maturing, and available land is going the way of the dinosaur. Although they're around, finding a single-family home at $100,000 or less takes some digging. The more typical price is up to $200,000, and some high-end properties reach a half-million or more, especially in the western foothills of the Catalina Mountains. But the choices are almost infinite — golf-course communities, manufactured housing, new apartment complexes, townhomes, retirement communities, custom mountainside homes with spectacular views and down-to-earth typical family-oriented neighborhoods with attractive tract homes and nearby schools.

The northwest is popular for several reasons. Land is still available for new housing, and home buyers have a broad choice among both older homes in established neighborhoods and brand new homes. For folks who commute often to Phoenix for business or for air travel, the proximity of I-10 is a great attraction. Likewise, the proximity of the freeway for commuters to downtown Tucson and the University means not having to battle crosstown traffic each day. And the Amphitheater School District, which serves the bulk of the northwest, draws families to this side of town.

Midvale Park

This was Tucson's first completely planned community, carved out of 1,300 acres known as Midvale Farms between the Santa Cruz River on the east, Mission Road on the west, Irvington Road on the north and the San Xavier reservation on the south. It was designed in the early 1980s to provide a complete mix of commercial, residential, educational and recreational offerings — shopping centers, office buildings, schools, parks and a variety of housing styles. Groves of cottonwood and pecan trees were left untouched by the builders, and landscaped boulevards and bike paths were integral to the design.

Annexed to the city in 1983, Midvale Park is an affordable area with single-family, multifamily and manufactured housing options. Close to Interstate 19, it's accessible to downtown, the airport and major employers such as Hughes and Burr-Brown. Homes can be purchased here for $40,000 to 50,000, and kids attend either Tucson Unified School District or the Sunnyside School District. One of its major claims to fame is the Balloon Fiesta, started in October 1984 and now an annual event.

Towns and a City

City of South Tucson

This is a small town surrounded by a city, a place where to be a minority is to be in the majority. It's one square mile of people with a strong sense of independence, pride and perseverance. After one thwarted attempt to incorporate to prevent the City of Tucson from annexing it, area residents successfully incorporated in 1939. The population today is about 80 percent Hispanic, 10 percent Anglo and 6 percent Indian, with the remainder black or Asian. Businesses tend to be small and family-run. Some of the best Mexican restaurants in Tucson are in South Tucson, particularly along S. 4th Avenue. Two of Tucson's main attractions are located here — Tucson Greyhound Park and the Fiesta de los Vaqueros, or the annual rodeo in February.

Generally, the people and Spanish-style houses of South Tucson have populated the area for generations. The residents fix up the homes, add to them or perhaps move to better housing, usually in the same area. Much of the residential property has been converted into small businesses — bakeries, restaurants and a variety of shops. Real estate is not in demand here except by existing residents of South Tucson, recent immigrants from Mexico or small-business owners. Most of the housing is small and Spanish-style, typically starting around $20,000 and probably in need of repair. A renovated or new house can be had for $100,000 or less. Its schools are part of the Tucson Unified School District.

Oro Valley

This incorporated town in the northwest had a population of 6,700 in 1990 that nearly tripled by 1995. Six miles north of Tucson's city limits along Oracle Road (Ariz. Highway 77), the valley is formed by the juncture of the Santa Cruz River and Gold Creek in the Santa Catalina Mountains. Originally incorporated in 1974, the town has grown to 24 square miles through annexation. Oro Valley has the image of being a small, sleepy bedroom community nestled in the foothills of the Catalinas, but in reality it's a growing town in a booming area of metro Tucson that could reach 50,000 by the century's end.

Housing in Oro Valley runs the gamut but tends toward the high end, because much of it is situated in the foothills, which is pricey property with a view. Very nice family-size houses are available for $150,000 while mountainside houses sell for $250,000 and more. The Amphitheater School District serves this area.

Marana

What started out as a small farming community just off I-10 about 15 miles northwest of Tucson had grown to a town of 65 square miles and a population of nearly 5,000 by 1995 with plans for more annexation to 190 square miles by the year 2020. In fact, Marana, Oro Valley, unincorporated areas of the northwest and the City of Tucson all seem to be in a battle to annex the vast northwest and close the gap between what today is the City of Tucson and the northwest towns.

The original town of Marana remains a rural area with low-end housing and manufactured housing, but Marana's character is definitely changing with its spread. For example, Continental Ranch, annexed by Marana in 1987, is an 1,800-acre master planned community off I-10 and Cortaro Farms Road calling for 4,000 homes (starting at about $80,000), a shopping center, golf course and large hotel. Another new project is Red Hawk, a 5,500-acre master planned community at the base of the Tortolita Mountains, where U.S. Homes is building its Heritage Highlands with homes starting in the low $100,000 range. Much of the residential real estate in Marana is more affordable than comparable housing in other areas of the metro area that are more centrally located. The Marana School District serves this town.

Green Valley

Often called one of the most successful retirement communities in the country, Green Valley is about 25 miles south of Tucson off I-19. This isn't a city or town but you'd never know it. It's an unincorporated area of Pima

County that took off in 1970 and continues to grow dramatically. The permanent population of 23,000 swells to 35,000 to 40,000 during the months of January through March with the arrival of winter visitors and seasonal homeowners. It has the atmosphere of a small town but provides all the services and commercial establishments anyone would need.

Although primarily a retirement community, a number of housing developments have no age restrictions, and kids attend the Continental School District. Villas can be purchased for $25,000 while more exclusive housing ranges up to $250,000. Spanish Colonial and territorial architectures prevail in Green Valley. It's famous for its golf courses (see the Golf chapter) and for nearby attractions including the Titan Missile Museum, Madera Canyon, Tubac and nearby Nogales, Mexico. (Look for more on Green Valley in the Retirement chapter.)

> **FYI**
>
> Unless otherwise noted, the area code for all phone numbers listed in this guide is 520.

Rentals

Apartments are as plentiful in Tucson as sunshine. In fact, it's largely because of our abundant sunshine that Tucson attracts so many visitors and newcomers who seek rental housing. There simply is not an area of Tucson — north, south, east or west, in the foothills or in the flatlands — that doesn't have something to rent. As of late 1997, Tucson had a glut (to use real estate jargon) of apartments with vacancy rates of 10 to 12 percent. This is good news for renters, because apartment owners tend to offer discounts and other move-in incentives when the supply of rentals exceeds the number of renters. Experts predict this glut will last at least through 1998.

Also as of late '97, the average monthly rent for apartments in the metro area was $492, excluding electricity, but luxury apartments in neighborhoods like the Catalina Foothills or Sabino Canyon can easily approach $1,000 for two or three bedrooms. Conversely, nice one- and two-bedroom apartments can be found for $350 but in less desirable neighborhoods and often on a main thoroughfare.

But apartments are not the only option for leasing. Many privately owned condos, town houses, patio homes and single-family homes are available for rent, often at not much more than a high-end apartment. The three best ways to find these rentals are to drive around neighborhoods and look for signs, check out the Sunday real estate section of the *Arizona Daily Star* or contact realty companies that also handle or locate rentals. (See the following section of real estate companies for ones handling rentals.)

With the mind-boggling array of rental choices, you might need a few good places to start. First, cruise around Tucson and decide on some areas you'd prefer to live; this will make your selection chore much easier no matter which resource you rely on. Next, read the real estate section of the Sunday *Arizona Daily Star* (the Sunday edition is most comprehensive), where rentals are broken down by type and geographic area.

Adobe Property Managers Inc.
4400 E. Broadway Blvd. • 325-6971

This agency provides strictly rentals and property management. The choices include apartments, condos, town houses and single-family homes but not mobile homes. All rentals require a six-month or annual lease and are unfurnished.

Apartment and Home Locators
1101 N. Wilmot Rd. • 296-3222
2400 N. Campbell Ave. • 323-2200
5501 N. Swan Rd. • 615-1000

This service is free to renters and boasts more than 35,000 apartments, condos, and townhomes and houses listed for rent, both furnished and unfurnished and month-to-month or longer term.

Video Apartments Guide
4500 N. Oracle Rd. • 887-7368

This service, located in Tucson Mall, handles about 800 rentals ranging from apartments to guesthouses and homes. Most are on a 12-month lease and most are unfurnished, but some carry shorter terms and come furnished. Many of the properties can be previewed by computer video. The service is free to renters.

Real Estate Companies

While Tucson certainly isn't one of the largest cities in the country, you'd never know that by looking up "real estate agents" in the phone book. The number of listings here probably rivals the Big Apple or the Bay area or L.A. This is a boom town in the desirable Southwest, and nothing signals a boom town more than real estate.

All the major nationwide real estate companies are represented here, and most have multiple offices across the metro area. In addition, there are a couple hundred local realty companies ranging in size from small to huge. Given the geographical size of Tucson and the size of its real estate market, it's almost a necessity to rely on a real estate professional, especially if you haven't zeroed in on a neighborhood you want or are unfamiliar with Tucson's many hidden communities.

Most real estate companies in Tucson, especially the biggies, don't specialize in any particular neighborhood or area, although individual agents within the company may; rather, they claim to be specialists in every area. And with access to the multiple listing service, which lists every property for sale by any realty company, this claim is pretty accurate. Nonetheless, it helps if the real estate agent you select really knows the neighborhood, not just what's for sale there. If you select one of the major companies, you can be assured that at least one of the many agents in one of their many offices will be a specialist in a given neighborhood. The **Tucson Association of Realtors** at 1622 N. Swan Road, 327-4812, can be a resource for inquiring about real estate companies.

The many real estate publications available nearly everywhere (grocery stores, shopping centers, libraries) for free will also help you choose a real estate agent. They often identify agents who specialize, for example in adult and golf communities, in the Catalina Foothills or in the northwest. Another clue to finding an area specialist is the location of the office; for example, the Century 21 office at 7780 North Oracle Road specializes in properties in Oro Valley and northwest Tucson. There's also a company that deals only in helping buyers find a new home in one of Tucson's 150-plus new subdivisions. You can also find real estate companies that specialize in modular or manufactured homes. And nearly every one of the major companies also has listings of lots if your choice is to build.

Century 21
2125 S. Craycroft Rd. • 790-7311
7780 N. Oracle Rd. • 297-8331
2725 N. Campbell Ave. • 881-8110
4641 E. Pima Rd. • 795-7031
7360 E. 22nd St. • 296-7143
8830 E. Speedway Blvd. • 296-5491

Although a national company, each office of Century 21 is independently owned and operated. All of the offices listed are full-service real estate agencies but some have specialties. For example, the S. Craycroft Road location specializes in speaking Spanish, while the office on Speedway Boulevard specializes in residential rentals. As part of the nationwide referral network of Century 21, they all deal with relocations to or from other places in the country. The company also has a rental hotline, 886-6188, listing apartments, condos and homes for rent.

Coldwell Banker Success Realty
5605 E. River Rd. • 577-7433
5340 E. Broadway Blvd. • 745-4545
6970 N. Oracle Rd. • 544-4545

With three offices strategically located around the metro area, this national company provides full-service real estate services to buyers and sellers across Tucson. They also rep-

---

INSIDERS' TIP

Free publications covering places to buy or rent in the metro area are just about everywhere — grocery stores, libraries and shopping centers. Look in the rental booklets — like Apartment Guide and Apartments For Rent — for discount coupons and other offers if you're planning to rent and want to save some bucks.

A string of chiles hangs outside the door of a home in the historic Fort Lowell neighborhood.

resent a number of new home developments and handle relocations nationally for people moving to or from Tucson.

del Oro Realty
8101 N. Thornydale Rd. • 744-1121

This realty company in the northwest is operated by a couple who are both brokers and owners and specialize in the northwest area of the valley. They deal in residential sales, land sales and property management, so they also have a list of rentals available in the northwest.

ERA Realty
6822 E. Sunrise Dr. • 577-4600
5656 E. Grant Rd. • 885-2500
7090 N. Oracle Rd. • 531-2200

The real estate agents in these offices provide residential sales, land sales and relocation assistance to both buyers and sellers. Although the offices are independently owned, they're connected with ERA offices across the country so they can provide electronic access to Tucson housing information from ERA offices anywhere.

Foothills Properties
6262 N. Swan Rd. • 299-2100

Despite the company's name, they don't focus just on the Foothills but cover the entire northern section of the valley. They offer full real estate services and manage about 400 properties in their rental portfolio, primarily houses and town houses ranging from $800 to $5,000 a month.

Long Realty Company
900 E. River Rd. • 888-8844

Tucson's largest realty company has been around since 1926 and is now also the area's exclusive affiliate of Sotheby's International Realty for those who are making an international relocation to or from southern Arizona.

INSIDERS' TIP

While visiting the El Presidio historic district downtown, stop by what has become a neighborhood institution — El Rapido. It's famous for its fast homemade Mexican food, prepared with fresh tortillas. And don't miss the opportunity to chat with owner Tony, reputed to be Tucson's (unofficial) best ambassador.

Locally, Long Realty's 11 offices cover the valley, while two more cover Green Valley and Bisbee. It's not likely you can drive down a residential street in Tucson without seeing a Long Realty sign in front of a house.

New Home Locators
4651 N. 1st Ave. • 292-0446

Unlike traditional real estate companies, this one represents the person interested in buying a new home in one of Tucson's nearly 200 new home subdivisions. The service is free to the buyer but can save a huge amount of time and effort by narrowing down the choices in location, price, amenities and so on while negotiating with the builder.

Northwest Properties
2120 W. Ina Rd. • 544-9927

As its name suggests, this agency specializes in the northwest. They offer full residential real estate services (including the multiple listing service) as well as short- and long-term rentals and property management.

The Prudential Aegis Realty
1760 E. River Rd. • 529-4144

In addition to the local corporate office, this national company also has three other Tucson offices, all independently owned and operated. They offer a full range of real estate services throughout the metro area.

RE/MAX
6377 E. Tanque Verde Rd. • 290-9500
5700 N. Swan Rd. • 577-3999
3450 E. Sunrise Dr. • 297-4545

The offices of this national company are independently owned and operated and all three offer full service real estate, including residential, commercial and relocation assistance through the national network.

Realty Executives of Tucson
2910 N. Swan Rd. • 321-7400

This national company has seven offices around Tucson plus another in Green Valley and is one of the area's major realty companies. The corporate office also has an international relocation services division.

Tucson Realty & Trust Co.
1890 E. River Rd. • 577-7400

This company is Tucson's oldest established real estate firm, having started business in 1911 during the territorial days. Although not the largest in Tucson, they are one of the best-known agencies for handling a huge range of properties, from modest homes to the most exclusive all over Tucson. In addition to the corporate office, the company has offices on the Eastside, northwest and the Foothills. Tucson Realty & Trust also has a relocation service as well as rentals for folks interested in renting a private residence.

Tucson Unified School District was the first public school district established in Arizona, and today it's the second largest in the state.

Education and Child Care

Keeping up with Tucson's growth is probably the biggest challenge the education system faces. Nearly all of the eight school districts serving the metro area are financially strapped and in need of new facilities to serve the growing population. On top of this, Arizona spends less on education than most other states do. As a result, Tucson has a vast number of private and charter schools as alternatives to public education.

Despite underfunding of public education, however, Tucson has some fine public schools and school districts. It also has some of the nation's best private schools and leads the nation in number of charter schools.

For youngsters who are not yet ready for school, Tucson has a vast array of child-care options, from day care operated by religious organizations or private businesses to preschools affiliated with the YMCA or local school districts. We also have nanny and babysitting services as well as excellent resources for finding the child care that's right for you and your child.

Opportunities for higher education in Tucson are almost limitless. Whether you're looking for a degree from a top-notch university, career training or just some courses to improve yourself, you'll find it here. We have the University of Arizona, ranked as one of the top in several fields of study, including anthropology, astronomy, pharmacy and creative writing. We have the nation's fifth-largest multicampus community college. And we have a slew of schools that offer training and degrees in nearly every career imaginable.

Here we provide a general overview of the school districts that serve Tucson as well as some of the private schools and charter schools in the area. You'll also find profiles of colleges, universities and other institutions of higher learning. Finally, we wrap up the chapter with a look at the child-care scene in Tucson.

Public School Districts

Tucson Unified School District
1010 E. 10th St. • 617-7233

Tucson Unified School District (TUSD) was the first public school district established in Arizona, and today it's the second largest in the state, encompassing the most populated part of the metropolitan area. It covers 228 square miles, has 63,000 students enrolled in 73 elementary, 19 middle or junior high and 11 high schools and transports about 15,000 children to school every day. (It's also the third largest employer in Pima County.)

Most of the district's schools operate on a traditional school-year calendar with summers off, but the school year coincides with that of the University of Arizona, so school ends early (by late May) and resumes early (mid-August). Eight of the district's schools, all elementary or middle, are on a year-round schedule with trimesters separated by three intercessions. The district offers all-day kindergarten in more than 50 of its elementary schools.

With about 42 percent of its student population of Hispanic background, TUSD places significant emphasis on bilingual education. The district has more than 700 bilingual teachers and support professionals in 40 elementary, 11 middle and five high schools. Nearly 18,000 kids are in dual English/Spanish instruction programs.

More than 1,600 TUSD students are American Indians, most of whom are Pascua Yaqui or Tohono O'odham. Approximately 1,000 students receive native language enrichment classes in seven district schools. And for the 4,000-plus African-American students, TUSD offers special programs for academic achievement and cultural awareness. Each summer, about 22 percent of the district's students attend summer enrichment classes.

About 6,000 students age 3 to 22, or almost 10 percent of the district enrollment, receive special-education services ranging from special facilities and transportation to physical, instructional and occupational support services. Four schools serve severely disabled students. About 3,500 gifted students in the district have access to self-contained classes (called GATE, for gifted and talented education) at several elementary and middle schools, including bilingual, or have access to itinerant teachers.

But one of the district's most unique and popular features may well be its magnet schools. A handful of schools at each level — elementary, middle and high — have been designated as magnet schools, meaning that they offer a special curriculum that's integrated throughout the school. Examples of these special curricula are math and science, engineering and technology, creative and performing arts, law, international studies, health, and aviation and aerospace. So if your child is a budding astronaut or artist or wants to be an engineer or computer programmer, check out the magnet programs offered by TUSD. If your child is gifted, he or she may want to attend University High, a school specifically for talented children that's located on the campus of Rincon High School.

Unless your child enrolls in a magnet school or needs special services offered at selected schools, he or she will be attending the school nearest to home. The school district operates a welcome center (at the previously listed address) that offers information on school and community resources as well as assessments, counseling and enrollment help.

Amphitheater Public Schools
701 W. Wetmore Rd. • 696-5000

Its first school was a five-room adobe building in 1893. Today the district has 19 schools and is growing by leaps and bounds along with the population of the Oro Valley and Catalina areas of the valley. The 109-square-mile district extends as far south as Grant Road, to the north it reaches the Pima County line, on the west is Shannon Road and east is the national forest of the Catalina Mountains. More than 16,000 students attend two high, one alternative high, one special-education, 12 elementary and three middle schools.

Also within this district is a privately operated extension program called PAL, 888-2727, that offers before- and after-school programs for students in the elementary schools. It's conducted at the elementary school sites, and fees include a registration of $40 plus hourly fees of about $2 depending on the number of hours the child attends. PAL is also available at selected school sites during holiday breaks and the summer.

Amphi is known as one of the best public school districts in the valley. On standardized test scores that compare it with other districts, Amphi students score among the highest. Their high schools also have outstanding athletic programs.

Some of the schools operate on a traditional calendar year that ends in late May and starts in mid-August, while others are on a modified year with a shorter summer vacation and several intercession breaks.

Catalina Foothills School District
2101 E. River Rd. • 299-6446

This school district only had 41 students in 1953 and didn't even build its second school until 1966. But the picture has changed dramatically since then. Its schools, new though they may be, are bursting at the seams. As the population of the foothills has grown, particularly on the eastern end of the district around Sabino Canyon and Ventana Canyon, the school populations have skyrocketed. This district traditionally has boasted an average class size that's the lowest in the state (about 24), but that record is under stress.

> **FYI**
> Unless otherwise noted, the area code for all phone numbers listed in this guide is 520.

Bounded roughly by the mountains to the north, Camino Seco to the east, Snyder Road to the south and 1st Avenue on the west, Catalina Foothills School District (CFSD), also commonly known as District 16, now has one high, four elementary, two middle schools and one preschool. Bus transportation is provided for most students.

CFSD's schools emphasize academics and the arts and have strict discipline policies. Students score in the top 4 percent of the nation and are among the highest in the state on standardized tests. The average CFSD student reads and computes one full year above grade level. Every new student takes reading and math placement tests.

The district operates several educational extension programs including GED, as well as an intergenerational orchestra — The Foothills Phil — open to all interested musicians. Its CARE program, based at each elementary school, is open to enrolled elementary students for before- and after-school enrichment and is especially valuable to families with both parents working. Its fee-based preschool can accommodate up to 16 three- and four-year-olds during morning or afternoon sessions.

Like most of the valley school districts, school starts in mid-August and ends in late May. The district offices (at the previously mentioned address) formerly housed its first school designed by famous local architect Joseph Joesler.

Flowing Wells School District
1556 W. Prince Rd. • 690-2200

Surrounded by the Amphitheater, Tucson and Marana School districts, Flowing Wells is geographically much smaller than the others. It covers 13 square miles between Grant and Ina roads and the Santa Cruz and Rillito rivers on Tucson's fast-growing northwest side. It has six elementary schools, one junior high and one high school, plus two alternative schools for kids who can't adjust or perform in a regular school setting.

About 6,000 kids are in the district, and buses transport all kindergarten students plus others who live more than a designated distance from their school (1 mile for elementary, 1.5 miles for junior and 2 miles for high school). Students have access to a comprehensive special-education program plus Army Junior ROTC, a center for academically talented students, summer school and after-school activity programs. Innovative curriculum offerings include vocational agriculture, fine arts, anthropology and environmental education. All the elementary schools offer an on-site daycare program, and Hendricks Elementary has an at-risk preschool.

At Flowing Wells High School the district operates a resource and wellness center to assist teens and their families with health, social and educational services. They provide pregnancy and teen-parent counseling, referrals to community services and medical care, and emergency food boxes.

The district has a good reputation for academics, and many of its schools have won state and national awards over the years. All schools are on the traditional school-year calendar, beginning in mid-August and concluding in late May.

Marana School District
11279 W. Grier Rd. • 682-3243

Geographically this school district covers a large area of the west and northwest valley — 550 square miles — but much of it is sparsely populated. It extends east from Shannon Road and the Tucson Mountains, north to the county line and south to where the Tucson Mountains end. It encompasses the town of Marana, the rapidly growing northwest residential areas along I-10 and west of downtown as well as the largely desert areas west and north of the Tucson Mountains. Marana's enrollment has more than doubled since 1984.

Approximately 11,000 students attend nine elementary, one intermediate, two junior high and two high schools, and 90 percent travel to school daily by bus (the district buses log 10,500 miles each day). The student achievement scores are typically well above county, state and national norms. The district has innovative programs in math, reading, spelling and written expression plus special-education, gifted-education and Indian-education programs. After-school tutoring is available at all secondary and most elementary schools, and high schools have a strong athletic program.

With about 16 percent of its enrollment Hispanic, most schools offer English as a second language. Marana also offers a preschool program for handicapped children ages 3 to 5. The district offices (see the previously listed address) are west of Exit 236 off I-10. The school year runs from mid-August to late May.

Sunnyside School District
2238 E. Ginter Rd. • 741-2500

This district covers 93 square miles in the south part of Tucson, including 2 miles of the Tohono O'odham Indian Reservation. More than 14,500 students attend 12 elementary, three middle and two high schools, plus one alternative school for grades 9 through 12. It's the third largest district in the county, and the 10th poorest one in the state. And like most districts in the booming Tucson area, its schools are overcrowded.

Despite the strains, it operates many good educational and enrichment programs. They include all-day kindergarten, bilingual education, Indian education, special education, a gifted and talented program and middle school intramural athletics. One of its elementary schools is not a neighborhood school but instead accepts students who want a more challenging and stringent educational environment (on a first-come basis). The district also has dropout prevention, a teenage parent program and health services that include immunization clinics in every school during October. In recent years, the graduation rate has increased and the dropout rate has decreased in the district. English as a second language and GED programs are available for adults.

Other unique offerings include a program for at-risk three- and four-year-olds and their parents and a preschool prevention program for minimal cost that includes child care and before- and after-school programs. District headquarters (at the previously listed address) is north of Valencia Road and west of Tucson Boulevard. The school year runs from mid-August to late May.

Tanque Verde School District
4201 N. Melpomene Wy. • 749-5751

Even though its first school opened more than 100 years ago, the schools in this small district on Tucson's far Eastside are relatively new, since this area was remote and largely unpopulated until the 1970s. Today 1,600 kids attend one junior high and two elementary schools in the district; the 400 high-school-age kids in the district are bussed to TUSD schools, although the district plans to build its own high school. Tanque Verde (which means "green tank") pays for the tuition and the transportation to a selected high school; otherwise, parents must provide transportation.

Tanque Verde has the reputation of one of the best districts in the area. Academically, students score above the norms, and the tax base for school funding enables small class sizes and top-notch instructional resources. Its boundaries encompass the upscale neighborhoods east of Sabino Canyon, the 49ers Country Club and the Reddington Pass and Old Spanish Trail areas.

The curriculum includes all the basics plus Spanish, fine arts, computers, band and chorus. Special education, gifted education, remedial reading and speech and language therapy are offered as needed. District offices are off Catalina Highway east of Houghton Road. Students attend classes from mid-August to late May.

Vail School District
13299 E. Colossal Cave Rd. • 762-5985

Situated in the far southeast and extending east from Wilmot Road and south from Irvington

---

INSIDERS' TIP

Each year, *The Arizona Daily Star* publishes an annual survey of private schools in Tucson. It offers good at-a-glance information, including tuition, so call the newspaper, 573-4400, for the latest survey or check the library. The newspaper publishes a similar profile of charter schools.

The A+ School Program honors schools for academic excellence. The State of Arizona only awards 10 per year.

Road, Vail School District covers a sparsely populated area but one that has seen a 126 percent increase in housing parcels in the past four years. Its eastern boundary is the Rincon Mountains and to the south it reaches the Santa Rita Mountains. It encompasses the Rita Ranch area as well as Corona de Tucson.

The district has one middle and two elementary schools with about 1,800 students. High school students either attend a charter school (described later in this chapter) or travel to a neighboring district. Because of a shortage of classroom space and a desire to keep class sizes small, the district operates on a multitrack calendar, utilizing the school space year round. Each of the four tracks have three trimesters, three of which start in July and one in August. The district plans to add a third elementary school and wants to add an additional school at each level (elementary, middle and high).

Private Schools

In addition to the 180 schools among the eight public school districts covered here, Tucson has more than 40 private schools, some of which have a religious affiliation, with tuition ranging from just less than $1,000 to $18,000 a year. So if your neighborhood public school doesn't suit your needs, there's a vast array of private schools to choose from. Some are considered among the top in the nation. Below we provide a brief profile of a few of the more prominent and popular ones.

Unless otherwise noted, all the schools listed here operate on the same school calendar (mid-August to late May) as most Tucson schools and offer some type of financial assistance.

Casas Adobes Baptist School
2131 W. Ina Rd. • 297-0922

Started in 1970, Casas Adobes is a Christian school that incorporates Bible study and prayer into the curriculum. Its academics emphasize problem solving, critical thinking and research skills. Reading takes a strong phonetic approach and grammar skills begin in grade 1. The school also has Spanish, music, art and computer learning. About 350 students attend in grades kindergarten through 8 with a class size of about 20.

Fenster School
8500 E. Ocotillo Dr. • 749-3340

It's by far the most costly private school in Tucson and has a reputation that matches. Located near Sabino Canyon on Tucson's Eastside, Fenster is a year-round coed college preparatory school with both boarding and day programs. Its 125 students in grades 9 through 12 represent a diverse population from all over the world. The student-to-faculty ratio is 8 to 1, and the school accepts underachievers as well as gifted students. Fenster offers sports including volleyball, baseball, basketball and soccer and has an outstanding equestrian program on site.

Green Fields Country Day School
6000 N. Camino de la Tierra • 297-2288

Founded in 1933 as a residential ranch school for boys, Green Fields is Arizona's oldest independent day school and today has a coed junior division for grades 4 to 7 and a coed high school (or senior division) for grades 8 through 12. Its 21-acre campus includes an extensive library, modern science labs, a computer lab, tennis, swimming and ball fields and a center for the performing arts that seats 300. Kids here can learn desktop publishing, pottery, print-making, drama and darkroom photography along with algebra, calculus, journalism, Spanish and French. They can participate in several interscholastic sports or intramural tennis. It's an outstanding school with about 220 students and a class size of about 21.

Kino School
6625 N. 1st Ave. • 297-7278

Located on 10 acres just north of the city limits, Kino is an independent coed school for grades kindergarten through 12 and has an early childhood program for three- and four-year-olds, all with waiting lists. Preschoolers learn language arts, environmental responsibilities, social and motor skills and self-expression. Older kids learn to think critically and creatively, be self-directed and take responsibility for their community. Kino considers the world to be a classroom and regularly exposes students to the environment and the arts through local and extended field trips. Students are involved in setting their own goals and evaluating their progress. Enrollment numbers about 100 with a ratio of one teacher to eight students. At present, no financial aid is available.

Salpointe Catholic High School
1545 E. Copper St. • 327-6581

This coed school for grades 9 through 12 has about 1,400 students representing a broad socioeconomic mix, about 22 percent of whom are not Catholic. This excellent college preparatory school requires courses in English, foreign language, math, theology, science and social studies as well as volunteerism. Electives include the fine arts, humanities, physical education and practical arts. Class size is about 22, and 98 percent of Salpointe graduates go directly to college, many on grants and scholarships. More than half the students participate in interscholastic sports including baseball, basketball, cross-country, football, golf, soccer, tennis, volleyball and swimming. Parish families get discounts on tuition.

Satori School
3801 N. 1st Ave. • 887-4003

Satori, a Japanese word describing the pursuit of learning, offers a preschool and elementary school for gifted children age 2½ through 5th grade. The self-directed curriculum, which includes math, art, dance and movement, drama, humanities, foreign language and computers and science, is designed to challenge the intellectual, emotional, behavioral and social needs of these children. Enrollment is about 150 with an average class size of six to 10. The school also offers summer camps for children ages 3 through 5th grade with science exploration, hands-on learning and field trips.

St. Gregory College Preparatory
3231 N. Craycroft Rd. • 327-6395

This is a nonsectarian coed day school for grades 6 through 12 located along the bank of the Rillito River near the Ft. Lowell historic area. The campus includes an indoor sports building that seats 400 or converts to a 250-seat theater, a 7,000-volume library with computer labs and a darkroom, and outdoor athletic facilities. Nearly all courses offered at the school are advanced placement or honors. In the sophomore year, students begin a college-planning program and, in their junior and senior years, meet with up to 100 college representatives during the school's annual college day. Students are encouraged to volunteer or take internships in the community. During summer, the school has enrichment programs of two to six weeks, some of which include studies in Mexico or Europe. Enrollment is 380, and class size is about 18. About 20 percent of the students receive financial assistance.

Tucson Hebrew Academy
3888 E. River Rd. • 529-3888

Located adjacent to the Jewish Community Center, the day school for grades 1 to 8 is a new and modern building facing the Santa Catalina foothills. It includes an auditorium for dining and theater events, a library, outdoor courtyard and state-of-the art classrooms with science, computer and art labs, and students have access to all the facilities at the community center. The general academic curriculum is integrated within a Judaic framework to provide both a secular and religious education. Enrollment averages about 170 with a class size of nine. The Academy also operates a preschool during the regular school year that includes early morning and late afternoon hours.

Turning Point School
2200 N. Dodge Blvd. • 326-3300

Turning Point is the only private day school specifically for learning disabled children in grades 1 to 8. It accommodates 80 students. The school accepts students who have reading, writing or spelling difficulties, are average or above in intelligence and have no behavior problems. Students receive the full range of academics along with special education in their particular learning disability. The school also offers a morning summer program during the month of June. It usually has a waiting list.

Charter Schools

In 1994, Arizona's legislature passed one of the nation's most lenient charter laws, and the state now leads the nation in the number of charter schools. These are "alternative" schools that are allowed to operate without the rigid education requirements attached to public schools except regarding health, safety, civil rights, special education, insurance and student assessment testing. Essentially, they are public schools under contract — or charter — from a public agency to a group of parents, teachers, a business or others who want to create alternatives and choice in education. Charters may be granted by the state or by individual school districts. The charter school then receives a per-student allocation (equivalent to the district's average cost per pupil) for each student enrolled plus some state monies allocated for capital needs. Typically, charter schools generate controversy (whether they should even exist as an alternative to public education), operate on minimal budgets and have not had their academic results tested over the long run.

During the 1996-97 school year, Tucson had nine charter schools with about 1,300 students and more opening each year. One such school is **Children's Academy**, 1346 N. Stone Avenue, 620-1100, which has a nontraditional curriculum with no grades that places students by skill level rather than by age. The student-to-staff ratio is 11 to 1. Like most money-strapped charter schools, it operates out of a nonschool building (a former government building) with used furniture. Another is **Khalsa Montessori Elementary School**, 3244 E. Camden Street, 325-3870, geared to parents who want a Montessori education for their kids without the private-school price tag. The Montessori philosophy holds that teachers need to give children the tools, environment and nurturing in which they can learn and grow.

Another is **Calli Ollin High School** (meaning "house of movement" in the Aztec language), where about 50 students who fail to fit in at traditional schools have a self-paced curriculum. It's operated by Chicanos por la Causa at 1525 N. Oracle Road, 882-3029. **Tucson Urban League** also operates a charter high school that's specifically for kids who are at risk of dropping out of a traditional school and never graduating. They also operate one middle and two elementary schools that are more traditional. The offices and two of the schools are at 2323 S. Park Avenue, 622-3651.

For more information on charter schools in Tucson, contact the Pima County Superintendent at 740-8451.

Higher Education

University of Arizona
University Blvd. and Park Ave.
• 621-2211

Although designated by the territorial legislature in 1885 (before Arizona was a state), the school existed only on paper until a saloon owner and two gamblers donated 40 acres. It opened in 1891 in its first building,

Old Main, with 32 students in agriculture and mining. Today it's one of the top-20 research universities in the country with an enrollment of 35,000-plus and covering 347 acres. It offers degrees in 131 undergraduate, 137 masters, 95 doctoral, three professional and five specialist programs. It boasts University Medical Center, a leading research and teaching hospital.

The University is first in the country in astronomy, optical sciences and applied mathematics. It's ranked in the top 10 in anthropology, East Asian studies, ecology and evolutionary biology, higher education, hydrology, linguistics, MIS, nursing, pharmacy, philosophy, planetary science, respiratory science, speech and hearing, radiology and sociology. It has 14 colleges, ranging from agriculture and architecture to medicine and law, and eight schools ranging from music and dance to public administration. A number of degrees can be obtained through the university's evening and weekend program.

The school year consists of two semesters, from August to December and January to May, with two five-week summer sessions available.

UA also has an Extended University that offers regular university credit courses off campus, noncredit courses and workshops both on and off campus, and high school and university correspondence courses. Call 621-8632 for details. The University's library system, which is also available to the public, contains an amazing seven million items, including three million books. In addition to the main library, at 4th Street and Cherry Avenue, there are separate science and engineering, music and medical libraries, the latter located at University Medical Center.

The University's athletic accomplishments rival its academic ones. It has 18 varsity sports teams, eight of which have placed in the top 15 nationally. Wildcats hold the PAC10 titles in basketball, baseball, women's softball, cross-country and women's golf and the NCAA championship for 1997 in men's basketball and women's softball — and this is just a partial list. The school is ranked in the top 10 overall in athletic program ratings.

And if it weren't for the University, Tucson's cultural and educational community would face a serious void. The school houses the Museum of Art with one of the best collections of Renaissance art in the Southwest. Centennial Hall, a major venue for performances in Tucson, is part of the University, as is the Arizona State Museum. Flandrau Science Center and Planetarium and its mineral museum are available to Tucsonans compliments of the University. UA also houses the Poetry Center and the Center for Creative Photography.

The University's benefits to the community go far beyond its cultural offerings. The Cooperative Extension, which has offices in every county in Arizona, assists farmers and supports natural resources statewide. UA operates southern Arizona's Public Broadcasting Station (KUAT) as well as one AM and two FM radio stations. For kids, UA's Extended University offers a variety of enrichment programs including SEEK (Summer Education and Enrichment for Kids) Saturdays for ages 5 and up and their parents, Science Saturdays for grades kindergarten through 5, and Spanish for four- and five-year-olds. The Extended University also has a Writing Works Center for Tucson writers and operates an Elderhostel.

It's highly unlikely that you can visit Tucson, and it's for sure you can't live here, without somehow being touched by the University. Maybe you'll use the University's library, attend performances at Centennial Hall or visit a museum. Perhaps you'll get medical care at UMC or one of several University Physician clinics around Tucson. Or you might visit the Campus Community Services Center (at the corner of Cherry Avenue and University Boulevard) for publications on the University. Maybe you'll take the kids to Spring Fling, a carnival on the mall featuring rides, eats and other fun. And most likely, you'll be watching the Wildcats compete in football, basketball and many other sports at McKale Center, Arizona Stadium or Frank Sancet Field.

Whether you're a prospective student, a visitor or a resident of Tucson, you'll want to take advantage of the Campus Community Service Center, 621-5130, which has an abundance of information. It offers a 1½-hour walking tour on Thursday and Saturday mornings September through May led by UA alumni docents and a monthly bus tour with wheelchair accessibility.

The 15-mile-per-hour school zone is strictly enforced.

Whatever reason you may be on campus, remember that pedestrians always have the right of way and finding parking can be difficult, especially for events. Inquire about the daily visitor parking permit ($3) sold at the Center.

Pima Community College
2202 W. Anklam Rd. • 206-6640

Since it opened in 1970, more than 400,000 students have enrolled at Pima, which today is the nation's fifth-largest multicampus community college. Its main campus is in the west on Anklam Road, but the college has four other campus locations scattered around Tucson and utilizes another 70 sites throughout the community for classes. Pima offers five associate degrees in more than 60 fields of study plus university transfer programs, career-oriented certificates and a multitude of noncredit classes. Degrees and certificates in health professions and hospitality and tourism are among the most popular. So whether you're a serious student looking for a degree and a career or a Pima County resident who simply wants to learn photography or dancing, PCC probably has a program to suit your needs.

Pima has three precollege programs, including one specifically for American-Indian students, where high schoolers can take classes at Pima. The college also makes special accommodations for disabled students and students who speak primarily Spanish. Tutoring, career counseling and job placement services are available as well.

Pima's full-semester courses cover 16 weeks with semesters beginning in August and January. Three summer sessions as well as some flexible-schedule classes throughout the year are available. Financial aid may be available in the form of scholarships, loans, grants and part-time employment. Free parking is available at all campuses, and most have cafeterias that are open all day during the week.

Extracurricular activities include a student

newspaper, literary magazines, student chorale, jazz band and music ensembles and student drama productions. Pima also offers more than 35 intramural and Junior College intercollegiate athletic program in sports such as baseball, golf, volleyball, softball, basketball, track, soccer and tennis. There's also club sports including wrestling, ice hockey and volleyball. The sports programs are primarily housed at the main west campus.

In truth, it would take an entire book to describe all that Pima offers (Pima's list of important telephone numbers is 12 pages long alone). In addition to the programs already mentioned, Pima offers college success courses for those wanting to improve their college experience, free workshops on subjects ranging from calculators to taking tests to career planning, career days that are open to the public, as well as customized educational services for businesses — to name a few. The college's west campus also houses the Proscenium Theater where performances by students and national troupes are offered throughout the year.

Other Colleges and Technical Schools

Tucson has a number of smaller colleges and specialty schools that offer degrees or career training. The **University of Phoenix**, 5099 E. Grant Road, 881-6512, is where working people can get an undergraduate or graduate degree by going to class evenings and weekends. They have degree programs in business, education and nursing plus nondegree graduate courses for school educators and administrators. **Tucson Open University**, 2030 E. Broadway Boulevard, 622-0170, is another school with evening classes, but its focus is on self-improvement, with offerings such as arts and crafts, languages, computers and wellness.

Prescott College at Tucson, 283 S. Scott Avenue, 622-8334, offers an adult-degree program where students of any age can earn a bachelor's degree in a unique individualized program that combines tutorial and traditional independent study. Areas of study include teacher education/certification, management, human services, psychology, counseling and environmental studies.

Chaparral College, 4585 E. Speedway Boulevard, 327-6866, emphasizes business and offers a bachelor's degree in business administration as well as several associate-degree (70 weeks) and career-training (30 and 50 weeks) programs. Tracks of study include accounting, computers, legal assistant, medical administration and travel and airline management. Students have a choice of day or evening classes, and financial aid is available.

Apollo College, 3870 N. Oracle Road, 888-5885, has diploma programs for medical and dental assistants, computerized office secretaries and pharmacy technicians as well as associate-degree programs for several health-related technicians. For a school that specializes in health fields, contact **Pima Medical Institute**, 3350 E. Grant Road, 326-1600. It has associate degrees in a number of health fields and career training in numerous medical, dental and veterinary assistant positions.

Two other schools that offer career training in business and technical fields are **ITT Technical Institute**, 1840 E. Benson Highway, 294-2944, and **Arizona Institute of Business and Technology**, 1844 S. Alvernon Way, 748-9799. The former offers associate and bachelor degree programs in fields such as electronics engineering and drafting. The latter offers medical, computer, banking, business, corrections, criminal justice, accounting and word processing training programs.

Both **Parks College**, 6992 E. Broadway Boulevard, 886-2295, and the **Institute of**

> **FYI**
> Unless otherwise noted, the area code for all phone numbers listed in this guide is 520.

INSIDERS' TIP

State law requires proof of immunization before any child can enroll in a school. Many post-secondary schools require it as well.

Word Processing, 40 N. Swan Road, 325-3050, provide career training in office skills such as word processing, computer software, legal secretarial, court reporting and transcription. Parks, an accredited business college, also has programs in hotel and restaurant management and business management.

For people pursuing a career in art, **The Art Center** at 2525 N. Country Club Drive, 325-0123, is a design college offering associate degrees and training in advertising art, desktop publishing and computer graphic design.

And if the food and beverage industry strikes your fancy, you can attend the **American Bartenders School**, 1058 North Campbell Avenue, 327-7332, during the day or evening and then have access to its nationwide job placement service. Or perhaps you want to become a professional chef and hone your skills at **Culinary Concepts**, 2930 N. Swan Road, 321-0968, which is located in Plaza Palomino.

Child Care

Tucson is a boom town and, like most comparable metropolitan areas, there is a significant demand for child care because of single-parent families and households with both parents working. Schools, churches, nonprofit organizations and private businesses all help meet this demand with a variety of day-care and pre-school programs. While there are too many to list here, we describe some of the options available to parents and resources for tracking down others. Average costs for child care range from $60 to $125 a week for full-time centers and $150 to $250 per week for full-time nannies.

When looking for child care, keep in mind that most school districts have before- and after-school programs either right at the school site or through nearby YMCAs. All YMCAs also operate day-care and after-school programs. Kids Forever Child Care Centers operates six locations around Tucson for infants through age 4. Another private enterprise is Discovery Learning Center with an east and northwest location. KIDCO, funded by the city's Parks and Recreation Department, offers a summer program at 37 schools for kids 5 to 12. It's a model program and free, so parents line up for hours just to get their kids enrolled. KIDCO also has an after-school program at schools citywide that's free for students enrolled in kindergarten through 6th grade.

Childcare Resource and Referral, 1010 N. Alvernon Way, 325-5778, provides information on child care, sitters, preschools and how to search for quality care. At local libraries and many stores catering to kids, you'll find the **Childcare Seekers Directory**, a free publication to help you get started. And each year, *Inside Tucson Business* publishes a list of the largest 20 child-care providers in the metro area. If you're a parent attending or affiliated with the University of Arizona, the college operates an **Office of Child Care Initiatives**, 621-5844, that helps select and evaluate all types of child-care options, including nannies and sitters. They also prepare a child-care guide, included as part of the University's annual Apartment Renters Handbook, which anyone will find very useful.

If you're a Tucson visitor or new in town and need a babysitter **A-1 Messner Sitter Service**, 881-1578, provides experienced adult sitters for four-hour minimums plus transportation costs. Expect to pay about $7 an hour, but more for more than one child or an infant. Sitters will come to your house or hotel. And any parent — resident or visitor — can get in a bind when a child becomes ill, so the **Tucson Association for Child Care**, a nonprofit agency, operates a sick child program, 795-2433, that provides quality on-call in-home care for ill children from birth through high school. Its fees are on a sliding scale, and all caregivers are carefully screened, trained and certified in skills such as CPR, first aid and healthcare.

You Deserve the Best!

When it comes to your health, only the finest hospital and physicians will do. University Medical Center and The University Physicians are consistently named among the nation's best in health care. Here are a few of our recognitions:

America's Best Hospitals, *U.S. News & World Report,* June 1997
The Best Doctors in America: Pacific Region, *Woodward/White, Inc.,* '96 -'97
The Country's Best Heart Doctors, *Good Housekeeping,* March 1996

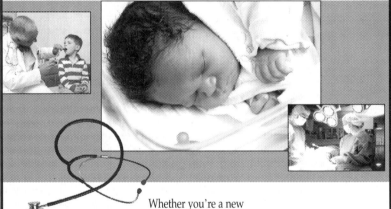

Whether you're a new resident in town or just visiting, you can choose us for your care. Call us to find out how easy it is.

We'd like to get to know you.

Information ▾ Appointments ▾ Referrals

The University
PHYSICIANS
University Medical Center

694-8888, ext. 10
All the Health Care You'll Ever Need.
Visit our web site at http://www.azumc.com

Healthcare

Forget the Hollywood Wild-West image of a cowtown with horse doctors serving the locals between ranch visits. Tucson is home to many top-shelf facilities in traditional medicine as well as the national headquarters of the Muscular Dystrophy Association. It is also quickly becoming a leader in alternative therapies. In fact, the city has become a mecca for wellness programs and health resorts. Most of the area hospitals devote a large part of their efforts to keeping seniors healthy, offering a variety of free classes and seminars that focus on health education and prevention programs.

Healthcare in Tucson officially began in 1880 when St. Mary's was established as the first hospital in the Arizona Territory. That same year, the Sisters of St. Joseph of Carondelet began their work to provide healthcare to the settlers of the area. Today, both hospitals are part of the Carondelet Health Care System, a nationwide network of hospitals.

During the 1920s, advertisements in East Coast newspapers promoted the dry climate and emerging health resorts, including DesertSan, a tuberculosis sanitarium (later to become Tucson Medical Center, southern Arizona's largest hospital), as cures for whatever ailed you.

Today, Tucson claims 11 major hospitals, a number of clinics with their own specialties, the only dedicated regional burn center in the area (St. Mary's Hospital), and the state's only hospital-based certified diabetes care center (St. Joseph's Hospital). Tucson has actually been criticized for having 1,000 more hospital beds and twice as many open-heart programs as a city this size needs, but you probably won't hear residents complaining. Tucson Medical Center and University Medical Center serve as the city's two trauma centers. And the Tucson Fire Department is currently training its staff to increase the number and quality of medical services that can be provided at the scene of an accident.

At University Medical Center, the teaching hospital for the University of Arizona, Dr. Andrew Weil, one of the world's best-known doctors and authors, is a leader in the wellness movement and director of UMC's new Integrative Medicine Center. Many HMOs in Arizona are providing funding for such alternative therapies, a sign that alternative medical approaches have reached the mainstream.

And rounding out the healthcare scene is an entrenched group of alternative wellness providers, health spas, fitness clubs and health-food stores ready to keep you healthy. We offer here the major players, as well as some phone numbers you'll want to keep handy during your stay in the Old Pueblo.

Hospitals

Carondelet St. Joseph's Hospital
350 N. Wilmot Rd. • 296-3211

St. Joseph's offers a number of inpatient, outpatient and home-care services, including care for cardiac and orthopedic patients as well as those with brain injuries. This 285-bed nonprofit facility on the Eastside has southern Arizona's only Regional Eye Center, the state's only hospital-based diabetes care center, an obstetrics unit and an emergency room. Laser surgery for improving eyesight and removing tattoos is available. The hospital is known for its magnetic resonance expertise and its hospital-based outpatient treatment facility for chemical dependence and detoxification, Carondelet Behavioral Health.

Carondelet St. Mary's Hospital
1601 W. St. Mary's Rd. • 622-5833

St. Mary's, the state's oldest hospital, is just west of downtown. The 394-bed nonprofit facility has comprehensive inpatient, outpatient and home-care medical services, including dialysis, occupational health and pediatrics. Other specialties include orthopedic surgery and sports medicine. St. Mary's is also home to Arizona's only dedicated burn unit and Tucson's busiest emergency room, which has a base for lifeline emergency response helicopters.

Columbia El Dorado Hospital
1400 N. Wilmot Rd. • 886-6361

Located on the Eastside, this 166-bed hospital is one of two Tucson hospitals operated by the Columbia Healthcare Corporation (Columbia Northwest Medical Center is the other). It offers full medical and surgical services, 24-hour emergency care and health seminars and classes. In addition to a center for pain management and home-care services, El Dorado operates a unit specializing in geriatric medical/psychiatric care.

Columbia Northwest Medical Center
6200 N. La Cholla Blvd. • 742-9000

A small 162-bed hospital in the valley's northwest, Columbia Northwest offers 24-hour emergency service and features birthing suites, cardiopulmonary services and radiation oncology facilities. It also hosts many free wellness and health classes for the local community, particularly for seniors.

Kino Community Hospital
2800 E. Ajo Wy. • 294-4471

A county-run hospital, Kino provides medical, surgical and emergency services, including pediatrics, obstetrics and gynecology, to the south-side community. The 196-bed facility has 700 full-time employees and offers a number of outpatient clinics, psychiatric services and professional social workers to counsel patients on personal and family issues related to their illness. It operates adult medicine, pediatric and dental clinics.

Tucson General Hospital
3838 N. Campbell Ave. • 318-6300

Known for its Westcenter, which specializes in addiction treatment, this 106-bed osteopathic hospital is centrally located. More than 250 physicians in 39 specialties practice at Tucson General. While the hospital is well-known for its family maternity center, other special services include health screenings, home health and mental health services targeting seniors. It also has an emergency room. A Bloodless Medicine Program is available at Tucson General for adult patients who do not wish to receive blood transfusions for religious or personal health reasons.

(For information about Westcenter, see "Mental and Behavioral Health" in this chapter.)

> **FYI**
> Unless otherwise noted, the area code for all phone numbers listed in this guide is 520.

Tucson Heart Hospital
4888 N. Stone Ave.
• 696-BEAT

Opened on October 1, 1997, this 60-bed facility has the single mission of providing highly specialized cardiology and cardiovascular services. The for-profit hospital offers a total heart-care environment for cardiac patients, ranging from prevention and wellness through surgery and rehabilitation, all with the latest technology. The emergency department is ready to treat not only acute coronary conditions, but also any emergency. To promote fitness, the hospital hosts the Walking Connection, which offers organized activities for people who wish to walk for health.

Tucson Medical Center
5301 E. Grant Rd. • 327-5461

Founded as a tuberculosis sanitarium in 1927, the facility was donated to the city in the 1940s to be run as a community hospital. Today it's a full-service facility spreading over 40 acres that offers maternal and child care as well as neuroscience, orthopedic, diagnostic and emergency services. TMC is considered to be a leader in the field of laser technology. This is one of Tucson's two trauma centers (UMC is the other). With 1,200 physicians on the medical staff and 620 beds, it's southern Arizona's largest hospital. The consumer health library at the Health Resources Center, which is available to the public for free, provides current medical and health information in the form of text, video and on-screen formats.

HEALTHCARE • 299

The VA Medical Center serves the needs of the large population of veterans in Tucson.

University Medical Center
University of Arizona, 1501 N. Campbell Ave. • 694-8888, ext.10

Part of the University of Arizona's medical school, this 365-bed hospital ranks among the top-five hospitals in the country for overall surgical survival rates according to a June 1997 report in *U.S. News & World Report*. *The Best Doctors in America: Pacific Region*, published in 1996, named 119 University physicians as the best in their fields. Five University physicians (out of seven from Arizona) were named as most expert in their fields in a report in the March 1996 issue of *Good Housekeeping*. The facility is one of the leading hospitals for corneal and liver transplants and is known for its open-heart surgery. World-renowned heart specialist Dr. Jack Copland is based here, as is Dr. Andrew Weil, integrative medicine guru. The cancer center is recognized nationwide for research and treatment. UMC is also one of only two trauma centers in the city.

As the primary teaching hospital for the University of Arizona College of Medicine, UMC is affiliated with several research projects including the Arizona Cancer Center, University Heart Center, Arizona Arthritis Center, Arizona Emergency Medicine Research Center, Respiratory Sciences Center and Arizona Aging Center.

INSIDERS' TIP

When you visit the alternative centers, health food stores and even some supermarkets, look for Tucson's local and statewide publications that deal with health issues. For a list of health-related publications, see the Media chapter.

Veterans Affairs Medical Center
3601 S. 6th Ave. • 792-1450

A 225-bed plus 120-bed nursing home facility, the medical center offers comprehensive inpatient and outpatient treatment in all specialties for area veterans. The VA hospital is known locally for its American Indian Veteran Program, which offers an American Indian traditional counselor to assist in addressing the spirit-body-mind balance. Other services include geriatric extended care, women's health programs, diagnostics with state-of-the-art imaging and a cardiology center. There is also a major outpatient psychiatric care center. The hospital's program for the visually impaired teaches mobility and manual and living skills as well as assists with housing, meals and equipment.

See this and many other Insiders' Guide® destinations online — in their entirety.

Visit us today!

Mental and Behavioral Health

Arizona's Children Association Center for Family Therapy
2820 S. 8th Ave. • 323-3877

As the name implies, this center addresses a variety of disorders in children and youth, including behavioral problems and drug addiction. Family treatment is conducted in the patient's home, or individuals can participate in group therapy at the center. The nonprofit center's staff includes psychologists and counselors.

CODAC Behavioral Health Services
333 W. Ft. Lowell Rd. • 327-4505

Well-known in Pima County since 1970, CODAC offers comprehensive drug, alcohol and mental health treatment services on an outpatient basis or as in-home support services. One program specializes in pregnant and postpartum women, their infants and young children.

The diversity of the nonprofit center's staff — case managers, counselors, nurses, psychiatrists and child care specialists — brings a well-rounded approach to treatment.

Cottonwood de Tucson
4110 W. Sweetwater Dr. • 743-0411

Cottonwood is a residential center with 59 beds for adults, 10 beds for adolescents and 5 detox rooms. The facility specializes in the treatment of alcohol and chemical dependency, family dysfunction, trauma, sexual abuses and behavioral problems. The center is staffed by psychiatrists, psychologists, counselors and therapists. Cottownwood also provides outpatient care through a center of the same name at 4742 N. Oracle Road, Suite 111.

Desert Hills Center for Youth and Families
2797 N. Introspect Dr. • 622-5437

At Desert Hills, children and adolescents with behavioral, emotional, mental, attention deficit or chemical dependency disorders can be treated in residential or day programs. An on-site school combines education and treatment for youth in these programs. Desert Hills also provides evaluations and emergency hospitalization for acute cases. Outpatient services are offered for youth and families.

La Frontera Center
502 W. 29th St. • 884-9920

The largest nonprofit community mental health provider in the state, La Frontera offers many services both at its main facility

---

INSIDERS' TIP

The Tucson Convention Center at 260 S. Church Street, 791-4266, hosts an average of 15 major events a month, and some of them are fairs specifically geared toward the health of women and seniors, alternative medicine or fitness equipment.

and at satellite facilities. La Frontera treats mental health and chemical dependency disorders in children, adolescents and adults, while its services for the seriously (or chronically) mentally ill include psychosocial and vocational rehabilitation and inpatient acute care. Most programs are outpatient, but it also operates a small hospital for the seriously mentally ill, a residential chemical dependency facility for adults and some in-home support services. Through its Child and Family Center, La Frontera has a preschool for developmentally disabled children, day treatment for adolescents and a therapeutic nursery program for infants at-risk due to prenatal substance abuse. La Frontera can accommodate Spanish-speaking patients.

Palo Verde Mental Health Services
2695 N. Craycroft Rd. • 324-4340

Palo Verde is a division of Tucson Medical Center and is adjacent to it. This psychiatric hospital treats youth, adults, seniors and families through inpatient or outpatient care for substance abuse, eating disorders, depression, anxiety and other psychiatric problems. Diagnostic evaluations and crisis care are available 24 hours.

Westcenter
2105 E. Allen Rd. • 795-0952

Affiliated with Tucson General Hospital and adjacent to it, Westcenter offers comprehensive treatment and recovery programs to adolescents, adults and seniors through inpatient, partial hospitalization and outpatient programs for behavioral health and substance abuse. It's substance abuse services are 12-step based and include detoxification, supervised interventions and codependency counseling. Westcenter also treats gambling addiction.

Rehabilitation

Direct Center for Independence, Inc.
1023 N. Tyndall Ave. • 624-6452 (voice/TDD)

Direct Center for Independence was the first agency in Arizona to find independent living arrangements for people with disabilities

The First of Its Kind

On August 4, 1997, The Center for Integrative Medicine opened as part of the University of Arizona's College of Medicine. The first of its kind in the United States, the center was founded by Andrew Weil, MD, best-selling author of *8 Weeks to Optimum Health*, *Spontaneous Healing* and several other books on natural health. For 20 years, Harvard-trained Dr. Weil has graced the covers of national magazines — from *Time* to *New Age Journal* — as America's best-known proponent of integrative medicine.

The approach melds the best of both conventional and alternative therapies and accepts the body's inherent ability to heal itself. At the clinic, patients are examined and interviewed for one hour about their lifestyles, diet, exercise, spiritual and emotional state and family-health history. The examining rooms have natural wood floors, vases of fresh flowers and soft lighting from floor lamps so patients will feel comfortable and secure.

At a follow-up appointment, patients receive the collective recommendations of Dr. Weil (program director), Dr. Tracy Gaudet (medical director), and four other physicians attending the fellowship program. From those recommendations an integrative combination of specific conventional and alternative holistic healing is suggested and overseen by Weil and his staff.

— continued on next page

As a leader in integrative medicine, Weil believes conventional medicine does some things very well, especially in the treatment of trauma and acute bacterial infections. In other words, conventional medicine is good at managing crises, but Weil's books are known for promoting prevention and wellness living that he believes in the long run can prevent many illnesses.

At this new center, he has assembled a small think tank of experts from a variety of fields to help create the curriculum for the fellowship program. They will also preform research on alternative therapies to develop a body of knowledge on what really works and why. The program will collaborate with the University of Arizona and visiting faculty in both laboratory and clinical research as well as track the comparative effectiveness and cost benefit of integrative medicine.

The clinic welcomes 16 new patients a week and is intent on training physicians in the whole range of alternative and natural therapies not currently taught in medical schools. A two-year postgraduate fellowship is the cornerstone of the program to train physicians who can later direct similar programs at other institutions. Because of the training aspect of the center, this is not a high-volume clinic, but the detail with which they look at the patient's mind/body connection makes this one of the most important new institutions in the United States healthcare system.

The Center for Integrative Medicine is on the sixth floor of University Medical Center, 1501 N. Campbell Avenue, 694-6555

Dr. Andrew Weil leads the Program in Integrative Medicine at the UA Health Sciences Center.

and teach the day-to-day skills they need to maintain independent lifestyles. Activities and classes include cooking, mobility training and household organization. Counselors help patients adjust to their disabilities, and advocates work for change within the community. Direct Center can even provide estimates and advice for making adaptations to homes or businesses, including bathroom modifications and ramps, and then provides a licensed and bonded contractor to do the work.

Riding and Rehabilitation Center
1373 Sunkist Rd. • 297-4771

The approach at this center is to saddle-up. It offers individual and group equine therapy for all ages and disabilities along with a good dose of fresh air.

Southern Arizona Rehabilitation Hospital
1921 W. Hospital Dr. • 742-2800

Offering inpatient and outpatient care, this facility deals with spinal injuries, strokes, arthritis, traumatic head injuries, pain management, cancer rehab, amputation and neurological problems using an interdisciplinary approach. The comprehensive services make use of physicians, nurses, therapists, psychologists and vocational workers as a team based on the special needs of each patient.

Hospices

Several hospitals in the area including Tucson Medical Center and Carondelet

Healthcare System operate hospices. Here are two that are not affiliated with a hospital.

Jacob C. Fruchthendler Jewish Community Hospice
5200 E. Grant Rd. • 881-5300

In association with Handmaker Jewish Services for the Aging, this nonsectarian hospice offers bereavement counseling, pain management, respite care and spiritual and emotional support to the terminally ill, their families and caregivers. Services are provided in the home, the hospital or nursing home.

TuNidito Children's Hospice
180 W. Ft. Lowell Rd. • 293-7738

This is southern Arizona's only children's hospice. The nonprofit TuNidito provides care for terminally ill children and counseling to their families in a home setting.

Alternative Therapy and Wellness

Tucsonans have a unique health advantage with a large community of alternative and wellness therapists to choose from including naturopaths, homeopaths, holistic healers, chiropractors and integrative medicine and Eastern medicine practitioners. Add to that an array of health-food stores, fitness clubs and vitamin shops and you have a town that has brought alternative medicine into the mainstream.

Here we offer a list of some of the most established centers and clinics in a wide range of recognized fields.

Cactus Flower Wellness Center
5813 N. Oracle Rd. • 293-3751

A one-stop wellness center, Cactus Flower offers a wide range of services including chiropractic medicine, acupuncture, massage therapy, naturopathy, Oriental medicine and counseling.

The Center for the Healing Arts
2550 E. Ft. Lowell Rd. • 322-5320

This is one of only eight homeopathic pharmacies in Arizona, and it offers an integrative approach to healing. Services include acupuncture, aromatherapy, breathwork, Reiki, chiropractic medicine, Oriental and herbal therapy and Shiatsu.

Complementary Medicine Association
4649 E. Malvern St. • 323-6291

This holistic organization will help you find an alternative therapist. It also publishes journals for the lay person and medical profession.

Desert Institute for the Healing Arts
125 E. 5th St. • 622-6234

Whether you need a good massage, Zen Shiatsu, or wish to be certified as a massage therapist, you'll find the services or classes you need here. Founded in 1982 to offer training for massage therapists, Desert Institute's many graduates have gone on to work at local spas and clinics. The center also has a bookstore.

Devine Healing Center
380 E. Ft. Lowell Rd., Ste. 205 • 882-9631

This center offers Merkabah light body activation, Reiki, distance healing, color chakra balancing, aromatherapy and light force work. Reiki classes are offered on-site.

Enchanted Gardens Healing Center
4659 E. North St. • 795-8198

Located on the Eastside near Swan and Grant roads, this natural health clinic has several practitioners specializing in everything from deep tissue massage and somato emotional release to spiritual healing. It offers free ongoing workshops that explain these healing techniques and what they can achieve.

Greenspring Wellness Center
5655 E. River Rd., Ste. 151 • 529-9668.

This Foothills center offers a variety of healing techniques for heart and blood vessel disease as well as other serious medical problems through its Rejuvenation Center. The center also helps patients combat aging through noninvasive anti-aging treatments.

IntegraMed
3402 E. Broadway Blvd. • 319-9074

IntegraMed combines allopathic medical doctors and alternative practitioners under one

304 • HEALTHCARE

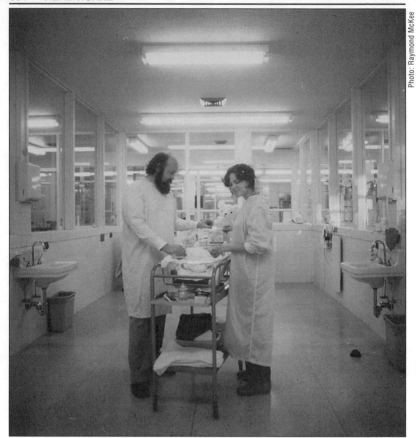

Tucson Medical Center is one of two trauma centers in Tucson.

roof. The integrative approach allows you to see a traditional doctor and discuss preventative health plans while also taking advantage of acupuncture, massage therapy and chiropractic services. Stop by for a tour of this new facility and the IntegraMed Health Products store.

Saguaro Clinic of Oriental Medicine
1640 N. Country Club Rd. • 319-9711

The practitioners at this clinic are National Board Certified and are committed to helping patients reach their optimum physical, psychological and spiritual health. Some of the techniques used include acupuncture, acupressure, Chinese herbs, Qi Gong, Tunia and holistic kinesiology.

Wellness Council of Tucson (WELCOT)
5301 E. Grant Rd. • 324-1414

WELCOT is the leading group involved in work-site wellness in Pima County. Healthcare providers conduct seminars at area businesses to improve lifestyles, health and productivity for workers and their families.

Wholistic Family Medicine
1601 N. Tucson Blvd., Ste. 37 • 322-8122

The doctors at this clinic provide naturopathic care, nutrition counseling, allergy testing, women's healthcare, acupuncture, alternative cancer therapy, chelation and metabolic vitamin therapy.

Need Help?

Ambulance, fire or police • 911
Alcoholics Anonymous • 624-4183, English; 624-5351, Spanish
American Cancer Society • 790-2600
American Diabetes Association of Southern Arizona
• 795-3711
American Heart Association
• 795-1403
American Parkinson Disease Association • 326-5400
Arizona Head Injury Foundation
• 747-7140
Arizona Kidney Foundation • 882-7604
Arizona Lions Eye Bank • 721-3854
Arizona Lung Association • 323-1812
Arthritis Foundation • 290-9090
Ask-A-Nurse • 544-2000
Community Outreach Program for the Deaf • 792-1906 (voice or TDD)
Council for Children and Adults with Attention Deficit Disorder • 797-2162
Crisis Pregnancy Center • 622-5774

HealthLine • 571-8744
HIV Testing • 791-7676
Information and Referral Service
• 881-1794
Muscular Dystrophy Association
• 529-2000
National Multiple Sclerosis, Southern Arizona Chapter • 290-1800
People with AIDS Coalition of Tucson
• 770-1710
Pima County Health Department
• 740-8866
Pima County Medical Society
• 795-7985
Planned Parenthood of Southern Arizona • 628-3074
Tucson Association for the Blind/Visually Impaired • 795-1331
Tucson Centers for Women and Children • 795-4266
Tucson Council on Alcoholism and Drug Dependence • 620-6615
Tucson Rape Crisis Center
• 327-1171, information; 327-7273, crisis

Arizona is second only to Florida in the number of seniors who move to the state.

Retirement

Ahhhhhh, retirement. No more punching the time clock, fighting the rush-hour traffic, dealing with office politics or waiting endlessly for that two-week vacation to roll around. You're finally free from decades of the workday world. But what to do with all that time? Well, if you're living or wintering in Tucson, your choices are almost infinite. Stroll through the many historic neighborhoods and parks or hike or bike along the rivers and washes. Play golf or tennis every day of the year if you want. Visit the many museums and art galleries around town. Explore fascinating attractions like Biosphere 2, Pima Air and Space Museum or Colossal Cave. Mingle with the wildlife at Arizona-Sonora Desert Museum or Reid Park Zoo. Go to a nearby senior center and make new friends. Volunteer at a local hospital or school.

And if you really want to get into the lifestyle of an active older adult, consider one of the many retirement communities for which Tucson is famous. They offer carefree living (as in "leave the driving and cooking to us"). Take your meals in elegant dining rooms, leave the housecleaning to the maids, forget about any household repairs or yard work, and simply hop on the van for weekly trips to the grocery store. But beyond that, they have activities galore — swimming, walking, playing shuffleboard, billiards or cards, dancing, learning crafts, putting on the green, working out in the exercise room, taking a group excursion or just finding a good book in the library — and lots of neighbors to share them with. All of this awaits you in one of Tucson's retirement apartment communities.

Or maybe you like the idea of having lots of activities and people to share them with but still want to own your own home. In that case, the Tucson area is a mecca of retirement communities or subdivisions. The Del Webb Corporation, famous for its Sun City (near Phoenix), created two similar communities here — Sun City Tucson and Sunflower. And don't forget about Green Valley just south of Tucson. It's a huge community with most subdivisions exclusively for older adults. And if you're a golfer, it's heaven. Still another option is adult communities that feature manufactured or prebuilt homes where you buy the house, lot and a carport or garage as a package and pay homeowner fees for maintenance of the common areas and facilities. You're still a homeowner, but the cost is usually less than buying in a regular senior subdivision.

There's even another option for adults who like the active lifestyle — living or wintering in your mobile home or RV. Tucson has many mobile communities exclusively for adults, complete with lots of activities and amenities to fill up your days and evenings. And if you don't own your own home on wheels, you can usually rent one of theirs.

While this chapter focuses on retirement abodes for people living independent lifestyles, it is by no means all there is. Many seniors can no longer live independently, and Tucson has a number of residential options for them. For example, some of the independent living apartments covered in this chapter also offer assisted living, in-home care or other related services. So you can choose to live in a retirement apartment and still get some daily help. There are many adult-care homes, nursing homes and in-home services available here as well. The nonsectarian Handmaker Jewish Services for the Aging is one agency that operates adult-care homes, assisted living apartments, a nursing home and home health services. Home Instead is one of a number of Tucson agencies providing a variety of in-home services for people who still live independently but need assistance with daily or weekly activities of a nonmedical nature.

Whatever lifestyle you're in search of — independent or assisted or just some ideas on how to spend your time constructively —

be sure to read the "Resource Roundup" section of the chapter. We present some important resources for older adults — places to contact for everything from Meals on Wheels to exercise classes and from nursing homes to in-home care. Older adults can often be the target of unscrupulous businesses, so it's critical to make informed choices and get advice and referrals from credible and upstanding sources.

Retirement Housing

Retirement housing choices in Tucson consist of apartments to rent or homes to buy (or privately owned homes the owners rent). While apartment communities are in all parts of the metro area, single-family housing communities are only in the northwest and southwest. And even though Tucson has well more than two dozen adult communities, the demand for them is high — many of the retirement apartments are usually full and housing subdivisions for adults sell out rather quickly. So once you've decided which one is right for you, get on a waiting list if the community is full. Also, be aware that in most of the communities, existing residents often have priority when a larger or more desirable unit opens up.

The apartment communities differ in many ways but have many similarities as well. Some are very secure, some are not. All meals may be included in the rent or some meals or none. Rules on owning pets vary. All offer cable-TV hookups but may or may not include cable TV in the rent. Rents may include all utilities (except phone) or some or none. While one-year leases are typical, some communities rent monthly. Be aware also that most of the rent prices quoted here are for one person in an apartment; a second occupant may mean a higher monthly rent. Rents change frequently (up is the way they usually go), so consider the rents given here as merely a guide. With all the variables, be sure to ask very specific questions when considering an adult community, including minimum age for occupancy.

One thing is fairly constant across all the communities: They want residents to have an array of both indoor and outdoor activities and amenities on-site, and they make it very easy to remain active, socialize and lead a nearly carefree lifestyle.

Broadway Proper
400 S. Broadway Pl. • 296-3238

"The Reuben sandwich is out of this world" might be a plaudit heard from residents of this 232-unit apartment complex, who generally speak highly of the dining hall's lunch offerings. But Broadway Proper has more going for it than the eats. Housed in a peach-colored Southwest-style three-story stucco elevator building are 10 floor plans of studio, one- and two-bedroom apartments surrounding a central courtyard and a beautifully landscaped .33-mile walk path. It isn't a gated community, but it is staffed around the clock. All the typical retirement apartment amenities are here: an elegant dining room, emergency call system in each apartment, lots of activities, weekly housekeeping and linen services and cable TV hookups. The staff puts out a great little newsletter that profiles all the upcoming activities for the next month or two, both on-site and excursions. The grounds are pleasantly green and palm-tree covered, and amenities include a library, beauty salon, pool and Jacuzzi (this is Arizona), free laundry facilities and off-street parking. A luxury air-conditioned and handicapped-accessible 26-passenger bus takes residents to scheduled activities. And right next door is a YMCA that residents can use for free. Four-footed friends can live here with owners who are age 62 or older.

> **FYI**
> Unless otherwise noted, the area code for all phone numbers listed in this guide is 520.

Monthly rents range from just more than $1,000 to just less than $1,500 and include just about everything described here plus basic utilities, breakfast and one additional meal daily. Assisted-living services are available to residents who need them for additional fees.

This complex is located in a busy area with lots of shopping, churches and hospitals nearby, but it's set back from the main roads enough to allow for privacy and quiet. The down side is that it's typically all filled up and has a waiting list of about six months. When you go searching for Broadway Proper, ignore the

RETIREMENT • 309

ManorCare Health Services℠

Quality People Improving Quality of Life®

Nursing & Rehab

The Support You Need.™

We offer skilled nursing care, rehabilitation, respite and posthospital/surgical care. Our dedicated staff strives to help residents achieve & maintain the highest degree of independence at all times.

- 24 hour skilled nursing care
- Alzheimer's services and support programs
- Rehabilitation services
- Social, recreational and therapeutic activities
- Respite care programs

3705 N. Swan Road
(520) 299-7088 Fax (520) 299-0038

Springhouse ManorCare Health Services℠

Assisted living

Springhouse is a gracious home, an Assisted Living Community designed specifically for older adults.

A place that gives residents control over their lives, encourages choices & independence. A place that enhances life through wellness programs activities, socialization & personal care services.
Our complete assisted living program is individually tailored-offering:

- Meals & snacks
- Housekeeping
- Daily activities
- Alzheimer's services
- Professional nurses 24 hours a day
- Scheduled transportation

3701 N. Swan Road
(520) 299-7755 Fax (520) 299-7827

www.manorcare.com

---

street address — it's not much help. Instead, look for the Hilton Hotel on Broadway Boulevard about two blocks east of Kolb Road and pretend you're going into the Hilton. It happens to be located behind the Hilton and shares the Hilton's entrance. Leisure Care, Inc., owns this property along with another one in Tucson and several dozen around the country.

Camlu Retirement Apartments
102 S. Sherwood Village Dr. • 298-9242

This one could be termed a homey resort — not too fancy but with all the necessities and more, plus a family-like atmosphere. It's owned by Camlu Corporation and has been here for 25 years. Like the Robin Hood of lore, Sherwood Village Drive is hidden away, but you'll find it just south of Broadway Boulevard and east of Pantano Road in southeast Tucson. It's a good location, with access to shopping, restaurants and medical services, but off the roadway enough to provide some peace and quiet in a middle-class residential neighborhood.

The 154 apartments are studios or one-bedrooms in a two-story building around a courtyard. And unlike many similar properties, no lease is required. For the monthly rent of $860 to $1,070, residents get three meals in the dining room, maid and linen service, scheduled transportation, laundry facilities, emergency call buttons, parking and lots of activities. Extras available on the property include a beauty shop, ministore and covered parking. Camlu can also accommodate overnight guests and guest dining. You won't find pets, a pool, a gated entry or a minimum age here. But Camlu does have a state-licensed assisted-living program with three care levels available for monthly rentals ranging from $1,265 to $1,675.

Campana del Rio
1550 E. River Rd. • 299-1941

If villa living is your cup of tea, this community, one of two in Tucson owned by Atria, may be one to consider. In addition to studio, one- and two-bedroom apartments in a three-story building, Campana del Rio has two-bedroom villas with one or two baths. The property has a total of 214 units, including assisted-living and memory-impaired units, with 40 more assisted living units under construction. Although the community is not gated, security is on duty 24 hours. Fine dining, complete with linens and flowers on the tables, is another hallmark of Campana del Rio, but they're not too formal to refuse diners a doggie bag for the delicious leftovers. And a private dining room can be reserved by residents who want a special gathering of friends or family.

For rents ranging from $1,035 to $2,200 a month (this includes assisted-living rates), residents receive breakfast and one main meal daily, weekly maid and linen service, free laundry facilities, scheduled van transportation, a pool, utilities and access to scads of activities such as aqua therapy, billiards, excursions and exercise equipment. Each apartment is equipped with emergency call buttons, and all the assisted-living units are handicapped-accessible with sit-in showers. The apartments and grounds are comfortable and clean, and the courtyard offers a tropical setting for walking, relaxing or swimming in the pool. The minimum age is 55, leases are required but negotiable for independent-living rentals, and small pets are OK.

Although Campana del Rio is in a scenic and convenient foothills area, it's also a congested area for traffic — something to keep in mind if you drive a lot. But it's also only about a furlough away from Rillito Racetrack if you're a horse race aficionado. The property itself is set back off River Road and hugs the north side of the Rillito "River" (for an explanation of the quotes here, see the Natural World chapter).

The Cascades
201 N. Jessica Ave. • 886-3171

This may be one of the only privately owned, as opposed to corporate owned, retirement communities in the area. An older but well-maintained complex of 240 apartments, The Cascades offers two types of apartments: independent and assisted. The former are one-bedroom apartments of 500 square feet with balconies that rent for $1,130 a month on a year's lease. This includes two meals a day in the dining room, weekly maid service, scheduled transportation and all on-site activities. Assisted living apartments are 350-square-foot studios renting for $1,700 and up. These residents get three meals, daily maid service and "lots of TLC." Special personal assistance is available to independent-living residents as well. The apartments are small but are handicapped-accessible with wide doorways and roomy showers.

The building is four stories with elevators and a central entrance. Apartments have emergency call buttons, and a security guard patrols at night. Amenities include a pool, game and activity rooms and a beauty salon. The minimum age is 65, and small pets are allowed. This is a convenient location in close-in east Tucson just off Broadway Boulevard between Wilmot Road and Kolb Road. The apartment complex is close to shopping and dining and nearly all other services but off the main road enough for quiet living. Oh, and it's very shaded — somewhat of a phenomenon in Tucson.

Catalina Village
5324 E. 1st St. • 327-4010

If you like being surrounded by green grass, roses and fruit trees and don't mind living in an older apartment, Catalina Village might suit you. Another plus is the rent, one of the most affordable of Tucson's retirement apartments. It's also in a close-in Eastside location only a short drive or taxi ride from nearly every kind of shop or service imaginable. Or if you prefer, hop onto the Catalina Village van for scheduled outings.

The 5-acre complex, which is gated but unlocked during the day, has 100 apartments in one-, two- and four-story buildings and casitas ranging in size from efficiency to two bedrooms for residents who live independently or need assistance (the staff prefers the term catered living). About one-third of the apartments are fully handicapped-accessible. Rents for independent living range from $485 to $785 and include maid and linen services and use of the clubhouse, pool, activities, equipped workout room, parking and scheduled transportation. Meals are available in the dining room but are not included with the rent. Catered-living rents range from $695 to $995 and include two meals daily. Apartments can be leased monthly by people older than 55, and small pets are permitted. The apartments have no emergency call buttons, however, which may be something to consider.

Copper Crest
7700 W. Bopp Rd. • 883-6670

This is a luxury senior community where you buy both the manufactured home and the lot it's on. It's much like being a homeowner in Sun City or Green Valley, except the home itself is pre-built. Opened in 1989, Copper Crest has 350 sites of various sizes on its 80 acres and only about half are sold. Complete packages — home, lot and carport or garage — start at about $80,000 and go to $140,000 with a maximum size of a fifth-acre. You'll also pay a monthly homeowner fee for maintenance of the common areas and facilities.

Among the facilities you'll find here for recreation and entertainment are a lap pool, spa, shuffleboard, bocce ball, horseshoes, putting green, exercise room, billiards, crafts center and a kitchen in the clubhouse for social gatherings. And since Copper Crest lies at the southwestern edge of the Tucson Mountains, there's plenty to do and see at the Arizona-Sonora Desert Museum, Old Tucson Studios and Tucson Mountain Park, all of which are nearby.

Country Club of La Cholla
8700 N. La Cholla Blvd. • 797-8700

The name is apt for this resort style retirement community — it's new, it's big, it's adjacent to Omni Tucson National Golf Course (in northwest Tucson), and it boasts a 30,000-square-foot clubhouse. And it's exclusively for independent adults older than 55 who can afford a monthly rent of $865 to $1,895. Lots of amenities and basics accompany the rent, including a few you'll find nowhere else in the Tucson area, but first you need to be lucky enough to be selected from the list of standbys — it's usually full with a waiting list.

For starters, you can choose from 200 bright apartments of 600 to 1,100 square feet, including casitas, but you'll need to sign a year's lease. Access is through a gated entrance that's locked at night, plus 24-hour security is on duty. The basics include breakfast and one meal daily, utilities, housekeeping, scheduled transportation, emergency call systems and either a patio or balcony with every unit. Country Club of La Cholla has not one but two dining rooms and an English Pub, complete with Friday happy hours. Contributing to your independent and active lifestyle are pool and spa, lots of on-site activities and outings, shuffleboard, a greenhouse available to residents, billiards, ballroom, exercise room, library, chapel and beauty salon. About the only drawback to this place is its lack of handicapped-accessible apartments.

The Fountains at La Cholla
2001 W. Rudasill Rd. • 797-2001

It would be possible to live here and never leave the 16 acres of grounds, so complete are the services and amenities at the Fountains. It also happens to be a beautiful setting — Southwestern-style buildings surrounded by the natural beauty of the desert and enhanced by lots of greenery, trees, flowers and fountains, of course. Living here is not cheap, but if you can afford the best, this is one place to find it. You can choose among 263 one- and two-bedroom apartments in a three-story complex, each with a balcony or patio, or 13 casitas (the Southwest term for patio homes) with two bedrooms and baths.

The clubhouse is elegant, the corridors are wide, and pets are not merely allowed, they're absolutely encouraged. That's because the Fountains subscribes to the "Eden alternative,"

INSIDERS' TIP

Find out beforehand if the adult-care home or nursing home you're looking into is licensed. The Department of Health Services, 628-6965, can tell you if the home is licensed and if any complaints have been registered against it.

which seems to prove that pets are indeed a boon to the elderly, emotionally as well as physically. But even if you don't have a furry friend, there's lots going on at the Fountains. In addition to all the standard amenities, there's a dance floor and stage, convenience store, on-site banking, wellness clinic, art gallery, spa and pool, library, beauty salon, outdoor gardening and on-site home-health agency.

Rents at this award-winning community range from $1,075 to $2,495 for independent-living apartments or casitas. But the Fountains also has assisted living, called The Inn and ranging from $1,985 to $2,650 monthly, and an Alzheimer's unit called The Gardens with a daily rate of $90 to $150. The apartments are typically full, and wannabees are placed on a wait list. The Fountains at La Cholla is about 10 years old, owned by a company also called The Fountains headquartered in Tucson. It's in the northwest of town with two hospitals and two nursing homes about a block away.

Green Valley, Arizona

Southern Arizona's most famous retirement community lies 25 miles south of Tucson off I-19. Although its population of 25,000 is not strictly older adults (11 of the subdivisions have no age restrictions and there are certainly signs of family life), this 30-something-year-old community is definitely populated primarily by 50-something-year-olds. Shuttle buses, golf carts, bicycles and wheelchairs bound about the streets, which feature specially designated "traffic" lanes. At 8 miles long and 2 miles wide, Green Valley isn't a town or city per se (it's unincorporated Pima County), but it sure seems like it. Nearly all the major services are right here — shopping, recreation, restaurants, medical and dental care — well more than 400 businesses in fact. It's also a golfing mecca, with at least seven of Southern Arizona's finest.

Green Valley has many appealing features for seniors. At an elevation slightly above Tucson's, the summer temperature is usually more tolerable and the rest of the year is lovely, so outdoor activities are often possible year round. Another plus is the beautiful environment — it's desert tempered with lots of lush landscaping and spectacular mountain views. Swimming pools, tennis courts, walk and bike paths and recreation centers throughout the community contribute to a fun lifestyle for active adults. And many older adults like this retirement area because it's not "big city," but big-city facilities and services are a mere 30-minute drive away.

You'll find many types of housing, whether for the winter season or for good and whether you want to rent or buy— single-family homes, apartments, condos and villas (or patio homes), both new and resale. Villas start around $25,000 and single-family homes go to $250,000 and more. Many housing subdivisions are located around golf courses. The best way to locate a place in Green Valley is through a local real estate agent or the Green Valley Chamber of Commerce, (520) 625-7575. Another source is For Rent, Inc., which manages privately owned housing that's available for short-term or long-term rent. Or just drive around and look for signs that signal something's for sale or for rent.

The Manor at Midvale
6250 S. Commerce Ct. • 294-3200

You can read all about Tucson's first master planned community of Midvale Park in the Neighborhoods and Real Estate chapter, which is where the Manor at Midvale is located. Specifically, Commerce Court is a squiggly street off Midvale Road north of Valencia Road on Tucson's southeast side and not far from I-19. One of its most desirable features is its proximity to services — major stores are a walk across the street and nearly everything else is nearby.

Owned by Holiday Retirement Corporation, the Manor is a fairly new retirement complex with Southwest-style architecture and lovely landscaping. Four two-story elevator apartment buildings and the clubhouse building form a square around a courtyard, all of which are connected with covered walkways and are handicapped-accessible. You need to be 55 or retired to live here but won't need to sign a yearlong lease. You can choose from 137 studio, one- or two-bedroom apartments of 500 to 980 square feet. The rent of $1,095 to 1,495 is a bit pricey for the middle-class and blue-collar community of Midvale Park, but you won't even have to cook one meal at home. It includes three dining-room meals daily, weekly housekeeping and linen, laundry facilities, local transportation, all utilities, emergency call buttons and amenities such as exercise classes, pool, spa and a homey and friendly atmosphere.

Saddlebrooke
64518 E. Saddlebrooke Blvd. • 791-7464

With more than 3000 residents and still growing, Saddlebrooke is by far the largest retirement community in the Tucson area. Unlike most of the other retirement properties in this chapter, this is a sprawling master-planned development, and the housing is for sale rather than rent. Although only 14 miles north of Tucson, it's actually situated in Pinal County, not Pima County, and abuts the northeast end of the Santa Catalina Mountains.

Buying a home here means you're likely to have great mountain views from nearly any spot plus an elevation of 3,300 feet, where temperatures are somewhat cooler than the city to the south. Although the setting is spectacular, the location is somewhat remote. Except for the few services available in Saddlebrooke, you'll be driving about 16 miles to the nearest hospital and at least half that far for groceries, restaurants, doctors and other services. Saddlebrooke does have a fire station with paramedics, however.

Robson Communities, the developer of Saddlebrooke, labels it a resort paradise, and that it certainly is. A multimillion-dollar rec center offers billiards, dining, a library, indoor/outdoor lap pool, weight room, tennis courts, spa and even massage and facial pampering. A 27-hole championship golf course with pro shop is strictly for Saddlebrooke residents and guests. Residents can hit the links every day of the year for just less than $1,400 or can pay as they play.

Because this is a fairly new development, it's only about half built with single-family, single-level homes that range from about $120,000 to $400,000 for 1,200 to nearly 3,500 square feet. They're available through the on-site sales office, while re-sale homes are sold through area real estate agents.

Santa Catalina Villas
7500 N. Calle Sin Envidia • 742-6242

Rancho Sin Vacas is an exclusive gated community in the Catalina foothills on Tucson's north side, which should tell you something about the retirement complex located there. It's exclusive, pricey and lovely. And there's usually a waiting list to rent one of its 160 independent-living apartments that range from studio to two-bedroom-and-two-bath units.

The apartments are located in 15 two-story buildings, each with only four to 16 apartments, so it resembles a villa (American Retirement Corporation, the owner, terms it campus style.) All have a patio or balcony, emergency call system, full kitchens, oversized bathrooms and weekly maid and linen services, but utilities and parking are extra. Some units are handicapped-accessible. The rents of $1,150 to $3,200 include 20 meals a month in the elegant dining room plus daily continental breakfast and amenities including scheduled van transportation, fitness center, free laundry rooms, pool, Jacuzzi, beauty salon and 24-hour security. The minimum age is 65, and one-year leases are required.

Because Santa Catalina Villas also has a nursing home on site, couples with one person needing nursing care and the other capable of independent living can still live in the same complex. The nursing center has 70 units that provide Alzheimer's, memory impairment and skilled nursing care. The community also operates its own in-home and companion services for independent-living residents who may need these services.

To reach Santa Catalina Villas, go north on either Campbell Avenue or Pima Canyon Road from Sunrise Drive, but be sure to call ahead. Rancho Sin Vacas is a gated area, and you'll need an appointment to get by the guard.

INSIDERS' TIP

Senior discounts are available just about anywhere in Tucson — from major attractions to restaurants and from golf to bus transportation. It's worth a query — you might save a few bucks.

Seniors make waves at a local retirement community.

Sun City Tucson
Oro Valley • (800) 422-8483

If you're at or near retirement age and haven't heard of Del Webb Corporation, you've possibly been living in a foreign country or in a cave. Del Webb was a pioneer in retirement communities and built one of the first, largest and most successful in the country — Sun City outside Phoenix. In early 1987, they opened Sun City Tucson within the larger master-planned community of Rancho Vistoso about 10 miles northwest of Tucson in what is now the town of Oro Valley. Within 10 years, the 2,500 homes covering Sun City Tucson's 1000 acres, ranging in price from the low $100,000s to $220,000, were sold out, but resales are on the market if you choose to live there.

Del Webb is renown for its amenities and activities for adults 55 and older, and Sun City Tucson is no exception. Multimillion-dollar recreation facilities include pools, tennis courts, an 18-hole golf course, restaurants and countless arts, crafts and sports offerings available to residents who own a home there and pay homeowner association fees. And surrounding Sun City Tucson is the larger community of Rancho Vistoso with shopping centers, medical and professional offices, shops, restaurants, churches, schools and additional sports and recreation facilities. (Rancho Vistoso's 7,555 acres contain developments by many builders, but only Sun City Tucson has an age qualification.)

Although Sun City Tucson is a bit remote from Tucson, nearly everything short of a hospital is available in Rancho Vistoso. Mountain views abound, as do wide streets, miles of walking paths, golf course views and a low crime rate. If you're an active adult who still wants to own (and care for) a home, contact an area real estate agent for homes available in Sun City Tucson. To find it, go north on Oracle Road to Rancho Vistoso Boulevard and look for the signs to Sun City Tucson.

Sunflower
7759 Goldbrook Dr. • 825-5888, (800) 433-5932

The word "sun" in the community's name is a good clue it's another Del Webb venture. The company's newest adult development in the Tucson area is located in the master-planned community of Continental Ranch in the Town of Marana to Tucson's northwest. Groundbreaking took place in late 1997, and eventually there will be 1000 homes on Sunflower's 245 acres ranging from 1,000 to 1,850 square feet and $80,000 to $130,000.

Like its sister communities, active lifestyle will be the byword. A central clubhouse area, with clusters of homes emanating from it like spokes of a wheel, offers pool, spa, tennis and tons of activities. The grounds will be abundant with walking and bicycling paths and the wide streets will be lined with hundreds of mesquite and palo verde trees along with all the customary desert vegetation. Although Sunflower is quite distant from the city of Tucson, both Continental Ranch and Marana are rapidly growing areas and will no doubt soon have major services to offer. To reach Sunflower, go west on Cortaro Farms Road from I-10 to Silverbell Road, then north to Twin Peaks Road and watch for the entrance.

Valley Manor
5549 E. Lee St. • 886-7937

This complex has undergone several transformations in its 30 years and now is operated by Atria as a retirement community with an adjacent nursing home. For couples with one needing nursing care and the other living independently, this type of community makes it possible to still be together. Although old, the buildings are spacious with wide hallways and large patios off the 67 apartments surrounding a pleasant courtyard. Valley Manor is located on a residential street one block south of Pima Street and east of Craycroft Road, a close-in Eastside neighborhood with major services nearby.

For apartments ranging from 400-square-foot efficiencies to 1,380-square-foot-two-bedroom-two-bath units, monthly rents are $795 to $1,595 and include continental breakfast and one main meal daily in the dining room, utilities and scheduled transportation. Maid and laundry services are available at an extra charge. The minimum age is 62, but the average age is 85. Yearly leases are required, and pets are allowed for an additional cost. Home healthcare is available also.

Mobile Home and RV Communities

Because Tucson is such a popular travel and retirement destination for older adults, many mobile home communities and RV resorts cater to this group. Retirees come here as winter visitors or permanent residents and set up housekeeping for the season or for good in one of Tucson's many mobile home or RV parks for adults. They get the benefits of a great climate without the responsibilities of maintaining a house or land and often can save money compared to renting in one of the area's retirement apartments. Most of these mobile and RV parks have all the trappings of a resort and offer residents ample activities and amenities along with the opportunity to make new friends with similar interests and lifestyles.

Mobile home communities differ from RV resorts (or parks) in that the homes and the residents tend to be more permanent while the RV parks tend to be more seasonal and more like resorts. Many of the mobile home and RV communities profiled here both sell and rent mobiles already set up on a space, or residents can wheel in their own and merely lease the space. Read on for a profile of some of the major mobile communities for adults.

Far Horizons Trailer Village
555 N. Pantano Rd. • 296-1234

Far Horizons has been offering RVers age 55 and older a lovely spot to visit or winter for the past 18 years. It's an excellent park on Tucson's Eastside, close to major services and attractions. More than 500 RV spaces are situated amidst beautiful desert landscaping, paved streets and views of the Rincon and Catalina Mountains. Activities include arts and crafts, weekly dances with live entertainment, Saturday morning jam sessions, hiking, miniature golf, shuffleboard, exercise classes, billiards, ping-pong and shuffleboard. For water fun, there's a pool and Jacuzzi. And if you need a break from the fun, you can always do the laundry.

The downside is that it's not easy getting space here. All the spots are usually rented by year-round residents at about $2,000 plus utilities. When these full-timers leave for periods of time, however, their spaces are available daily ($24), weekly ($143) or monthly ($430). However, spaces usually aren't available during the peak months of January through March.

Mission View Mobile Home and RV Resort
31 W. Los Reales Rd. • 741-1945

This is an adult community that offers both a mobile home park and an RV park —the former is called Club Estates and the latter Mission View RV Resort. (There's even a third section, called Mission View Manor, but it's a family mobile home park, so we don't have to confuse you further by covering it here; suffice it to say that the adult sections are off limits to the youngsters.) The community is located on the part of the Tohono O'odham reservation that's called the San Xavier reservation, although it's not operated by the Indian tribe and is directly east of the San Xavier Mission. (Hence the name Mission View, and a lovely view it is.)

The adult mobile home park has just less than 200 spaces that lease for $235 to $250 a month plus utilities, but you're not likely to get a spot here unless you're on a waiting list and someone vacates. The RV park has 150-plus spaces that are 40x60 feet, big enough to accommodate just about anything; they have gravel, cement patios and picnic tables. These spaces rent from $22 daily to $1,900 yearly, but the months of January through March are usually reserved by the previous September. Both the mobile and RV parks are surrounded by fence and have a single entrance, but it's not secured. Desert landscaping and paved streets surround the rental spaces.

The two adult communities are for people age 55 or older and share facilities and amenities — most notably an indoor tropical pool and spa. There are shower and laundry facilities in addition to the customary clubhouse and outdoor activities.

If you'd like to check out Mission View, ignore the address. Instead, take I-19 south from Tucson to Exit 92, which is San Xavier Road. Go east about a mile to the RV resort.

Quail Ridge Estates
15301 N. Oracle Rd. • 824-9088

The Catalina or Tortolita Mountains are the backdrops for the terraced homesites in this manufactured home community situated in Tucson's far northwest on gently sloping desert land. It boasts a layout in which 91 percent of the 130 homesites are corner lots and a 1996 national award as manufactured home community of the year. Not many spaces are available, but they rent for $283 a month on a one-year lease. All the homes are double-wide and you can buy a new one from the community or a resale for around $70,000 and up.

To qualify for Quail Ridge, each home must have one person 55 or older and no one younger than 18. The residents are active adults who take advantage of the community's offerings — pool and spa, putting green, shuffleboard, horseshoes, crafts and lots of social gatherings. Quail Ridge is off Oracle Road north of the Rancho Vistoso area, so it's quite a trek from Tucson. But the area of Catalina is nearby with shops, restaurants and medical services.

Rincon Country RV Resort West
4555 S. Mission Rd. • 294-5608, (800) RV2-PARK

This is the sister resort to Rincon Country East but is much larger, probably the second-largest RV resort in Tucson. It's on Tucson's southwest side in a still somewhat rural area but within easy reach of major roads and all the west side attractions, including San Xavier Mission, Tucson Mountain Park, Arizona-Sonora Desert Museum and Old Tucson Studios. Its 80 acres contain 1,100 spaces that usually are filled in the high season of January through March. Both short-term visitors and year-round residents are welcome, but you must be 55 or older. Pets are allowed, but

> **FYI**
> Unless otherwise noted, the area code for all phone numbers listed in this guide is 520.

there are restricted areas where they can be walked. Spaces go for $25 daily, $455 monthly and $2,200 yearly, with some utilities extra. The resort has a perimeter fence, and gated entry at night is by card or code.

With Rincon Country's amazing array of amenities and activities, boredom should never be a factor. An activities director arranges crafts, classes and social gatherings to suit just about anyone. Or you can swim in the pool, bask in the indoor or outdoor Jacuzzi, practice on the putting green, throw horseshoes or play tennis, shuffleboard or billiards.

Rincon Country rents and sells "park models," which are 400 square feet with one bedroom, or you can wheel in your own RV for as short or long a time as you want. Opened in 1983, it's an attractive RV park with active and community-spirited residents.

Rincon Country RV Resort East
8989 E. Escalante Rd. • 886-8431

Located on Tucson's southeast side near the eastern end of Davis-Monthan Air Force Base, this is the smaller of the two Rincon Country resorts, so it only has one Jacuzzi. Otherwise, the number of activities and amenities rivals its sister resort on the west side. Here you will find 400 spaces that rent for $149 a week, $445 a month or $2,035 a year. Spaces are usually unavailable in the high season without reservations years in advance. This resort also rents and sells park model RVs. Don't be frightened off by the proximity to the base — the airstrips are miles away on the base's west end. But you probably will have a view of the aircraft graveyard on Davis-Monthan's eastern end.

Swan Lakes Estates
4550 N. Flowing Wells Rd. • 887-9292

At first glance, you may be put off by the neighborhood surrounding this mobile home community — it's older and definitely not upscale. But if you look closer, you'll see a lovely and well-maintained community with a beautiful lake in its center, complete with ducks and fish and maybe even a swan. And residents can fish in it, too. There are 279 spaces but not many are available. Swan Lakes sells mobile homes but doesn't rent them and leases sites for $265 a month plus utilities. The community is fenced in, and a nightly security guard controls access through the entrance gate. For fun and recreation, there's an extensive social and activities calendar plus two heated pools and a Jacuzzi.

Trails West
8401 S. Kolb Rd. • 574-0298

This manufactured home community is on the southeast edge of Tucson just off I-10 and adjacent to Voyager RV Resort. It's a pleasant, well-maintained community in a rural area with major services only about 10 minutes away. About 80 percent of the residents stay here year round (the others escape for the summer), but spaces are available because Trails West is expanding beyond its present 380 lots. At least one person in the home must be 55 or older and all others must be older than 18.

Preowned homes are for sale, or you can buy a home from Trails West all set up for about $25,000 or more. Spaces lease for $210 to $270 a month with most utilities extra. Your rent includes 24-hour gated security, access to laundry facilities and a clubhouse with activities including social and craft gatherings, billiards, a library, a dance floor, occasional entertainment on the stage and a TV lounge. Outdoor fun includes a heated pool and Jacuzzi, barbecue areas and shuffleboard.

Voyager RV Resort
8701 S. Kolb Rd. • 574-5000,
(800) 424-9191

Voyager has been voted best in the nation and has as much if not more to offer than the poshest resort anywhere. And you need not be older than 55 to live here, just 19 or older. You can bring in your own RV or buy one of their 400-square-foot park models and lease one of the 1,500 spaces for $31 a night to $2,611 a year (plus electricity). As you might guess, however, Voyager is full during the high season and mighty popular the rest of the year as well.

And here are some of the things that make it so popular. Start off with 150 acres of lush landscaping, well-lighted streets and walkways, plenty of parking and spacious lots with cement patios. Toss in one nine-hole golf course with a lake, putting green, driving range and pro shop.

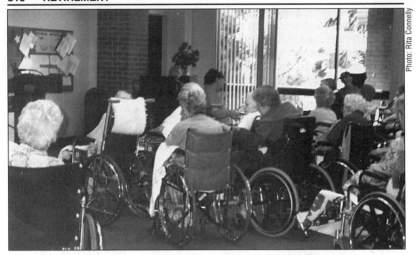
Seniors can find quality care and a variety of services citywide.

Add two heated swimming pools, two heated spas, two saunas, 16 shuffleboard courts, lighted tennis courts, volleyball courts, square, round and ballroom dancing with instructions, billiards, card rooms, a slew of arts and crafts and deep pit barbecues complete with cookouts. Round it out with a restaurant and general store (in-season), chapel and library. There's not much more anyone could want except possibly mountain views, and Voyager has that as well.

Western Way RV Resort
3100 S. Kinney Rd. • 578-1715

Kinney Road winds along the western side of the Tucson Mountains, and that's where Western Way is. With the mountains as a backdrop, the 12-year-old RV park offers residents and visitors a heated swimming pool, spa, ballroom (and dancing), card and game rooms, library, billiards and bingo. Directly across the street is Tucson Mountain Estates, a huge mobile home community with a private 18-hole golf course where residents of Western Way can play for a fee. Also within walking distance are several restaurants, beauty salons, stores and a post office. Nearby are some of Tucson's most popular attractions: Arizona-Sonora Desert Museum, Old Tucson Studios, Justin's Water World and San Xavier Mission. And Tucson Mountain Park is great for desert hiking and picnicking.

Western Way doesn't have RVs for sale or rent, so bring your own. Spaces lease for $27 daily, $177 weekly and $506 monthly with utilities included. Annual spaces go for $2,240 to $2,340 plus electricity. Of the park's 300 spaces, however, only about 80 are not occupied by year-round renters. The busy season is fall through spring, and the peak is January through March. The park has a perimeter wall with only one entrance, but it's not secured.

Resource Roundup

Arizona is second only to Florida in the number of seniors who move to the state. So you might surmise, correctly so, that Tucson has lots of resources and services for older adults. For example, Tucson has 37 nursing homes and about 200 adult-care homes licensed by the state's Department of Health Services. Whether you're seeking a place to ballroom dance or swim in a heated pool, or whether you're in need of meals on wheels or in-home healthcare, this section of the chapter will point you in the right direction.

Senior Resource Network, which is part of a nonprofit agency called Information and Referral Services, may be your best single source for senior information and assistance in town. They can help you find anything — from a place to dance or swim or socialize with other seniors to a place to live if you can't live independently. There's no charge to use the service. This is a private nonprofit agency that knows what's available or will find out for you. Their expertise is especially valuable if you're looking for some type of healthcare or a place to live that provides daily assistance and don't want to make a wrong choice. They're wise, and they're willing, so call them at 795-7480 for assistance.

The **Pima Council on Aging**, 790-7262, is a private nonprofit agency that offers a variety of information and help for seniors. Their many services include advocacy on senior issues, respite care, Medicare insurance counseling, housing referrals, places to socialize, how to get meals delivered and more. Most of their services are free (with donations welcomed) or available on a sliding scale. They have excellent knowledge of the area's senior resources and can usually lend a helping hand. The **Tucson Interfaith Coalition on Aging**, 798-3839, is another good resource for seniors needing information or assistance, as is the **Northwest Interfaith Council**, 297-6049, which focuses on the Oro Valley area.

There are several private agencies that make referrals to adult-care homes, nursing homes and retirement communities. One of these is **Anderson's Referral** at 577-2267. This agency is particular about the places it recommends and conducts inspections before making a referral. They'll help you locate in-home care, respite care, assisted-living residences, adult-care homes and nursing homes. A similar agency is **Adult Care Home Placement Services**, 748-4351, which specializes in matching residents to one of Tucson's many adult-care homes. When choosing this type of referral agency, look for one that's staffed by health professionals (registered nurse or social worker, for example). Both of these are.

For seniors looking for a place to socialize, exercise, play bingo, learn arts and crafts or maybe even get a noon meal, both the City of Tucson and Pima County operate senior citizens programs (or centers) around town, and they're free. There are 13 such programs, many held at park buildings, plus one in Green Valley. Your best source for locating one of these senior programs and finding out what it offers is the Pima Council on Aging.

Print publishing in Tucson covers everything from coffee to poetry.

Media

Print publishing is on an upswing in Tucson, with many new specialty newspapers and magazines — covering everything from coffee to poetry — popping up each year. For a city of less than 1 million, the Old Pueblo has more than its share of small book publishers supporting the growing number of professional writers who have settled here during the last decade (see the "Literary Arts" in the Arts and Culture chapter).

Though Tucson Newspaper, Inc. operates both daily newspapers, *The Arizona Daily Star* and the *Tucson Citizen* are distinctly different in scope and political leanings. Two papers — *The Star* and the *Tucson Weekly* — both operate their own Internet website networks, giving media junkies even more material to browse.

This chapter gives descriptions of the major papers, magazines, radio and television stations available in Tucson. But keep your eyes open during your stay since more papers and magazines arrive every year, and you're bound to stumble upon some new ones.

Newspapers

Dailies

The Arizona Daily Star
4850 S. Park Ave. • 573-4400

Considered the state's first daily newspaper, the roots of *The Star* date back to 1877 when the *Daily Bulletin* began publishing with a firm Democratic slant. After going through a triweekly stage and then a weekly one, the paper, as we know it today, was finally entrenched in the publishing world in 1885.

Today, the city's morning newspaper is published seven days a week, with a Friday "Starlight" section that serves as a weekly arts and entertainment guide. The Sunday edition includes "Home," "Travel" and editorial comment sections. The Monday "Startech" section covers high-technology issues. Watch for regular supplements geared toward everything from wedding planning to senior health. It also operates StarNet, an electronic cyberspace version of the paper that allows you to read a story and then jump to other sites for more information at a cost of $20 per month. The paper is 50¢ on the street, but *The Star* offers a variety of subscription packages ranging from $5.75 a week to $8 for four weeks of Sunday editions only. Daily circulation is 96,198; Sunday is 178,820.

Arizona Daily Wildcat
University of Arizona • 621-1714

Founded in 1914 (two years after Arizona became a state), this daily college paper has a following off campus as well. It can be found around the University area. The *Wildcat* is free and contains well-written articles and editorials on local, state and national politics as well as campus news. It's also a great source for information and schedules regarding games, seminars and concerts at the University.

The Daily Territorial
3280 E. Hemisphere Loop • 294-1200

This is Pima County's legal newspaper of record and contains some business and legal news. But primarily it's a list of legal notices filed within the county. The paper was started in 1966 and currently has a circulation of 1,000. A year's subscription is $90, or you can pur-

---

INSIDERS' TIP

When searching for Tucson's free publications, check the independent bookstores, large supermarkets and libraries.

Tucson Citizen
4850 S. Park Ave. • 573-4400

Established in 1870 by Republican Richard McCormick, the original *Arizona Citizen* was published as a weekly until the *Arizona Daily Citizen* was established in 1879. The final name change came in 1903 when the owners dubbed it the *Tucson Citizen*. Now the city's Gannett afternoon paper publishes six times a week. There is no Sunday paper, but the Saturday edition acts as a weekend paper and is available early Saturday morning with comics and other trappings of a "Sunday" paper. On Thursday, it publishes the Calendar, a weekly guide to entertainment, the arts and activities. An annual, home-delivered subscription is $185. Issues are 35¢ a day on the street. Daily circulation is 46,062.

Other Papers — Weekly, Semiweekly, Semimonthly, Monthly

Arizona Jewish Post
3812 E. River Rd. • 529-1500

Published since 1946, this semimonthly Jewish-interest paper keeps the community up-to-date on events, news and people. The *Post* is only distributed through subscription, which runs $18 per year.

Arizona Senior World
4621 N. 1st. Ave., #10 • 887-2900

This statewide monthly is the essential publication for those retiring in Arizona. The free paper contains news, an events calendar and features geared toward those in their golden years. You'll typically find copies distributed in area restaurants and at the library branches.

The Awareness Journal
P.O. Box 57130, Tucson 85732
• 749-6041

Published in Tucson, this monthly New Age publication is distributed statewide and in New Mexico and California. It covers the growing metaphysical interests of the Southwest and includes human potential, healing arts, spiritual and environmental issues as well as a statewide calendar of events. The paper is distributed free in bookstores and restaurants. Or you can obtain a year's subscription for $25.

Aztec Press
Pima Community College,
2202 W. Anklam Rd.
• 884-6800

Aztec Press is the student-run weekly paper distributed on Wednesdays at the city's community college. It's free and covers news pertinent to the campus.

Bear Essential News
2919 E. Broadway Blvd., Ste. 201
• 795-9930

This lively free monthly is a great kid's publication, especially if your child likes to work puzzles, play games, enter contests or actually write articles. Parents will find a lot of useful information about day care, events and even places to eat with little guys. There is also a "Kid Times" section that is written mostly by middle school students and by members of a local Young Reporters Program. This paper can be found all over town at eating establishments, bookstores and the Children's Museum.

Coffee Times
2818 N. Campbell Ave., #156 • 531-4721

This little newspaper is published six times a year and can be picked up free at any of Tucson's coffee boutiques. With short articles and poetry, it's designed to be companion reading over a hot cup of joe.

Dateline Downtown
P.O. Box 1493, Tucson 85702
• 629-9920

You can only find this free monthly if you venture to downtown Tucson. The paper was created to support the rejuvenation of the downtown area and contains business news, events calenders and history features.

FYI

Unless otherwise noted, the area code for all phone numbers listed in this guide is 520.

MEDIA • 323

DesertLeaf
4720 E. Mission Hill Dr. • 299-7508

DesertLeaf is more magazine than award-winning tabloid-size paper, running only feature stories. Targeting the Catalina Foothills community, the monthly paper is delivered free to some 35,000 households in the area as well as distributed free at select bookstores. The regular features include travel, arts, nature, history, people, restaurant listings, gallery listings and desert gardening. People outside the foothills can subscribe for a mere $12 a year.

The Explorer
7925 N. Oracle Rd. • 797-4384

This weekly community newspaper targets the residents of the fast-growing northwest corridor, providing a local focus of news, politics, reviews and meeting updates as well as a variety of columnists, both local and national. The paper is primarily delivered by subscription ($23.95 per year), but it has recently begun to place boxes in the area where you can by individual copies for 50¢. The company also publishes an Oro Valley edition.

Good News
3222 S. Richey Ave. • 790-2440

Published by Good News Radio Broadcasting, Inc. (KVOI/KGMS radio), this free monthly tabloid "explores social issues and ministry topics." The slant leans toward the teachings of Jesus Christ and family values. The paper covers everything from music to restaurants and subscribes to the Evangelical Press News Service. You'll find it in street boxes around the city.

Healthy Times
5425 E. Broadway Blvd., #145 • 760-9228

From the publishers of *The Awareness Journal*, this monthly keeps readers up-to-date on integrative medicine, health and fitness. You can pick this up free at health food stores or receive it in the mail for $25 per year.

Inside Tucson Business
3280 E. Hemisphere Loop • 294-1200

Inside is the weekly business publication of professionals in Tucson. The paper is the only one devoted entirely to business news. It costs $1 from street boxes or at newsstands or $35 per year with a subscription.

Sagi's Outdoor News
7014 E. Golf Links Rd., #313 • 795-8544

If you hunt, fish, boat, camp or just want to keep up-to-date on news about the Arizona Game and Fish Commission, this independent monthly publication is a must. It's geared primarily to sport hunters and anglers and is free at bookstores and sporting good stores. You can also subscribe for $13 a year.

Sports Stuff
P.O. Box 18681, Tucson 85731
• 571-0139

This free monthly is distributed at sports bars, restaurants, sporting goods stores, bowling centers, golf courses and tennis centers. You'll find regional sports news, puzzles, trivia and more.

Tailwinds
630 N. Craycroft Rd. • 745-2033

Published six times a year by The Perimeter Bicycling Association of America, this magazine-style newspaper covers everything related to biking in Arizona, including races and equipment. Though you can find it free at selected locations (upscale bicycle shops), the publishers are pushing to make it a subscription-only paper at $15 a year.

Tucson Comic News
P.O. Box 510, Tucson 85702 • 320-5105

A monthly tabloid-size paper, *Comic News* is about as irreverent as they come. If you love the comics in your local Sunday paper, you'll be in heaven when you see this rag that is a collection of original and syndicated political cartoons. The laughs are 50¢ and distributed through street boxes, bookstores and restaurants.

The Tucson Poet
228 N. 4th Ave. • 206-9244

Published eight times a year, this paper is the newest support publication for Tucson's exploding literary scene (see our Arts and Culture chapter). *TP* lists coffeehouses that have poetry readings, and it contains local poetry submissions. Though it's available for free in coffeehouses and bookstores, you can sign on for a year's subscription for $20.

Tucson Theater Scene
P.O. Box 57722, Tucson 85732 • 722-1731

This new monthly newspaper covers Tucson's booming performing arts scene, offering a calendar of events, news, theater reviews, audition listings and more. It's distributed free in bookstores, theater and performance center lobbies, cafes and restaurants.

Tucson Tourist News
2225 E. Broadway Blvd. • 721-1181

Published every other Thursday and distributed free in virtually every hotel, RV center, sporting goods shop as well as the airport and the Visitors Bureau, this newspaper is packed with information for those visiting southern Arizona. Most of the articles are short and to the point, covering walking tours, golf, arts and entertainment, attractions, shopping, dining and outdoor activities. One issue alone could give a visitor to Tucson more than enough to do.

Tucson Weekly
201 W. Cushing St. • 792-3630

Tucson's free alternative weekly paper is published on Thursdays, distributed through street boxes and restaurants and contains articles on local politics as well as music reviews, club listings and even a section supporting local book authors. "The Weekly" also maintains DesertNet, a cyberspace version of the paper, and publishes an annual reader's poll of the Best of Tucson each September.

The Weekly Observer
P.O. Box 50733, Tucson 85703 • 622-7176

This free weekly paper supports and offers news about the region's gay and lesbian community. Besides local stories, it also carries national news. The advertising covers all the gay nightspots, which are pretty much the only places you'll find this 24-page newspaper. Also included are notices about events and benefits, information regarding safe sex, commentary and classified ads.

Magazines

Arizona Golfer
6987 N. Oracle Rd., #542 • 575-0025

Arizona's only monthly golf publication, this magazine highlights golf throughout Arizona, including golf vacations and resorts. An annual subscription is $14, or you can pick up a copy at area golf shops.

Artlife
P.O. Box 36777, Tucson 85740
• 797-1271

This pocket-size, carry-along quarterly guidebook is essential for those planning to do some art gallery hopping. The full-color publication with lots of maps includes a complete gallery, art services and museum listing as well as a cross-listing of artists showing within the entire southern Arizona region. You can find it free at most galleries, museums and many independent bookstores.

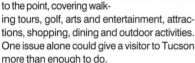

Fitness Plus
3402 E. Kleindale Rd. • 881-6696

As the title suggests, this free monthly magazine covers all aspects of keeping fit, including nutrition and health. Packed with ads from fitness clubs, the publication is very advertiser-driven but contains a full range of articles covering the fitness lifestyle in both Tucson and Phoenix. It's available through street boxes and at sporting goods stores.

Tucson Guide Quarterly
2730 E. Broadway Blvd., #250 • 322-0895

From the largest magazine-publishing house in Arizona, Madden Publishing, *TGQ* is a classy, full-color quarterly guide to the city that has excellent feature articles, such as a regular "101 Things to Do" column and a calendar of "Festivals & Fiestas." The publication is $3.50 at newsstands and anywhere magazines are sold. A one-year subscription is $12.95.

Tucson Lifestyle
7000 E. Tanque Verde Rd. • 721-2929

This monthly "City Book" covers

Jimmy Stewart, KVOA's morning weatherman, tracks the weather on state-of-the-art computers.

Tucson's lifestyle, real estate, fashion and society-related topics. A regular feature is the City Guide: "Where to Shop — Where to Dine — What to See." The newsstand price is $2.95; a one-year subscription is $14.

Tucson Monthly
2730 E. Broadway Blvd. • 322-0895

The latest offering from Madden Publishing, the state's largest magazine publishing house, this monthly presents meaty articles on everything from local politics to home improvements. The full-color magazine's regular columns include a calendar of events, weekend getaways, restaurant reviews and historical anecdotes. This publication's journalistic and graphic arts standards make it one of the city's more popular magazines. *Tucson Monthly* is found at magazine stands all over town, and the street price is $2.95 per monthly issue. A one-year subscription costs $19.45. It's $34.90 for two years.

Tucson Visitor
5132 N. Pueblo Villas Dr. • 888-1009

Distributed at hotels monthly in July and August and biweekly September through June, this little full-color magazine is a good starting point for anyone visiting the area. With short articles and reviews as well as easy-to-read maps, the free magazine targets visitors to the area who want their information fast.

Tucson's Film Industry

The film industry has had a solid foothold in Tucson with Old Tucson Studios, dubbed "Hollywood in the Desert." Since it was built in 1939 as a re-creation of 1860s Tucson for the movie *Arizona*, the 160-acre site has been the location of more than 200 movies, TV shows and commercials (see our Attractions chapter). The facility is the most popular Old West location in the United States. But southern Arizona, in general, has become popular as well, with film crews shooting movies and TV shows like *A Star is Born*, *Highway to Heaven*, *Alice Doesn't Live Here Anymore,* and others that have yet to be released.

Such activity sprouted the Tucson Film Commission to coordinate filming activities and offer professional support services. But Tucson also has an active independent film community with its own International Film Festival (see our Festivals and Events chapter); art films shown regularly at The Loft, 3233 E. Speedway Boulevard (see our Arts and Culture chapter); and the popular World Cinema series at the University of Arizona.

For those making videos, the not-for-profit Tucson Community Cable Corp. has one of the best production facilities in the country due to generous funding from the local commercial cable operators, and the company is always looking for volunteer producers! (See the "Cable Companies" section.)

Television

Present-day KOLD, Tucson's first TV station, went on the air February 1, 1953 as KOPO. The station was owned by Gene Autry, and the population of the city was 48,774. It took a while for the unrefined electronic stranger to catch on in Tucson. At the time TVs were selling for between $199 and $599, not much different from today until you consider a solid middle-class income was $5,000.

Today, Tucson not only has a full complement of network affiliates and independent stations, but also several cable operators. Though People's Choice can be received anywhere in the city due to its wireless operation, the other pay cable operators are somewhat geographical in their distribution, depending on what part of the city you settle in.

- KGUN Channel 9 (ABC)
- KHRR Channel 40 (Telemundo)
- KOLD Channel 13 (CBS)
- KMSB Channel 11 (Fox)
- KQBN Channel 14 (Telenoticias)
- KTTU Channel 18 (UPN)
- KUAT Channel 6 (PBS)
- KVOA Channel 4 (NBC)
- KWBA Channel 58 (WBN)

Cable Companies

The cable TV companies serving Tucson have their own distinct geographical areas, so depending on where you stay in town — or where you choose to live — you will be somewhat limited by which company you can order.

Jones Intercable
8251 N. Cortaro Rd. • 744-1000

This cable operator offers 40 basic channels and 10 premium channels including HBO, Showtime, Cinemax and others. The company carries the local Pima County Education and Community Service Channel and the Jones Computer and Product Information Network. The company has been serving Pima County since 1982, but it only serves the area outside the Tucson City limits, such as the Catalina Foothills, northwest areas, far eastern area and far southern area. Jones Intercable also offers free cable radio when you hook in to an FM receiver, which enables you to hear many commercial-free music as well as stations from around the country.

People's Choice
5311 E. Broadway Blvd.
• 750-9900

This wireless operation has become popular around the country because it offers virtually outage-free service using an antenna delivery system rather than a cable. The downside is that People's Choice offers substantially fewer channels (about 30).

Tucson Cable Inc. (TCI)
1440 E. 15th St. • 884-0133

If you live within the city limits, such as downtown, the University area, Davis-Monthan AFB or central Tucson, this is the cable company that will serve you. TCI offers more than 50 channels. The company also carries several local channels, including a Tucson Arts channel, four channels from the City of Tucson, local education channels and four public access channels produced at Tucson Community Cable Corp. TCI offers Digital Music Express, a form of cable radio with noncommercial music, but it will cost another $5 per month.

Tucson Community Cable Corporation
124 E. Broadway Blvd. • 624-9833

City, county and FCC agreements mandated that the commercial operators in the city should provide funds for a nonprofit, public access operation. Today this corporation is

---

FYI

Unless otherwise noted, the area code for all phone numbers listed in this guide is 520.

a training ground for up-and-coming TV and video producers, and it is one of the best production facilities of its kind in the country. It offers classes, digital editing booths, sound stages and even equipment loans to members. The public access channels this organization produces are offered only through TCI.

Radio

KTUC (1400 AM), Tucson's first radio station, went on the air July 10, 1926, as KGAR. The call letters were later changed to KTUC when the owners realized that "KGAR" was a bit too close to a Spanish word that had a rather unsavory meaning.

Today, Tucson is unusual in that, for a city this size, there isn't much format-war-type competition among radio stations. That's because there is virtually one station for each major format: one rock, one Top 40, one country hits, etc.

KIIM-FM (Country) has been the No. 1 station practically since it went on the air in 1983 and is the only major family-owned station in this market.

For those desiring an alternative to the commercial, KAMP-AM, a student-run station at the University of Arizona, offers an eclectic fare, as does the community station KXCI-FM. The University of Arizona also runs a professional public radio jazz station and a classical station, both broadcasting the National Public Radio programs heard around the country.

But you won't be seeing new offerings any time soon. The radio frequency allocations from the FCC have all been spoken for. Of course, there is an occasional "Pirate Radio" station that pops up at 103.3 FM (Radio Limbo) during some evenings. But there's no telling how long the station will maintain its broadcasts.

Included here is a complete list of the stations on the dial in Tucson.

Adult Contemporary
KMXZ 94.9 FM
KZPT 104.1 FM (Modern)

Christian
KVOI 690 AM (Christian Talk/News)
KFLT 830 AM (Christian)
KEVT 1030 AM (Spanish Christian)
KFLR 88.5 FM
KGMS 97.1 and 102.3 FM (Christian hits)

Classical
KUAT 90.5 FM

College Radio
KAMP 1570 AM (Eclectic/Univ. of Ariz.)

Community Radio
KXCI 91.3 FM (Eclectic)

Country
KCUB 1290 AM (Traditional country)
KSJM 97.5 FM
KIIM 99.5 FM (Contemporary country)

Jazz
KUAZ 89.1 FM (Jazz/National Public Radio/Univ. of Ariz.)
KJZZ 98.9 FM (NPR News/Talk/Evening jazz)
KUAT 1550 AM (Jazz/National Public Radio/Univ. of Ariz.)

News/Talk
KNST 790 AM (News/Talk/Sports/UA football, baseball and softball games)
KTKT 990 AM (News/Talk/Sports)
KTUC 1400 AM (Talk/Sports/News)
KFFN 1490 AM (Sports talk)

Latin
KQTL 1210 AM (Spanish Language)
KXEW 1600 AM (Mexican Country)
KOHT 98.3 FM (Spanish Contemporary Hits)
KZLZ 107.5 FM (Spanish Contemporary)

Oldies
KSAZ 580 AM (Adult Standards)
KCEE 940 AM (Standards)
KGVY 1080 AM (Big Band)

Rock
KFMA 92.1 FM/106.3 FM (Alternative Rock)
KWFM 92.9 FM (Rock Oldies)
KLPX 96.1 FM
KHYT 107.5 FM (70s Rock)

Top 40
KRQQ 93.7 FM

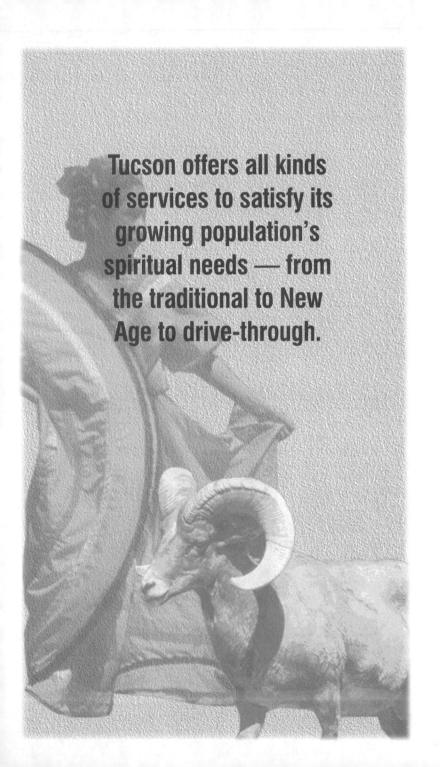

Tucson offers all kinds of services to satisfy its growing population's spiritual needs — from the traditional to New Age to drive-through.

Worship

Forget the Old West stereotypes of lawlessness, liquor and loose ladies. Today, Tucson offers all kinds of services to satisfy its growing population's spiritual needs — from the traditional to New Age to drive-through.

Since Father Francisco Kino arrived in the area in the late 1680s (see our History chapter), the native peoples of southern Arizona have had exposure to organized western Christian religion. As the area grew during the late 1800s, the Old Pueblo saw a steady influx of religious organizations representing several different denominations. The first influences were from the Catholic church in the form of missionaries. A Mormon battalion moved through the area in 1846 but didn't stay to organize. Protestant preachers arrived in the 1860s, and the city's first Presbyterian church was built by 1878. In 1881, the first Methodist church was completed, as was Grace Episcopal Church.

By 1910 Tucson had grown to 13,000 people with Presbyterian, Congregational, Episcopal, Baptist, Catholic, Methodist, Lutheran, First Church of Christ and First Christian Church all represented. Another population boom from the late 1920s through the late 1940s saw the establishment of a Mormon congregation; St. Demetrios Greek Orthodox Church, 1145 E. Ft. Lowell Road; Christian Science Church, 150 S. Scott Avenue; Immaculate Heart Novitiate at 4100 Sabino Canyon Road; and what is today the largest conservative Jewish synagogue in southern Arizona, Congregation Anshei Israel at 550 E. 5th Street, which serves more than 900 families and offers kindergarten, preschool and adult education. As the area grows, so do the number of churches.

Tucson's religious centers offer much more than worship services. The Jewish Community Center, 3800 E. River Road, plays a major role in not just local Jewish life, but also the life of the entire community. A modern facility, it offers a long list of activities, including recreation, athletics, child care and classes for all ages, as well as camps, senior programs and even a dating service. Next door, the Jewish Federation of Southern Arizona, organized in 1946, serves as the umbrella organization for the Jewish Community Center, Handmaker Jewish Services for the Aging, Jewish Family & Children's Services and the Tucson Hebrew Academy. It also supports the rescue of Jews in the former Soviet Union and elsewhere.

Many area churches provide hospice services, camps, preschools and after-school programs. St. Philips in the Hills at 4440 N. Campbell Avenue, one of the 12 largest parishes in the Episcopal Church in the country, is particularly innovative in its services to the community and the events it sponsors. The 6.4-acre site contains a patio and garden, an art gallery and music rooms, as well as a preschool and kindergarten. Adult programs range from the arts to sports and Bible study to support groups. The church's Gay & Lesbian Spirituality Group is open to everyone, regardless of faith. Like St. Philips and the Jewish Community Center, the Unitarian Universalist Church of Tucson, 4831 E. 22nd Street, offers an array of activities ranging from poetry workshops to music to open forums. Because the church offers so much, its newsletter is published twice a month to cover all the activities.

Other spiritual centers in the area revolve around a common goal as opposed to an or-

INSIDERS' TIP

Some churches devote specific times for a Spanish-language mass.

The Holocaust Memorial is in front of the Jewish Community Center on River Road.

ganized faith or religion. The Pima County Interfaith Council, 3227 N. 1st Avenue, serves the community under the slogan "Faith, Power, Action." It offers strategies to address the challenges Tucson faces during the remainder of the century, which the council views as welfare reform, crime prevention and the economy. Through a series of programs geared toward youth, the Interfaith Council focuses on the full development of human potential, inner-city urban renewal and the creation of jobs.

Historically and architecturally speaking, there are some magnificent religious structures in Tucson. Dove of Peace Lutheran Church, 665 W. Roller Coaster Road, was designed in the 1960s and won an honor award from the American Association of Architects. Unlike most churches, the altar is in the middle, with pews surrounding it and a skylight above. Saint Augustine Cathedral, 192 S. Stone Avenue, was established in 1863 as Tucson's first Catholic parish. The present location downtown is actually the third site for St. Augustine parish (built in 1897 and refurbished in 1967). In 1975 it was designated a National Historic Landmark. Tucson and the Catholic diocese grew up together, and today there are 25 parishes in Tucson alone. Saint Augustine, reminiscent of European church architecture, is the flagship cathedral. Another example of religion but not in the form of a building is El Tiradito, located downtown next to El Minuto Cafe, 345 S. Main Avenue, a shrine listed as a National Historic Place. It is said that wishes are granted here. (See our Neighborhoods, Neighboring Towns and Real Estate chapter for more information about the shrine.)

Perhaps the most cherished religious structure in the area, however, is Mission San Xavier Del Bac, 1950 W. San Xavier Road. Located 19 miles south of downtown Tucson and known as the "white dove of the desert," it's considered to be the finest example of mission architecture in the United States and one of southern Arizona's most striking landmarks. Founded by Father Francisco Kino in 1700, the current structure was opened for services in 1797. Fredrick Remington preserved it in an 1885 painting, and the U.S. Postal Service celebrated it with a commemorative stamp in 1971. The seals of both the City of Tucson and Pima County are adorned with its image. The entire structure is a series of domes and arches, and no surface is left unadorned. Masses are offered daily except Monday at the mission. (See our Attractions chapter for more about the Mission.)

Though we take great pride in the past and more traditional forms of worship, we are also open to less-mainstream forms of spirituality. The Church of Cosmic Christ, 2620 N. Dodge Boulevard, is a nondogmatic metaphysical Christian church acting as a support and "a center of light, life and love" for those seeking a New Age view in their religious experiences. Park Avenue Christian Church, 4635 S. Park Avenue, is Tucson's only drive-in church, offering regular services without the pews. Twice on Sunday, drivers pull into a lot and listen to a minister (accompanied by an organist) address the congregation.

Bodhisattva Institute, 3901 E. Kleindale Road, provides information on the Buddhist religion. Members worship in the Kagyu tradition of Tibetan Buddhists. The institute is building a temple on 8.2 acres of land, but until it's completed, members meet at other locations, including the Unitarian Universalist Church, previously mentioned in this chapter.

We cannot possibly list every worship service and religious center here. But we do have a few suggestions on where to look for places of worship and religious information during your stay in Tucson.

The Saturday edition of *The Arizona Daily Star* has a section devoted to area houses of worship and the times for their services. And whether you lean toward Christian, New Age or the Jewish faith, there is probably a publication covering your interests in Tucson. Check our Media chapter for information on papers such as *Good News*, *The Awareness Journal* and the *Jewish Post*. Also, three radio stations — KFLT (830 AM), KVOI (690 AM) and KGMS (97.1 or 102.3 FM) — offer music and information with a religious message.

Index of Advertisers

Albertsons	97
Elysian Grove Market — A Bed & Breakfast Inn	43
Flandrau Science Center	117
Hacienda del Desierto	43
Hawthorn Suites Ltd.	29
International Wildlife Museum	119
Lodge on the Desert	33
Manor Care Health Services	309
Metropolitan Tucson Convention and Visitors Bureau	17
Papagayo Restaurant	59
Racer's Edge Bicycles	221
Sunstone	26
The Cactus Quail	43
The Congenial Quail	43
Tubac Golf Resort	31
University Medical Center	296
Zocalo	94

Index

Symbols

1880's Cowboy Mercantile 104

A

A-1 Messner Sitter Service 295
a.k.a. Theater 158
Access Tucson Gallery 174
Adobe Property Managers Inc. 280
Adobe Rose Inn 41
Adult Care Home Placement Services 319
Advance Reservations &
    Old Pueblo Homestays 41
Ain't Nobody's Bizness 89
Aires Flamencos 161
Airport Lounge 86
Ajo Bikes 226
Alamo Woodworkers Gallery 174
Alejandro's Tortilla Factory 96
America West Arena 234
American Bartenders School 295
American Cinema 91
Americas Gallery 95
Amerikan Hoodoo Theatreworks 161
Amerind Foundation 257
Amphitheater Public Schools 286
Amtrak 18
Anderson's Referral 319
Annual Quilter's Guild Show 144
Anthony's in the Catalinas 69
Antigone Books 110
Antigua de Mexico 103
Antique Center of Tucson 113
Antique Mall 113
Apartment and Home Locators 280
Apollo College 294
Archaeology For All 131
Arcosanti 253, 263
Arizona Bookstore 110
Arizona Cardinals 239
Arizona Commission on the Arts 156
Arizona Contemporary Dance Festival 144
Arizona Cycle & Sport 226

INDEX • 333

Arizona Daily Star, The 321
Arizona Daily Wildcat 321
Arizona Diamondbacks 238
Arizona Early Music Society 167
Arizona Earthworks Trading Company 104
Arizona Golfer 324
Arizona Hatters 104
Arizona Historical Society 2, 115, 131
Arizona Humanities Council 156
Arizona Inn 28, 69, 86
Arizona Institute of Business
    and Technology 294
Arizona International Film Festival 147
Arizona Jewish Post 322
Arizona Media Arts Center 171
Arizona Opera Company 5, 163
Arizona Pathfinders Hispanic Theater 158
Arizona Repertory Singers 163
Arizona Repertory Theater 158
Arizona Rose Theater Company 158
Arizona Senior World 322
Arizona Stadium 234
Arizona State Museum 116
Arizona Symphonic Winds 164
Arizona Theater Company 5, 158
Arizona Trails B&B Reservation Service 41
Arizona Trains 140
Arizona Youth Theater 135, 159
Arizona-Sonora Desert Museum 115, 134
Arizona-Sonora Desert Museum Press 178
Arizona's Children Association Center 300
Armory Park 269
Aroma Caffe, The 67
Art Center, The 295
Art Company, The 174
Art! 174
Arthur Pack Golf Course 208
Artlife 324
Artsreach 176
Asarco Mineral Discovery Center 116
Aspen Mills Bread 96
Audubon Nature Shop 112
Avra Valley Airport 17
Awareness Journal, The 322
AZ Stixx 62
Aztec Press 322
Azteca Mexican Imports 103

B

B & B Cactus Farm 100
Baby's Away 141
Bach's Greenhouse Cactus Nursery 100
Baggin's 64
Bahti Indian Arts 95
Ballet Arts Foundation 162
Ballet Continental 162
Ballet Folklorico Mexica 162
Balloon America 199
Balloon Glo 152
Bank One Tucson International
    Mariachi Conference 148
Barbea Williams Performing Company 162
Bargain Basement Bikes 226
Barksdale Gallery, The 174

Barrio Historico 269
Bear Essential News 322
Benson 256
Berger Performing Arts Center 157
Berky's Bar 87
Bero Gallery 174
Bertrand's Books 110
Best Western Executive Inn 28
Best Western Ghost Ranch Lodge 28
Best Western Inn 28
Best Western InnSuites Hotel 28
Best Western Royal Sun 28
Bianco Children's Theatre 159
Bicycles West 226
Bicycling 219
Bicycling Magazine 219
Big A, The 65
Big House, The 42
Bike & Bus Program 220
Bike Rights 224
Biking Events 224
Biking, Retail Shops and Repair 226
Biosphere 2 117, 132
Bisbee 257
Bison Witches 65
Bloodhut Productions 159
Blue Willow Restaurant Bakery &
    Poster Gallery 73
Bog Springs 50
Book Mark 110
Bookman's 110
Boom Boom's 90
Boomers Childrens Boutique 141
Boondocks Lounge 87
Borderlands Theater 159
Borders Books and Music 110
Boyce Thompson Southwestern
    Arboretum 247
Breakaway to the Border Bike Tour 150, 226
Breakers Water Park 137
Breckenridge Brewery & Pub 63, 91
Broadway Bicycles 227
Broadway Proper 308
Broadway Village 105
Brooklyn Pizza 80
Buddy's Grill 58
Buffalo Kids 141
Bum Steer, The 66
Bushwacker's Dancehall and Saloon 88
Bwiya-Toli 164

C

Cactus Cards & Gifts 104
Cactus Country RV Resort 50
Cactus Flower Wellness Center 303
Cactus Forest Loop 222
Cactus Moon 88
Cactus Quail Bed and Breakfast, The 42
Cafe Magritte 67
Cafe Paraiso 67
Cafe Poca Cosa 76
Cafe Sweetwater 68, 87
Cafe Terra Cotta 59
Cage, The 90

334 • INDEX

Calli Ollin High School 291
Camlu Retirement Apartments 309
Campana del Rio 309
Candlelight Suites 29
Canoa Hills Golf Course 217
Canyon Golf Course 211
Canyon Lake 260
Canyon Ranch Spa 36
Canyon State Collectibles 113
Capriccio's 74
Car-Mar's Southwest Bed and Breakfast 42
Carondelet St. Joseph's Hospital 297
Carondelet St. Mary's Hospital 297
Carter's for Kids 141
Caruso's 75
Casa Alegre Bed and Breakfast 42
Casa De La Cultura International 156
Casa Grande Ruins National Monument 260
Casa Tierra Adobe Bed and Breakfast Inn 44
Casas Adobes Baptist School 289
Casas Adobes Plaza 105
Casbah Tea House, The 68
Cascades, The 310
Casino of the Sun 118
Catalina Bicycle Shop 227
Catalina Chamber Orchestra 164
Catalina Cineplex 91
Catalina Foothills School District 286
Catalina Foothills, The 274
Catalina Park Inn 44
Catalina State Park 195, 203
Catalina State Park Campground 50
Catalina Village 310
Cele Peterson's 111
Celebrity Tennis Classic 237
Centennial Hall 157
Center for Creative Photography 169
Center for Intergrative Medicine, The 302
Center for the Healing Arts, The 303
Central Arts Collective 174
Century 21 281
Century Gateway 12 91
Century Park 16 92
Chancel Choir 165
Chaparral College 294
Chaparral Lounge 89
Charles 70
Chicago Bar, The 88
Childcare Resource and Referral 295
Childcare Seekers Directory 295
Children's Academy 291
Children's Memorial Park 196
Chiricahua Mountains 258
Chiricahua National Monument 258
Chow Bella 72, 96
Christine's Curiosity Shop & Doll Museum 113
Chuck E Cheese's 140
Cielos 70
Cinco de Mayo 149
City Grill, The 59
City of South Tucson 279
City of Tucson Parks and
    Recreation Department 199
Civic Orchestra of Tucson 165
Clarion Hotel 29

Clarion Santa Rita Hotel and Suites 29
Cliff Manor Inn 29
Cliff Valley Golf Course 212
Climb "A" Mountain 144
Club 21 77
Club Congress 86
Cochise County 256
Cochise's Stronghold 258
Cocoraque Ranch Cattle Drive 200
CODAC Behavioral Health Services 300
Coffee Plantation 86
Coffee Times 322
Coldwell Banker Success Realty 281
Coleccion Mexicana 103
Colossal Cave 118
Columbia El Dorado Hospital 298
Columbia Northwest Medical Center 298
Complementary Medicine Association 303
Congenial Quail Bed and Breakfast, The 44
Conquistador Stables 203
Continental Ranch 279
Copper Crest 311
Copper Queen Hotel 257
Copper Queen Mine 257
Corona de Tucson 276
Corona Ranch 44
Coronado National Forest 194
Corral Western Wear, The 104
Cosanti 253
Cottonwood Club 87
Cottonwood de Tucson 300
Country Club of La Cholla 311
Country Suites By Carlson 30
Courtyard by Marriott 30
Cowtown Boots 104
Coyote Crossing Bed and Breakfast 44
Coyote Ramblers 159
Coyote's Voice Books 110
Craig Fine Arts 174
Cross Creek Riding Club 203
Crossroads Festival 92, 105
Crowder Hall 157
Culinary Concepts 295
Cup, The 68
Cuppuccino's Coffee House 68
Curves Cabaret 92
Cushing Street Bar & Grill 60, 86
Cycle Spectrum 227

D

Daily Territorial, The 321
Dakota Cafe & Catering Co. 60
Damesrocket Theater Company 159
Dancing Gecko, The 104
Daniel's 75
Dateline Downtown 322
DaVinci's Italian Restaurant and Pizza 75
Davis-Monthan Air Force Base 119, 241
Day Star Farm Bed and Breakfast 45
Days Inn 30
De Anza Drive-In 92
De Grazia Gallery in the Sun 169
del Oro Realty 282
Delectables 74

INDEX • 335

Dell Urich Municipal Golf Course 209
Desert Artisans' Gallery 174
Desert Artists Guild 171
Desert Bluegrass Association 167
Desert Diamond Casino 119
Desert High Country Stables, Inc. 204
Desert Hills Center for Youth and Families 300
Desert Institute for the Healing Arts 303
Desert Players Community Theater 159
Desert Son 95
Desert Survivors 102
Desert Voices 165
DesertLeaf 323
Devine Healing Center 303
Dinnerware Artists' Cooperatve Gallery 174
Direct Center for Independence, Inc. 301
Discount Agate House 104
Discovery Zone Funcenter 138
Dish, The 68
Don's Restaurant 57
Dorado Country Club 276
Dorado Golf Course 209
Double Zero 87
DoubleTree Guest Suites 30
DoubleTree Hotel 31

E

Eastside Artist Series 165
eegee's 66
Egg Connection, The 58
El Adobe Ranch 45
El Charro Cafe 77
El Con Mall 105
El Corral 82
El Dorado Cineplex 92
El Encanto 273
El Greco's Grecian Gardens 73
El Mercado 106
El Minuto 77
El Presidio 268
El Presidio Bed and Breakfast 45
El Presidio Gallery 174
El Rio Bakery 98
El Rio Municipal Golf Course 209
El Saguarito 78
El Torero 78
El Tour de Tucson 151, 224, 226
Eleanor Jeck Galleries of
  Contemporary Art 174
Elysian Grove Market Bed & Breakfast Inn 45
Embassy Suites Hotel and Conference Center 31
Embassy Suites Hotel Broadway 31
Enchanted Earthworks Gallery 174
Enchanted Gardens Healing Center 303
Epic Cafe, The 68
ERA Realty 282
Etherton Gallery 174
Executive Terminal, Tucson Int. Airport 16
Explorer, The 323

F

F.L. Wright Gallery 175
Fair Wheel Bikes 227
Family Golf Centers Inc. 214
Far Horizons Trailer Village 315
Feig's Kosher Foods Market & Delicatessen 72
Fenster School 289
Fiesta Bowl Basketball Classic 239, 239
Fine Print 111
Finger Rock Canyon 202
Firecracker 62
Firehouse Antique Center 113
Firenze Boutique 111
Fisher Books 178
Fitness Plus 324
Flandrau Science Center and
  Planetarium 120, 132
Flowing Wells School District 287
Flying V Bar & Grill 70
Flying V Ranch 35
Foothills Cineplex 92
Foothills Mall 106
Foothills Phil, The 165
Foothills Properties 282
Fort Bowie 258
Fort Lowell 271
Fort Lowell Museum 120
Fort Lowell Park 197, 201
Forty-niners Country Club 276
Fountains at La Cholla, The 311
Fourth Avenue Spring Street Fair 147
Fourth Avenue Winter Street Fair 152
Fourth of July Fireworks 149
Fred Enke Municipal Golf Course 209
Friends of Western Art 171
Frog & Firkin 91
Fuego 60
Full Cycle 227
Fundacion Por Herencia Mexicana 156
Funtastiks 138

G

G & L Import Export 98
Galen Press, Ltd. 179
Garden of Gethsemane 120
Garland, The 74
Gaslight Theater, The 159
Gavi 75
General Hitchcock 54
Gentle Ben's Brewing Company 64, 91
Geronimo 4
Geronimoz' Restaurant & Bar 66
Ghini's French Caffe 71
Gila Monsters 232
Gila River Rafting 248
Glenwood 259
Gold Room, The 70
Golden Dragon 63
Goldfield Ghost Town 260
Golf 207
Golf Club at Vistoso, The 210
Golf 'N Stuff 138
Golf Practice Ranges 214
Good News 323
Goofy Gallery 113
Gourmet Emporium and Cheese Shop 98
Govinda's 74

336 • INDEX

Grande Tortilla Factory 98
Grandma Tony's Pizza 80
Greater Arizona Bicycling Association 219, 224
Greek Festival 150
Green Fields Country Day School 290
Green Valley 215
Greenspring Wellness Center 303
Grey Dog Trading Company 95
Greyhound 18
Grill at Hacienda del Sol, The 60
Grill, The 69
Grossman's Bake Shop 98
Group for Photographic Intentions 171
Gus Balon's 58
Gymboree Store, The 141

H

Hacienda del Desierto Bed and Breakfast 45
Hacienda del Sol Guest Ranch Resort 37
Hampton Inn 31
Haven Public Golf Course and
    Tortuga Golf Course 216
Hawthorn Suites 31
Healthy Times 323
Heard Museum 260
Heavy Metal Brass Quintet 165
Heritage Highlands Golf Club 210
Hi Corbett Field 235
Hidden Valley Inn 82
High Chiva Loop 222
High Desert Convoys, Inc. 204
Himmel Park 197, 201
Holiday Inn City Center 32
Holiday Inn Express 32
Honeybaked Ham Company 98
Hotel Congress 32
Hotel Park Tucson 32
Hours 90
Howard Johnson Lodge 32

I

IBT's 90
Iceoplex 136, 204
Iguana Cafe 69
Ilsa's Konditorei & Bakery 99
Inca Dove Bed and Breakfast 45
InnSuites Hotels 32
Inside Tucson Business 323
Insight.Com Bowl 152, 232
Institute of Word Processing 294
IntegraMed 303
International Mariachi Conference 167
International Wildlife Museum 122
Invisible Theater 159
Ironwood Cactus Nursery 102
ITT Technical Institute 294

J

Jack Conrad's Practice Range 214
Jacob C. Fruchthendler Jewish
    Community Hospital 303
Jacobs Park 198
Janos 61
Jeremiah Inn Bed and Breakfast, The 46
Jerome 264
Jewish Film Festival 143
John Jacob's El Parador 77
John Jacobs' Golf Schools 216
Jones Intercable 326
Juneteenth Festival 149
Justin's Water World 123, 137

K

Kaibab Courtyard Shops 106
Keaton's 81
Kennedy Park 198
Khalsa Montessori Elementary School 291
KIDCO 199
Kingfisher 81
Kino Community Hospital 298
Kino School 290
Kino Springs Golf Course 217
Kitt Peak National Observatory 123
Kore Press, Inc. 179

L

La Buena Mexican Foods 99
La Buhardilla 103
La Casa del Libro Bookstore 111
La Fiesta de los Chiles 150
La Fiesta de los Vaqueros 146
La Fiesta de San Augustin 149
La Frontera Center 300
La Mariposa Club 214
La Mesa Tortillas 99
La Parilla Suiza 79
La Posada del Valle 46
La Quinta Inn and Suites 33
La Quinta Inn 32
Laff's Comedy Club 88
Lakeview 52
Last Territory Steakhouse and Saloon, The 82
Lazy K Bar Ranch 35
Lemmon Park Trail 223
Lil Abner's Steakhouse 83
Little Anthony's Diner 58, 140
Live Theater Workshop 160
Lodge at Ventana Canyon
    Golf and Racquet Club 37, 210
Loft Cinema, The 92
Long Realty Company 282
Lost Barrio 108
Luminaria Nights 152

M

Mac's Indian Jewelry 96
Madera Canyon 248
Magpie's Gourmet Pizza 80
Maine Course 81
Malibu Grand Prix Family
    Entertainment Center 139
Malkia African Arts and Gifts 113
Manor at Midvale, The 312
Marana School District 287

INDEX • 337

Marana Skydiving Center 205
Marathon Art Gallery 175
Marlene's Hungry Fox Restaurant 58
Marriott University Park 33
Maxwell's Restaurant 61
Maya Palace 111
McKale Center 235
Medicine Man Gallery 175
Metro Grill, The 59
Mexican Rule 2
Meyer House, The 46
Mi Nidito Cafe 79
Midvale Park 278
Millennium Theatre Company 160
Mills-Touche 111
Minds in Motion 141
Mission San Xavier del Bac 123
Mission View Mobile Home and RV Resort 316
Mix & Match 109
Mogollon 260
Molino Basin 53
Montezuma Castle 263
Montezuma Well 264
Morning Star Traders 96
Mount Lemmon 195
Mountain Biking 221
Mountain Golf Course 211
Mountain View Adventures 204
Mrs. Tiggy Winkle's 141
Mt. Lemmon 223
Mt. Lemmon Oktoberfest 150
Multiple Sclerosis Society 226
Munson's Tucson Date Company 99
Music in the Canyon 153
Music Under the Stars 150

N

National League of American Penwomen 176
National Society of Arts & Letters 157
Native Seeds/SEARCH 102
New Delhi Palace 63
New Home Locators 283
New West 93
Nimbus Brewery 64
Nogales, Mexico 250
Northwest Interfaith Council 319
Northwest Properties 283
Nova Graphics Gallery 175

O

Oak Creek Canyon 264
Obsidian Gallery 175
Office of Child Care Initiatives 295
OK Corral 83
Old Pueblo Archaeology Center 199
Old Pueblo Playwrights 176
Old Pueblo Traders 109
Old Pueblo Trolley 125, 132
Old Town Artisans 108
Old Tucson Studios 5, 125, 132, 325
Old-Time Fiddle Contest 146
Olive Tree, The 73
O'Malley's 88

Omni Tucson National
   Golf Resort and Spa 37, 211
Organ Pipe Cactus National Monument 261
Oro Valley 279
Orts Theater of Dance 162
Outback, The 90
Oven's Restaurant 61

P

Paintball Headquarters, Inc. 204
Palo Verde Mental Health Services 301
Papagayo 79
Park Mall 106
Parks College 294
Patagonia Lake State Park 54, 251
Patrice Press, The 179
Pat's Drive In 66
Penelope's 71
People's Choice 326
Peppersauce 54
Peppertrees Bed and Breakfast Inn, The 46
Perimeter Bicycling Association
   of America, The 224, 226
Philabaum Contemporary Art Glass 175
Phoenix 260
Phoenix Coyotes 239
Phoenix Mercury 238
Phoenix Suns 238
Picacho Peak State Park 55
Pie Allen Neighborhood 272
Pima Air and Space Museum 125, 133
Pima Canyon 202
Pima Community College 293
Pima Council on Aging 319
Pima County Community Center
   for the Arts 157
Pima County Fair 147
Pima County Parks and Recreation 199
Pima Medical Institute 294
Pink Adobe Gallery 175
Pinnacle Peak Steakhouse 83
Players, The 135
Plaza Hotel and Conference Center 33
Plaza Palomino 106
Poets Alive! 177
Practice Tee, The 215
Prescott 264
Prescott College at Tucson 294
Presidio Grill 61
Prudential Aegis Realty, The 283
Puerto Penasco 261
Pusch Ridge Brewing 64, 91
Pusch Ridge Golf Course 213
Pusch Ridge Stables 204

Q

Quail Canyon Golf Course 212
Quail Ridge Estates 316
Quality Hotel and Suites 34
Que Bonita 103

338 • INDEX

R

R&R Bicycle 227
R.W. Webb Winery 126
Racer's Edge Bicycles 227
Ramada Palo Verde 34
Ramsey Canyon Preserve 257
Rancho Quieto Bed and Breakfast 46
Rancho Vistoso 210
Randolph North Municipal Golf Course 212
Randolph Park 198
Randolph Skatepark 136
Randolph Tennis Center 201
Rascon Imports 103
Raven Golf Club at Sabino Springs 212
Rawhide 260
RBC's Cafe 61
RE/MAX 283
Realty Executives of Tucson 283
Reay's Markets 72
Red Hawk 279
Redhouse Dancers 162
Reid Park 198
Reid Park Zoo 126, 135
Repp Big and Tall 112
Rex Allen Cowboy Museum 258
Riding and Rehabilitation Center 302
Rillito Downs 233
Rillito River Park 196, 220
Rimrock West Hacienda
    Studio and Gallery 175
Rincon Country RV Resort East 317
Rincon Country RV Resort West 316
Rincon Market 72, 100
Rincon Mountain Wilderness 194, 203
Rio Rico 261
Rio Rico Resort Golf Course 217
Rita Ranch 276
River Center 107
Rochelle K 112
Rocking M Ranch 46
Rocks and Ropes 200
Rocky Point, Mexico 261
Roma Imports 100
Rose Canyon 54
Rosequist Galleries, Inc. 176
Rum Runner Wine and Cheese Company 100
Ryan Airfield 17

S

Sabino Canyon 195, 275
Sabino Cycles 227
Saddlebrooke 313
Sagi's Outdoor News 323
Saguaro Clinic of Oriental Medicine 304
Saguaro National Park 193
Saguaro National Park East 194, 203, 222
Saguaro National Park West 201
Sahuaro Vista Guest Ranch
    Bed and Breakfast 47
Sakura 63
Salpointe Catholic High School 290
Sam Hughes 271
Samurai 63
San Augustin del Tucson 268
San Ignacio Golf Club 216
San Pedro and Southwest Railroad 256
San Xavier del Bac Mission 146
San Xavier Mission Shops 96
San Xavier Wa:k Pow Wow 146
Sanchez Burrito Co. 79
Santa Catalina Villas 313
Santa Cruz River Park 196, 220
Santa Fe Kids 141
Santa Rita Golf Course 212
Satori School 290
Sausage Deli, The 66
Savvy Boutique 112
Scordato's 76
Screening Room, The 92
Sedona 264
Senior Resource Network 318
Senior Sports Classic 144
Serenity Books 111
Shadow Mountain Ranch Bed and Breakfast 47
Shari's First Avenue Drive-In 67
Shelter, The 87
Sheraton El Conquistador Resort
    and Country Club 37, 213
Show, The 215
Silver City 258
Silverbell Municipal Golf Course 213
Silverbell Park 198
Silverbell Trading 96
"Simon Peter" Passion Play of Tucson 147
Skate Country East 136
Skate Country North 137
Ski Valley 24, 204
Smuggler's Inn 34
Society of Southwestern Authors 177
Solarium, The 82
Sonora Tourism Office 263
Sons of Orpheus 165
Southern Arizona Balloon Excursions 200
Southern Arizona Clay Artists 173
Southern Arizona Hiking Club 201
Southern Arizona Square/Round Dance and
    Clogging Festival 143
Southern Arizona Symphony Orchestra 165
Southern Arizona Watercolor Guild 173
Southern Arizona Woodworkers
    Association 173
Southwest Designs 104
Southwestern International Raceway 233
Spanish Trail Outfitters, Inc. 200
Speedway Bikes 227
Spencer Canyon 54
Sports Stuff 323
Spring Training 230
St. Gregory College Prepatory 290
St. Patrick's Catholic Church 257
St. Patrick's Day Parade and Festival 147
St. Philip's Plaza 107
Starr Pass 39
Starr Pass Golf Resort 213
Stewart Theater of Puppetry 160
Summit Hut 112
Sumner Suites 34
Sun City Tucson 314

INDEX • 339

Sun Devil Stadium 236
Sun Tran 16, 24, 220
Sun Tran Customer Service Center 224
Sunflower 315
Sunnyside School District 288
Sunrise Golf Course 213
Sunset Strip 92
Sunshine Jeep Tours 204
Sunstone Guest Ranch 36
Superstition Mountains 260
Swan Lakes Estates 317

T

Tack Room, The 71
Tailwinds 224, 323
Taliesin West 251
Tanger Factory Outlet Center 109
Tania's Tortillas and Mexican Food 100
Tanque Verde Greenhouses 103
Tanque Verde Ranch 36
Tanque Verde School District 288
Tanque Verde Swap Meet 109
TD's Showclub 93
Ted's Country Store 100
Temple of Music and Art 157
Ten's Nightclub 93
Tenth Street Danceworks 162
Terra Nova Restaurant and Bakery 74
Texas Canyon 257
Third Stone Bar and Grill, The 62, 88
Third Street Kids 135, 160
Titan Missile Museum 127
Tohono Chul Park 128, 198
Tohono Chul Park Gallery 176
Tohono Chul Tearoom 62
Tombstone 256
Tony's Italian Style Butcher Shop & Restaurant 73
Torres Blancas Golf Club 216
Tour for Tucson's Children 225
Tour of the Tucson Mountains 147, 225
Trail Dust Jeep Tours 204
Trail Dust Town 107, 140
Trails West 317
Treasure Chest Books 179
Triple B "BBB" Bed & Breakfast 47
Tubac 251
Tubac Golf Resort 217
Tucson Arizona Boys Chorus 165
Tucson Art Theater 160
Tucson Arts and Crafts Association 173
Tucson Arts Brigade 173
Tucson Arts Coalition 173
Tucson Arts District Partnership, Inc. 157
Tucson Association for Child Care 295
Tucson Association of Realtors 281
Tucson Bicycles 227
Tucson Bike Week 225
Tucson Blues Festival 150
Tucson Blues Society 168
Tucson Book Publishing Association 177
Tucson Botanical Gardens 128
Tucson Cable Inc. (TCI) 326
Tucson Center for the Performing Arts 158

Tucson Children's Museum 134
Tucson Chrysler Golf Classic 144
Tucson Citizen 322
Tucson Comic News 323
Tucson Community Cable Corporation 326
Tucson Convention Center 158
Tucson Country Club 274
Tucson Electric Park 236
Tucson Folk Festival 149
Tucson Friends of Traditional Music 168
Tucson Gem and Mineral Show 144
Tucson General Hospital 298
Tucson Girls Chorus 166
Tucson Goodtime Singers 166
Tucson Greyhound Park 233
Tucson Guide Quarterly 324
Tucson Guitar Society 168
Tucson Heart Hospital 298
Tucson Hebrew Academy 291
Tucson Interfaith Coalition on Aging 319
Tucson International Airport 15
Tucson Jazz Society 168
Tucson Kitchen Musicians Association 168
Tucson Lifestyle 324
Tucson Mall 107
Tucson Marathon 152
Tucson Masterworks Chorale 166
Tucson Medical Center 298
Tucson Metropolitan Dance Company 162
Tucson Mountain Park 194, 201
Tucson Museum of Art 5, 170
Tucson Musical Arts Club 169
Tucson Open University 294
Tucson Parks and Recreation Community Theater 160
Tucson Philharmonia Youth Orchestra 166
Tucson Poet, The 323
Tucson Poetry Festival 146
Tucson Poetry Festival Committee 178
Tucson Pops Orchestra 166
Tucson Raceway Park 233
Tucson Realty & Trust Co. 283
Tucson Regional Ballet 163
Tucson Rodeo 146
Tucson Screenwriting Group 178
Tucson Sidewinders 230
Tucson Symphony Orchestra 136, 166
Tucson Theater Scene 324
Tucson Tourist News 324
Tucson Unified School District 285
Tucson Urban League 291
Tucson Visitor 325
Tucson Weekly 324
Tucson Writer's Project 178
Tucson-Pima County Bicycle Advisory Committee 219, 224
Tucson/Pima Arts Council 173
Tucson's Map and Flag Center 111
Tumacacori 252
TuNidito Children's Hospice 303
Turning Point School 291
Turquoise Skies 96

U

UA Icecats 232
UA Poetry Center 178
UA Presents 167
UA Wildcats 229, 231, 232
UA Writing Works Center 178
Udall Park 199
United States Handball Association 201
University Bicycles 227
University Medical Center 299
University of Arizona 291
University of Arizona Balalaika Orchestra 167
University of Arizona Dance Division 163
University of Arizona Mineral Museum 129
University of Arizona Museum of Art 170
University of Arizona Press 179
University of Arizona School of
    Music & Dance 167
University of Phoenix 294
Upstairs Theater Company 160

V

Vail School District 288
Valencia Vista 92
Valley Manor 315
Valley of the Moon 139
Ventana Canyon 275
Venture Fine Arts Gallery 176
Venture Up 200
Verde Valley 263
Veterans Affairs Medical Center 300
VF Factory Outlet 110
Video Apartments Guide 280
Village at Coffee Etc., The 69
Viro's Real Italian Bakery 100
Viscount Suite Hotel 34
Vivace Restaurant 76
Voyager RV Resort 317

W

Waila Festival 149
Walking Winds Stables 204
Wayward Winds Lodge 34
Weekly Observer, The 324
Welch's/Circle K Championship
    LPGA Golf Tournament 146, 212
Wellness Council of Tucson (WELCOT) 304
West Center 301
Western Music Association 169
Western Music Festival 151
Western Warehouse 104
Western Way RV Resort 318
Westin La Paloma Resort and
    Country Club 39, 214
Westward Look Resort 39
Whipple Observatory 129
White Stallion Ranch 36
Whitewater Canyon 259
Whiz Kids Books and Toys 141
Wholistic Family Medicine 304
Wild Horse Ranch 36
Willcox 258
Windmill Inn at St. Philip's Plaza 34
Winterhaven 273
Winterhaven Festival of Lights 152
WomanKraft Castle Art Center 176

Y

Yikes Toys 141
Young Artists Community Ballet 163
Young Audiences of Southern Arizona 157

Z

Zachary's 81
Zenith Dance Collective 163

Going Somewhere?

Insiders' Publishing Inc. presents 48 current and upcoming titles to popular destinations all over the country (including the titles below) — and we're planning on adding many more. To order a title, go to your local bookstore or call (800) 582-2665 and we'll direct you to one.

Adirondacks	Minneapolis/St. Paul, MN
Atlanta, GA	Mississippi
Bermuda	Myrtle Beach, SC
Boca Raton and the Palm Beaches, FL	Nashville, TN
Boulder, CO, and Rocky Mountain National Park	New Hampshire
Bradenton/Sarasota, FL	North Carolina's Central Coast and New Bern
Branson, MO, and the Ozark Mountains	North Carolina's Mountains
California's Wine Country	Outer Banks of North Carolina
Cape Cod, Nantucket and Martha's Vineyard, MA	The Pocono Mountains
Charleston, SC	Relocation
Cincinnati, OH	Richmond, VA
Civil War Sites in the Eastern Theater	Salt Lake City
Colorado's Mountains	Santa Fe
Denver, CO	Savannah
Florida Keys and Key West	Southwestern Utah
Florida's Great Northwest	Tampa/St. Petersburg, FL
Golf in the Carolinas	Tucson
Indianapolis, IN	Virginia's Blue Ridge
The Lake Superior Region	Virginia's Chesapeake Bay
Las Vegas	Washington, D.C.
Lexington, KY	Wichita, KS
Louisville, KY	Williamsburg, VA
Madison, WI	Wilmington, NC
Maine's Mid-Coast	Yellowstone

Insiders' Publishing Inc. • P.O. Box 2057 • Manteo, NC 27954
Phone (919) 473-6100 • Fax (919) 473-5869 • www.insiders.com